The Prentice Hall Guide for Student Writers
Canadian Edition

Stephen Reid
Colorado State University

Enid Gossin
Seneca College

Susan Stancer
Seneca College

Prentice
Hall

Toronto

Canadian Cataloguing in Publication Data

Stephen Reid, 1940–
    The Prentice Hall guide for student writers

Canadian ed.
Includes index.
ISBN 0-13-022270-4

1. English language — Rhetoric. 2. College readers. 3. Report writing. I. Gossin, Enid, 1950– .
II. Stancer, Susan, 1937– . III. Title.

PE1408.R44 2002 808'.042   C2001-930506-0

ISBN 0-13-022270-4

Vice-President, Editorial Director: Michael Young
Editor-in-Chief: David Stover
Marketing Manager: Sharon Loeb
Executive Developmental Editor: Marta Tomins
Production Editor: Joe Zingrone
Copy Editor: Ann McInnis
Production Coordinator: Peggy Brown
Page Layout: Jansom
Art Director: Mary Opper
Cover/Interior Design: Amy Harnden
Cover Image: Kamil Vojnar/Photonica

1 2 3 4 5   05 04 03 02

Printed and bound in Canada.

"To the partners and progeny with our love and appreciation."

—*Enid Gossin and Susan Stancer*
Seneca College

BRIEF CONTENTS

1   Writing Myths and Rituals   1

2   Purposes and Processes for Writing   14

3   Reading   38

4   Observing   83

5   Remembering   115

6   Investigating   143

7   Explaining   178

8   Evaluating   223

9   Arguing   261

10 Responding to Literature   307

11 Writing a Research Paper   372

Appendix: Writing Under Pressure   434

Handbook   442

CONTENTS

PREFACE xiii

1 WRITING MYTHS AND RITUALS 1
WRITING FITNESS: RITUALS AND PRACTICE 3
Place, Time, and Tools 4
Energy and Attitude 5
Keeping a Journal 6
"On Keeping a Journal" by Roy Hoffman 10

2 PURPOSES AND PROCESSES FOR WRITING 14
"Memoirs and Diaries" by Ting-xing Ye 16
PURPOSES FOR WRITING 17
Writer-Based Purposes 17
Subject- and Audience-Based Purposes 18
Combinations of Purposes 18
Subject, Purpose, and Thesis 19
PURPOSE AND AUDIENCE 19
Audience Analysis 20
The Writing Situation 21
PURPOSE AND AUDIENCE IN TWO ESSAYS 22
"His Name Was Sander, and He Was My Best Friend" by Sandy Wolofsky ... 22
"I'm O.K., but You're Not" by Robert Zoellner 25
DIMENSIONS OF THE PROCESS 27
Collecting 28
Shaping 28
Drafting 28
Revising 28
The Whole Process 29
A WRITING PROCESS AT WORK: COLLECTING AND SHAPING ... 30
"Athletes and Education" by Neil H. Petrie 30
"On Writing 'Athletes and Education'" by Neil H. Petrie 34

3 READING 38
TECHNIQUES FOR WRITING ABOUT READING 40
How Readers Read 41
SUMMARIZING AND RESPONDING TO AN ESSAY 41
"Teach Diversity—With a Smile" by Barbara Ehrenreich 42
Summarizing 45
Responding 46
"Some Don't Like Their Blues at All" by Karyn M. Lewis .. 49
"IBM and *The X-Files*" by Susan Douglas 52

READING AND WRITING PROCESSES 55

Choosing a Subject 56
"Children and Violence in America" by Dudley Erskine Devlin 56
Collecting 59
Guidelines for Class Discussion 62
Shaping 63
Outlines for Summary/Response Essays 67
Drafting 68
Revising 69
"How Male and Female Students Use Language Differently" by Deborah Tannen 70
"A Response to Deborah Tannen's Essay" by Jennifer Koester 77
"Is Deborah Tannen Convincing?" by Sonja H. Browe 79

4 OBSERVING 83
TECHNIQUES FOR WRITING ABOUT OBSERVATIONS 85

Observing People 86
from *The Way of a Boy* by Ernest Hillen 86
Observing Places 87
Observing Objects 88
Observing Events 88
"The Snake" by Annie Dillard 90
"Observing Wolves" by Farley Mowat 94
OBSERVING: THE WRITING PROCESS 102

Choosing a Subject 102
Collecting 103
Shaping 105
from "The Pleasures of Love" by Robertson Davies 108
Drafting 111
Revising 112

5 REMEMBERING 115
TECHNIQUES FOR WRITING ABOUT MEMORIES 116

Remembering People 117
from *Wordstruck* by Robert McNeil 117
Remembering Places 118
from *The Street* by Mordecai Richler 118
Remembering Events 120
from *Inside Memory* by Timothy Findley 120
"The Day Language Came Into My Life" by Helen Keller 120
"Beauty: When the Other Dancer Is the Self" by Alice Walker 124
REMEMBERING: THE WRITING PROCESS 132

Choosing a Subject 133
Collecting 133

Shaping 135
from *My Life and Hard Times* by James Thurber 138
Drafting 140
Revising 141

6 INVESTIGATING 143
TECHNIQUES FOR INVESTIGATIVE WRITING 144
Summary of a Book or Article 145
"Date Rape: Familiar Strangers" by Jeff Meer 145
Investigation Using Multiple Sources 147
"The Personality Pill" by Anastasia Toufexis 147
Profile of a Person: Wayne Gretzky 150
"Asking for Directions" by Chris Garbutt 151
INVESTIGATING: THE WRITING PROCESS 161
Choosing a Subject 162
Collecting 163
Shaping 170
Drafting 172
Revising 172
"My Friend Michelle, an Alcoholic" by Bridgid Stone 173

7 EXPLAINING 178
TECHNIQUES FOR EXPLAINING 180
Explaining *What* 181
Explaining *How* 183
Explaining *Why* 185
from *Illiterate America* by Jonathan Kozol 186
"Welcome to Cyberspace" by Philip Elmer-DeWitt 187
"The Global Village Finally Arrives" by Pico Iyer 195
EXPLAINING: THE WRITING PROCESS 200
Choosing a Subject 200
Collecting 201
Shaping 203
Drafting 209
Revising 210
"English Only" by Christine Bishop 211
"Anorexia Nervosa" by Nancie Brosseau 219

8 EVALUATING 223
TECHNIQUES FOR WRITING EVALUATIONS 224
"The Belvedere" by John Gilchrist 225
Evaluating Commercial Products or Services 227
"DVD Moves Into the Mainstream" by Grant Buckler 228

Evaluating Performances   232

"Oprah . . . Oscar; Oscar . . . Oprah" by Peter Travers   232

"Watching the Eyewitless News" by Elayne Rapping   234

"Omigawd! Canadian Optimism!" by Patrick Watson   241

"Not Available in Stores" by Mark Kingwell   245

EVALUATING: THE WRITING PROCESS   251

Choosing a Subject   251

Collecting   252

Shaping   254

Drafting   256

Revising   256

The Red Violin by Roger Ebert   257

9   ARGUING   261

TECHNIQUES FOR WRITING: ARGUMENT   262

from "Active and Passive Euthanasia" by James Rachels   263

Claims for Written Argument   264

from "A Case of Severe Bias" by Patricia Raybon   264

from *The Plug-In Drug: Television, Children, and the Family* by Marie Winn 266

from "College Is a Waste of Time and Money" by Caroline Bird   266

Appeals for Written Argument   268

from "Letter from Birmingham Jail" by Martin Luther King, Jr.   271

Rogerian Argument   272

from "Animal Rights Versus Human Health" by Albert Rosenfeld   274

"The Ethics of Endorsing a Product" by Mike Royko   275

"The Gift of Fame" by Tyler Cowen   277

"In Praise of Hero Worship" by Norman Doidge   284

"The Internet: A Clear and Present Danger?" by Cathleen A. Cleaver   286

"Fields of Broken Dreams" by Sharon Butala   293

ARGUING: THE WRITING PROCESS   297

Choosing a Subject   297

Collecting   298

Shaping   300

Drafting   303

Revising   303

10 RESPONDING TO LITERATURE   307

"The Story of an Hour" by Kate Chopin   309

TECHNIQUES FOR RESPONDING TO LITERATURE   312

PURPOSES FOR RESPONDING TO LITERATURE   313

RESPONDING TO SHORT FICTION   314

Responding as a Reader   314
Reading with a Writer's Eye   315
"The Boat" by Alistair MacLeod   317
"The Wednesday Circle" by Sandra Birdsell   335
"Eyes" by Clark Blaise   345
"The Light of Distant Planets" by Stephen Guppy   352
RESPONDING TO LITERATURE: THE WRITING PROCESS   366
Collecting   366
Shaping   368
Drafting   369
Revising   370

11 WRITING A RESEARCH PAPER   372
TECHNIQUES FOR WRITING A RESEARCH PAPER   373
Using Purpose, Audience, and Form as Guides   374
Finding the Best Sources   375
Using Sources to Make Your Point   376
Documenting Your Sources   376
PREPARING YOURSELF FOR THE RESEARCH PROCESS   376
Research Notebook   377
Research Timetable   379
Documentation Format: MLA and APA Styles   380
RESEARCH PAPER: THE WRITING PROCESS   381
Choosing a Subject   381
Collecting   384
Shaping   400
Drafting   401
Revising   405
Documenting Sources   406
"Spies in the Sixties: The Conflicting Themes of Ian Fleming and
John le Carré" by John Polanszky   422

APPENDIX: WRITING UNDER PRESSURE   434
KNOW YOUR AUDIENCE   435
ANALYZE KEY TERMS   435
MAKE A SKETCH OUTLINE   436
KNOW THE MATERIAL   437
PRACTISE WRITING   438
PROOFREAD AND EDIT   438
SAMPLE ESSAY QUESTIONS AND RESPONSES   438

HANDBOOK   442
SECTION 1 - REVIEW OF BASIC SENTENCE ELEMENTS   449
SECTION 2 - SENTENCE STRUCTURE AND GRAMMAR   458
SECTION 3 - DICTION AND STYLE   476
SECTION 4 - PUNCTUATION AND MECHANICS   490

LITERARY CREDITS   507

INDEX   511

PREFACE

As we venture into this new millennium, we continue to witness dramatic changes in the contexts for the teaching of writing. The ongoing expansion of World Wide Web sites, the increasing speed of access to the Internet, and the expanding number of computer classrooms and terminals available to student writers have revolutionized the teaching and practice of writing. On the Internet, writers now access an incredible range of information, both about specific subjects and about the process of writing and revising. On local networks, students continue conversations started in print media or in the classroom, get and receive peer advice about drafting and revision, and access teacher response. Distance learning in this brave new century is a practical reality, as students sitting at computers in different cities or countries can communicate as easily as students sitting at adjoining computers.

The more things change, however, the more they remain the same. Writers still need to learn critical reading skills. They still need to assess rhetorical contexts, establish rhetorical purpose, consider their audiences and readers, develop and organize their ideas, and learn how to revise and edit their writing to meet the rhetorical situation. They still need to learn to work cooperatively and collaboratively to create a writing community. Computers and networks are merely electronic means for communicating—for putting people in contact with people, writers in contact with readers. Computers and networks can continue teachers' efforts to communicate with their students and to centre their curriculum on the students' reading, writing, and revising.

The Prentice Hall Guide for Student Writers, Canadian Edition, retains an emphasis on aims and purposes for reading and writing, on a clear sequence of chapters that move from expressive to argumentative writing, and on extensive, integrated writing process advice that helps students learn to read, write, and revise. Providing ongoing support for both students and teachers during the reading, writing, and revising processes remains the overriding goal of this text.

Continued also is an emphasis on critical reading and responding to texts. Chapter 3, "Reading," uses the summary/response essay as a means to teach active and critical reading, accurate summarizing, and focussed responding to texts. Drawing on reader-response theories and psycholinguistic research, Chapter 3 provides a variety of activities to promote active reading and critical responding. Useful information about the Internet explains how to use it and how it affects writing and learning. Second, an expanded section on locating, evaluating, and documenting Internet and Web sources—using the latest MLA guidelines—help students use electronic resources in their writing. The work of student writers appears at key points.

KEY FEATURES

The Prentice Hall Guide for Student Writers offers a wide range of noteworthy features:

Logical Sequence of Purpose-Based Chapters

Aims and purposes, not rhetorical strategies, guide each writing assignment. Early chapters focus on invention strategies (reading, observing, remembering, and investigating), while later chapters emphasize exposition and argumentation (explaining, evaluating, and arguing).

Focus on Writing Processes

Every major chapter contains professional and student samples, rhetorical techniques, reading and writing activities, collaborative activities, and revision suggestions designed to assist students with their work-in-progress.

An Introduction to Myths and Rituals for Writing

Chapter 1, "Writing Myths and Rituals," discounts some common myths about college and university writing courses, introduces the notion of writing rituals, and outlines the journal writing process. Rituals are crucial for all writers but especially so for novice writers. Effective rituals are simply those behavioural strategies that complement the cognitive and social strategies of the writing process.

An Orientation to the Rhetorical Situation and to Writing Processes

Chapter 2, "Purposes and Processes for Writing," bases the writing process in the rhetorical situation (writer, subject, purpose, text, and audience). It restores the writer's intent or purpose (rather than a thesis sentence or a rhetorical strategy) as the driving force during the writing process. It demonstrates how meaning evolves from a variety of recursive, multidimensional, and hierarchical activities that we call the writing process. Finally, it reassures students that, because individual writing and learning styles differ, they will be encouraged to discover and articulate their own processes from a range of appropriate possibilities.

Aims and Purposes for Writing

The text then turns to specific purposes and assignments for writing. Chapters 3 through 6 ("Reading," "Observing," "Remembering," and "Investigating") focus on invention strategies. These chapters illustrate how writing to learn is a natural part of learning to write. To promote reading, writing, discussing, revising, and learning, these chapters introduce four sources of invention—reading and responding to texts; observing people, places, objects, and events; remembering people, places, and events; and investigating information through interviews, surveys, and written sources. Although students write essays intended for a variety of audiences in each of these chapters, the emphasis is on invention strategies and on writer-based purposes for writing. Although this text includes expressive and transactional elements in every assignment, the direction of the overall sequence of assignments is from the more personal forms of discourse to the more public forms.

Chapters 7 through 9 ("Explaining," "Evaluating," and "Arguing") emphasize subject and audience-based purposes. The sequence in these chapters moves the student smoothly from exposition to argumentation (acknowledging the obvious overlapping), building on the skills and strategies of the previous chapters. The teacher may, in fact, use Chapters 7 through 9 as a mini-course in argument, teaching students how to develop and argue claims of fact, claims of cause and effect, claims about values, and claims about solutions or policies.

Responding to Literature

Chapter 10 guides students through the process of writing interpretive essays about short fiction, using many of the critical reading strategies, invention techniques, and shaping strategies practised in the earlier chapters. This chapter contains five short fiction works.

Research Paper

Chapter 11 ("Writing a Research Paper") draws on all the cognitive and social strategies presented in the first 10 chapters. Research papers are written for specific purposes and audiences, too, but the invention, composing, and revising processes are more extended. This chapter helps students select and plan their projects, use the library, find Internet sources, evaluate and document electronic and print sources, record their progress, and test ideas in research logs—learning all the while to integrate the information they gather with their own experiences and ideas.

Handbook

A brief handbook includes a review of basic sentence elements, sentence structure and grammar, diction and style, and punctuation and mechanics.

PREFACE TO THE CANADIAN EDITION

The adapted Canadian edition reflects the philosophy and tone of Stephen Reid's approach to teaching writing through active reading and critical responding. As community college teachers, we recognize that we must meet the needs of a growing and diverse population of students seeking post-secondary education: high school and university graduates, first-year university and college students, and mature students returning to school after many years. These students are required to take a composition course, the goal of which is to refine their reading, writing, and critical thinking skills, all necessary for success in the world of work. We have limited the material by approximately 150 pages so that teachers and students can use as many of the readings and exercises as possible, given the reality of the academic schedule in a post-secondary institution. Finally, this Canadian edition not only highlights good writing by Canadians but also provides further insights into Canadian culture and ideas.

On the basis of our own experience and in response to suggestions from reviewers, we have made the following changes:

- Many examples and essays by Canadians about the Canadian experience are included. Chapter 10, "Responding to Literature," features four Canadian short stories.
- References, examples, and readings come from all across Canada; some concern experiences that are specifically regional, others, uniquely Canadian, and still others, universal.
- Our focus is on familiarizing students with a broad sampling of published Canadian writers.
- Chapter 3, "Reading," was moved from its position as Chapter 5 in the U.S. edition to reinforce at the outset the relationship between active reading, critical thinking, and writing.
- Journal writing remains as a model in Chapter 1. Subsequent journal exercises have been moved to the Instructor's Manual to be used at the discretion of the instructor.
- Peer collaboration can be a valuable activity in giving and receiving constructive feedback; a Peer Response exercise in Chapter 5 serves as a model to be used at the instructor's discretion.

The Canadian edition is soft-covered, slim, easy to carry, reasonably priced, and is bound so that it will lie flat as you read. Teachers and students can cover the material in one semester, making choices among a variety of engaging readings, discussion topics, and writing exercises. The text offers its users the opportunity to meet required learning outcomes in a context which highlights Canada's uniqueness.

SUPPLEMENTARY MATERIAL FOR INSTRUCTORS AND STUDENTS

Instructor's Manual

The accompanying Instructor's Manual gives support to teachers with ESL students in their classes. All major chapters contain ESL teaching tips, designed to alert teachers to possible ESL problems and their solutions.

Critical Thinking Skills Journal

Available for a nominal fee, the Critical Thinking Skills Journal provides students with additional exercises and freewriting activities, as well as opportunities to consider and respond to opposing viewpoints.

Companion Website

A unique FREE Online Study Resource . . . the Companion Website™ at **www.prenhall.com/reid**. Prentice Hall's exclusive Companion Website™ that accompanies the corresponding U.S. edition of *The Prentice Hall Guide for Student Writers* offers unique tools and support that make it easy for students and instructors to integrate this online study guide with the text. The site is a comprehensive resource that is organized according to the chapters within the text and features a variety of learning and teaching modules. The Companion Website™ makes integrating the Internet into your course exciting and easy. Join us online at the above address and enter a new world of teaching and learning possibilities and opportunities.

ACKNOWLEDGMENTS

This textbook builds on the work of hundreds of teachers and researchers. Its most obvious and immediate debts are to James Kinneavy, Frank D'Angelo, Donald Murray, Rise Axelrod and Charles Cooper, Jeanne Fahnestock and Marie Secor, Linda Flower and John Hayes, Patricia Bizzell, Frank Smith, Louise Rosenblatt, and Lynn Troyka.

Since teaching writing is always a situated enterprise, I would like to thank the members of the composition faculty and staff at Colorado State University whose teaching expertise and enthusiasm have improved every page of the text and the teacher's manual: Kate Kiefer, Mike Palmquist, Donna LeCourt, Laura Thomas, Brenda Edmands, Stephanie Wardrop, and Laurel Nesbitt. Many of the innovative teaching strategies and resources developed by Colorado State University composition faculty members are available at **www.ColoState.edu/Depts/WritingCenter**.

In addition, the following teachers offered excellent advice about changes and additions for this edition: Avon Crismore, Indiana University, Purdue University; Sylvia Stacey, Oakton Community College; Christopher Gould, University of North Carolina, Wilmington; Susan Latta, University of Detroit, Mercy; Gay Lynn Crossley, Marian College. I wish to thank them for their thorough, honest, and professional advice.

For the expert crew at Prentice Hall, I am especially grateful. Phil Miller, a fine editor and friend, has enthusiastically supported this text from the first edition. Leah Jewell provided ongoing revision and editorial support, and Patricia Castiglione handled the daily chores with care and courtesy. On the shortest of timelines, Randy Pettit did the expert and careful editing that made the book possible. To Gina Sluss, I can only say thanks for being so professional—and for being such a good friend.

Finally, I wish to thank my family—Joy, Shelley, Michael, Gus, and Loren—for their continued patience and active support.

—*Stephen Reid*
Colorado State University

We appreciate the recommendations made by the reviewers of this text. They are Alexandra MacLennan; Crystal Hurdle, Capilano College, Vancouver; Susan Lieberman, Grant MacEwan College, Edmonton; Ilona Ryder, Grant MacEwan College; Betsy Sargent, University of Alberta; and Pat Rogin, Durham College, Oshawa. Many thanks to the team at Pearson Education Canada — including acquisitions editor, David Stover; developmental editor, Marta Tomins; and production editor, Joe Zingrone. We are also grateful for the efforts of our tireless copy editor, Ann McInnis. Working together has been a joy. In adapting this text we have been inspired by our students and the richness and diversity of our Canadian literary talent.

—Enid Gossin and Susan Stancer
Seneca College

WRITING MYTHS
AND RITUALS

LEARNING OUTCOMES

After reading this chapter you will have learned that

- negative myths prevent you from writing
- useful rituals help you start writing
- a positive attitude helps in all your writing

As you begin a college writing course, you need to get rid of some myths about writing that you may have been packing around for some time. Don't allow misconceptions to ruin a good experience. Here are a few common myths about writing, followed by some facts compiled from the experiences of working writers.

Myth: "Good writers are born, not made. A writing course really won't help my writing."

Fact: *Writers acquire their skills the same way athletes do—through practice and hard work.* There are very few "born" writers. Most writers—even professional writers and journalists—are not continually inspired to write. In fact, they often experience "writer's block"—the stressful experience of staring helplessly at a piece of paper, unable to think or to put words down on paper. A writing course will teach you how to cope with your procrastination, anxiety, lack of "inspiration," and false starts by focussing directly on solving the problems that occur during the writing process.

Myth: "Writing courses are just a review of boring grammar and punctuation. When teachers read your writing, the only thing they mark is that stuff, anyway."

Fact: *Learning and communicating—not grammar and punctuation—come first in college writing courses.* Knowledge of grammar, spelling, punctuation, and usage is essential to editing, but it is secondary to discovering ideas, thinking, learning, and communicating. In a writing course, students learn to revise and improve the content and organization of each other's writing. *Then* they help each other edit for grammar, punctuation, or spelling errors.

Myth: "College writing courses are really 'creative writing,' which is not what my program requires."

Fact: *Writing courses emphasize rhetoric.* Rhetoric involves practising the most effective means or strategies for informing or persuading an audience. All writing—even technical or business writing—is "creative." Deciding what to write, how to write it, how best to get your reader's attention, and how to inform or persuade your reader requires creativity and imagination. Every subject requires the skills that writing courses teach: exploring new ideas, learning concepts and processes, communicating with others, and finding fresh or creative solutions to problems.

Myth: "Writing courses are not important in college or the real world. I'll never have to write, anyway."

Fact: *Writing courses do have a significant effect on your success in college or university, on the job, and in life.* Even if you don't have frequent, formal writing assignments in other courses, writing improves your note taking, reading comprehension, and thinking skills. When you do have other written tasks or assignments, a writing course teaches you to *adapt* your writing to a variety of different purposes and audiences—whether you are writing a lab report in biology, a letter to an editor, a complaint to the Better Business Bureau, or a memorandum to your boss. Taking a writing course helps you express yourself more clearly, confidently, and persuasively—a skill that comes in handy whether you're writing a psychology essay, a job application, or a love letter.

The most important fact about writing is that *you are already a writer.* You have been writing for years. A writer is someone who writes, not someone who writes a nationally syndicated newspaper column, publishes a bestseller, or wins a Pulitzer Prize. To be an effective writer, you don't have to earn a million dollars; you just have to practise writing often enough to get acquainted with its personal benefits for you and its value for others.

■ WARM-UP EXERCISE: FREEWRITING   Put this book aside—right now—and take out pencil or pen and a piece of paper. Use this free exercise (private, unjudged, ungraded) to remind yourself that you are already a writer. Time yourself for five minutes. Write on the first thing that comes to mind—*anything whatsoever.* Write nonstop. Keep writing even if you have to write, "I can't think of anything to say. This feels stupid!" When you get an idea, pursue it.

When five minutes are up, stop writing and reread what you have written. Whether you write about a genuinely interesting topic or about the weather, freewriting is an excellent way to warm up, to get into the habit of writing, and to establish a writing ritual.

WRITING FITNESS: RITUALS AND PRACTICE

Writing is no more magic or inspiration than any other human activity that you admire: figure skating at the Olympics, rebuilding a car engine, cooking a gourmet meal, or acting in a play. Behind every human achievement are many unglamorous hours of practice—working and sweating, falling flat on your face, and picking yourself up again. You can't learn to write just by reading some chapters in a textbook or by memorizing other people's advice. You need help and advice, but you also need practice. Consider the following parable about a Chinese painter:

> A rich patron once gave money to the painter Chu Ta, asking him to paint a picture of a fish. Three years later, when he still had not received the painting, the patron went to Chu Ta's house to ask why the picture was not done. Chu Ta did not answer but dipped a brush in ink and with a few strokes drew a splendid fish. "If it is so easy," asked the patron, "why didn't you give me the picture three years ago?" Again, Chu Ta did not answer. Instead, he opened the door of a large cabinet. Thousands of pictures of fish tumbled out.

Most writers develop little rituals that help them practise their writing. A ritual is a *repeated pattern of behaviour* that provides structure, security, and a sense of progress to the one who practises it. Creating your own writing rituals and making them part of your regular routine will help reduce that dreaded initial panic and enable you to call upon your writing process with confidence when you need it.

PLACE, TIME, AND TOOLS

Some writers work best in pen and ink, sprawled on their beds in the afternoon while pets snooze on nearby blankets. Others start at 8 A.M. and rely on hard chairs, clean tables, and a handful of pencils sharpened to needle points. Still others are most comfortable with their keyboards and word processors at their desks or in the computer lab. Legal-sized pads help some writers produce, while others feel motivated by spiral notebooks with pictures of mountain streams on the covers. Only you can determine which place, time, and tools give you the best support as a writer.

The place where you write is also extremely important. If you are writing in a computer lab, you have to adapt to that place, but if you write a draft in longhand or on your own word processor, you can choose the place yourself. In selecting a place, keep the following tips in mind:

- **Keep distractions minimal.** Some people simply can't write in the kitchen, where the refrigerator is distractingly close, or in a room that has a TV in it. On the other hand, a public place—a library, an empty classroom, a cafeteria—can be fine as long as the surrounding activity does not disturb you.

- **Control interruptions.** If you can close the door to your room and work without interruptions, fine. But even then, other people often assume that you want to take a break when they do. Choose a place where you can decide when it's time to take a break.

- **Have access to notes, journal, textbooks, sources, and other materials.** If the place is totally quiet but you don't have room to work or access to important notes or sources, you still may not make much progress. Whatever you need—a desk to spread your work out on, access to notes and sources, extra pens, or computer disks—make sure your place has it.

The time of day you write and the tools you write with can also affect your attitude and efficiency. Some people like to write early in the morning, before their busy days start; others like to write in the evening, after classes or work. Whatever time you choose, try to write regularly—at least three days a week—at about the same time. If you're trying to get in shape by jogging, swimming, or doing aerobics, you wouldn't exercise for five straight hours on Monday and then take four days off. Like exercise, writing requires regular practice and conditioning.

Your writing tools—pen, pencil, paper, legal pads, four by six inch index cards, notebooks, computer—should also be comfortable for you. Some writers like to make notes with pencil and paper and write drafts on computers; some like to do all composing on computers. As you try different combinations of tools, be aware of how you feel and whether your tools make you more effective. If you feel comfortable, it will be easier to establish rituals that lead to regular practice.

Rituals are important because they help you with the most difficult part of writing—getting started. So use your familiar place, time, and tools to trick yourself into getting some words down on paper. Your mind will devise clever schemes to avoid writing those first 10 words—watching TV, balancing your chequebook, drinking some more coffee, or calling a friend and whining together about all the writing you have to do. But if your body has been through the ritual before, it will walk calmly to your favourite place, where all your tools are ready (perhaps bringing the mind kicking and screaming all the way). Then, after you get the first 10 words down, the mind will say, "Hey, this isn't so bad—I've got something to say about that!" And off you'll go.

Each time you perform your writing ritual, the *next* time you write will be that much easier. Soon, your ritual will let you know: *"This is where you write. This is when you write. This is what you write with."* No fooling around. Just writing.

ENERGY AND ATTITUDE

Once you've tricked yourself into the first 10 words, you need to keep your attitude positive and your energy high. When you see an intimidating wall starting to form in front of you, don't ram your head into it; figure out a way to sneak around it. Try these few tricks and techniques:

- **Start anywhere, quickly.** No law says that when you sit down to write a draft, you have to "begin at the beginning." If the first sentence is hard to write, begin with the first thoughts that come to mind. Or begin with a good example from your experience. Use that to get you going; then come back and rewrite your beginning after you've figured out what you want to say.

- **Write the easiest parts first.** Forcing yourself to start a piece of writing by working on the hardest part first is a sure way to make yourself hate writing. Take the path of least resistance. If you can't get your thesis to come out right, jot down more examples. If you can't think of examples, go back to brainstorming.

- **Keep moving.** Once you've plunged in, write as fast as you can—whether you are scribbling ideas out with a pencil or hitting the keys of a typewriter or a computer. Maintain your momentum. Reread if you need to, but then plunge ahead.

- **Quit when you know what comes next.** When you do have to quit for the day, stop at a place where you know what comes next. Don't drain the well dry; stop in the middle of something you know how to finish. Make a few notes about what you need to do next and circle them. Leave yourself an easy place to get started next time.

One of the most important strategies for every writer is to *give yourself a break from the past and begin with a fresh image.* In many fields—mathematics, athletics, art, engineering—some people are late bloomers. Don't let that C or D you once got in English hold you back now like a ball and chain. Imagine yourself cutting the chain and watching the ball roll away for good. Now you are free to start fresh with a clean slate. Your writing rituals should include only positive images about the writer you are right now and realistic expectations about what you can accomplish.

- **Visualize yourself writing.** Successful athletes know how to visualize a successful tennis swing, a basketball free throw, or a baseball swing. When you are planning your activities for the day, visualize yourself writing at your favourite place. Seeing yourself doing your writing will enable you to start writing more quickly and maintain a positive attitude.

- **Discover and emphasize the aspects of writing that are fun for you.** Emphasize whatever is enjoyable for you—discovering an idea, getting the organization of a paragraph to come out right, clearing the unnecessary words and junk out of your writing. Concentrating on the parts you enjoy will help you make it through the tougher parts.

- **Set modest goals for yourself.** Don't aim for the stars; just work on a sentence. Don't measure yourself against some great writer. Compare what you write to what *you* have written before.

- **Congratulate yourself for the writing you do.** Writing is hard work; you're using words to create ideas and meanings literally out of nothing. So pat yourself on the back occasionally. Keep in mind the immortal words of comedian and playwright Steve Martin: "I think I did pretty well, considering I started out with nothing but a bunch of blank paper."

KEEPING A JOURNAL

Many writers keep some kind of notebook in which they write down their thoughts for later use. Some writers call it a *journal,* a place for their day-to-day thoughts. Other writers call it a *daybook,* a place to record ideas, collected information, possible outlines, titles, questions—anything related to the process of writing, thinking, and learning. Scientists and social scientists keep daily logs in which they record data or describe behaviour. The word *journal* is the general term referring to "a place for daily writing." Whatever you call it, it should become part of your writing ritual. In it should go all kinds of writing. Bits and pieces of experience or memory that might come in handy later. Summary/responses of essays you read. In-class write-to-learn entries. Plans for writing your essays. A log of your writing plans and the writing problems you face. Postscripts on your writing process. Your journal is a place to practise, a closet where all your "fish paintings" go.

As the following list indicates, there are many kinds of journal entries, but they fall into three categories: *Reading Entries, Write-to-Learn Entries,* and *Writing Entries.* Reading entries help you understand and actively respond to student or professional writing. Write-to-learn entries help you summarize, react to, or question ideas or essays discussed in class. Writing entries help you warm up, test ideas, make writing plans, practise rhetorical strategies, or solve specific writing problems. All three kinds of journal writing, however, take advantage of the unique relationship between thinking, writing, and learning. Simply put, writing helps you learn what you know (and don't know) by shaping your thoughts into language.

Reading Entries

- **Prereading journal entries.** Before you read an essay, read the head-note and write for five minutes on the topic of the essay—what you know about the subject, what related experiences you have had, and what opinions you hold. After you write your entry, the class can discuss the topic before you read the essay. The result? Your reading will be more active, engaged, and responsive.

- **Double-entry logs.** Draw a line vertically down a sheet of paper. On the left-hand side, summarize key ideas as you reread an essay. On the right-hand side, write down your reactions, responses, and questions. Writing while you read helps you understand and respond more thoroughly.

- **Essay annotations.** Writing your comments in the margin as you read is sometimes more efficient than writing separate journal entries.

- **Vocabulary entries.** Looking up unfamiliar words in a dictionary and writing out definitions in your journal will make you a much more accurate reader. Often an essay's thesis, meaning, or tone will hinge on the meanings of a few key words.

- **Summary/response entries.** Double-entry logs help you understand while you reread, but a short one-paragraph summary and one-paragraph response after you finish your rereading helps you focus on both the main ideas of a passage and your own key responses.

Write-to-Learn Entries

- **Lecture/discussion entries.** At key points in a class lecture or discussion, your teacher may ask you to write for five minutes by responding to a few questions: What is the main idea of the discussion? What one question would you like to ask? How does the topic of discussion relate to the essay that you are currently writing?

- **Responses to essays.** Before discussing an essay, write for a few minutes to respond to the following questions: What is the main idea of this essay? What do you like best about the essay? What is confusing, misleading, or wrong in this essay? What strategies illustrated in this essay will help you with your own writing?

- **Time-out responses.** During a controversial discussion or argument about an essay, your teacher may stop the class, take time out, and ask you to write for five minutes to respond to several questions: What key issue is the class debating? What are the main points of disagreement? What is your opinion? What evidence, either in the essay or in your experience, supports your opinion?

Writing Entries

- **Warming up.** Writing, like any other kind of activity, improves when you loosen up, stretch, get the kinks out, practise a few lines. Any daybook or journal entry gives you a chance to warm up.

- **Collecting and shaping exercises.** Some journal entries will help you collect information by observing, remembering, or investigating people, places, events, or objects. You can also record quotations or startling statistics for future writing topics. Other journal entries suggested in each chapter of this book will help you practise organizing your information. Strategies of development, such as comparison/contrast, definition, classification, or process analysis will help you discover and shape ideas.

- **Writing for a specific audience.** In some journal entries, you need to play a role. Imagine that you are in a specific situation, writing for a defined audience. For example, you might write a letter of application for a job or letter to a friend explaining why you've chosen a certain program.

- **Revision plans and postscripts.** Your journal is also the place to keep a log—a running account of your writing plans, revision plans, problems, and solutions. Include your research notes, peer responses, and postscripts on your writing process in this log.

- **Imitating styles of writers.** Use your journal to copy passages from writers you like. Practise imitating their styles on different topics. Also, try simply transcribing a few paragraphs. Even copying effective writers' words will reveal some of their secrets for successful writing.

- **Writing free journal entries.** Use your journal to record ideas, reactions to people on campus, events in the news, reactions to controversial articles in the campus newspaper, conversations after class or work, or just your private thoughts.

For each of these writing entries, let your ideas flow easily. Don't stop to fix spelling or punctuation. Focus on key images from your train of thought.

Below is a sample of a freewriting entry. The author, Terri Ciccarello, had originally decided to write about a bumper sticker that she had seen, but the more she wrote, the more it suggested related ideas to her. Although she never wrote an essay about that bumper sticker, the theme of being an individual and wanting to make the world a better place was an undercurrent in several of her essays. Articulating these questions helped her discover what she wanted to write about.

I just bought a bumper sticker, white writing on black that reads, "Are we having fun yet?" It struck me as funny. The purpose of that bumper sticker for those who display it is to make a statement about a way of life. Are we having fun yet? It conveys a sense of dissatisfaction at the way life is supposed to be. It's an attitude. Why does it have to be structured the way it is? Does everyone have to fit in? Is this it? Is this all? Are we having fun yet? Are we supposed to be? When do I get to do what I want to do? Why don't things go my way? Can't I play by my own rules?

That seems like a lot of "message" in one little saying, but when I read it for the first time, that's what it brought to my mind. So, I was part of the audience. I think a lot of people, especially young people are the intended audience for this sticker. Young people who are still idealistic; who think that maybe there is still time to change the world. Young people who are brought into society they didn't organize and if they had, it would have been done differently. Young people who want to be individuals when they "grow up," not just another nameless faceless joe blow on the street. Are we having fun yet? When is it our turn to run the show?

Terri Ciccarello

■ WARMING UP: JOURNAL EXERCISES   Choose three of the exercises below and write for 10 minutes on each. Date and number each entry.

1. Make an "authority" list of activities, subjects, ideas, places, people, or events that you already know something about. List as many topics as you can. If your reaction is "I'm not really an *authority* on anything," then imagine you've met someone from another school, province, country, or historical period. With that person as your audience, what are you an "authority" on?

2. Choose one activity, sport, or hobby that you do well and that others might admire you for. In the form of a letter to a friend, describe the steps or stages of the process through which you acquired that skill or ability.

3. In two or three sentences, complete the following thought: "I have trouble writing because . . ."

4. In a few sentences, complete the following thought: "In my previous classes and from my own writing experience, I've learned that the three most important rules about writing are . . ."

5. Describe your own writing rituals. *When, where,* and *how* do you write best?

6. Write an open journal entry. Describe events from your day, images, impressions, bits of conversation—anything that catches your interest. For possible ideas for open journal entries, read the following essay by Roy Hoffman.

PROFESSIONAL WRITING

ON KEEPING A JOURNAL
ROY HOFFMAN

In a Newsweek on Campus *essay, Roy Hoffman describes his own experience, recording events and trying out ideas just as an artist doodles on a sketch pad. Your own journal entries about events, images, descriptions of people, and bits of conversation will not only improve your writing but also become your own personal time capsule, to dig up and reread in the year 2020.*

Wherever I go I carry a small notebook in my coat or back pocket for thoughts, observations and impressions. As a writer I use this notebook as an artist would a sketch pad, for stories and essays, and as a sporadic journal of my comings and goings. When I first started keeping notebooks, though, I was not yet a professional writer. I was still in college. **(1)**

I made my first notebook entries . . . just after my freshman year, in what was actually a travel log. A buddy and I were setting out to trek from our Alabama hometown to the distant tundra of Alaska. With unbounded enthusiasm I began: "Wild, crazy ecstasy wants to wrench my head from my body." The log, written in a university composition book, goes on to chronicle our adventures in the land where the sun never sets, the bars never close and the prepipeline employment prospects were so bleak we ended up taking jobs as night janitors. **(2)**

When I returned to college that fall I had a small revelation: the world around me of libraries, quadrangles, Frisbees and professors was as rich with material for my journals and notebooks as galumphing moose and garrulous fishermen. **(3)**

These college notebooks, which built to a pitch my senior year, are gold mines to me now. Classrooms, girlfriends, cups of coffee and lines of poetry—from mine to John Keats's—float by like clouds. As I lie beneath these clouds again, they take on familiar and distinctive shapes. **(4)**

Though I can remember the campus's main quadrangle, I see it more vividly when I read my description of school on a visit during summer break: "the muggy, lassitudinal air . . . the bird noises that can not be pointed to, the summer emptiness that grows emptier with a few students squeaking by the library on poorly oiled bicycles." An economics professor I fondly remember returns with less fondness in my notebooks, "staring down at the class with his equine face." And a girl I had a crush on senior year, whom I now recall mistily, reappears with far more vitality as "the ample, slightly-gawky, whole-wheat, fractured object of my want gangling down the hall in spring heat today." **(5)**

When, in reading over my notebooks, I am not peering out at quadrangles, midterm exams, professors or girlfriends, I see a portrait of my parents and hometown during holidays and occasional weekend breaks. Like a wheel, home revolves, each turn regarded differently depending on the novel or political essay I'd been most influenced by the previous semester. **(6)**

Mostly, though, in wandering back through my notebooks, I meet someone who could be my younger brother: the younger version of myself. The younger me seems moodier, more inquisitive, more fun-loving and surprisingly eager to stay up all night partying or figuring out electron orbitals for a 9 A.M. exam. The younger me wanders through a hall of mirrors of the self, writes of "seeing two or three of myself on every corner," and pens long meditations on God and society before scribbling in the margin, "what a child I am." The younger me also finds humor in trying to keep track of this hall of mirrors, commenting in ragged verse. (7)

I hope that one day
Some grandson or cousin
Will read these books,
And know that I was
Once a youth
Sitting in drugstores with
Anguished looks.
And poring over coffee,
And should have poured
The coffee
Over these lines. (8)

I believe that every college student should attempt to keep some form of notebook, journal or diary. A notebook is a secret garden in which to dance, sing, muse, wander, perform handstands, even cry. In the privacy of this little book, you can make faces, curse, turn somersaults and ask yourself if you're *really* in love. A notebook or journal is one of the few places you can call just your own. (9)

. . . Journal writing suffers when you let someone, in your mind, look over your shoulder. Honesty wilts when a parent, teacher or friend looms up in your imagination to discourage you from putting your *true* thoughts on the page. Journal writing also runs a related hazard: the dizzying suspicion that one day your private thoughts, like those of Samuel Pepys or Virginia Woolf, will be published in several volumes and land up required reading for English 401. How can you write comfortably when the eyes of all future readers are upon you? Keep your notebooks with the abandon of one who knows his words will go up in smoke. Then you might really strike fire a hundred years or so from now if anyone cares to pry. (10)

By keeping notebooks, you improve your writing ability, increasing your capacity to communicate both with yourself and others. By keeping notebooks, you discover patterns in yourself, whether lazy ones that need to be broken or healthy ones that can use some nurturing. By keeping notebooks, you heighten some moments and give substance to others: even a journey to the washateria offers potential for some offbeat journal observations. And by keeping notebooks while still in college, you chart a terrain that, for many, is more dynamically charged with ideas and discussions than the practical, workaday world just beyond. Notebooks, I believe, not only help us remember this dynamic charge, but also help us sustain it. **(11)**

Not long ago, while traveling with a friend in Yorktown, Va., I passed by a time capsule buried in the ground in 1976, intended to be dug up in 2076. Keeping notebooks and journals is rather like burying time capsules into one's own life. There's no telling what old rock song, love note, philosophical complaint or rosy Saturday morning you'll unearth when you dig up these personal time capsules. You'll be able to piece together a remarkable picture of where you've come from, and may well get some important glimmers about where you're going. **(12)**

PURPOSES AND PROCESSES FOR WRITING

LEARNING OUTCOMES

After reading this chapter you will have learned that

- purpose guides the writing process

- the stages of writing are distinct: collecting, shaping, drafting, and revising

- the "rules" of writing vary with purpose, audience, occasion, and genre

The writing for this course (and the structure of this textbook) starts with the premise that effective communication begins with learning. It also assumes that learning results—at least in part—from your written efforts to make connections and see relationships between your own observations and experience and the written or collected knowledge of others. There are four important sources for learning, writing, and communication:

- observing and describing the world around you
- remembering and drawing on your experiences
- reading and responding to textual material
- investigating knowledge through interviews, surveys, and library sources

Writing, as a means of learning and communicating, begins with what you see and have experienced. It then makes use of what you're reading in texts, hearing in lectures, finding out at work, or learning from friends and family.

■ FREEWRITING: INVENTORY OF YOUR WRITING

Before you read further in this chapter, take out a pen or pencil and a piece of paper and inventory what you have written in the last year or two. Brainstorm a list of everything you can think of: grocery lists, letters, wedding invitations, reports, school essays, notes to friends, applications for jobs, memos to your boss. Then for one of your longer writing projects, jot down several sentences describing the situation that called for that piece of writing—*when* you did it, *whom* you wrote it for, *what* its purpose was, *where* you wrote it, and *how* you went about writing it.

Most good writing has a personal dimension. It may be about the writer personally or it may address a subject or an idea the writer cares about. It begins with honesty, curiosity, inquiry, and even vulnerability. Good writers assert themselves, knowing that they are vulnerable to other people's criticism. They take risks—sometimes writing on subjects they don't completely understand—knowing that taking their thoughts to a public forum is one way to actively engage the information that threatens to overwhelm them. By continually probing and learning, being honest with themselves, and accepting risks, writers can use their writing to teach themselves as well as their readers.

PROFESSIONAL WRITING

MEMOIRS AND DIARIES
TING-XING YE

Ting-xing Ye is the author of A Leaf in the Bitter Wind *which chron-icles the story of her life in China. In the following essay she explains her reason for writing this memoir. Now a Canadian citizen, Ye lives in Orillia, Ontario, with author William Bell.*

After my memoir, *A Leaf in the Bitter Wind* was published, my friends asked me how I felt about revealing my personal life for all to see. Was I comfortable with questions from TV interviewers, radio hosts? Weren't reviews and analyses in the press intrusive?

As an English interpreter for the government of China who had frequent contact with foreigners, I knew the English word "pri-vacy," and I knew there is no equivalent word in Chinese. Privacy to me was an unheard-of luxury in a country where everybody knows everything about everybody else. It was not until my defec-tion to Canada in 1987 that I truly understood the concept of pri-vacy and the safeguards people erect to defend it.

None of which, however, made *A Leaf in the Bitter Wind* easy to write. In fact, the book began as a record of my life written for my daughter Qi-meng, whose father has kept her from me since I split with him in 1987, when she was six years old. The bare record I began one spring day soon blossomed. Jotted notes became para-graphs; pages grew into chapters as I remembered detail and dia-logue; chapters called for yet more chapters. Early in the process my husband, writer William Bell, convinced me that my life story would be interesting to others, and that I should try to publish it.

On my computer screen I saw myself as a young girl in a queue outside a Shanghai hospital on a windy fall afternoon, waiting to receive the small wooden tablet that would gain me admittance to see my mother, who had just undergone an operation for stomach cancer. I relived my grief and dread when I was denied entry because I couldn't remember her bed number.

I experienced once more the debilitating guilt I had felt on the prison farm where, at seventeen years of age, under psychological torture and interrogation, I betrayed friends accused of "engaging in counter revolutionary activities." It was here that the pain of writing a memoir was most keenly felt. I couldn't leave events out of the story because they cast me in a dark light.

Now, looking back at that painful two-year process, during which I often had to move away from my desk so my tears wouldn't drop onto the keyboard, I realize I came through it with reasonable calm. The manuscript weighed heavily in my hand; there was a great deal for Qi-meng to read, and for interested readers to discover. As for me, I found peace with my past, especially the guilt I carried with me all my life—for a childhood wish and for the estrangement of friends.

PURPOSES FOR WRITING

Getting a good grade, making a million dollars, or contributing to society may be among your motives for writing. However, as a writer, you also have more specific purposes for writing. These purposes help you make key decisions about content, structure, and style. When your main purpose is to *express* your feelings, you may write a private entry in your journal. When your main purpose is to *explain* how your sales promotion increased the number of your company's customers, you may write a factual report to your boss. When your main purpose is to *persuade* others to see a movie that you like, you may write a review for the local newspaper. In each case, the intended purpose—your desired effect on your audience—helps determine what you write and how you write it.

WRITER-BASED PURPOSES

Because writing is, or should be, for yourself first of all, everything you write involves at least some purpose that benefits you. Of course, expressing yourself is a fundamental purpose of all writing. Without the satisfaction of expressing your thoughts, feelings, reactions, knowledge, or questions, you might not make the effort to write in the first place.

A closely related purpose is learning: Writing helps you discover what you think or feel, simply by using language to identify and compose your thoughts. Writing not only helps you form ideas but actually promotes observing and remembering. If you write down what you observe about people, places, or things, you can actually "see" them more clearly. Similarly, if you write down facts, ideas, experiences, or reactions to your readings, you will remember them longer. Writing and rewriting facts, dates, definitions, impressions, or personal experiences will improve your powers of recall on such important occasions as examinations and job interviews.

SUBJECT- AND AUDIENCE-BASED PURPOSES

Although some writing is intended only for yourself—such as entries in a diary, lists, class notes, reminders—much of your writing will be read by others, by those readers who constitute your "audience."

- You may write to *inform* others about a particular subject—to tell them about the key facts, data, feelings, people, places, or events.

- You may write to *explain* to your readers what something means, how it works, or why it happens.

- You may write to *persuade* others to believe or do something—to convince others to agree with your judgment about a book, record, or restaurant, or to persuade them to take a certain class, vote for a certain candidate, or buy some product you are advertising.

- You may write to *explore* ideas and "truths," to examine how your ideas have changed, to ask questions that have no easy answers, and then to share your thoughts and reflections with others.

- You may write to *entertain*—as a primary purpose in itself or as a purpose combined with informing, explaining, persuading, or exploring. Whatever your purposes may be, good writing both teaches and pleases. Remember, too, that your readers will learn more, remember more, or be more convinced when your writing contains humour, wit, or imaginative language.

COMBINATIONS OF PURPOSES

In many cases, you write with more than one purpose in mind. Purposes may appear in combinations, connected in a sequence, or actually overlapping. Initially, you may take notes about a subject to learn and remember, but later you may want to inform others about what you have discovered. Similarly, you may begin by writing to express your feelings about a movie that you loved or that upset you; later, you may wish to persuade others to see it—or not to see it.

Purposes can also contain each other, like Chinese boxes, or overlap, blurring the distinctions. An explanation of how an automobile works will contain information about that vehicle. An attempt to persuade someone to buy an automobile may contain an explanation of how it handles and information about its body style or engine. Usually, writing to persuade others will contain explanations and basic information, but the reverse is not necessarily true; you can write simply to give information, without trying to persuade anyone to do anything.

SUBJECT, PURPOSE, AND THESIS

The *thesis, claim,* or *main idea* in a piece of writing is related to your purpose. As a writer, you usually have a purpose in mind that serves as a guide while you gather information about your subject and think about your audience. However, as you collect and record information, impressions, and ideas you gradually narrow your subject to a specific topic and thus clarify your purpose. You bring your purpose into sharper and sharper focus—as if progressing on a target from the outer circles to the bull's-eye—until you have narrowed your purpose down to a central thesis. The thesis is the dominant idea, explanation, evaluation, or recommendation that you want to impress upon your readers.

The following examples illustrate how a writer moves from a general subject, guided by purpose, to a specific thesis or claim.

Subject	Purpose	Thesis, Claim, or Main Idea
Childhood experiences	To *express* your feelings and explain how one childhood experience was important.	The relentless competition between my sisters and me distorted my easygoing personality.
Heart disease	To *inform* readers about relationships between Type A personalities and heart attacks.	Type A personalities do not necessarily have an abnormally high risk of suffering heart attacks.
The death penalty	To *persuade* readers that the death penalty should be used.	Despite our belief that killing is wrong, the death penalty is fair, just, and humane.

PURPOSE AND AUDIENCE

Writing for yourself is relatively easy; after all, you already know your audience and can make spontaneous judgments about what is essential and what is not. However, when your purpose is to communicate to other readers, you need to analyze your audience. Your writing will be more effective if you can anticipate what your readers know and need to know, what they are interested in, and what their beliefs or attitudes are. As you write for different readers, you will select different kinds of information, organize it in different ways, or write in a more formal or less formal style.

■ FREEWRITING: WRITING FOR DIFFERENT AUDIENCES

Before you read further, get a pen or pencil and several sheets of paper and do the following exercise:

1. For your eyes only, write about your college cafeteria. Write for four minutes.

2. On a second sheet of paper, describe the cafeteria for the members of your class; you will read it aloud to the class. Stop after four minutes.

3. On a third sheet of paper, write a letter to the president of the college describing the cafeteria. Stop after four minutes.

AUDIENCE ANALYSIS

If you are writing to communicate to other readers, analyzing your probable audience will help you answer some basic questions:

  • How much information or evidence is enough? What should I assume my audience already knows? What should I not tell them? What do they believe? Will they readily agree with me or will they be antagonistic?

  • How should I organize my writing? How can I get my readers' attention? Can I just describe my subject and tell a story or should I analyze everything in a logical order? Should I put my best examples or arguments first or last?

  • Should I write informally, with simple sentences and easy vocabulary, or should I write in a more elaborate or specialized style, with technical vocabulary?

Analyze your audience by considering the following questions. As you learn more about your audience, the possibilities for your own role as a writer will become clearer.

1. **Audience profile.** How narrow or broad is your audience? Is it a narrow and defined audience—a single person, such as your Aunt Mary, or a group with clear common interests, such as the zoning board in your city or the readers of *Cottage Life?* Is it a broad and diverse audience: educated readers who wish to be informed on current events, Canadian voters as a whole, or residents of your province? Do your readers have identifiable roles? Can you determine their age, sex, economic status, ethnic background, or occupational category?

2. **Audience-subject relationship.** Consider what your readers know about your subject. If they know very little about it, you'll need to explain the basics; if they already know quite a bit, you can go straight to more dif-

ficult or complex issues. Also estimate their probable attitude toward this subject. Are they likely to be sympathetic or hostile?

3. **Audience-writer relationship.** What is your relationship with your readers? Do you know each other personally? Do you have anything in common? Will your audience be likely to trust what you say, or will they be skeptical about your judgments? Are you the expert on this particular subject and the readers the novices? Or are you the novice and your readers the experts?

4. **Writer's role.** To communicate effectively with your audience, you should also consider your own role or perspective. Of the many roles that you could play (friend, big sister or brother, business student, music fan, employee of a fast-food restaurant, and so on), choose one that will be effective for your purpose and audience. If, for example, you are writing to sixth-graders about nutrition, you could choose the perspective of a concerned older brother or sister. Your writing might be more effective, however, if you assume the role of a person who has worked in fast-food restaurants for three years and knows what goes into hamburgers, french fries, and milkshakes.

Writers may write to real audiences, or they may create audiences. Sometimes the relationship between writer and reader is real (sister writing to brother), so the writer starts with a known audience and writes accordingly. Sometimes, however, writers begin and gradually discover or create an audience in the process of writing. Knowing the audience guides the writing, but the writing may construct an audience as well.

THE WRITING SITUATION

Taken together, the writer's purpose or aim, the subject, and the probable audience (whether yourself or others) define the writing situation. Sometimes an instructor or employer assigns you a specific writing situation. At other times, you yourself construct a situation from scratch.

The components of the writing situation—writer, subject, purpose, thesis, and audience—are so interrelated that a change in one may affect the other three. As you write, therefore, you do not always follow a step-by-step order. You may begin, for example, with a specific audience on which you wish to make an impression; as you analyze the audience, you decide what subject and purpose would be most appropriate. Conversely, you may start with an interesting subject but no clear sense of purpose or audience. Or you may be asked to write for a certain audience, and then you discover that its needs and expectations have led you to discover or modify your purpose or subject. In short, subject, purpose, thesis, and audience are all modified, reconsidered, and revised as you write.

The following example illustrates how subject, purpose, and audience combine to define a writing situation.

> In response to a request by an editor of a college marketing pamphlet, a student decides to write an essay explaining the advantages of the social and academic life at his college. According to the editor, the account needs to be realistic but should also promote the college. It shouldn't be too academic and stuffy—the college catalogue itself contains all the basic information—but it should give high school graduates a flavour of college life. The student decides to write a narrative account of his most interesting experiences during his first week at college.

PURPOSE AND AUDIENCE
IN TWO ESSAYS

The two short essays that follow appeared as articles in newspapers. Both relate the writers' own experiences. They are similar in form but have different purposes and appeal to different kinds of readers. As you read each essay, decide which one you find more interesting—and why.

PROFESSIONAL WRITING

HIS NAME WAS SANDER,
AND HE WAS MY BEST FRIEND
SANDY WOLOFSKY

"I'm calling to warn you," my friend at CTV whispered through the phone lines last Tuesday. "The first images just came in, and I'm running them in the second block." (1)

"Make sure," I managed to say through my hyperventilating sobs, "you pronounce his last name right. It's TOO-Nes. Okay? TOO-Nes." (2)

He didn't answer. (3)

If I had forgotten why I hated working in daily news, the memory was reignited within 15 minutes. Somewhere stuck amid a hodgepodge of superfluity on the network's newscast was 10 seconds of my best friend in the entire world—his foot, his notebook, and a voice-over that included the words "believed to be a Dutch journalist." For almost 24 hours CTV's *N1 News* used the same images with the same misrepresented copy. (4)

He *was* a journalist, he *was* Dutch, and it *was* Sander's body. There was no "believed to be" anywhere to be found in the equation. In describing him that way, the script dishonoured a colleague, a moral human being who died at the age of 30 in East Timor in pursuit of a moral cause—a cause, I might add, that news networks are more than willing to exploit. (5)

As a journalist, I am always being told: People are tired of world tragedies. Can't you put something happy on the news? Can't you put something about people solving problems in the news? (6)

That's exactly what Sander was trying to do: solve problems. He was a journalist with a genuine sense of morality. Like so many other grads of Massachusetts' Hampshire College, he believed that every one of us shares a responsibility to help make the world a better place. He believed that if he told the story of human suffering passionately enough, and often enough, there would be changes. He was a great believer in the "if nobody reports on a massacre, did it really happen?" theory of journalism. So he went back to East Timor the minute he heard that the United Nations troops were landing. (7)

When he left a message on my machine a week ago Sunday, it was simply to say: "Hey, Sandy, haven't talked since the elections started, just checking in to see how you are and hoping that you are okay." There was nothing about East Timor. (8)

On Tuesday afternoon I had this sudden urge, despite work, to write him an E-mail. "Sander . . . thinking of you every day . . . don't do anything stupid, okay? Hope you are not heading back into Timor . . . And Jerk, if you do, FOLLOW THE PACK!!!! I know it's against our religion—the pack journalism thing. I know you know better. I know you know that those are not the 'real' stories. WE ALL KNOW THAT. But please. Stay behind the UN folk and be a drone for once please. Okay? Luv ya, s." (9)

A couple of hours later I picked up my home phone to hear the familiar clicks of a faraway Third World phone line. It was Ian, Sander's friend, with the horrific news. As I was writing my E-mail, Sander was crawling away from Indonesian militiamen (a.k.a. thugs) intent on mutilating his body. It was as if my thoughts of him came from him thinking of me as he lay dying. (10)

Sander and I had been friends since our very first day at Hampshire College in 1987. Together we progressed from school to "real life" as journalists in Moscow. **(11)**

It was 4 a.m. in Moscow when I screamed uncontrollably into his ex-girlfriend's answering machine: *"Angela, wake up! Wake up! Sander's been killed in East Timor. Angela, waaake up!"* **(12)**

My sweet, darling, cherubic Sander. The person who, when I had mononucleosis, drove me home to Montreal instead of letting me lie miserably in a stuffy dorm room. The person who stood by me and accompanied me to KGB headquarters when they wanted to revoke my visa and kick me out of Russia for a story I had written. **(13)**

But for a few seconds on the CTV *National News* he was nothing but a foot and a notebook. The message sent was that this death is really not all that important: that nobody in Canada knows who he is, he doesn't have any important friends, so we don't really have to care what his name is and neither should you. **(14)**

Well, this nameless body so unceremoniously displayed on millions of Canadian TV sets had plenty of Canadian friends. For all the years he and I went to school together in Massachusetts, he spent his holidays in Montreal with my friends and family. In Toronto live a whole group of former Moscow correspondents who knew and loved Sander. They would have known his name. And in Ottawa, up and down the hallowed diplomatic halls of Foreign Affairs, the list of people who dined, partied or travelled with Sander are too numerous to count. **(15)**

From London, Jakarta, Paris, Amsterdam, Darwin, Moscow, Utrecht, New Orleans, Toronto and Ottawa came calls from journalist and diplomat friends. From Miami, Amherst, San Francisco and just about every major American city came phone calls and E-mails from school friends. All this for one blond-haired, bullet-ridden dead "kid" who didn't merit the dignity of a name. **(16)**

In this age of big business and big news, names like Monica, JFK, Jr., and Diana Ross grab the headlines. The image of the journalist has become one of a faceless parasite intruding on families' private lives. It has skewed the reality that many journalists, like Sander Thoenes, are intrepid, courageous young minds in search of social justice and the truth. Unfortunately, exposing injustice is not a major money-maker, so these efforts are rarely disseminated to a larger community. Thus, when the journalists themselves become victims, they, like so many victims of injustice, are deemed unworthy of a face or a name. **(17)**

Sander knew nobody in the "Western world" really cared about Indonesia, let alone East Timor. But he did. He told me once that "you know the corruption here puts Russia to shame . . . but I really like the people. I feel like I've gotta do the reporting even if no one out there cares." **(18)**

That's why he was in East Timor, and why he was nowhere near the other journalists. Following the pack meant you got only what the officials wanted you to get. He was always one of the few to risk telling what "the people" had to say. He was off on his own to give dignity, a name and a human face to those who were suffering. He not only believed in the "if a massacre happens and nobody is there" theory, but practised it. He was never one to let victims remain nameless and faceless. **(19)**

And that's why I'm writing this story. To let everyone know that his name was Sander Thoenes and he was my best friend. I will miss him forever. **(20)**

PROFESSIONAL WRITING

I'M O.K., BUT YOU'RE NOT
ROBERT ZOELLNER

The American novelist John Barth, in his early novel, *The Floating Opera*, remarks that ordinary, day-to-day life often presents us with embarrassingly obvious, totally unsubtle patterns of symbolism and meaning—life in the midst of death, innocence vindicated, youth versus age, etc. **(1)**

The truth of Barth's insight was brought home to me recently while having breakfast in a lawn-bordered restaurant on College Avenue near the Colorado State University campus. I had asked to be seated in the smoking section of the restaurant—I have happily gone through three or four packs a day for the past 40 years. **(2)**

As it happened, the hostess seated me—I was by myself—at a little two-person table on the dividing line between the smoking and non-smoking sections. Presently, a well-dressed couple of advanced years, his hair a magisterial white and hers an electric blue, were seated in the non-smoking section five feet away from me. **(3)**

It was apparent within a minute that my cigarette smoke was bugging them badly, and soon the husband leaned over and asked me if I would please stop smoking. As a chronic smokestack, I normally comply, out of simple courtesy, with such requests. Even an addict such as myself can quit for as long as 20 minutes. **(4)**

But his manner was so self-righteous and peremptory—he reminded me of Lee Iacocca boasting about Chrysler—that the promptings of original sin, always a problem with me, took over. I quietly pointed out that I was in the smoking section—if only by five feet—and that that fact meant that I had met my social obligation to non-smokers. Besides, the idea of morning coffee without a cigarette was simply inconceivable to me—might as well ask me to vote Republican. **(5)**

The two of them ate their eggs-over-easy in hurried and sullen silence, while I chain-smoked over my coffee. As well as be hung for a sheep as a lamb, I reasoned. Presently they got up, paid their bill, and stalked out in an ambiance of affronted righteousness and affluent propriety. **(6)**

And this is where John Barth comes in. They had parked their car—a diesel Mercedes—where it could be seen from my table. And in the car, waiting impatiently, was a splendidly matched pair of pedigreed poodles, male and female. **(7)**

Both dogs were clearly in extremis, and when the back door of the car was opened, they made for the restaurant lawn in considerable haste. Without ado (no pun intended), the male did a doo-doo that would have done credit to an animal twice his size, and finished off with a leisurely, ruminative wee-wee. The bitch of the pair, as might be expected of any well-brought-up female of Republican proclivities, confined herself to a modest wee-wee, fastidious, diffident, and quickly executed. **(8)**

Having thus polluted the restaurant lawn, the four of them marshalled their collective dignity and drove off in a dense cloud of blue smoke—that lovely white Mercedes was urgently in need of a valve-and-ring job, its emission sticker an obvious exercise in creative writing. **(9)**

As I regretfully watched them go—after all, the four of them had made my day—it seemed to me that they were in something of a hurry, and I uncharitably wondered if the husband was not anxious to get home in order to light the first Fall fire in his moss-rock fireplace, or apply the Fall ration of chemical fertilizer to his doubtlessly impeccable lawn, thus adding another half-pound of particulates to the local atmosphere and another 10 pounds of nitrates and other poisons to the regional aquifers. But that, of course, is pure and unkindly speculation. **(10)**

In any case, the point of this real-life vignette, as John Barth would insist, is obvious. The current controversy over public smoking in Fort Collins is a clear instance of selective virtue at work, coming under the rubric of, what I do is perfectly OK, but what you do is perfectly awful. **(11)**

Questions for Writing and Discussion

1. Choosing only one adjective to describe your main reaction to each essay, answer the following question: "When I finished the _____ [Wolofsky/Zoellner] essay, I was _____ [intrigued, bored, amused, irritated, curious, confused, or _____] because _____. Explain your choice of adjectives in one or two sentences.

2. Referring to specific passages, explain the purpose and state the thesis or main point of each essay.

3. What personality or role does each writer project? Drawing from evidence in the essay, describe what you think both writers would be like if you met them.

4. Both of these essays appeared in newspapers. What kind of reader would find each essay interesting? What kind of reader would not enjoy each essay? For each essay, find examples of specific sentences, word choices, vocabulary, experiences, or references to culture or politics that would appeal to one reader but perhaps irritate another.

DIMENSIONS OF THE PROCESS

Processes for writing vary from one writer to the next and from one writing situation to the next. Most writers, however, can identify four basic stages, or dimensions, of their writing process: collecting, shaping, drafting, and revising. The writing situation may precede these stages—particularly if you are assigned a subject, purpose, audience, and form. Usually, however, you continue to narrow your subject, clarify your purpose, meet the needs of your audience, and modify your form as you work through the dimensions of your writing process.

COLLECTING

You may collect firsthand information, or you may rely on the data, experience, or expertise of others. In any case, writers constantly collect facts, impressions, opinions, and ideas that are relevant to their subjects, purposes, and audiences. Collecting involves observing, remembering, imagining, thinking, reading, listening, writing, investigating, talking, taking notes, and experimenting. Collecting also involves thinking about the relationships among the bits of information that you have collected.

SHAPING

Writers focus and organize the facts, examples, and ideas that they have collected into the recorded, linear form that is written language. A chronological order is just one of the shapes that a writer may choose to develop and organize experience. Such shaping strategies also help writers collect additional information and ideas. Reconstructing a chronological order may suggest some additional details.

DRAFTING

At some point, writers actually write down a rough version of what will evolve into the finished piece of writing. Drafting processes vary widely from one writer to the next. Some writers prefer to reread their collecting and shaping notes, find a starting point, and launch themselves—figuring out what they want to say as they write it. Other writers start with a plan—a mental strategy, a short list, or an outline—of how they wish to proceed. Whatever approach you use in your draft, write down as much as possible: You want to see whether the information is clear, whether your overall shape expresses and clarifies your purpose, and whether your content and organization meet the needs and expectations of your audience.

REVISING

When writers revise rough drafts, they literally "resee" their subjects—and then modify drafts to fit new visions. Revision is more than just tinkering with a word here and there; revision leads to larger changes—new examples or details, a different organization, or a new perspective. You accomplish these changes by adding, deleting, substituting, or reordering words, sentences, and paragraphs. Although revision begins the moment you get your first idea, most revisions are based on the reactions—or anticipated reactions—of the audience to your draft. You often play the role of audience yourself by putting the draft aside and rereading it later when you have some distance from your writing. Wherever you feel readers might not get your point, you revise to make it clearer. As a result of your rereading, you may change your thesis or write for an entirely different audience.

Editing—in contrast to revising—focusses on the minor changes that you make to improve the accuracy and readability of your language. You usually edit your essay to improve word choice, grammar, usage, or punctuation. You also use a computer spell-check program and proofread to catch typos and other surface errors.

THE WHOLE PROCESS

In practice, a writer's process rarely follows the simple, consecutive order that these four stages or dimensions suggest. The writing process is actually recursive: It begins at one point, goes on to another, comes back to the first, jumps to the third, and so forth. A stage may last hours or only a second or two. While writing a letter to a friend, you may collect, shape, revise, and edit in one quick draft; a research paper may require repeated shaping over a two-week period. As writers draft, they may correct a few mistakes or typos, but they may not proofread until many days later. In the middle of reorganizing an essay, writers often reread drafts, go back and ask more questions, and collect more data. Even while editing, writers may throw out several paragraphs, collect some additional information, and draft new sections.

In addition to the recursive nature of the writing process, keep in mind that writing often occurs during every stage, not just during drafting and revising. During collecting, you will be recording information and jotting down ideas. During shaping, you will be writing out trial versions that you may use later when you draft or revise. Throughout the writing process, you use your writing to modify your subject, purpose, audience, and form.

The most important point to keep in mind is that the writing process is unique to each writer and to each writing situation. What works for one writer may be absolutely wrong for you. Some writers compose nearly everything in their heads. Others write only after discussing the subject with friends or drawing diagrams and pictures.

During the writing process, you need to experiment with several collecting, shaping, and drafting strategies to see what works best for you and for a particular piece of writing. As long as your process works, however, it's legitimate—no matter how many times you backtrack and repeat stages. When you are struggling with a piece of writing, remember that numerous revisions are a normal part of the writing process—even for most professionals.

WRITING WITH COMPUTERS

The computer can assist you both as a writing tool and as a networking tool. Listed in the left-hand column are writing activities that a stand-alone computer provides. Listed in the right-hand column are the additional capabilities of computers tied into a network.

THE COMPUTER AS A WRITING TOOL	THE COMPUTER AS A NETWORKING TOOL
• Freewriting	• Access to bulletin boards
• Brainstorming	• E-mail messages
• Double-entry reading log	• E-mail essays or files
• Answers to "Wh" questions	• "Chat" dialogues
• Insert/delete sentences	• Postings to Class Forum
• Move paragraphs	• Access to online library catalogues
• Style/usage checkers	• Access to the Internet and the World Wide Web
• Thesaurus	
• Spelling checker	
• Print preview	

A WRITING PROCESS AT WORK: COLLECTING AND SHAPING

PROFESSIONAL WRITING

ATHLETES AND EDUCATION

NEIL H. PETRIE

In the following essay, which appeared in The Chronicle of Higher Education, *Neil H. Petrie argues that schools have a hypocritical attitude toward student athletes. Although most universities claim that their athletes—both male and female—are there to get a good education, in reality, the pressures on athletes compromise their academic careers. The problem, Petrie argues, is not the old cliché that jocks are dumb, but the endless hours devoted to practice or spent on road trips, which drain even the good student-athlete's physical and mental energies. Schools point with pride to a tiny number of athletes who become professionals, but much more frequently the system encourages athletes to settle for lower grades and incomplete programs. In far too many cases, athletes never graduate. These are the students whom, as Petrie says, "the system uses and then discards after the final buzzer."*

I have spent all my adult life in academe, first as a student and then as a professor. During that time I have seen many variations in the role of intercollegiate athletics in the university, and I've developed sharply split opinions on the subject. On one hand, I despise the system, clinging as it does to the academic body like a parasite. On the other hand, I feel sympathy and admiration for most of the young athletes struggling to balance the task of getting an education with the need to devote most of their energies to the excessive demands of the gym and the field. **(1)**

My earliest experiences with the intrusion of athletics into the classroom came while I was still a freshman at the University of Colorado. While I was in my English professor's office one day, a colleague of hers came by for a chat. Their talk turned to the football coach's efforts to court the favor of the teachers responsible for his gladiators by treating them to dinner and a solicitous discussion of the academic progress of the players. I vividly recall my professor saying, "He can take me out to dinner if he wants, but if he thinks I'll pass his knuckleheads just because of that, he'd better think again." **(2)**

Later, as a graduate teaching fellow, a lecturer, and then an assistant professor of English, I had ample opportunity to observe a Division I university's athletics program. I soon discovered that the prevailing stereotypes did not always apply. Athletes turned out to be as diverse as any other group of students in their habits, tastes, and abilities, and they showed a wide range of strategies for coping with the stress of their dual roles. **(3)**

Some of them were poor students. An extreme example was the All-American football player (later a successful pro) who saw college only as a step to a six-figure contract and openly showed his disdain for the educational process. Others did such marginal work in my courses that I got the feeling they were daring me to give them D's or F's. One woman cross-country star, who almost never attended my composition class, used to push nearly illiterate essays under my office door at odd hours. **(4)**

Yet many athletes were among the brightest students I had. Not so surprising, when you consider that, in addition to physical prowess, success in athletics requires intelligence, competitive drive, and dedication—all qualities that can translate into success in the classroom as well as on the field. The trouble is that the grinding hours of practice and road trips rob student athletes of precious study time and deplete their reserves of mental and physical energy. A few top athletes have earned A's; most are content to settle for B's or C's, even if they are capable of better. (5)

The athletes' educational experience can't help being marred by their numerous absences and divided loyalties. In this respect, they are little different from the students who attempt to go to college while caring for a family or working long hours at an outside job. The athletes, however, get extra help in juggling their responsibilities. Although I have never been bribed or threatened and have never received a dinner invitation from a coach, I am expected to provide extra time and consideration for athletes, far beyond what I give other students. (6)

Take the midterm grade reports, for example. At my university, the athletic department's academic counselor sends progress questionnaires to every teacher of varsity athletes. While the procedure shows admirable concern for the academic performance of athletes, it also amounts to preferential treatment. It requires teachers to take time from other teaching duties to fill out and return the forms for the athletes. (No other students get such progress reports.) If I were a cynic it would occur to me that the athletic department might actually be more concerned with athletes' eligibility than with their academic work. (7)

Special attendance policies for athletes are another example of preferential treatment. Athletes miss a lot of classes. In fact, I think the road trip is one of the main reasons that athletes receive a deficient education. You simply can't learn as much away from the classroom and the library as on the campus. Nevertheless, professors continue to provide make-up tests, alternative assignments, and special tutoring sessions to accommodate athletes. Any other student would have to have been very sick or the victim of a serious accident to get such dispensations. (8)

It is sad to see bright young athletes knowingly compromise their potential and settle for much less education than they deserve. It is infuriating, though, to see the ones less gifted academically exploited by a system that they do not comprehend and robbed of any possible chance to grow intellectually and to explore other opportunities. (9)

One specific incident illustrates for me the worst aspects of college athletics. It wasn't unusual or extraordinary—just the all-too-ordinary case of an athlete not quite good enough to make a living from athletics and blind to the opportunity afforded by the classroom. **(10)**

I was sitting in my office near the beginning of a term, talking to a parade of new advisees. I glanced up to see my entire doorway filled with the bulk of a large young man, whom I recognized as one of our basketball stars from several seasons ago who had left for the pros and now apparently come back. **(11)**

Over the next hour I got an intensive course on what it's like to be a college athlete. In high school, John had never been interested in much outside of basketball, and, like many other indifferent students, he went on to junior college on an athletic scholarship. After graduating, he came to the university, where he played for two more years, finishing out his eligibility. He was picked in a late round of the N.B.A. draft and left college, but in the end he turned out to be a step too slow for the pros. By that time he had a family to support, and when he realized he could never make a career of basketball, he decided to return to college. **(12)**

We both knew that his previous academic career hadn't been particularly focused, and that because of transferring and taking minimum course loads during the basketball season, he wouldn't be close to a degree. But I don't think either one of us was prepared for what actually emerged from our examination of his transcripts. It was almost as if he had never gone beyond high school. His junior-college transcript was filled with remedial and nonacademic courses. **(13)**

Credit for those had not transferred to the university. Over the next two years he had taken a hodgepodge of courses, mostly in physical education. He had never received any advice about putting together a coherent program leading to a degree. In short, the academic side of his college experience had been completely neglected by coaches, advisers, and, of course, John himself. **(14)**

By the time we had evaluated his transcripts and worked out a tentative course of study, John was in shock and I was angry. It was going to take him at least three years of full-time study to complete a degree. He thanked me politely for my time, picked up the planning sheets, and left. I was ashamed to be a part of the university that day. Why hadn't anyone in the athletic department ever told him what it would take to earn a degree? Or at least been honest enough to say, "Listen, we can keep you eligible and give you a chance to play ball, but don't kid yourself into thinking you'll be getting an education, too." **(15)**

I saw John several more times during the year. He tried for a while. He took classes, worked, supported his family, and then he left again. I lost track of him after that. I can only hope that he found a satisfying job or completed his education at some other institution. I know people say the situation has improved in the last few years, but when I read about the shockingly low percentages of athletes who graduate, I think of John. **(16)**

Colleges give student athletes preferential treatment. We let them cut classes. We let them slide through. We protect them from harsh realities. We applaud them for entertaining us and wink when they compromise themselves intellectually. We give them special dorms, special meals, special tutors, and a specially reprehensible form of hypocrisy. **(17)**

I can live with the thought of the athletes who knowingly use the college-athletics system to get their pro contracts or their devalued degrees. But I have trouble living with the thought of the ones whom the system uses and then discards after the final buzzer. **(18)**

PROFESSIONAL WRITING

ON WRITING "ATHLETES AND EDUCATION"

NEIL H. PETRIE

In the following postscript on his writing process, Neil Petrie describes why he wanted to write the paper, how he collected material to support his argument, and how he shaped and focussed his ideas as he wrote. His comments illustrate how his purpose—to expose the hypocrisies of college athletics—guided his writing of the essay. In addition, Petrie explains that other key questions affected the shape of his essay: how he should begin, where he should use his best example, and what words he should choose.

This essay has its origin, as all persuasive writing should, in a strongly held opinion. I'm always more comfortable if I care deeply about my subject matter. As a teacher, I hold some powerful convictions about the uneasy marriage of big-time athletics and higher education, and so I wanted to write an essay that would expose what I think are the dangers and hypocrisies of that system. **(1)**

At the beginning of my essay, I wanted to establish some authority to lend credibility to my argument. Rather than gather statistics on drop-out rates of student athletes or collect the opinions of experts, I planned to rely on my own experiences as both a student and teacher. I hoped to convince my readers that my opinions were based on the authority of firsthand knowledge. In this introduction I was also aware of the need to avoid turning off readers who might dismiss me as a "jock hater." I had to project my negative feelings about the athletic system while maintaining my sympathy with the individual student athletes involved in that system. The thesis, then, would emerge gradually as I accumulated the evidence; it would be more implied than explicitly stated. **(2)**

Gathering the material was easy. I selected a series of examples from my personal experiences as a college student and instructor, as well as anecdotes I'd heard from other instructors. Most of these stories were ones that I had shared before, either in private discussions with friends or in classrooms with students. **(3)**

Shaping the material was a little tougher. As I began thinking about my examples and how to order them, I saw that I really wanted to make two main points. The first was that most colleges give preferential treatment to athletes. The second point was that, despite the extra attention, the success of the athlete's academic career is often ignored by all parties involved. Many of my examples, I realized, illustrated the varieties of pressures put upon both athletes and instructors to make sure that the students at least get by in class and remain eligible. These examples seemed to cluster together because they showed the frustrations of teachers and the reactions of athletes trying to juggle sports and academics. This group would make a good introduction to my general exposé of the system. But I had one more example I wanted to use that seemed to go beyond the cynicism of some athletes or the hypocrisy of the educators. This was the case of John, an athlete who illustrated what I thought were the most exploitative aspects of varsity athletics. I originally planned on devoting the bulk of my essay to this story and decided to place it near the end where it would make my second point with maximum emotional effect. **(4)**

A two-part structure for the essay now emerged. In the first segment following my introductory paragraph, I gave a series of shorter examples, choosing to order them in roughly chronological order (paragraphs 2–4). I then moved from these specific details to a more general discussion of the demands placed upon both students and teachers, such as lengthy practice time, grade reports, road trips, and special attendance policies. This concluded my description of the way the system operates (paragraphs 5–8). **(5)**

Then it was time to shift gears, to provide a transition to the next part of my essay, to what I thought was my strongest example. I wanted the story of John to show how the system destroyed human potential. To do this, I needed to increase the seriousness of the tone in order to persuade the reader that I was dealing in more than a little bureaucratic boondoggling. I tried to set the tone by my word choice: I moved from words such as "sad," "compromise," and "settle" to words with much stronger emotional connotations such as "infuriating," "exploited," and "robbed," all in a single short transitional paragraph (paragraph 9). **(6)**

I then introduced my final extended example in equally strong language, identifying it as a worst-case illustration (paragraph 10). I elaborated on John's story, letting the details and my reactions to his situation carry the more intense outrage that I was trying to convey in this second part of the essay (paragraphs 10–16). The first version that I tried was a rambling narrative that had an overly long recounting of John's high school and college careers. So I tightened this section by eliminating such items as his progress through the ranks of professional basketball and his dreams of million-dollar contracts. I also cut down on a discussion of the various courses of study he was considering as options. The result was a sharper focus on the central issue of John's dilemma: the lack of adequate degree counseling for athletes. **(7)**

After my extended example, all that was left was the conclusion. As I wrote, I was very conscious of using certain devices, such as the repetition of key words and sentence patterns in paragraph seventeen ("We let them . . . We let them . . . We protect them . . . We applaud them . . . We give them . . .") to maintain the heightened emotional tone. I was also conscious of repeating the two-part structure of the essay in the last two paragraphs. I moved from general preferential treatment (paragraph 17) to the concluding and more disturbing idea of devastating exploitation (paragraph 18). **(8)**

On the whole, I believe that this essay effectively conveys its point through the force of accumulated detail. My personal experience was the primary source of evidence, and that experience led naturally to the order of the paragraphs and to the argument I wished to make: that while some athletes knowingly use the system, others are used and exploited by it. **(9)**

Questions for Writing and Discussion

1. In your notebook, describe how your extracurricular activities (athletics, jobs, clubs, or family obligations) have or have not interfered with your education. Recall one specific incident that illustrates how these activities affected your classwork—either positively or negatively.

2. Describe Petrie's audience and purpose for this essay. What sentences reveal his intended audience? What sentences reveal his purpose? What sentences contain his thesis, claim, or main idea? Do you agree with that thesis? Why or why not?

3. Reread Petrie's postscript. Based on his comments and on your reading of the essay, how does Petrie describe or label each of the following sections of his essay:

   paragraphs 1–4

   paragraphs 5–8

   paragraph 9

   paragraphs 10–16

   paragraphs 17–18.

4. Who do you think is most to blame for the situation that Petrie describes: The athletes themselves? The colleges for paying their scholarships and then ignoring them when they drop out? The students and alumni who pay to see their teams win?

5. Petrie does not explicitly suggest a solution to the problem that he describes. Assume, however, that he has been asked by the president of his university to propose a solution. Write the letter that you think Petrie would send to the president.

READING

LEARNING OUTCOMES

After reading this chapter you will have learned how to

- read actively and critically
- summarize and respond to an essay

At first glance, a chapter on reading in a textbook on writing may catch you by surprise. This chapter, however, is not about learning your abc's or about reading *The Cat in the Hat*. It is about learning to read texts actively and critically. It is about learning how to summarize and respond to what you read. It is about using reading—along with observing and remembering—as a source for your writing.

At the beginning of this chapter, we need to define two key terms: *texts* and *reading*. Normally, when you think about a text, you may think of a textbook. A text, however, can be any graphic matter—a textbook, an essay, a poem, a story, a newspaper editorial, a graph, a design, or an advertisement. Some people expand the definition of *texts* to include any thing or phenomenon in the world. In this widest sense, the layout of a restaurant, the behaviour of children on a playground, or clouds in the sky could be "texts" that can be read.

Similarly, the term *reading* has both narrow and broad senses. In a narrow sense, reading is just understanding words on a page. But reading has a variety of wider meanings as well. Reading can mean analyzing, as when an architect "reads" blueprints and knows how to construct a roof. Reading can mean interpreting, as when a sailor "reads" the sky and knows that the day will bring winds and rough weather. Reading can also mean examining media or cultural patterns and perceiving textual messages of sexism or racism. All of these "readings" require close, repeated observation of the text and an ability to engage, analyze, respond to, and interpret the text.

In this chapter, you will practise a fairly specific kind of textual reading. Most of the texts are essays on academic topics, and your reading will be active, critical, and responsive. Implied in active, critical reading is writing. Reading and writing work together to make reading more active and writing more effective. Reading and writing are so inseparable that we sometimes use the phrase "reading/writing" to discuss any reading activity. In addition, there is an essential third dimension to critical reading: discussion. This third dimension can take a variety of forms—sharing ideas in small groups, engaging in a class conversation, posting e-mail responses, or taking sides in a debate. Reading, writing, and discussing are all "reading" activities. We may be able to read the words on a page and write out our reactions, but we must also engage other readers' reactions and points of view in order to fully grasp the possible meanings of a text.

This chapter will show you how to use reading/writing/discussing strategies for three important tasks. First, you will learn how to write short critiques or summary/response essays that are frequent college and university writing assignments. Second, you will practise reading student and professional writing actively and critically. Third, you will use critical reading to find information and generate ideas for expository or argumentative essays. Just as observing gives you descriptive strategies and remembering helps you to practise drawing on your personal experience, reading will help you critically analyze ideas, facts, statistics, and arguments—a skill that you will need for many writing assignments.

TECHNIQUES FOR WRITING ABOUT READING

As you approach your assignments in this chapter, remember that reading, writing, and discussing are all interrelated and interactive strategies. Writing assists reading, discussing, and rereading. Reading and rereading help you discuss and write. Conversations (written and oral) among readers and writers are integral to reading/writing. Focus on the techniques that follow as you write your summary/response or critique.

- **Using active and responsive reading/writing/discussing strategies.** Preview the author's background and the writing context. Prewrite about your own experiences with the subject. Read initially for information and enjoyment. As you reread, make annotations, write questions, or do a double-entry log. Discuss the text with other readers.

- **Summarizing the main ideas or features of the text.** A summary should *accurately* and *objectively* represent the key ideas. Summaries cite the author and title, accurately represent the main ideas, quote directly key phrases or sentences, and describe main features of the text.

- **Responding to or critiquing the ideas in the text.** A response should focus on your ideas and reactions. Types of responses include *analysis* of the argument, organization, or evidence in the text; *agreement or disagreement* with the author/text; or *interpretation* of the text.

- **Supporting the response with evidence.** As supporting evidence for the response, writers should analyze key features of the text, cite evidence from other relevant texts, and/or use examples from personal experience.

- **Combining summary and response into a coherent essay.** Usually, the summary appears first, followed by the reader's response, but be sure to *integrate* the two parts. Focus early on a main idea for your response. Use transitions between the summary and the response.

As you work on these techniques, don't simply read the text, discuss it in class, and then write out your critique. Instead, write notes as you read. Reread the text after class discussion. Reread and discuss the text after you have written your draft. Use the interactive powers of reading/writing/discussing to help you throughout your writing process.

HOW READERS READ

One of the purposes of this chapter is to show you how readers read. If you know how readers read and how they construct meaning from a text, you will become a more active reader and a more effective writer.

Reading, some theorists believe, involves a three-part process. First, readers bring their *prior experience* (about the subject, about language, and about culture) to their reading. Second, based on their prior experience, readers make *guesses* about how each passage relates to their prior experience and *predictions* about where the text is headed. Finally, as readers continue to read or reread, they *make meaning of* or *comprehend* the text by testing (confirming or rejecting) the guesses and predictions that they have made. If readers have limited experience with the subject or the language, making accurate predictions can be difficult. If readers have a good deal of prior experience, they are more likely to make accurate predictions.

If this theory of reading and comprehension is true, it has three important lessons for any reader/writer:

- **First, prior knowledge about a text and its subject is extremely important.** As a reader, you should activate your prior knowledge *before* reading the text. Doing a prereading journal exercise and discussing the subject with others are excellent strategies to access what you already know.

- **Second, making guesses and predictions enables readers to make meaning.** Making wrong guesses is just as important as making right guesses. Don't worry about making wrong guesses—they are a crucial part of the active reading process.

- **Third, learning to read actively will make you a better writer.** Good writers know the problems that readers have making meaning. Good writers activate their readers' prior knowledge by using examples from their own experience. Good writers preview their main ideas so that their readers can make better guesses. Good writers use transitions or signals to help readers make meaning.

SUMMARIZING AND RESPONDING TO AN ESSAY

Following is an essay by Barbara Ehrenreich, "Teach Diversity—With a Smile." First, write for five minutes on the suggested Prereading Journal Entry that precedes the essay. The purpose of the journal entry is to allow you to collect your thoughts about the subject *before* you read Ehrenreich's essay. You will be a much more responsive reader if you reflect on your experiences and articulate your opinions *before* you are influenced by the author and her text. If possible, discuss your experiences and opinions with your classmates after you write your entry but before you read the essay. Next, read the introductory note about Barbara Ehrenreich to understand her background and the context for the essay. Finally, practise active reading techniques as you read. Read first for information and enjoyment. Then, reread with a pen in your hand. Either write your comments and questions directly in the text or do a double-entry log, summarizing the main ideas on one side of a piece of paper and writing your questions and reactions on the other.

■ **PREREADING EXERCISE**   Describe the ethnic groups of people who live in your neighbourhood. List all the groups you can recall. Then choose one of the following terms and briefly explain what it means: *diversity, multiculturalism,* or *political correctness.* Finally, describe one personal experience that taught you something about diversity or political correctness. What was the experience and how did you react?

PROFESSIONAL WRITING

TEACH DIVERSITY—WITH A SMILE
BARBARA EHRENREICH

Barbara Ehrenreich received a Ph.D. from Rockefeller University. She has been a health policy adviser and a professor of health sciences, but since 1974, she has spent most of her time writing books and articles about socialist and feminist issues. She has received a Ford Foundation award and a Guggenheim fellowship for her writings, which include Fear of Falling: The Inner Life of the Middle Class *(1989),* The Worst Years of Our Lives: Irreverent Notes From a Decade of Greed *(1990), and* The Snarling Citizen: Essays *(1995). Her articles and essays have appeared in* Esquire, Mother Jones, Ms., New Republic, The New York Times Magazine, *and* Time. *The following essay on cultural diversity appeared in* Time *magazine.*

Something had to replace the threat of communism, and at last a workable substitute is at hand. "Multiculturalism," as the new menace is known, has been denounced in the media recently as the new McCarthyism, the new fundamentalism, even the new totalitarianism—take your choice. According to its critics, who include a flock of tenured conservative scholars, multiculturalism aims to toss out what it sees as the Eurocentric bias in education and replace Plato with Ntozake Shange and traditional math with the Yoruba number system. And that's just the beginning. The Jacobins of the multiculturalist movement, who are described derisively as P.C., or politically correct, are said to have launched a campus reign of terror against those who slip and innocently say "freshman" instead of "freshperson," "Indian" instead of "Native American" or, may the Goddess forgive them, "disabled" instead of "differently abled." **(1)**

So you can see what is at stake here: freedom of speech, freedom of thought, Western civilization and a great many professorial egos. But before we get carried away by the mounting backlash against multiculturalism, we ought to reflect for a moment on the system that the P.C. people aim to replace. I know all about it; in fact it's just about all I *do* know, since I—along with so many educated white people of my generation—was a victim of monoculturalism. **(2)**

American history, as it was taught to us, began with Columbus's "discovery" of an apparently unnamed, unpeopled America, and moved on to the Pilgrims serving pumpkin pie to a handful of grateful red-skinned folks. College expanded our horizons with courses called Humanities or sometimes Civ, which introduced us to a line of thought that started with Homer, worked its way through Rabelais and reached a poignant climax in the pensées of Matthew Arnold. Graduate students wrote dissertations on what long-dead men had thought of Chaucer's verse or Shakespeare's dramas; foreign languages meant French or German. If there had been high technology in ancient China, kingdoms in black Africa or women anywhere, at any time, doing anything worth noticing, we did not know it, nor did anyone think to tell us. **(3)**

Our families and neighborhoods reinforced the dogma of monoculturalism. In our heads, most of us '50s teenagers carried around a social map that was about as useful as the chart that guided Columbus to the "Indies." There were "Negroes," "whites" and "Orientals," the latter meaning Chinese and "Japs." Of religions, only three were known—Protestant, Catholic and Jewish—and not much was known about the last two types. The only remaining human categories were husbands and wives, and that was all the diversity the monocultural world could handle. Gays, lesbians, Buddhists, Muslims, Malaysians, Mormons, etc. were simply off the map. **(4)**

So I applaud—with one hand, anyway—the multiculturalist goal of preparing us all for a wider world. The other hand is tapping its fingers impatiently, because the critics are right about one thing: when advocates of multiculturalism adopt the haughty stance of political correctness, they quickly descend to silliness or worse. It's obnoxious, for example, to rely on university administrations to enforce P.C. standards of verbal inoffensiveness. Racist, sexist and homophobic thoughts cannot, alas, be abolished by fiat but only by the time-honored methods of persuasion, education and exposure to the other guy's—or, excuse me, woman's—point of view. **(5)**

And it's silly to mistake verbal purification for genuine social reform. Even after all women are "Ms." and all people are "he or she," women will still earn only 65¢ for every dollar earned by men. Minorities by any other name, such as "people of color," will still bear a hugely disproportionate burden of poverty and discrimination. Disabilities are not just "different abilities" when there are not enough ramps for wheelchairs, signers for the deaf or special classes for the "specially" endowed. With all due respect for the new politesse, actions still speak louder than fashionable phrases. **(6)**

But the worst thing about the P.C. people is that they are such poor advocates for the multicultural cause. No one was ever won over to a broader, more inclusive view of life by being bullied or relentlessly "corrected." Tell a 19-year-old white male that he can't say "girl" when he means "teen-age woman," and he will most likely snicker. This may be the reason why, despite the conservative alarms, P.C.-ness remains a relatively tiny trend. Most campuses have more serious and ancient problems: faculties still top-heavy with white males of the monocultural persuasion; fraternities that harass minorities and women; date rape; alcohol abuse; and tuition that excludes all but the upper fringe of the middle class. **(7)**

So both sides would be well advised to lighten up. The conservatives ought to realize that criticisms of the great books approach to learning do not amount to totalitarianism. And the advocates of multiculturalism need to regain the sense of humor that enabled their predecessors in the struggle to coin the term P.C. years ago—not in arrogance but in self-mockery. **(8)**

Beyond that, both sides should realize that the beneficiaries of multiculturalism are not only the "oppressed peoples" on the standard P.C. list (minorities, gays, etc.). The "unenlightened"—the victims of monoculturalism—are oppressed too, or at least deprived. Our educations, whether at Yale or at State U, were narrow and parochial and left us ill-equipped to navigate a society that truly is multicultural and is becoming more so every day. The culture that we studied was, in fact, *one* culture and, from a world perspective, all too limited and ingrown. Diversity is challenging, but those of us who have seen the alternative know it is also richer, livelier and ultimately more fun. **(9)**

SUMMARIZING

The purpose of a summary is to give a reader a condensed and objective account of the main ideas and features of a text. Usually, a summary has between one and three paragraphs or 100 to 300 words, depending on the length and complexity of the original essay and the intended audience and purpose. Typically, a summary will do the following:

- **Cite the author and title of the text.** In some cases, the place of publication or the context for the essay may also be included.

- **Indicate the main ideas of the text.** Accurately representing the main ideas (while omitting the less important details) is the major goal of a summary.

- **Use direct quotation of key words, phrases, or sentences.** *Quote* the text directly for a few key ideas; *paraphrase* the other important ideas (that is, express the ideas in your own words).

- **Include author tags** ("according to Ehrenreich" or "as Ehrenreich explains") to remind the reader that you are summarizing the author and the text, not giving your own ideas. *Note:* Instead of repeating "Ehrenreich says," choose verbs that more accurately represent the purpose or tone of the original passage: "Ehrenreich argues," "Ehrenreich explains," "Ehrenreich warns," "Ehrenreich asks," "Ehrenreich advises."

- **Avoid summarizing specific examples or data** unless they help illustrate the thesis or main idea of the text.

- **Report the main ideas as objectively as possible.** Represent the author and text as accurately and faithfully as possible. Do not include your reactions; save them for your response.

Summary of "Teach Diversity—With a Smile"

Following is a summary of Ehrenreich's essay. Do *not* read this summary, however, until you have tried to write your own. After you have made notes and written a draft for your own summary, you will more clearly understand the key features of a summary. *Note*: There are many ways to write a good summary. If your summary conveys the main ideas and has the features described previously, it may be just as good as the following example. (Key features of a summary are annotated in the margin.)

Title and author

Main idea

Paraphrase

Context for essay

Author tag

Direct quotations

Main idea
Paraphrase

Author tag
Main idea
Paraphrase

In "Teach Diversity—with a Smile," journalist Barbara Ehrenreich explains the current conflict between people who would like to replace our Eurocentric bias in education with a multicultural approach and those critics and conservative scholars who are leading the backlash against multiculturalism and "political correctness." Writing for readers of *Time* magazine, Ehrenreich uses her own experience growing up in the 1950s to explain that her narrow education left her a "victim of monoculturalism," ill-equipped to cope with America's growing cultural diversity. Ehrenreich applauds multiculturalism's goal of preparing people for a culturally diverse world, but she is impatient at the "haughty stance" of the P.C. people because they mistake "verbal purification for genuine social reform" and they arrogantly bully people and "correct" their language. Since actions speak louder than words, Ehrenreich argues, the multiculturalists should focus more on genuine social reform—paying equal salaries to men and women, creating access for people with disabilities, and reducing date rape and alcohol abuse. The solution to the problem, according to Ehrenreich, is for both sides to "lighten up." The conservatives should recognize that criticizing the great books of Western civilization is not totalitarian, and the multiculturalists should be less arrogant and regain their sense of humour.

RESPONDING

A response requires your reaction and interpretation. Your own perspective—your experiences, beliefs, and attitudes—will guide your particular response. Your response may be totally different from another reader's response, but that does not necessarily make yours better or worse. Good responses say what you think, but then they *show why* you think so. They show the relationships between your opinions and the text, between the text and your experience, and between this text and other texts.

Depending on its purpose and intended audience, a response to a text can take several directions. Responses may focus on one or more of the following strategies. Consider your purpose and audience or check your assignment to see which type(s) you should emphasize.

Types of Responses

- **Analyzing the effectiveness of the text.** In this case, the response analyzes key features such as the clarity of the main idea, the organization of the argument, the quality of the supporting evidence, and/or the effectiveness of the author's style, tone, and voice.

- **Agreeing and/or disagreeing with the ideas in the text.** Often responders react to the ideas or the argument of the essay. In this case, the responders show why they agree and/or disagree with what the author/text says.

- **Interpreting and reflecting on the text.** The responder explains key passages or examines the underlying assumptions or the implications of the ideas. Often, the responder reflects on how his or her own experiences, attitudes, and observations relate to the text.

Analyzing, agreeing/disagreeing, and interpreting are all slightly different directions that a response may take. But regardless of the direction, responses must be supported by evidence, examples, facts, and details. A responder cannot simply offer an opinion or agree or disagree. Good responses draw on several kinds of supporting evidence.

Kinds of Evidence

- **Personal experience.** Responders may use *examples* from their personal experiences to show why they interpreted the text as they did, why they agreed or disagreed, or why they reacted to the ideas as they did.

- **Evidence from the text.** Responders should cite *specific phrases* or sentences from the text to support their explanation of a section, their analysis of the effectiveness of a passage, or their agreement or disagreement with a key point.

- **Evidence from other texts.** If appropriate, responders may bring in ideas and information from other relevant essays, articles, books, or graphic material.

Not all responses use all three kinds of supporting evidence, but all responses *must* have sufficient examples to support the responder's ideas, reactions, and opinions. Responders should not merely state their opinions. They must give evidence to *show* how and why they read the text as they did.

One final—and crucial—point about responses: A response should make a coherent, overall main point. It should not be just a laundry list of reactions, likes, and dislikes. Sometimes the main point is that the text is not convincing because it lacks evidence. Sometimes the overall point is that the text makes an original statement even though it is difficult to read. Perhaps the basic point is that the author/text stimulates the reader to reflect on his or her experience. Every response should focus on a coherent main idea.

Response to "Teach Diversity—With a Smile"

Following is one possible response to Ehrenreich's essay. Before you read this response, however, write out your own reactions. You need to decide what you think before other responses influence your reading. There are, of course, many different but legitimate responses to any given essay. As you read this response, note the marginal annotations indicating the different types of responses and the different kinds of evidence this writer uses.

Analyzing effectiveness of text

Responder's main point

What I like best about Barbara Ehrenreich's article is her effective use of personal experience to clarify the issues on both sides of the multiculturalism debate. However, her conclusion, that we should "lighten up" and accept diversity because it's "more fun," weakens her argument by ignoring the social inequalities at the heart of the debate. The issue in this debate, I believe, is not just enjoying diversity, which is easy to do, but changing cultural conditions, which is much more difficult.

Evidence from text

Evidence from text

Ehrenreich effectively uses her own experiences—and her common sense—to let us see both the virtues and the excesses of multiculturalism. When she explains that her monocultural education gave her a social map that was "about as useful as the chart that guided Columbus to the 'Indies,'" she helps us understand how vital multicultural studies are in a society that is more like a glass mosaic than a melting pot. Interestingly, even her vocabulary reveals—perhaps unconsciously—her Western bias: *Jacobins, pensées, fiat,* and *politesse* are all words that reveal her Eurocentric education. When Ehrenreich shifts to discussing the P.C. movement, her commonsense approach to the silliness of excessive social correctness ("the other guy's—or, excuse me, woman's—point of view") makes us as readers more willing to accept her compromise position.

Reflecting on the text

Personal experience

Evidence from other texts

My own experience with multiculturalism certainly parallels Ehrenreich's impatience with the "haughty stance" of the P.C. people. Of course, we should avoid racist and sexist terms and use our increased sensitivity to language to reduce discrimination. But my own backlash began several years ago when a friend said I shouldn't use the word *girl.* I said, "You mean, not ever? Not even for a 10-year-old female child?" She replied that the word had been so abused by people referring to a "woman" as a "girl" that the word *girl* now carried too many sexist connotations. Although I understood my friend's point, it seems that *girl* should still be a perfectly good word for a female child under the age of 12. Which reminds me of a book I saw recently, *The Official Politically Correct Dictionary.* It is loaded with examples of political correctness out of control: Don't say *bald,* say *hair disadvantaged.* Don't use the word *pet,* say *nonhuman companion.* Don't call someone *old,* say that they are *chronologically gifted.* One humorous example even suggested that George Bush Sr. was "electorally slighted" when he was not reelected.

Ehrenreich does recommend keeping a sense of humour about the P.C. movement, but the conclusion to her essay weakens her argument. Instead of focussing on her earlier point that "it's silly to mistake verbal purification for genuine social reform," she advises both sides to lighten up and have fun with the diversity around us. Instead, I wanted her to conclude by reinforcing her point that "actions still speak louder than fashionable phrases." Changing the realities of illiteracy, poverty, alcohol abuse, and sexual harassment should be the focus of the multiculturalists. Of course, changing language is crucial to changing the world, but the language revolution has already happened—or at least begun. Ehrenreich's article would be more effective, I believe, if she concluded her essay with a call for both sides to help change cultural conditions rather than with a reference to the silly debate about what to call a teenage woman.

Analyzing effectiveness of text

Responder's main point

Summarizing and Responding to an Advertisement

Summarizing and responding to graphic material, such as advertisements, is an excellent way to practise responding to texts. In this case, a summary must observe and describe the key features of the advertisement (layout, colour, proportion, images, and copy). The response then "reads" the advertisement for the message, selling tactics, cultural stereotypes, or other implications. The focus of the response may be to analyze and explain the persuasive tactics, to interpret cultural values or stereotypes, to judge the effectiveness of the ad, and/or to reflect on assumptions and implications.

The following summary/response is to an advertisement for Fila jeans. Notice how the student writer, Karyn M. Lewis, carefully describes key features of the advertisement so her readers can clearly visualize it.

STUDENT WRITING

SOME DON'T LIKE THEIR BLUES AT ALL
KARYN M. LEWIS

He strides toward us in navy and white, his body muscled and heavy-set, one arm holding his casually flung jeans jacket over his shoulder. A man in his prime, with just the right combination of macho and sartorial flair.

He is also black.

She is curled and giggling upon a chair, her hair loose and flowing around her shoulders, leaning forward innocently—the very picture of a blossoming, navy flower.

She is white.

They are each pictured on a magazine page of their own, situated opposite each other in a complementary two-page spread. They are stationed in front of a muted photograph which serves as a background for each one. They both merit their own captions: bold indigo letters presiding over them in the outer corners of each page.

His says: SOME LIKE THEIR BLUES HARD.

Hers says: SOME LIKE THEIR BLUES SOFT.

His background depicts a thrusting struggle between a quarterback and a leaping defender, a scene of arrested violence and high tension.

Her background is a lounging, bikini-clad goddess, who looks at the camera with intriguing, calm passion. She raises her hand to rest behind her head in a languid gesture as she tries to incite passion within the viewer.

At the bottom of the page blazes the proud emblem of the company that came up with this ad: FILA JEANS.

This advertisement blatantly uses stereotypes of men and women to sell its product. It caters to our need to fit into the roles that society has deemed right for the individual sexes ever since patriarchal rule rose up and replaced the primitive worship of a mother goddess and the reverence for women. These stereotypes handed down to us throughout the centuries spell out to us that men are violence and power incarnate, and that the manly attitude has no room for weakness or softness of nature. And we find our role model of women in the compliant and eager female who obeys her man in all things, who must not say no to a male, and who is not very bright—someone who flutters her eyelashes, giggles a lot, and uses tears to get her way.

This ad tells us, by offering the image of a hard, masculine male, who is deified in violence, that he is the role model men should aspire to, and that for women, their ideal is weak but sexual, innocent and at the same time old enough to have sex. In viewing this ad, we see our aspirations clothed in Fila jeans, and to be like them, we must buy the clothes pictured here. This ad also suggests that a man can become hard and powerful (or at least look it) dressed in these jeans; a woman can become sexually intense and desirable dressed in Fila's clothing.

The words of the captions tantalize with their sexual innuendo. The phrase "Some like their blues hard" hints at male sexual prowess. Most men and women in this country are obsessed with males' need to prove their virility, and Fila plays on this obsession. Females too have their own stereotype of what constitutes their sexuality. "Some like their blues soft" exemplifies this ideal: A woman should be soft and yielding. Her soft, sensuous body parts, which so excite her partners, have been transformed into her personal qualities. By using the term *soft*, Fila immediately links the girl with her sexuality and sexual organs.

We are shown by the models' postures that men and women are (according to Fila) fundamentally different and total antonyms of one another. He is standing and walking with purpose; she sits, laughing trivially at the camera. Even the background hints at separation of the sexes.

The football players on the man's page are arranged in a diagonal line which starts at the upper left-hand corner and runs to the opposite corner, which is the centre of the ad. On her page, the enchanting nymph in the bathing suit runs on a diagonal, beginning where his ends, and traveling up to the upper right-hand corner of her page. These two photos in effect create a *V*, which both links the two models and suggests movement away from one another. Another good example of their autonomy from one another is their skin color. He is a black man, she's white. Black is the opposite color of white on an artist's color wheel and palette and symbolizes dynamically opposed forces: good and evil, night and day, man and woman. This ad hits us with the idea that men and women are not parallel in nature to one another but are fundamentally different in all things. It alienates the sexes from each other. Opposites may attract, but there is no room for understanding a nature completely alien to your own.

So in viewing this ad, and reading its captions, the consumer is left with the view that a woman must be "soft" and sensual, a male's sexual dream, and must somehow still retain her innocence after having sex. She must be weak, the opposite of the violence which contrasts with her on the opposite page. The men looking at this ad read the message that they are supposed to be well-dressed and powerful and possess a strength that borders on violence. As we are told by the caption, men should be "hard." Furthermore, men and women are opposite creatures, as different as two sides of a coin.

This ad is supposed to cause us to want to meet these requirements, but it fills me with a deep-rooted disgust that we perpetu-
ate the myth that men are unyielding creatures of iron and women
are silly bits of fluff. The ad generates no good role models to aspire
to, where men and women are equal beings, and both can show
compassion and still be strong. Fila may like their blues hard and
soft, but I don't like their blues at all.

IBM AND *THE X-FILES*
SUSAN DOUGLAS

*Susan Douglas is a professor of American studies at the University of
Michigan. Following her first book,* Inventing American Broadcasting
(1987), Douglas published the popular and controversial study, Where
the Girls Are: Growing Up Female with the Mass Media *(1994),
in which she examines images of women in the media in the 1970s. She
has published articles on the media in* The New York Times, *the*
Washington Post, Women's Review of Books, *and* New York *magazine. She is currently a media and culture critic for* The Progressive.
In the following article from The Progressive, *Douglas reads the cultural and ideological messages in a popular television series.*

My job in this magazine, and my inclination in general, is to
point out the various ways rightwing ideologies costume themselves and parade seductively through the mass media. A colleague
who knows this recently challenged me with the following: "So,
how do you account for *The X-Files?* It's one of the most subversive shows on television," he said. **(1)**

He's got a point. Sunday-in and Sunday-out, twenty million
viewers tune in to episodes about FBI and CIA cover-ups, government disinformation, human abductions, alien visitations, and
secret plots to test unknown substances on unsuspecting citizens.
Shadowy lighting and oboes in minor keys intensify the paranoid
atmosphere. *Walker, Texas Ranger* it ain't. No celebration of traditional authority figures here, no deification of state power. Instead,
government officials at the highest level are incompetents, or liars,
or murderous anti-democratic conspirators out to hoodwink every
single American and violate the Constitution. **(2)**

This fall's much anticipated season premiere gave an analysis of the Cold War that would have done Noam Chomsky proud. Archival footage of the 1940s and 1950s accompanied the words of a government agent as he explained that the entire Cold War was a fabrication designed to sustain America's war industries. "The business of America is not business," he tells Mulder, "it's war." Since the military wanted to spend money, "when there wasn't a war we called it a war anyway," he says. The military's postwar goal? "Global domination through the capability of total annihilation." (3)

The agent's history lesson went like this: When Robert Oppenheimer tried to stop the arms race, "we silenced him." And after Joe McCarthy, Americans ate up the Cold War ideology "with a big spoon." More recently, he continued, "the biological weapons used in the Gulf War were so ingenious as to be almost undetectable," adding that they were "developed right in this very building." Reported alien abductions were and are really citizens being taken against their will and used by the government as guinea pigs for all sorts of life-threatening tests. Whew! (4)

Having just taken this in, it's time to cut to the commercials, which make you feel like you're being slammed around in ideological bumper cars. Time now to stop questioning authority and instead acquiesce to it. IBM's new Lotus campaign stands out as one of the more aggressive sets of ads in recent memory, designed to ridicule the anti-authoritarian tendencies the audience might have. (5)

The IBM ads take aim at those who believe in the democratic potential of the Internet. Many regular users envision a new public sphere where people can escape the one-way, top-down communication of the mass media and, instead, participate in chat groups, put up their own web pages, and establish ties based on cultural, personal, and political interests. (6)

Dennis Leary, a comedian known for his obnoxious sarcasm, is IBM's pitch man. He sprawls in a chair with neo-punk guitars blaring as various people gush about the Internet. "It will create a new utopia," says one, "make us all smile," says another, and "fix everything that's wrong in the world," says a third. (7)

"Stop before I get sick," he yells at them, his lip curled. (8)

"I just sent my first e-mail," says a grandma-type, to which he sarcastically responds, "That's nice." (9)

"We're creating a virtual pet," report two school children, which elicits a disgusted, "That's useful." (10)

By now, our slacker capitalist has had enough. "Hey!" he yells to a roomful of computer users. "What are you chuckleheads doing?" **(11)**

Cut to a CEO-type who announces that Chrysler has used Lotus and the web to save $1.2 billion. Finally! A *productive* use of this technology. **(12)**

"That's a start," he says. **(13)**

The implication: People who want to use the web to level America's hierarchies are stupid, misguided, even, in a nice twist, selfish. **(14)**

Another ad in the series shows our hero visiting a store that sells Communist memorabilia. Even here, computers expedite sales and inventory, because, as the owner puts it, "We're Marxists, but we gotta make a buck like everybody else." **(15)**

In yet another, Leary berates a boy's enthusiasm for making friends over the web because the boy doesn't appreciate how much his parents had to pay for the computer, nor does he understand that the main purpose of computers is to maximize profits. **(16)**

The subversive message of *The X-Files* melts into anti-government, procapitalist pabulum when you view the show along with the commercials. *The X-Files* says the government is inept and/or venal. IBM says communications technologies are best left in the hands of corporate oligopolies unfettered by government and naïve, obstructionist technophiles. I mean, isn't this what Microsoft keeps saying in its ongoing campaign to fight long over-due antitrust proceedings? **(17)**

I suspect Rupert Murdoch, owner of Fox, would be delighted with this mix of *X-Files* subversion and IBM hectoring. **(18)**

Vocabulary

Write down the meaning of the following words:

- right-wing *ideologies* **(1)**
- most *subversive* shows **(1)**
- no *deification* of state power **(2)**
- *acquiesce* to it **(5)**
- America's *hierarchies* **(14)**

- pro-capitalist *pabulum* (**17**)
- corporate *oligopolies* (**17**)
- obstructionist *technophiles* (**17**)
- IBM *hectoring* (**18**)

Questions for Writing and Discussion

1. If you are a regular viewer of *The X-Files*, write a summary and response to a show you have seen recently. What was the subject of the episode? Did it take a subversive look at government and authority, or was there another focus? What advertisements were shown during the show? Did they appeal to regular viewers of *The X-Files?* Explain.

2. Summaries of media performances may be different from summaries of academic texts, but they should still contain accurate and objective information about the program, including the title, plot line, key characters and events, and main idea of the episode. Which paragraphs in Douglas's essay give the background and summary? Which paragraphs contain analysis and interpretation? Is her article an effective summary/response essay? Explain.

3. Reread Douglas's article. Is her thesis that *The X-Files* is *not* a subversive drama? Is it that the IBM advertisement counters and thus dilutes the subversive nature of *The X-Files?* Is her point that viewers should consider a show's advertisements an integral part of the show itself? Write out her thesis in your own words. Does she persuade you that her thesis is correct?

4. Using Douglas's essay as a guide, write a summary and critique of another television show, film, news broadcast, Web site, newspaper, or other media text or event. If possible, videotape the program so you can watch it more than once. Focus on interpreting the assumptions, implications, or ideology of the media text.

READING AND WRITING PROCESSES

■ ASSIGNMENT FOR READING/WRITING   Write an essay that summarizes and then responds to one or more essays, articles, or advertisements. As you review your particular assignment, make sure you understand what text or texts you should respond to, how long your summary and response should be, and what type(s) of responses you should focus on.

Your purpose for this assignment is to represent the text(s) accurately and faithfully in your summary and to explain and support your response. Taken together, your summary and response should be a coherent essay, with a main idea and connections between summary and response. Assume that your audience is other members of the class, including the instructor, with whom you are sharing your reading.

CHOOSING A SUBJECT

Suggested processes, activities, and strategies for reading and writing will be illustrated in response to the following essay by Dudley Erskine Devlin.

PROFESSIONAL WRITING

CHILDREN AND VIOLENCE IN AMERICA

DUDLEY ERSKINE DEVLIN

Originally trained as a scientist, Dudley Erskine Devlin currently teaches English at Colorado State University and writes columns and editorials on contemporary problems. The targets for his editorials are often the large and complicated issues of the day, such as education, violence, health care, and the media. "My first goal as a writer," Devlin said in a recent interview, "is to provoke response. If just one reader is angry enough to write me a letter of response, then my time is not wasted." As you read Devlin's essay, note places where you agree or disagree with his ideas. How would you reply to Devlin's argument?

Violence seems to be everywhere in America, but increasingly both the victims and the perpetrators are likely to be children and teenagers. According to a recent Department of Education study, 81 percent of the victims of violent crimes are now preteens and teenagers. Teenagers also lead adults in the number of serious crimes committed. As if to prove this point, recently a stray bullet from gang violence in Denver struck a 10-month-old child who was visiting the zoo. In another incident, a 13-year-old boy accidently shot his friend, and then in despair shot and killed himself. Even this morning's newspaper carries the story of a 15-year-old boy who accidentally shot his 9-year-old sister while showing her how to load and unload his father's .22 semi-automatic handgun. The gun went off, and the bullet shattered her spine. The 9-year-old girl is now paralyzed. When people read these shocking and unbelievable stories, they begin to wonder about the causes of the problem. Why are children so frequently the victims or the perpetrators of violence? **(1)**

The debate in America today is about the causes of violence involving children. But what exactly is the basic, underlying cause? Conventional explanations take an either/or approach: Either the cause lies in TV programs which promote violence or the cause is a society riddled with family instability, drugs, and poverty. It's a classic chicken-or-the-egg question: Does TV and movie violence promote social violence, or is social violence merely reflected in violent movies and television programs? **(2)**

I believe that we should not be fooled by this either/or logic. There is, after all, a third possible answer. Instead of the primary cause being TV violence or the decline in family values, I believe that the news media themselves are the underlying cause of our crisis. The truth is that the liberal media—particularly newspapers and network TV news—have cleverly staged this crisis of violence by hyping a few statistics and isolated cases of violence. To prove this claim, I need to review the conventional arguments. **(3)**

First, let's analyze the belief that violence on TV and in the movies is causing increased violence among children and teenagers. The self-appointed liberal reformers usually trot out a bunch of statistics and examples like the following:

- By the age of 18, the average American child will have seen 200,000 violent acts on television, including 40,000 murders. By the time an American child has left elementary school, he or she has witnessed 8,000 murders on TV.

- Today, television programs and films strive for high body counts, not high morals. *Terminator 2* seems like one long machine-gunning. In *RoboCop*, 32 people are killed. *Die Hard 2* may have the unofficial record with 264 people killed.

- In 1950, approximately 15 percent of America's homes had television; by 1990, 93 percent of America's homes had television. In that 40-year period, the murder rate per 100,000 people jumped from 5.3 to 10.2. That's almost a 100 percent increase in murders.

Using examples like these, the TV and media critics like Tipper Gore argue that children confuse images on TV with the real world, that they become desensitized to repeated acts of violence, and that they say that "it's fun" to do violence to others. Researchers like University of Illinois psychologists Leonard Eron and Rowell

Huesmann argue that violence on TV does cause violent behavior: "Television violence affects youngsters of all ages, of both genders, at all socioeconomic levels. It cannot be denied or explained away." (4)

On the other side of this either/or argument are those who believe that social violence causes violent behavior in children and teenagers. Those who make this argument point to drug use, poverty, and the decline in family values. Their best evidence is that violence already exists in our children's public schools. They like to cite figures released by the National Education Association (NEA) that show that violence is an everyday part of every child's education. Every school day, the NEA claims, at least 100,000 students bring guns to school; 40 are hurt or killed by firearms; 6,250 teachers are threatened with bodily injury; and 260 teachers are physically assaulted. Everywhere, schools are installing metal detectors and police are stationed in the hallways. (5)

Obviously, each of these arguments represents a half-truth. Possibly there is some TV and movie violence that adds to the culture of violence in America. And yes, we can believe that there are a few, isolated pockets of violence in society and schools. But the real truth is that the newspaper media and the network news have actually invented this epidemic of violence in order to promote their product and frighten the public. Every day, reporters search for a few examples of violence to teens and children, plaster them on the front page, and blow the whole thing out of proportion. (6)

To be sure, there are violent TV shows and movies that a few people watch, but there are also family shows like *Home Improvement* and *Home Alone* that don't get the publicity of *RoboCop* or *Terminator 2*. There are, of course, one or two cities in America, like Los Angeles and Washington, D.C., where there is occasional violence on the streets and in children's schools. But the liberal establishment press has done its thing again, trying to scare the daylights out of the public in order to sell newspapers and raise their Neilsen ratings. (7)

So when you pick up your paper in the morning or turn on the TV news and see another story about teenage violence, take it with a big lump of salt and don't believe everything you read. As they say, one swallow doesn't make a summer, and one infant shot in the Denver Zoo does not mean that we have this huge crisis of violence. In terms of "telling it like it is," you'll find more truth if you turn to the comics and check out "Peanuts." When Lucy hits Charlie Brown, at least you know it's make-believe. (8)

COLLECTING

Once a text or texts has been selected or assigned for your summary and response, try the following reading/writing/discussing activities.

■ **PREREADING EXERCISE**   In your notebook, write what you already know about the subject of the essay. For an essay about children and violence, for example, the following questions will help you to recall your prior experiences and think about your own opinions before you read the essay. The purpose of this entry is to think about your own experiences and opinions *before* you are influenced by the arguments of the essay.

What experiences have you had with guns and violence?

What acts of violence to or by children can you recall?

What seems to be the cause of these violent acts?

What would you do to solve the problem?

Text Annotation   Most experts on reading and writing agree that you will learn more and remember more if you actually write out your comments, questions, and reactions in the margins of the text you are reading. Writing your responses helps you begin a conversation with the text. Reproduced below are one reader's marginal responses to paragraphs 6 and 7 of Devlin's essay.

There's a lot of violence on TV and in society

Obviously, each of these arguments represents a half-truth. Possibly there is some TV and movie violence that adds to the culture of violence in America. And yes, we can believe that there are a few, isolated pockets of violence in society and schools. But the real truth is that the newspaper media and the network news have actually invented this epidemic of violence in order to promote their product and frighten the public. Every day, reporters search for a few examples of violence to teens and children, plaster them on the front page, and blow the whole thing out of proportion.

I think that both areas contribute to violence

TV news does this every night

? Network news didn't invent it, but they do hype it.

Home Alone was filled with violence

Showing violence on TV does

To be sure, there are violent TV shows and movies that a few people watch, but there are also family shows like *Home Improvement* and *Home Alone* that don't get the publicity of *RoboCop* or *Terminator 2*. There are, of course, one or two cities in America, like Los Angeles and Washington, D.C., where there is occasional violence on the streets and in children's schools. But the liberal establishment press has done its thing again, trying to scare the daylights out of the public in order to sell newspapers and raise their Neilsen ratings.

Huh? Violence exists in every city in America

Reading Log   A reading log, like text annotation, encourages you to interact with the author/text and write your comments and questions as you read. While text annotation helps you identify specific places in the text for commentary, a reading log encourages you to write out longer, more thoughtful responses. In a reading log, you can keep a record of your thoughts *while you read and reread* the text. Often, reading-log entries help you focus on a key idea to develop later in your response.

Below is one reader's response to Devlin's claim in paragraphs 6 and 7 that the violence is isolated in just a few cities.

> When Devlin says that violence happens in only a few cities like L.A. or D.C., I really disagree. One would never expect to hear of violence in a sparsely populated state like Montana, but it does happen there. Peers in my school bring weapons daily—guns, knives, and the like. So far, only threats have been made, but everyone lives in fear that one day someone will get hurt. Schools don't have to be in the slums to have violence. Three years ago, a boy walked into his classroom in Lewistown, Montana, and killed his teacher and wounded two others. This student went to a safe school, in a safe city, but somehow the violence found a way into this haven.

Double-Entry Log   One of the most effective strategies to promote active reading is a double-entry log. Draw a line down the middle of a page in your notebook. On the left-hand side, keep a running summary of the main ideas and features that you notice in the text. On the right-hand side, write your questions and reactions. A double-entry log, especially if used with the Rereading Guide that follows, can help you quickly organize your ideas for a summary/response essay.

Author and Title:

Summary Comments: Main Ideas and Key Features	Response: Comments, Reactions, and Questions

Rereading Guide   After you've read an essay once, let the following set of questions guide your *rereadings* of the text. The questions on the left-hand side will help you summarize and analyze the text; the questions on the right-hand side will help focus your response.

Description	Response
I. Purpose • Describe the author's overall *purpose* (to inform, explain, explore, evaluate, argue, negotiate, or other purpose). • How does the author/text want to affect or change the reader?	• Is the overall purpose clear or muddled? • Was the actual purpose different from the stated purpose? • How did the text actually affect you?

Description	Response

II. Audience/Reader

- Who is the *intended* audience?
- What *assumptions* does the author make about the reader's knowledge or beliefs?
- From what *point of view* or *context* is the author writing?

- Are you part of the intended audience?
- Does the author misjudge the reader's knowledge or beliefs?
- Do you share the author's point of view on this subject?

III. Thesis and Main Ideas

- What key *question* or *problem* does the author/text address?
- What is the author's *thesis?*
- What *main ideas* support the thesis?
- What are the key passages or key moments in the text?

- Where is the thesis stated?
- Are the main ideas related to the thesis?
- Where do you agree or disagree?
- Does the essay have contradictions or errors in logic?
- What ideas or arguments does the essay omit or ignore?
- What experience or prior knowledge do you have about the topic?
- What are the implications or consequences of the essay's ideas?

IV. Organization and Evidence

- Where does the author *preview* the essay's organization?
- How does the author *signal* new sections of the essay?
- What kinds of *evidence* does the author use (personal experience, descriptions, statistics, interviews, other authorities, analytical reasoning, or other)?

- At what point could you accurately predict the organization of the essay?
- At what points were you confused about the organization?
- What evidence was most or least effective?
- Where did the author rely on assertions rather than on evidence?
- Which of your own personal experiences did you recall as you read the essay?

V. Language and Style

- What is the author's *tone* (casual, humorous, ironic, angry, preachy, academic, or other)?
- Are *sentences* and *vocabulary* easy, average, or difficult?
- What key *words* or *images* recur throughout the text?

- Did the tone support or distract from the author's purpose or meaning?
- Did the sentences and vocabulary support or distract from the purpose or meaning?
- Did recurring words or images relate to or support the purpose or meaning?

Remember that not all these questions will be relevant to any given essay or text, but one or two of these questions may suggest a direction or give a *focus* to your overall response. When one of these questions suggests a focus for your response to the essay, *go back to the text, to other texts, and to your experience* to gather *evidence* and *examples* to support your response.

Discussion and Rereading   After you have recorded your initial reactions in your reading log or double-entry log, discuss your reactions in small groups. Do a collaborative annotation of the text by recording your group's best responses in the margins of a photocopy of the text. Or your class or small group may want to debate the strengths and weaknesses of the text. After your class or small-group discussion activity, however, take time to enter your responses to the following questions:

What do you need to change in your summary?

What new responses did you hear?

Which of your original responses have you revised?

What will be the new focus or main emphasis of your response?

GUIDELINES FOR CLASS DISCUSSION

Class discussions are an important part of the reading/writing/discussing process. Often, however, class discussions are not productive because not everyone knows the purpose of the discussion or how to discuss openly and fairly. Following is a suggested list of goals for class discussion. Read them carefully. *Make notes about any suggestions, revisions, or additions for your class.* Your class will then review these goals and agree to adopt, modify, or revise them for your own class discussions for the remainder of the semester.

Discussion Goals

1. To understand and *accurately represent* the views of the author(s) of an essay. The first discussion goal should be to summarize the author's views fairly.

2. To understand how the views and arguments of individual authors *relate* to each other. Comparing and contrasting different authors' views help clarify each author's argument.

3. To encourage all members of the class to articulate their *understanding* of each essay and their *response* to the ideas in each essay. Class discussions should promote multiple responses rather than focus on a single "right" interpretation or response.

4. To hear class members' responses in an *open forum.* All points of view must be recognized. *Discussions in class should focus on ideas and arguments, not on individual class members.* Class members may attack ideas but not people.

5. To relate class discussions to the *assigned reading/writing task*. What effective writing strategies are illustrated in the essay the class is discussing? How can class members use any of these strategies in writing their own essays?

SHAPING

Summaries and responses have several possible shapes, depending on the writer's purpose and intended audience. Keep in mind, however, that in a summary/response essay or critique, *the summary and the response should be unified by the writer's overall response.* The summary and the response may be organized or drafted separately, but they are still parts of one essay, focussed on the writer's most important or overall response.

Summary Shaping   Summaries should convey the main ideas, the essential argument, or the key features of a text. The purpose should be to represent the author's/text's ideas as accurately and as faithfully as possible. Summaries rely on description, paraphrase, and direct quotation. Below are definitions and examples for each of these terms.

Description   The summary should *describe* the main features of an essay, including the author and title, the context or place of publication of the essay (if appropriate), the essay's thesis or main argument, and any key text features, such as sections, chapters, or important graphic material.

> In an editorial entitled "Children and Violence in America," Dudley Erskine Devlin documents the increasing violence in America done to children and by children. In addressing the question of why the violence has increased, he reports on the debate between those people who think that television violence is the main cause and those who think that the decline of social values is the cause. Devlin suggests that each of these arguments represents only a half-truth. In fact, Devlin argues, the news media have largely invented this crisis of violence.

Paraphrase   A paraphrase restates a passage or text in different words. The purpose of a paraphrase is to recast the author's/text's words in your own language. A good paraphrase retains the original meaning without plagiarizing from the original text.

Original: But the real truth is that the newspaper media and the network news have actually invented this epidemic of violence in order to promote their product and frighten the public.

Paraphrase: Television and print media have created an illusion that violence is widespread simply to attract anxious viewers and readers to their programs and news stories.

As you can see, a paraphrase does not necessarily condense a passage. Actually, the paraphrase may be nearly as long as the original. A summary includes occasional paraphrasing of a few, selected, main ideas.

Direct Quotation

Often, summaries directly quote a few key phrases or sentences from the source. *Remember: Any words or phrases within the quotation marks must be accurate, word-for-word transcriptions of the original.* Guidelines for direct quotation and examples are as follows. Use direct quotations sparingly to convey the key points in the essay:

> Devlin's essay addresses a simple but difficult question: "Why are children so frequently the victims or the perpetrators of violence?"

Use direct quotations when the author's phrasing is more memorable, more concise, or more accurate than your paraphrase might be:

> Devlin argues that media reporters are trying to "scare the daylights out of the public" in order to sell their stories.

Use direct quotations for key words or phrases that indicate the author's attitude, tone, or stance:

> Television and the news media, Devlin claims, have "invented" this crisis of violence.

Don't quote long sentences. Condense the original sentence to the most important phrases. Use just a short phrase from a sentence or use an ellipsis (three spaced periods . . .) to indicate words that you have left out.

Original: But the real truth is that the newspaper media and the network news have actually invented this epidemic of violence in order to promote their product and frighten the public.

Condensed quotation: "The real truth," according to Devlin, is that the media "have actually invented this epidemic . . . to promote their product and frighten the public."

Sample Summaries

Following are summaries of Devlin's essay written by two different readers. Notice that while both convey the main ideas of the essay by using description, paraphrase, and direct quotation, they are not identical. Check each summary to see how well it meets these guidelines:

- Cite the author and title of the text.

- Indicate the main ideas of the text.

- Use direct quotation of key words, phrases, or sentences.

- Include author tags.

- Do not summarize most examples or data.

- Be as accurate, fair, and objective as possible.

Summary No. 1

In "Children and Violence in America," Dudley Erskine Devlin takes a different approach to explaining the apparent increase of violence involving children. Devlin begins by describing several cases of children and violence, and then he outlines the two major explanations for violence that most social analysts subscribe to. The first is that television promotes violence, and the second is that the decline in family values causes children to kill children. Devlin then offers his theory—that there is no real increase in child violence. The apparent increase is, in fact, caused by the liberal media "blowing the whole thing out of proportion." Devlin closes by urging the reader to think before jumping to conclusions about the causes of teenage violence.

Summary No. 2

Dudley Erskine Devlin's editorial, "Children and Violence in America," attempts to refute the claims of some people that violence on television and in movies leads to violence involving young people in real life. Devlin also argues against the idea that family instability, drugs, and poverty cause violence among young Americans. While Devlin agrees that "possibly there is some TV and movie violence that adds to the culture of violence in America," he argues that the media have "actually invented this epidemic of violence" to "frighten the public" and thus sell their stories. In actuality, Devlin claims, there is no problem with violence among young people in America. It is just something made up by the media to promote business.

Response Shaping   Strategies for organizing a response depend on the purpose of the response. Typically, responses include one or more of the following three purposes:

- Analyzing the effectiveness of the text.

- Agreeing and/or disagreeing with the ideas in the text.

- Interpreting and reflecting on the text.

As the following explanations illustrate, each of these types of responses requires supporting evidence from the text, from other texts, and/or from the writer's own experience.

Analyzing

Analysis requires dividing a whole into its parts in order to better understand the whole. In order to analyze a text for its effectiveness, start by examining key parts or features of the text, such as the purpose, the intended audience, the thesis and main ideas, the organization and evidence, and the language and style. Notice how the following paragraph analyzes Devlin's illogical use of *evidence.*

> Devlin's essay has some clear problems with supporting evidence. In one case, his evidence does not support his argument, and in another the evidence he gives refutes his main point. In Devlin's opening paragraph, two of his examples involve shooting *accidents,* not violent crimes. The boy who accidentally shot his friend and the boy who accidentally shot his sister did not commit "violent crimes." To support his point in the first paragraph, Devlin needs examples showing children as victims and perpetrators of violent crime. Another obvious problem with supporting evidence occurs later in the essay. Devlin argues in paragraph 4 that TV and movie violence is not a major cause of teenage violence, but then he goes on to cite several convincing examples and statistics linking TV shows and movies with violence. In this case, Devlin gives plenty of evidence, but it supports the argument that he dismisses both in this paragraph and at the end of the essay.

Agreeing/Disagreeing

Often, a response to a text focuses on agreeing and/or disagreeing with its major ideas. Responses may agree completely, disagree completely, or agree with some points but disagree with others. Responses that agree with some ideas but disagree with others are often more effective because they show that the responder sees both strengths and weaknesses in an argument. In the following paragraphs, notice how the responder agrees and disagrees and then supports each judgment with evidence.

> I agree with the author that the news media blow many stories out of proportion. It seems that every time I see a story about a child-related violent crime on the news, I am always told to stay tuned for more information. They keep going back to the same reporter, giving the same information. They usually have a special "follow-up report" on the next night. The more violent the crime, the more attention it gets. For example, if there is a high-speed chase involving a teenager, it will be mentioned on the news. If the chase ends in a crash, however, the story will be repeated in depth for several days. The media can stretch one incident into a crime story that lasts all week. The media always dwell on the

bad. If a news story mentions a teenager on a good note, it is shown just once, not shown or reprinted the rest of the week.

I have to disagree with the author as well. Violent TV shows can lead to an increase in violent crimes. To see the effects of violent movies, you don't have to look any farther than the toy store or your local Wal-Mart. For every movie such as *RoboCop* or *Terminator 2,* there is a new line of violent toys. As children grow up playing with these toys, they begin associating violent objects with fun. As they grow older, they begin looking for more violent "toys." Pretty soon you have a 16-year-old kid holding a real 9-mm pistol to his best friend's head.

Interpreting and Reflecting Many responses contain interpretations of passages that might be read from different points of view or reflections on the assumptions or implications of an idea. An interpretation says, "Here is what the text says, but let me explain what it means, what assumptions the argument carries, or what the implications might be." Here is a paragraph from an interpretive response to Devlin's essay on children and violence:

Finally, Devlin's closing line about Lucy hitting Charlie Brown really made me stop and think. Statistics show that 90 percent of domestic violence is perpetrated by men, not women. This example helped me realize that the real problem of violence goes deeper than the media. TV and movies only reflect a deeper culture of sexism in America. Movies constantly depict knifings and rapes and murders, most of them against women. Men will accept violence in the media as long as it's played out against women and children, but never, never against themselves. The movie *Thelma and Louise* created a firestorm of controversy simply because it showed a woman shooting a rapist. Until the day comes when women and children are treated as equals to men, and not their property, there will be violence in this country.

OUTLINES FOR
SUMMARY/RESPONSE ESSAYS

Three common outlines for summary/response essays are as follows. Select or modify one of these outlines to fit your audience, purpose, and kind of response. Typically, a summary/response will take the following form:

I.   Introduction to text(s)

II.   Summary of text(s)

III. Response(s)

    A. Point 1

    B. Point 2

    C. Point 3, etc.

IV. Conclusion

A second kind of outline focusses initially on key ideas or issues and then examines the text or texts for their contribution to these key ideas. This outline begins with the issues, then summarizes the text(s), and then moves to the reader's responses:

I.   Introduction to key issues

II. Summary of relevant text(s)

III. Response(s)

    A. Point 1

    B. Point 2

    C. Point 3, etc.

IV. Conclusion

A third outline integrates the summary and the response. It begins by introducing the issue and/or the text, gives a brief overall idea of the text, but then summarizes and responds point-by-point.

I.   Introduction to issues and/or text(s)

II. Summary of text's Point 1/response to Point 1

III. Summary of text's Point 2/response to Point 2

IV. Summary of text's Point 3/response to Point 3, etc.

V. Conclusion

DRAFTING

If you have been reading actively, you have been writing throughout the reading/writing/discussing process. At some point, however, you will gather your best ideas, have a rough direction or outline in mind, and begin writing a draft. Some writers like to have their examples and evidence ready when they begin drafting. Many writers have outlines in their heads or on paper. Perhaps you like to put your rough outline on the computer and then just expand each section as you write. Finally, most writers like to skim the text and *reread their notes* immediately before they start their drafts, just to make sure everything is fresh in their minds.

Once you start drafting, keep interruptions to a minimum. Because focus and concentration are important to good writing, try to keep writing as long as possible. If you come to a spot where you need an example that you don't have at your fingertips, just put in parentheses—(put the example about cosmetics and animal abuse here)—and keep on writing. Concentrate on making all your separate responses add up to a focussed, overall response.

REVISING

Revision means, literally, *reseeing*. Revising requires rereading the text and rewriting your summary and response. While revision begins as you read and reread the text, it continues until—and sometimes after—you turn in a paper or send it to its intended audience.

Guidelines for Revision

- **Review the purpose and audience for your assignment.** Is your draft addressed to the appropriate audience? Does it fulfill its intended purpose?

- **Continue to use your active reading/writing/discussing activities as you revise your draft.** If you are uncertain about parts of your summary or response, reread the text, check your notes, or discuss your draft with a classmate.

- **Reread your summary for key features.** Make sure your summary indicates author and title, cites main ideas, uses an occasional direct quotation, and includes author tags. Check your summary for accuracy and objectivity.

- **Check paraphrases and direct quotations.** If you are paraphrasing (without quotation marks), you should put the author's ideas into your own language. If you are quoting directly, make sure the words within the quotation marks are accurate, word-for-word transcriptions.

- **Review the purpose of your response.** Are you analyzing, agreeing/disagreeing, interpreting, or some combination of all three? Do your types of responses fit the assignment or address your intended audience and satisfy your purpose?

- **Amplify your supporting evidence.** Summary/response drafts often need additional, relevant evidence. Be sure you use sufficient personal experience, evidence from the text, or examples from other texts to support your response.

- **Focus on a clear, overall response.** Your responses should all add up to a focussed, overall reaction. Delete or revise any passages that do not maintain your focus.

- **Revise sentences to improve clarity, conciseness, emphasis, and variety.** (See Handbook.)

- **Edit your final version.** Use the spelling checker on your computer. Have a friend help proofread. Check the Handbook for suspected problems in usage, grammar, and punctuation.

HOW MALE AND FEMALE STUDENTS USE LANGUAGE DIFFERENTLY

DEBORAH TANNEN

Everyone knows that men and women communicate differently, but Deborah Tannen, a linguist at Georgetown University, has spent her career studying how and why their conversational styles are different. Tannen's books include Conversational Style: Analyzing Talk Among Friends *(1984) and her best-selling* You Just Don't Understand: Women and Men in Conversation *(1990). In the following article from* The Chronicle of Higher Education, *Tannen applies her knowledge of conversational styles to the classroom. How do men and women communicate differently in the classroom? What teaching styles best promote open communication and learning for both sexes? As you read her essay, think about your own classes. Do the men in your classes talk more than the women? Do men like to argue in large groups, while women prefer conversations in small groups? How clearly—and convincingly—does Tannen explain discussion preferences and their effects in the classroom?*

When I researched and wrote my latest book, *You Just Don't Understand: Women and Men in Conversation,* the furthest thing from my mind was reevaluating my teaching strategies. But that has been one of the direct benefits of having written the book. **(1)**

The primary focus of my linguistic research always has been the language of everyday conversation. One facet of this is conversational style: how different regional, ethnic, and class backgrounds, as well as age and gender, result in different ways of using language to communicate. *You Just Don't Understand* is about the conversational styles of women and men. As I gained more insight into typically male and female ways of using language, I began to suspect some of the causes of the troubling facts that women who go to single-sex schools do better in later life, and that when young women sit next to young men in classrooms, the males talk more. This is not to say that all men talk in class, nor that no women do. It is simply that a greater percentage of discussion time is taken by men's voices. **(2)**

The research of sociologists and anthropologists such as Janet Lever, Marjorie Harness Goodwin, and Donna Eder has shown that girls and boys learn to use language differently in their sex-separate peer groups. Typically, a girl has a best friend with whom she sits and talks, frequently telling secrets. It's the telling of secrets, the fact and the way that they talk to each other, that makes them best friends. For boys, activities are central: their best friends are the ones they do things with. Boys also tend to play in larger groups that are hierarchical. High-status boys give orders and push low-status boys around. So boys are expected to use language to seize center stage: by exhibiting their skill, displaying their knowledge, and challenging and resisting challenges. **(3)**

These patterns have stunning implications for classroom interaction. Most faculty members assume that participating in class discussion is a necessary part of successful performance. Yet speaking in a classroom is more congenial to boys' language experience than to girls', since it entails putting oneself forward in front of a large group of people, many of whom are strangers and at least one of whom is sure to judge speakers' knowledge and intelligence by their verbal display. **(4)**

Another aspect of many classrooms that makes them more hospitable to most men than to most women is the use of debate-like formats as a learning tool. Our educational system, as Walter Ong argues persuasively in his book *Fighting for Life* (Cornell University Press, 1981), is fundamentally male in that the pursuit of knowledge is believed to be achieved by ritual opposition: public display followed by argument and challenge. Father Ong demonstrates that ritual opposition—what he calls "adversativeness" or "agonism"—is fundamental to the way most males approach almost any activity. (Consider, for example, the little boy who shows he likes a little girl by pulling her braids and shoving her.) But ritual opposition is antithetical to the way most females learn and like to interact. It is not that females don't fight, but that they don't fight for fun. They don't *ritualize* opposition. **(5)**

Anthropologists working in widely disparate parts of the world have found contrasting verbal rituals for women and men. Women in completely unrelated cultures (for example, Greece and Bali) engage in ritual laments: spontaneously produced rhyming couplets that express their pain, for example, over the loss of loved ones. Men do not take part in laments. They have their own, very different verbal ritual: a contest, a war of words in which they vie with each other to devise clever insults. **(6)**

When discussing these phenomena with a colleague, I commented that I see these two styles in American conversation: many women bond by talking about troubles, and many men bond by exchanging playful insults and put-downs, and other sorts of verbal sparring. He exclaimed: "I never thought of this, but that's the way I teach: I have students read an article, and then I invite them to tear it apart. After we've torn it to shreds, we talk about how to build a better model." (7)

This contrasts sharply with the way I teach: I open the discussion of readings by asking, "What did you find useful in this? What can we use in our own theory building and our own methods?" I note what I see as weaknesses in the author's approach, but I also point out that the writer's discipline and purposes might be different from ours. Finally, I offer personal anecdotes illustrating the phenomena under discussion and praise students' anecdotes as well as their critical acumen. (8)

These different teaching styles must make our classrooms wildly different places and hospitable to different students. Male students are more likely to be comfortable attacking the readings and might find the inclusion of personal anecdotes irrelevant and "soft." Women are more likely to resist discussion they perceive as hostile, and, indeed, it is women in my classes who are most likely to offer personal anecdotes. (9)

A colleague who read my book commented that he had always taken for granted that the best way to deal with students' comments is to challenge them; this, he felt it was self-evident, sharpens their minds and helps them develop debating skills. But he had noticed that women were relatively silent in his classes, so he decided to try beginning discussion with relatively open-ended questions and letting comments go unchallenged. He found, to his amazement and satisfaction, that more women began to speak up. (10)

Though some of the women in his class clearly liked this better, perhaps some of the men liked it less. One young man in my class wrote in a questionnaire about a history professor who gave students questions to think about and called on people to answer them: "He would then play devil's advocate . . . *i.e.,* he debated us. . . . That class *really* sharpened me intellectually. . . . We as students do need to know how to defend ourselves." This young man valued the experience of being attacked and challenged publicly. Many, if not most, women would shrink from such "challenge," experiencing it as public humiliation. (11)

A professor at Hamilton College told me of a young man who was upset because he felt his class presentation had been a failure.

The professor was puzzled because he had observed that class members had listened attentively and agreed with the student's observations. It turned out that it was this very agreement that the student interpreted as failure: since no one had engaged his ideas by arguing with him, he felt they had found them unworthy of attention. **(12)**

So one reason men speak in class more than women is that many of them find the "public" classroom setting more conducive to speaking, whereas most women are more comfortable speaking in private to a small group of people they know well. A second reason is that men are more likely to be comfortable with the debate-like form that discussion may take. Yet another reason is the different attitudes toward speaking in class that typify women and men. **(13)**

Students who speak frequently in class, many of whom are men, assume that it is their job to think of contributions and try to get the floor to express them. But many women monitor their participation not only to get the floor but to avoid getting it. Women students in my class tell me that if they have spoken up once or twice, they hold back for the rest of the class because they don't want to dominate. If they have spoken a lot one week, they will remain silent the next. These different ethics of participation are, of course, unstated, so those who speak freely assume that those who remain silent have nothing to say, and those who are reining themselves in assume that the big talkers are selfish and hoggish. **(14)**

When I looked around my classes, I could see these differing ethics and habits at work. For example, my graduate class in analyzing conversation had twenty students, eleven women and nine men. Of the men, four were foreign students: two Japanese, one Chinese, and one Syrian. With the exception of the three Asian men, all the men spoke in class at least occasionally. The biggest talker in the class was a woman, but there were also five women who never spoke at all, only one of whom was Japanese. I decided to try something different. **(15)**

I broke the class into small groups to discuss the issues raised in the readings and to analyze their own conversational transcripts. I devised three ways of dividing the students into groups: one by the degree program they were in, one by gender, and one by conversational style, as closely as I could guess it. This meant that when the class was grouped according to conversational style, I put Asian students together, fast talkers together, and quiet students together. The class split into groups six times during the semester, so they met in each grouping twice. I told students to regard the groups as examples of interactional data and to note the different ways they participated in the different groups. Toward the end of the term, I gave them a questionnaire asking about their class and group participation. **(16)**

I could see plainly from my observation of the groups at work that women who never opened their mouths in class were talking away in the small groups. In fact, the Japanese woman commented that she found it particularly hard to contribute to the all-woman group she was in because "I was overwhelmed by how talkative the female students were in the female-only group." This is particularly revealing because it highlights that the same person who can be "oppressed" into silence in one context can become the talkative "oppressor" in another. No one's conversational style is absolute; everyone's style changes in response to the context and others' styles. **(17)**

Some of the students (seven) said they preferred the same-gender groups; others preferred the same-style groups. In answer to the question "Would you have liked to speak in class more than you did?" six of the seven who said yes were women; the one man was Japanese. Most startlingly, this response did not come only from quiet women; it came from women who had indicated they had spoken in class never, rarely, sometimes, and often. Of the eleven students who said the amount they had spoken was fine, seven were men. Of the four women who checked "fine," two added qualifications indicating it wasn't completely fine: One wrote in "maybe more," and one wrote, "I have an urge to participate but often feel I should have something more interesting/relevant/wonderful/intelligent to say!!" **(18)**

I counted my experiment a success. Everyone in the class found the small groups interesting, and no one indicated he or she would have preferred that the class not break into groups. Perhaps most instructive, however, was the fact that the experience of breaking into groups, and of talking about participation in class, raised everyone's awareness about classroom participation. After we had talked about it, some of the quietest women in the class made a few voluntary contributions, though sometimes I had to ensure their participation by interrupting the students who were exuberantly speaking out. **(19)**

Americans are often proud that they discount the significance of cultural differences: "We are all individuals," many people boast. Ignoring such issues as gender and ethnicity becomes a source of pride: "I treat everyone the same." But treating people the same is not equal treatment if they are not the same. **(20)**

The classroom is a different environment for those who feel comfortable putting themselves forward in a group than it is for those who find the prospect of doing so chastening, or even terrifying. When a professor asks, "Are there any questions?" students who can formulate statements the fastest have the greatest opportunity to respond. Those who need significant time to do so have not really been given a chance at all, since by the time they are ready to speak, someone else has the floor. **(21)**

In a class where some students speak out without raising hands, those who feel they must raise their hands and wait to be recognized do not have equal opportunity to speak. Telling them to feel free to jump in will not make them feel free; one's sense of timing, of one's rights and obligations in a classroom, are automatic, learned over years of interaction. They may be changed over time, with motivation and effort, but they cannot be changed on the spot. And everyone assumes his or her own way is best. When I asked my students how the class could be changed to make it easier for them to speak more, the most talkative woman said she would prefer it if no one had to raise hands, and a foreign student said he wished people would raise their hands and wait to be recognized. **(22)**

My experience in this class has convinced me that small-group interaction should be part of any class that is not a small seminar. I also am convinced that having the students become observers of their own interaction is a crucial part of their education. Talking about ways of talking in class makes students aware that their ways of talking affect other students, that the motivations they impute to others may not truly reflect others' motives, and that the behaviors they assume to be self-evidently right are not universal norms. **(23)**

The goal of complete equal opportunity in class may not be attainable, but realizing that one monolithic classroom-participation structure is not equal opportunity is itself a powerful motivation to find more diverse methods to serve diverse students—and every classroom is diverse. **(24)**

Vocabulary

Write down the meanings of the following words:

- ritual opposition is *antithetical* **(5)**

- personal *anecdotes* **(8)**

- *conducive* to speaking **(13)**

- *ethics* of participation **(14)**
- *monolithic* classroom-participation structure **(24)**

Questions for Writing and Discussion

1. Reread Tannen's essay, noting places where your experiences as a student match or do not match her observations. In what contexts were your experiences similar to or different from Tannen's? Explain what might account for the different observations.

2. In her essay, Tannen states and then continues to restate her thesis. Reread her essay, underlining all the sentences that seem to state or rephrase her main idea. Do her restatements of the main idea make her essay clearer? Explain.

3. Explaining essays may explain *what* (describe and define), explain *how* (process analysis), and/or explain *why* (causal analysis). Find one example of each of these strategies in Tannen's essay. Which of these three is the dominant shaping strategy? Support your answer with references to specific sentences or paragraphs.

4. Does the style of Tannen's essay support her thesis that men and women have different ways of communicating? Does Tannen, in fact, use a "woman's style" of writing that is similar to women's conversational style? Examine Tannen's tone (her attitude toward her subject and audience), her voice (the projection of her personality in her language), and her supporting evidence (her use of facts and statistics or anecdotal, contextual evidence). Cite specific passages to support your analysis.

S T U D E N T   W R I T I N G

TWO RESPONSES TO DEBORAH TANNEN
JENNIFER KOESTER AND SONJA H. BROWE

The two essays reprinted here were written in response to the essay by Deborah Tannen, "How Male and Female Students Use Language Differently." Jennifer Koester and Sonja H. Browe have opposite responses to Tannen's essay. Jennifer Koester, a political science major at Colorado State University, argues that Tannen's essay is effective because she uses sufficient evidence and organizes her essay clearly. On the other hand, Sonja Browe, an English education major at the University of Wyoming, writes an essay that is critical of Deborah Tannen's focus and supporting evidence.

A RESPONSE TO
DEBORAH TANNEN'S ESSAY

JENNIFER KOESTER

Deborah Tannen's "How Male and Female Students Use Language Differently" addresses how male and female conversational styles influence classroom discussions. Tannen asserts that women speak less than men in class because often the structure of discussion is more "congenial" to men's style of conversing. (1)

Tannen looks at three differences between the sexes that shape classroom interaction: classroom setting, debate format, and contrasting attitudes toward classroom discussion. First, Tannen says that during childhood, men "are expected to seize center stage: by exhibiting their skill, displaying their knowledge, and challenging and resisting challenge." Thus, as adults, men are more comfortable than women when speaking in front of a large group of strangers. On the other hand, women are more comfortable in small groups. (2)

Second, men are more comfortable with the debate format. Tannen asserts that many classrooms use the format of putting forth ideas followed by "argument and challenge." This too coincides with men's conversational experiences. However, Tannen asserts that women tend to "resist discussion they perceive as hostile." (3)

Third, men feel it is their duty to think of things to say and to voice them. On the other hand, women often regulate their participation and hold back to avoid dominating discussion. (4)

Tannen concludes that educators can no longer use just one format to facilitate classroom discussion. Tannen sees small groups as necessary for any "non-seminar" class along with discussion of differing styles of participation as solutions to the participation gap between the sexes. (5)

Three things work together to make Deborah Tannen's essay "How Male and Female Students Use Language Differently" effective: the qualifications of her argument, the evidence used, and the parallel format of comparison/contrast. (6)

First, Tannen's efforts to qualify her argument prevent her from committing logical errors. In the first paragraphs of her essay, she states, "This is not to say that all men talk in class, nor that no women do. It is simply that a greater percentage of discussion time is taken by men's voices." By acknowledging exceptions to her claim, Tannen avoids the mistake of oversimplification. She also strengthens her argument because this qualification tells the reader that she is aware of the complexity of this issue. **(7)**

Later, Tannen uses another qualification. She says, "No one's conversational style is absolute; everyone's style changes in response to the context and others' styles." Not only does this qualification avoid a logical fallacy, but it also strengthens Tannen's argument that classroom discussion must have several formats. By acknowledging that patterns of participation can change with the setting, Tannen avoids oversimplifying the issue and adds to her argument for classroom variety. **(8)**

Second, Tannen's evidence places a convincing argument before her reader. In the beginning of her essay, Tannen states that a greater percentage of discussion time in class is taken by men and that those women who attend single-sex schools tend to do better later in life. These two pieces of evidence present the reader with Tannen's jumping-off point. These statistics are what Tannen wants to change. **(9)**

In addition, Tannen effectively uses anecdotal evidence. She presents the reader with stories from her colleagues and her own research. These stories are taken from the classroom, a place which her audience, as educators, are familiar with. Her anecdotal evidence is persuasive because it appeals to the common sense and personal experiences of the audience. While some might question the lack of hard statistics throughout the essay, the anecdotal evidence serves Tannen best because it reminds her audience of educators of their own experiences. When she reminds the audience of their experiences, she is able to make them see her logic. **(10)**

Third, the parallel format of comparison/contrast between the genders highlights for the reader Tannen's main points. Each time Tannen mentions the reactions of one gender, she follows with the reaction of the other gender. For example, Tannen states, "So one reason men speak in class more than women is that many of them find the 'public' classroom setting more conducive to speaking, whereas most women are more comfortable speaking in private to a small group of people they know well." Here, Tannen places the tendencies of men and of women together, thus preventing the reader from having to constantly refer back to another section of the essay. **(11)**

In an earlier example, Tannen discusses men's comfort with the debate format in class discussion. The majority of that paragraph relates why men feel comfortable with that format. After explaining this idea, Tannen then tells the reader how women feel about the debate structure. Because how men and women feel about the debate format is placed within a paragraph, the readers easily see the difference between the genders. Tannen's use of the parallel format in the above examples and the rest of the essay provides a clear explanation of the differences in men's and women's interactions in the classroom. **(12)**

Tannen writes her essay effectively. She makes the essay convincing by qualifying her claims about gender participation. This strengthens her argument that just as the classroom is diverse, so should the format be diverse. Her supporting evidence is convincing because it comes from Tannen's own experience, reminds the audience of its own experiences, and appeals to the audience's common sense. Finally, her parallel format for discussing the differences between men and women enhances the reader's understanding. Overall, Tannen's essay is effective because she qualifies her argument, uses convincing evidence, and makes clear how men and women use language differently through a parallel comparison/contrast format. **(13)**

IS DEBORAH TANNEN CONVINCING?

SONJA H. BROWE

In her article entitled "How Male and Female Students Use Language Differently," Deborah Tannen explores the issue of gender as it affects the way we use language to communicate. Specifically, she discusses how differences in the way males and females are socialized to use language affect their classroom interactions. She explains that as females are growing up, they learn to use language to talk to friends, and to tell secrets. She states that for females, it is the "telling of secrets, the fact and the way they talk to each other, that makes them best friends." Boys, on the other hand, are "expected to use language to seize center stage: by exhibiting their skill, displaying their knowledge, and challenging and resisting challenge." **(1)**

According to Tannen, these differences make classroom language use more conducive to the way males were taught to use language. Tannen suggests that speaking in front of groups and the debatelike formats used in many classrooms are more easily handled by male students. **(2)**

Finally, Tannen describes an experiment she conducted in her own classroom which allowed students to evaluate their own conversation transcripts. From this experience, she deduced that small-group interaction is essential in the classroom because it gives students who don't participate in whole-class settings the opportunity for conversation and interaction. (3)

Though Tannen's research is a worthwhile consideration and provides information which could be of great interest to educators, this particular article lacks credibility and is unfocused. The points she is trying to make get lost in a world of unsupported assertions, and she strays from her main focus, leaving the reader hanging and confused. (4)

Tannen does take some time at the beginning of her article to establish her authority on linguistic analysis, but we may still hold her accountable for supporting her assertions with evidence. However, Tannen makes sweeping declarations throughout the essay, expecting the reader to simply accept them as fact. For example, when discussing the practice of the teacher playing devil's advocate and debating with the students, she states that "many, if not most women would shrink from such a challenge, experiencing it as public humiliation." Following such an assertion, we expect to see some evidence. Whom did Tannen talk to? What did they say? What percentage of women felt this way? This sort of evidence is completely lacking, so that what Tannen states as fact appears more like conjecture. (5)

Tannen makes another such unsupported pronouncement when she discusses the debatelike formats used in many classrooms. She explains that this type of classroom interaction is in opposition to the way that females, in contrast to males, approach learning. She states that "it is not that females don't fight, but that they don't fight for fun. They don't ritualize opposition." Again, where is Tannen's evidence to support such a claim? (6)

When Tannen does bother to support her assertions, her evidence is trite and unconvincing. For example, she reviews Walter Ong's work on the pursuit of knowledge, in which he suggested that "ritual opposition . . . is fundamental to the way males approach almost any activity." Tannen supports this claim of Ong's in parentheses, saying, "Consider, for example, the little boy who shows he likes a little girl by pulling her braids and shoving her." This statement may serve as an example but is not enough to convince the reader that ritual opposition is fundamental to the way males approach "almost any activity." (7)

Other evidence which Tannen uses to support her declarations comes in the form of conversations she has had with colleagues on these issues. Again, though these may provide examples, they do not represent a broad enough database to support her claims. **(8)**

Finally, Tannen takes three pages of her article to describe in detail an experiment she conducted in her classroom. Though the information she collected from this experiment was interesting, it strayed from the main point of the essay. Originally, Tannen's article was directed specifically at gender differences in communication. In this classroom activity, she looked at language-use differences in general, including cultural differences. She states that some people may be more comfortable in classes where you are expected to raise your hand to speak, while others prefer to be able to talk freely. She makes no mention of gender in regard to this issue. **(9)**

Finally, at the close of her essay, where we can expect to get the thrust of her argument or at least some sort of summary statement which ties into her main thesis, Tannen states that her experience in her classroom convinced her that "small-group interaction should be a part of any classroom" and that "having students become observers of their own interaction is a crucial part of their education." Again, these are interesting points, but they stray quite a bit from the original intention of the article. **(10)**

In this article, Tannen discusses important issues of which those of us who will be interacting with students in the classroom should be aware. However, her article loses a great deal of its impact because she does not stay focused on her original thesis and fails to support her ideas with convincing evidence. **(11)**

Questions for Writing and Discussion

1. Do your own double-entry log for Tannen's essay. On the left-hand side of a piece of paper, record Tannen's main points. On the right-hand side, write your own questions and reactions. Compare your notes to Koester's and Browe's responses. Whose response most closely matches your own? Where or how does your response differ from each?

2. Koester and Browe use different strategies for writing their summaries of Tannen's essay. Describe how the two summaries are different. Which summary is more accurate? Why?

3. Responses to texts may analyze the effectiveness of the text, agree or disagree with the ideas in the text, and/or interpret or reflect on the text.

What kinds of responses do Koester and Browe give? Would a different kind of response work better for either writer? Why or why not?

4. Koester focusses on three writing strategies that Tannen uses to make her essay more effective. What are they? What weaknesses of Tannen's essay does Koester ignore or downplay?

5. Browe's response focusses on two criticisms of Tannen's essay. What are they? In which paragraphs does Browe develop each criticism? What strengths of Tannen's essay does Browe ignore or downplay?

6. Neither Browe nor Koester uses personal experience as supporting evidence. Think of one experience that you have had in a specific class illustrating the conversational preferences of men and women. Write out that specific example. Could either Browe or Koester use such a specific example? Where might each writer use it in her response?

O B S E R V I N G

Observing is essential to good writing. Whether you are writing in a journal, doing a laboratory report for a science class, dashing off a memo at work, or writing a letter to the editor of a newspaper, keen observation is essential. Writing or verbalizing what you see helps you discover and learn more about your environment. Sometimes your purpose is limited to yourself: You observe and record to help you understand your world or yourself better. At other times, your purpose extends to a wider audience: You want to share what you have learned with others to help them learn as well. No matter who your audience is or what your subject may be, however, your task is to see and to help your readers see.

Of course, observing involves more than just "seeing." Good writers draw on all their senses: sight, smell, touch, taste, hearing. In addition, however, experienced writers also notice what is *not* there. The smell of food that should be coming from the kitchen but isn't. A friend who usually is present but now is absent. The absolute quiet in the air that precedes an impending storm. Writers should also look for *changes* in their subjects—from light to dark, from rough to smooth, from bitter to sweet, from noise to sudden silence. Good writers learn to use their previous *experiences* and their *imaginations* to draw comparisons and create images. Does a sea urchin look and feel like a pincushion with the pins stuck in the wrong way? Does the room feel as cramped and airless as the inside of a microwave oven? Finally, good writers write from a specific point of view or role: a student describing basic laws of physics or an experienced worker in a mental health clinic describing the clientele.

Depending on your purpose and audience, writing from observation can be relatively *objective,* as when you record what is actually, demonstrably there; or it can be more *subjective,* as when you suggest how you feel, think, or react to a subject. For example, you might describe a bicycle objectively as a "secondhand blue Bridgestone MB-3 mountain bike with a 25-inch Ritchey Logic frame, Shimano Deore DX derailleurs, a Shimano crank, Dia Compe brakes, and an Avocet saddle." You might need to communicate that kind of objective information to a prospective buyer or to an employee in a cycle repair shop. On the other hand, you may wish to communicate the bicycle's subjective feel—how easily it pedals; how it cranks up steep, rocky trails; or how solid it feels on rough terrain. In most situations, however, good writers describe their subjects both objectively and subjectively. They use some objectivity for accuracy and specific detail and some subjectivity to suggest the value or relevance of their subjects in a human environment.

The key to effective observing is to *show* your reader the person, place, event, or object through *specific detail.* Good description allows the reader to draw general conclusions based on specific detail. Rather than just telling a reader, "This bicycle has good technical components," the writer should show or describe how it feels as she rides it. If your reader is going to learn from your observations, you need to give the *exact details that you learned from,* not just your conclusions or generalizations. Even in writing, experience is the best teacher, so use specific details to communicate the feel, the data, the sights and sounds and smells. Whether you are a tourist describing the cliff dwellings at Mesa Verde, a salesperson analyzing consumer preferences for your boss, a physicist presenting data on a new superconducting material to other physicists, or a social worker putting together the details of a child abuse case, your first task is to describe your subject—to show your readers, to make them *see*.

TECHNIQUES FOR WRITING ABOUT OBSERVATIONS

The short passages that follow all use specific techniques for observing people, places, objects, or events. Some emphasize objective detail; some recreate subjective reactions or feelings. In all the passages, however, the writer *narrows* or *limits* the scope of the observation and selects specific details. The result is some *dominant idea*. The dominant idea reflects the writer's purpose for that particular audience. As you read these excerpts, notice how the authors use the following six techniques for recording vivid observations:

- **Giving sensory details (sight, sound, smell, touch, taste).** Also include *actual dialogue* and *names of things* where appropriate. Good writers often "zoom in" on crucial details.

- **Using comparisons and images.** To help readers visualize the unfamiliar (or see the commonplace in a new light), writers often draw comparisons and use evocative images.

- **Describing what is *not* there.** Sometimes keen observation requires stepping back and noticing what is absent, what is not happening, or who is not present.

- **Noting changes in the subject's form or condition.** Even when the subject appears static—a landscape, a flower, a building—good writers look for evidence of changes, past or future: a tree being enveloped by tent worms, a six inch purple-and-white iris that eight hours earlier was just a green bud, a sandstone exterior of a church being eroded by acid rain.

- **Writing from a distinct point of view.** Good writers assume distinct roles; in turn, perspective helps clarify what they observe. A lover and a botanist, for example, see entirely different things in the same red rose. *What* is seen depends on *who* is doing the seeing.

- **Focussing on a dominant idea.** Good writers focus on those details and images that clarify the main ideas or discoveries. Discovery often depends on the *contrast* between the reality and the writer's expectations.

These six techniques are illustrated in the following two paragraphs by Karen Blixen, who wrote *Out of Africa* under the pen name Isak Dinesen. A Danish woman who moved to Kenya to start a coffee plantation, Blixen knew little about the animals in Kenya Reserve. In this excerpt from her journals, she describes a startling change that occurred when she shot a large iguana. (The annotations in the margin identify all six observing techniques.)

Role: A newcomer to the Reserve

In the Reserve I have sometimes come upon the Iguana, the big lizards, as they were sunning themselves upon a flat stone in a riverbed. They are not pretty in shape, but nothing can be imagined more beautiful than their coloring. They shine like a heap of precious stones or like a pane cut out of an old church window. When, as you approach, they swish away, there is a flash of azure, green and purple over the stones, the color seems to be standing behind them in the air, like a comet's luminous tail.

Comparisons and images

Sensory details
Comparisons and images

Once I shot an Iguana. I thought that I should be able to make some pretty things from his skin. A strange thing happened then, that I have never afterwards forgotten. As I went up to him, where he was lying dead upon his stone, and actually while I was walking the few steps, he faded and grew pale, all color died out of him as in one long sigh, and by the time that I touched him he was grey and dull like a lump of concrete. It was the live impetuous blood pulsating within the animal, which had radiated out all that glow and splendor. Now that the flame was put out, and the soul had flown, the Iguana was as dead as a sandbag.

Changes in condition
Sensory detail

What is not there
Dominant idea: now colourless and dead

When writers describe people, places, objects, and events, they zero in on specific details that fit overall patterns or impressions. Ernest Hillen uses this technique in his memoir, *The Way of a Boy.*

OBSERVING PEOPLE

Manang smelled of different kinds of smoke. He never hurried and I liked being near him: it was restful. My father and the other men used to return from the tea gardens in shirts dark with sweat, their faces wet. Not Manang. He never looked hot. Manang wore faded khaki shorts that used to be my father's, no shirt, and a straw hat that hid his eyes. His large flat feet had spaces between the toes because he didn't have to wear shoes. I had felt the bottoms of those feet and they were hard and covered with deep, dry, criss-cross cuts which he said didn't hurt. I wanted feet like that, and his shiny brown skin, and I tried to walk bow-legged like him. Manang usually worked squatting, slowly moving along in

the quiet warm air like a duck. That's how he chopped at the lawn
with a long knife, that's how he weeded or dug or planted. That's
how, from bamboo and from a certain soft wood, he would carve
guns, knives, arrows, whatever we needed; we had only to ask.
And that's how, from half peanut shells, splinters of wood, and
bits of banana leaf, he built boats to sail on a puddle; you lay on
your stomach and blew the boat from shore to shore. Manang
almost never seemed to need to stand. He didn't often say much,
and I don't know if he had a wife or children or where he lived,
but he let me stay near him.

OBSERVING PLACES

Our new camp, Tjihapit, held about 15 000 prisoners, three times
as many as Bloemenkamp. Bigger in size, it was also a lot more
crowded. It swallowed neighbours and friends; many I never saw
again: Mrs. Witte and Mieke, Dirk, and Mrs. Plomp. Since Aunt
Ina, Erik, Ineke, and Hanneke were allotted a room some distance
from us we seldom visited.

At first, in Tjihapit, time moved fast: everything and everybody
was new. Eleven other families lived in our house and it had one
toilet. Our room (which in her way our mother at once made a
safe space) was about the same size as the one in Bloemenkamp—
the mattresses just fit—but it had a window. We looked out on
the back yard over a round flower bed, as high and wide as a truck
tire, thick with orange and pink hibiscus, and on to a clump of
short fruitless palm trees.

Jerry and I went to explore. Besides the palms growing in a tight
circle, which formed a decent cave, the garden held two low,
climbable trees, and more useless flower beds. Never mind if
Johnny Tomato might also move to Tjihapit, the beds would have
to be dug up and planted with vegetables. An overgrown lawn
ringed the house and in the rear, on our side, it stretched a dozen
steps to the edge of a stinking sewer; on the other side of the
ditch rose the camp's bamboo fence. Open sewers ran behind all
the houses but were usually hidden by man-high whitewashed
walls topped with spikes or shards of glass to stop thieves. The
foot-wide ditches, with a walkway on either side for cleaners
(before the war), made a network of alleys throughout the camp.
After a rainstorm, the sewers, not built to service the thousands
now crammed into that small section of Bandung, quickly over-
flowed and the alleys turned into narrow foaming rivers. Some

people threw garbage, broken glass, wrecked furniture and appliances, used-up bicycles, anything at all, over those walls. So, when the sun came out and the water level sank, there could be interesting finds amongst the steaming debris; flies, snakes, rats, snails, ravens, and frogs that honked in the night thought so, too. It was stupid to forage there on bare feet and we clappered walking in *klompen*, pieces of wood carved to fit soles and held on by strips of rubber tire across the toes. One girl didn't and stepped on a nail: awful poisons raced through her body and she soon died.

Ours was a corner house on a hilly street that climbed towards us and stopped short at the camp's wall. Beyond it was the "outside," from which in the quiet of the evening sometimes drifted sounds, faint and unreal: horseshoes on pavement, a *betja* bell, a vendor's cry nearing and fading. Camp streets were busy with women and teenagers walking to and from work or fetching food, children playing, women pushing the creaking moving vans, and, infrequently, soldiers on bicycles or in a car or truck. Already grass and weeds sprouted from Tjihapit's cracked sidewalks and pitted streets, cut telephone lines drooped from poles, and scum crusted the surface of clogged roadside ditches. Except for vegetable patches, gardens grew wild beneath wash lines strung up helter-skelter. Houses showed broken windows, doors and shutters askew, dangling eavestroughs, peeling paint, sunken roofs, and holes knocked into outside walls as additional entrances; inside, plaster crumbled, roofs leaked, and electrical wiring, plumbing, and gas piping had failed. It would get worse, but we wouldn't notice.

OBSERVING OBJECTS

But when I woke up that day, there was a traditional Dutch birthday chair, a chair she'd borrowed (we didn't have one) all decorated with flowers and bits of coloured paper stuck on with the glue-like porridge we were fed. The two of them sang Happy Birthday. On the chair's seat, each with a bit of white ribbon around it, were a pencil and a child's drawing pad. My mother handed me a cup of fruit salad. "There's more tonight," she promised. Who knows how she got the fruit, the presents, and the ribbon.

OBSERVING EVENTS

As the train clattered through the night down towards the sea, heat returned and with it high humidity. In the moist air you could almost taste our stink. I'd heard adults say that compared to Batavia's wet heat, Bandung was dry and cool. When dawn broke, the lookouts said we were nearing Batavia. The usual three-hour Bandung–Batavia run had taken us about twenty.

The train slowed down, halted with a jerk; after the night of stops and starts, most of us stayed stiff and in place. Another small station. But this time, the watchers reported, guards were running up and down the platform. We could hear them yelling. Fear rose again. Were we there? What now? Mothers shook children awake, yanked at luggage; some people stood up. My mother said, "Let's not rush." Then the doors screaked open and soldiers' heads stuck through grey light and bawled at us to come out. *Lekas! Lekas!* People staggered and slithered across the coach's filthy floor, banging into each other, falling, children howling. *Lekas! Lekas!* Out on the platform we huddled in a warm drizzle, a tired, frightened, smelly group, licking rain from our hands and arms. Soldiers carted several old women and a limp child out of the train and laid them down one next to the other. "Dead," I said. My mother nodded. Some women leaned on others, children held tight to legs and handbags. The guards prodded us into a line-up and started to count—until an officer screamed impatiently and we were rushed off the platform, stumbling, clutching each other, and into canvas covered military trucks. The still figures and a broken suitcase were left on the platform.

The truck's rear flap was struck down tightly, and we were once again all riding, standing up, through an unknown outside, unseeing in the dark. Our truck drove fast, tires sizzling, honking a lot, so it was probably in the lead. The trip lasted about half an hour. The truck stopped, turned sharply, throwing many off their feet, and backed up a bit. I heard the other trucks roaring up, stopping, turning, and reversing. Our flap was slung open and we could see a few yards away a wide gate made of bamboo poles strung with barbed wire: you could look right through it. On either side, though, rounding away from view, ran the familiar high dense *bilik* wall. Where were we? In the air hung a smell like that in the railroad car. Soldiers yelled at us to come down—*Lekas! Lekas!* Off to the side, a small thin officer, legs in shiny boots wide apart, stood watching us from under his umbrella. Behind him I could see a corner of the wide veranda of a grey stone house and some purple bougainvillaea. Clambering off the truck I kept my eyes on the man because, in a very un-Japanese way, his face showed expression: the small mouth looked as if it was smiling.

PROFESSIONAL WRITING

THE SNAKE

ANNIE DILLARD

Annie Dillard was born in Pittsburgh in 1945 and received her B.A. and M.A. degrees from Hollins College. She has published a book of poetry, Tickets for a Prayer Wheel *(1974); columns and essays for* Living Wilderness, Harper's, *and the* Atlantic; *and several books, including* An American Childhood *(1987),* A Writing Life *(1989), and* Modern American Memoirs *(1995). In the following selection from* Pilgrim at Tinker Creek *(1974), Dillard carefully observes a snake, a poisonous copperhead, as it lies on a sandstone quarry ledge at twilight. To her surprise, a mosquito alights on the snake and goes about its business of drilling through the scaly skin and sucking the snake's blood. Observing this bizarre episode, Dillard wonders about the laws of biological survival: "A little blood here, a chomp there, and still we live, trampling the grass? Must everything whole be nibbled?"*

There was a snake at the quarry with me tonight. It lay shaded by cliffs on a flat sandstone ledge above the quarry's dark waters. I was thirty feet away, sitting on the forest path overlook, when my eye caught the dark scrawl on the rocks, the lazy sinuosity that can only mean snake. I approached for a better look, edging my way down the steep rock cutting, and saw that the snake was only twelve or thirteen inches long. Its body was thick for its length. I came closer still, and saw the unmistakable undulating bands of brown, the hourglasses: copperhead. **(1)**

I never step a foot out of the house, even in winter, without a snakebite kit in my pocket. Mine is a small kit in rubber casing about the size of a shotgun shell; I slapped my pants instinctively to fix in my mind its location. Then I stomped hard on the ground a few times and sat down beside the snake. **(2)**

The young copperhead was motionless on its rock. Although it lay in a loose sprawl, all I saw at first was a camouflage pattern of particolored splotches confused by the rushing speckles of light in the weeds between us, and by the deep twilight dark of the quarry pond beyond the rock. Then suddenly the form of its head emerged from the confusion: burnished brown, triangular, blunt as a stone ax. Its head and the first four inches of its body rested on airy nothing an inch above the rock. I admired the snake. Its scales shone with newness, bright and buffed. Its body was perfect, whole and unblemished. I found it hard to believe it had not just been created on the spot, or hatched fresh from its mother, so unscathed and clean was its body, so unmarked by any passage. (3)

Did it see me? I was only four feet away, seated on the weedy cliff behind the sandstone ledge; the snake was between me and the quarry pond. I waved an arm in its direction: nothing moved. Its low-forehead glare and lipless reptile smirk revealed nothing. How could I tell where it was looking, what it was seeing? I squinted at its head, staring at those eyes like the glass eyes of a stuffed warbler, at those scales like shields canted and lapped just so, to frame an improbable, unfathomable face. (4)

Yes, it knew I was there. There was something about its eyes, some alien alertness . . . what on earth must it be like to have scales on your face? All right then, copperhead. I know you're here, you know I'm here. This is a big night. I dug my elbows into rough rock and dry soil and settled back on the hillside to begin the long business of waiting out a snake. (5)

The only other poisonous snake around here is the timber rattler, *Crotalus horridus horridus.* These grow up to six feet long in the mountains, and as big as your thigh. I've never seen one in the wild; I don't know how many have seen me. I see copperheads, though, sunning in the dust, disappearing into rock cliff chinks, crossing dirt roads at twilight. Copperheads have no rattle, of course, and, at least in my experience, they do not give way. You walk around a copperhead—if you see it. Copperheads are not big enough or venomous enough to kill adult humans readily, but they do account for far and away the greatest number of poisonous snakebites in North America: there are so many of them, and people, in the Eastern woodlands. It always interests me when I read about new studies being done on pit vipers; the team of herpetologists always seems to pick my neck of the woods for its fieldwork. I infer that we have got poisonous snakes as East Africa has zebras or the tropics have orchids—they are our specialty, our stock-in-trade. So I try to keep my eyes open. But I don't worry: you have to live pretty far out to be more than a day from a hospital. And worrying about getting it in the face from a timber rattler is like worrying about being struck by a meteorite: life's too short. Anyway, perhaps the actual bite is painless. . . . (6)

The copperhead in front of me was motionless; its head still hung in the air above the sandstone rock. I thought of poking at it with a weed, but rejected the notion. Still, I wished it would do something. Marston Bates tells about an English ecologist, Charles Elton, who said, with his Britishness fully unfurled, "All cold-blooded animals . . . spend an unexpectedly large proportion of their time doing nothing at all, or at any rate nothing in particular." That is precisely what this one was doing. **(7)**

I noticed its tail. It tapered to nothingness. I started back at the head and slid my eye down its body slowly: taper, taper, taper, scales, tiny scales, air. Suddenly the copperhead's tail seemed to be the most remarkable thing I had ever seen. I wished I tapered like that somewhere. What if I were a shaped balloon blown up through the tip of a finger? **(8)**

Here was this blood-filled, alert creature, this nerved rope of matter, really here instead of not here, splayed soft and solid on a rock by the slimmest of chances. It was a thickening of the air spread from a tip, a rush into being, eyeball and blood, through a pin-hole rent. Every other time I had ever seen this rock it had been a flat sandstone rock over the quarry pond; now it hosted and bore this chunk of fullness that parted the air around it like a driven wedge. I looked at it from the other direction. From tail to head it spread like the lines of a crescendo, widening from stillness to a turgid blast; then at the bulging jaws it began contracting again, diminuendo, till at the tip of its snout the lines met back at the infinite point that corners every angle, and that space once more ceased being a snake. **(9)**

While this wonder engaged me, something happened that was so unusual and unexpected that I can scarcely believe I saw it. It was ridiculous. **(10)**

Night had been rising like a ground vapor from the blackened quarry pool. I heard a mosquito sing in my ear; I waved it away. I was looking at the copperhead. The mosquito landed on my ankle; again, I idly brushed it off. To my utter disbelief, it lighted on the copperhead. It squatted on the copperhead's back near its "neck," and bent its head to its task. I was riveted. I couldn't see the mosquito in great detail, but I could make out its lowered head that seemed to bore like a well drill through surface rock to fluid. Quickly I looked around to see if I could find anyone—any hunter going to practice shooting beer cans, any boy on a motorbike—to whom I could show this remarkable sight while it lasted. **(11)**

To the best of my knowledge, it lasted two or three full minutes; it seemed like an hour. I could imagine the snake, like the frog sucked dry by the giant water bug, collapsing to an empty bag of skin. But the snake never moved, never indicated any awareness. At last the mosquito straightened itself, fumbled with its forelegs about its head like a fly, and sluggishly took to the air, where I lost it at once. I looked at the snake; I looked beyond the snake to the ragged chomp in the hillside where years before men had quarried stone; I rose, brushed myself off, and walked home. **(12)**

Is this what it's like, I thought then, and think now: a little blood here, a chomp there, and still we live, trampling the grass? Must everything whole be nibbled? Here was a new light on the intricate texture of things in the world, the actual plot of the present moment in time after the fall: the way we the living are nibbled and nibbling—not held aloft on a cloud in the air but bumbling pitted and scarred and broken through a frayed and beautiful land. **(13)**

Vocabulary

Write down the meanings of the following words:

- the lazy *sinuosity* **(1)**
- *undulating* bands **(1)**
- team of *herpetologists* **(6)**
- *splayed* soft and solid **(9)**
- lines of a *crescendo* **(9)**
- *diminuendo* **(9)**
- in time after the *fall* **(13)**

Questions for Writing and Discussion

1. If you have ever seen a snake or reptile up close, describe the snake (and the experience) in a paragraph.

2. Using only the details and description provided by Dillard, write a paragraph describing and characterizing the copperhead. Now, compare the paragraph you wrote in Question 1 with the details that Dillard gives. What does she describe that you did not? What did you notice that she doesn't?

3. Reread Dillard's essay, annotating for sensory details, images, descriptions of what is not there, and changes in her subject. Cite two specific examples (phrases or sentences) for each of these four observing techniques. Which of these techniques does she use most frequently? Which does she use most effectively?

4. In addition to observing her subject, Dillard describes herself and her relationship to the snake. Find three specific instances of this strategy. If she omitted these descriptions of herself, would her essay be more effective? Explain.

5. Observing essays focus on a discovery, a dominant idea, or a perceived general law. What facts does Dillard observe? What general law does she perceive? In which sentences does Dillard connect observed facts with her general law or dominant idea?

OBSERVING WOLVES
FARLEY MOWAT

Farley Mowat was born in Ontario in 1921 and received a B.A. from the University of Toronto. He has published over fifty books of fiction and nonfiction, including People of the Deer *(1952),* Never Cry Wolf *(1963), and* Woman in the Mists: The Story of Dian Fossey and the Mountain Gorillas of Africa *(1987).* Never Cry Wolf *(1963), from which "Observing Wolves" was taken, describes how the Canadian government sent Mowat to the Keewatin Barren Lands in the Northwest Territories to prove that the wolves were decimating the caribou herds—and thus should be exterminated. After observing wolves for a few short days, however, Mowat realized that "the centuries-old and universally accepted human concept of wolf character was a palpable lie. . . . I made my decision that, from this hour onward, I would go open-minded into the lupine world and learn to see and know the wolves, not for what they were supposed to be, but for what they actually were." In the first scene, Mowat learns how wolves establish territories; in the second, he discovers something about their diet. Mowat also gives names to each wolf that he observes: Angeline is a female wolf, George is her mate, and Uncle Albert is a male attached to the group.*

I

During the next several weeks I put my decision into effect with the thoroughness for which I have always been noted. I went completely to the wolves. To begin with I set up a den of my own as near to the wolves as I could conveniently get without disturbing the even tenor of their lives too much. After all, I *was* a stranger, and an unwolflike one, so I did not feel I should go too far too fast. **(1)**

Abandoning Mike's cabin (with considerable relief, since as the days warmed up so did the smell) I took a tiny tent and set it up on the shore of the bay immediately opposite to the den esker. I kept my camping gear to the barest minimum—a small primus stove, a stew pot, a teakettle, and a sleeping bag were the essentials. I took no weapons of any kind, although there were times when I regretted this omission, even if only fleetingly. The big telescope was set up in the mouth of the tent in such a way that I could observe the den by day or night without even getting out of my sleeping bag. (2)

During the first few days of my sojourn with the wolves I stayed inside the tent except for brief and necessary visits to the out-of-doors which I always undertook when the wolves were not in sight. The point of this personal concealment was to allow the animals to get used to the tent and to accept it as only another bump on a very bumpy piece of terrain. Later, when the mosquito population reached full flowering, I stayed in the tent practically all of the time unless there was a strong wind blowing, for the most bloodthirsty beasts in the Arctic are not wolves, but the insatiable mosquitoes. (3)

My precautions against disturbing the wolves were superfluous. It had required a week for me to get their measure, but they must have taken mine at our first meeting; and, while there was nothing overtly disdainful in their evident assessment of me, they managed to ignore my presence, and indeed my very existence, with a thoroughness which was somehow disconcerting. (4)

Quite by accident I had pitched my tent within ten yards of one of the major paths used by the wolves when they were going to, or coming from, their hunting grounds to the westward; and only a few hours after I had taken up residence one of the wolves came back from a trip and discovered me and my tent. He was at the end of a hard night's work and was clearly tired and anxious to go home to bed. He came over a small rise fifty yards from me with his head down, his eyes half-closed, and a preoccupied air about him. Far from being the preternaturally alert and suspicious beast of fiction, this wolf was so self-engrossed that he came straight on to within fifteen yards of me, and might have gone right past the tent without seeing it at all, had I not banged my elbow against the teakettle, making a resounding clank. The wolf's head came up and his eyes opened wide, but he did not stop or falter in his pace. One brief, sidelong glance was all he vouchsafed to me as he continued on his way. (5)

It was true that I wanted to be inconspicuous, but I felt uncomfortable at being so totally ignored. Nevertheless, during the two weeks which followed, one or more wolves used the track past my tent almost every night—and never, except on one memorable occasion, did they evince the slightest interest in me. **(6)**

By the time this happened I had learned a good deal about my wolfish neighbours, and one of the facts which had emerged was that they were not nomadic roamers, as is almost universally believed, but were settled beasts and the possessors of a large permanent estate with very definite boundaries. **(7)**

The territory owned by my wolf family comprised more than a hundred square miles, bounded on one side by a river but otherwise not delimited by geographical features. Nevertheless there *were* boundaries, clearly indicated in wolfish fashion. **(8)**

Anyone who has observed a dog doing his neighbourhood rounds and leaving his personal mark on each convenient post will have already guessed how the wolves marked out *their* property. Once a week, more or less, the clan made the rounds of the family lands and freshened up the boundary markers—a sort of lupine beating of the bounds. This careful attention to property rights was perhaps made necessary by the presence of two other wolf families whose lands abutted on ours, although I never discovered any evidence of bickering or disagreements between the owners of the various adjoining estates. I suspect, therefore, that it was more of a ritual activity. **(9)**

In any event, once I had become aware of the strong feeling of property rights which existed amongst the wolves, I decided to use this knowledge to make them at least recognize my existence. One evening, after they had gone off for their regular nightly hunt, I staked out a property claim of my own, embracing perhaps three acres, with the tent at the middle, and *including a hundred-yard long section of the wolves' path.* **(10)**

Staking the land turned out to be rather more difficult than I had anticipated. In order to ensure that my claim would not be overlooked, I felt obliged to make a property mark on stones, clumps of moss, and patches of vegetation at intervals of not more than fifteen feet around the circumference of my claim. This took most of the night and required frequent returns to the tent to consume copious quantities of tea; but before dawn brought the hunters home the task was done, and I retired, somewhat exhausted, to observe results. **(11)**

I had not long to wait. At 0814 hours, according to my wolf log, the leading male of the clan appeared over the ridge behind me, padding homeward with his usual air of preoccupation. As usual he did not deign to glance at the tent; but when he reached the point where my property line intersected the trail, he stopped as abruptly as if he had run into an invisible wall. He was only fifty yards from me and with my binoculars I could see his expression very clearly. **(12)**

His attitude of fatigue vanished and was replaced by a look of bewilderment. Cautiously he extended his nose and sniffed at one of my marked bushes. He did not seem to know what to make of it or what to do about it. After a minute of complete indecision he backed away a few yards and sat down. And then, finally, he looked directly at the tent and at me. It was a long, thoughtful, considering sort of look. **(13)**

Having achieved my object—that of forcing at least one of the wolves to take cognizance of my existence—I now began to wonder if, in my ignorance, I had transgressed some unknown wolf law of major importance and would have to pay for my temerity. I found myself regretting the absence of a weapon as the look I was getting became longer, yet more thoughtful, and still more intent. **(14)**

I began to grow decidedly fidgety, for I dislike staring matches, and in this particular case I was up against a master, whose yellow glare seemed to become more baleful as I attempted to stare him down. **(15)**

The situation was becoming intolerable. In an effort to break the impasse I loudly cleared my throat and turned my back on the wolf (for a tenth of a second) to indicate as clearly as possible that I found his continued scrutiny impolite, if not actually offensive. **(16)**

He appeared to take the hint. Getting to his feet he had another sniff at my marker, and then he seemed to make up his mind. Briskly, and with an air of decision, he turned his attention away from me and began a systematic tour of the area I had staked out as my own. As he came to each boundary marker he sniffed it once or twice, then carefully placed his mark on the outside of each clump of grass or stone. As I watched I saw where I, in my ignorance, had erred. He made *his* mark with such economy that he was able to complete the entire circuit without having to reload once, or, to change the simile slightly, he did it all on one tank of fuel. **(17)**

The task completed—and it had taken him no longer than fifteen minutes—he rejoined the path at the point where it left my property and trotted off towards his home—leaving me with a good deal to occupy my thoughts. **(18)**

II

After some weeks of study I still seemed to be as far as ever from solving the salient problem of how the wolves made a living. This was a vital problem, since solving it in a way satisfactory to my employers was the reason for my expedition. (19)

Caribou are the only large herbivores to be found in any numbers in the arctic Barren Lands. Although once as numerous as the plains buffalo, they had shown a catastrophic decrease during the three or four decades preceding my trip to the Barrens. Evidence obtained by various Government agencies from hunters, trappers and traders seemed to prove that the plunge of the caribou toward extinction was primarily due to the depredations of the wolf. It therefore must have seemed a safe bet, to the politicians-cum-scientists who had employed me, that a research study of wolf–caribou relationships in the Barrens would uncover incontrovertible proof with which to damn the wolf wherever he might be found, and provide a more than sufficient excuse for the adoption of a general campaign for his extirpation. (20)

I did my duty, but although I had searched diligently for evidence which would please my superiors, I had so far found none. Nor did it appear I was likely to. (21)

Toward the end of June, the last of the migrating caribou herds had passed Wolf House Bay heading for the high Barrens some two or three hundred miles to the north, where they would spend the summer. (22)

Whatever my wolves were going to eat during those long months, and whatever they were going to feed their hungry pups, it would not be caribou, for the caribou were gone. But if not caribou, what *was* it to be? (23)

I canvassed all the other possibilities I could think of, but there seemed to be no source of food available which would be adequate to satisfy the appetites of three adult and four young wolves. Apart from myself (and the thought recurred several times) there was hardly an animal left in the country which could be considered suitable prey for a wolf. Arctic hares were present; but they were very scarce and so fleet of foot that a wolf could not hope to catch one unless he was extremely lucky. Ptarmigan and other birds were numerous; but they could fly, and the wolves could not. Lake trout, arctic grayling and whitefish filled the lakes and rivers; but wolves are not otters. (24)

About this time I began having trouble with mice. The vast expanses of spongy sphagnum bog provided an ideal milieu for several species of small rodents who could burrow and nest-build to their hearts' content in the ready-made mattress of moss. **(25)**

They did other things too, and they must have done them with great frequency, for as June waned into July the country seemed to become alive with little rodents. The most numerous species were the lemmings, which are famed in literature for their reputedly suicidal instincts, but which, instead, *ought* to be hymned for their unbelievable reproductive capabilities. Red-backed mice and meadow mice began invading Mike's cabin in such numbers that it looked as if *I* would soon be starving unless I could thwart their appetites for my supplies. *They* did not scorn my bread. They did not scorn my bed, either; and when I awoke one morning to find that a meadow mouse had given birth to eleven naked offspring inside the pillow of my sleeping bag, I began to know how Pharaoh must have felt when he antagonized the God of the Israelites. **(26)**

I suppose it was only because my own wolf indoctrination had been so complete, and of such a staggeringly inaccurate nature, that it took me so long to account for the healthy state of the wolves in the apparent absence of any game worthy of their reputation and physical abilities. The idea of wolves not only eating, but actually thriving and raising their families on a diet of mice was so at odds with the character of the mythical wolf that it was really too ludicrous to consider. And yet, it was the answer to the problem of how my wolves were keeping the larder full. **(27)**

Angeline tipped me off. **(28)**

Late one afternoon, while the male wolves were still resting in preparation for the night's labours, she emerged from the den and nuzzled Uncle Albert until he yawned, stretched and got laboriously to his feet. Then she left the den site at a trot, heading directly for me across a broad expanse of grassy muskeg, and leaving Albert to entertain the pups as best he could. **(29)**

There was nothing particularly new in this. I had several times seen her conscript Albert (and on rare occasions even George) to do duty as a babysitter while she went down to the bay for a drink or, as I mistakenly thought, simply went for a walk to stretch her legs. Usually her peregrinations took her to the point of the bay farthest from my tent where she was hidden from sight by a low gravel ridge; but this time she came my way in full view and so I swung my telescope to keep an eye on her. **(30)**

She went directly to the rocky foreshore, waded out until the icy water was up to her shoulders, and had a long drink. As she was doing so, a small flock of Old Squaw ducks flew around the point of the Bay and pitched only a hundred yards or so away from her. She raised her head and eyed them speculatively for a moment, then waded back to shore, where she proceeded to act as if she had suddenly become demented. (31)

Yipping like a puppy, she began to chase her tail; to roll over and over among the rocks; to lie on her back; to wave all four feet furiously in the air; and in general to behave as if she were clean out of her mind. (32)

I swung the glasses back to where Albert was sitting amidst a gaggle of pups to see if he, too, had observed this mad display, and, if so, what his reaction to it was. He had seen it all right, in fact he was watching Angeline with keen interest but without the slightest indication of alarm. (33)

By this time Angeline appeared to be in the throes of a manic paroxysm, leaping wildly into the air and snapping at nothing, the while uttering shrill squeals. It was an awe-inspiring sight, and I realized that Albert and I were not the only ones who were watching it with fascination. The ducks seemed hypnotized by curiosity. So interested were they that they swam in for a closer view of this apparition on the shore. Closer and closer they came, necks outstretched, and gabbling incredulously among themselves. And the closer they came, the crazier grew Angeline's behaviour. (34)

When the leading duck was not more than fifteen feet from shore, Angeline gave one gigantic leap towards it. There was a vast splash, a panic-stricken whacking of wings, and then all the ducks were up and away. Angeline had missed a dinner by no more than inches. (35)

This incident was an eye-opener since it suggested a versatility at food-getting which I would hardly have credited to a human being, let alone to a mere wolf. However, Angeline soon demonstrated that the charming of ducks was a mere side line. (36)

Having dried herself with a series of energetic shakes which momentarily hid her in a blue mist of water droplets, she padded back across the grassy swale. But now her movements were quite different from what they had been when she passed through the swale on the way to the bay. (37)

Angeline was of a rangy build, anyway, but by stretching herself so that she literally seemed to be walking on tiptoe, and by elevating her neck like a camel, she seemed to gain several inches in height. She began to move infinitely slowly upwind across the swale, and I had the impression that both ears were cocked for the faintest sound, while I could see her nose wrinkling as she sifted the breeze for the most ephemeral scents. **(38)**

Suddenly she pounced. Flinging herself up on her hind legs like a horse trying to throw its rider, she came down again with driving force, both forelegs held stiffly out in front of her. Instantly her head dropped; she snapped once, swallowed, and returned to her peculiar mincing ballet across the swale. Six times in ten minutes she repeated the straight-armed pounce, and six times she swallowed—without my having caught a glimpse of what it was that she had eaten. The seventh time she missed her aim, spun around, and began snapping frenziedly in a tangle of cotton grasses. This time when she raised her head I saw, quite unmistakably, the tail and hind quarters of a mouse quivering in her jaws. One gulp, and it too was gone. **(39)**

Although I was much entertained by the spectacle of one of this continent's most powerful carnivores hunting mice, I did not really take it seriously. I thought Angeline was only having fun; snacking, as it were. But when she had eaten some twenty-three mice I began to wonder. Mice are small, but twenty-three of them adds up to a fair-sized meal, even for a wolf. **(40)**

It was only later, by putting two and two together, that I was able to bring myself to an acceptance of the obvious. The wolves of Wolf House Bay, and, by inference at least, all the Barren Land wolves who were raising families outside the summer caribou range, were living largely, if not almost entirely, on mice. **(41)**

Vocabulary

Write down the meanings of the following words:

- the den *esker* **(2)**
- *superfluous* **(4)**
- somehow *disconcerting* **(4)**
- *preternaturally* **(5)**
- *evince* the slightest interest **(6)**
- *lupine* **(9)**
- *extirpation* **(20)**
- her *peregrinations* **(30)**

Questions for Writing and Discussion

1. Describe what you knew about wolves before you read Mowat's description. Which parts of Mowat's description agreed with your preconceptions? Which parts gave you new information or a different opinion?

2. What equipment and habits of observation does the narrator employ in his study of wolves?

3. *What* is observed depends on *who* is doing the observing. Describe the narrator's behaviour and personality. How do his preconceptions affect what he observes? Should a scientific observer interfere with the lives of the wolves, as the narrator does? What does the narrator learn?

4. Four keys to effective description are repeated observation, attention to sensory details, noticing changes in the subject or the subject's behaviour, and noticing what is not present. Find examples of each of these four strategies in this essay.

5. Reread Dillard's "The Snake." What are the similarities and differences between Mowat's and Dillard's methods of observation, their voices as observers, and their discoveries?

OBSERVING: THE WRITING PROCESS

■ **ASSIGNMENT FOR OBSERVING**   Do a piece of writing in which you observe a specific person, place, object, or event. Your goal is to show how specific, observed details create dominant ideas about the person, place, object, or event. Your initial purpose is to use your writing to help you observe, discover, and learn about your subject; your final purpose will be to show your reader what you have seen and learned.

Important: Repeated observation is essential. Choose some *limited* subject—a person or small group of people, a specific place, a single object or animal, or a recurring event—that *you can reobserve over a period of several days during the writing process.*

CHOOSING A SUBJECT

If one of your journal entries suggested an interesting subject, try the collecting and shaping strategies. If none of those exercises caught your interest, consider the following ideas:

• Think about your current classes. Do you have a class with a laboratory—chemistry, physics, biology, engineering, animal science, horticulture, industrial sciences, physical education, social work, drawing, pottery—in which you have to make detailed observations? Use this assignment to help you in one of those classes: Write about what you observe and learn during one of your lab sessions.

- Seek out a new place on campus that is off your usual track. Check the college catalogue for ideas about places you haven't yet seen: a theatre where actors are rehearsing, a greenhouse, a physical education class in the martial arts, a studio where artists are working, a computer laboratory, or an animal research centre. Or visit a class you wouldn't take for credit. Observe, write, and learn about what's there and what's happening.

- Get a copy of the Yellow Pages for your town or city. Open to a page at random and place your finger on the page. If it lands on an advertisement for a nearby store, take your notebook there for a visit. Describe the chocolate mousse at a restaurant, an expensive wine at a liquor store, a new car at a dealership, a headstone at a burial-monument company, a twelve-string guitar at a music shop—whatever you would like to learn about through careful observation.

As you write on your subject, consider a tentative audience and purpose. Who might want to know what you learn from your observations? What do you need to explain? What will readers already know? Jot down tentative ideas about your subject, audience, and purpose. Remember, however, that these are not cast in concrete: You may discover some new idea, focus, or angle as you write.

COLLECTING

Once you have chosen a subject from your journal or elsewhere, begin collecting information. Depending on your purpose, your topic, or even your personal learning preferences, some activities will work better than others. However, you should *practise* all of these activities to determine which is most successful for you and most appropriate to your topic. During these collecting activities, go back and *reobserve your subject*. The second or third time you go back, you may see additional details or more actively understand what you're seeing.

Sketching   Begin by *drawing* what you see. Your drawing doesn't have to be great art to suggest other details, questions, or relationships that may be important. Instead of trying to cover a wide range of objects, try to focus on one limited subject and draw it in detail.

Here's an example. Writing student Brad Parks decided to visit an Eskimo art display at a local gallery. As part of his observing notes, he drew these sketches of Eskimo paintings. As he drew, he made notes in the margins of his sketches and zoomed in for more detail on one pair of walruses.

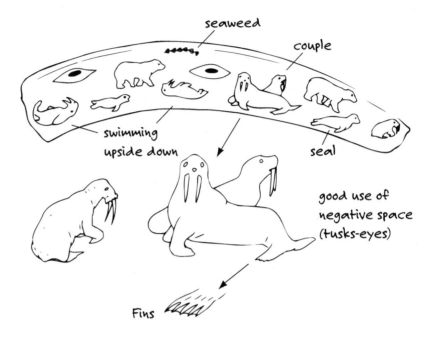

Taking Double-Entry Notes   Taking notes in a double-entry format is a simple but effective system for recording observed details. Draw a
vertical line down the middle of a page in your notebook. On the left-hand
side, record bits of description and sensory details. On the right-hand side,
jot down your reactions, thoughts, or ideas. On the left-hand side, make your
observed details as *objective* as possible. Comments on the right-hand side
will be more *subjective*, noting your impressions, reactions, comparisons, and
images, as well as additional questions and ideas.

Sensory Details, Facts, Data	Impressions, Reactions, Ideas, Questions
size, colour, shape, sounds, smell, touch, taste, actions, behaviour	impressions, associations, feelings, reactions, ideas, images, comparisons, related thoughts, questions

Answering Questions   To help you describe the person, place, object,
or event, write a short response in your journal to each of the following
questions:

- What exactly is it? Can you *define* this person, place, object, or
  event? If it's an object, are its parts related? Who needs it, uses it, or
  produces it?

- How much could it change and still be recognizable?

- Compare and contrast it. How is it similar to or different from other comparable people, places, things, or events?

- From what points of view is it usually seen? From what point of view is it rarely seen?

Freewriting   Freewriting means exactly what it says. Write about your subject, nonstop, for five to ten minutes. Sometimes you may have to write, "I can't think of anything" or "This is really stupid," but keep on writing. Let your words and ideas suggest other thoughts and ideas. For observing, the purpose of freewriting is to let your *imagination* work on the subject, usually *after* you have observed and recorded specific details. Freewriting on your subject will also develop more *associations* or *comparisons* for the right-hand side of your double-entry log. It should also help you to identify a dominant idea for your details.

SHAPING

To focus once again on the shaping process, consider your subject, purpose, and audience. Has your purpose changed? Can you narrow your subject to a specific topic? You may know the answers to some questions immediately; others you may not know until after you complete your first draft. Jot down your current responses to the following questions:

- *Subject:* What is your general subject?

- *Specific topic:* What aspect of your subject are you interested in? Try to *narrow* your field or limit your focus.

- *Purpose:* Why is this topic interesting or important to you or to others? From what point of view will you be writing? What is the *dominant idea* you are trying to convey?

- *Audience:* Who are your readers? What are these readers like, and why might they be interested in this topic? How can you direct your description of your subject to your particular audience?

With answers to these questions in mind, you should experiment with several of the following shaping strategies. These strategies will not only organize your specific examples but may also suggest related ideas to improve your description.

As you practise these strategies, try to *focus* on your subject. In a profile of a person, for example, focus on key facial features or revealing habits or mannerisms. If you're writing about a place or an event, narrow the subject. Describe, for instance, the street at night, a spider spinning a web in a windowsill, a man in a laundromat banging on a change machine, a bird hovering in midair, a photograph, a fish. Write in depth and detail about a *limited* subject.

With a limited subject, a shaping strategy such as spatial order, classification, or comparison/contrast will organize all the specific details for your audience. Shaping strategies give you ways of seeing relationships among the many bits of your description and of presenting them in an organized manner for your reader. Seeing these relationships will also help you discover and communicate the *dominant idea* to your reader.

Spatial Order

Spatial order is a simple way to organize your descriptive details. Choose some sequence—left to right, right to left, bottom to top—and describe your observed details in that sequence. In the following description of his "trashed" dorm room, Dale Furnish, a student who was the victim of a prank, uses spatial order. The italicized words illustrate the spatial order.

> As I walked in the door, I could hardly believe that this scene of destruction used to be my room. *Along the left hand wall*, nearly hiding my desk and mirror, was a pile of beer cans and bottles, paper cups, and old crumpled newspapers. The small window *on the far wall* was now covered with the mattress of the bed, and the frame of the bunk bed stood on end. The clothes closet, *to the right of the window*, looked as though it were a giant washing machine which had just gone through spin cycle—clothes were plastered all over, and only four hangers remained, dangling uselessly on the pole. *On the right wall*, where the bed had been, was the real surprise. Tied to the heating pipe was a mangy looking sheep. I swear. It was a real sheep. As I looked at it, it turned to face me and loudly and plaintively said, "Baaaa." *Behind me*, in the hall, everyone began laughing. I didn't know whether to laugh or cry.

Chronological Order

Chronological order is simply the time sequence of your observation. In the following passage, Gregory Allen, writing from his point of view as a five-foot-six-inch guard on a basketball team, describes sights, sounds, and his feelings during a pickup game. The italicized words emphasize the chronological order.

> The game *begins*. The guy checking me is about 6'1", red hair, freckles, and has no business on the court. He looks slow, so I decide to run him to tire him. I dribble twice, pump fake, and the guy goes for it, thinking that he's going to block this much smaller guy's shot. *Then* I leap, flick my wrist, and the ball glides through the air and flows through the net with a swish as the net turns upside down. I come down and realize that I have been scratched. *Suddenly*, I feel a sharp pain as sweat runs into the small red cut. I wipe the blood on my shorts and *continue playing*

the game. *After* that first play, I begin to hear the common song of
the game. There's the squeak of the high-top Nike sneakers, the
bouncing ball, the shuffle of feet. *Occasionally,* I hear "I'm open!"
"Pass the ball!" "Augghh!" And *then,* "Nice play, man!"

Comparison/Contrast   If what you've observed and written about
your subject so far involves seeing similarities or differences, you may be able
to use comparison/contrast as a shaping strategy—either for a single paragraph or for a series of paragraphs. The following two paragraphs, for example, are taken from Albert Goldman's biography of Elvis Presley, entitled
Elvis. In these paragraphs, Goldman's dominant idea depends on the striking contrast between what he finds on the front lawn of Graceland, the rock
star's mansion in Memphis, and what he notices when he steps through the
front door.

> Prominently displayed on the front lawn is an elaborate creche.
> The stable is a full-scale adobe house strewn with straw. Life-
> sized are the figures of Joseph and Mary, the kneeling shepherds
> and Magi, the lambs and ewes, as well as the winged annunciatory
> angel hovering over the roof beam. Real, too, is the cradle in
> which the infant Jesus sleeps.
>
> When you step through the ten-foot oak door and enter the
> house, you stop and stare in amazement. Having just come from
> the contemplation of the tenderest scene in the Holy Bible, imag-
> ine the shock of finding yourself in a *whorehouse!* Yet there is no
> other way to describe the drawing room of Graceland except to say
> that it appears to have been lifted from some turn-of-the-century
> bordello down in the French Quarter of New Orleans. . . . The
> room is a gaudy melange of red velour and gilded tassels, Louis
> XV furniture and porcelain bric-a-brac, all informed by the kind of
> taste that delights in a ceramic temple d'amour housing a miniature
> Venus de Milo with an electrically simulated waterfall cascading
> over her naked shoulders.

Examine once again your collecting notes about your subject. If there are
striking similarities or differences between the two parts or between various
aspects of your subject, perhaps a comparison or contrast structure will organize your details.

Classification   Classifying people, events, or things by *types* may provide a shape that you can use for either a paragraph or a whole essay. In the
following paragraph from "Speedway," an essay on racing at the
Indianapolis 500, cultural critic Paul Fussell categorizes spectators into
three social classes: the middle classes, or "middles"; the high proletarians,
or "high proles"; and the "uglies."

I'd say the people can be divided into three social classes: the middles, who on race day tend, in homage to the checkered flag, to dress all in black and white and who sit in reserved seats; the high proles, who watch standing or lolling in the infield, especially at the turns, "where the action is"; and the uglies, the overadvertised, black-leathered, beer-sodden, pot-headed occupiers of that muddy stretch of ground in the infield at the first turn, known as the Snake Pit. These are the ones who, when girls pass, spiritlessly hold up signs reading "Show Us Your T___s." The uglies are sometimes taken to be the essence of Indy, and they are the people who, I think, Frank Deford has in mind when he speaks of "barbarians." But they are not the significant Indy audience. The middle class is all those people arriving at the Speedway in cars bearing Purdue and Indiana State stickers.

Classification is often a useful method of shaping description. To see if it is appropriate for your subject, ask, "What types do you observe?" The answer may lead to categories or types that you had failed to observe, and the categories may provide a shape you can adopt.

Definition   Definition is the essence of observation. Defining a person, place, or object requires stating its exact meaning and describing its basic qualities. Literally, a definition sets the boundaries, indicating, for example, how an apple is distinct from an orange or how a canary is different from a sparrow. *Definition*, however, is a catchall term for a variety of strategies. It uses classification and comparison as well as description. It often describes a thing by negation—by saying what it is not. For example, in "The Pleasures of Love," Robertson Davies begins to describe love by defining what it is not.

Let us understand one another at once: I have been asked to discuss the pleasures of love, not its epiphanies, its ecstasies, its disillusionments, its duties, its burdens or its martyrdoms—and therefore the sexual aspect of it will get scant attention here. So if you have begun this piece in hope of fanning the flames of your lubricity, be warned in time.

Nor is it my intention to be psychological. I am heartily sick of most of the psychologizing about love that has been going on for the past six hundred years. Everybody wants to say something clever, or profound, about it, and almost everybody has done so. Only look under "Love" in any book of quotations to see how various the opinions are.

Alas, most of this comment is wide of the mark; love, like music and painting, resists analysis in words. It may be described, and some poets and novelists have described it movingly and well; but it does not yield to the theorist. Love is the personal experience of lovers. It must be felt directly.

My own opinion is that it is felt most completely in marriage, or some comparable attachment of long duration. Love takes time. What are called "love affairs" may afford a wide, and in retrospect, illuminating variety of emotions; not only fierce satisfactions and swooning delights, but the horrors of jealousy and the desperation of parting attend them; the hangover from one of these emotional toots may be long and dreadful.

But rarely have the pleasures of love an opportunity to manifest themselves in such riots of passion. Love affairs are for emotional sprinters; the pleasures of love are for the emotional marathoners.

Clearly, then, the pleasures of love are not for the very young.

At this stage in the writing process, you have already been defining your subject simply by describing it. But you may want to use a deliberately structured definition, as Davies does, to shape your observations.

Simile, Metaphor, and Analogy
Simile, metaphor, and analogy create vivid word pictures or *images* by making *comparisons*. These images may take up only a sentence or two, or they may shape several paragraphs.

- A *simile* is a comparison using *like* or *as:* A is like B. "Rashid eats his food like a vacuum cleaner."

- A *metaphor* is a direct or implied comparison suggesting that A is B: "At the dinner table, Rashid is a vacuum cleaner."

- An *analogy* is an extended simile or metaphor that builds a point-by-point comparison into several sentences, a whole paragraph, or even a series of paragraphs. Writers use analogy to explain a difficult concept, idea, or process by comparing it with something more familiar or easier to understand. If the audience, for example, knows about engines but has never seen a human heart, a writer might use an analogy to explain that a heart is like a simple engine, complete with chambers or cylinders, intake and exhaust valves, and hoses to carry fuel and exhaust.

As an illustration of simile and metaphor, notice how Joseph Conrad, in the following brief passage from *Heart of Darkness*, begins with a simile and then continues to build on his images throughout the paragraph. Rather than creating a rigid structural shape for his details (as classification or comparison/contrast would do), the images combine and flow like the river he is describing.

Going up that river was like travelling back to the earliest beginnings of the world, when vegetation rioted on the earth and the big trees were kings. An empty stream, a great silence, an impenetrable forest. The air was warm, thick, heavy, sluggish. There was no joy in the brilliance of sunshine. The long stretches of the waterway ran on, deserted, into the gloom of overshadowed distances. On silvery sandbanks hippos and alligators sunned themselves side by side. The broadening waters flowed through a mob of wooded islands; you lost your way on that river as you would in a desert, and butted all day long against shoals, trying to find the channel, till you thought yourself bewitched and cut off for ever from everything you had known once—somewhere—far away—in another existence perhaps.

An analogy helps shape the following paragraph by Carl Sagan, author of *The Dragons of Eden* and *Cosmos.* To help us understand a difficult concept, the immense age of the Earth (and, by comparison, the relatively tiny span of human history), Sagan compares the lifetime of the universe to something simple and familiar: the calendar of a single year.

The most instructive way I know to express this cosmic chronology is to imagine the fifteen-billion year lifetime of the universe . . . compressed into the span of a single year. . . . It is disconcerting to find that in such a cosmic year the Earth does not condense out of interstellar matter until early September; dinosaurs emerge on Christmas Eve; flowers arise on December 28th; and men and women originate at 10:30 P.M. on New Year's Eve. All of recorded history occupies the last ten seconds of December 31; and the time from the waning of the Middle Ages to the present occupies little more than one second.

Consider whether a good analogy would help you shape one or more paragraphs in your essay. Ask yourself, "What is the most difficult concept or idea I'm trying to describe?" Is there an extended point-by-point comparison—an analogy—that would clarify it?

Title, Introduction, and Conclusion

Depending on your purpose and audience, you may want a *title* for what you're writing. At the minimum, titles—like labels—should accurately indicate the contents in the package. In addition, however, good titles capture the reader's interest with some catchy phrasing or imaginative language—something to make the reader want to "buy" the package. Annie Dillard uses the simple label, "The Snake," for her essay. If a title is appropriate for your observation, write out several possibilities in your journal.

The introduction should set up the context for the reader—*who, what, when, where,* and *why*—so that readers can orient themselves. Depending on your audience and purpose, introductions can be very brief, pushing the reader quickly into the scene, or they can take more time, easing readers into the setting. Annie Dillard begins with a dramatic sentence: "There was a snake at the quarry with me tonight."

Conclusions should wrap up the observation, providing a sense of completeness. Conclusions vary, depending upon a writer's purpose and audience, but they tend to be of two types or have two components: a *summary* and a *reference* to the introduction. Dillard's final paragraph is of the first type. She states the whole point of her discovery: "Is this what it's like, I thought then, and think now. . . . Must everything whole be nibbled?" Mowat uses both components when he concludes his essay. Part II of his essay ends by referring to and then answering the central question of his expedition, that is: How do wolves survive? "The wolves of Wolf House Bay" Mowat tells us, "were living largely, if not almost entirely, on mice."

As you work on shaping strategies and drafting, make notes about possible titles, appropriate introductions, or effective conclusions for your written observations.

DRAFTING

Reread Notebook Entries and Notes from Collecting and Shaping   Before you start drafting, review your material so you aren't writing cold. Stop and reread everything you've written on your subject. You're not trying to memorize particular sentences or phrases; you're just getting it all fresh in your mind, seeing what you still like and discarding details that are no longer relevant.

Reobserve Your Subject   If necessary, go back and observe your subject again. One more session may suggest an important detail or idea that will help you get started writing.

Reexamine Purpose, Audience, Dominant Idea, and Shape
After all your writing and rereading, you may have some new ideas about your purpose, audience, or dominant idea. Take a minute to jot these down in your journal. Remember that your specific details should show the main point or dominant idea, whether you state it explicitly or not.

Next, if the shaping strategies suggested an order for your essay, use it to guide your draft. You may, however, have only your specific details or a general notion of the dominant idea you're trying to communicate to your reader. In that case, you may want to begin writing and work out a shape or outline as you write.

Create a Draft   With the above notes as a guide, you are ready to start drafting. Work on establishing your ritual: Choose a comfortable, familiar place with the writing tools you like. Make sure you'll have no interruptions. Try to write non-stop. If you can't think of a word, substitute a dash. If you can't remember how to spell a word, don't stop to look it up now—keep writing. Write until you reach what feels like the end. If you do get stuck, *reread* your last few lines or some of your writing process materials. Then go back and pick up the thread. Don't stop to count words or pages. You should shoot for more material than you need because it's usually easier to cut material later, when you're revising, than to add more if you're short.

REVISING

Gaining Distance and Objectivity   Revising, of course, has been going on since you put your first sentence down on paper. You've changed ideas, thought through your subject again, and observed your person, place, object, or event. After your rough draft is finished, your next step is to revise again to resee the whole thing. But before you do, you need to let it sit at least 24 hours, to get away from it for a while, to gain some distance and perspective. Relax. Congratulate yourself.

About the time you try to relax, however, you may get a sudden temptation—even an overwhelming urge—to have someone else read it—immediately! Usually, it's better to resist that urge. Chances are, you want to have someone else read it either because you're bubbling with enthusiasm and you want to share it or because you're certain that it's all garbage and you want to hear the bad news right away. Most readers will not find it either as great as you hope *or* as awful as you fear. As a result, their offhand remarks may seem terribly insensitive or condescending. In a day or so, however, you'll be able to see your writing more objectively: Perhaps it's not great yet, but it's not hopeless, either. At that point, you're ready to get some feedback and start your revisions.

| PEER | RESPONSE |

The instructions below will help you give and receive constructive advice about the rough draft of your observing essay. You may use these guidelines for an in-class workshop, a take-home review, or a computer e-mail response.

Writer: Before you exchange drafts with another reader, write out the following information about your rough draft:

1. What is the dominant impression that you want your description to make? What overall idea or impression do you want your reader to have?

2. What paragraph(s) contains your best and most vivid description? What paragraph(s) still needs some revision?

3. Explain one or two things you would like your reader to comment on as he or she responds to your draft.

Reader: First, without making any marks, read the entire draft from start to finish. As you *reread* the draft, answer the following questions.

1. What *dominant impression* does the draft create? Does the dominant impression you received agree with the writer's own idea? If not, how might the writer better achieve that overall impression?

2. Look at the writer's responses to Question 2. Does the writer, in fact, use vivid description in his or her best paragraph(s)? How might the paragraph(s) that the writer says needs revision be improved? Review the six techniques for descriptive writing at the beginning of this chapter. Where or how might the writer improve the *sensory details, images,* descriptions of what is *not there, changes* in the subject, or *point of view?* Offer specific suggestions.

3. Reread the assignment for this essay. Explain how this essay should be revised to more clearly *meet the assignment.*

4. List the *two most important things* this writer should work on as he or she revises this draft. Explain why these are important.

Guidelines for Revision

As you revise your essay, keep the following tips and checklist questions in mind:

- **Reexamine your purpose and audience.** Are you doing what you intended? If your purpose or audience has changed, what other changes do you need to make as you revise?

- **Consider your point of view.** Would changing to another point of view clarify what you are describing?

- **Consider your vantage point.** Do you have a bird's-eye view, or are you observing from a low angle? Do you zoom in for a close-up of a person or object? Would a different vantage point fit your purpose and audience?

- **Make sure you are using sensory details where appropriate.** Remember, you must *show* your reader the details you observe. If necessary, reobserve your subject.

- **Do all your details and examples support your dominant idea?** Reread your draft and omit any irrelevant details.

- **What is *not* present in your subject that might be important to mention?**

- **What changes occur in the form or function of your subject?** Where can you describe those changes more vividly?

- **Make comparisons if they will help you or your reader understand your subject better.** Similes, metaphors, or analogies may describe your subject more vividly.

- **Does what you are observing belong to a class of similar objects?** Would classification organize your writing?

- **Be sure to cue or signal your reader with appropriate transition words.** Transitions will improve the coherence or flow of your writing.

  - *Spatial order:* on the left, on the right, next, above, below, higher, lower, farther, next, beyond

  - *Chronological order:* before, earlier, after, afterward, thereafter, then, from then on, the next day, shortly, by that time, immediately, slowly, while, meanwhile, until, now, soon, within an hour, first, later, finally, at last

  - *Comparison/contrast:* on one hand, on the other hand, also, similarly, in addition, likewise, however, but, yet, still, although, even so, nonetheless, in contrast.

- **Revise sentences for clarity, conciseness, emphasis, and variety.**

- **When you have revised your essay, edit your writing for correct spelling and appropriate word choice, punctuation, usage, and grammar.**

REMEMBERING

EARNING OUTCOMES

fter reading this chapter you will have
earned how to

tell a story to make a point

use specific examples from experience
and observation

The human brain is a pack rat: Nothing is too small, obscure, or mundane for the brain's collection. Often the brain collects and discards information without regard to our wishes. Out of the collection may arise, with no warning, the image of windblown whitecaps on a lake you visited more than five years ago, the recipe for Uncle Joe's incomparable chili, or even the right answer to an exam question that you've been staring at for the past 15 minutes.

Remembering is sometimes easy, sometimes difficult. Often careful concentration yields nothing, while the most trivial occurrence—an old song on a car radio, the acrid smell of diesel exhaust, the face of a stranger—will trigger a flood of recollections. Someone tells a story and you immediately recall incidents, funny or traumatic, from your own life. Some memories, however, are nagging and troublesome, keeping you awake at night, daring you to deal with them. You pick at these memories. Why are they so important? You write about them, usually to probe that mystery of yesterday and today. Sights, sounds, or feelings from the present may draw you to the past, but the past leads, just as surely, back to the present.

Direct observations are important to learning and writing, but so are your memories, experiences, and stories. You may write an autobiographical account of part of your life, or you may recall a brief event, a person, or a place just as an example to illustrate a point. Whatever form your writing from memory takes, however, your initial purpose is to remember experiences so that you can understand yourself and your world. The point is not to write fiction, but to practise drawing on your memories and to write vividly enough about them so that you and others can discover and learn.

The value of remembering lies exactly here: Written memories have the power to teach you and, through *empathy* with your readers, to inform or convince them as well. At first, you may be self-conscious about sharing your personal memories. But as you reveal these experiences, you realize that your story is worth telling—not because you're such an egotist, but because sharing experiences helps everyone learn.

TECHNIQUES FOR WRITING ABOUT MEMORIES

Writing vividly about memories includes all the skills of careful observing, but it adds several additional narrative strategies. Listed below are five techniques that writers use to compose effective remembering essays. As you read the essays that follow in this chapter, notice how each writer uses these techniques. Then, when you write your own remembering essay, use these techniques in your own essay. Remember: Not all writing about memories uses all five techniques, but one or two of them may transform a lifeless or boring account into an effective narrative.

- Using *detailed observation* of people, places, and events. Writing vividly about memories requires many of the skills of careful observation. Give actual dialogue where appropriate.

- Creating specific scenes set in time and space. Show your reader the actual events; don't just tell about events. Narrate specific incidents as they actually happened. Avoid monotonously summarizing events or presenting just the conclusions (for instance, "those experiences really changed my life").

- Noting *changes, contrasts,* or *conflicts.* Changes in people or places, contrasts between two different memories or between memories of expectations and realities, and conflicts between people or ideas— any of these may lead to the meaning or importance of a remembered person, place, or event.

- Making *connections* between past events, people, or places and the present. The main idea of a narrative often grows out of changes and conflicts or arises from the connections you make between past and present.

- Discovering and focussing on a main idea. A remembering essay is not a random narrative of the writer's favourite memories. A narrative should have a clear main point, focus on a main idea, or make a discovery. The essay should clearly show why the memories are important.

All of these techniques are important, but you should also keep several other points in mind. Normally, you should write in the *first person,* using *I* or *we* throughout the narrative. Although you will usually write in *past tense,* sometimes you may wish to lend immediacy to the events by retelling them in the *present tense,* as if they are happening now. Finally, you may choose straightforward *chronological order,* or you may begin near the end and use a *flashback* to tell the beginning of the story.

The key to effective remembering, however, is to get beyond *generalities and conclusions* about your experiences ("I had a lot of fun—those days really changed my life"). Your goal is to recall *specific incidents set in time and place* that *show* how and why those days changed your life. The specific incidents should show your *main point* or *dominant idea.*

REMEMBERING PEOPLE

In the following passage from *Wordstruck,* Robert McNeil describes his parents. Focussing specifically on the musical and dramatic qualities of his mother's voice, McNeil reveals his feelings through this memory.

> My parents loved books, and the Depression left them too hard
> up for much other diversion. My mother would weep over a book,
> my father lose himself in one for hours.

All this combined to fashion a childhood which made words important. Pleasure was another matter. The pleasures of children were not as aggressively consulted—or exploited—then as now; the child as a consumer had yet to be invented. I did not consciously come to love the language, and to know I did, until much later, until late adolescence. But in these years all the seeds of love were planted.

The words were spoken into my ears by my Nova Scotian mother, in a musical voice which inclined towards British intonations. It was not an English accent; it was cultured Haligonian, a variety of the distinctive, close-lipped Nova Scotian dialect. It was multi-hued, like glass fused of many bottles in a fire, with wisps of Lowland Scots and Highland Gaelic, Irish, Hanoverian German, Acadian French and the many flavours of English deposited by generations of British soldiers and sailors. My mother's words sounded Nova Scotian, but the lilt and music of the speech—its rise and fall and its rhythms— were English. My father's speech, acquired in Montreal, was more flatly Canadian. He was the constant reader and collector of books, but for much of my childhood he was away at sea. It was my mother who read to me and my two younger brothers.

She read with enthusiasm and delight. If reading the childish stories bored her, she never showed it. She sounded as enthralled, as full of wonder and close-rivetted attention as I was. She had a sense of dramatic situation and character and played the parts to the hilt. She felt the descriptive passages and gave them full value; the uplifting and poetic moments got a reading worthy of them.

REMEMBERING PLACES

In the following passage from *The Street,* Mordecai Richler remembers the liveliness of his Montreal neighbourhood.

If the Main was a poor man's street, it was also a dividing line. Below, the French Canadians. Above, some distance above, the dreaded WASPS. On the Main itself there were some Italians, Yugoslavs and Ukrainians, but they did not count as true Gentiles. Even the French Canadians, who were our enemies, were not entirely unloved. Like us, they were poor and coarse with large families and spoke English badly.

Looking back, it's easy to see that the real trouble was there was no dialogue between us and the French Canadians, each elbowing the other, striving for WASP acceptance. We fought the French Canadians stereotype for stereotype. If many of them believed that the St. Urbain Street Jews were secretly rich, manipulating the black market, then my typical French Canadian was a moronic gum-chewer. He wore his greasy black hair parted down the middle and also affected an eyebrow moustache. His zoot trousers were belted just under the breastbone and ended in a peg hugging his ankles. He was the dolt who held up your uncle endlessly at the liquor commission while he tried unsuccessfully to add three figures or, if he was employed at the customs office, never knew which form to give you. Furthermore, he only held his liquor commission or customs or any other government job because he was the second cousin of a backwoods notary who had delivered the village vote to the Union Nationale for a generation. Other French Canadians were speed cops, and if any of these ever stopped you on the highway you made sure to hand him a folded two dollar bill with your licence.

Actually, it was only the WASPS who were truly hated and feared. "Among them," I heard it said, "with those porridge faces, who can tell what they're thinking?" It was, we felt, their country, and given sufficient liquor who knew when they would make trouble?

We were a rude, aggressive bunch round the Main. Cocky too. But bring down the most insignificant, pinched WASP fire insurance inspector and even the most arrogant merchant on the street would dip into the drawer for a ten spot or a bottle and bow and say, "Sir."

After school we used to race down to the Main to play snooker at the Rachel or the Mount Royal. Other days, when we chose to avoid school altogether, we would take the No. 55 streetcar as far as St. Catherine Street, where there was a variety of amusements offered. We could play the pinball machines and watch archaic strip-tease movies for a nickel at the Silver Gameland. At the Midway or the Crystal Palace we could see a double feature and a girlie show for as little as thirty-five cents. The Main, at this juncture, was thick with drifters, panhandlers, and whores. Available on both sides of the street were "Tourists Rooms by Day and Night," and everywhere there was the smell of french fried potatoes cooking in stale oil. Tough, unshaven men in checked shirts stood in knots outside the taverns and cheap cafés. There was the promise of violence.

As I recall it, we were always being warned about the Main. Our grandparents and parents had come there by steerage from Rumania or by cattleboat from Poland by way of Liverpool. No sooner had they unpacked their bundles and cardboard suitcases than they were planning a better, brighter life for us, the Canadian-born children. The Main, good enough for them, was not to be for us, and that they told us again and again was what the struggle was for. The Main was for *bummers*, drinkers, and (heaven forbid) failures.

REMEMBERING EVENTS

In the following excerpt from *Inside Memory,* Timothy Findley's recollection of the Atlantic House Hotel is forever bound up with the picture of former Governor General Jules Léger in a ferocious thunderstorm.

The Atlantic House Hotel is now a thing of the past. They have torn it down and put up condominiums for millionaires. Consequently, I will never see that bit of the Atlantic shore again. But as long as I live, so will my memories of sand and sea and a white clapboard haven.

One of the keenest images—never to be forgotten—comes from the last summer spent there by our former Governor General Jules Léger. On an August afternoon, the beach was hit by a sudden and typically violent thunderstorm. Inside the hotel, all the lights went out. The sky was green. The wind—and the waves it caused—were quite alarming. Everyone remembered the hurricanes of '54 and '38. When I glanced out the window, I saw a tall, gaunt figure standing on the lawn, his sand-coloured raincoat whipping around his legs and one arm dangling free—the arm that had been paralysed by a stroke. It was Jules Léger.

For once, he was not surrounded by the small children who seemed to instantly collect wherever he went. He stood alone, facing the sea and drinking in the wind—defying all the worst the elements had to offer. He went down onto the sand and, choosing his place with some deliberation, he stood there amidst the waves until the storm was over. So far as I am concerned—he is standing there still; just as is the Atlantic House Hotel—for those of us who loved it.

PROFESSIONAL WRITING

THE DAY LANGUAGE CAME INTO MY LIFE

HELEN KELLER

At the age of 18 months, Helen Keller (1880–1968) lost her sight and hearing as a result of illness. During the next five years of her childhood, Keller became increasingly wild and unruly as she struggled against her dark and silent world. In "The Day Language Came Into My Life," Keller remembers how, at age seven, her teacher, Anne Sullivan, arrived and taught her the miracle of language. After learning sign language and braille, Keller began her formal schooling and—with continued help from Sullivan—eventually graduated with honours from Radcliffe College. In her adult years, Keller became America's best-loved ambassador for the blind and disabled. She met nearly every American president, travelled to dozens of countries to speak on behalf of blind and deaf people, and wrote several books, including The Story of My Life *(1903),* The World I Live In *(1908), and* Midstream: My Later Life *(1930). The story of Anne Sullivan's teaching is told in William Gibson's Pulitzer Prize–winning play,* The Miracle Worker.

The most important day I remember in all my life is the one on which my teacher, Anne Mansfield Sullivan, came to me. I am filled with wonder when I consider the immeasurable contrast between the two lives which it connects. It was the third of March 1887, three months before I was seven years old. **(1)**

On the afternoon of that eventful day, I stood on the porch, dumb, expectant. I guessed vaguely from my mother's signs and from the hurrying to and fro in the house that something unusual was about to happen, so I went to the door and waited on the steps. The afternoon sun penetrated the mass of honeysuckle that covered the porch and fell on my upturned face. My fingers lingered almost unconsciously on the familiar leaves and blossoms which had just come forth to greet the sweet southern spring. I did not know what the future held of marvel or surprise for me. Anger and bitterness had preyed upon me continually for weeks and a deep languor had succeeded this passionate struggle. **(2)**

Have you ever been at sea in a dense fog, when it seemed as if a tangible white darkness shut you in, and the great ship, tense and anxious, groped her way toward the shore with plummet and sounding-line, and you waited with beating heart for something to happen? I was like that ship before my education began, only I was without compass or sounding-line and had no way of knowing how near the harbor was. "Light! give me light!" was the wordless cry of my soul, and the light of love shone on me in that very hour. **(3)**

I felt approaching footsteps. I stretched out my hand as I supposed to my mother. Someone took it, and I was caught up and held close in the arms of her who had come to reveal all things to me, and, more than all things else, to love me. **(4)**

The morning after my teacher came she led me into her room and gave me a doll. The little blind children at the Perkins

Institution had sent it and Laura Bridgman had dressed it; but I did not know this until afterward. When I had played with it a little while, Miss Sullivan slowly spelled into my hand the word "d-o-l-l." I was at once interested in this finger play and tried to imitate it. When I finally succeeded in making the letters correctly I was flushed with childish pleasure and pride. Running downstairs to my mother I held up my hand and made the letters for doll. I did not know that I was spelling a word or even that words existed; I was simply making my fingers go in monkeylike imitation. In the days that followed I learned to spell in this uncomprehending way a great many words, among them *pin, hat, cup* and a few verbs like *sit, stand* and *walk*. But my teacher had been with me several weeks before I understood that everything has a name. (5)

One day, while I was playing with my new doll, Miss Sullivan put my big rag doll into my lap also, spelled "d-o-l-l" and tried to make me understand that "d-o-l-l" applied to both. Earlier in the day we had had a tussle over the words "m-u-g" and "w-a-t-e-r." Miss Sullivan had tried to impress it upon me that "m-u-g" is *mug* and that "w-a-t-e-r" is *water*, but I persisted in confounding the two. In despair she had dropped the subject for the time, only to renew it at the first opportunity. I became impatient at her repeated attempts and, seizing the new doll, I dashed it upon the floor. I was keenly delighted when I felt the fragments of the broken doll at my feet. Neither sorrow nor regret followed my passionate outburst. I had not loved the doll. In the still, dark world in which I lived there was no strong sentiment or tenderness. I felt my teacher sweep the fragments to one side of the hearth, and I had a sense of satisfaction that the cause of my discomfort was removed. She brought me my hat, and I knew I was going out into the warm sunshine. This thought, if a wordless sensation may be called a thought, made me hop and skip with pleasure. (6)

We walked down the path to the well-house, attracted by the fragrance of the honeysuckle with which it was covered. Someone was drawing water and my teacher placed my hand under the spout. As the cool stream gushed over one hand she spelled into the other the word *water*, first slowly, then rapidly. I stood still, my whole attention fixed upon the motions of her fingers. Suddenly I felt a misty consciousness as of something forgotten—a thrill of returning thought; and somehow the mystery of language was revealed to me. I knew then that "w-a-t-e-r" meant the wonderful cool something that was flowing over my hand. The living word awakened my soul, gave it light, hope, joy, set it free! There were barriers still, it is true, but barriers that could in time be swept away. (7)

I left the well-house eager to learn. Everything had a name, and each name gave birth to a new thought. As we returned to the house every object which I touched seemed to quiver with life. That was because I saw everything with the strange, new sight that had come to me. On entering the door I remembered the doll I had broken. I felt my way to the hearth and picked up the pieces. I tried vainly to put them together. Then my eyes filled with tears; for I realized what I had done, and for the first time I felt repentance and sorrow. **(8)**

I learned a great many new words that day. I do not remember what they all were; but I do know that *mother, father, sister, teacher* were among them—words that were to make the world blossom for me, "like Aaron's rod, with flowers." It would have been difficult to find a happier child than I was as I lay in my crib at the close of that eventful day and lived over the joys it had brought me, and for the first time longed for a new day to come. **(9)**

Vocabulary

Write down the meanings of the following words:

- I stood on the porch, *dumb* **(2)**

- a deep *languor* **(2)**

- with *plummet* and *sounding-line* **(3)**

- no strong *sentiment* **(6)**

- like *Aaron's rod* **(9)**

Questions for Writing and Discussion

1. Write for five minutes, recalling your earliest memories with reading, speaking, or writing. Focus on one specific incident. How old were you? Where were you? What were you reading or writing?

2. Helen Keller's books have been translated into more than 50 languages. Explain why you believe her story, as illustrated in this essay, has such universal appeal.

3. In paragraph 3, Keller uses an analogy to explain her feelings and her state of mind before language opened her life. Identify the extended comparison. What "difficult concept" does Keller explain through her analogy?

4. In paragraph 8, Keller says, "Everything had a name, and each name gave birth to a new thought." Explain what Keller means by using examples of the names of things from your own life.

5. Contrast Keller's actions and feelings before she discovers language to her actions and feelings afterward. In addition to learning words, how do her feelings and personality change?

6. A century ago, when Helen Keller was learning to read and speak, people who were blind and deaf were classified by the law as "idiots." Describe one experience you have had with a disabled person. Based on that experience, explain how our attitudes toward people with some disability have (or have not) improved.

PROFESSIONAL WRITING

BEAUTY: WHEN THE OTHER DANCER IS THE SELF
ALICE WALKER

The author of the Pulitzer Prize–winning novel The Color Purple *(1983), Alice Walker has written works of fiction and poetry, including* Love and Trouble: Stories of Black Women *(1973),* Meridian *(1976), and* Revolutionary Petunias and Other Poems *(1973). "Beauty: When the Other Dancer Is the Self" originally appeared in* Ms. *magazine and was revised and published in Walker's collection of essays,* In Search of Our Mother's Gardens *(1983). Walker, a former editor of* Ms., *refers in this essay to Gloria Steinem and an interview published in* Ms. *entitled "Do You Know This Woman? She Knows You—A Profile of Alice Walker." As you read the essay reprinted here, consider Walker's purpose: Why is she telling us—total strangers—about a highly personal and traumatic event that shaped her life?*

It is a bright summer day in 1947. My father, a fat, funny man with beautiful eyes and a subversive wit, is trying to decide which of his eight children he will take with him to the county fair. My mother, of course, will not go. She is knocked out from getting us ready: I hold my neck stiff against the pressure of her knuckles as she hastily completes the braiding and then beribboning of my hair. (1)

My father is the driver for the rich old white lady up the road. Her name is Miss Mey. She owns all the land for miles around, as well as the house in which we live. All I remember about her is that she once offered to pay my mother thirty-five cents for cleaning her house, raking up piles of her magnolia leaves, and washing her family's clothes, and that my mother—she of no money, eight children, and a chronic earache—refused it. But I do not think of this in

1947. I am two-and-a-half years old. I want to go everywhere my daddy goes. I am excited at the prospect of riding in a car. Someone has told me fairs are fun. That there is room in the car for only three of us doesn't faze me at all. Whirling happily in my starchy frock, showing off my biscuit polished patent leather shoes and lavender socks, tossing my head in a way that makes my ribbons bounce, I stand, hands on hips, before my father. "Take me, Daddy," I say with assurance, "I'm the prettiest!" **(2)**

Later, it does not surprise me to find myself in Miss Mey's shiny black car, sharing the backseat with the other lucky ones. Does not surprise me that I thoroughly enjoy the fair. At home that night I tell all the unlucky ones about the merry-go-round, the man who eats live chickens, and the abundance of Teddy bears, until they say: that's enough, baby Alice. Shut up now, and go to sleep. **(3)**

It is Easter Sunday, 1950. I am dressed in a green, flocked scalloped-hem dress (handmade by my adoring sister Ruth) that has its own smooth satin petticoat and tiny hot-pink roses tucked into each scallop. My shoes, new T-strap patent leather, again highly biscuit polished. I am six years old and have learned one of the longest Easter speeches to be heard in church that day, totally unlike the speech I said when I was two: "Easter lilies / pure and white / blossom in / the morning light." When I rise to give my speech I do so on a great wave of love and pride and expectation. People in the church stop rustling their new crinolines. They seem to hold their breath. I can tell they admire my dress, but it is my spirit, bordering on sassiness (womanishness), they secretly applaud. **(4)**

"That girl's a little *mess*," they whisper to each other, pleased. **(5)**

Naturally I say my speech without stammer or pause, unlike those who stutter, stammer, or, worst of all, forget. This is before the word "beautiful" exists in people's vocabulary, but "Oh, isn't she the *cutest* thing!" frequently floats my way. "And got so much sense!" they gratefully add . . . for which thoughtful addition I thank them to this day. **(6)**

It was great fun being cute. But then, one day, it ended. **(7)**

I am eight years old and a tomboy. I have a cowboy hat, cowboy boots, checkered shirt and pants, all red. My playmates are my brothers, two and four years older than I. Their colors are black and green, the only difference in the way we are dressed. On Saturday nights we all go to the picture show, even my mother; Westerns are her favorite kind of movie. Back home, "on the ranch," we pretend we are Tom Mix, Hopalong Cassidy, Lash LaRue (we've even named one of our dogs Lash LaRue); we chase each other for hours rustling cattle, being outlaws, delivering damsels from distress. Then my parents decide to buy my brothers guns. These are not "real" guns. They shoot "BBs," copper pellets my brothers say will kill birds. Because I am a girl, I do not get a gun. Instantly I am relegated to the position of Indian. Now there appears a great distance between us. They shoot and shoot at everything with their new guns. I try to keep up with my bow and arrows. (8)

One day while I am standing on top of our makeshift "garage"—pieces of tin nailed across some poles—holding my bow and arrow and looking out toward the fields, I feel an incredible blow in my right eye. I look down just in time to see my brother lower his gun. (9)

Both brothers rush to my side. My eye stings, and I cover it with my hand. "If you tell," they say, "we will get a whipping. You don't want that to happen, do you?" I do not. "Here is a piece of wire," says the older brother, picking it up from the roof; "say you stepped on one end of it and the other flew up and hit you." The pain is beginning to start. "Yes," I say. "Yes, I will say that is what happened." If I do not say this is what happened, I know my brothers will find ways to make me wish I had. But now I will say anything that gets me to my mother. (10)

Confronted by our parents we stick to the lie agreed upon. They place me on a bench on the porch and I close my left eye while they examine the right. There is a tree growing from underneath the porch, that climbs past the railing to the roof. It is the last thing my right eye sees. I watch as its trunk, its branches, and then its leaves are blotted out by the rising blood. (11)

I am in shock. First there is intense fever, which my father tries to break using lily leaves bound around my head. Then there are chills: my mother tries to get me to eat soup. Eventually, I do not know how, my parents learn what has happened. A week after the "accident" they take me to see a doctor. "Why did you wait so long to come?" he asks, looking into my eye and shaking his head. "Eyes are sympathetic," he says. "If one is blind, the other will likely become blind too." (12)

This comment of the doctor's terrifies me. But it is really how I look that bothers me most. Where the BB pellet struck there is a glob of whitish scar tissue, a hideous cataract, on my eye. Now when I stare at people—a favorite pastime, up to now—they will stare back. Not at the "cute" little girl, but at her scar. For six years I do not stare at anyone because I do not raise my head. **(13)**

Years later, in the throes of a mid-life crisis, I ask my mother and sister whether I changed after the "accident." "No," they say, puzzled. "What do you mean?" **(14)**

What do I mean? **(15)**

I am eight, and for the first time, doing poorly in school, where I have been something of a whiz since I was four. We have just moved to the place where the "accident" occurred. We do not know any of the people around us because this is a different county. The only time I see the friends I knew is when we go back to our old church. The new school is the former state penitentiary. It is a large stone building, cold and drafty, crammed to overflowing with boisterous, ill-disciplined children. On the third floor there is a huge circular imprint of some partition that has been torn out. **(16)**

"What used to be here?" I ask a sullen girl next to me on our way past it to lunch. **(17)**

"The electric chair," says she. **(18)**

At night I have nightmares about the electric chair, and about all the people reputedly "fried" in it. I am afraid of the school, where all the students seem to be budding criminals. **(19)**

"What's the matter with your eye?" they ask, critically. **(20)**

When I don't answer (I cannot decide whether it was an "accident" or not), they shove me, insist on a fight. **(21)**

My brother, the one who created the story about the wire, comes to my rescue. But then brags so much about "protecting" me, I become sick. **(22)**

After months of torture at the school, my parents decide to send me back to our old community to my old school. I live with my grandparents and the teacher they board. But there is no room for Phoebe, my cat. By the time my grandparents decide there is room, and I ask for my cat, she cannot be found. Miss Yarborough, the boarding teacher, takes me under her wing, and begins to teach me to play the piano. But soon she marries an African—a "prince," she says—and is whisked away to his continent. **(23)**

At my old school there is at least one teacher who loves me. She is the teacher who "knew me before I was born" and bought my first baby clothes. It is she who makes my life bearable. It is her presence that finally helps me turn on the one child at the school who continually calls me "one-eyed bitch." One day I simply grab him by his coat and beat him until I am satisfied. It is my teacher who tells me my mother is ill. **(24)**

My mother is lying in bed in the middle of the day, something I have never seen. She is in too much pain to speak. She has an abscess in her ear. I stand looking down on her, knowing that if she dies, I cannot live. She is being treated with warm oils and hot bricks held against her cheek. Finally a doctor comes. But I must go back to my grandparents' house. The weeks pass, but I am hardly aware of it. All I know is that my mother might die, my father is not so jolly, my brothers still have their guns, and I am the one sent away from home. **(25)**

"You did not change," they say. **(26)**

Did I imagine the anguish of never looking up? **(27)**

I am twelve. When relatives come to visit I hide in my room. My cousin Brenda, just my age, whose father works in the post office and whose mother is a nurse, comes to find me. "Hello," she says. And then she asks, looking at my recent school picture which I did not want taken, and on which the "glob" as I think of it is clearly visible, "You still can't see out of that eye?" **(28)**

"No," I say, and flop back on the bed over my book. **(29)**

That night, as I do almost every night, I abuse my eye. I rant and rave at it, in front of the mirror. I plead with it to clear up before morning. I tell it I hate and despise it. I do not pray for sight. I pray for beauty. **(30)**

"You did not change," they say. **(31)**

I am fourteen and baby-sitting for my brother Bill who lives in Boston. He is my favorite brother and there is a strong bond between us. Understanding my feelings of shame and ugliness, he and his wife take me to a local hospital where the "glob" is removed by a doctor named O. Henry. There is still a small bluish crater where the scar tissue was, but the ugly white stuff is gone. Almost immediately I become a different person from the girl who does not raise her head. Or so I think. Now that I've raised my head, I win the boyfriend of my dreams. Now that I've raised my head, I have plenty of friends. Now that I've raised my head, classwork comes from my lips as faultlessly as Easter speeches did, and I leave high school as valedictorian, most popular student and *queen*, hardly believing my luck. Ironically, the girl who was voted most beautiful in our class (and was) was later shot twice through the chest by a male companion, using a "real" gun, while she was pregnant. But that's another story in itself. Or, is it? **(32)**

"You did not change," they say. **(33)**

It is now thirty years since the "accident." A beautiful journalist comes to visit and to interview me. She is going to write a cover story for her magazine that focuses on my last book. "Decide how you want to look on the cover," she says. "Glamorous, or whatever." **(34)**

Never mind "glamorous," it is the "whatever" that I hear. Suddenly all I can think of is whether I will get enough sleep the night before the photography session: if I don't, my eye will be tired and wander, as blind eyes will. **(35)**

At night in bed with my lover I think up reasons why I should not appear on the cover of a magazine. "My meanest critics will say I've sold out," I say. "My family will now realize I write scandalous books." **(36)**

"But what's the real reason you don't want to do this?" he asks. **(37)**

"Because in all probability," I say in a rush, "my eye won't be straight." **(38)**

"It will be straight enough," he says. Then, "Besides, I thought you'd made your peace with that." **(39)**

And I suddenly remember that I have. **(40)**

I remember:

I am talking to my brother Jimmy, asking if he remembers anything unusual about the day I was shot. He does not know I consider that day the last time my father, with his sweet home remedy of cool lily leaves, "chose" me, and that I suffered and raged inside because of this. "Well," he says, "all I remember is standing by the side of the highway with Daddy, trying to flag down a car. A white man stopped, but when Daddy said he needed somebody to take his little girl to the doctor, he drove off." **(41)**

I remember:

I am in the desert for the first time. I fall totally in love with it. I am so overwhelmed by its beauty, I confront for the first time, consciously, the meaning of the doctor's words years ago: "Eyes are sympathetic. If one is blind, the other will likely become blind too." I realize I have dashed about the world madly, looking at this, looking at that, storing up images against the fading of the light. But I might have missed seeing the desert! The shock of that possibility—and gratitude for over twenty-five years of sight—sends me literally to my knees. Poem after poem comes—which is perhaps how poets pray.

On Sight

I am so thankful I have seen

The Desert

And the creatures in the desert

And the desert Itself.

The desert has its own moon

Which I have seen

With my own eye

There is no flag on it.

Trees of the desert have arms

All of which are always up

That is because the moon is up

The sun is up

Also the sky

The stars

Clouds

None with flags.

If there were flags, I doubt

the trees would point.

Would you? (42)

But mostly, I remember this:

I am twenty-seven, and my baby daughter is almost three. Since her birth I have worried over her discovery that her mother's eyes are different from other people's. Will she be embarrassed? I wonder. What will she say? Every day she watches a television program called "Big Blue Marble." It begins with a picture of the earth as it appears from the moon. It is bluish, a little battered-looking, but full of light, with whitish clouds swirling around it. Every time I see it I weep with love, as if it is a picture of Grandma's house. One day when I am putting Rebecca down for her nap, she suddenly focuses on my eye. Something inside me cringes, gets ready to try to protect myself. All children are cruel about physical differences, I know from experience, and that they don't always mean to be is another matter. I assume Rebecca will be the same. **(43)**

But no-o-o-o. She studies my face intently as we stand, her inside and me outside her crib. She even holds my face maternally between her dimpled little hands. Then, looking every bit as serious and lawyerlike as her father, she says, as if it may just possibly have slipped my attention: "Mommy, there's a *world* in your eye." (As in, "Don't be alarmed, or do anything crazy.") And then, gently, but with great interest: "Mommy, where did you *get* that world in your eye?" **(44)**

For the most part, the pain left then. (So what if my brothers grew up to buy even more powerful pellet guns for their sons and to carry real guns themselves. So what if a young "Morehouse man" once nearly fell off the steps of Trevor Arnett Library because he thought my eyes were blue.) Crying and laughing I ran to the bathroom, while Rebecca mumbled and sang herself off to sleep. Yes indeed, I realized, looking into the mirror. There *was* a world in my eye. And I saw that it was possible to love it; that in fact, for all it had taught me, of shame and anger and inner vision, I *did* love it. Even to see it drifting out of orbit in boredom, or rolling up out of fatigue, not to mention floating back at attention in excitement (bearing witness, a friend has called it), deeply suitable to my personality, and even characteristic of me. **(45)**

That night I dream I am dancing to Stevie Wonder's song "Always" (the name of the song is really "As," but I hear it as "Always"). As I dance, whirling and joyous, happier than I've ever been in my life, another bright-faced dancer joins me. We dance and kiss each other and hold each other through the night. The other dancer has obviously come through all right, as I have done. She is beautiful, whole and free. And she is also me. **(46)**

Vocabulary

Write down the meanings of the following words:

- a subversive wit **(1)**
- rustling their new *crinolines* **(4)**
- Eyes are *sympathetic* **(12)**
- a hideous *cataract* **(13)**
- *boisterous*, ill-disciplined children **(16)**
- bearing *witness* **(45)**

Questions for Writing and Discussion

1. Why does Alice Walker share this story with us? What memories from your own life did her story trigger? Write them down.

2. What does Walker discover or learn about herself? As a reader, what did you learn about your own experiences by reading this essay?

3. Reread the essay, looking for examples of the following techniques for writing about memories: (1) using detailed observations; (2) creating specific scenes; (3) noting changes, contrasts, or conflicts; and (4) seeing relationships between past and present. In your opinion, which of these techniques does she use most effectively?

4. What is Walker's main idea in this autobiographical account? State it in your own words. Where in the essay does she state it most explicitly?

5. How many scenes or episodes does Walker recount? List them according to her age at the time. Explain how each episode relates to her main idea.

6. Walker also uses images of sight and blindness to organize her essay. The story begins with a description of a father who has "beautiful eyes" and ends with her dancing in her dream to a song by Stevie Wonder. Catalogue the images of sight and blindness from each scene or episode. Explain how, taken together, these images reinforce Walker's main idea.

7. Walker writes her essay in the present tense, and she uses italics not only to emphasize ideas but also to indicate the difference between past thoughts and events and the present. List the places where she uses italics. Explain how the italicized passages reinforce her main point.

REMEMBERING: THE WRITING PROCESS

■ **ASSIGNMENT FOR REMEMBERING**   Write an essay about an important person, place, and/or event in your life. Your purpose is to recall and then use specific examples that *recreate* this memory and *show why* it is so important to you.

As you begin writing, assume that you are writing for yourself or for a small audience of good friends who are interested in your life. Let your writing recreate the experience vividly enough so that your readers can see the main idea that you wish to convey.

CHOOSING A SUBJECT

Consider the following ideas:

- Interview (in person or over the phone) your parents, a brother or sister, or a close friend. What events or experiences do they remember that were important to you?

- Get out a map of your town, city, province, or country and spend a few minutes doing an inventory of places you have been. Make a list of trips you have taken, with dates and years. Which of those places is the most memorable for you?

- Dig out a school yearbook and look through the pictures and the inscriptions that your classmates wrote. Whom do you remember most clearly? What events do you recall most vividly?

- Go to the library and look through news magazines or newspapers from 5 to 10 years ago. What were the most important events of those years? What do you remember about them? Where were you and what were you doing when these events occurred? Which events had the largest impact on your life?

- Choose an important moment in your life, but write from the *point of view* of another person—a friend, family member, or stranger who was present. Let this person narrate the events that happened to you.

Note: Avoid choosing overly emotional topics such as the recent death of a close friend or family member. Ask yourself if you can emotionally distance yourself from the subject. If you received a C for the essay, would you feel devastated?

COLLECTING

Once you have chosen a subject for your essay, try the following collecting strategies:

Brainstorming   Brainstorming is merely jotting down anything and everything that comes to mind that is remotely connected to your subject: words, phrases, images, or complete thoughts. You can brainstorm by yourself or in groups, with everyone contributing ideas and one person recording them.

Looping   Looping is a method of controlled freewriting that generates ideas and provides focus and direction. Begin by freewriting about your subject for 8 to 10 minutes. Then pause, reread what you have written, and *underline* the most interesting or important idea in what you've written so far. Then, using that sentence or idea as your starting point, write for 8 to 10 minutes more. Repeat this cycle, or "loop," one more time. Each loop should add ideas and details from some new angle or viewpoint, but overall you will be focussing on the most important ideas that you discover.

Clustering   Clustering is merely a visual scheme for brainstorming and free-associating about your topic. It can be especially effective for remembering because it helps you sketch relationships among your topics and subtopics. As you can see from the sample sketch, the sketch that you make of your ideas should help you see relationships between ideas or get a rough idea about an order or shape you may wish to use.

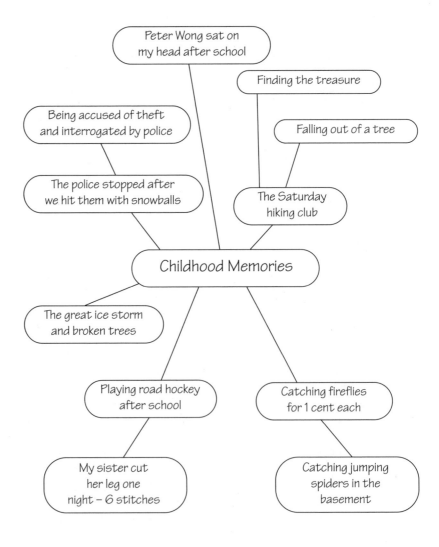

SHAPING

First, reconsider your purpose; then jot down tentative answers for the following questions. If you don't have an answer, go on to the next question.

- *Subject:* What is your general subject?

- *Specific topic:* What aspect of your subject are you interested in?

- *Purpose:* Why is this topic interesting or important to you or your readers?

- *Main idea:* What might your main idea be?

- *Audience:* For whom are you writing this? What is your reader like, and why might he or she be interested in this topic?

Narrow and focus your subject. If you're going to write a three-page essay, don't try to cover everything in your life. Focus on one person, one episode, one turning point, one day, even one *part* of one day, and do that in depth and detail.

As you start your shaping activities, use the observing strategies discussed in Chapter 4. *Spatial order* may help you shape your description of a place you are remembering; *classification* or *definition* can shape your memories of people, places, or events. *Similes, metaphors,* and *analogies* will make your writing more vivid and may also suggest a shape or help you develop your subject.

In addition, use the following strategies for shaping written memories. Try each strategy to see if it works for your subject. Although some strategies may not be appropriate, others will work naturally, suggesting ways to shape and develop your writing.

Chronological Order   If you are writing about remembered events, you will probably use some form of chronological order. Try making a *chronological list of the major scenes or events*. Then go through the list, deciding what you will emphasize by telling about each item in detail and what you will pass over quickly. Normally, you will be using a straightforward chronological order, but you may wish to use a flashback, starting in the middle or near the end and then returning to tell the beginning. In his paragraph about a personal relationship, for example, a student writer begins the story at the most dramatic point, returns to tell how the relationship began, and then concludes the story.

> Her words hung in the air like iron ghosts. "I'm pregnant," she said as they walked through the park, the snow crackling beneath their feet. Carol was looking down at the ground when she told him, somewhat ashamed, embarrassed, and defiant all at once. Their relationship had only started in September, but both had felt the

uneasiness surrounding them for the past months. She could remember the beginning so well and in such favour, now that the future seemed so uncertain. The all-night conversations by the bay window, the rehearsals at the university theatre—where he would make her laugh during her only soliloquy, and most of all the Christmas they had spent together in Vermont. No one else had existed for her during those months. Yet now, she felt duped by her affections—as if she had become an absurd representation of a tragic television character. As they approached the lake, he put his arm around her, "Just do what you think is best, babe. I mean, I think you know how I feel." At that moment, she knew it was over. It was no longer "their" decision. His hand touched her cheek in a benedictorial fashion. The rest would only be form now. Exchanging records and clothes with an aside of brief conversa-tion. She would see him again, in the market or at a movie, and they would remember. But like his affection in September, her memory of him would fade until he was too distant to see.

Comparison/Contrast   Although you may be comparing or contrast-ing people, places, or events from the past, you will probably also be comparing or contrasting the past to the present. You may do that at the beginning, noting how something in the present reminds you of a past per-son, place, or event. You may do it at the end. You may do it both at the beginning and at the end. You may even contrast past and present through-out, as Alice Walker does in "Beauty: When the Other Dancer Is the Self." Comparing or contrasting the past with the present will often clarify your dominant idea.

Image   Sometimes a single mental picture or recurring image will shape a paragraph or two in an essay. Consider how novelist George Orwell, in his essay "Shooting an Elephant," uses the image of a puppet or dummy to describe his feeling at a moment when he realized that, against his better judgment, he was going to have to shoot a marauding elephant in order to satisfy a crowd of 2000 Burmese who had gathered to watch him. The ital-icized words emphasize the recurring image.

> Suddenly I realized that I should have to shoot the elephant after all. The people expected it of me and I had got to do it; I could feel their *two thousand wills pressing me forward,* irresistibly. And it was at this moment, as I stood there with the rifle in my hands, that I first grasped the hollowness, the futility of the white man's dominion in the East. Here was I, the white man with his gun, standing in front of the unarmed native crowd—*seemingly the leading actor* of the piece; but in reality I was only an absurd *pup-pet pushed to and fro* by the will of those yellow faces behind. I per-

ceived in this moment that when the white man turns tyrant it is his own freedom that he destroys. He becomes a sort of *hollow, posing dummy,* the *conventionalized figure* of a sahib. For it is the condition of his rule that he shall spend his life in trying to impress the "natives" and so in every crisis he has got to do what the "natives" expect of him. He *wears a mask,* and his face grows to fit it. I had got to shoot the elephant. I had committed myself to doing it when I sent for the rifle. *A sahib has got to act like a sahib;* he has got to appear resolute, to know his own mind and do definite things.

Voice and Tone   When you have a personal conversation with someone, the way you look and sound—your body type, your voice, your facial expressions and gestures—communicates a sense of personality and attitude, which in turn affects how the other person reacts to what you say. In written language, although you don't have those gestures, expressions, or the actual sound of your voice, you can still create the sense that you are talking directly to your listener.

The term *voice* refers to a writer's personality as revealed through language. Writers may use emotional, colloquial, or conversational language to communicate a sense of personality. Or they may use abstract, impersonal language either to conceal their personalities or to create an air of scientific objectivity.

Tone is a writer's attitude toward the subject. The attitude may be positive or negative. It may be serious, humorous, honest, or ironic; it may be skeptical or accepting; it may be happy, frustrated, or angry. Often voice and tone overlap, and together they help us hear a writer talking to us. In the following passage, we hear a student writer talking to us directly; we hear a clear, honest voice telling the story. His tone is not defensive or guilty: He openly admits he has a "problem."

> Oh no, not another trash day. Every time I see all those trash containers, plastic garbage bags and junk lined up on the sidewalks, it drives me crazy. It all started when I was 16. I had just received my driver's licence and the most beautiful Ford pickup. It was Wednesday as I remember and trash day. I don't know what happened. All of a sudden I was racing down the street swerving to the right, smashing into a large green Hefty trash bag filled with grass clippings. The bag exploded, and grass clippings and trash flew everywhere. It was beautiful and I was hooked. There was no stopping me.
>
> At first I would smash one or two cans on the way to school. Then I just couldn't get enough. I would start going out the night before trash day. I would go down the full length of the street and

wipe out every garbage container in sight. I was the terror of the neighbourhood. This was not a bad habit to be taken lightly. It was an obsession. I was in trouble. There was no way I could kick this on my own. I needed help.

I received that help. One night after an evening of nonstop can smashing, the police caught up with me. Not just one or a few but the whole department. They were willing to set me on the right path, and if that didn't work, they were going to send me to jail. It was a long, tough road to rehabilitation, but I did it. Not alone. I had the support of my family and the community.

Persona   Related to voice and tone is the *persona*—the "mask" that a writer can put on. Sometimes in telling a story about yourself, you may want to speak in your own "natural" voice. At other times, however, you may change or exaggerate certain characteristics in order to project a character different from your "real" self. Writers, for example, may project themselves as braver and more intelligent than they really are. Or to create a humorous effect, they may create personas who are more foolish or clumsy than they really are. This persona can shape a whole passage. In the following excerpt, James Thurber, a master of autobiographical humour, uses a persona—along with chronological narrative—to shape his account of a frustrating botany class.

I passed all the other courses that I took at my university, but I could never pass botany. This was because all botany students had to spend several hours a week in a laboratory looking through a microscope at plant cells, and I could never see through a microscope. I never once saw a cell through a microscope. This used to enrage my instructor. He would wander around the laboratory pleased with the progress all the students were making in drawing the involved and, so I am told, interesting structure of flower cells, until he came to me. I would just be standing there. "I can't see anything," I would say. He would begin patiently enough, explaining how anybody can see through a microscope, but he would always end up in a fury claiming that I could too see through a microscope but just pretended that I couldn't. "It takes away from the beauty of flowers anyway," I used to tell him. "We are not concerned with beauty in this course," he would say. "We are concerned solely with the mechanics of flowers." "Well," I'd say, "I can't see anything." "Try it just once again," he'd say, and I would put my eye to the microscope and see nothing at all, except now and again a nebulous milky substance—a phenomenon of maladjustment. You were supposed to see a vivid, restless clockwork of sharply defined plant cells. "I see what looks like a lot of milk," I would tell him. This, he claimed, was the result of my not having adjusted the microscope properly, so he would readjust it for me, or rather, for himself. And I would look again and see milk. I finally took a deferred pass, as they called it, and waited a year and tried again. (You had to pass one of the biological sciences or you couldn't graduate.) The professor had come back from vacation brown as a berry, bright-eyed, and eager to explain cell-structure again to his classes. "Well," he said to me, cheerily, when we met in the first laboratory hour of the semester, "we're going to see cells this time, aren't we?" "Yes, sir," I said. Students to the right of me and to the left of me and in front of me were seeing cells; what's more, they were quietly drawing pictures of them in their notebooks. Of course, I didn't see anything.

"We'll try it," the professor said to me, grimly, "with every adjustment of the microscope known to man. As God is my witness, I'll arrange this glass so that you see cells through it or I'll give up teaching. In twenty-two years of botany, I—" He cut off abruptly for he was beginning to quiver all over, like Lionel Barrymore, and he genuinely wished to hold onto his temper; his scenes with me had taken a great deal out of him.

So we tried it with every adjustment of the microscope known to man. With only one of them did I see anything but blackness or the familiar lacteal opacity, and that time I saw, to my pleasure and amazement, a variegated constellation of flecks, specks, and dots. These I hastily drew. The instructor, noting my activity, came back from an adjoining desk, a smile on his lips and his eyebrows high in hope. He looked at my cell drawing. "What's that?" he demanded, with a hint of a squeal in his voice. "That's what I saw," I said. "You didn't, you didn't, you didn't!" he screamed, losing control of his temper instantly, and he bent over and squinted into the microscope. His head snapped up. "That's your eye!" he shouted. "You've fixed the lens so that it reflects! You've drawn your eye!"

Dialogue   Dialogue, which helps to *recreate* people and events rather than just tell about them, can become a dominant form and thereby shape your writing. Recreating an actual conversation, you could possibly write a whole scene using nothing but dialogue. More often, however, writers use dialogue occasionally for dramatic effect. In the account of his battle with the microscope, for instance, Thurber uses dialogue in the last two paragraphs to dramatize his conclusion:

"We'll try it," the professor said to me, grimly, "with every adjustment of the microscope known to man. As God is my witness, I'll

arrange this glass so that you see cells through it or I'll give up teaching. In twenty-two years of teaching botany, I—" . . .
"What's that?" he demanded. . . . "That's what I saw," I said. "You didn't, you didn't, you didn't!" he screamed. . . . "You've fixed the lens so that it reflects! You've drawn your eye!"

Title, Introduction, and Conclusion Sketch out several possible titles you might use. You may want a title that is merely an accurate label, such as "Main Street," but you may prefer something less direct that gets your reader's attention. As a reader, what do you think about Alice Walker's title, "Beauty: When the Other Dancer Is the Self"?

Introductions or beginning paragraphs take several shapes. Some writers plunge the reader immediately into the action and then later fill in the scene and context. Others announce the subject and then take the reader from the present to the past and the beginning of the story. At some point, however, readers do need to know the context—the *who, what, when,* and *where* of your account.

Conclusions are also of several types. In some, writers will return to the present and discuss what they have learned. Some, like Alice Walker, end with an image or even a dream. Some writers conclude with dramatic moments, as James Thurber does, or with an emotional scene. But many writers will try to tie the conclusion back to the beginning. Experiment with several possibilities until you find one that works for your subject.

DRAFTING

When you have experimented with the above shaping strategies, reconsider your purpose, audience, and main idea. Have they changed? Reexamine the notes you made before trying the shaping activities. If necessary, revise your statements about purpose, audience, or main idea based on what you have actually written.

Working from your notes and from your collecting and shaping activities, draft your essay. It is important *not* to splice different parts together or just recopy and connect segments, for they may not fit or flow together. Instead, reread what you have written, and then start with a clean sheet of paper. If you're working on a computer file, you can start with your list of events or one of your best shaping strategies and expand that file as you draft. Concentrate on what you want to say and write as quickly as possible.

To avoid interruptions, choose a quiet place to work. Follow your own writing rituals. Try to write non-stop. If you cannot think of the right word, put a line or a dash, but keep on writing. When necessary, go back and reread what you have previously written.

REVISING

Revising begins, of course, when you get your first idea and start collecting and shaping. It continues as you redraft certain sections of your essay and rework your organization. Use the guidelines below to give constructive advice about a remembering essay draft.

Guidelines for Revision

- **Reexamine your purpose and audience.** Are you doing what you intended?

- **Revise to make the main idea of your account clearer.** You don't need a "moral" to the story or a bald statement saying, "This is why this person was important." Your reader, however, should know clearly why you wanted to write about the memory that you chose.

- **Revise to clarify the important *relationships* in your story.** Consider relationships between past and present, between you and the people in your story, between one place and another place, between one event and another event.

- **Close and detailed observation is crucial.** *Show,* don't just tell. Can you use any of the collecting and shaping strategies for observing discussed in Chapter 4?

- **Revise to show crucial changes, contrasts, or conflicts more clearly.** Keller's and Walker's essays, for instance, illustrate how *conflict* and *change* are central to an effective remembering essay. See if their strategies will work in your essay.

- **Have you used a straight chronological order?** If it works, keep it. If not, would another order be better? Should you begin in the middle and do a flashback? Do you want to move back and forth from present to past or stay in the past until the end?

  If you are using a chronological order, cue your reader by occasionally using transitional words to signal changes: *then, when, first, next, last, before, after, while, as, sooner, later, initially, finally, yesterday, today.*

- **Be clear about point of view.** Are you looking back on the past from a viewpoint in the present? Are you using the point of view of yourself as a child or at some earlier point in your life? Are you using the point of view of another person or object in your story?

- **What are the key images in your account?** Should you add or delete an image to show the experience more vividly?

- **What voice are you using?** Does it support your purpose? If you are using a persona, is it appropriate for your audience and purpose?

- **Revise sentences to improve clarity, conciseness, emphasis, and variety.**

- **Check your dialogue for proper punctuation and indentation.** See the essay by Alice Walker in this chapter for a model.

- **When you are relatively satisfied with your draft, edit for correct spelling, appropriate word choice, punctuation, and grammar.**

CHAPTER SIX

INVESTIGATING

LEARNING OUTCOMES

After reading this chapter, you will have learned to

- report about a subject or inform a reader
- represent objectively the facts, ideas, and information from your sources
- use online, library-based, and field-based sources of information

Investigating begins with questions. What causes the greenhouse effect? How does illiteracy affect a person's life? How was the World Wide Web created? How does rape affect the lives of women in Canada? How do colleges recruit applicants? What can you find out about a famous person's personality, background, and achievements? At what age do children first acquire simple mathematical abilities? What kind of employee is most likely to be promoted? Why are sunsets yellow, then orange, red, and finally purple?

Investigating also carries an assumption that probing for answers to such questions—by observing and remembering, researching sources, interviewing key people, or conducting surveys—will uncover truths not generally known or accepted. As you dig for information, you learn *who, what, where,* and *when.* You may even learn *how* and *why.*

The purpose of investigating is to uncover or discover facts, opinions, and reactions for yourself and then to *report* that information to other people who want to know. A report strives to be as objective and informative as possible. It may summarize other people's judgments, but it does not editorialize. It may represent opposing viewpoints or arguments, but it does not argue for one side or the other. A report is a window on the world, allowing readers to see the information for themselves.

TECHNIQUES FOR INVESTIGATIVE WRITING

Investigative writing begins with asking questions and finding informed sources: published material, knowledgeable people, or both. In most cases, collecting information in an investigation requires the ability to use a library and then to summarize, paraphrase, and quote key ideas accurately from other people's writing. In addition, personal interviews are often helpful or necessary. For an investigation, you might talk to an expert or an authority, an eyewitness or participant in an event, or even the subject of a personality profile. Finally, you may wish to survey the general public to determine opinions, trends, or reactions. Once you have collected your information, you must then present your findings in a written form suitable for your audience, with clear references in the text to your sources of information.

Investigative writing uses the following techniques:

- **Beginning with an interesting title and a catchy lead sentence or paragraph.** The first few sentences arouse your readers' *interest* and focus their attention on the subject.

- **Giving background information by answering relevant who, what, when, where, and why questions.** Answering the *reporter's "Wh" questions* ensures that readers have sufficient information to understand your report.

- **Stating the main idea, question, or focus of the investigation.** The purpose of a report is to convey information as *clearly* as possible. Readers shouldn't have to guess the main idea.

- **Summarizing or quoting information from written or oral sources; citing sources in the text.** Quote *accurately* any statistics, data, or sentences from your sources. Cite authors and titles.

- **Writing in a readable and interesting style appropriate for the intended audience.** Clear, direct, and readable language is essential in a report. Use graphs and charts as appropriate.

The following reports illustrate three common types of investigative writing: the *summary* of a single book or article, the *investigation* of a controversial issue (using multiple sources), and the *profile* of a person. The three types may overlap (the investigation of a controversial issue may contain a personality profile, for instance), and all three types may use summaries of written material, questionnaires, and interviews. While some investigative reports are brief, intended to be only short news items, others are full-length features.

The intended audience for each report is often determined by the publication in which the report appears: *Psychology Today* assumes that its readers are interested in personality and behaviour; *Discover* magazine is for readers interested in popular science; readers of *Ms.* magazine expect coverage of contemporary issues concerning women.

SUMMARY OF A BOOK OR ARTICLE

The following report from *Psychology Today,* by journalist Jeff Meer, summarizes information taken from an article by Charlene L. Muehlenhard and Melaney A. Linton that appeared in *Journal of Counseling Psychology.* Although the *Psychology Today* report summarizes only that one article, it demonstrates several key features of an investigative report.

PROFESSIONAL WRITING

DATE RAPE: FAMILIAR STRANGERS
JEFF MEER

Attention-getting title

By now, everyone knows the scenario. Boy meets girl, they go to a party, get drunk, return to his apartment, and he forces her to have sex. **(1)**

Lead-in paragraph

Focus of investigation or report

Most people assume that date rape occurs on a first or second date between relative strangers. But new research supports a different conclusion: The individuals involved generally know each other fairly well. (2)

Who, what, where questions answered

Psychologist Charlene L. Muehlenhard and undergraduate Melaney A. Linton asked more than 600 college men and women about their most recent dates, as well as their worst experience with "sexual aggression"—any time a woman was forced to participate in acts, ranging from kissing to intercourse, against her will. More

Summary of results

than three quarters of the women and more than half of the men admitted to having an experience with sexual aggression on a date, either in high school or in college. And nearly 15 percent of the women and 7 percent of the men said they had intercourse against the woman's will. (3)

Summary of results

The researchers found that when a man initiated the date, drove to and from and paid for the date, sexual aggression was more likely. They also found that if both people got drunk (at a party, for example) and "parked," or found themselves in the man's dorm room or apartment, the date was more likely to end with the woman being forced to perform against her wishes. Men and women who thought of themselves as having traditional values and those who were more accepting of violence were also more likely to have been involved in date rape. (4)

Summary of results

But contrary to what one might expect, date rape and sexual aggression were much more likely to happen between partners who knew each other. On average, students said they had known the partner almost a year before the incident. "If women were more

Quotation

aware of this, they might be less surprised and more prepared to deal with sexual aggression by someone they know well," Muehlenhard says. (5)

Summary

She points out that communication is often a big problem on dates during which there is sexual aggression. Both men and women reported that the man had felt "led on" during such dates. Men said that women desired more sexual contact on these dates than had others on previous dates. Women said that they had desired less sexual contact than usual. (6)

Quotation

Muehlenhard believes that a direct approach, such as a woman saying "I don't want to do anything more than kiss," might clear up confusion better than simply saying "No." (7)

INVESTIGATION USING
MULTIPLE SOURCES

Most investigative reports draw on multiple sources: books and articles, research studies, and interviews. The following article, which appeared in *Time* magazine, has all the key features of an interesting investigative report. The author, Anastasia Toufexis, focusses on the popular but controversial psychiatric drug Prozac. She catches our interest with personal case histories. She asks probing questions about the medical and psychological effects of the drug. She focusses her report on a best-selling book by Peter Kramer, but she also weaves in several interviews with other authorities on Prozac. Despite the controversial nature of her topic, however, Toufexis remains as neutral as possible. She presents the background information and lets the experts debate the issues so that her readers can judge for themselves.

PROFESSIONAL WRITING

THE PERSONALITY PILL
ANASTASIA TOUFEXIS

Susan Smith has everything going for her. A self-described workaholic, she runs a Cambridge, Massachusetts, real estate consulting company with her husband Charles and still finds time to cuddle and nurture their two young kids, David, 7, and Stacey, 6. What few people know is that Susan, 44, needs a little chemical help to be a supermom: she has been taking the antidepressant Prozac for five years. (1)

Smith never had manic depression or any other severe form of mental illness. But before Prozac, she suffered from sharp mood swings, usually coinciding with her menstrual periods. "I would become highly emotional and sometimes very angry, and I really wasn't sure why I was angry," she recalls. Charles will never forget the time she threw her wedding band at him during a spat. Now, says Susan, "the lows aren't as low as they were. I'm more comfortable with myself." And she has no qualms about her long-term relationship with a psychoactive pill: "If there's a drug that makes you feel better, you use it." (2)

Millions agree, making Prozac the hottest psychiatric drug in history. Since its introduction five years ago, 5 million Americans—

and 10 million people worldwide—have used it. The drug is much more than a fad: it is a medical breakthrough that has brought unprecedented relief to many patients with severe depressions, phobias, obsessions and compulsions. But it is also increasingly used by people with milder problems, and its immense popularity is raising some unsettling questions. When should Prozac be prescribed? How does a doctor draw the line between illness and normal behavior? If you feel better after taking Prozac, were you ill before? When does drug therapy become drug abuse? Will Prozac become the medically approved feel-good drug, a cocaine substitute without the dangerous highs and lows? **(3)**

At medical meetings or dinner parties, the talk turns more and more often to Prozac, and what frequently sets off the discussion is a provocative book about the drug—*Listening to Prozac: A Psychiatrist Explores Antidepressant Drugs and the Remaking of the Self* by Dr. Peter Kramer of Brown University. Having quickly become a must-read, the book has perched near the top of the bestseller lists for three months. **(4)**

The author, who uses Prozac in his private practice, is both impressed by the drug and uneasy about what its widespread use may portend for human society. In case after case, he contends, Prozac does more than treat disease; it has the power to transform personality, instill self-confidence and enhance a person's performance at work and play. One of the patients profiled in the book, an architect named Sam, claims that the drug made him "better than well." His depression lifted, and he became more poised and thoughtful, with keener concentration and a more reliable memory than ever before. Prozac, writes Kramer, seems "to give social confidence to the habitually timid, to make the sensitive brash, to lend the introvert the social skills of a salesman." **(5)**

The psychiatrist maintains that the power of Prozac challenges basic assumptions about the origins and uniqueness of individual personalities. They may be less the result of experiences and more a matter of brain chemistry. If temperament lies in a tablet, is there an essential, immutable Self? Ultimately, Kramer muses, society could enter a new era of "cosmetic psychopharmacology," in which changing personality traits may be as simple as shampooing in a new hair color. "Since you only live once, why not do it as a blond?" he asks, and "why not as a peppy blond?" Already, pharmaceutical houses are churning out a whole new class of similar drugs, including Paxil and Zoloft, that mimic the effects of Prozac. **(6)**

So what makes Prozac any different from all the other popular mood-altering potions down through history, from alcohol, opium and marijuana to widely prescribed "mother's little helpers" such as Librium and Valium? Unlike the typical street drug, which sends people soaring and then crashing, Prozac has an effect that is even and sustained. And it seems safer and has fewer bothersome side effects than previous medicines prescribed to lift people out of depression. Prozac is what scientists call a "clean" drug. Instead of playing havoc with much of the brain's chemistry, the medication has a very specific effect: it regulates the level of serotonin, a crucial compound that carries messages between nerve cells. "Prozac makes people feel different without making them feel drugged," notes Kramer. (7)

Patients don't all react the same way, of course; some don't feel a bit better. And many psychiatrists and patients don't agree with Kramer about the drug's transformative powers. "I have my ability to not snap at people back, my energy back," notes a rabbi who recently started taking Prozac for mild depression. But, he adds, "I don't feel like Superman, and I still can't stand parties." (8)

"There's a lot less than meets the eye with Prozac," says Dr. Daniel Auerbach of the Veterans Health Administration in Sepulveda, California. "Nothing changes personality. What gets changed is symptoms of a disease." In other words, Prozac enables a person's true personality, often imprisoned by illness, to come out. Contends Dr. Hyla Cass, a psychiatrist in Santa Monica, California: "I don't think Prozac is manipulating people, turning them into feel-goods. It is correcting an imbalance, allowing people to be who they can be." (9)

But, counters Kramer, doesn't that broaden the boundaries of mental illness to include any condition that responds to Prozac? If a person responds to an antidepressant, does that necessarily mean that he or she is suffering from depression? Kramer questions whether the "imbalances" cured by the drug are always bad; maybe they are just frowned upon by current society. Are the vivacity and blithe spirits often produced by Prozac superior to shyness and a touch of melancholy? Do decisiveness and vigor have more merit than reticence and calmness? Should a business executive who lacks aggressiveness feel compelled to take a pill? (10)

Most psychiatrists argue that while Prozac may be abused, it is still a long way from being overused. A study by the National Institute of Mental Health shows that 40% to 50% of people with major depression are not receiving any kind of therapy. (11)

> With so many still going untreated, Kramer's book may do a service by alerting some of them to Prozac's potential benefits. But Kramer may also be raising expectations too high. Says Dr. Glen Gabbard, director of the Menninger Memorial Hospital in Topeka, Kansas: "We should not send patients rushing to their corner pharmacy in hopes of getting a magic chemical that will solve all their problems." For most people, happiness does not come packaged in a pill. (12)

PROFILE OF A PERSON

The following passage is a *profile* of a person—a biographical sketch intended to give a sense of the person's history, behaviour, character, and accomplishments. These paragraphs are part of a profile of hockey legend Wayne Gretzky.

THE GREAT ONE

Every "hockey parent" who has loaded children and their equipment into a car at six in the morning on a bitter cold Saturday in February, and who has felt the joy and pain of their successes and disappointments on the ice, understands why Wayne Gretzky is called The Great One: The skating, stick-handling skills and the intuitive "feel" for the game that distinguish the ordinary from the extraordinary player are a rare gift. Gretzky's father put skates on a two-year-old and observed a remarkable connection between the boy and the ice.

Gretzky was born on January 26, 1961, in Brantford, Ontario. By the time he was three, his father had built a rink in the backyard so that the boy could practise close to home and the father could watch him from the window of their warm kitchen. Playing with the Atom League in Brantford, Gretzky had scored 378 goals by the time he was ten, a record unbroken to this day.

At 17, in his first year playing professional hockey with the Edmonton Oilers in the World Hockey Association, Gretzky was named rookie of the year with 46 goals and 110 points to his credit. Many trophies were to follow. He holds more than 60 NHL records; Gretzky won four Stanley Cup titles in five seasons with the NHL Oilers. Over his memorable career, he scored a total of 2857 points.

Off the ice, Gretzky's positive image as a sportsman and gentleman has made him a role model for both youths and adults. As a spokesperson for hockey or arthritis sufferers, he brings not only his celebrity but also a credibility born from trustworthiness.

On December 19, 1998, Gretzky played his last game at Toronto's Maple Leaf Gardens and on April 15, 1999, his final game in Canada at the Corel Centre in Ottawa. At the press conference to follow, a tearful Gretzky admitted, "Obviously, it's an emotional time for me; it's an experience I'll never forget tonight." And in Madison Square Garden in New York, on April 18, 1999, the first number in history never again to be worn by an NHL player was declared: No. 99.

In his book *The Great One: The Life and Times of Wayne Gretzky*, Andrew Podnieks praises Gretzky's professionalism and patriotism: "Some of Gretzky's greatest moments have now, with time and their exceptionality, become part of the game's lexicon, its history, its glory . . . " and "The Gretzky I cherished was the one who always said *yes* to Canada. He played with a pride and dignity. . . . He recognized the honour involved in international competition, never presumed to be above his country's endeavours, and represented Canada with passion and, yes success."

PROFESSIONAL WRITING

ASKING FOR DIRECTIONS
CHRIS GARBUTT

In his exploration of today's masculinity, first published in the March 2000 issue of Canadian Forum, *Chris Garbutt, publisher of* Write Magazine, *provides information on traditional views of maleness, gender roles, and feminism. In writing his investigation, Garbutt interweaves personal experience and observations with references to pop culture, interviews, and books.*

It is a warm late-summer day in Montreal. My wife takes the Atwater exit off Route 20. Unfortunately, the exit doesn't actually take you to Atwater, and there are no signs. So we guess at which way to turn, and immediately know we're lost when the road curves west, away from where we're going. **(1)**

"Ask that guy for directions," my wife says, slowing down next to a young man on the sidewalk. **(2)**

"Ummm . . . how would I do that in French?" I respond. **(3)**

"Just ask," she says. But the man steps into a doorway and is gone. **(4)**

"Let's just stop and try to figure it out," I say. "If I just have a minute to get my bearings, I'll know how to get downtown." (5)

My wife is getting annoyed. At a stoplight a car pulls up next to us, and she shouts across, "Excusez-moi!" The light turns green, we move forward, but as our two cars travel parallel to each other, the woman in the other car gives us a complete set of directions that will take us back to Atwater. (6)

Men's reluctance to ask for directions is an old joke, but the story is true. And the story is true. Am I just too stubborn to allow anyone to think I'm not in control of the situation? Is my need to be methodical so strong that I will ignore an obvious solution? It's probably a little of both. In any case, the story goes to the heart of where men seem to be in the turn-of-the-millennium year. In the wake of incredible economic and social change, men are a little lost in a familiar place, and unable to ask for directions. (7)

———

In the late 1980s and early 1990s, I was a twentysomething pro-feminist male. I regularly read *Ms.* magazine, nodded with understanding when my women friends talked of the horrors of being female in a patriarchal culture, made fun of men who acted macho, and I warned my female friends against guys who seemed to be sensitive but were only being feminists as a way to get women into bed. I also hid my love for professional hockey, and kept in check comments I wanted to make about attractive women. (8)

Around the age of 28, I looked at my life and wondered why I was so lonely. I had a lot of friends, but they were all women. Perhaps I was playing the odds—surround myself with a lot of women that I like, and I'll have to end up in a relationship with at least one of them. I was an excellent listener. I told my female friends that I understood, that they could call me any time. The truth is, though, that I can't fully understand what it's like to be a woman. There was a lack of balance in my life. I had rejected everything traditionally masculine as sexist and dangerous and accepted everything feminine as caring and loving. (9)

Although it's safe and fashionable to insult men as a group, I decided to stop. I would loudly protest when I heard the ubiquitous "Men are pigs." The response from many women was, "Oh, but you're different." Or, even more painful, "But you're not a *man*." (10)

But I am a man, and here I sit, a white male heterosexual at a time of tremendous change. Feminism and economic conditions have left the old idea of masculinity in tatters. In my memories of the 1970s, men seemed mostly bemused by feminism, but a little afraid as well. Over the last couple of decades, the promise of the postwar years—everyone with their own house, a chicken in every pot, a car in every driveway—was shown to be unsustainable (and for a lot of us, not wholly desirable), and this has hit men particularly hard. Men have taken most of their identity from their work, and when jobs traditionally held by men are being lost or devalued, so are the men. Yet, as much as things have changed in the world, men still expect and are usually expected to be the primary breadwinners of the family. (11)

So I wondered whether there's a different kind of masculinity. A way of being a man that isn't dictated by women, but doesn't exclude them either. Something with balance, allowing guys to be strong sometimes and vulnerable other times. Well, I couldn't just continue sitting here. I had to ask for directions. (12)

Women dominate the gender discussion, even when the subject is men. The biggest hype relating to men's issues last year surrounded the release of Susan Faludi's book *Stiffed: The Betrayal of the American Man*. Faludi was in the papers and on the cover of *Newsweek*, and she was interviewed repeatedly in the broadcast media. Her book is a massive undertaking in reportage, in which she relays the stories told to her by dozens of broken-down American men—from members of a small group of Promise Keepers to Rambo himself, Sylvester Stallone. Most of the men in her book have been rocked by a changing economic climate in which traditional male jobs—manual labour, mostly—have been moved overseas or made redundant by machines. (13)

But her analysis is incomplete. She finds that the culture of consumerism is as oppressive to men as women, and that feminism offers lessons in how to bring about change. Fair enough. However, she completely avoids an obvious question: what about the effects of a movement that repeatedly says that men as a group are the problem? She brushes off men who claim that women have power as missing the point. I felt as if I read dispatches from a foreign correspondent who had gathered a whole lot of facts, but never understood the context. (14)

We can find some clues to the context in pop culture. One example is a full-page newspaper ad for Tag Heuer watches featuring German tennis superstar Boris Becker. Rivet holes are drilled in an arc across his forehead, showing a ground metallic texture.

Engraved into a metallic surface below the face are the words "Inner Strength" and below that, "I drew my strength from fear. Fear of losing. I don't remember the games I won only the ones I lost." (15)

Fear of failure doesn't seem like much to pin your manhood on, but it is one of the masculine stereotypes provided by professional sports. There are others. A few years ago, I was talking to a guy at a party about the Toronto Maple Leafs. It was a light conversation that turned ugly when I told him I felt there was too much fighting in hockey. He started making fists and threatening to hit me, because "maybe you need to see a real fight!" He didn't calm down until the woman he was with called him off. I still don't fully understand the meaning of that experience, but it wasn't the first time I had been threatened with violence for a stupid reason. (16)

To understand men and professional sports, or men at all, we must go back at least as far as the industrial revolution. I realized this first when I tried to read *Iron John* by mythopoetic men's movement guru Robert Bly. I couldn't finish because I found Bly's pseudopoetic writing style too annoying, but I hung in long enough to come across this line: "The love unit most damaged by the industrial revolution has been the father–son bond." (17)

A book by Varda Burstyn, *The Rites of Men: Manhood, Politics and the Culture of Sport*, adds more depth. *The Rites of Men* is one of the best books on men and masculinity I have read. In it, Burstyn points out that today's major sports were set in place during the nineteenth century, a time when "adult males left the family household en masse and abandoned their traditional roles in socializing children to take on duties in far-away places. Sport emerged as an institution for social fatherhood to provide training in manly pursuits of war, commerce, and government." (18)

When I reached Burstyn on the telephone, she told me she got interested in the subject after she saw a cover of *Sports Illustrated* featuring a picture of American football star Walter Payton, who had just broken a rushing record. The look on his face was not victorious, Burstyn said, but one of pain. She decided that, as a feminist to understand issues such as violence against women, one had to come to terms with the violence among men. (19)

Sports played a major role in filling the gap of the absent father. But, Burstyn says, "It has antisocial qualities. It has created an ideal of hypermasculinity that's all based on higher-faster-stronger." Thus emerges the ideal male body of our time—a machine-like physical specimen, with chiselled muscles and no body hair. It's as impossible an ideal as the skinny but large-breasted supermodels that women are offered. The sports superstar, much like the female supermodel, becomes an image of himself. This explains Mark McGwire's odd statement after breaking Roger Maris's single-season home run record in 1998: "I am in awe of myself." McGwire, a (legal) pill-popping, intense weight-training athlete, could barely see this as a personal accomplishment. **(20)**

Hypermasculinity can be seen literally growing over the course of the late twentieth century. Basketball players, for example, went from skinny to supermuscular. Injuries in the field and in the arena are increasing: according to the National Football Players Association, six times in every American football game an injured player is carried off the field. In the sports world, the ideal man makes lots of money, keeps his body hard, gives 110 percent (exerts himself to the point of injury) and lives through the pain. The model is old-school masculinity at its most extreme: make the money, and don't give up, even if it hurts. **(21)**

Rather than feeling our masculinity from within, we've given it over to our tough guys, our sports superstars. It's an institutionalized passivity. Slogans for Canadian sports channel TSN have included "Real Life. Real TV" and "See it. Live it." Susan Faludi refers to this as "ornamental consumer culture." How else would you describe a slogan that equates seeing something on television with living it in real life? What is real about a world where professional athletes set impossible standards for physical prowess, and make more money in a year than most men will in a lifetime? **(22)**

I decided I couldn't get much further without understanding my own situation. So I started at the beginning: I talked to my father and asked him how he learned to be a man. **(23)**

During the Depression and through the Second World War, his family lived in poverty on a farm in what is now suburban Toronto. "In my family's case, especially during the war, my father was away," he said. "We would see him maybe once a month." My grandfather worked seven days a week, leaving before the children got up and arriving home after they were in bed. My grandmother discouraged my father from physical work, and regularly said to him, "Remember you're not strong." Once upon a time this was true: he suffered a debilitating bout of pneumonia when he was six. But the "not strong" label stuck, and it was his three younger brothers who took up traditionally masculine pursuits such as carpentry and sports. **(24)**

"When I was growing up, I wouldn't put my hand on a tool, because other people would say, 'Look, let me do that,'" my father says. When he eventually settled into teaching as a profession, he never felt as if his family saw it as real work. At 37, he got a position at a high school and was given his own room. He asked a staff member how he should set things up, and the response was, "I don't care. It's your room." It was the first time someone had enough confidence in him to allow him to take charge of something. **(25)**

Compared to his own father, my father was a devoted parent and very present in our home. Nevertheless, he remembers the years in which I was growing up with a measure of guilt towards my mother. "In those days, the husband was the final answer, and didn't want to hear about smaller decisions," he said. "I didn't understand how hard she had it with you guys." In a later conversation, I had with both my parents, he said he was "lazy" as a father. "Not lazy," my mother interjected. "Just absent." **(26)**

I had problems with bullies in school, especially when I entered grade two and my mentally retarded sister started her first year of kindergarten. Kids hit my sister and made fun of her until she came home soaking wet—from being pushed into a ditch, from crying her face wet, from wetting her pants in fear. I just tried to get in between. I took punches, kicks and insults, absorbing them like a sponge. I learned very early one of the lessons all men are taught, and have been taught for centuries: protect your women. **(27)**

Where were my parents during this time? Another lesson of masculinity, protect your children, didn't seem to apply here. I don't know what my parents ought to have done—drive me to school, sue the school board—but they weren't there to protect me because my mother had a baby to take care of at home and my father had already left for work. In spite of his "sickly" status as a boy, he was quick to pick up the traditional male role of leaving the home and making money. **(28)**

I felt close to my father as a young child, but as I got older—and ironically, as he was actually spending more time around the house—we became more distant. The distance peaked when I was in my twenties, when I would call home and he would assume I didn't want to speak to him. "Hang on a second, I'll get your mother," he would say. We didn't hug or even shake hands when we saw each other. It has only been in the last year that he and I have regularly had real conversations that go beyond politics or sports. **(29)**

My father helped me a lot in understanding where I came from, but he's as confused as I am about masculinity. So when I saw a poster for a men's group last fall, I was interested. Five years ago I would have scoffed at such a thing, and even a few months earlier I would have ignored it. The group is run by Karl (I'm changing the names of the people in the group to protect their privacy), who told me it was a nontherapeutic discussion group. I'm not sure what I expected from it. Perhaps I thought it would be a group like the one lampooned in the pseudofeminist hit television show *Ally McBeal*, in which men confess their chauvinism. Or maybe I expected an intellectual discussion on broad political issues. **(30)**

As we introduced ourselves at the first meeting, I took the intellectual approach: "I've been pro-feminist for a long time, but I'm trying to integrate masculinity into my worldview." After I had finished, we moved to Mike. He looked a bit like a tough guy, and I wondered if he was there to talk sports, or maybe to trash women. Mike opened his mouth and said simply, "I'm here because I'm lonely." **(31)**

The group consists of men who are all somehow adrift: a mature student who is questioning whether to drop out, a man who is afraid of social situations, a man who wants to find love but ends up being abused in his relationships. We've had a few dropouts too, including a gay man whose partner was "so perfect" that he never felt worthy and an astoundingly attractive criminal lawyer, a self-proclaimed "stud" who told us of his successes with women and then talked about how women were the source of all his problems. **(32)**

At the end of a particularly intense meeting, Karl said we had done some "good sharing." I bristled at the word. Once when I was celebrating Christmas with co-workers over lunch, a guy wanted chocolate cake for dessert but didn't think he could eat it all, so he asked if anyone wanted to split it. "I'll have some," I said. The woman next to me turned to me with a horrified look. "Guys don't share dessert!" she said. **(33)**

It's not just dessert that guys don't share. Guys don't share much of anything. What is often referred to as "male bonding"—watching and discussing sports together, talking about women, arguing politics—isn't really bonding at all. It does connect men on a certain level, but it also serves to keep them distant. As Peter Davidson, a founding member of Men for Change in Halifax, told me, "We can watch an entire hockey game together and learn nothing about our souls." **(34)**

A common topic of conversation in the group is how much we envy women for being able to talk openly with one another. I realized that when Karl used the word "share," it felt like it was a word for women only. When I thought I was so "in touch with my feelings," in my twenties, I was actually in touch with women's feelings. To share my true feelings would once in a while require me to be critical, even angry, towards women—which in this era is considered unacceptable, misogynistic and dangerous. What this group gave me was a chance to express these feelings in an environment safe from rebuke ("Guys don't share!") and free from the fear that I might be making women uncomfortable. **(35)**

Michael Kaufman is a writer and public educator on men's issues who argues in his book *Cracking the Armour* that thousands of years of patriarchy have harmed women but have also created a great deal of unexpressed pain for men. "Most grandly," Kaufman told me, "we are living through the biggest revolution in human history." Men have had "enormous privilege" for centuries because they have not had to worry about domestic life. But with that privilege has come loss:

> The paradox of patriarchal culture is that men suffer too.
> A lot of men find that they've worked their whole lives to
> pursue their career, and then they retire and they don't have
> the job or the family that they've worked for. **(36)**

Since the 1960s, men's privilege has been challenged by women, and the changes are impressive. Feminists, Kaufman argued, did men a favour. This is most evident in the gradually increasing role men are playing in raising children. "The next generation of men are increasingly growing up with strong images of men in nurturing roles," he said. "Just take the example of the fact that 30 years ago, it was still rare for a man to attend the birth of his children. Now 98 per cent are there for the birth." Kaufman also points out changes in attitudes towards violence against women and increases in parental leave and increased numbers of women in the workforce. A few examples of a revolutionary change in values and a "broadening of the range of definitions of manhood." **(37)**

But if this is true, I asked Kaufman, why do we still see narrow images of men in the media? Why do we see still see men as rugged, and not nurturing? **(38)**

"Keep in mind we're up against a system that's probably 8,000 years old," he said. Even more important is that change will not happen the way it did with the women's movement: "I think that changes happen in pretty peculiar ways, and a lot of those changes are going to happen in our own lives. It's important for men to try to live the changes." (39)

In response to the 1989 Montreal Massacre, Kaufman and Toronto city councillor Jack Layton founded the White Ribbon Campaign, which encourages men to wear a ribbon in the week leading up to December 6, the anniversary of the massacre, as a commitment to not commit or condone violence against women. The campaign also conducts seminars, mostly in schools. (40)

Layton is a tough man to reach, but I finally tracked him down on his cell phone between a council meeting and a staff party. "One of the things the Montreal Massacre seemed to produce was a tendency for women to tell their stories," Layton said. As a politician, he began to hear horror stories from women in his constituency, and even from his own wife. "We're not trying to become pure," Layton said, "but how can we change so we are treating our sisters better?" (41)

The sisters were not altogether with White Ribbon at first. Last year, in her column in the *Toronto Star*, Michele Landsberg described a glitzy fundraiser held by White Ribbon and pointed out that women's groups feel an "edge of unease" with the campaign. "In 25 years of the women's movement, not a single anti-violence women's organization could ever have filled a ballroom with so much money and influence," she wrote. (42)

During the campaign's first year, Layton said, women's groups were extremely upset about it. They felt that a bunch of guys had co-opted a women's issue: "The message we heard was, 'Don't take our day.'" (43)

White Ribbon seemed to fade out of the public eye for a few years, but it's actually growing. Kaufman has been travelling the world to help set up similar organizations in countries as diverse as Finland, Nepal and Namibia. And at the memorial held in Montreal on the tenth anniversary of the massacre, white ribbons were being worn by both men and women. (44)

While I am a fan of the White Ribbon campaign, I worry that it only addresses part of the issue. Violence is so pervasive in masculine culture that we take it for granted. We abhor violence against women, yet we encourage and expect violence against men. We read a statistic that says more than half of women have experienced violence or sexual assault in their lives. We almost never see in the mainstream press that a man is twice as likely to be a victim of a violent attack as a woman. **(45)**

In my search for masculinity, I have spoken to men and women, friends and colleagues, feminists, "equalists" and people who are just plain angry. Every single one of them—from men who felt liberated by radical feminism to divorced fathers who can't see their kids— had intelligent, useful things to say. It was refreshing, since so many of the gender discussions I have witnessed have degraded into "more victimized than thou" arguments. **(46)**

The old models of masculinity and femininity are gone. Indeed, these terms are a kind of Holy Grail. It's the quest that matters, and much to my surprise, I found many men out there searching. In the words of David Shackleton, the editor of *Everyman*, a journal on personal and political issues relating to men, we need to find a new kind of interdependence, in which we value, respect and rely on both the masculine and the feminine. Shackleton feels that since the 1940s, the masculine has been represented as the dark side of humanness, and the feminine as the light. **(47)**

Does this mean, then, as my friend Rhea asked me, that we should not be looking at the world in terms of male and female, but in terms of human? I wonder. It would be nice, though I think that as long as we have different bodies we will continue to ascribe different sets of expectations on the sexes. Perhaps we need a new, less salacious defi- nition of "Vive la différence!" Perhaps we will not need words such as masculine and feminine, if men and women allow themselves to be vulnerable to each other and strong for themselves and each other. I'm still looking. I'm less afraid to ask for directions. And even when I don't ask for help, that doesn't mean I'm completely lost. **(48)**

Vocabulary

Write down the meanings of the following words:
- *patriarchal* culture **(8)**
- shown to be *unsustainable* **(11)**
- *en masse* **(18)**
- *scoffed* **(30)**
- *lampooned* **(30)**
- *pervasive* **(45)**
- *salacious* **(48)**

Questions for Writing and Discussion

1. Investigative essays focus on answering at least one key question. The question for Chris Garbutt's article might be "What is masculinity at the beginning of the new millennium?" What is Garbutt's answer to this question? Explain why you find his answer satisfying or unsatisfying.

2. Garbutt writes in the first person. Refer to two specific examples from his personal experience and discuss how each adds to the quality of his investigation.

3. What reference does Garbutt make to historical views of masculinity? Why are these important in his investigation?

4. What does Garbutt's investigation of each of the following contribute to his search: sports, men's groups, the White Ribbon Campaign? Suggest another source he could have mined for additional perspectives on his subject.

5. Write a list of Garbutt's sources (books, interviews, etc.).

6. Investigating essays should begin with a "lead" or introduction to grab the reader's interest and attention. Turn to Chapter 7, "Explaining," and read the section on "Introductions and Lead-Ins." Of the kinds of lead-ins illustrated, which type does Garbutt use? Is it effective in getting your attention? Which other types of lead-ins might be equally effective? Explain.

7. In Deborah Tannen's essay, "How Male and Female Students Use Language Differently," (Chapter 3, "Reading"), what comments on male language use corroborate Garbutt's conclusions about traditional male behaviour?

8. Write an investigation of femininity in the new millennium. Use your personal experience, observations. Interview other people about their views. Assume that your article will appear in a local or campus newspaper/magazine.

INVESTIGATING: THE WRITING PROCESS

■ **ASSIGNMENT FOR INVESTIGATING**   Choose a subject to investigate: one aspect of a current social or political policy, a scientific discovery or principle, an historical event, a profile of a controversial public figure, or perhaps just an ordinary event, person, process, or place that you find interesting. Your initial purpose should be to discover or learn about your subject. Then, with a specific audience in mind, report your findings. A report presents the information that you find; it should not argue for or against any idea or plan. With the final copy of your investigative report, you must turn in photocopies of any sources you have summarized or cited, notes from your interview(s), and/or copies of questionnaires that you used.

CHOOSING A SUBJECT

Consider the following ideas. If you already have a subject, go on to the collecting and shaping strategies.

- Choose some idea, principle, process, or theory discussed in a class that you are currently taking. Begin by interviewing classmates, graduate students, or a professor about how to investigate the history, development, or personalities behind this idea. With information from the interview, continue your investigation in the library, looking in appropriate magazines, books, or journals. As you read, focus your question on one narrow or specific area.

- Investigate and report on a campus or community service organization. Choose any academic, minority, cultural, or community organization. Visit the office. Interview an official. Read the organization's literature. Talk to students or community members who have used the service. Check the library for background information. Find people who are dissatisfied with or critical of the organization. Select an audience who might use this service or who might be interested in volunteering for the organization, and report the relevant who, what, when, where, why, and/or how information.

- At your workplace, investigate how something does or does not work, research how the business (or your part of the business) is organized, do a profile of a co-worker, or survey your customers to find out what they like best or least about your store or company.

- Write an investigation of some aspect of your favourite hobby. No matter what the subject is, you will find several magazines in the library devoted to it: fashion, cars, rock climbing, music, cooking, fly fishing, photography, scuba diving, interior decorating, health foods, and so on. Find several magazines and browse through them. Based on what you find in the magazines, interview and/or survey other people interested in this subject. Focus your survey or interview on one specific aspect of this topic.

- For practice, investigate one of the following questions on the Internet and/or in the library (be prepared to explain your answers to your class members): How can you minimize jet lag? Can aspirin prevent heart attacks? How expensive is television advertising? What is a wind tunnel used for? Why is the Antarctic ice shelf melting?

How do endorphins work? What is a melanoma? What causes seasonal affective disorder? How does a "Zamboni" work? What effects does the Young Offender's Act have? Do Canadians spend more money on cosmetics than on education? What are the newest ways to repair torn ACLs (Anterior Cruciate Ligament) in your knee? What is computer morphing, and how does it work?

COLLECTING

The collecting strategies discussed in Chapters 3, 4, and 5 (brainstorming, clustering, looping, mapping, sketching, reading, summarizing, taking double-entry notes) may be useful as you collect ideas. Other strategies particularly useful for investigating are suggested here. Try each of the following collecting strategies for your subject.

Asking Questions   Asking the *right questions* is crucial to investigative writing. Sets of questions (often called *heuristics*) will help you narrow and focus your subject and tailor your approach to the expectations or needs of your audience. You don't know what information you need to collect until you know what questions your investigation needs to answer.

1. The "reporter's" or the familiar "Wh" questions are one basic heuristic:

    Who? What? When? Where? Why?

    Asking these questions of a topic ensures that you're not leaving out any crucial information. If, for example, you are investigating recreational opportunities in your city or on campus, you might ask the following questions to focus your investigation (remember to ask the *negative* version of each question, too):

    - *Whom* is the recreation for?
    - *Who* runs the programs?
    - *Who* is excluded from the programs?
    - *Who* pays for the programs?
    - *What* is the program?
    - *What* sports are included in the program?
    - *What* sports are not included?
    - *What* is the budget for these programs?
    - *When* are these opportunities available or not available?
    - *Where* do the activities take place?
    - *Where* are they restricted?

- *Why* are these programs offered?
- *Why* are certain activities not offered?
- *Why* have activities been changed?

These questions might lead you to focus your investigation on the scheduling, on why soccer has been excluded, or on why participants are charged a fee for one class or program but not for another.

2. The classical "topics" provide a second set of questions for an investigation.

Definition: What is it?
Comparison: What is it like or unlike?
Relationship: What caused it? What are its consequences?
Testimony: What has been said or written about it?

These questions can be used in conjunction with the reporter's questions to focus an investigation. Applied to the topic on recreational opportunities, the questions might be as follows:

Definition: What activities exist?
How can the activities be described, classified,
or analyzed?
Comparison: What are similarities to or differences from other
programs?
Relationship: What caused these programs to be offered?
What causes people to use or avoid these activities?
What are the consequences of these programs?
Testimony: What do students think about these activities?
What do administrators think?
What have other schools done?
What does research show?
What proverbs or common sayings apply here?

These two sets of questions will *expand* your information, helping you collect facts, data, examples, and ideas—probably more than you can use in a short essay. Once you have all of this information, you can then *narrow* your topic.

Using the Library   Knowing how to use a library is crucial for most investigations. For this essay, you will not need to do exhaustive research on your topic, but you will need some background information, statistics, or information about current research, public opinion trends, or recent discoveries. Chapter 11, "Writing a Research Paper," will answer your research questions in more depth, but you can get information quickly in a library by using a few key sources.

- **Ask librarians for assistance.** Every library has librarians stationed at information desks, checkout counters, or reference desks whose job is to answer your questions. Be sure to ask for their advice when you need it. Because frustration is the number-one enemy of research projects, ask for assistance early in your investigation. The best procedure is simply to explain your project—what you intend to do and have done so far—and ask for advice or help. *There are no stupid questions in a library.*

- **Acquaint yourself with the basic sources of information in the library.** Most libraries offer group tours that familiarize their users with the location and use of the following:

  The online catalog

  CD-ROM access

  Internet and Web access

  Microfilm and microfiche room

  Current periodical room

  Basic references such as encyclopedias, almanacs, and dictionaries

Using the Internet and the Web   In the library, in a computer lab, or at home, you may be able to access the Internet to get information about your possible topic. Your browser—such as Netscape—will usually allow you quick access to a number of search engines, such as AltaVista, Magellan, Lycos, Excite, Net Search, Google, or Yahoo. Be sure to try a search on one of these, such as AltaVista or Yahoo. There are some additional search tools that you may need a URL address to locate on your system. Below are some research sites you should definitely check out.

- *The Electric Library* at **www.elibrary.com** will give you access to articles on popular topics that you can usually *print out* right at your computer.

- *The Internet Public Library* at **www.ipl.org** will give you access to a library environment that looks like your public library.

- *The Internet Services List* at **www.spectracom.com/islist** is a Top 5% Point and Magellan 3 Star site that provides an excellent starting point for investigating a new topic.

- *The WWW Virtual Library* at **www.w3.org/pub/DataSources/by Subject/Overview.html** will get you to one of the best investigating sites on the Web.

For additional Web sites for investigating topics, see Chapter 11.

Using Written and Electronic Sources

- **When printed copies are not available directly from your computer access, make photocopies of relevant articles.** The small amount of money you spend on copies will enable you to reread articles if necessary, quote or paraphrase from them accurately, and cite them accurately as references. (The money you spend is also excellent anti-frustration insurance, in case you return to the library stacks and discover that someone else has checked out your magazine or book.) On your photocopies, be sure to write *source information:* magazine or book title, author, publisher, date and place of publication, volume, and page numbers. For this investigative report, remember that you must turn in photocopies of any pages of articles or books you use.

- **Make notes and summaries from your photocopied sources.** As you collect information from photocopied sources, jot down key facts, ideas, and direct quotations. For every note you take, record the author, title, publishing information, and page numbers. You may *paraphrase* another writer's ideas, examples, sentences, or short passages by writing them in your own words. Use *direct quotation* when words or phrases in a source are more striking than your paraphrase might be. You may edit a direct quotation by (1) deleting any irrelevant or unnecessary words or phrases by using ellipsis points (three spaced periods) to indicate the deleted words and by (2) inserting your own words in square brackets [ ] if you need to clarify a quoted passage. Otherwise, the words within the quotation marks must accurately reproduce the original: No altered spellings, changed words, or rephrasings are allowed.

- **Avoid plagiarism.** Use quotation marks whenever you quote more than a word or two from your source. Paraphrase in your own words rather than stringing together phrases and sentences written by someone else. Give credit for ideas, facts, and language by citing your sources. In informal investigative writing, you may simply mention the author and title of written sources, citing page numbers of direct quotations in parentheses. (All formal research papers and some investigative essays cite sources in full in a "Works Cited" section at the end. See Chapter 11, "Writing a Research Paper," for more details.)

Summarizing   As explained in Chapter 3, a *summary* is a concise explanation of the main and supporting ideas in a passage, report, essay, book, or speech. It is usually written in the present tense. It identifies the author and title of the source; it may refer to the context or the actual place where the study took place; it contains the passage's main ideas; and it may quote directly a few forceful or concise sentences or phrases. It will not usually cite the author's examples. A *paraphrase* usually expresses all the information in the passage—including examples—in your own words. Summary, paraphrase, and direct quotation often occur together as you use sources. (See Chapter 3 for more details.)

Citing Sources in Your Text   As you collect information, you should note authors, titles of books or magazines, dates of publication, publishers, and page numbers to give proper credit to your sources. For some journalistic writing, you may need to cite only the author, the title of your source, or both. For a more formal, academic context, the MLA (Modern Language Association) requires that the author and page numbers be given, in parentheses, at the end of the sentence. However, if you refer to the author in the sentence that contains the citation, indicate just the page numbers in parentheses. For additional information on formal, in-text citation, consult Chapter 11, "Writing a Research Paper."

Interviewing   After you have done some initial research, interviews are a logical next step. Remember that the more you know about the subject (and the person you're interviewing), the more productive the interview will be. In planning an interview, keep the following steps in mind:

1. Make an *appointment* with the person you wish to interview. Although you may feel hesitant or shy about calling or e-mailing someone for an interview, remember that most people are flattered that someone else is interested in them and wants to hear their opinions or learn about their areas of expertise.

2. Make a *list of questions,* in an appropriate *sequence,* that you can ask during the interview. The interview itself will generate additional topics, but your list will jog your memory if the interview gets off the track. Begin with relatively objective or factual questions and work your way, gradually, to the more subjective questions or controversial issues. Try to phrase your questions so that they require more than a yes or no answer.

3. Begin the interview by introducing yourself and describing *your* investigation. Keep your biases or opinions out of the questions. Be sure to *listen* carefully and ask follow-up questions: "What information do you have on that? What do the statistical studies suggest? In your opinion, do these data show any trends? What memorable experiences have you had relating to this topic?" Like a dog with a good bone, a reporter doesn't drop a topic until the meat's all gone.

4. During the interview, *take notes,* and, if appropriate, use a tape recorder to ensure accuracy. Don't hesitate to ask your interviewee to repeat or clarify a statement. Remember: People want you to get the facts right and quote them accurately. Especially if you're doing a personality profile, describe notable features of your interviewee: hair colour, facial features, stature, dress, gestures, and nervous habits, as well as details about the room or surroundings. Finally, don't forget to ask your interviewee for additional leads or sources. At the conclusion of the interview, express your thanks and ask if you can check with him or her later, perhaps by e-mail, for additional details or facts.

5. Immediately after the interview, go over your notes. If you recorded the interview, listen to the tape and transcribe important responses. List other questions you may still have.

Writing Questionnaires   Questionnaires are useful when you need to know the attitudes, preferences, or opinions of a large group of people. If you are surveying customers in your business, you may discover that 39 percent of those surveyed would prefer that your business stay open an additional hour, from 5 P.M. to 6 P.M. If you are surveying students to determine their knowledge of geography, you might discover that only 8 percent can correctly locate Beirut on a map of the Middle East. The accuracy and usefulness of a survey depend on the kinds of questions you ask, on the number of people you survey, and on the sample of people you select to respond to your questionnaire.

Open questions are easy to ask, but the answers can be difficult to interpret. For example, if you want to survey customers at a department store where you work, you might ask questions requiring a short written response:

- What is your opinion of the service provided by clerks at the Bay?

- What would make your shopping experience at the Bay more enjoyable?

While these questions may give you interesting—and often reliable—responses, the results may be difficult to tabulate. Open questions are often valuable in initial surveys because they can help you to determine specific areas or topics for further investigation.

Closed questions are more typical than open questions in surveys. They limit the responses so that you can focus on a particular topic and accurately tabulate the responses. Following are several types of closed questions:

- *Yes/no questions:* Have you shopped at the Bay in the last three months?

  _____ Yes

  _____ No

- *Multiple choice:* How far did you travel to come to the Bay?

  _____ 0–5 kilometres

  _____ 5–10 kilometres

  _____ 10–15 kilometres

  _____ Over 15 kilometres

- How would you characterize the salespeople at the Bay?

  _____ Exceptionally helpful

  _____ Helpful

  _____ Indifferent

  _____ Occasionally rude

  _____ Usually rude

- *Checklists:* Which departments at the Bay do you usually visit?

  _____ Women's Wear

  _____ Sporting Goods

  _____ Children's Wear

  _____ Lingerie

  _____ Men's Wear

  _____ Household Goods

- *Ranking lists:* Rank the *times* you prefer to shop (1 indicates most convenient time, 2 indicates slightly less convenient, and so on).

  _____ 9 A.M.–11 A.M.

  _____ 11 A.M.–1 P.M.

  _____ 1 P.M.–4 P.M.

  _____ 4 P.M.–8 P.M.

As you design, administer, and use your questionnaire, keep the following tips in mind:

- Limit and focus your questions so that respondents can fill out the questionnaire quickly.

- Avoid loaded or biased questions. For example, don't ask, "How do you like the high-quality merchandise in the Bay's sports department?"

- At the top of your questionnaire, write one or two sentences describing your study and thanking participants.

- Pretest your questionnaire by giving it to a few people. Based on their oral and written responses, focus and clarify your questions.

- Use a large sample group. Thirty responses will give you more accurate information about consumer attitudes than will three responses.

- Make your sample as *random* or as evenly representative as possible. Don't survey customers on only one floor, in only one department, or at only one time of day.

- Be sure to include a copy of your questionnaire with your article or essay.

Note: If you intend to do a formal study using questionnaires, check your library for additional sources to help you design and administer statistically reliable surveys.

SHAPING

As you begin shaping your material, reconsider your purpose and audience. Limit your subject to create a *narrowed* and *focussed* topic. Don't try to cover everything; focus on the *most interesting questions and information*. Take the time to write out a statement of your topic, key questions, purpose, and audience. Then try the following strategies.

Inverted Pyramid   A common form for reports, especially in journalism, is the *inverted pyramid*. The writer begins with a succinct but arresting title, opens the story with a sentence or short paragraph that answers the reporter's "Wh" questions, and then fills in the background information and details in order of importance, from the *most important* to the *least important*.

Writers use the inverted pyramid when concrete information and the convenience of the reader are most important. The advantage of the inverted pyramid is that a hurried reader can quickly gather the most important information and determine whether the rest of the story is worth reading. The disadvantage is that some details or information may be scattered or presented out of clear sequence. In investigative writing, therefore, writers often supplement the inverted pyramid with other forms of development: chronological order, definition, classification, or comparison/contrast.

"Wh" question lead: Who, What, When, Where, Why
Most important information and details

Important information and details

Least important
information and
details

Chronological Order   Often, writers present their information in the order in which they discovered it, enabling the reader to follow the research as if it were a narrative or a story. In this format, the writer presents the steps of the investigation, from the earliest incidents, to the discoveries along the way, to the final pieces of information.

Definition   Definitions are central to investigating and reporting, whether they shape a sentence or two, several paragraphs, or, as in Garbutt's investigation of today's masculinity, an expression of what may be an answer to his question. His definition of "a different kind of masculinity" establishes what he hopes to discover in his exploration:

> So I wondered whether there's a different kind of masculinity. A way of being a man that isn't dictated by women, but doesn't exclude them either. Something with balance, allowing guys to be strong sometimes and vulnerable other times.

Comparison and Contrast   Comparison and contrast are as essential to investigating and reporting as they are to observing and remembering. Consider how Lance Morrow uses comparison to shape the opening paragraphs of a *Time* magazine essay on AIDS. In this essay, entitled "The Start of a Plague Mentality," Morrow notes the similarities between attitudes created by a plague 200 years ago and contemporary attitudes toward AIDS.

> An epidemic of yellow fever struck Philadelphia in August 1793. Eyes glazed, flesh yellowed, minds went delirious. People died, not individually, here and there, but in clusters, in alarming patterns. A plague mentality set in. Friends recoiled from one another. If they met by chance, they did not shake hands but nodded distantly and hurried on. The very air felt diseased. People dodged to the windward of those they passed. They sealed themselves in their houses. The deaths went on, great ugly scythings. . . .

> In the past four years, some 6000 people have died of AIDS in the U.S. From a statistical point of view, AIDS is not a major plague. Still, one begins to detect a plague mentality regarding the disease and those who carry it.

Analysis   In the process of investigating any subject, writers frequently use analysis to organize or shape their writing. Analysis simply involves dividing a whole into its parts. In order to explain how the web works, a writer used *analysis* to shape his article: The computer's server, he explains, breaks the URL down "into its parts, much like a mailing address." Those key parts, he explains, are the protocol (**http**), the address name (as in *www.yahoo.com*), and the directory path (as in **/headlines/pl/story.html**).

Additional Shaping Strategies   Other shaping strategies, discussed in previous chapters, may be useful for your investigation, too. *Classifying people, places,* or *things* may help organize your investigation. *Simile, metaphor,* or *analogy* may develop and shape parts of your article. Even in investigative reporting, writers may create an identifiable *persona* or adopt a humorous tone.

Title, Introduction, and Conclusion   Especially in an investigative report, a catchy title is important to help get your readers' interest and attention. Jot down several ideas for titles now and add to that list *after* you've drafted your essay.

In your introductory paragraph(s), answering the "Wh" questions will help focus your investigation. Other types of lead-ins, such as a short *description*, a *short narrative*, a *question*, a *statement of a problem*, a *startling fact* or *statistic*, or an arresting *quotation*, may get the reader's interest and focus on the main idea you wish to investigate. (See Chapter 7 for additional examples of lead-ins.)

The conclusion should resolve the question or questions posed in the investigation, summarize the most important information (useful primarily for long or complicated reports), and give the reader a sense of completion, often by picking up an idea, fact, quotation, narrative, or bit of description used in the introduction.

Some writers like to have a title and know how they're going to start a piece of writing before they begin drafting. However, if you can't think of the perfect title or introduction, begin drafting, and continue working on the title, the introduction, and the conclusion after the first draft.

DRAFTING

Before you begin a first draft, reconsider your purpose in writing and further focus your questions, sense of audience, and shaping strategies.

The actual drafting of an investigative essay requires that you have all your facts, statistics, quotations, summaries, notes from interviews, or results of surveys ready to use. Organize your notes, decide on an overall shaping strategy, or write a sketch outline. In investigative writing, a primary danger is postponing writing too long in the mistaken belief that, if you read just one more article or interview just one more person, you'll get the information you need. At some point, usually *before* you feel ready, you must begin writing. (Professional writers rarely feel they know enough about their subject, but deadlines require them to begin.) Your main problem, you'll quickly discover, will be having too much to say rather than not enough. If you have too much, go back to your focussing questions and see whether you can narrow your topic further.

REVISING

After you have drafted your essay, you may wish to get some feedback from your peers about your work in progress. When you read other students' drafts or ideas, be as constructively critical as possible. Think carefully about the assignment. Be honest about your own reactions as a reader. What would make the draft better?

Guidelines for Revision

As you add, delete, substitute, or rearrange materials, keep the following tips in mind:

- **Reexamine your purpose and audience:** Are you doing what you intended? You should be *reporting* your findings; you should *not* be arguing for or against any idea.

- **Is the form of your essay or report responsive to audience needs and expectations?** Use samples of other writing for your audience (from newspapers, magazines, or journals) as models.

- **Can you add any of your own observations or experiences to the investigation?** Remember that your own perceptions and experiences as a reporter are also relevant data.

- **Review the reporter's "Wh" questions.** Are you providing your readers with relevant information *early* in the report and also catching their interest with a key statistic, fact, quotation, example, question, description, or short narrative?

- **Recheck your summaries, paraphrases, or direct quotations.** Are they accurate, and have you cited these sources in your text?

- **Use signals, cues, and transitions to indicate your shaping strategies:**

  - *Chronological order:* before, then, afterward, next, soon, later, finally, at last

  - *Comparison/contrast:* likewise, similarly, however, yet, even so, in contrast

  - *Analysis:* first, next, third, fourth, finally

- **Revise sentences for directness, clarity, and conciseness.** Avoid unnecessary passive voice.

- **Edit your report for appropriate word choice, usage, and grammar.** Check your writing for problems in spelling and punctuation.

STUDENT WRITING

MY FRIEND MICHELLE, AN ALCOHOLIC

BRIDGID STONE

Bridgid Stone decided to write her investigative essay on alcoholism. In the library, she was able to find quite a lot of information and statistics about alcohol. In her friend, Michelle, she had a living example of the consequences of alcohol abuse. The question, however, was how to com-bine the two. As you read her essay, notice how she interweaves descrip-tion and dialogue with facts and statistics.

Five million teenagers are problem drinkers, according to *Group* magazine's article "Sex, Drugs, and Alcohol." One of these five mil-lion teenagers is my friend, Michelle.

"I can't wait to go out tonight and get drunk," Michelle announces as she walks into my dorm room. I just sigh and shake my head. Michelle has been drunk every night since Wednesday. In the last three days, she has been to more fraternity parties than classes.

We leave a few hours later for a Sig Tau party. Even though I have been attending these parties for weeks now, the amount of alco-hol present still amazes me. Almost everyone is walking around with a twelve-pack of beer. Others are carrying fifths of vodka or Jack Daniels whiskey. As cited in *Fraternities and Sororities on the Contemporary College Campus,* 73 percent of fraternity advisers believe that alcohol is a problem in fraternities. I wish the other 27 percent could be here now. Fraternities are synonymous with drinking.

Michelle and I both have innocent-looking squeeze bottles, but inside are very stiff screwdrivers. They probably have more vodka than orange juice. Michelle finishes her drink before I am halfway through mine. So she finishes off mine, too, before disappearing into the throng of people at the party. The next time I see her, she is holding a beer in each hand. Her speech is slurred, and she can barely stand up on her own.

We head back to the dorm when Michelle starts vomiting. Once we are in her room, I help her undress and put her to bed.

"Bridgid, I am so sorry," Michelle cries, "I promise never to drink again."

"Okay, just get some sleep," I tell her as I leave.

It's Thursday night and Michelle is ready to party again.

"I haven't been to my Friday 8:00 class in a month. Do you think I should just stay up all night after the party and go to class drunk? Or should I just not go to class and sleep in?" Michelle asks.

"Don't go out and get drunk. Stay home tonight and get up and go to your classes tomorrow," I advise.

"I am just going to sleep in," Michelle informs me as she leaves for the party.

Like Michelle, an estimated 4.6 million adolescents experience negative consequences of alcohol abuse, such as poor school performance. This was reported in a survey conducted by NIAAA for a United States Congressional report.

Early Friday morning, I get a phone call from the on-duty resident adviser. Michelle has passed out in the lobby of the Towers Complex. She couldn't remember her phone number or even what floor she lived on, but I had written my phone number on Michelle's hand, so she could call me if she got into any trouble. The R.A. had seen my number and decided to call, since Michelle was too drunk to dial the four digits.

"Could you please escort your friend up to your room?" the R.A. asks. She doesn't sound very happy.

"Sure, I will be down in a few minutes," I promise. It takes me and another girl from our floor to get Michelle onto the elevator. She keeps lying down or passing out. Thirty minutes later, we get Michelle into bed. She is mumbling incoherently, and she reeks of alcohol. Needless to say, Michelle doesn't make it to her 8:00 A.M. class, again.

Saturday afternoon, I confront Michelle about the Thursday night incident. This is rather hard to do, since she doesn't remember any of it.

"I just drink to loosen up. I'm much more fun if I've been drinking," Michelle tells me.

"You are not much fun when you are puking or passing out," I reply. A desire to loosen up is one of the main reasons that teenagers drink, reports *Group* magazine. Other reasons include a need to escape and to rebel.

"I have to release steam every once in a while," she argues. "School is really stressing me out."

"Michelle, you don't even go to class," I tell her.

"Everyone else drinks!" she says. "Why are you picking on me?" She stomps out of my room.

Michelle was partially correct, though, when she stated, "Everyone else drinks." As reported in *Alcohol and Youth*, more than 80 percent of all college students surveyed had been drinking in the previous month. But this doesn't mean that what Michelle is doing is any less serious. In all probability, Michelle is an alcoholic.

A test that is often used to determine if someone has a drinking problem can be found in *Getting Them Sober,* by Toby Rice Andrews. There are twenty questions on the test. A "yes" answer to two of the questions indicates a possible drinking problem. Questions include: "Do you miss time from school or work due to drinking?" "Do you drink to escape from worries or troubles?" "Do you drink because you are shy?" "Have you ever had a memory loss due to drinking?" Michelle would probably have answered "yes" to all of the above questions.

I moved out of the dorm at the beginning of the second semester, so I haven't seen much of Michelle. The last time I saw her was about three weeks ago. She had gotten arrested while in New Orleans for spring break. Apparently, Michelle had been out drinking and eventually had been arrested for public drunkenness.

"It wasn't that bad," she told me. "I don't even remember being in the jail cell. I was pretty trashed."

WORKS CITED

Andrews, Toby Rice. *Getting Them Sober.* South Plainfield, N. J.: Bridge Publishing, 1980.

Barnes, Grace. *Alcohol and Youth.* Westport, Conn.: Greenwood Press, 1982.

Pruett, Harold, and Vivian Brown. *Crisis Intervention and Prevention.* San Francisco: Jossey-Bass Inc., 1987.

"Sex, Drugs, and Alcohol." *Group,* February 1992: 17–20.

Van Pelt, Rich. *Intensive Care.* Grand Rapids, Mich.: Zondervan Publishing House, 1988.

Winston, Roger, William Nettles III, and John Opper, Jr. *Fraternities and Sororities on Contemporary College Campuses.* San Francisco: Jossey-Bass Inc., 1987.

Questions for Writing and Discussion

1. Investigative reports should remain as objective as possible. Describe how Stone's essay affected you. Does Stone remain objective, or does she become emotionally involved? Where is she most objective? Where does her point of view colour her report? How successfully does Stone maintain her reportorial stance?

2. Who is Stone's audience for her essay? Where would you recommend that Stone send her essay for possible publication? List two possible publication sources (magazines or newspapers), and explain your choices.

3. If Stone were revising her essay, what advice would you give her about balancing statistics and personal experience? Should she have more statistics? Should she have more narrative? Refer to specific paragraphs and examples in your response.

4. Stone's use of the present tense adds dramatic impact to her essay. Reread her essay, noticing where she uses the present tense and where she shifts to the past tense. Where was the use of the present tense most effective? Did her tense shifting confuse you at any point? Where?

EXPLAINING

LEARNING OUTCOMES

After reading this chapter, you will have learned to

- analyze an object or phenomenon and show the relationships of the parts

- explain the subject from your viewpoint

- focus on what, how, why, or perhaps all three

Explaining and demonstrating relationships is a frequent purpose for writing. Explaining goes beyond investigating the facts and reporting information; it analyzes the component parts of a subject and then shows how the parts fit in relation to one another. Its goal is to clarify for a particular group of readers *what* something is, *how* it happened or should happen, and/or *why* it happens.

Explaining begins with *analysis:* You divide a thing or phenomenon (object, person, place, feeling, belief, event, process, or cause) into its various parts. Explaining how to learn to play the piano, for example, begins with an analysis of the parts of the learning process: playing scales, learning chords, getting instruction from a teacher, sight reading, and performing in recitals. Explaining why two automobiles collided at an intersection begins with an analysis of the contributing factors: the nature of the intersection, the number of cars involved, the condition of the drivers, and the condition of each vehicle. Then you bring the parts together and show their *relationships:* You show how practising scales on the piano fits into the process of learning to play the piano; you demonstrate why one small factor—such as a faulty turn signal—combined with other factors to cause an automobile accident.

The emphasis you give to the *analysis* of the object or phenomenon and the time you spend explaining *relationships* of the parts depends on your purpose, subject, and audience. If you want to explain how a flower reproduces, for example, you may begin by identifying the important parts, such as the pistil and stamen, that most readers need to know about before they can understand the reproductive process. However, if you are explaining the process to a botany major who already knows the parts of a flower, you might spend more time discussing the key operations in pollination or the reasons why some flowers cross-pollinate and others do not. In any effective explanation, analyzing parts and showing relationships must work together for that particular group of readers.

Because its purpose is to teach the reader, *expository writing*, or writing to explain, should be as clear as possible. Explanations, however, are more than organized pieces of information. Expository writing contains information that is focussed by your point of view, by your experience, and by your reasoning powers. Thus, your explanation of a thing or phenomenon makes a point or has a thesis: This is the *right* way to define *happiness*. This is how one *should* bake lasagne or do a calculus problem. These are the *most important* reasons why the mayor of Edmonton was elected. To make your explanation clear, you show what you mean by using specific support: facts, data, examples, illustrations, statistics, comparisons, analogies, and images. Your thesis is a *general* assertion about the relationships of the *specific* parts. The support helps your reader identify the parts and see the relationships. Expository writing teaches the reader by alternating of general and specific examples.

TECHNIQUES FOR EXPLAINING

Explaining requires first that you assess your subject and your audience. Although you will need to draw on your own observations and memories about this subject, you may also need to do some reading or perhaps interview an expert. As you consider your subject, keep in mind that while an explanation (involving both analysis and showing relationships) focusses on what, how, or why, it may involve all three. Following are five important techniques for writing clear explanations.

- **Getting the reader's attention and stating the thesis.** Devise an accurate but interesting *title*. Use an attention-getting *lead-in*. State the *thesis* clearly.

- **Defining key terms and describing *what* something is.** Analyze and *define* by describing, comparing, classifying, and giving examples.

- **Identifying the steps in a process and showing *how* each step relates to the overall process.** Describe how something should be done or how something typically happens.

- **Describing causes and effects and showing *why* certain causes lead to specific effects.** Analyze how several causes lead to a single effect, or show how a single cause leads to multiple effects.

- **Supporting explanations with specific evidence.** Use descriptions, examples, comparisons, analogies, images, facts, data, or statistics to *show* what, how, or why.

In *Spirit of the Valley: Androgyny and Chinese Thought*, psychologist Sukie Colgrave illustrates many of these techniques as she explains an important concept from psychology: the phenomenon of *projection*. Colgrave explains how we "project" attributes missing in our own personality onto another person—especially someone we love:

Explaining what:
Definition example

Explaining why:
Effects of projection

A one-sided development of either the masculine or feminine principles has [an] unfortunate consequence for our psychological and intellectual health: it encourages the phenomenon termed "projection." This is the process by which we project onto other people, things, or ideologies, those aspects of ourselves which we have not, for whatever reason, acknowledged or developed. The most familiar example of this is the obsession which usually accompanies being "in love." A person whose feminine side is unrealised will often "fall in love" with the feminine which she or he "sees" in another person, and similarly with the masculine. The experience of being "in love" is one of powerful dependency. As long as the projection appears to fit its object nothing awakens the person to the reality of the projection. But sooner or later the lover usually becomes aware of certain discrepancies between her or his desires and the person chosen to satisfy them. Resentment, disappointment, anger and rejection rapidly follow, and often the relationship disintegrates. . . . But if we can explore our own psyches we may discover what it is we were demanding from our lover and start to develop it in ourselves. The moment this happens we begin to see other people a little more clearly. We are freed from some of our needs to make others what we want them to be, and can begin to love them more for what they are.

Explaining how: The process of freeing ourselves from dependency

EXPLAINING *WHAT*

Explaining *what* something is or means requires showing the relationship between it and the *class* of beings, objects, or concepts to which it belongs. *Formal definition*, which is often essential in explaining, has three parts: the thing or term to be defined, the class, and the distinguishing characteristics of the thing or term. The thing being defined can be concrete, such as a turkey, or abstract, such as democracy.

THING OR TERM	CLASS	DISTINGUISHING CHARACTERISTICS
A turkey is a	bird	that has brownish plumage and a bare, wattled head and neck; it is widely domesticated for food.
Democracy is	government	by the people, exercised directly or through elected representatives.

Frequently, writers use *extended definitions* when they need to give more than a mere formal definition. An extended definition may explain the word's etymology or historical roots, describe sensory characteristics of something (how it looks, feels, sounds, tastes, smells), identify its parts, indicate how something is used, explain what it is not, provide an example of it, and/or note similarities or differences between this term and other words or things. The following extended definition of *democracy* begins with the etymology and then explains—using analysis, comparison, example, and description—what democracy is and what it is not:

Since democracy is government of the people, by the people, and for the people, a democratic form of government is not fixed or static. Democracy is dynamic; it adapts to the wishes and needs of the people. The term *democracy* derives from the Greek word

Formal definition

Description: What democracy is

Etymology: Analysis of the word's roots

demos, meaning "the common people," and *-kratia,* meaning "strength or power" used to govern or rule. Democracy is based on the notion that a majority of people creates laws and then everyone agrees to abide by those laws in the interest of the common good.

Comparison: What democracy is not

In a democracy, people are not ruled by a king, a dictator, or a small group of powerful individuals. Instead, people elect officials who use the power temporarily granted to them to govern the society. For

Example

example, the people may agree that their government should raise money for defence, so the officials levy taxes to support an army. If enough people decide, however, that taxes for defence are too high, then they request that their elected officials change the laws or they

Formal definition

elect new officials. The essence of democracy lies in its responsiveness: Democracy is a form of government in which laws and lawmakers change as the will of the majority changes.

Figurative expressions—vivid word pictures using similes, metaphors, or analogies—can also explain what something is. During World War II, for example, the Writer's War Board asked E. B. White (author of *Charlotte's Web* and many *New Yorker* magazine essays, as well as other work) to provide an explanation of democracy. Instead of giving a formal definition or etymology, White responded with a series of imaginative comparisons showing the *relationship* between various parts of American culture and the concept of democracy:

> Surely the Board knows what democracy is. It is the line that forms on the right. It is the don't in Don't Shove. It is the hole in the stuffed shirt through which the sawdust slowly trickles; it is the dent in the high hat. Democracy is the recurrent suspicion that more than half of the people are right more than half of the time. It is the feeling of privacy in the voting booths, the feeling of communion in the libraries, the feeling of vitality everywhere. Democracy is the score at the beginning of the ninth. It is an idea which hasn't been disproved yet, a song the words of which have not gone bad. It's the mustard on the hot dog and the cream in the rationed coffee. Democracy is a request from a War Board, in the middle of a morning in the middle of a war, wanting to know what democracy is.

Sometimes we think that technical subjects are by nature objective and denotative, but some of these subjects also use definitions that contain images and metaphors. Consider the following definition of Web robots—so-called "bots"—by Andrew Leonard writing in *Wired* magazine:

> Web robots—spiders, wanderers, and worms. Cancelbots, Lazarus, and Automoose. Chatterbots, soft bots, userbots, taskbots, knowbots, and mailbots. . . . In current online parlance,

the word "bot" pops up everywhere, flung around carelessly to describe just about any kind of computer program—a logon script, a spellchecker—that performs a task on a network. Strictly speaking, all bots are "autonomous"—able to react to their environments and make decisions without prompting from their creators; while the master or mistress is brewing coffee, the bot is off retrieving Web documents, exploring a MUD, or combatting Usenet spam. . . . Even more important than function is behavior—bona fide bots are programs with personality. Real bots talk, make jokes, have feelings—even if those feelings are nothing more than cleverly conceived algorithms.

EXPLAINING *HOW*

Explaining *how* something should be done or how something happens is usually called *process analysis*. One kind of process analysis is the "how-to" explanation: how to cook a turkey, how to tune an engine, how to get a job. Such recipes or directions are *prescriptive:* You typically explain how something *should* be done. In a second kind of process analysis, you explain how something happens or is typically done—without being directive or prescriptive. In a *descriptive* process analysis, you explain how some natural or social process typically happens: how cells split during mitosis, how hailstones form in a cloud, how students react to the pressure of examinations, or how political candidates create their public images. In both prescriptive and descriptive explanations, however, you are analyzing a *process*—dividing the sequence into its parts or steps—and then showing how the parts contribute to the whole process.

Cookbooks, automobile-repair manuals, instructions for assembling toys or appliances, and self-improvement books are all examples of *prescriptive* process analysis. Writers of recipes, for example, begin with analyses of the ingredients and the steps in preparing the food. Then they carefully explain how the steps are related, how to avoid problems, and how to serve mouthwatering concoctions. Farley Mowat, naturalist and author of *Never Cry Wolf*, gives his readers the following detailed—and humorous—recipe for creamed mouse. Mowat became interested in this recipe when he decided to test the nutritional content of the wolf's diet. "In the event that any of my readers may be interested in personally exploiting this hitherto overlooked source of excellent animal protein," Mowat writes, "I give the recipe in full":

SOURIS À LA CRÈME

Ingredients:

One dozen fat mice	Salt and pepper	One cup white flour
Cloves	One piece sowbelly	Ethyl alcohol

Skin and gut the mice, but do not remove the heads; wash, then place in a pot with enough alcohol to cover the carcasses. Allow to marinate for about two hours. Cut sowbelly into small cubes and fry slowly until most of the fat has been rendered. Now remove the carcasses from the alcohol and roll them in a mixture of salt, pepper and flour; then place in frying pan and sauté for about five minutes (being careful not to allow the pan to get too hot, or the delicate meat will dry out and become tough and stringy). Now add a cup of alcohol and six or eight cloves. Cover the pan and allow to simmer slowly for fifteen minutes. The cream sauce can be made according to any standard recipe. When the sauce is ready, drench the carcasses with it, cover and allow to rest in a warm place for ten minutes before serving.

Explaining *how* something happens or is typically done involves a *descriptive* process analysis. It requires showing the chronological relationship between one idea, event, or phenomenon and the next—and it depends on close observation. In *Lives of the Cell*, biologist and physician Lewis Thomas explains that ants are like humans: While they are individuals, they can also act together to create a social organism. Although exactly how ants communicate remains a mystery, Thomas explains how they combine to form a thinking, working organism:

[Ants] seem to live two kinds of lives: they are individuals, going about the day's business without much evidence of thought for tomorrow, and they are at the same time component parts, cellular elements, in the huge, writhing, ruminating organism of the Hill, the nest, the hive. . . .

A solitary ant, afield, cannot be considered to have much of anything on his mind; indeed, with only a few neurons strung together by fibers, he can't be imagined to have a mind at all, much less a thought. He is more like a ganglion on legs. Four ants together, or ten, encircling a dead moth on a path, begin to look more like an idea. They fumble and shove, gradually moving the food toward the Hill, but as though by blind chance. It is only when you watch the dense mass of thousands of ants, crowded together around the Hill, blackening the ground, that you begin to see the whole beast, and now you observe it thinking, planning, calculating. It is an intelligence, a kind of live computer, with crawling bits for its wits.

At a stage in the construction, twigs of a certain size are needed, and all the members forage obsessively for twigs of just this size. Later, when outer walls are to be finished, thatched, the size must change, and as though given new orders by telephone, all the workers shift the search to the new twigs. If you disturb the arrangement of a part of the Hill, hundreds of ants will set it vibrating, shifting, until it is put right again. Distant sources of food are somehow sensed, and long lines, like tentacles, reach out over the ground, up over walls, behind boulders, to fetch it in.

EXPLAINING *WHY*

"Why?" may be the question most commonly asked by human beings. We are fascinated by the reasons for everything that we experience in life. We ask questions about natural phenomena: Why is the sky blue? Why does a teakettle whistle? Why do some materials act as superconductors? We also find human attitudes and behaviour intriguing: Why is chocolate so popular? Why do some people hit small leather balls with big sticks and then run around a field stomping on little white pillows? Why are Canada's family farms economically depressed? Why is the Internet so popular?

Explaining *why* something occurs can be the most fascinating—and difficult—kind of expository writing. Answering the question "why" usually requires analyzing *cause-and-effect relationships*. The causes, however, may be too complex or intangible to identify precisely. We are on comparatively secure ground when we ask *why* about physical phenomena that can be weighed, measured, and replicated under laboratory conditions. Under those conditions, we can determine cause and effect with precision.

Fire, for example, has three *necessary* and *sufficient* causes: combustible material, oxygen, and ignition temperature. Without *each* of these causes, fire will not occur (each cause is "necessary"); taken together, these three causes are *enough* to cause fire (all three together are "sufficient"). In this case, the cause-and-effect relationship can be illustrated by an equation:

CAUSE 1 + **CAUSE 2** + **CAUSE 3** = **EFFECT**
(combustible material)　(oxygen)　(ignition temperature)　(fire)

Analyzing both necessary and sufficient causes is essential to explaining an effect. You may say, for example, that wind shear (an abrupt downdraft in a storm) "caused" an airplane crash. In fact, wind shear may have *contributed* (been necessary) to the crash but was not by itself the total (sufficient) cause of the crash: An airplane with enough power may be able to overcome wind-shear forces in certain circumstances. An explanation of the crash is not complete until you analyze the full range of necessary *and* sufficient causes, which may include wind shear, lack of power, mechanical failure, and even pilot error.

Sometimes, explanations for physical phenomena are beyond our analytical powers. Astrophysicists, for example, have good theoretical reasons for believing that black holes cause gigantic gravitational whirlpools in outer space, but they have difficulty explaining why black holes exist—or whether they exist at all.

In the realm of human cause and effect, determining causes and effects can be as tricky as explaining why black holes exist. Why, for example, do some children learn math easily while others fail? What effect does failing at math have on a child? What are necessary and sufficient causes for divorce? What are the effects of divorce on parents and children? Although you may not be able to explain all the causes or effects of something, you should not be satisfied until you have considered a wide range of possible causes and effects. Even then, you need to qualify or modify your statements, using such words as *might, usually, often, seldom, many,* or *most,* and then giving as much support and evidence as you can.

In *Illiterate America,* Jonathan Kozol explains the multiple effects of a single cause: illiteracy. He supports his explanation by citing specific ways that illiteracy affects the lives of people:

Illiterates cannot read the menu in a restaurant.

They cannot read the cost of items on the menu in the window of the restaurant before they enter.

Illiterates cannot read the letters that their children bring home from their teachers. They cannot study school department circulars that tell them of the courses that their children must be taking if they hope to pass the SAT exams. They cannot help with homework. They cannot write a letter to the teacher. They are afraid to visit in the classroom. They do not want to humiliate their child or themselves. . . .

Many illiterates cannot read the admonition on a pack of cigarettes. Neither the Surgeon General's warning nor its reproduction on the package can alert them to the risks. Although most people learn by word of mouth that smoking is related to a number of grave physical disorders, they do not get the chance to read the detailed stories which can document this danger with the vividness that turns concern into determination to resist. They can see the handsome cowboy or the slim Virginia lady lighting up a filter cigarette; they cannot heed the words that tell them that this product is (not "may be") dangerous to their health. Sixty million men and women are condemned to be the unalerted, high-risk candidates for cancer. . . .

Illiterates cannot travel freely. When they attempt to do so, they encounter risks that few of us can dream of. They cannot read traffic signs and, while they often learn to recognize and to decipher symbols, they cannot manage street names which they haven't seen before. The same is true for bus and subway stops. While ingenuity can sometimes help a man or woman to discern directions from familiar landmarks, buildings, cemeteries, churches, and the like, most illiterates are virtually immobilized. They seldom wander past the streets and neighborhoods they know. Geographical paralysis becomes a bitter metaphor for their entire existence. They are immobilized in almost every sense we can imagine. They can't move up. They can't move out. They cannot see beyond.

PROFESSIONAL WRITING

WELCOME TO CYBERSPACE

PHILIP ELMER-DEWITT

Philip Elmer-DeWitt was born in Boston and educated at Oberlin College, Columbia University, and the University of California at Berkeley. Elmer-DeWitt writes for Time *magazine, where he has been since 1982. He has written several hundred articles, often on computer-related issues, including several* Time *cover stories, such as "Computer Viruses" (1988), "Supercomputers" (1988), "Cyberpunk" (1993), "Bards of the Internet" (1994), and "The Internet" (1994). "Welcome to Cyberspace" appeared as a* Time *magazine cover story in 1995. In this essay, Elmer-DeWitt explains what cyberspace is, how the Internet got started, and what questions we still have about future commercial and personal uses of the Net.*

It started, as the big ideas in technology often do, with a science-fiction writer. William Gibson, a young expatriate American living in Canada, was wandering past the video arcades on Vancouver's Granville Street in the early 1980s when something about the way the players were hunched over their glowing screens struck him as odd. "I could see in the physical intensity of their postures how *rapt* the kids were," he says. "It was like a feedback loop, with photons coming off the screens into the kids' eyes, neurons moving through their bodies and electrons moving through the video game. These kids clearly *believed* in the space the games projected." **(1)**

That image haunted Gibson. He didn't know much about video games or computers—he wrote his breakthrough novel *Neuromancer* (1984) on an ancient manual typewriter—but he knew people who did. And as near as he could tell, everybody who worked much with the machines eventually came to accept, almost as an article of faith, the reality of that imaginary realm. "They develop a belief that there's some kind of actual space behind the screen," he says. "Some place that you can't see but you know is there." **(2)**

Gibson called that place "cyberspace," and used it as the setting for his early novels and short stories. In his fiction, cyberspace is a computer-generated landscape that characters enter by "jacking in"—sometimes by plugging electrodes directly into sockets implanted in the brain. What they see when they get there is a three-dimensional representation of all the information stored in "every computer in the human system"—great warehouses and sky-scrapers of data. He describes it in a key passage in *Neuromancer* as a place of "unthinkable complexity," with "lines of light ranged in the non-space of the mind, clusters and constellations of data. Like city light, receding. . . ." (3)

In the years since, there have been other names given to that shadowy space where our computer data reside: the Net, the Web, the Cloud, the Matrix, the Metaverse, the Datasphere, the Electronic Frontier, the information superhighway. But Gibson's coinage may prove the most enduring. By 1989 it had been bor-rowed by the online community to describe not some science-fiction fantasy but today's increasingly interconnected computer systems—especially the millions of computers jacked into the Internet. (4)

Now hardly a day goes by without some newspaper article, some political speech, some corporate press release invoking Gibson's imaginary world. Suddenly, it seems, everybody has an E-mail address, from Hollywood moguls to the Holy See. Billy Graham has preached on America Online; Vice President Al Gore has held forth on CompuServe; thousands chose to celebrate New Year's this year with an online get-together called First Night in Cyberspace. . . . (5)

One result of this drum roll is a growing public appetite for a place most people haven't been to and are often hard-pressed to define. In a *Time*/CNN poll of 800 Americans conducted in January by Yankelovich Partners, 57% didn't know what cyberspace meant, yet 85% were certain that information technology had made their life better. They may not know where it is, but they want des-perately to get there. The rush to get online, to avoid being "left behind" in the information revolution, is intense. Those who find fulfillment in cyberspace often have the religious fervor of the recently converted. (6)

These sentiments have been captured brilliantly in an IBM ad on TV showing a *phalanx* of Czech nuns discussing—of all things—the latest operating system from Microsoft. As they walk briskly through a convent, a young *novice* mentions IBM's compet-ing system, called Warp. "I just read about it in *Wired*," she gushes.

"You get true multitasking . . . easy access to the Internet." An older sister glances up with obvious interest; the camera cuts to the mother superior, who wistfully confesses, "I'm dying to surf the Net." Fade as the pager tucked under her habit starts to beep. **(7)**

Cybernuns. **(8)**

What is cyberspace? According to John Perry Barlow, a rock-'n-roll lyricist turned computer activist, it can be defined most succinctly as "that place you are in when you are talking on the telephone." That's as good a place to start as any. The telephone system, after all, is really a vast, global computer network with a distinctive, audible presence (crackling static against an almost inaudible background hum). By Barlow's definition, just about everybody has already been to cyberspace. It's marked by the feeling that the person you're talking to is "in the same room." Most people take the spatial dimension of a phone conversation for granted—until they get a really bad connection or a glitchy overseas call. Then they start raising their voice, as if by sheer volume they could propel it to the outer reaches of cyberspace. **(9)**

Cyberspace, of course, is bigger than a telephone call. It encompasses the millions of personal computers connected by modems—via the telephone system—to commercial online services, as well as the millions more with high-speed links to local area networks, office E-mail systems and the Internet. It includes the rapidly expanding wireless services: microwave towers that carry great quantities of cellular phone and data traffic; communications satellites strung like beads in a geosynchronous orbit; low-flying satellites that will soon crisscross the globe like angry bees, connecting folks too far-flung or too much on the go to be tethered by wires. Someday even our television sets may be part of cyberspace, transformed into interactive "teleputers" by so-called full-service networks like the ones several cable-TV companies (including Time Warner) are building along the old cable lines, using fiber optics and high-speed switches. **(10)**

But these wires and cables and microwaves are not really cyberspace. They are the means of conveyance, not the destination: the information superhighway, not the bright city lights at the end of the road. Cyberspace, in the sense of being "in the same room," is an experience, not a wiring system. It is about people using the new technology to do what they are genetically programmed to do: communicate with one another. It can be found in electronic mail exchanged by lovers who have never met. It emerges from the endless debates on mailing lists and message boards. It's that bond that knits together regulars in electronic chat rooms and news-groups. It is, like Plato's plane of ideal forms, a metaphorical space, a virtual reality. **(11)**

But it is no less real for being so. We live in the age of information, as Nicholas Negroponte, director of M.I.T.'s Media Lab, is fond of pointing out, in which the fundamental particle is not the atom but the bit—the binary digit, a unit of data usually represented as a 0 or a 1. Information may still be delivered in magazines and newspapers (atoms), but the real value is in the contents (bits). We pay for our goods and services with cash (atoms), but the ebb and flow of capital around the world is carried out—to the tune of several trillion dollars a day—in electronic funds transfers (bits). **(12)**

At this point, however, cyberspace is less about commerce than about community. The technology has unleashed a great rush of direct, person-to-person communications, organized not in the top-down, one-to-many structure of traditional media but in a many-to-many model that may—just may—be a vehicle for revolutionary change. In a world already too divided against itself—rich against poor, producer against consumer—cyberspace offers the nearest thing to a level playing field. **(13)**

Take for example, the Internet. Until something better comes along to replace it, the Internet *is* cyberspace. It may not reach every computer in the human system, as Gibson imagined, but it comes very close. And as anyone who has spent much time there can attest, it is in many ways even stranger than fiction. **(14)**

Begun more than 20 years ago as a Defense Department experiment, the Internet escaped from the Pentagon in 1984 and spread like Kudzu during the personal-computer boom, nearly doubling every year from the mid-1980s on. Today 30 million to 40 million people in more than 160 countries have at least E-mail access to the Internet; in Japan, New Zealand and parts of Europe the number of Net users has grown more than 1000% during the past three years. **(15)**

One factor fueling the Internet's remarkable growth is its resolutely grass-roots structure. Most conventional computer systems are hierarchical and proprietary; they run on copyright software in a pyramid structure that gives dictatorial powers to the system operators who sit on top. The Internet, by contrast, is open (non-proprietary) and rabidly democratic. No one owns it. No single organization controls it. It is run like a commune with 4.8 million fiercely independent members (called hosts). It crosses national boundaries and answers to no sovereign. It is literally lawless. **(16)**

Although graphics, photos and even videos have started to show up, cyberspace, as it exists on the Internet, is still primarily a text medium. People communicate by and large through words, typed and displayed on a screen. Yet cyberspace assumes an astonishing array of forms, from the utilitarian mailing list (a sort of junk E-mail list to which anyone can contribute) to the rococo MUDS, or Multi-User Dungeons (elaborate fictional gathering places that users create one "room" at a time). All these "spaces" have one thing in common: they are egalitarian to a fault. Anybody can play (provided he or she has the requisite equipment and access), and everybody is afforded the same level of respect (which is to say, little or none). Stripped of the external trappings of wealth, power, beauty and social status, people tend to be judged in the cyberspace of the Internet only by their ideas and their ability to get them across in terse, vigorous prose. On the Internet, as the famous *New Yorker* cartoon put it, nobody knows you're a dog. . . . **(17)**

The Internet is far from perfect. Largely unedited, its content is often tasteless, foolish, uninteresting or just plain wrong. It can be dangerously habit-forming and, truth be told, an enormous waste of time. Even with the arrival of new point-and-click software such as Netscape and Mosaic, it is still too hard to navigate. And because it requires access to both a computer and a high-speed telecommunications link, it is out of reach for millions of people too poor or too far from a major communications hub to participate. **(18)**

But it is remarkable nonetheless, especially considering that it began as a cold war postapocalypse military command grid. "When I look at the Internet," says Bruce Sterling, another science-fiction writer and a great champion of cyberspace, "I see something astounding and delightful. It's as if some grim fallout shelter had burst open and a full-scale MardiGras parade had come out. I take such enormous pleasure in this that it's hard to remain properly skeptical." **(19)**

There is no guarantee, however, that cyberspace will always look like this. The Internet is changing rapidly. Lately a lot of the development efforts—and most of the press attention—have shifted from the rough-and-tumble Usenet newsgroups to the more passive and consumer-oriented "home pages" of the World Wide Web—a system of links that simplifies the task of navigating among the myriad offerings on the Internet. The Net, many oldtimers complain, is turning into a shopping mall. But unless it proves to be a total bust for business, that trend is likely to continue. (20)

The more fundamental changes are those taking place underneath our sidewalks and streets, where great wooden wheels of fiber-optic cable are being rolled out one block at a time. Over the next decade, the telecommunications systems of the world will be rebuilt from the ground up as copper wires are ripped up and replaced by hair-thin fiber-optic strands. (21)

The reason, in a word, is bandwidth, the information-carrying capacity of a medium (usually measured in bits per second). In terms of bandwidth, a copper telephone wire is like a thin straw, too narrow to carry the traffic it is being asked to bear. By contrast, fiber-optic strands, although hair-thin, are like great fat pipes, with an intrinsic capacity to carry tens of thousands of times as many bits as copper wire. (22)

It's not just the Internet surfers who are crying for more bandwidth. Hollywood needs it to deliver movies and television shows on demand. Video game makers want it to send kids the latest adventures of Donkey Kong and Sonic the Hedgehog. The phone companies have their eyes on what some believe will be the next must-have appliance: the videophone. (23)

There is a broad consensus in government and industry that the National Information Infrastructure, as the Clinton Administration prefers to call the info highway, will be a broadband, switched network that could, in theory, deliver all these things. But how it will be structured and how it will be deployed are not so clear. For example, if cable-TV and telephone companies are allowed to roll out the new services in only the richest neighborhoods—a practice known as "cream skimming"—that could exacerbate the already growing disparity between those who have access to the latest information and the best intelligence and those who must be content with what they see on TV. (24)

An even trickier question has to do with the so-called upstream capacity of the network. Everybody wants to build a fat pipeline going into the home; that's the conduit by which the new information goods and services will be delivered. But how much bandwidth needs to be set aside for the signal going from the home back into the network? In some designs that upstream pathway is quite narrow—allowing just enough bits to change the channel or order a zirconium ring. Some network activists argue that consumers will someday need as much bandwidth going out of the home as they have coming in. Only then can ordinary people become, if they choose, not just consumers of media but producers as well, free to plug their camcorders into the network and broadcast their creations to the world. (25)

How these design issues are decided in the months ahead could change the shape of cyberspace. Will it be bottom up, like the Internet, or top down, like broadcast television? In the best case, says Mitch Kapor, cofounder (with John Perry Barlow) of the Electronic Frontier Foundation, we could collectively invent a new entertainment medium, one that taps the creative energies of a nation of midnight scribblers and camcorder video artists. "In the worst case," he says, "we could wind up with networks that have the principal effect of fostering addiction to a new generation of electronic narcotics." (26)

If Kapor seems to be painting these scenarios in apocalyptic terms, he is not alone. There is something about cyberspace that sets people's imaginations blazing. Much of what has been written about it—in the press and on the networks—tends to swing from one extreme to the other, from hype and romanticism to fear and loathing. It may be that the near-term impact of cyberspace is being oversold. But that does not mean that real change isn't in the works. As a rule of thumb, historians say, the results of technological innovation always take longer to reach fruition than early champions of change predict. But when change finally comes, its effect is likely to be more profound and widespread and unanticipated than anyone imagined—even the guys who write science fiction. (27)

Vocabulary

Write down the meanings of the following words:

- *phalanx* of Czech nuns (7)

- a young *novice* (7)

- defined most *succinctly* (9)

- a *geosynchronous* orbit (10)

- *rococo* MUDS (17)

- *egalitarian* to a fault (17)

- *postapocalypse* military command grid (19)

- *exacerbate* the already growing *disparity* (24)

- longer to reach *fruition* (27)

Questions for Writing and Discussion

1. Most readers of Elmer-DeWitt's article already know the basics about the Internet and the Web. In the form of a double-column log, write in the left-hand column what you already knew about the Internet. In the right-hand column, list the information that you learned from reading Elmer-DeWitt's article. Based on your list, do you think you are included in Elmer-DeWitt's target audience? Explain.

2. Explaining essays typically explain what something means (definition), how something works or was created (process analysis), and/or why something happens (cause-and-effect analysis). List the paragraph numbers of passages illustrating all three of these types of analysis (definition, process, cause/effect). Which of these types does Elmer-DeWitt rely on most frequently?

3. In his essay, Elmer-DeWitt defines key terms as he introduces them. The central word of the essay, *cyberspace,* Elmer-DeWitt defines several times. Identify the different paragraphs in which he defines *cyberspace.* Elmer-DeWitt also defines the following technical terms in the course of his essay: *feedback loop, bit, hierarchical and proprietary, hosts, MUDS, bandwidth,* and *upstream capacity.* List the paragraph numbers in which each of these is defined. Overall, how effective is Elmer-DeWitt at defining key terms for his readers?

4. Elmer-DeWitt organizes his essay into clear sections. Referring to specific paragraph numbers, indicate where the following major divisions of the article begin and end.

   I.   Introduction to cyberspace and William Gibson

   II. The growing popularity of cyberspace today

   III. Extended definition of cyberspace

   IV. The Internet and its history

   V.   The future of cyberspace and the Internet

   What clues did you use to discover Elmer-DeWitt's organization? Is his organization effective, or does it need clarification in places? Explain.

5. Explaining essays should use clear transitions between paragraphs to signal to the reader how the previous paragraph and the new paragraph topics are related. Choose any four consecutive paragraphs. Underline any transitional words or phrases (usually in the first sentence of each paragraph) that help the reader move from one paragraph to the next. Which transitions are effective? Which ones could be improved? Explain.

6. Write your own essay explaining some new technique for navigating the Web or some other aspect of the Internet or computer technology. Decide on your audience (novices, average computer users, or experts). Define key terms, explain processes, or analyze causes and effects.

PROFESSIONAL WRITING

THE GLOBAL VILLAGE FINALLY ARRIVES

PICO IYER

Born in 1957 in Oxford, England, to Indian parents, Pico Iyer was educated at Eton, Oxford, and Harvard Universities. In addition to his regular features in Time *magazine, Iyer has published a novel and several travel books, including* The Lady and the Monk: Four Seasons in Kyoto *(1991),* Falling Off the Map *(1993), and* Tropical Classical: Essays from Several Directions *(1997). Although Iyer is noted for his travel books, he is not a travel guide like Frommer or Fodor. Always his goal is to tell a story about cultural differences, in the narrative style of an "intimate letter to a stranger." In "The Global Village Finally Arrives," Iyer explains—relying on immediate details, striking contrasts, and metaphors—the new multicultural village we all inhabit.*

This is the typical day of a relatively typical soul in today's diversified world. I wake up to the sound of my Japanese clock radio, put on a T-shirt sent me by an uncle in Nigeria and walk out into the street, past German cars, to my office. Around me are English-language students from Korea, Switzerland and Argentina—all on this Spanish-named road in this Mediterranean-style town. On TV, I find, the news is in Mandarin; today's baseball game is being broadcast in Korean. For lunch I can walk to a sushi bar, a tandoori palace, a Thai café or the newest burrito joint (run by an old Japanese lady). Who am I, I sometimes wonder, the son of Indian parents and a British citizen who spends much of his time in Japan (and is therefore—what else?—an American permanent resident)? And where am I? **(1)**

I am, as it happens, in Southern California, in a quiet, relatively uninternational town, but I could as easily be in Vancouver or Sydney or London or Hong Kong. All the world's a rainbow coalition, more and more; the whole planet, you might say, is going global. When I fly to Toronto, or Paris, or Singapore, I disembark in a world as hyphenated as the one I left. More and more of the globe looks like America, but an America that is itself looking more and more like the rest of the globe. Los Angeles famously teaches 82 different languages in its schools. In this respect, the city seems only to bear out the old adage that what is in California today is in America tomorrow, and next week around the globe. (2)

In ways that were hardly conceivable even a generation ago, the new world order is a version of the New World writ large: a wide-open frontier of polyglot terms and postnational trends. A common multiculturalism links us all—call it Planet Hollywood, Planet Reebok or the United Colors of Benetton. *Taxi* and *hotel* and *disco* are universal terms now, but so too are *karaoke* and *yoga* and *pizza*. For the gourmet alone, there is *tiramisù* at the Burger King in Kyoto, echt angel-hair pasta in Saigon and enchiladas on every menu in Nepal. (3)

But deeper than mere goods, it is souls that are mingling. In Brussels, a center of the new "unified Europe," one new baby in every four is Arab. Whole parts of the Paraguayan capital of Asunción are largely Korean. And when the prostitutes of Melbourne distributed some pro-condom pamphlets, one of the languages they used was Macedonian. Even Japan, which prides itself on its centuries-old socially engineered uniculture, swarms with Iranian illegals, Western executives, Pakistani laborers and Filipina hostesses. (4)

The global village is defined, as we know, by an international youth culture that takes its cues from American pop culture. Kids in Perth and Prague and New Delhi are all tuning in to *Santa Barbara* on TV, and wriggling into 501 jeans, while singing along to Madonna's latest in English. CNN (which has grown 70-fold in 13 years) now reaches more than 140 countries; an American football championship pits London against Barcelona. As fast as the world comes to America, America goes round the world—but it is an America that is itself multi-tongued and many hued, an America of Amy Tan and Janet Jackson and movies with dialogue in Lakota. (5)

For far more than goods and artifacts, the one great influence being broadcast around the world in greater numbers and at greater speed than ever before is people. What were once clear divisions are now tangles of crossed lines: there are 40 000 "Canadians" resident in Hong Kong, many of whose first language is Cantonese. And with people come customs: while new immigrants from Taiwan and Vietnam and India—some of the so-called Asian Calvinists—import all-American values of hard work and family closeness and entrepreneurial energy to America, America is sending its values of upward mobility and individualism and melting-pot hopefulness to Taipei and Saigon and Bombay. (6)

Values, in fact, travel at the speed of fax; by now, almost half the world's Mormons live outside the U.S. A diversity of one culture quickly becomes a diversity of many: the "typical American" who goes to Japan today may be a third-generation Japanese American, or the son of a Japanese woman married to a California serviceman, or the offspring of a Salvadoran father and an Italian mother from San Francisco. When he goes out with a Japanese woman, more than two cultures are brought into play. (7)

None of this, of course, is new: Chinese silks were all the rage in Rome centuries ago, and Alexandria before the time of Christ was a paradigm of the modern universal city. Not even American eclecticism is new: many a small town has long known Chinese restaurants, Indian doctors and Lebanese grocers. But now all these cultures are crossing at the speed of light. And the rising diversity of the planet is something more than mere cosmopolitanism: it is a fundamental recoloring of the very complexion of societies. Cities like Paris, or Hong Kong, have always had a soigné, international air and served as magnets for exiles and émigrés, but now smaller places are multinational too. Marseilles speaks French with a distinctly North African twang. Islamic fundamentalism has one of its strongholds in Bradford, England. It is the sleepy coastal towns of Queensland, Australia, that print their menus in Japanese. (8)

The dangers this internationalism presents are evident: not for nothing did the Tower of Babel collapse. As national borders fall, tribal alliances, and new manmade divisions, rise up, and the world learns every day terrible new meanings of the word Balkanization. And while some places are wired for international transmission, others (think of Iran or North Korea or Burma) remain as isolated as ever, widening the gap between the haves and the have-nots, or what Alvin Toffler has called the "fast" and the "slow" worlds. Tokyo has more telephones than the whole continent of Africa. (9)

Nonetheless, whether we like it or not, the "transnational" future is upon us: as Kenichi Ohmae, the international economist, suggests with his talk of a "borderless economy," capitalism's allegiances are to products, not places. "Capital is now global," Robert Reich, the

Secretary of Labor, has said, pointing out that when an Iowan buys a Pontiac from General Motors, 60% of his money goes to South Korea, Japan, West Germany, Taiwan, Singapore, Britain and Barbados. Culturally we are being re-formed daily by the cadences of world music and world fiction: where the great Canadian writers of an older generation had names like Frye and Davies and Laurence, now they are called Ondaatje and Mistry and Skvorecky. **(10)**

As space shrinks, moreover, time accelerates. This hip-hop mishmash is spreading overnight. When my parents were in college, there were all of seven foreigners living in Tibet, a country the size of Western Europe, and in its entire history the country had seen fewer than 2000 Westerners. Now a Danish student in Lhasa is scarcely more surprising than a Tibetan in Copenhagen. Already a city like Miami is beyond the wildest dreams of 1968; how much more so will its face in 2018 defy our predictions of today? **(11)**

It would be easy, seeing all this, to say that the world is moving toward the *Raza Cosmica* (Cosmic Race), predicted by the Mexican thinker Jose Vasconcelos in the '20s—a glorious blend of mongrels and mestizos. It may be more relevant to suppose that more and more of the world may come to resemble Hong Kong, a stateless special economic zone full of expats and exiles linked by the lingua franca of English and the global marketplace. Some urbanists already see the world as a grid of 30 or so highly advanced city-regions, or technopoles, all plugged into the same international circuit. **(12)**

The world will not become America. Anyone who has been to a baseball game in Osaka, or a Pizza Hut in Moscow, knows instantly that she is not in Kansas. But America may still, if only symbolically, be a model for the world. *E Pluribus Unum,* after all, is on the dollar bill. As Federico Mayor Zaragoza, the director-general of UNESCO, has said, "America's main role in the new world order is not as a military superpower, but as a multicultural superpower." **(13)**

The traditional metaphor for this is that of a mosaic. But Richard Rodriguez, the Mexican-American essayist who is a psalmist for our new hybrid forms, points out that the interaction is more fluid than that, more human, subject to daily revision. "I am Chinese," he says, "because I live in San Francisco, a Chinese city. I became Irish in America. I became Portuguese in America." And even as he announces this new truth, Portuguese women are becoming American, and Irishmen are becoming Portuguese, and Sydney (or is it Toronto?) is thinking to compare itself with the "Chinese city" we know as San Francisco. **(14)**

Vocabulary

Write down the meanings of the following words:

- a rainbow *coalition* (2)
- a world as *hyphenated* (2)
- frontier of *polyglot* terms (3)
- *postnational* trends (3)
- socially engineered *uniculture* (4)
- with dialogue in *Lakota* (5)
- *entrepreneurial* energy (6)
- Alexandria . . . was a *paradigm* (8)
- American *eclecticism* (8)
- a *soigné*, international air (8)
- new meanings of the word *Balkanization* (9)
- the *cadences* of world music (10)
- glorious blend of mongrels and *mestizos* (12)
- the *lingua franca* of English (12)

Questions for Writing and Discussion

1. The purpose of Iyer's essay is to explain the multicultural dimensions of our new global village. But in explaining these dimensions, he actually *recreates* them by referring to over 30 countries, 30 cities, and 10 languages. Make a list of these countries, cities, and languages. (Can you find these countries and cities on a map?) What effect does Iyer wish to create by including so many geographical and language references?

2. Unfamiliar vocabulary in Iyer's essay is a crucial part of the content, since Iyer's purpose is to explain and recreate the "wide open frontier of polyglot terms" that is "itself multi-tongued and many hued." Look up the words in the vocabulary list. Then reread the essay, looking for other words you do not know. Look them up in your dictionary. What effect does Iyer wish to create by using his polyglot or multicultural vocabulary?

3. In your own words, express the thesis of Iyer's essay. What is he trying to explain? Find at least three sentences from Iyer's essay that may suggest this thesis. How do these sentences each express a different aspect of the thesis? How are these sentences thematically related? Explain.

4. In paragraph 14, Iyer says that the traditional metaphor for the new transnational, multicultural world order is the mosaic. But taking his cue

from Richard Rodriguez, Iyer suggests that the multicultural interaction is "more fluid than that, more human." In what other paragraphs does Iyer suggest the fluidity and humanity of the global village? Explain.

5. Iyer's essay celebrates the global village that technology has created, but he also points to potential dangers. What dangers does he cite? What other dangers exist? How might the technologies that have created the global village (television, fax, telephones, cell phones and pagers, airplanes, the Internet, and so forth) help solve these problems?

EXPLAINING: THE WRITING PROCESS

■ ASSIGNMENT FOR EXPLAINING   Explain *what* something means or is, *how* it should be done or how it occurs, and/or *why* something occurs. Choose from your personal experiences, talents, or interests, or choose from ideas, concepts, theories, or strategies that you are learning in other courses. Your purpose is to explain something as clearly as possible for your audience by analyzing, showing relationships, and demonstrating with examples, facts, illustrations, data, or other information.

CHOOSING A SUBJECT

If you need an interesting subject, consider the following suggestions:

- Reread your authority list or the most interesting journal entries from previous chapters. Do they contain ideas that you might define or explain, processes suitable for how-to explanations, or causes or effects that you could analyze and explain for a certain audience?

- Brainstorm a list of the five most important things that you've done in the last three years. Focus on one thing, event, or idea. Now imagine that your audience is someone like you, only three years younger. Explain this topic.

- Reread your notes from another class in which you have an upcoming examination. Select some topic, idea, principle, process, famous person, or event from the text or your notes. Investigate other texts, popular magazines, or journals for information on that topic. If appropriate, interview someone or conduct a survey. Explain this principle or process to a member of your writing class.

COLLECTING

Questions   Once you have a tentative subject and audience in mind, consider which of the following will be your primary focus (all three may be relevant):

- *What* something means or is
- *How* something occurs or is done (or should be done)
- *Why* something occurs or what its effects are

To explain *what* something is, jot down answers to each of the following questions. The more you can write on each question, the more details you'll have for your topic.

- What are its class and distinguishing characteristics?
- What is its etymology?
- How can you describe it?
- What examples can you give?
- What are its parts or its functions?
- What is it similar to? What is it *not?*
- What figurative comparisons apply?
- How can it be classified?
- Which of the above is most useful to your audience?

To explain *how* something occurs or is done, answer the following questions:

- What are the component parts or steps in the whole process?
- What is the exact sequence of steps or events?
- Are several of the steps or events related?
- If steps or events were omitted, would the outcome change?
- Which steps or events are most crucial?
- Which steps or events does your audience most need to know?

To explain *why* something occurs or what its effects are, consider the following issues:

- Which are the necessary or sufficient causes?
- Which causes are remote in time, and which are immediate?

- What is the order or sequence of the causes? Do the causes occur simultaneously?

- What are the effects? Do they occur in a sequence or simultaneously?

- Do the causes and effects occur in a "chain reaction"?

- Is there an action or situation that would have prevented the effect?

- Are there comparable things or events that have similar causes or effects?

- Which causes or effects need special clarification for your audience?

Branching   Often, *branching* can help you visually analyze your subject. Start with your topic and then subdivide each idea into its component parts. The resulting analysis will not only help generate ideas but may also suggest ways to shape an essay:

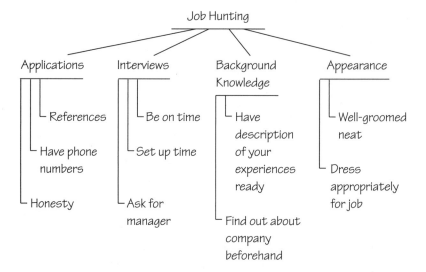

Observing   If you can observe your subject, try drawing it, describing it, or taking careful notes. Which senses can you use to describe it—sight, sound, touch, smell, taste? If it is a scientific experiment that you can reproduce or a social situation you can reconstruct, go through it again and observe carefully. As you observe it, put yourself in your readers' shoes: What do you need to explain it to them?

Remembering   Your own experience and memory are essential for explaining. *Freewriting, looping,* and *clustering* may all generate detailed information, good examples, and interesting perspectives that will make your explanation clearer and more vivid. (See Chapter 5 for an explanation of looping and clustering.)

Reading   When you find written texts about your subject, be sure to use your active reading strategies. You may need only a few sources if you reread them carefully. Write out a short summary for each source. Respond to each source by analyzing its effectiveness, agreeing or disagreeing with its ideas, or interpreting the text. The quality of your understanding is more important than the sheer number of sources you cite.

Investigating   Use sources available in the library, textbooks containing relevant information, or interviews with teachers, participants, or experts. Interview your classmates about their own subjects for this assignment: Someone else's subject may trigger an idea that you can write about or may suggest a fresh approach to the subject that you have already chosen.

SHAPING

As you collect information and generate ideas from your collecting activities, be sure to *narrow* and *focus* your subject into a topic suitable for a short essay. You will not be able to cover everything you've read, thought, or experienced about your subject. Choose the most interesting ideas—for you and for your audience—and shape, order, and clarify those ideas. In addition to *spatial order* and *comparison/contrast*, which are discussed in Chapters 4 and 5, one of the following shaping strategies may help you organize your essay.

Definition and Classification   An essay explaining *what* something means or is can be shaped by using a variety of definition strategies or by classifying the subject.

Definition itself is not a single organizing strategy; it supports a variety of strategies that may be useful in shaping your essay: description, analysis of parts or function, comparison/contrast, development by examples, or figures of speech such as simile, metaphor, and analogy.

Classification, on the other hand, is a single strategy that can organize a paragraph or even a whole essay quickly. Observers of human behaviour, for example, love to use classification. Grocery shoppers might be classified by types: racers (the ones who seem to have just won 45 seconds of free shopping and run down the aisles filling their carts as fast as possible), talkers (the ones whose phone must be out of order because they stand in the aisles gossiping forever), penny-pinchers (who always have their calculators out and read the unit price labels for everything), party shoppers (who camp out in the junk food aisles, filling their carts with potato chips, dip, candy, peanuts, and drink mixers), and dawdlers (who leave their carts crosswise in the aisles while they read 29 different soup can labels). You can write a sentence or two about each type or devote a whole paragraph to explaining a single type.

Example   Development by example can effectively illustrate what something is or means, but it can also help explain how or why something happens.

Usually, an example describes a specific incident, located at a certain place and occurring at a particular time, that *shows* or *demonstrates* the main idea. In the following paragraph from *Mediaspeak,* Donna Woolfolk Cross explains what effects soap operas can have on addicted viewers. This paragraph is developed by several examples—some described in detail, others referred to briefly:

> Dedicated watchers of soap operas often confuse fact with fiction. . . . Stars of soap operas tell hair-raising stories of their encounters with fans suffering from this affliction. Susan Lucci, who plays the promiscuous Erica Kane on "All My Children," tells of a time she was riding in a parade: "We were in a crowd of about 250 000 traveling in an antique open car moving ver-r-ry slowly. At that time in the series I was involved with a character named Nick. Some man broke through, came right up to the car and said to me, 'Why don't you give me a little bit of what you've been giving Nick?'" The man hung onto the car, menacingly, until she was rescued by the police. Another time, when she was in church, the reverent silence was broken by a woman's astonished remark, "Oh, my god, Erica prays!" Margaret Mason, who plays the villainous Lisa Anderson in "Days of Our Lives," was accosted by a woman who poured a carton of milk all over her in the supermarket. And once a woman actually tried to force her car off the Ventura Freeway.

Voice and Tone   Writers also use voice and tone to shape and control whole passages, often in combination with other shaping strategies. In the following paragraph, Toni Bambara, author of *The Salt Eaters* and numerous short stories, explains *what* being a writer is all about. This paragraph is shaped both by a single extended example and by Bambara's voice talking directly to the reader:

> When I replay the tapes on file in my head, tapes of speeches I've given at writing conferences over the years, I invariably hear myself saying—"A writer, like any other cultural worker, like any other member of the community, ought to try to put her/his skills in the service of the community." Some years ago when I returned south, my picture in the paper prompted several neighbors to come visit. "You a writer? What all you write?" Before I could begin the catalogue, one old gent interrupted with—"Ya know Miz Mary down the block? She need a writer to help her send off a letter to her grandson overseas." So I began a career as the neighbourhood scribe—letters to relatives, snarling letters to the traffic chief about the promised stop sign, nasty letters to the utilities, angry letters to the principal about that confederate flag hanging in front of the school, contracts to transfer a truck from seller to buyer, etc. While my efforts have been graciously appreciated in the form of sweet

potato dumplings, herb teas, hair braiding, and the like, there is still much room for improvement—"For a writer, honey, you've got a mighty bad hand. Didn't they teach penmanship at that college?" Another example, I guess, of words setting things in motion. What goes around, comes around, as the elders say.

Chronological Order and Process Analysis   Writers use chronological order in expository writing to help explain how to do something or how something is typically done. In her essay "Anorexia Nervosa," student writer Nancie Brosseau uses transitional words to signal the various stages of anorexia. In the following sentences, taken from the third paragraph of her essay, the *italicized* words mark the chronological stages of her anorexia:

> Several serious health problems bombarded me, and it's a wonder I'm still alive. . . . *As my weight plummeted,* my circulation grew *increasingly worse.* . . . My hair *started* to fall out, and my whole body took on a very skeletal appearance. . . . I would force myself to vomit *as soon as possible* if I was forced to eat. The enamel on my teeth *started to be eaten away* by the acid in the vomit, and my lips cracked and bled regularly. I *stopped* menstruating completely because I was not producing enough estrogen. . . . *One time,* while executing a chain of back handsprings, I broke all five fingers on one hand and three on the other because my bones had become so brittle. . . . I chose to see a psychologist, and she helped me sort out the emotional aspects of anorexia, *which in turn* solved the physical problems.

Causal Analysis   In order to explain *why* something happens or what the effects of something are, writers often use one of the following three patterns of cause and effect to shape their material:

CAUSE 1 + CAUSE 2 + CAUSE 3 . . . + CAUSE n → EFFECT

In the case of fire, for example, we know that three causes lead to a single effect. These causes do not occur in any special sequence; they must all be present at the same time. For historical events, however, we usually list causes in chronological order.

Sometimes one cause has several effects. In that case, we reverse the pattern:

CAUSE → EFFECT 1 + EFFECT 2 + EFFECT 3 . . . + EFFECT n

For example, an explanation of the collapse of the economy following the stock market crash of 1929 might follow this pattern. The crash (itself a symptom of other causes) led to a depreciated economy, widespread unemployment, bankruptcy for thousands of businesses, foreclosures on farms, and so forth. An essay on the effects of the crash might devote one or two paragraphs to each effect.

In the third pattern, causes and effects form a pattern of chain reactions. One cause leads to an effect that then becomes the cause of another effect, and so on:

CAUSE 1 → EFFECT 1 (CAUSE 2) → EFFECT 2 (CAUSE 3) → EFFECT 3

We could analyze events in the Middle East prior to the Persian Gulf War as a series of actions and reactions in which each effect becomes the cause of the next effect in the chain of skirmishes, car bombings, air raids, terrorist hijackings, and kidnappings. An essay on the chain reaction of events in the Middle East might have a paragraph or two on each of the links in this chain.

Introductions and Lead-Ins

Often, the first sentences of the introductory paragraph of an essay are the hardest to write. You want to get your reader's attention and focus on the main idea of your essay, but you don't want to begin, boringly, with your thesis statement. Below are several kinds of opening sentences designed to grab your reader's interest. Consider your topic—see if one of these strategies will work for you.

A PERSONAL EXAMPLE

I knew my dieting had gotten out of hand, but when I could actually see the movement of my heart beating beneath my clothes, I knew I was in trouble.

—"Anorexia Nervosa," Nancie Brosseau

A DESCRIPTION OF A PERSON OR PLACE

Manang wore faded khaki shorts that used to be my father's, no shirt, and a straw hat that hid his eyes. His large flat feet had spaces between the toes because he didn't have to wear shoes.

—*The Way of a Boy*, Ernest Hillen

AN EXAMPLE FROM A CASE STUDY

Susan Smith has everything going for her. A self-described workaholic, she runs a Cambridge, Massachusetts, real estate consulting company with her husband Charles and still finds time to cuddle and nurture their two young kids, David, 7, and Stacey, 6. What few people know is that Susan, 44, needs a little chemical help to be a supermom: she has been taking the antidepressant Prozac for five years.

—"The Personality Pill," Anastasia Toufexis

A STARTLING STATEMENT, FACT, OR STATISTIC

Embalming is indeed a most extraordinary procedure, and one must wonder at the docility of Americans who each year pay hundreds of millions of dollars for its perpetuation, blissfully ignorant of what it is all about, what is done, how it is done.

—"To Dispel Fears of Live Burial," Jessica Mitford

A STATEMENT FROM A BOOK

The American novelist John Barth, in his early novel *The Floating Opera,* remarks that ordinary, day-to-day life often presents us with embarrassingly obvious, totally unsubtle patterns of symbolism and meaning—life in the midst of death, innocence vindicated, youth versus age, etc.

—"I'm O.K., but You're Not," Robert Zoellner

Lead-In, Thesis, and Essay Map   The introduction to an explaining essay—whether one paragraph or several—usually contains the following features:

- *Lead-In:* Some example, description, startling statement, statistic, short narrative, allusion, or quotation to get the reader's interest *and* focus on the topic you will explain.

- *Thesis:* Statement of the main idea; a "promise" to the reader that the essay fulfills.

- *Essay Map:* A sentence, or part of a sentence, that *lists* (in the order in which the essay discusses them) the main subtopics for the essay.

In her essay on anorexia nervosa at the end of this chapter, Nancie Brosseau's introductory paragraph has all three features:

I knew my dieting had gotten out of hand, but when I could actually see the movement of my heart beating beneath my clothes, I knew I was in trouble. At first, the family doctor reassured my parents that my rapid weight loss was a "temporary phase among teenage girls." However, when I, at fourteen years old and five feet tall, weighed in at sixty-three pounds, my doctor changed his diagnosis from "temporary phase" to "anorexia nervosa." Anorexia nervosa is the process of self-starvation that affects over 100 000 young girls each year. Almost 6 000 of these girls die every year. Anorexia nervosa is a self-mutilating disease that affects its victim both physically and emotionally.

The essay map is contained in the phrase "both physically and emotionally": The first half of the essay discusses the physical effects of anorexia nervosa; the second half explains the emotional effects. Like a road map, the essay map helps the reader anticipate what topics the writer will explain.

Paragraph Transitions and Hooks   Transition words and paragraph hooks are audience cues that help the reader shift from one paragraph to the next. These connections between paragraphs help the reader see the relationships of the various parts. Transition words—*first, second, next, another, last, finally,* and so forth—signal your reader that a new idea or a new part of the idea is coming up. In addition to transition words, writers often tie paragraphs together by using a key word or idea from a previous paragraph in the opening sentence of the following paragraph to "hook" the paragraphs together. The following paragraphs from Philip Elmer-DeWitt's essay "Welcome to Cyberspace" illustrate how transition words and paragraph hooks work together to create smooth connections between paragraphs.

. . . By Barlow's definition, just about everybody has already been to cyberspace. It's marked by the feeling that the person you're talking to is "in the same room." Most people take the spatial dimension of a phone conversation for granted—until they get a really bad connection or a glitchy overseas call. Then they start raising their voice, as if by sheer volume they could propel it to the outer reaches of cyberspace.

Hooks: "Cyberspace,"
"telephone call"

Cyberspace, of course, is bigger than a telephone call. It encompasses the millions of personal computers connected by modems—via the telephone system—to commercial online services, as well as the millions more with high-speed links to local area networks, office E-mail systems and the Internet. It includes the rapidly expanding wireless services: microwave towers that carry great quantities of cellular phone and data traffic; communications satellites strung like beads in a geosynchronous orbit; low-flying satellites that will soon crisscross the globe like angry bees, connecting folks too far-flung or too much on the go to be tethered by wires. Someday even our television sets may be part of cyberspace, transformed into interactive "teleputers" by so-called full-service networks like the ones several cable-TV companies (including Time Warner) are building along the old cable lines, using fiber optics and high-speed switches.

Transition: "But"
Hooks: "Wires," "cables,"
and "microwaves"
Hook: "Cyberspace"

Hook to first paragraph:
"In the same room"

But these wires and cables and microwaves are not really cyberspace. They are the means of conveyance, not the destination: the information superhighway, not the bright city lights at the end of the road. Cyberspace, in the sense of being "in the same room," is an experience, not a wiring system. . . .

Body Paragraphs   Body paragraphs in expository writing are the main paragraphs in an essay, excluding any introductory, concluding, or transition paragraphs. They often contain the following features:

- *Topic sentence:* To promote clarity and precision, writers often use topic sentences to announce the main ideas of paragraphs. The main idea should be clearly related to the writer's thesis. A topic sentence usually occurs early in the paragraph (first or second sentence) or at the end of the paragraph.

- *Unity:* To avoid confusing readers, writers focus on a single idea for each paragraph. Writing unified paragraphs helps writers—and their readers—concentrate on one point at a time.

- *Coherence:* To make their writing flow smoothly from one sentence to the next, writers supplement their shaping strategies with coherence devices: repeated key words, pronouns referring to key nouns, and transition words.

The following body paragraph from Elmer-DeWitt's essay illustrates these features. The paragraph begins with a topic sentence that focusses on the Internet's "resolutely grass-roots structure." It has unity because every sentence in the paragraph discusses what that grass-roots or democratic structure is (and how that differs from conventional computer systems). It uses transitions, pronouns, repeated key words, and repeated sentence patterns to promote coherence:

One factor fueling the Internet's remarkable growth is its resolutely grass-roots structure. Most conventional computer systems are hierarchical and proprietary; they run on copyright software in a pyramid structure that gives dictatorial powers to the system operators who sit on top. The Internet, by contrast, is open (non-proprietary) and rabidly democratic. No one owns it. No single organization controls it. It is run like a commune with 4.9 million fiercely independent members (called hosts). It crosses national boundaries and answers to no sovereign. It is literally lawless.	*Topic sentence* *Repeated key words:* *"The Internet"* *Transition: "By contrast"* *Repeated pronoun:* *"It" Repeated sentence patterns*

DRAFTING

Before you begin drafting, reconsider your purpose and audience. What you explain depends on what your audience needs to know or what would demonstrate or show your point most effectively.

As you work from an outline or from an organizing strategy, remember that all three questions—*what, how,* and *why*—are interrelated. If you are writing about causes, for example, an explanation of *what* the topic is and *how* the causes function may also be necessary to explain your subject clearly.

As you write, balance your sense of plan and organization with a willingness to pursue ideas that you discover as you write. While you need to have a plan, you should be ready to change course if you discover a more interesting idea or angle.

REVISING

As you revise your explaining essay, concentrate on making yourself perfectly clear, on illustrating with examples where your reader might be confused, and on signalling the relationship of the parts of your essay to your reader.

Guidelines for Revision

- **Compare your thesis sentence with what you say in your conclusion.** You may have a clearer statement of your thesis near the end of your paper. Revise your original thesis sentence to make it clearer, more focussed, or more in line with what your essay actually says.

- **Explaining means *showing* and *demonstrating* relationships.** Be sure to follow general statements with *specific examples, details, facts, statistics, memories, dialogues,* or other *illustrations.*

- **In a formal definition, be sure to include the class of objects or concepts to which the term belongs.** Avoid ungrammatical writing, such as "Photosynthesis is *when* plants absorb oxygen" or "The lymphatic system is *where* the body removes bacteria and transports fatty cells."

- **Avoid introducing definitions with "Webster says . . ."** Instead, read definitions from several dictionaries and give the best or most appropriate definition.

- **Remember that you can modify the dictionary definition of a term or concept to fit your particular context.** For example, to you, *heroism* may mean having the courage to *say* what you believe, not just to endanger your life through selfless actions.

- **Don't mix categories when you are classifying objects or ideas.** If you are classifying houses *by floor design* (ranch, bilevel, split-level, two-storey), don't bring in other categories, such as passive-solar, which could be incorporated into any of those designs.

- **In explaining *how* something occurs or should be done, be sure to indicate to your audience which steps are *most important.***

- **In cause-and-effect explanations, avoid *post hoc* fallacies.** This term comes from the Latin phrase *post hoc, ergo propter hoc:* "After this, therefore because of this." For example, just because Event B occurred after Event A, it does not follow, necessarily, that A caused B. If, for example, statistics show that traffic fatalities in your province actually declined after the speed limit on highways was increased, you should not conclude that higher speeds actually caused the reduction in fatalities. Other causes—increased radar patrols, stiffer drunk-driving penalties, or more rigorous vehicle-maintenance laws—may have been responsible for the reduction.

- **As you revise to sharpen your meaning or make your organization clearer, use appropriate transitional words and phrases to signal the** *relationships among the various parts of your subject.*

  - *To signal relation in time:* before, meanwhile, later, soon, at last, earlier, thereafter, afterward, by that time, from then on, first, next, now, presently, shortly, immediately, finally

  - *To signal similarity:* likewise, similarly, once again, once more

  - *To signal difference:* but, yet, however, although, whereas, though, even so, nonetheless, still, on the other hand, on the contrary

  - *To signal consequences:* as a result, consequently, therefore, hence, for this reason

STUDENT WRITING

ENGLISH ONLY

CHRISTINE BISHOP

Christine Bishop decided to write on "English Only" as one of her semester portfolio topics. She had become interested in the topic in a previous year when she went to a speech tournament that debated the English-only issue. She wrote the following essay as the first step in her semester portfolio project. Following this explaining essay, she wrote a persuasive essay, arguing against English-only legislation. For this initial essay, however, she focussed on reading key articles about English only, exploring the issues in each article, and explaining key arguments on both sides. Her goal was not to argue for one side or the other, but to explore the issues and explain the arguments on both sides of the English-only debate. As you read her essay, see if she explains the major arguments for both sides in a clear and balanced manner.

PREWRITING FOR TOPIC PROPOSAL

The English-only issue is a very controversial issue. Some say America should adopt an official language policy. Others think that this is a very racist idea. I have been reviewing reports of a recent vote on making Puerto Rico a state. Part of the legislation centered on making the people of Puerto Rico (which is predominantly Spanish-speaking) adopt English as their official language. Supporters of this bill claim that it is necessary that the Puerto Ricans learn English to become Americanized. Other people feel this will take away their language rights. Some people speculate that the English-only movement is a xenophobic reaction to the 1960 immigration amendments. These amendments made it illegal to restrict citizenship to America based on race. With this new amendment, there has been an influx in immigrants from diverse places. This influx of people could lead to xenophobia (fear of strangers or foreigners). I feel this speculation may be true. In 1921, when New Mexico became a state, it was allowed to keep Spanish as its official language provided that English was also an official language. Why such a radical change in policy when Puerto Rico applies to be a state? Is America afraid that it will lose its identity to non–English-speaking people? America started out as a conglomerate of immigrants who did not all speak the same language. What now?

I would like to explore this topic more. The two main positions on English-only legislation are as follows:

1. English needs to be the official language of the United States because we need one unifying language. Without English-only laws, immigrants will not learn English and will not contribute to society.

2. It is unfair to expect current citizens in the United States to learn English. Making English official will make people not learn other languages.

I know some about this subject, but I haven't done much research on my own. The questions I have are whether I could tie this into racism and whether I will be able to get enough information in the library and on the Internet.

FIRST DRAFT

The issue has been raised that the United States needs to make English the official language of the nation. Currently, the Senate is reviewing a proposal to require Puerto Rico to adopt English as its official language before considering it for statehood. While everyone agrees that it is important for all Americans to speak English, there is disagreement as to whether the government should adopt an official language policy. Those who support an official language policy (such as Richard Rodriguez) believe that without a policy, immigrants to America will not learn English. Those who do not support this policy believe that there is enough pressure on immigrants, and that they have enough desire to learn English quickly on their own. Some who oppose an official English policy believe that this policy will alienate immigrants and that Americans who support this policy are having a xenophobic reaction to recent immigrants from more diverse cultures initiated by 1960s immigration laws. I would like to explain exactly what these opposing positions are, using essays written by Richard Rodriguez, Samuel Hayakawa, James Crawford, and James Fallows.

As a champion of English Only legislation, Richard Rodriguez believes that without the government to push them into learning English, immigrants will not learn the language. In "Aria: A Memoir of a Bilingual Childhood," Mr. Rodriguez states, "What I did not believe was that I could speak a single public language. . . . It would have pleased me to hear my teachers address me in Spanish. . . . But I would have delayed—for how long postponed?—having to learn the language of public society [English]." Although Richard was born in the United States, being the son of migrant workers, he had not been exposed to English until he had entered school. Without the church (he attended a Catholic school) to force him to learn English, Richard believes he would never have learned to speak English. Like all people on both sides of the issue, Rodriguez believes that it is necessary to speak English to succeed in the United States. Because Rodriguez was not motivated to speak English as a child, he feels that it is imperative for the government to push immigrants to learn English by making English the official language of the United States. People opposing English being the official language believe immigrants desire to learn English.

Both James Fallows, in "Viva Bilingualism," and James Crawford, author of *Hold Your Tongue: Bilingualism and the Politics of English Only*, oppose English-only legislation. Fallows, an English-speaking American who lived in Japan, feels that his experiences are contradictory to these beliefs. While living in Japan—a country that "makes many more accommodations to the English language than America does to Spanish"—Fallows found that most English-speaking people learned Japanese in order to participate in society. In America, Fallows thinks the incentives for immigrants to learn English are greater. The only way to get any kind of white-collar job or to attend college, according to Fallows, is through learning English. English is how communities in America are built.

Other English-only supporters, like former Senator Samuel Hayakawa, feel that a common language in the United States would better unite Americans. Hayakawa uses the example of Chinese- and Japanese-Americans, who didn't get along during World War II. Now they have begun to form Asian-American groups. Hayakawa believes this is the result of having learned English. Hayakawa states, "A common tongue encourages trust while reducing racial hostility and bigotry." Hayakawa believes that unless the United States implements an English-only policy, we will head the way of Quebec or India—"a chaotic mess which has led to countless problems in the government's efforts to manage the nation's business." According to Hayakawa, this problem is already apparent. He blames the 50 percent dropout rate among Hispanic students on the current bilingual policy.

People who do not support English only, like James Crawford, do not believe that the differences in language will cause chaos. They further believe that an official English policy will separate Americans. In his book, James Crawford quotes Raul Yzaguirre, President of the National Council of La Raza, as saying: "U.S. English is to Hispanics as the Ku Klux Klan is to blacks." Crawford says that this is the consensus among Latino leaders. Crawford goes on to say that Latino leaders believe English only "is a Xenophobic, intolerant act."

Because I believe that Rodriguez's experience might be unique and that there are many other people's experiences pointing the other way—including my own—I think Hayakawa's argument may be shaky. Possibly, Crawford and Fallows, because of their experience, may be correct. Crawford has spent ten years researching the issue, which gives his argument credibility. I think that although it is quite debatable, the new push for English as an official language may be due to a backlash against the recent influx of more diverse groups into the United States. But determining exactly how government laws might affect the motivation of immigrants to learn English is difficult. We seem to have different personal testimonies: Hayakawa and Rodriguez think an English-only policy will encourage immigrants to learn English; Fallows and Crawford think immigrants already have enough incentives to learn English.

FINAL DRAFT

ENGLISH ONLY

English-only laws have been in the news again, with a recent debate in the Senate over a requirement that Puerto Rico adopt English as its official language before being allowed to become a state (Gugliotta 1). In the United States, English-only laws currently exist in twenty-three states—having passed recently in Alaska and Missouri—but they suffered a setback in Arizona, where the United States Supreme Court upheld a decision that struck down an Arizona law that passed originally in 1988 (Denniston 1). Basically, English-only laws such as Arizona's state that "this state and all political subdivisions of this state shall act in English and no other language" (Denniston 2). While everyone agrees that it is important for all Americans to speak English, there is disagreement as to whether state governments should adopt an official language policy. **(1)**.

The debate over "English only" continues as groups such as U.S. English try to promote language laws in every state. Those who support an official language policy believe that without a policy, immigrants will not learn English. Those who oppose an official English policy believe that English-only laws alienate immigrants and that Americans who support these laws are having a xenophobic reaction to the flood of recent immigrants from more diverse cultures. In order to explain what this debate is about and what the major issues are on both sides, I will look primarily at four authors who have written about English-only laws. Two writers who support English only are the late Senator Samuel Hayakawa and Richard Rodriguez, author of *Hunger of Memory*. Two authors who oppose English only are James Fallows, Washington editor of *Atlantic* magazine, and John Crawford, author of *Hold Your Tongue: Bilingualism and the Politics of English Only*. **(2)**

Those who support an English-only policy feel that it will encourage immigrants and non–English-speaking Americans to speak English. In his essay, "Bilingualism in America: English Should Be the *Only* Language," Hayakawa uses the example of Chinese- and Japanese-Americans, who didn't get along during World War II. Now they have begun to form Asian-American groups (252). Hayakawa believes this is the result of having learned English. Hayakawa states, "A common tongue encourages trust while reducing racial hostility and bigotry" (252). Hayakawa, one of the original founders of U.S. English, believes that unless the United States implements an English-only policy, we will head the way of Quebec or India: India's "ten official languages" have created a situation that is "a chaotic mess which has led to countless problems in the government's efforts to manage the nation's business" (253). According to Hayakawa, the problem in the United States is already apparent. He blames the 50 percent dropout rate among Hispanic students on the current bilingual policy (254). Writers such as Hayakawa forecast a Tower of Babel. They believe that unless we adopt an English-only policy, immigrants will not learn English and U.S. citizens will not be able to communicate with each other. Of course, Hayakawa's analogy with Quebec and India may be difficult to support, because immigrants to the United States have always learned English, whereas in Quebec and India, people have always spoken different languages. **(3)**

As a champion of English-only legislation, Richard Rodriguez, like the late Senator Hayakawa, believes that without the government to push immigrants into learning English, they will not learn English. In "Aria: A Memoir of a Bilingual Childhood," Mr. Rodriguez states, "What I needed to learn in school was that I had the right, and the obligation, to speak the public language. . . . It would have pleased me to hear my teachers address me in Spanish. . . . But I would have delayed—postponed for how long?—having to learn the language of public society" (270). Although Rodriguez was born in the United States, the son of migrant workers, he was not exposed to English until he entered school. Without his Catholic schoolteachers' forcing him to learn English, Rodriguez believes that he would never have learned to speak the public language (271). Like people on both sides of the English-only issue, Rodriguez believes that to succeed in the United States, it is necessary to be proficient in English. Because Rodriguez was not motivated to speak English as a child, he feels that it is imperative for the government to push immigrants to learn English by making English the official language of the United States. **(4)**

In addition, the website for U.S. English agrees with Hayakawa and Rodriguez that without English-only legislation, immigrants will "fail to learn English and separate into linguistic enclaves. This division of the United States into separate language groups contributes to racial and ethnic conflicts" (*U.S. English* 1). This is, of course, a controversial position because many other people believe that immigrants have plenty of incentive to learn English on their own, and those people have history to cite as evidence. **(5)**

On the other side of the English-only debate, James Fallows, a Washington editor of *Atlantic* magazine and author of "Viva Bilingualism," believes that there are enough incentives for immigrants to learn English without adding pressure to the situation. Fallows, an English-speaking American who lived in Japan, feels that his experiences show that English-only laws are unnecessary. When living in Japan, a country that "makes many more accommodations to the English language than America does to Spanish," Fallows found that he, as well as most English-speaking people, needed to learn Japanese to participate in society (262). In America, Fallows thinks the incentives for immigrants to learn English are greater. The only way to get a white-collar job or to attend college, according to Fallows, is to learn English. As Fallows puts it, in America, you can't take the SATs in Spanish or even watch *David Letterman* (262). **(6)**

Writers such as James Fallows who do not support an English-only policy do not believe that the differences in language will cause chaos. However, some believe that an official English-only policy will actually separate Americans. James Crawford, author of *Hold Your Tongue: Bilingualism and the Politics of English Only*, argues that English-only laws are racist and xenophobic. Crawford quotes Raul Yzaguirre, President of the National Council of La Raza, as saying, "U.S. English is to Hispanics as the Ku Klux Klan is to blacks" (1). Crawford says that this is the consensus among Latino leaders. Crawford goes on to say that Latino leaders believe English only is a xenophobic, intolerant act (1). When Spanish leaders are saying that English only is similar to something extreme like the KKK, something has to be wrong. That Latino leaders link English only to the KKK, coupled with the fact that immigrants have always learned English on their own, seems to be compelling evidence that many people think English-only laws are unnecessary and possibly destructive. **(7)**

If there is any middle ground in this debate, I find it difficult to explain. Often, arguments on both sides seem to come down to personal experiences. Rodriguez thinks his experiences show that there should be the pressure of English-only laws; Fallows's experiences in Japan persuade him that there are already sufficient pressures to encourage immigrants to learn English. Hayakawa does point to real problems in countries such as Canada and India, but his statistics may be shaky. Hayakawa quotes Hispanics as having a 50 percent dropout rate, saying that this could be due to the lack of English proficiency, and then later states that 90 percent of the

Hispanics in the United States are fluent in English (254, 255). These two statements are contradictory and weaken Hayakawa's position. Crawford and Fallows, because of their experience, do have legitimate points. Crawford spent ten years of research on the issue, which adds to his credibility. In addition, Fallows has personal experience similar to my own. When I was living in a foreign country, I felt continual pressure to learn the language spoken in my host country, and because I did not have my family around, I couldn't hide from the new language and culture. (8)

It is difficult to determine the long-term effects of English-only legislation. I haven't found any evidence that the laws in twenty-three states have increased the number of immigrants who speak English, but I have found evidence that the debate about these laws can be heated and divisive. Although this issue is certainly debatable, I believe that the new push for English as an official language may be due to a backlash against the recent influx of more diverse groups into the United States. If state governments continue to support that backlash, it may further alienate our new citizens. On the other hand, many immigrants don't learn English very quickly, and they survive in linguistic enclaves, separated by language barriers from mainstream American culture. Possibly the economic pressures of earning a living will have a far greater effect on encouraging immigrants to learn English than any official English laws. If the momentum for English-only laws persists in state legislatures, we will continue to see arguments from both sides used in the debate. (9)

WORKS CITED

Crawford, John. *Hold Your Tongue: Bilingualism and the Politics of English Only.* Reading, MA: Addison Wesley, 1992. 24 Sept. 1998 <http://ourworld. compuserve.com/homepages/JWCRAWFORD/home.html>.

Denniston, Lyle. "English-Only Measure Dealt Blow." *Baltimore Sun* 12 Jan. 1998. 11 Jan. 1999 <http://www.sunspot.net/cgi-bin/editorial>.

Fallows, James. "Viva Bilingualism." *Exploring Language.* Ed. Gary Goshgarian. 8th ed. New York: Addison Wesley Longman, 1998. 259–63.

Gugliotta, Guy. "House Passes Puerto Rico Bill." *Washington Post Online* 5 March 1998. 24 Sept. 1998 <http://ourworld.compuserve.com/homepages/ JWCRAWFORD/WPOST4.html>.

Hayakawa, S. I. "Bilingualism in America: English Should Be the *Only* Language." *Exploring Language.* Ed. Gary Goshgarian. 8th ed. New York: Addison Wesley Longman, 1998. 251–56.

Rodriguez, Richard. "Aria: A Memoir of a Bilingual Childhood." *Exploring Language.* Ed. Gary Goshgarian. 8th ed. New York: Addison Wesley Longman, 1998. 266–75.

U.S. English Page. 13 Jan. 1999 <http://www.us-english.org/why.htm>.

Questions for Writing and Discussion

1. Compare Bishop's first and revised drafts. What information and explanations did she add in the revised version? How did she reorganize her essay for the revised version? Explain.

2. Bishop's purpose in this first essay for her portfolio was to explore the arguments on each side of the English-only debate and then explain these arguments to her reader. She did *not* want to argue for or against English only until the final essay in her portfolio. What paragraphs does she devote to the advocates of the English-only movement? What paragraphs explain the arguments of those who oppose English only. Does she balance the arguments without taking sides herself? Explain.

3. Explaining essays should define key terms, concepts, or ideas. What terms or ideas does Bishop explain or define? Are there other terms or ideas that she needed to define? Explain.

4. In this chapter, read Pico Iyer's essay, "The Global Village Finally Arrives." What side might Iyer take in this English-only debate? Assume you are Pico Iyer, and write a response—to Bishop or any of the authors she cites—explaining how you react to these English-only issues. In a postscript, indicate how your own personal views might differ from the views of Pico Iyer.

STUDENT WRITING

ANOREXIA NERVOSA
NANCIE BROSSEAU

In her essay on anorexia nervosa, Nancie Brosseau writes from her own experience, explaining what anorexia nervosa is and what its effects are. Her essay succeeds not only because it is organized clearly, but also because it is so vivid and memorable. Relying on specific details, her explanation shows the effects of anorexia on her life.

I knew my dieting had gotten out of hand, but when I could actually see the movement of my heart beating beneath my clothes, I knew I was in trouble. At first, the family doctor reassured my parents that my rapid weight loss was a "temporary phase among teenage girls." However, when I, at fourteen years old and five feet tall, weighed in at sixty-three pounds, my doctor changed his diagnosis from "temporary phase" to "anorexia nervosa." Anorexia nervosa is the process of self-starvation that affects over 100 000 young girls each year. Almost 6 000 of these girls die every year. Anorexia nervosa is a self-mutilating disease that affects its victim both physically and emotionally. **(1)**

As both a gymnast and a dancer, I was constantly surrounded by lithe, muscular people, all of them extremely conscious about their weight. Although I wasn't overweight to begin with, I thought that if I lost five to ten pounds I would look, feel, dance, and tumble better. I figured the quickest way to accomplish this was by drastically limiting my intake of food. By doing this, I lost ten pounds in one week and gained the approval of my peers. Soon, I could no longer control myself, and ten pounds turned into twenty, twenty into forty, and so on, until I finally ended up weighing fifty-eight pounds. **(2)**

Several serious health problems bombarded me, and it's a wonder I'm still alive. Because my body was receiving no nourishment at all, my muscles and essential organs, including my heart, liver, kidneys, and intestines, started to compensate by slowly disintegrating. My body was feeding on itself! As my weight plummeted, my circulation grew increasingly worse. My hands, feet, lips, and ears took on a bluish-purple tint, and I was constantly freezing cold. My hair started to fall out and my whole body took on a very skeletal appearance. My eyes appeared to have sunken into my face, and my forehead, cheekbones, and chin protruded sharply. My wrists were the largest part of my entire arm, as were my knees the widest part of my legs. My pants rubbed my hips raw because I had to wear my belts at their tightest notch to keep them up. I would force myself to vomit as soon as possible if I was forced to eat. The enamel on my teeth started to be eaten away by the acid in the vomit, and my lips cracked and bled regularly. I stopped menstruating completely because I was not producing enough estrogen. Instead of improving my skills as a dancer and a gymnast, I drastically reduced them because I was so weak. One time, while executing a chain of back handsprings, I broke all five fingers on one hand and three on the other because my bones had become so brittle. My doctor realized the serious danger I was in and told me I either had to see a psychologist or be put in the hospital. I chose to see a psychologist, and she helped me sort out the emotional aspects of anorexia which in turn solved the physical problems. **(3)**

The emotional problems associated with anorexia nervosa are equally disastrous to the victim's health. Self-deception, lying, and depression are three examples of the emotions and actions an anorexic often experiences. During my entire bout with anorexia, I deceived myself into thinking I had complete control over my body. Hunger pains became a pleasant feeling, and sore muscles from overexercising just proved to me that I still needed to lose more weight. When my psychologist showed me pictures of girls that were of normal weight for my age group, they honestly looked obese to me. I truly believed that even the smallest amount of food would make me extremely fat. (4)

Another problem, lying, occurred most often when my parents tried to force me to eat. Because I was at the gym until around eight o'clock every night, I told my mother not to save me dinner. I would come home and make a sandwich and feed it to my dog. I lied to my parents every day about eating lunch at school. For example, I would bring a sack lunch and sell it to someone and use the money to buy diet pills. I always told my parents that I ate my own lunch. I lied to my doctor when he asked if I was taking an appetite suppressant. I had to cover one lie with another to keep from being found out, although it was obvious that I was not eating by looking at me. (5)

Still another emotion I felt, as a result of my anorexia, was severe depression. It seemed that, no matter how hard I tried, I kept growing fatter. Of course, I was getting thinner all the time, but I couldn't see that. One time, I licked a postage stamp to put on a letter and immediately remembered that there was 1/4 of a calorie in the glue on the stamp. I punished myself by doing 100 extra situps every night for one week. I pinched my skin until it bruised as I lay awake at night because I was so ashamed of the way I thought I looked. I doomed myself to a life of obesity. I would often slip into a mood my psychologist described as a "blue funk." That is, I would become so depressed, I seriously considered committing suicide. The emotional instabilities associated with anorexia nervosa can be fatal. (6)

Through psychological and physical treatment, I was able to overcome anorexia nervosa. I still have a few complications today due to anorexia, such as dysmenorrhea (severe menstrual cramps) and the tendency to fast. However, these problems are minute compared to the problems I would have had if I hadn't received immediate help. Separately, the physical and emotional problems that anorexia nervosa creates can greatly harm its victim. However, when the two are teamed together, the results are deadly. (7)

Questions for Writing and Discussion

1. Without looking back at this essay, jot down the specific examples that you found most memorable. How would you describe these examples: tedious and commonplace, eye-opening, shocking, upsetting, persuasive? Explain.

2. Identify the thesis statement and essay map. Referring to paragraph numbers, show how the essay map sets up the organization of the essay.

3. Reread the opening sentences of each body paragraph. Identify one opening sentence that creates a smooth transition from the previous paragraph. Identify one opening sentence in which the transition could be smoother. Revise this sentence to improve the transition with a paragraph hook.

4. In this essay, Brosseau defines anorexia nervosa, explains its physical and emotional effects (and hints at its causes), and analyzes the process of the disorder, from its inception to its cure. Identify passages that illustrate each of these strategies: definition, cause-and-effect analysis, and process analysis.

EVALUATING

LEARNING OUTCOMES

After reading this chapter, you will have learned to

- make a value judgment using clear standards and specific evidence

- persuade others to accept your judgment

Hardly a day passes when we do not express our likes or dislikes. We constantly pass judgment on people, places, objects, events, ideas, and policies in the world around us: "Sue is a wonderful person." "The food in this cafeteria is horrible." "That movie we saw Saturday night ought to get an Oscar nomination for best picture." "The Young Offenders Act is a good piece of legislation." At the same time, we are constantly exposed to the opinions of our friends, family members, teachers, and business associates. And, of course, the media barrage us with claims about products, famous personalities, and candidates for public office.

A claim or opinion, however, is not an *evaluation*. Your reaction to a person, a sports event, a meal, a movie, or a public policy becomes an evaluation *only* when you support your value judgment with clear standards and specific evidence. Your goal in evaluating something is not only to express your viewpoint, but also to *persuade* others to accept your judgment. You convince your readers by indicating the standards for your judgment and then supporting it with evidence: "The food in this cafeteria is horrible [your claim]. I know that not all cafeteria food tastes great, but it should at least be sanitary [one standard of judgment]. Yesterday, I had to dig a piece of green mould out of the meat loaf, and just as I stuck my fork into the green salad, a large black roach ran out [evidence]."

Most people interested in a subject agree that certain standards are important, for example, that a cafeteria be clean and pest-free. The standards that you share with your audience are the *criteria* for your evaluation. You convince your readers that something is good or bad, ugly or beautiful, tasty or nauseating by analyzing your subject in terms of your criteria. For each separate criterion, you support your judgment with specific *evidence:* descriptions, statistics, testimony, or examples from your personal experience. If your readers agree that your standards or criteria are appropriate, and if you supply detailed evidence, your readers should be convinced. They will take your evaluation seriously—and think twice about eating at that roach-infested cafeteria.

TECHNIQUES FOR WRITING EVALUATIONS

Any writing that requires a *value judgment* uses the techniques of evaluating—whether you're writing about consumer products or services, works of art, or performances by people. Effective evaluations use the following techniques:

- **Stating an** *overall claim* **about your subject.** This statement serves as the *thesis* for your evaluation.

- **Describing the person, place, object, text, event, service, or performance being evaluated.** Readers need basic information—*who, what, when,* and *where*—to form a clear judgment.

- **Clarifying the *criteria* for your evaluation.** A criterion is a standard of judgment that most people interested in your subject agree is important. A criterion serves as a yardstick against which you measure your subject.

- **Stating a *judgment* for each criterion.** The overall claim is based on your judgment of each separate criterion. Include both positive *and* negative judgments.

- **Supporting each judgment with *evidence*.** Support can include detailed description, facts, examples, testimony, or statistics.

- **Balancing your evaluation with both positive and negative judgments about your subject.** Evaluations that are all positive are merely advertisements; evaluations that are entirely negative may seem too harsh or mean-spirited.

In the following evaluation of a restaurant in Calgary, Alberta, journalist and critic John Gilchrist illustrates the main features of an evaluation:

PROFESSIONAL WRITING

THE BELVEDERE
JOHN GILCHRIST

The biggest buzz in the restaurant industry right now is about the *Belvedere*, a brand-new, top-end restaurant at 107 - 8 Ave SW. The buzz is about the quality of the food, the beauty of the room, and the height of the prices. All three are quite exceptional. **(1)**

Location

Overall claim

The Belvedere has revived yet another old bank building, this time the Union Bank, and they have done an excellent job on the space. It is not huge—there's a 60-seat non-smoking dining room in the back and a 40-seat smoker-friendly lounge out front divided by a plush floor-to-ceiling curtain. The dining room is wide enough to allow for three rows of tables, placed fairly close together. **(2)**

Criterion #1: Setting
Judgment: Excellent with one exception

The décor is part retro with exposed overhead beams and a big skylight, part contemporary with mirrored panels, and part 50's dinner club with plush accoutrements. However, where they could

Evidence

go a little more plush is in the dining room chairs. They are nice, unpadded hard wood chairs that get a bit uncomfortable after a few hours. **(3)**

And a few hours you will need. The Belvedere falls into the Dining Experience category, lunch in an hour is tight, and dinner is a 2–3 hour event. **(4)**

Criterion #2:
Unique dishes
Judgment: Excellent

Take your time. It's worth it. The Belvedere features the work of chef Alan Groom, former executive chef at Vancouver's Wedgewood Hotel. He has created a seasonal menu of what I would describe as contemporary global fusion. This is the kind of food that adventurous chefs around the world are doing these days—lots of fresh local ingredients, vaguely continental preparations, a certain amount of Asian sensibility and unusual combinations like ahi tuna and foie gras, duck confit with a potato terrine, Riesling glaze, wild rice gnocchi. **(5)**

Evidence

At a recent dinner I had a buffalo oxtail soup with madeira and orange oil and those wild rice gnocchi: dense, beefy flavours lightened with the citrus and madeira. Light, fluffy gnocchi—every spoonful was a treat. **(6)**

Next was a grilled arctic char fillet with saffron risotto and various roasted vegetables. A beautiful plate of food, nicely presented, the flavours and textures balancing off each other. My wife had a rack of lamb in a black olive crust with a barley and squash risotto with sautéed spinach and pomegranate juice—exceptional. One of our guests had sea bass in a porcini mushroom crust with a wasabi risotto. Very nice ideas. **(7)**

Criterion #3: Prices

Judgment: High

The Belvedere does not do skimpy portions either. You get a serious plate of food. And the prices? Well, we're into a whole different category here. The soup is $6, the salad $7, a carpaccio appetizer $12. Entrees start at $17 for a grilled vegetable and ricotta polenta, pass through the sea bass at $24 and osso bucco at $25 and end up at the rack of lamb for $29. **(8)**

Evidence

By international major city standards these are not bad prices. These same entrées in New York or London would be at least $10 higher. But we are used to pretty reasonably priced menus here. Dinner for the two of us with a bottle of wine was $130 when all was said and done. That's a bit high compared to Calgary's other better restaurants. **(9)**

But the Belvedere is not lacking for customers. Reservations are a must and most nights it can be difficult to get in, the food is that good. **(10)**

And the service supports it. Very skilled, professional staff. Very well-run room. **(11)**

Criterion #4: Service Judgment: Professional with some exceptions Evidence

Complaints? Very few. The tables are too small to accommodate the plates, especially when they squeeze four people into a table meant for two. Second, when the menu touts preserved lemon and wild honeycomb in a salad dressing there should be some evidence of it. Third, a thing that drives me to distraction. When the staff announce the daily specials they should include the price. On both my visits I had to ask the price of the special; unnecessary. And if there is any shortcoming to the food, it's that the desserts are not exceptional. They are very good—I enjoyed the brioche bread pudding, but they are not quite the pinnacle of dining that they should be after such an exquisite dinner. **(12)**

Regardless, the Belvedere rates a very solid **9 out of 10**. At 107 – 8 Ave SW it is open Mon. to Fri. for lunch and daily for dinner. Pricey, but it is an experience. **(13)**

Overall claim restated

EVALUATING COMMERCIAL PRODUCTS OR SERVICES

Writers frequently evaluate commercial products or services. Consumer magazines test and rate every imaginable product or service—from cars and dishwashers to peanut butter and brokerage houses. Guidebooks evaluate tourist spots, restaurants, colleges, and fishing lodges. Specialty magazines, such as *Modern Photography, Road and Track, Skiing,* and *Wired,* often rate products and services of interest to their readers. To qualify as evaluation— and not just advertising—the authors and the publishers must maintain an independent status, uninfluenced by the manufacturers of the products or services they are judging.

Consider, first, the following "evaluation" of a wine, found on a bottle of Cabernet Sauvignon:

> This Cabernet Sauvignon is a dry, robust, and complex wine whose hearty character is balanced by an unusual softness.

This "evaluative" language is so vague and esoteric that it may mean very little to the average consumer who just wants some wine with dinner. *Dry:*

How can a liquid be dry? *Robust:* Does this refer to physique? *Soft:* Wine is not a pillow, though it might put you to sleep. *Complex:* Are they describing a wine or conducting a psychological analysis? While an independent evaluator may legitimately use these terms for knowledgeable wine drinkers, this particular description suggests that the wine is absolutely everything the buyer would like it to be—dry yet robust, hearty but at the same time soft. Apparently, the writer's purpose here is not to evaluate a product but to flatter readers who imagine themselves connoisseurs of wine.

Now consider the following report on DVDs. The writer illustrates a more objective evaluation of a consumer product.

PROFESSIONAL WRITING

DVD MOVES INTO THE MAINSTREAM
GRANT BUCKLER

Feel like watching a movie on your personal computer? Want games with more realistic video images? Just don't feel like shuffling several CD-ROMs when you install new software? A Digital Video Disc Read-Only Memory (DVD-ROM) drive might be just what you need. (1)

DVD discs offer much higher capacity than CDs—up to 17 gigabytes (earlier DVD discs held only 4.7 gigs) compared to a CD's 650 megabytes. Computers equipped with DVD drives can play movies recorded on DVDs—and a quick tour through any video store will show you the selection of movies on DVD has grown rapidly. DVD drives can also read ordinary CD-ROM discs, so if you have a DVD drive you don't need a separate CD drive. (2)

The main reasons to want a DVD drive today are to play movies on your computer and to use games that take advantage of DVD to offer better video quality. (3)

But DVD's higher capacity also makes it possible to pack bulky software packages onto one disc instead of several. For instance, Microsoft's *Encarta* encyclopedia is currently available on several CDs or a single DVD disc, with the obvious advantage that you don't have to switch discs as you move around within the encyclopedia. (4)

That's not a big deal today, since software vendors are only beginning to offer their wares on DVD. It may be the best reason to look for a DVD drive when you buy a new computer, though. (5)

If you have an older computer without a CD drive, you've undoubtedly run into the problem of installing new software that is no longer available on diskettes. As software companies move toward DVD, that same problem will probably repeat itself with DVD versus CD drives. **(6)**

So, if you buy a new computer today with a CD drive, you may need to upgrade in a couple of years to get access to new software. The good news is that a DVD drive fits in the same bay as the CD drive and replaces it, so upgrading is at least possible, which is more than you can say about getting CD drives into older notebooks not designed for them. **(7)**

So, whether you're looking for an upgrade DVD drive for your existing computer or as a feature in a new computer, what do you look for? **(8)**

Like CD drives, DVD drives have different speeds that are stated as multiples of the basic transfer rate—2×, 4× and so forth. Most of the DVD drives sold today are 6× or 8×, but 12× drives are on the market and 16× drives will be here very soon. **(9)**

By the way, don't try to compare the speeds of DVD versus CD drives using these numbers. A 36× CD drive is not in fact six times as fast as a 6× DVD. The specifications for a drive should include two transfer rates—one for DVD and another, higher number for CD. **(10)**

MOVIE SOFTWARE

Assuming that playing DVD movies is one reason for buying a DVD drive, find out what software comes with the drive to help you do this. Some drives come with player software that makes it simpler to play movies on your computer screen, with features such as pause and rewind. **(11)**

You may also want to display your DVD movies on a television screen instead of on your computer. You can do this provided your DVD drive has a TV-out connection that lets you feed the signal straight from the drive to a TV set. **(12)**

When choosing a DVD drive, one option to consider is a model that combines DVD technology with the ability to handle rewritable compact discs, or CD-RW. Toshiba, Ricoh, Hewlett-Packard and Samsung all have such drives. They are a bit more expensive, but let you write data to rewritable compact discs. **(13)**

The typical retail price for a DVD drive on its own is around $200, though shortages of components have pushed that price up in recent months, according to Matthew Ki, product manager at Samsung Electronics Canada in Toronto. Major PC vendors' brand-name products are likely to cost more. In fact, a quick survey of prices at the end of March found price tags as high as $500 for faster, brand-name models. Ki says the part shortages have been mostly resolved and prices are expected to settle back down. **(14)**

It's one thing to buy a computer already equipped with a DVD drive—you can assume the PC's hardware and software are adequate to take advantage of the device. If you're purchasing a drive as an upgrade for an existing computer, though, there are a few things to bear in mind. **(15)**

Obviously, you need a bay in which to install the unit. That should not usually be a problem, since you can remove an existing CD drive if you have one. If the computer has no CD drive, you can probably assume it is too old to support DVD anyway—PC users need at least a Pentium running at 166 to 200 megahertz, a VGA graphics adapter, and Windows 95. **(16)**

With a basic Pentium chip, you will need a graphics adapter that handles Motion Picture Experts Group (MPEG) video encoding in hardware because your processor will not have the power to do it adequately in software, warns Robert Kwong, marketing manager for data storage products at Panasonic Canada in Toronto. Some newer video adapters decode MPEG in software, which is great if you have at least a 250-MHz Pentium II chip but won't work well with anything slower. Your computer should also have a minimum of 32 megs of memory to handle DVD playback, Ki says. **(17)**

Then there's the display. If you plan to watch movies on your computer, this will make a big difference to your enjoyment. Essentially any monitor will work, but Kwong recommends at least a 17-inch unit for a watchable picture. The resolution of the monitor is not critical. Ki adds that if your video adapter does not have enough memory, the video signal may be jerky. **(18)**

SOUND QUALITY

The picture goes hand in hand with the sound. There is no minimum requirement for sound—even the cheapest speakers will work—but movies and games will sound much better if your computer is equipped with good quality speakers including a sub-woofer. In general, the better the display and sound hardware, the better the results. **(19)**

Installing a DVD drive is not terribly complicated. It's essentially like putting in a CD drive or a magnetic drive—you need to connect a power cable and data cable and fit the unit into its bay. If you've had any experience messing around inside a PC, you won't find this difficult. If not, it may be best to have your dealer do the installation for you. **(20)**

The obvious reason to buy a DVD drive as an upgrade is that you want to put it in an existing PC. However, even if you're buying a new PC it may be worth looking at alternatives. DVD tends to be standard equipment on higher-priced models. Rather than buy a fancier PC just to get DVD, it could make sense to buy a lower-end model and purchase a DVD drive separately. **(21)**

And what about rewritable DVD technology? There are two competing rewritable DVD standards, called DVD-RW and DVD-RAM. Today, their high prices and the uncertainty over standards mean the average buyer is probably better off avoiding them. **(22)**

DVD-RAM drives are available today for around $1000, Kwong says, and the discs go for about $50 for a single-sided version that holds 2.6 gigs of data and about $60 for a double-sided, 5.2-gig disc. For the time being, Kwong says, "based on price point it's not going to the consumer level." The DVD-RW standard is similar to DVD-RAM, but the discs hold three gigs per side. **(23)**

A standard DVD drive can read the single-sided 2.6-gig DVD-RAM discs, but not the double-sided DVD-RAM discs or DVD-RW discs. Full compatibility is expected to come, but anyone buying one of these rewritable drives now should be very careful about this issue. **(24)**

These rewritable drives could be good for archiving large amounts of data, especially for backup purposes, but at today's prices only larger organizations and those with specific needs are more likely to use them on a daily basis. **(25)**

The prices will probably come down eventually, so the new DVD-ROM drive you buy this year may be replaced in the near future with a drive that can both read and write the discs. **(26)**

EVALUATING PERFORMANCES

Evaluating live, recorded, or filmed performances of people in sports, dance, drama, debate, public meetings or lectures, and music may involve practical criteria, such as the prices of tickets to sports events or rock concerts. However, there are also aesthetic criteria that apply to people and their performances. In film evaluations, for example, the usual criteria are good acting and directing, an entertaining or believable story or plot, memorable characters, dramatic special effects, and so forth.

In the following review of *Beloved,* film critic Peter Travers evaluates the film itself, the directing by Jonathan Demme, and the acting of Oprah Winfrey and her supporting cast.

PROFESSIONAL WRITING

OPRAH . . . OSCAR; OSCAR . . . OPRAH
PETER TRAVERS

The Oscar race, led by Steven Spielberg's *Saving Private Ryan,* heats up with Jonathan Demme's triumphant *Beloved.* This film of shocking immediacy and surpassing tenderness doesn't flinch at taking on a big book (Nobel laureate Toni Morrison's 1988 Pulitzer Prize winner), a big subject (slavery) and the big expectations that arise when TV phenom Oprah Winfrey serves as star and producer. It's not surprising that the film suffers some structural damage while trying to wrestle the muscular lyricism of Morrison's prose into a straight narrative. What is surprising—remarkable even—is that *Beloved* arrives onscreen with a minimum of dull virtue, gagging uplift, and slick Hollywood gloss. Credit Winfrey, who's been struggling for ten years to get the film made, for not playing it safe. The movie takes nearly three draining, devastating hours to relate the reconstruction of Sethe, a former slave who works menial jobs to feed her children in rural Ohio circa 1873. Neighbors avoid Sethe's run-down house, and for good reason: It's haunted by the horrors of her slave past and the spiteful ghost of her murdered baby. Winfrey's pitch-perfect performance as Sethe, besides being the stuff for which Oscars are molded, resonates with beauty, terror and the kind of truth that invades dreams. Detractors who resent her TV success as the anti-Jerry Springer, her wealth, her book clubs, her influence over popular culture will just have to shut up and eat crow. She's that good. **(1)**

And Demme, directing his first film since 1993's *Philadelphia,* is in peak form. Moving from exploitation cheapies (*Caged Heat*) to blockbusters (*The Silence of the Lambs*) and documentaries (*Haiti Dreams of Democracy*), Demme has never viewed a sense of fun and a sense of purpose as being mutually exclusive. His films brim over with the messy sprawl of humanity, and *Beloved* is no exception. It's maudlin gush that Demme can't abide. Unlike Spielberg's film of Alice Walker's *The Color Purple*, which earned Winfrey a deserved supporting-actress Oscar nomination, *Beloved* doesn't do your crying for you. The film is a knot of fierce emotions that is left for the viewer to untangle. Make the effort. Although the by-committee screenplay from Akosua Busia, Richard LaGravenese and Adam Brooks can't match Morrison's flights into magic realism, it doesn't sink to pat sermonizing, either. **(2)**

A terrific cast keeps adding grace notes. As Paul D, a slave who, like Sethe, endured abuse on the Sweet Home plantation in Kentucky, Danny Glover radiates compassion and commands an anger that is blissfully free of smack-my-bitch-up clichés. After eighteen years, Paul D finds Sethe in the hope of starting a new life. Sethe's two older sons have been scared off by the ghost, and her daughter Denver, who is thrillingly played by star-in-the-making Kimberly Elise, can't bear to go outside. **(3)**

Flashbacks detail Sethe's beatings, her sexual abuse, and the loss of her husband. Lisa Gay Hamilton invests her scenes as the young Sethe with agonizing expressiveness. And cinematographer Tak Fujimoto—a Demme regular—paints so hypnotically with light that the images become indelible. There's the joy when Sethe, a pregnant runaway, delivers Denver with the help of a white girl and escapes across the river. And the madness when Sethe, mistakenly believing that her four children are about to be captured, tries to kill them in a woodshed, succeeding only in cutting the throat of the two-year-old girl she calls Beloved. **(4)**

It is this tragedy that defines Sethe's future, keeps Denver a prisoner in her house and reduces *Beloved*, in the view of critic Stanley Crouch, to a black-holocaust novel that uses Sethe as an "Aunt Medea." The film resists such harsh comparisons through Winfrey's subtle immersion in Sethe's pain and her community's matter-of-fact acceptance of the dead as a contentious presence in life. **(5)**

This is not to say that Demme experiences no difficulty in bringing a clanking literary symbol to life onscreen. He begins by showing Beloved as a red, undulating light that moves furniture, shatters mirrors, and possesses the family dog. With the arrival of Paul D, Beloved takes human form: a vengeful two-year-old in the body of a woman who wreaks havoc with Sethe and Denver, and drags Paul D to bed ("Touch me on the inside"). It is not the fault of the gifted Thandie Newton, who plays her with a siren's seductiveness and the croak of a child demon out of *The Exorcist*, that Beloved remains more of a concept than a character. But when the guilt-racked Sethe says she welcomes her lost child and Beloved answers with tenderness, "I know," Newton pierces the heart. **(6)**

Demme, with the help of seamless editing from Carol Littleton and Andy Keir, lets slavery and freedom collide with a thunder that rings true. The past that weighs so heavily on Sethe can be lightened: by the spirit of her mother-in-law, Baby Suggs (the superb Beah Richards), who preached about "flesh that weeps and flesh that can laugh"; by the community of women who exorcise Beloved with their prayer chants; by Paul D, who tenderly kisses the tree of scars that whips have left on Sethe's back; and by Denver, who finally steps off her front porch—a transcendent moment—into a world beyond her imagining, or Sethe's. Winfrey and Elise achieve an alchemy as mother and daughter that goes beyond acting. Their sweet, leaping courage lets *Beloved* soar. **(7)**

PROFESSIONAL   WRITING

WATCHING THE EYEWITLESS NEWS

ELAYNE RAPPING

Culture critic Elayne Rapping is a professor of communications at Adelphi University and is the author of several books, including The Looking Glass World of Nonfiction TV *(1987),* Mediations: Forays into the Culture and Gender Wars *(1994), and* The Culture of Recovery: Making Sense of the Self-Help Movement in Women's Lives *(1996). She has also published dozens of articles about a variety of social, cultural, and media-related issues. "Watching the Eyewitless News," which originally appeared as a column in* The Progressive, *evaluates the local "Eyewitness" news programs featured daily in regional television markets.*

Jimmy Cagney, the ultimate street-smart wise guy, used to snap, "Whadya hear? Whadya know?" in the days of black-and-white movies and READ ALL ABOUT IT! headlines. But that was then and this is now. Today, when gangsta rap has replaced gangster movies, and television has replaced newsprint as the primary source of information (for two-thirds of us, the *only* source), Cagney's famous question is not only antiquated, it is beside the point. What we hear when we consume "the news" has only the most marginal relationship to what we *know* about anything. (1)

I'm not referring here to CNN or the "evening news" on the national broadcast networks. I'm referring here to what passes for news in the homes and minds of the vast majority of Americans today: The Eyewitless, Happy Talk local newscasts that run in many cities for as much as an hour and a half to two hours a day, on as many as seven or eight different channels. (2)

The rise of local news, the infotainment monster that ate the news industry, is a long and painful story about a key battle-front in the endless media war between capitalism and democracy, between the drive for profits and the constitutional responsibility of those licensed to use the airwaves to serve the public interest. We know who's winning, of course. The game was rigged from the start.... (3)

Local news as we know it was invented in 1970, the brainchild of a marketing research whiz hired by the industry to raise ratings by finding out what audiences "wanted to see." The Jeffersonian notion that public media should cover what citizens "need to know" was not a big consideration. Nor was it a concern to respect the audience's intelligence or diversity. (4)

The researchers offered a limited, embarrassingly vapid list of choices of formats and subjects, while ignoring the possibility that different groups might want different kinds of information and analysis. More annoying still, they ignored the possibility that individual viewers, of all kinds, might want and need different things at different times for different reasons. Nope, said the marketing whizzes, this master model of "The News" will buy us the most overall-ratings bang per buck. Wrap it up and send it out. (5)

And it worked. Their invention has conquered the TV world. The set, the news lineups, the anchors, the weather maps, the sports features—all developed for a New York City market— quickly became a universal formula, sent out to every network affiliate and independent station in America, complete with fill-in-the-blanks guidelines for adaptation to any community, no matter how large or small, urban or rural. Local news today is the single most profitable form of nonfiction television programming in the country and, for most stations, the only thing they actually produce.

Everything else comes from the networks. As time went by, this tendency toward cookie-cutter formulas, exported far and wide from a central media source, reached ever more depressing depths. The trend has led to ever more nationally produced, generic features exported to local stations to be passed off as "local." (6)

So today we have a phenomenon euphemistically called "local news," although it is anything but, filled with images of a pseudo-community called "America," which is actually closer to Disney World in its representation of American life. But why should that surprise us, in a national landscape now filled, from coast to coast, with identical, mass-produced shopping malls that pass for town marketplaces, and hotels and airports that pass for village inns? In postmodern America, after all, this kind of brand-name synthetic familiarity appears to be the only thing that holds us—a nation of endlessly uprooted and mobile strangers—together. (7)

When you turn on the news, whether at home or in an airport or Holiday Inn in some totally strange locale, you see a predictable, comforting spectacle. The town or city in question, whether Manhattan or Moose Hill, Montana, is presided over by a group of attractive, charming, well-dressed performers—whose agents, salaries, and movements up and down the ladder of media success, gauged by the size of the "market" they infiltrate, are chronicled each week in *Variety*. They seem to care endlessly for each other and us. "Tsk, tsk," they cluck at news of yet another gang rampage or Congressional scandal. "Ooh," they sigh, at news of earthquakes and plane crashes, far and near. (8)

IF IT BLEEDS, IT LEADS is the motto of the commercial news industry and local news. Its endless series of fires, shootouts, collapsing buildings, and babies beaten or abandoned or bitten by wild dogs is the state-of-the-art showcase for the industry. As Don Henley once put it, in a scathing song about the local news phenomenon, "It's interesting when people die." And it's especially interesting when they die in bizarre or inhuman situations, when their loved ones are on camera to moan and wail, when a lot of them die at once. And since so much of our news is indeed personally terrifying and depressing, we need to have it delivered as cleverly and carefully as possible. And so we have the always smiling, always sympathetic, always confidently upbeat news teams to sugarcoat the bad news. (9)

Not that local news ignores the politically important stories. Well, not entirely anyway. When wars are declared or covered, when elections are won or lost, when federal budgets and plant closings do away with jobs and services or threaten to put more and more of us in jail, for less and less cause, the local news teams are there to calm our jagged nerves and reassure us that we needn't worry. **(10)**

This reassurance is sometimes subtle. National news items typically take up less than two minutes of a half-hour segment. And what's said and seen in that brief interlude is hardly enlightening. On the contrary, the hole for "hard news" is generally filled with sound bites and head shots, packaged and processed by the networks, from news conferences with the handful of movers and shakers considered "newsworthy"—the President and his key henchmen and adversaries, mostly. **(11)**

But even local issues of serious import are given short shrift on these newscasts. Hard news affecting local communities takes up only a minute or two more airtime than national events. And local teams are obsessed with "man-on-the-street" spot interviews. Neighbors on local TV are forever gasping and wailing the most clichéd of reflex responses to actual local horrors, whether personal or social. **(12)**

"It's so horrible," they say over and over again, like wind-up dolls with a limited repertoire of three-word phrases, when asked about a local disaster. And when the crisis affects them directly—a school budget cut or neighborhood hospital closing, for example—their on-air responses are equally vapid. "I don't know what we're going to do without any teachers or books," they say with puzzled, frenzied expressions as they try desperately to articulate some coherent reply to a complex issue they've just heard about. **(13)**

I am not suggesting that the news should not feature community residents' views and experiences. Of course it should. But the local news teams' way of presenting such community responses is deliberately demeaning and fatuous. No one could say much worth saying in such a format. And if someone managed to come up with something serious and intelligent, rest assured it would be cut in favor of a more sensational, emotional response. **(14)**

But real news, even about cats in trees or babies in wells, is hardly what takes up the most airtime. "Don't bother too much about that stuff," say the guys and gals in the anchor chairs. Here's Goofy Gil with the weather, or Snappy Sam with the sports—the two features which, on every local newscast, are given the longest time slots and the most elaborate and expensive props. The number and ornateness of the weather maps on local news, and the endlessly amazing developments in special-effects technology to observe climate changes and movements of impending "fronts" is truly mind-boggling. **(15)**

Who needs this stuff? But we're forgetting that this is not the question to ask. "Who wants it?" is the criterion for news producers, and it is, understandably, the weather and sports that most people, most of the time, are likely to sit still for. If local news is meant to be a facsimile of a sunny Disneyesque community of happy, cozy campers, in which the bothersome bad guys and events of the day are quickly dealt with so that community harmony may once more reign, at least for the moment—and that *is* the intended fantasy— then what better, safer, kind of information than weather reports. Historically, after all, the weather is the standard small-talk item for people wishing to be pleasant and make contact without getting into anything controversial or heavy. It is the only kind of news we can all share in—no matter what our race, class, gender, or political differences—as members of a common community. **(16)**

The researchers are not entirely wrong, after all, about what people in this kind of society want. They do want comfort, reassurance, and a community where they belong and feel safe. And why shouldn't they? They find precious little of those things in the streets and buildings they traverse and inhabit in their daily lives. In my urban neighborhood, parents warn children never to make eye contact with anyone on the street or subway; never to speak to anyone, even in case of tragedy or emergency; never to look at or listen to the pathetic souls who regularly beg for money or ramble incoherently in the hope that someone, anyone, will take pity and respond. **(17)**

Remember when California was God's country, the Promised Land of Milk and Honey, to which people migrated for clean air, good jobs, and single-dwelling homes? Try to find these things in overpopulated, polluted, socially vexed and violent LA today. . . . But if we can't all dream of moving to sunny California anymore, there's always TV, where something resembling that innocent dream still exists. Eyewitness News and its various clones allow us to believe, just for a moment, that there really is a Santa Claus, a Mary Poppins, a Good Samaritan giving away fortunes to the needy, a spirit of Christmas Past to convert the most cold-hearted of corporate Scrooges. Indeed, this kind of "good news" is another staple of the genre. Charities, celebrations, instances of extraordinary good luck or good works by or for local residents are ever-present on local newscasts. Every day, in the midst of even the most dreadful and depressing news, there are legions of friends and neighbors to mourn and console each other, offering aid, bringing soup and casseroles to the victims of natural and man-made disasters, stringing lights and hanging balloons for festive neighborhood gatherings. **(18)**

The news teams themselves often play this role for us. They march at the head of holiday parades and shake hands and kiss babies at openings of malls and industrial parks. They are the neighbors—often thought of as friends by the loneliest among us—we wish we had in real life, there to do the right thing on every occasion. That is their primary function. They are not trained in journalism. They often cannot pronounce the local names and foreign words they read from teleprompters. But they sure can smile. . . . **(19)**

Sociologist Joshua Gamson has suggested, in an insightful essay, that there is a lesson to be learned from the enormous popularity of tabloid television—a category in which I would certainly include local news. The lesson is not that people are stupid, venal, "addicted," or otherwise blameworthy for their fascinated interest in junk TV. On the contrary, it is those responsible for the quality of our public life who are more deserving of such terms of contempt and opprobrium. For it is, says Gamson, "Only when people perceive public life as inconsequential, as not their own, [that] they readily accept the invitation to turn news into play." And people most certainly do perceive public life as inconsequential and worse these days, whether outside their doors or in Washington or on Wall Street. **(20)**

Only I don't think it is primarily the desire to "play" that drives people in droves to local newscasts, or even the trashier tabloid shows like *Hard Copy*. What people are getting from local newscasts—and here the researchers were right on the money, literally—is indeed what they want, in the most profound and sad sense of that phrase. They are getting what they always sought in fantasy and fiction, from *The Wizard of Oz* to *As the World Turns*. They are getting, for a brief moment, a utopian fantasy of a better, kinder, more decent and meaningful world than the one that entraps them. **(21)**

It is not only that public life is inconsequential, after all. It is, far more tragically, that public and private life today are increasingly unjust, inhumane, painful, even hopeless, materially and spiritually, for many of us. And there is no relief in sight except, ironically, on the local newscasts that are a respite from reality. Only, unlike the utopian villages of soap opera and fairy tale, these "imagined communities" are supposed to be, pretend to be, real and true. And for that reason they are more troubling than the trashiest or silliest of pop-culture fictions. **(22)**

Vocabulary

Write down the meanings of the following words:

- is not only *antiquated* (**1**)
- *euphemistically* called "local news" (**7**)
- are given short *shrift* (**12**)
- a limited *repertoire* (**13**)
- equally *vapid* (**13**)
- demeaning and *fatuous* (**14**)
- be a *facsimile* (**16**)
- a *utopian* fantasy (**21**)

Questions for Writing and Discussion

1. When you finish reading Elayne Rapping's essay, write out your personal responses. Did you agree or disagree with her analysis? Did you find her essay humorous or were you angry at her pronouncements? Were her judgments believable? Did her judgments fit with your own experiences watching your local news programs? Write out your reactions as fully as possible.

2. Reread Rapping's essay, identifying the criteria behind her judgments. In this case, criteria are statements describing what an ideal news program should be; for example, "Good news programs should provide what the people need, not necessarily what they want." Find and list as many of these criteria as you can. Then make a three-column log for this essay, indicating the judgment that Rapping makes about each criterion and the supporting evidence that she provides.

3. Referring to the three-column log from Question 2, above, assess Rapping's use of supporting evidence—specific examples from local news shows illustrating her point. Which of Rapping's judgments have supporting evidence? Which are merely unsupported assertions? Based on your analysis, do you think Rapping has written an effective evaluative essay? Explain.

4. Observe a local news program. If possible, videotape the program. As you replay your videotape, list each segment of the news: local events, national news, weather, sports, business news, international news, medical and health issues, and so forth. Note any transitional sections (segues) that contain small talk among the anchors. Next to each segment, record the length of time. Next, indicate your opinion about quality or depth of coverage. Finally, record any evidence about the newscasters' personalities,

on-camera style, or journalistic ability. Based on your observations and evidence, write an essay responding to Elayne Rapping. How accurately do her observations apply to the case you have observed? What other general conclusions about Rapping's article or about local news programs might you make?

5. Using Rapping's method of cultural analysis, observe and then analyze/evaluate a particular social, cultural, or media-related event. You might choose hall or club meetings at your university, lecture or lab classes, sports events, class registration rituals, TV sitcoms, Internet home pages—the list is bounded only by your imagination. (Be sure to focus on only one particular kind of cultural event or media program.) Your purpose is both to evaluate these cultural "events" and to explain why the cultural event itself is or is not constructed to avoid limited, stereotypical visions of reality or of people.

PROFESSIONAL WRITING

OMIGAWD! CANADIAN OPTIMISM!

PATRICK WATSON

Patrick Watson is one of Canada's most celebrated broadcasters. He earned his M.A. at the University of Toronto, taught at Queen's University in Kingston, and did his doctoral studies at the University of Michigan. Since 1988 he has been the Creative Director and principal writer of the CRB Foundation's Heritage Minutes *project, dramatizations of moments from Canada's past, appearing daily on TV screens nationwide. Watson's television and documentary productions have involved his conceiving, writing, producing, directing, and sometimes hosting such programs as* This Hour Has Seven Days, Close-Up, The Struggle for Democracy, *and* The Watson Report. *He has received several national and international television and documentary awards. In 1981, Watson was named an Officer of The Order of Canada. Patrick Watson is currently commissioning editor and host of History Television's series* The Canadians: Biographies of a Nation *and a contributing reviewer to* The Globe and Mail. *His most recent book is* The Struggle for Democracy *(Key Porter: Toronto).*

In his review of Myrna Kostash's book The Next Canada, *Watson evaluates the author's documentation of her "odyssey" to discover what young Canadians feel about their country. Typically, book reviews have a dual purpose: to* inform *readers about the main ideas of the book and to* evaluate *the work's accuracy, interest level, and style. As you read Watson's review, think about your own feelings about being Canadian.*

It seems that every age throws up a body of Regretters, usually older people whose understanding and appraisal of present change is impaired by their compulsive failure to escape an embellished and sanitized view of the past, with its illusions of stability and security, and by Right Thinking. And in this present phase of the Television Age, where the posture of broadcast journalism is cynicism and superficiality in the service of ratings, rather than enlightenment, it is not surprising that today's Regretters find a lot to talk about. **(1)**

The conventional wisdom that fuels today's litany of regret portrays the new generation as one preoccupied with physical possessions, conspicuous consumption, comfort and convenience: restless kids who know nothing of their past and culture and are loyal to nothing. If a historian—Jack Granatstein, say—publishes another lament in which it is shown that millions of young Canadians can't name our first Prime Minister, the response in editorials and letters to the editor is a string of tut-tuts stretching from Salmon Arm to Signal Hill. **(2)**

Myrna Kostash is a prolific and irrepressible writer from Alberta. Among her many books are a prize-winning study of the culture of teenage girls and another of the Canadian bloodlines that flow from Eastern Europe. Teacher, journalist, playwright, short-story writer—she has been published in just about every Canadian magazine most of us can name, with pieces on feminism, travel, ethnicity, censorship, erotica and literature, and the list goes on and on. **(3)**

Now she has produced a richly documented book responding to Regretters' Complaint, a disease that seems momentarily to have infected Kostash herself. She was writer-in-residence at the Regina Public Library when she became aware that the high school students she was meeting with were puzzled by her references to luminosities of our recent past such as Margaret Laurence or the War Measures Act. So she decided to take a closer and more rigorous look at what Canadians, especially young people, are saying and thinking about the state of the country and its values, and the extent, if any, of their commitment to being Canadian. **(4)**

The book is a kind of odyssey, and at the start of her journey log she sets the tone of her inquiry with a quote from the late George Grant's *Lament for a Nation* (1965): "But a nation does not remain a nation only because it has roots in the past. Memory is never enough to guarantee that a nation can articulate itself in the present. There must be a thrust of intention into the future." **(5)**

So in search of both memory and thrust, Kostash set out across the country and talked to farmers and students and the editors of and contributors to hip, non-establishment periodicals, the front-line "digerati," the on-line "zine-freaks." She watched more TV than is good for a healthy person, and clipped the papers voraciously. She sent out an assistant with a browser on the 'Net. She investigated the dogmas of the gay communities, including the more radically doctrinaire lesbians. **(6)**

She spent more time with writers and editors and activists than she did with stockbrokers or marketing managers, but she did talk extensively with a couple of grizzled veterans of the parliamentary press gallery. These latter seem a little, well, intrusive, in this particular company of young Canadians, but their presence may help the Regretters to consider seriously Kostash's intriguing findings. The Regretters aren't going to like this book a whole lot, and without some conventional authority figures like these two established commentators, they might not trust it at all. **(7)**

Kostash confesses that as she set out on her quest she expected to find a generation whose sense of nationhood "had been dissolved in the saturating soup of borderless, denationalized media, and whose continuity with familial, class and cultural memory had been broken, along with the communities that transmitted them." **(8)**

And indeed, she finds plenty of reason why there should be discontinuity and disengagement. She is a sort of old lefty of the late sixties outlook. She feels strongly the general downgrading of that essential old civic idea of the public good. She is struck by its absence from the discourse of our national leaders. She notes the ways in which corporate marketing has moved in on our once-treasured and protected institutions of public education, where exclusive campus contracts for Coca-Cola, or ad-laden screensavers and TV in the classrooms, are doing their best to crowd out the idea that critical thinking is a vital part of the educational process. **(9)**

There are times when this reader found the sheer accumulation of detail in the form of quotes and anecdotes a bit daunting. Sometimes, *The Next Canada* reads more like a reference book than an essay with a clear thrust and point. There are in-depth excursions into the doctrinaire jargon of some self-marginalized folk that—while useful material for the satirist—may be fatiguing for the rest of us. But I expect that many readers will find all this detail to be an extended network of veins to be mined, territory in which to go prospecting after their own particular ores and interests. **(10)**

But what did she, Kostash, make of it all, in terms of memory and thrust and the survival of the civil society? Not all good, by any means. She found a lot of distressing evidence of the deeply set persistence of racism, and of community division by what used to be called "class." Despite the liberality of the public prints and airwaves in sexual matters, she found drastically alienated sexual minorities. **(11)**

These are not surprising matters; what they do is to temper and caution the refreshing and infectious optimism all that research produced in her, that "astonishing series of conversations that have made me a Canadian all over again." Legions of young people know perfectly well that TV sucks and that being part of a nation is not about prosperity and lower taxes, not even about health care, but about giving meaning to or finding it in the word "we." Here is one young man who rejoices in his sense of being "embedded" in North York, Ont., and another who calls his Manitoba forebears "Founding Nation . . . even of this space, this weather." (Kostash even says she found an Albertan who says he "freaks out" on *The Globe and Mail!*) **(12)**

In sum, she says, there is a tremendous community of young people who are struggling to be Canadian and to declare for their country, "telling our stories to each other, keeping the plot going." **(13)**

The Next Canada is not what you would call a great read, not the book to settle down with comfortably in front of the fire for a tidy and reassuring dose of inspirational rhetoric. But I think it is an important work that would convey a message of real value to the governing class, were they interested. They should know about what Kostash has found out—if they have genuine interest in the survival of this Canadian experiment at tinkering with and cobbling together a genuine civil society. For, she says, there is "a coherent narrative after all—a narrative of pure desire. Somehow, at the turn of the millennium, we have in our midst yet another generation of Canadians who have found a way to dig deep enough that they have struck their own roots. The next Canadians are right here, they are at home, and they call it Canada." **(14)**

Vocabulary

Write down the meanings of the following words:

- references to *luminosities* **(4)**
- *doctrinaire* **(6)**

- *discontinuity and disengagement* (9)
- *cobbling* together (14)

Questions for Writing and Discussion

1. Underline Watson's major claim. According to Watson, what was Kostash's purpose in writing this book? What does she conclude about Canadians? With which of her conclusions do you agree or disagree? Explain.

2. What implied criteria does Watson use to evaluate Kostash's book? Does his evaluation sufficiently represent the book's strengths and weaknesses? Explain.

3. Watson does not cite authorities to question or refute Kostash's ideas, evidence or methods. Is this omission a flaw in his evaluation? Why? Why not?

4. Write an outline of Watson's review. Where is his introduction? Identify the kind of lead-in Watson uses (Chapter 7). Do you find it effective? Why? Why not? Choose three consecutive paragraphs in the body of Watson's review. What phrases, transitions, or ideas does he use to signal the connections between paragraphs? Where is his conclusion? Explain why it is effective or ineffective.

5. Write an evaluation of Watson's review. As guides, use the list of the six evaluating techniques at the beginning of this chapter and your answers to the questions above. Organize your material into an article with an introduction, body, and conclusion.

PROFESSIONAL WRITING

NOT AVAILABLE IN STORES
MARK KINGWELL

According to Michael Ignatieff, Kingwell is . . . "interesting because he seems to know things about popular culture while also knowing something about Aristotle [and] . . . he has a sense of humour." Mark Kingwell has commented on topics ranging from the nature of happiness to the appeal of Melrose Place; *from Princess Diana's death to the millennium.*

Kingwell graduated from the University of Toronto with a B.A., attended the University of Edinburgh where he received a Master's degree in literature and philosophy, and then earned a Ph.D. in philosophy at Yale. Currently, he is Assistant Professor of Philosophy at the

University of Toronto. He has published four books, the most recent, The
World We Want *(September 2000), as well as academic articles in several journals. His writing can also be found in a variety of periodicals
such as* Descant, Shift, Gravitas, Adbusters, The Globe and Mail,
The Canadian Forum, *and* Harper's.

"Not Available in Stores" first appeared as a column in Saturday Night
*magazine in 1998. In his essay, Kingwell evaluates traditional infomer-
cials and their more recent counterparts. Is newer better?*

It begins like one of those cosy Women's Television Network
chat shows, complete with bad lighting, fuzzy lenses, and warm
looks. The host is an attractive, soft-spoken woman of a certain age.
She purrs at the camera. She and her guests are here to tell you
about what she chucklingly calls "Hollywood's breast-kept secret."
Yes, it's true: Accents, the Plasticine bust enhancers favoured by
movie stars and models alike, are now available to you, the lowly
viewer. No surgery. No hideous contraptions. You don't even have
to leave home to get them. **(1)**

And what a difference they make! Soon a line-up of gorgeous
but slightly flat-chested women are being transformed before your
eyes into jiggly supermodels or "Baywatch" lifeguards. These flesh-
coloured slabs of silicone gel that "fit into any underwire bra" and
"within minutes warm to your natural body temperature" can actually be used in the swimming pool! At the end of the half-hour, the
ever-smiling host and her guests admit that *they are all wearing
Accents themselves*! Well, shut my mouth. **(2)**

"Accents" is only the most outrageous of the current crop of
television infomercials: those over-the-top attempts to hawk make-
up, cleaning products, and ab-flexers under the guise of a genial talk
show ("Kathie Lee Talks") or breathless science programme
("Amazing Discoveries!"). Turn on your television late at night or
on a weekend afternoon—even, these days, at midmorning—and
the good-natured hosts, a has-been actress (Ali McGraw) or never-
was celeb (Ed McMahon), are touting cosmetics or miracle car wax
as if they are doing us a public service. Information + commercial =
infomercial. Line up the word, and the phenomenon, next to those
long advertising features in newspapers and magazines, often slyly
imitating the publication's actual typeface and design, known as
"advertorials." **(3)**

Patently absurd, maybe, but if emerging trends continue,
infomercials will not remain what they have been so far: a marginal
and benign, if irritating, television presence. With the loosening of

CRTC regulations, the explosion of cable channels, and the crude economics that can make them more lucrative than regular programming for network affiliates, infomercials are showing up in more and more places on the TV schedule, elbowing aside such popular quality fare as Sunday-afternoon sports, syndicated comedies, and old movies. They are also getting more and more sophisticated, as big-name companies with mainstream products—Ford Motor Co., Procter & Gamble, Apple Canada—enter the infomercial market. **(4)**

And if, as enthusiasts in the business press insist, this is the future of TV advertising, then that is very bad news indeed for television and its viewers. But not because there is anything inherently wrong with infomercials, at least not as they have existed until now. The delicate pact between ads and shows that makes television possible has always been able to withstand the amateurish, ad-becomes-show genre they represent. But when infomercials are everywhere, and especially when they go high market, that pact is in danger of being overturned, and the thin line between entertainment and pitch may be erased for good. **(5)**

Blame Ron Popeil. Blame him a lot, and at length. Blame him until his smiling, trout-like face is imprinted on your mind as the fount of all evil. Because Popeil is the one who started the sort of television hard sell that reaches its tacky terminus in today's infomercials. Founder of Ronco, restless inventor of the Popeil Pocket Fisherman, the Patti-Stacker, and other cheesy "labour-saving" devices too numerous to mention, Popeil is the guy who all but invented television shopping. In the 1970s he discovered that people got very excited, and very willing to spend, at the thought that you need never leave your couch to have the entire Ronco or K-Tel product line delivered to your home. His favourite author was the guy who came up with *Call this toll-free number now*. **(6)**

Popeil has recently come out from behind the camera to appear in his own convection-oven and pasta-machine infomercials. Looking like an also-ran from a professional tanning competition, he slops flour and water into slowly spinning machines that disgorge brightly coloured goo for thirty minutes. Your own fresh pasta every night! Operators are standing by! **(7)**

It isn't hard to decipher what makes these and other low-end infomercials so successful. Potential buyers are never made to feel bad, even as their baser desires are being pandered to. For example, we are told at least four times that Accents "are shipped confidentially" and arrive at your door in (get this) "a beautiful designer chest that will look great on your vanity." The Accents people even muster expert opinion, the *sine qua non* of the TV hard sell. In this case, it's a panel of Hollywood make-up artists and photographers. "I tried everything," says one. "Foam pads, wires, push-up bras, duct tape. Nothing works like Accents." (Duct tape?) **(8)**

The same forms of reassurance are visible on all the successful infomercials now airing, from The Stimulator to the Ab-Roller Plus. The Stimulator—a small syringe-like device that is supposed to kill pain by means of mild electric shock, a sort of mini stun gun—also produces what has to be the funniest infomercial moment of all time. Evel Knievel, the all-but-forgotten daredevil of the 1970s, shares, over footage of his famous Caesar's Palace motorcycle crash, his belief in the pain-relieving properties of The Stimulator. "If it hepped me," Knievel twangs, "it can hep you." Now that's expert opinion.

This is so silly that it is easy to imagine a kind of self-parody operating, of the sort in the hilarious "Money Show" spots on CBC's *This Hour Has 22 Minutes*: "Gus, I want to pay less in taxes, but I'm not sure how." "Marsha, it couldn't be easier; stop filing your returns!" But that would misread the intentions of the makers—and the attitudes of the audience, whose response to infomercials has been wholehearted. Canadians spent $100-million on infomercial products in 1995, up thirty-four percent from 1994. One Ontario company, Iona Appliances Inc., quadrupled annual sales of its "dual-cyclonic" vacuum cleaner when it started marketing via infomercial. **(10)**

In fact, the point of infomercials has so far been their lack of sophistication. The niche is still dominated by the charmingly inept likes of Quality Special Products, the Canadian company responsible for such thoroughly trailer-park items as the Sweepa ("The last broom you'll ever have to buy!") and the Sophist-O-Twist hair accessory ("French braids made easy!"). **(11)**

Most current efforts eschew the cleverness and quality visible on more traditional commercial spots in favour of the low-ball aesthetic of public-access cable. Instead of competing with shows for our attention—and therefore being pushed to find better writing, multimillion-dollar budgets, and gilt-edged directorial talent—infomercials becomes the shows. Yet they do so in ways so obviously half-hearted that nobody, not even the quintessential couch-potato viewer, could actually be fooled. The talk-show cover story is really nothing more than a tacit agreement between marketer and viewer that they're going to spend half an hour in each other's company, working over a deal. **(12)**

And this is what many critics miss: most infomercials, as they now appear, aren't really trying to dupe the viewer. They are instead the bottom-feeding equivalent of the irony observable in many regular commercials. Bargain-basement infomercials offer a simpler form of customer complicity than the crafty self-mockery and self-reference that appeals to young, kitsch-hungry viewers. Infomercials are a pure game of "let's pretend," taken straight from the carnival midway. **(13)**

That's why the entry of high-end marketers into the field is so alarming. Big-money companies are not content to maintain the artless façade that now surrounds infomercials. They break the carny-style spell of cheap infomercials, where we know what we see is fake, but we go along anyway, and offer instead the high production quality, narrative structure, and decent acting of actual shows. **(14)**

A recent Apple Canada effort, for example, which aired last year in Toronto, Calgary, and Vancouver, is set up as a saccharine half-hour sitcom about a white-bread family deciding to buy a home computer ("The Marinettis Bring Home a Computer"). It is reminiscent of "Leave It To Beaver" or "The Wonder Years," complete with Mom, Pop, Gramps, the family dog, and an annoying pre-teen narrator named TJ. Gramps buys the computer, then bets grumpy Pop that the family will use it enough to justify the expense. Soon TJ is bringing up his slumping math grades, Mom is designing greeting cards for profit, and Gramps is e-mailing fellow opera buffs. It's nauseating, but effective. Heather Hutchison, marketing communications manager for Apple Canada, explains the company's decision to enter the infomercial universe this way: "Having produced something of higher quality," she says, "there's a recognition at—I hesitate to use the word 'subconscious,' but at a lower level—that it says something about the quality of the product. The Canadian market responds well to this kind of softer sell." **(15)**

We all know that television, as it now operates, is primarily a vehicle for the delivery of advertising. That is, we know that if it weren't for ads, nobody would get to spend a million dollars on a single episode of an hour-long drama or employ some of the best dramatic writers and directors now working. True, this symbiosis is uneasy at best, with good shows all but free-riding on the masses of dreck that keep the advertisers happily reaching their targets. That's fine—or at least not apocalyptic. We can accept that advertising is the price we have to pay (every seven minutes) for good television. **(16)**

But slick infomercials, unlike their cheapo forebears, threaten to destroy this shaky convenant. Only a moron could mistake a low-end infomercial for a real show. (And only a condescending jerk could think that all people who buy Sweepas and Abdomenizers are, in fact, morons.) Up-market infomercials have a much greater potential to muddy the waters between advertising and programming. It may be that, without the cheesy aesthetics and side-show barker style, these new infomercials won't find an audience. But it's more likely that big companies with big budgets and top advertising talent will be able to suck even non-morons into these narrative ads that masquerade as entertainment. The new corporate offerings, in other words, may actually do what Ron Popeil couldn't: strip TV of extraneous effects like quality programming so that it finally reveals its essential nature—selling things, selling things, and selling things. **(17)**

When that's true, maybe it's time to turn the damn thing off for good. **(18)**

Vocabulary

Write down the meanings of the following words:

- *sine qua non* **(8)**
- *niche* **(11)**
- most current efforts *eschew* **(12)**
- *kitsch* **(13)**
- artless *façade* **(14)**

Questions for Writing and Discussion

1. Think about your response to television advertising. Do you sit and watch commercials or do you use them as a chance to get a snack or see what is on other channels? What is your favourite commercial? Your least favourite?

2. In order to express his opinion about infomercials, Kingwell needs to describe what they are. In which paragraphs does the author describe infomercials? Which paragraphs describe the background of infomercials? Why are these paragraphs necessary or helpful in Kingwell's evaluation of infomercials? Explain.

3. What criteria does Kingwell use to evaluate traditional infomercials? What criteria does he use to evaluate the "up-market," newer infomercials?

4. Kingwell repeats his claim about infomercials throughout his essay. What sentences state or restate his thesis most clearly? How is his thesis revealed in the examples he relates?

5. Although Kingwell makes some serious points, his sense of humour is apparent in this essay. Cite some examples you find amusing and explain how the humour is effective.

6. What is his final evaluation of infomercials?

EVALUATING: THE WRITING PROCESS

■ ASSIGNMENT FOR EVALUATING   With a specific audience in mind, evaluate a product or service, a work of art, or a performance. Choose a subject that is *reobservable*—that you can revisit or re-view as you write your essay. Select criteria appropriate for your subject and audience. Collect evidence to support or determine a judgment for each criterion.

CHOOSING A SUBJECT

If you have already settled on a possible subject, try the following collecting and shaping strategies. If you have not found a subject, consider these ideas:

- Evaluating requires some expertise about a particular person, performance, place, object, or service. You generate expertise not only through experience but also through writing, reading, and rewriting. Review your authority list from Chapter 1. Which of those subjects could you evaluate? Have you observed or investigated some person, place, or thing that you could write about for the purpose of evaluating it?

- Comparing and contrasting leads naturally to evaluation. For example, compare two places you've lived, two friends, or two jobs. Compare two newspapers for their coverage of international news, local features, sports, or business. Compare two famous people from the same profession. Compare your expectations about a person, place, or event with the reality. The purpose of your comparison is to determine, for a specific audience, which is "better," based on the criteria you select and the evidence you find.

COLLECTING

Once you have a tentative subject and audience in mind, ask the following questions to focus your collecting activities:

- Can you narrow, restrict, or define your subject to focus your paper?

- What *criteria* will you use to evaluate your subject?

- What *evidence* might you gather? As you collect evidence, focus on three questions:

   What *comparisons* can you make between your subject and similar subjects?

   What are the *uses* or *consequences* of this subject?

   What *experiments* or *authorities* might you cite for support?

- What initial *judgments* are you going to make?

Observing   Observation and description of your subject are crucial to a clear evaluation. In most cases, your audience will need to know *what* your subject is before they can understand your evaluation.

- Examine a place or object repeatedly, looking at it from different points of view. Take notes. Describe it. Draw it, if appropriate. Analyze its component parts. List its uses. To which senses does it appeal—sight, sound, touch, smell, taste? If you are comparing your subject to other similar subjects, observe them carefully. Remember: The second or third time you observe your subject, you will see even more key details.

- If you are evaluating a person, collect information about this person's life, interests, abilities, accomplishments, and plans for the future. If you are able to observe the person directly, describe his or her physical features, write down what he or she says, and describe the person's environment.

- If you are evaluating a performance or an event, a tape recording or videotape can be extremely useful. If possible, choose a concert, film, or play on tape so that you can stop and re-view it if and when necessary. If a tape recording or videotape is not available, attend the performance or event twice.

Making notes in a *three-column log* is an excellent collecting strategy for evaluations. Using the following example from John Gilchrist's evaluation of the Belvedere restaurant, list the criteria, evidence, and judgments for your subject:

Subject: The Belvedere Restaurant

CRITERIA	EVIDENCE	JUDGMENT
Attractive setting	Exposed overhead beams Mirrored panels Plush accoutrements	Excellent
Good service	Very skilled Professional	Prices of specials not communicated

Remembering   You are already an authority on many subjects, and your personal experiences may help you evaluate your subject. Try *freewriting*, *looping*, *branching*, or *clustering* your subject to help you remember relevant events, impressions, and information. In evaluating appliances for consumer magazines, for example, reporters often use products over a period of months, recording data, impressions, and experiences. Those experiences and memories are then used to support criteria and judgments. Evaluating a film often requires remembering similar films that you have liked or disliked. An evaluation of a great athlete may include your memories of previous performances. A vivid narrative of those memories can help convince an audience that a performance is good or bad.

Reading   Some of the ideas and evidence for your evaluation may come from reading descriptions of your subject, other evaluations of your subject, or the testimony of experts. Be sure you read these texts critically: Who is the intended audience for the text? What evidence does the text give? What is the author's bias? What are other points of view? Read your potential sources critically.

Investigating   All evaluations involve some degree of formal or informal investigation as you probe the characteristics of your subject and seek evidence to support your judgments.

Using the Library or the Internet Check the library and Internet resources for information on your subject, for ideas about how to design and conduct an evaluation of that subject, for possible criteria, for data in evaluations already performed, and for a sense of different possible audiences. In its evaluation of chocolate chip cookies, for example, *Consumer Reports* suggests criteria and outlines procedures. The magazine rated some two dozen popular store-bought brands, as well as four "boutique" or freshly baked varieties, on "strength of chocolate flavor and aroma, cookie and chip texture, and freedom from sensory defects." When the magazine's evaluators faced a problem sampling the fresh cookies in the lab, they decided to move the lab: "We ended up loading a station wagon with scoresheet, pencils, clipboards, water containers, cups, napkins . . . and setting off on a tasting safari to shopping malls."

Gathering Field Data You may want to supplement your personal evaluation with a sample of other people's opinions by using *questionnaires* or *interviews*. (See Chapter 6.) If you are rating a film, for example, you might give people leaving the theatre a very brief *questionnaire*, asking for their responses on key criteria relating to the movie that they just saw. If you are rating a class, you might want to *interview* several students in the class to support your claim that the class was either effective or ineffective. The interviews might also give you some specific examples: descriptions of experiences that you can then use as evidence to support your own judgments.

SHAPING

While the shaping strategies that you have used in previous essays may be helpful, the strategies that follow are particularly appropriate for shaping evaluations.

Analysis by Criteria   Often, evaluations are organized by criteria. You decide which criteria are appropriate for the subject and audience, and then you use those criteria to outline the essay. Your first few paragraphs of introduction establish your thesis or overall claim and then give background information: what the subject is, why you are evaluating it, what the competition is, and how you gathered your data. Then you order the criteria according to some plan: chronological order, spatial order, order of importance, or another logical sequence.

Comparison and Contrast   Many evaluations compare two subjects in order to demonstrate why one is preferable to another. Books, films, restaurants, courses, music, writers, scientists, historical events, sports—all can be evaluated by means of comparison and contrast. In evaluating two Asian restaurants, for example, student writer Chris Cameron uses a comparison-and-contrast structure to shape her essay. In the following body paragraph from her essay, Cameron compares two restaurants, the Unicorn and the Yakitori, on the basis of her first criterion—an atmosphere that seemed authentically Asian:

> Of the two restaurants, we preferred the authentic atmosphere of the Unicorn to the cultural confusion at the Yakitori. On first impression, the Yakitori looked like a converted truck stop, sparsely decorated with a few bamboo slats and Japanese print fabric hanging in slices as Bruce Springsteen wailed loudly in the ears of the customers. The feeling at the Unicorn was quite the opposite as we entered a room that seemed transported from Chinatown. The whole room had a red tint from the light shining through the flowered curtains, and the place looked truly authentic, from the Chinese patterned rug on the wall to the elaborate

dragon on the ceiling. Soft oriental music played as the customers sipped tea from small porcelain cups and ate fortune cookies.

Cameron used the following *alternating* comparison-and-contrast shape for her whole essay:

- Introductory paragraph(s)
- Thesis: Although several friends recommended the Yakitori, we preferred the Unicorn for its more authentic atmosphere, courteous service, and well-prepared food.
- Authentic atmosphere: Yakitori versus Unicorn
- Courteous service: Yakitori versus Unicorn
- Well-prepared food: Yakitori versus Unicorn
- Concluding paragraph(s)

On the other hand, Cameron might have used a *block* comparison-and-contrast structure. In this organizational pattern, the outline would be as follows:

- Introductory paragraph(s)
- Thesis: Although several friends recommended the Yakitori, we preferred the Unicorn for its more authentic atmosphere, courteous service, and well-prepared food.
- The Yakitori: atmosphere, service, and food
- The Unicorn: atmosphere, service, and food as compared to the Yakitori's
- Concluding paragraph(s)

Chronological Order   Writers often use chronological order, especially in reviewing a book or a film, to shape parts of their evaluations. Film reviewers rely on chronological order to sketch the main outlines of the plot as they comment on the quality of the acting, directing, or cinematography.

Causal Analysis   Analyzing the *causes* or *effects* of a place, object, event, or policy can shape an entire evaluation. Evaluations of works of art or performances, for example, often measure the *effect* on the viewers or audience.

Title, Introduction, and Conclusion   Titles of evaluative writing tend to be short and succinct, stating what product, service, work of art, or performance you are evaluating ("Watching the Eyewitless News") or suggesting a key question or conclusion in the evaluation ("DVD Moves Into the Mainstream").

Introductory paragraphs provide background information and description and usually give an overall claim or thesis. In some cases, however, the overall claim comes last, in a concluding "Recommendations" section or in a final summary paragraph. If the overall claim appears in the opening paragraphs, the concluding paragraph may simply review the strengths or weaknesses or may just advise the reader: This *is* or *is not* worth seeing, reading, watching, doing, or buying.

DRAFTING

With your criteria in front of you, your data or evidence at hand, and a general plan or sketch outline in mind, begin writing your draft. As you write, focus on your audience. If your evaluation needs to be short, you may have to use only those criteria that will appeal most effectively to your audience. As you write, check occasionally to be sure that you are including your key criteria. While some parts of the essay may seem forced or awkward as you write, other parts will grow and expand as you get your thoughts on paper. As in other papers, don't stop to check spelling or worry about an occasional awkward sentence. If you stop and can't get going, reread what you have written, look over your notes or sketch outline, and pick up the thread again.

REVISING

Remember that revision is not just changing a word here and there or correcting occasional spelling errors. Make your evaluation more effective for your reader by including more specific evidence, changing the order of your paragraphs to make them clearer, cutting out an unimportant point, or adding a point that one of your readers suggests.

Guidelines for Revision

During your revision, keep the following tips in mind:

- **Criteria are *standards of value*.** They contain categories and judgments, as in "good fuel economy," "good reliability," or "powerful use of light and shade in a painting." Some categories, such as "price," have clearly implied judgments ("low price"), but make sure that your criteria refer implicitly or explicitly to a standard of value.

- **Examine your criteria from your audience's point of view.** Which criteria are most important in evaluating your subject? Will your readers agree that the criteria you select are indeed the most important ones? Will changing the order in which you present your criteria make your evaluation more convincing?

- **Include both positive and negative evaluations of your subject.** If all of your judgments are positive, your evaluation will sound like an advertisement. If all of your judgments are negative, your readers may think you are too critical.

- **Be sure to include supporting evidence for each criterion.** Without any data or support, your evaluation will be just an opinion that will not persuade your reader.

- **Avoid overgeneralizing in your claims.** If you are evaluating only three software programs, you cannot say that Lotus 1-2-3 is the best business program around. You can say only that it is the best among the group or the best in the particular class that you measured.

- **Unless your goal is humour or irony, compare subjects that belong in the same class.** Comparing a Yugo to a BMW is absurd because they are not similar cars in terms of cost, design, or purpose.

- **If you need additional evidence to persuade your readers, review the questions at the beginning of the "Collecting" section of this chapter.** Have you addressed all the key questions listed there?

- **If you are citing other people's data or quoting sources, check to make sure your summaries and data are accurate.**

- *Signal* **the major divisions in your evaluation to your reader using clear transitions, key words, and paragraph hooks.** At the beginning of new paragraphs or sections in your essay, let your reader know where you are going.

- **Revise sentences for directness and clarity.**

- **Edit your evaluation for correct spelling, appropriate word choice, punctuation, usage, and grammar.**

PROFESSIONAL WRITING

THE RED VIOLIN
ROGER EBERT

Here Roger Ebert, movie critic for The Chicago Sun-Times *and host of the television show* Ebert & Roeper and the Movies, *reviews the award winning Canadian film* The Red Violin. *Film reviewers often need to walk a tightrope. They should give the basic information about key characters and plot—without revealing too much about the story; they should analyze and evaluate the film—without so much analysis that the reader is bored. As you read the review, decide how successful Ebert is at both informing and entertaining the reader.*

There is a kind of ideal beauty that reduces us all to yearning for perfection. "The Red Violin" is about that yearning. It traces the story of a violin ("the single most perfect acoustical machine I've ever seen," says a restorer) from its maker in 17th century Italy to an auction room in modern Montreal. The violin passes from the rich to the poor, from Italy to Poland to England to China to Canada. It is shot, buried, almost burned and stolen more than once. It produces music so beautiful that it makes you want to cry. **(1)**

The film is heedlessly ambitious. In a time of timid projects and easy formulas, "The Red Violin" has the kind of sweep and vision that we identify with elegant features from decades ago—films that followed a story thread from one character to another, such as "Tales of Manhattan" or "La Ronde." There really is a little something here for everyone: music and culture, politics and passion, crime and intrigue, history and even the backstage intrigue of the auction business. Not many films can encompass a British aristocrat who likes to play the violin while he is having sex and a Chinese woman who risks her life to protect a violin from the martinets of the Cultural Revolution. **(2)**

The violin is crafted in Cremona, Italy, in 1681—made by the craftsman Nicolo Bussotti (Carlo Cecchi) for his unborn son. But his wife, Anna (Irene Grazioli), dies in childbirth after hearing a series of prophecies from a village crone who reads the tarot deck. The cards provide a structure for flash-forwards to the future adventures of the violin, and at the same time there is a flashback structure, as bidders arrive at the auction house in Montreal and we learn why they desire the instrument. **(3)**

The film is easy to follow, and yet reveals its secrets slyly. The story of the violin is a series of stories involving the people who own it over a period of 300 years. Then there is another story, hinted at, slowly revealing itself, involving an expert evaluator of instruments (Samuel L. Jackson). He is the person who proves that this is indeed Bussotti's famous red violin and solves the mystery of its color. He is also perhaps the person best equipped to appreciate how rare and wonderful the instrument is—but, like many passionate connoisseurs, he lacks the wealth to match his tastes. His plans for the instrument supply a suspenseful ending to a movie that has already given us just about everything else. **(4)**

The film was directed by the Canadian François Girard and written by him and actor-director Don McKellar. They also co-wrote Girard's brilliant first film, "32 Short Films About Glenn Gould" (1994), which considered the life and work of the great Canadian pianist in 32 separate episodes. "The Red Violin" uses a similar approach, spinning stories and tones out of the central thread. **(5)**

After the opening sequence involving Bussotti, the violin drifts into the hands of an order of monks, and we rejoin it 100 years later at their orphanage. They dote on a young prodigy named Kasper (Christoph Koncz), who plays with the purity of an angel. The musician Poussin (Jean-Luc Bideau), expert but poor, hears the boy play and adopts him on the spot, despite the doubts of his wife. This sequence develops tenderly, as the old couple grow to love the boy—who sleeps with his violin. **(6)**

Flash-forward. The violin is in the possession of gypsies (I am not revealing the details of the transfers). It is played by many hands and travels from Poland to England, where in the 19th century, it is heard by a rich virtuoso named Frederick Pope (Jason Flemyng), who incorporates it into his concerts and into his lovemaking with his mistress Victoria (Greta Scacchi). It is she who fires a bullet at it. The violin next surfaces in a pawn shop in Shanghai, where during the Cultural Revolution, it stands as a symbol of Western decadence. It's defended by a brave musician, who points out that Beethoven and Prokofiev were revolutionaries, but is saved only when a music lover (Sylvia Chang) risks her life. Eventually the now-capitalist Chinese government sends it off to Montreal, where it attracts the attention of the Samuel L. Jackson character. **(7)**

A brief outline doesn't begin to suggest the intelligence and appeal of the film. The story hook has been used before. "Tales of Manhattan" followed an evening coat from person to person, and "The Yellow Rolls-Royce" followed a car. Max Ophul's "La Ronde" (1950), Luis Buñuel's "The Phantom of Liberty" (1974) and Richard Linklater's "Slacker" (1991) all follow chains of characters, entering a scene with one person and exiting with another. **(8)**

Such structures take advantage of two contradictory qualities of film: It is literal, so that we tend to believe what we see, and it is fluid, not tied down to times and places. All of those titles more or less observe time and place, however; "The Red Violin" follows not a person or a coat, but an idea: the idea that humans in all times and places are powerfully moved, or threatened, by the possibility that with our hands and minds we can create something that is perfect. **(9)**

Questions for Writing and Discussion

1. Profile yourself as a typical reader of this review: Give your age, note whether you frequently go to movies, describe the kinds of films you enjoy, and indicate whether or not you have seen *The Red Violin*. With

these notes, come to class prepared to discuss whether or not Ebert's review succeeded. Does it make you want to see the movie? If you've seen the film already, is his evaluation convincing? Is it entertaining?

2. Write a review of a movie you have seen recently. Remember to comment on the acting and directing, the story or plot, the characters, the dramatic special effects, and so on.

ARGUING

LEARNING OUTCOMES

After reading this chapter, you will have
learned that

- argumentation emphasizes logical reasoning
  and a fair countering of opposing positions

- argumentation is determined by four kinds
  of claims

- Rogerian argumentation contains elements
  of personal narrative and problem solving

When people argue with each other, they often become highly emotional or confrontational. Remember the last heated argument you had with a friend or family member: At the end of the argument, one person stomped out of the room, slammed the door, and didn't speak to the other for days. In the aftermath of such a scene, you felt angry at the other person and angry at yourself. Nothing was accomplished. Neither of you came close to achieving what you wanted when you began the argument. Rather than understanding each other's point of view and working out your differences, you effectively closed the lines of communication.

When writers construct arguments, however, they try, through reason and use of evidence, to avoid the emotional outbursts that often turn verbal arguments into displays of temper. Strong feelings may energize an argument—few of us make the effort to argue without emotional investment in the subject—but written argument stresses a fair weighing of pros and cons. While you advocate one position, you keep the lines of communication open by acknowledging and evaluating opposing arguments. Because written arguments are public, they take on a civilized manner. They implicitly say, "Let's be reasonable about this. Let's look at the evidence for *both* sides. Let's not shout or fight; let's be as objective as we can."

As writers construct written arguments, they carefully consider their audiences. Does the audience know about this controversy, or does it need background information? Do the readers hold an opposing viewpoint, or are they likely to listen to both sides and decide what to believe? What arguments will they find most persuasive? A written argument creates an atmosphere of reason, which encourages readers to examine their own views clearly and dispassionately. When successful, such argument convinces rather than alienates an audience. It changes people's minds or persuades them to adopt a recommended course of action.

TECHNIQUES FOR WRITING: ARGUMENT

A written argument is similar to a public debate—between lawyers in a court of law or members of Parliament who represent different political parties. It begins with a *debatable* issue: Is this a good bill? Should we vote for it? In such debates, one person argues for a position or proposal, while the other argues against it. The onlookers (the members of Parliament, the jury, or the public) then decide what to believe or what to do. *Written argument imitates this situation by examining the opinions both for and against a position and then advocating one of the positions or proposing a solution.* Written argument evaluates the conflicting positions and then uses reasons and evidence to support the writer's claim. The writer represents the opposing arguments, responds to them, and advocates his or her own position. A sound written argument uses the following techniques:

- **Focussing on a *debatable* proposition or claim.** This claim becomes your thesis.

- *Analyzing the audience.* Knowing what your audience believes will help you convince them of your position or persuade them to act on your thesis.

- **Representing and evaluating the *opposing points of view* on the issue fairly and accurately.** The key to a successful arguing paper is anticipating and responding to the most important opposing positions.

- **Arguing reasonably *against the opposition* and *for your claim*.** State and refute opposing arguments. Present the best arguments supporting your claim. Argue reasonably and fairly.

- **Supporting your claims with *sufficient* evidence.** Use firsthand observations; examples from personal experience; statistics, facts, and quotations from your reading; and results of surveys and interviews.

In an article entitled "Active and Passive Euthanasia," James Rachels claims that active euthanasia may be defensible for patients with incurable and painful diseases. The following paragraphs from that article illustrate the key features of argument:

The distinction between active and passive euthanasia is thought to be crucial for medical ethics. The idea is that it is permissible, at least in some cases, to withhold treatment and allow a patient to die, but it is never permissible to take any direct action designed to kill the patient. This doctrine seems to be accepted by most doctors. . . .	*Opposing position*
However, a strong case can be made against this doctrine. In what follows I will set out some of the relevant arguments, and urge doctors to reconsider their views on this matter.	*Claim* *Audience*
To begin with a familiar type of situation, a patient who is dying of incurable cancer of the throat is in terrible pain, which can no longer be satisfactorily alleviated. He is certain to die within a few days, even if present treatment is continued, but he does not want to go on living for those days, since the pain is unbearable. So he asks the doctor for an end to it, and his family joins in the request.	*Argument for claim* *Example*

Example

Argument against opposition

Suppose the doctor agrees to withhold treatment, as the conventional doctrine says he may. The justification for his doing so is that the patient is in terrible agony, and since he is going to die anyway, it would be wrong to prolong his suffering needlessly. But now notice this. If one simply withholds treatment, it may take the patient longer to die, and so he may suffer more than he would if more direct action were taken and a lethal injection given. This fact provides strong reason for thinking that, once the initial decision not to prolong his agony has been made, active euthanasia is actually preferable to passive euthanasia, rather than the reverse. To say otherwise is to endorse the option that leads to more suffering rather than less, and is contrary to the humanitarian impulse that prompts the decision not to prolong his life in the first place.

CLAIMS FOR WRITTEN ARGUMENT

The thesis of your argument is a *debatable claim*. Opinions on both sides of the issue must have some merit. Claims for a written argument usually fall into one of four categories: claims of fact, claims about cause and effect, claims about value, and claims about solutions and policies. A claim may occasionally fall into several categories or may even overlap categories.

Claims of Fact

- Grades do not measure intelligence or achievement.
- Polygraph tests do not accurately detect lies.
- Women face serious discrimination in the job market.

These claims are about matters of "fact" that are not easily measured or agreed upon. If I claim that a Lhasa apso was an ancient Chinese ruler, you can check a dictionary and find out that I am wrong. A Lhasa apso is, in fact, a small Tibetan dog. There is no argument. But people do disagree about some *supposed* "facts": Do grades measure achievement? Are polygraph tests accurate? They also disagree about matters of "degree": Sexual discrimination exists in the marketplace, but is it "serious"? How prevalent and extreme are the economic inequities? What is "discrimination," anyway? *Definition* is a key to claims of fact: What do we mean by "detect lies"? Does "accurate" mean 100 percent of the time? 90 percent? 80 percent? What does "serious discrimination" mean? Does the fact that female workers currently earn only 73 cents for every dollar that male workers earn qualify as "serious discrimination"?

In an excerpt from a *Newsweek* column entitled "A Case of Severe Bias," Patricia Raybon makes a claim of fact when she argues that the news media's portrayal of black America is inaccurate, biased, and stereotyped:

This is who I am not. I am not a crack addict. I am not a welfare mother. I am not illiterate. I am not a prostitute. I have never been in jail. My children are not in gangs. My husband doesn't beat me. My home is not a tenement. None of these things defines who I am, nor do they describe the other black people I've known and worked with and loved and befriended over these 40 years of my life.

Nor does it describe most of black America, period.

Yet in the eyes of the American news media, this is what black America is: poor, criminal, addicted and dysfunctional. Indeed, media coverage of black America is so one-sided, so imbalanced that the most victimized and hurting segment of the black community—a small segment, at best—is presented not as the exception but as the norm. It is an insidious practice, all the uglier for its blatancy.

In recent months, oftentimes in this very magazine, I have observed a steady offering of media reports on crack babies, gang warfare, violent youth, poverty and homelessness—and in most cases, the people featured in the photos and stories were black. At the same time, articles that discuss other aspects of American life—from home buying to medicine to technology to nutrition— rarely, if ever, show blacks playing a positive role, or for that matter, any role at all.

Day after day, week after week, this message—that black America is dysfunctional and unwhole—gets transmitted across the American landscape. Sadly, as a result, America never learns the truth about what is actually a wonderful, vibrant, creative community of people.

Claims About Cause and Effect

- Cigarettes cause lung cancer.
- Capital punishment does not deter violent crime.
- Rock music weakens the moral fibre of Canada's youth.

Unlike the claim "Grades affect admission to college," these claims about cause and effect are debatable. The claim that cigarettes cause lung cancer is, of course, less debatable than it was 20 years ago, before the evidence demonstrating the link became overwhelming. The deterring effect of capital punishment is still an arguable proposition with reasonable arguments on both sides. The argument that rock music weakens the moral fibre of youth is certainly debatable; the writer would have to counter the argument that rock music sometimes raises social consciousness and fights world hunger.

In a selection from her book *The Plug-In Drug: Television, Children, and the Family*, Marie Winn argues that television has a negative effect on family life. In her opening paragraphs, she sets forth both sides of the controversy and then argues that the overall effect is negative:

> Television's contribution to family life has been an equivocal one. For while it has, indeed, kept the members of the family from dispersing, it has not served to bring them *together*. By its domination of the time families spend together, it destroys the special quality that depends to a great extent on what a family does, what special rituals, games, recurrent jokes, familiar songs, and shared activities it accumulates.
>
> "Like the sorcerer of old," writes Urie Bronfenbrenner, "the television set casts its magic spell, freezing speech and action, turning the living into silent statues so long as the enchantment lasts. The primary danger of the television screen lies not so much in the behavior it produces—although there is danger there—as in the behavior it prevents: the talks, the games, the family festivities and arguments through which much of the child's learning takes place and through which his character is formed. Turning on the television set can turn off the process that transforms children into people."
>
> Yet parents have accepted a television-dominated family life so completely that they cannot see how the medium is involved in whatever problems they might be having.

Claims About Value

- Boxing is a dehumanizing sport.
- The Ford Edsel is the ugliest automobile ever built in America.
- Margaret Atwood is a great Canadian novelist.

Claims about value lead to evaluative essays. All the strategies discussed in Chapter 8 apply here, with the additional requirement that you must anticipate and respond to alternate or opposing arguments. The argumentative essay that attempts to prove that boxing is dehumanizing must respond to the argument that boxing is merely another form of competition that promotes athletic excellence. Arguing that Atwood is a great Canadian novelist requires setting criteria for great Canadian novels and then responding to critics who argue that Atwood's work does not reach those standards.

In "College Is a Waste of Time and Money," teacher and journalist Caroline Bird argues that many students go to college simply because it is the "thing to do." For those students, Bird claims, college is not a good idea:

Nowadays, says one sociologist, you don't have to have a reason for going to college; it's an institution. His definition of an institution is an arrangement everyone accepts without question; the burden of proof is not on why you go, but why anyone thinks there might be a reason for not going. The implication is that an 18-year-old . . . should listen to those who know best and go to college.

I don't agree. I believe that college has to be judged not on what other people think is good for students, but on how good it feels to the students themselves.

I believe that people have an inside view of what's good for them. If a child doesn't want to go to school some morning, better let him stay at home, at least until you find out why. Maybe he knows something you don't. It's the same with college. If high-school graduates don't want to go, or if they don't want to go right away, they may perceive more clearly than their elders that college is not for them. It is no longer obvious that adolescents are best off studying a core curriculum that was constructed when all educated men could agree on what made them educated, or that professors, advisors, or parents can be of any particular help to young people in choosing a major or a career. High-school graduates see college graduates driving cabs and decide it's not worth going. College students find no intellectual stimulation in their studies and drop out.

Claims about Solutions or Policies

- Pornography on the Internet should be censored.
- The penalty for drunk driving should be a mandatory jail sentence and loss of driver's licence.
- To reduce exploitation and sensationalism, the news media should not be allowed to interview victims of crime or disaster.

Claims about solutions or policies sometimes occur *along with* claims of fact, cause and effect, or value. Because grades do not measure achievement (argue that this is a fact), they should be abolished (argue for this policy). Boxing is a dehumanizing sport (argue this claim of value); therefore, boxing should be banned (argue for this solution). Claims about solutions or policies involve all the strategies used for problem solving, but with special emphasis on countering opposing arguments: "Although advocates of freedom of speech suggest that we cannot suppress pornography on the Internet, in fact, we already have self-monitoring devices in other media that could help reduce pornography on the Internet."

In *When Society Becomes an Addict*, psychotherapist Anne Wilson Schaef argues that our society has become an "Addictive System" that has many characteristics in common with alcoholism and other addictions. Advertising becomes addictive, causing us to behave dishonestly; the social pressure to be "nice" can become addictive, causing us to lie to ourselves. Schaef argues that the solution for our social addictions begins when we face the reality of our dependency:

> We cannot recover from an addiction unless we first admit that we have it. Naming our reality is essential to recovery. Unless we admit that we are indeed functioning in an addictive process in an Addictive System, we shall never have the option of recovery. Once we name something, we own it. . . . Remember, to name the system as addict is not to condemn it: it is to offer it the possibility of recovery.

> Paradoxically, the only way to reclaim our personal power is by admitting our powerlessness. The first part of Step One of the AA [Alcoholics Anonymous] Twelve-Step Program reads, "We admitted we were powerless over alcohol." It is important to recognize that admitting to powerlessness over an addiction is not the same as admitting powerlessness as a person. In fact, it can be very powerful to recognize the futility of the illusion of control.

APPEALS FOR WRITTEN ARGUMENT

To support claims and respond to opposing arguments, writers use *appeals* to the audience. Argument uses three important types of appeals: to *reason* (logic and evidence support the claim), to *character* (the writer's good character itself supports the claim), and to *emotion* (the writer's expression of feelings about the issue may support the claim). Effective arguments emphasize the appeal to reason but may also appeal to character or emotion.

Appeal to Reason   An appeal to reason depends most frequently on *inductive logic,* which is sometimes called the *scientific method.* Inductive logic draws a general conclusion from personal observation or experience, specific facts, reports, statistics, testimony of authorities, and other bits of data.

Experience is the best teacher, we always say, and experience teaches inductively. Suppose, using biologist Thomas Huxley's famous example, you pick a green apple from a tree and take a bite. Halfway through the bite you discover that the apple is sour and quickly spit it out. But, you think, perhaps the next green apple will be ripe and will taste better. You pick a second green apple, take a bite, and realize that it is just as sour as the first. However, you know that some apples—like the Granny Smith—look green even when they're ripe, so you take a bite out of a third apple. It is also sour. You're beginning to draw a conclusion. In fact, if you taste a fourth or fifth apple, other people may begin to question your intelligence. How many green apples from this tree must you taste before you get the idea that all of these green apples are sour?

Experience, however, may lead to wrong conclusions. You've tasted enough of these apples to convince *you* that all these apples are sour, but will others think that these apples are sour? Perhaps you have funny taste buds. You may need to ask several friends to taste the apples. Or perhaps you are dealing with a slightly weird tree—in fact, some apple trees are hybrids, with several different kinds of apples grafted onto one tree. Before you draw a conclusion, you may need to consult an expert in order to be certain that your tree is a standard, single-variety apple tree. If your friends and the expert also agree that all of these green apples are sour, you may use your experience *and* their testimony to reach a conclusion—and to provide evidence to make your argument more convincing to others.

In inductive logic, a reasonable conclusion is based on a *sufficient* quantity of accurate and reliable evidence that is selected in a *random* manner to reduce human bias or to take into account variation in the sample. The definition of *sufficient* varies, but generally the number must be large enough to convince your audience that your sample fairly represents the whole subject.

Let's take an example to illustrate inductive reasoning. Suppose you ask a student, one of 50 in a Psychology I class, a question of value: "Is Professor X a good teacher?" If this student says, "Professor X is the worst teacher I've ever had!" what conclusion can you draw? If you avoid taking the class based on a sample of one, you may miss an excellent class. So you decide to gather a *sufficient sample* by polling 20 of the 50 students in the class. But which 20 do you interview? If you ask the first student for a list of students, you may receive the names of 20 other students who also hate the professor. To reduce human or accidental bias, then, you choose a random method for collecting your evidence: As the students leave the class, you give a questionnaire to two out of every five students. If they all fill out the questionnaires, you probably have a *sufficient* and *random* sample.

Finally, if the responses to your questionnaire show that 15 out of 20 students rate Professor X as an excellent teacher, what *valid conclusion* should you draw? You should not say, categorically, "X is an excellent teacher." Your conclusion must be restricted by your evidence and the method of gathering it: "Seventy-five percent of the students polled in Psychology I believe that Professor X is an excellent teacher."

Most arguments use a shorthand version of the inductive method of reasoning. A writer makes a claim and then supports it with *reasons* and representative *examples* or *data:*

Claim:	Professor X is an excellent psychology teacher.
Reason #1:	Professor X is an excellent teacher because she gives stimulating lectures that students rarely miss.
Evidence:	Sixty percent of the students polled said that they rarely missed a lecture. Three students cited Professor X's lecture on "assertiveness" as the best lecture they'd ever heard.
Reason #2:	Professor X is an excellent teacher because she gives tests that encourage learning rather than sheer memorization.
Evidence:	Seventy percent of the students polled said that Professor X's essay tests required thinking and learning rather than memorization. One student said that Professor X's tests always made her think about what she'd read. Another student said he always liked to discuss Professor X's test questions with his classmates and friends.

Appeal to Character   An appeal based on your good character as a writer can also be important in argument. (The appeal to character is frequently called the *ethical appeal* because readers make a value judgment about the writer's character.) In a written argument, you show your audience—through your reasonable persona, voice, and tone—that you are a person who abides by moral standards that your audience shares: You have a good reputation, you are honest and trustworthy, and you argue "fairly."

A person's reputation often affects how we react to a claim, but *the argument itself* should also establish the writer's trustworthiness. You don't have to be a Mahatma Gandhi or a Mother Teresa to generate a strong ethical appeal for your claim. Even if your readers have never heard your name before, they will feel confident about your character if you are knowledgeable about your subject, present the pros and cons fairly, and support your own claim with sufficient, reliable evidence.

If your readers have reason to suspect your motives or think that you may have something personal to gain from your argument, you may need to bend over backward to be fair. If you do have something to gain, lay your cards on the table. Declare your vested interest but explain, for example, how your solution would benefit everyone equally. Similarly, don't try to cover up or distort the opponents' arguments; acknowledge the opposition's strong arguments and refute the weak ones.

Appeal to Emotion   Appeals to emotion can be tricky because, as we have seen, when emotions come in through the door, reasonableness may fly out the window. Argument emphasizes reason, not emotion. We know, for example, how advertising plays on emotions, by means of loaded or exaggerated language or through images of famous or sexy people. Emotional appeals designed to *deceive* or *frighten* people or to *misrepresent* the virtues of a person, place, or object have no place in rational argument. But emotional appeals that illustrate a truth or movingly depict a reality are legitimate and effective means of convincing readers.

Combined Appeals   Appeals may be used in combination. Writers may appeal to reason and, at the same time, establish trustworthy characters and use legitimate emotional appeals. The following excerpt from Martin Luther King, Jr.'s "Letter from Birmingham Jail" illustrates all three appeals. He appeals to reason, arguing that, historically, civil rights reforms are rarely made without political pressure. He establishes his integrity and good character by treating the opposition (in this case, the Birmingham clergy) with respect and by showing moderation and restraint. Finally, he uses emotional appeals, describing his six-year-old daughter in tears and recalling his own humiliation at being refused a place to sleep. King uses these emotional appeals legitimately; he is not misrepresenting reality or trying to deceive his readers.

One of the basic points in [the statement by the Birmingham clergy] is that the action that I and my associates have taken in Birmingham is untimely. Some have asked: "Why didn't you give the new city administration time to act?" The only answer that I can give to this query is that the new Birmingham administration must be prodded about as much as the outgoing one, before it will act. We are sadly mistaken if we feel that the election of Albert Boutwell as mayor will bring the millennium to Birmingham. While Mr. Boutwell is a much more gentle person than Mr. Connor, they are both segregationists, dedicated to the maintenance of the status quo. I have hoped that Mr. Boutwell will be reasonable enough to see the futility of massive resistance to desegregation. But he will not see this without pressure from devotees of civil rights. My friends, I must say to you that we have not made a single gain in civil rights without determined legal and nonviolent pressure. Lamentably, it is an historical fact that privileged groups seldom give up their privileges voluntarily. Individuals may see the moral light and voluntarily give up their unjust posture; but, as Reinhold Niebuhr has reminded us, groups tend to be more immoral than individuals.

Appeal to character and appeal to reason

Appeal to reason

Evidence

We know through painful experience that freedom is never voluntarily given by the oppressor; it must be demanded by the oppressed. Frankly, I have yet to engage in a direct-action campaign that was "well timed" in the view of those who have not suffered unduly from the disease of segregation. For years now I have heard the word "Wait!" It rings in the ear of every Negro with piercing familiarity. This "Wait" has almost always meant "Never." We must come to see, with one of our distinguished jurists, that "justice too long delayed is justice denied."

Appeal to character and reason

We have waited for more than 340 years for our constitutional and God-given rights. . . . Perhaps it is easy for those who have never felt the stinging darts of segregation to say, "Wait." But

Appeal to emotion

Evidence

Appeal to emotion

Evidence

Appeal to emotion

Evidence

Appeal to character

when you have seen vicious mobs lynch your mothers and fathers at will and drown your sisters and brothers at whim; when you have seen hate-filled policemen curse, kick, and even kill your black brothers and sisters; when you see the vast majority of your twenty million Negro brothers smothering in an airtight cage of poverty in the midst of an affluent society; when you suddenly find your tongue twisted and your speech stammering as you seek to explain to your six-year-old daughter why she can't go to the public amusement park that has just been advertised on television, and see tears welling up in her eyes when she is told that Funtown is closed to colored children . . . when you take a cross-country drive and find it necessary to sleep night after night in the uncomfortable corners of your automobile because no motel will accept you; when you are humiliated day in and day out by nagging signs reading "white" and "colored"; when your first name becomes "nigger," your middle name becomes "boy" (however old you are) and your last name becomes "John" . . . —then you will understand why we find it difficult to wait. There comes a time when the cup of endurance runs over, and men are no longer willing to be plunged into the abyss of despair. I hope, sirs, you can understand our legitimate and unavoidable impatience.

ROGERIAN ARGUMENT

Traditional argument assumes that people are most readily convinced or persuaded by a confrontational "debate" on the issue. In a traditional argument, the writer argues reasonably and fairly, but the argument becomes a kind of struggle or "war" as the writer attempts to "defeat" the arguments of the opposition. The purpose of a traditional argument is thus to convince an undecided audience that the writer has "won a fight" and emerged "victorious" over the opposition.

In fact, however, there are many situations in which a less confrontational and less adversarial approach to argument is more effective. Particularly when the issues are highly charged or when the audience that we are trying to persuade is the opposition, writers may more effectively use negotiation rather than confrontation. *Rogerian argument*—named after psychologist Carl Rogers—is a kind of negotiated argument where understanding and compromise replace the traditional, adversarial approach. Rogerian, or *non-threatening* argument, opens the lines of communication by reducing conflict. When people's beliefs are attacked, they instinctively become defensive and strike back. As a result, the argument becomes polarized: The writer argues for a claim, the reader digs in to defend his or her position, and no one budges.

Crucial to Rogerian argument is the fact that convictions and beliefs are not abstract but reside in people. If people are to agree, they must be sensitive to each other's beliefs. Rogerian argument, therefore, contains a clear appeal to character. While Rogerian argument uses reason and logic, its primary goal is not to "win" the argument but to open the lines of communication. To do that, the writer must be sympathetic to different points of view and willing to modify his or her claims in response to people who hold different viewpoints. Once the reader sees that the writer is open to change, the reader may become more flexible.

Once both sides are more flexible, a compromise position or solution becomes possible. As Rogers says, "This procedure gradually achieves a mutual communication. Mutual communication tends to be pointed toward solving a problem rather than toward attacking a person or group." Rogerian argument, then, imitates not a courtroom debate but the mutual communication that may take place between two people. Whereas traditional argument intends to change the actions or the beliefs of the opposition, Rogerian argument works toward changes *in both sides* as a means of establishing common ground and reaching a solution.

If you choose Rogerian argument, remember that you must actually be willing to change your beliefs. Often, in fact, when you need to use Rogerian argument most, you may be least inclined to use it—simply because you are inflexible on an issue. If you are unwilling to modify your own position, your reader will probably sense your basic insincerity and realize that you are just playing a trick of rhetoric.

Rogerian argument is appropriate in a variety of sensitive or highly controversial situations. You may want to choose Rogerian argument if you are an employer requesting union members to accept a pay cut in order to help the company avoid bankruptcy. Similarly, if you argue to husbands that they should assume responsibility for half the housework, you may want to use a Rogerian strategy. By showing that you empathize with the opposition's position and are willing to compromise, you create a climate for mutual communication.

Rogerian argument makes a claim, considers the opposition, and presents evidence to support your claim, but in addition, it avoids threatening or adversarial language and promotes mutual communication and learning. A Rogerian argument uses the following strategies:

- **Avoiding** a *confrontational stance*. Confrontation threatens your audience and increases their defensiveness. Threat hinders communication.

- **Presenting** your *character* as someone who understands and can empathize with the opposition. Show that you understand by restating the opposing position accurately.

- **Establishing** *common ground* with the opposition. Indicate the beliefs and values that you share.

- **Being willing** *to change your views.* Show where your position is not reasonable and could be modified.

- **Directing your argument toward** *a compromise or workable solution.*

Note: An argument does not have to be either entirely adversarial or entirely Rogerian. You may use Rogerian techniques for the most sensitive points in an argument that is otherwise traditional or confrontational.

In his essay "Animal Rights Versus Human Health," biology professor Albert Rosenfeld illustrates several features of Rogerian argument. Rosenfeld argues that animals should be used for medical experiments, but he is aware that the issues are emotional and that his audience is likely to be antagonistic. In these paragraphs, Rosenfeld avoids threatening language, represents the opposition fairly, grants that he is guilty of *speciesism,* and says that he sympathizes with the demand to look for alternatives. He indicates that his position is flexible: Most researchers, he says, are delighted when they can use alternatives. He grants that there is some room for compromise, but he is firm in his position that some animal experimentation is necessary for advancements in medicine.

States opposing position fairly and sympathetically

It is fair to say that millions of animals—probably more rats and mice than any other species—are subjected to experiments that cause them pain, discomfort, and distress, sometimes lots of it over long periods of time. . . . All new forms of medication or surgery are tried out on animals first. Every new substance that is released into the environment, or put on the market, is tested on animals. . . .

States opposing position fairly

In 1975, Australian philosopher Peter Singer wrote his influential book called *Animal Liberation,* in which he accuses us all of "speciesism"—as reprehensible, to him, as racism or sexism. He freely describes the "pain and suffering" inflicted in the "tyranny of human over nonhuman animals" and sharply challenges our biblical license to exercise "dominion over the fish of the sea, and over the fowl of the air, and over every living thing that moveth upon the Earth."

Acknowledges common ground

Sympathetic to opposing position

Well, certainly we are guilty of speciesism. We do act as if we had dominion over other living creatures. But domination also entails some custodial responsibility. And the questions continue to be raised: Do we have the right to abuse animals? To eat them? To hunt them for sport? To keep them imprisoned in zoos—or, for that matter, in our households? Especially to do experiments on these creatures who can't fight back?

Suggests compromise position

Hardly any advance in either human or veterinary medicine—cure, vaccine, operation, drug, therapy—has come about without experiments on animals. . . . I certainly sympathize with the demand that we look for ways to get the information we want without using animals. Most investigators are delighted when they can get their data by means of tissue cultures or computer simulations. But as we look for alternative ways to get information, do we meanwhile just do without?

PROFESSIONAL WRITING

THE ETHICS OF
ENDORSING A PRODUCT

MIKE ROYKO

The following essay by columnist Mike Royko appeared in the Chicago Tribune.

The man from an advertising agency had an unusual proposition. His agency does the TV commercials for a well-known chain of Mexican restaurants in Chicago.

"You may have seen our commercials," he said. "They include a cameo appearance by Lee Smith and Leon Durham of the Cubs. It shows them crunching into a tortilla."

No, I somehow missed seeing that.

"Well, anyway, we'd like to have you in a commercial."

Doing what?

"Crunching into a tortilla."

I thought tortillas were soft. I may be wrong, but I don't think you can crunch into a tortilla. Maybe you mean a taco.

"Well, you'd be biting into some kind of Mexican food."

What else would I have to do?

"That's it. It would be a cameo appearance. You'd be seen for about four seconds. You wouldn't have to say anything."

I'd just bite into a piece of Mexican food?

"Right. For a fee, of course."

How big a fee?

He named a figure. It was not a king's ransom, but it was more than walking-around money.

"It would take about 45 minutes to film," he said.

Amazing. In my first newspaper job almost 30 years ago, I had to work 12 weeks to earn the figure he had mentioned.

It was a small, twice-a-week paper, and I was the only police reporter, the only sports reporter, the only investigative reporter, the assistant political writer, and on Saturday I would edit the stories going into the entertainment page. The publisher believed in a day's work for an hour's pay.

Now I could make the same amount just for spending 45 minutes biting into a taco in front of a TV camera.

"Well, what do you think?" he asked.

I told him that I would think about it and get back to him.

So I asked Slats Grobnik, who has sound judgment, what he thought of the deal.

"That's a lot of money just to bite a taco on TV. For that kind of scratch, I'd bite a dog. Grab the deal."

But there is a question of ethics.

"Ethics? What's the ethics in biting a taco? Millions of people bite tacos every day. Mexicans have been biting them for hundreds of years. Are you saying that Mexicans are unethical? Careful, some of my best friends are Mexicans."

No, I'm not saying that at all. I like Mexicans, too, although I'm opposed to bullfighting.

"Then what's unethical?"

The truth is, I can't stand tacos.

"What has that got to do with it? I can't stand work, but I do it for the money."

It has everything to do with it. If I go on TV and bite into a taco, won't I be endorsing that taco?

"So what? You've endorsed politicians and I've never met a politician that I liked better than a taco."

But endorsing a taco I didn't like would be dishonest.

"Hey, that's the American way. Turn on your TV and look at all the people who endorse junk. Do you think they really believe what they're saying?"

Then it's wrong. Nobody should endorse a taco if they don't like a taco.

"Then tell them you'll bite something else. A tortilla or an enchilada."

But I don't like them, either. The truth is, I can't stand most Mexican food. The only thing I really like is the salt on the edge of a margarita glass.

"Can't you just bite the taco and spit it out when the camera is turned off?"

That would be a sham. Besides, even if I liked tacos or tortillas, what does it matter? Why should somebody eat in a restaurant because they see me biting into that restaurant's taco? Am I a taco expert? What are my credentials to tell millions of people what taco they should eat? I'm not even a Mexican.

"You're as Mexican as Jane Byrne, and she's doing it."

To get the Hispanic vote, she would go on TV and eat a cactus.

"Well, you're a sucker to turn it down. Why, it's almost un-American. Do you think that in Russia any newsman would ever have an opportunity to make that much money by biting into a pirogi?"

That may be so.

But maybe someday a food product will come along that I can lend my name to, something I can truly believe in.

"I doubt it. Not unless they start letting taverns advertise shots and beers on TV."

PROFESSIONAL WRITING

THE GIFT OF FAME
TYLER COWEN

Tyler Cowen is a professor of economics at George Mason University and author of In Praise of Commercial Culture *and* What Price Fame?, *both published by Harvard University Press. "The Gift of Fame," excerpted here from the latter book, appeared in the* National Post, *May*

27, 2000. In his argument, Cowen distinguishes celebrities from heroes, arguing that "the much-maligned celebrity is central to nothing less than progress itself." Cowen supports his claim with an accumulation of evidence, current and historical. His discussion is lively and informed, qualities which do not necessarily ensure that you will be persuaded by his argument or that his reasons and evidence are flawless. Before you read Cowen's essay, be sure to review the discussions and techniques, claims, and appeals for written argument in the opening sections of this chapter. Be prepared to evaluate Cowen's argument and the counterargument by Norman Doidge that follows.

Ours is a culture steeped in fame. We have famous musicians, actors, athletes, artists, designers, architects, scientists, charitable benefactors, cooks, critics, fashion models, CEOs and even famous intellectuals. **(1)**

Today's famous are typically celebrities, who are distinct from heroes. Heroes command widespread respect and adulation for something they have done, typically in a leadership role. Celebrities are merely well known, often for entertaining us. Nelson Mandela is a hero, Paul McCartney is a celebrity. Bob Geldof, of Live Aid and the Boomtown Rats, is both. **(2)**

Many intellectuals have attacked celebrity and valourized heroes. Their arguments, which are as old as Plato, transcend the usual political spectrum and come from both the left and the right. **(3)**

To give one example, Daniel Boorstin, in his 1961 book *The Image*, famously complained that the "pseudo-event" was replacing the real event, and that celebrities were replacing heroes. More generally, critics charge that the commercial production of publicity cheapens our culture and corrupts our morals. Pondering the perceived lack of giants in modern society, Winston Churchill asked in 1932: "Can modern communities do without great men? Can they dispense with hero worship?" Churchill openly asked if nations can "remain healthy . . . in a world whose brightest stars are film stars." **(4)**

Contrary to the critics, I am an optimist about celebrities. Fame encourages individuals to seek stardom, as nearly everyone wants recognition in one form or another. Writing more than two centuries ago, economist Adam Smith viewed the search for approval as "the end of half the labours of human life." By making more fame and more stardom possible, we spur creative performances. We have more music, more movies—and more science and entrepreneurship—than any previous era. We use fame to reward stars, thus helping to draw forth a dazzling and unprecedented array of diverse achievements. The much-maligned celebrity, in short, is central to nothing less than progress itself. **(5)**

Celebrity is simply commercialized fame. We commercialize fame so corporations will help us produce more of it by promoting stars for profit. The chain is simple: More profit means more fame, which in turn means more achievement. **(6)**

Modern technology has intensified the reach for fame and its commercialization. Modern notions of fame and celebrity date from the 1920s and 1930s, when radio, recording, and motion pictures gave stars greater ability to project their personae to wide audiences. Today, television, the compact disc and the Internet make the projection even easier. These technologies are driven by the profit motive and commercialization. The market in fame brings fans together with stars. **(7)**

Celebrities serve many useful functions. Fans use stars to advertise their tastes, distinguish themselves from others and signal their social status. **(8)**

Fans also use stars as a point of reference, such as when women ask their hairdressers for a Princess Di cut, or men tell corporate fashion consultants they wish to look like Lee Iacocca, the former CEO of Chrysler Corp. Celebrities now stand among our most important commonly shared public experiences. **(9)**

Celebrity endorsements also help markets function more effectively. Vince Carter of the Toronto Raptors, for example, is starting to endorse a wide variety of products, even though he knows little or nothing about many of them. Stars' agents are keen to make sure their clients project the appropriate image and avoid disappointing their fans. An agent such as Carter's, therefore, will have seen to it his star endorses only "the right" products. **(10)**

Fans thus expect a product of a certain kind when they see Carter's endorsement. The company, Carter and the fans are all better off. Even people who do not like Carter, basketball or male sports culture are better off: They know which products to stay away from. **(11)**

The world of celebrity also satisfies the expressive dimensions of the human psyche. Stars provide a realm in which arbitrary and subjective prejudices are given free reign to rule opinion. In many cases, fans take pleasure in judging the famous by especially harsh standards. They love the booing and the mocking. As Jonathan Swift noted, "Censure is the Tax a Man pays to the Publick for being Eminent." **(12)**

Finally, a world with fame and celebrity is likely to be a diverse world. Fame means it is easier for producers to reach audiences, and this includes relatively small audiences. **(13)**

A fame-intensive world is a world where niche audiences are brought together and served. The modern world produces many kinds of renown, not just the celebrity of Alanis Morissette or Jim Carrey. More than ever before, we have niche audiences who know a good deal about film director David Cronenberg, industrial band Skinny Puppy or writer-intellectual John Ralston Saul. **(14)**

In modern commercial society, the notion of celebrity has displaced the idea of the hero. A Web poll of the most popular Canadians (defined as "favourite") yields a steady stream of entertainers, but no heroes in the traditional sense. Mike Myers, Alanis Morissette, Bryan Adams and Matthew Perry topped the list. **(15)**

This trend is not cause for concern. The lack of hero-worship reflects the sophistication of a culture rather than its poverty. Cultural discernment will likely lead to skepticism about heroes. Hence Canadians' perfect willingness to embrace celebrities, whom they need not take so seriously as moral exemplars. **(16)**

It is no accident that heroes tend to be oversimplified images of parodies of themselves. An individual becomes a hero when millions of fans co-ordinate on granting that person collective homage. Large numbers of people can co-ordinate more easily on relatively obvious matters, leading to the tendency for heroes to acquire simplistic images, whether intentionally or not. To use an American example, George Washington was not a simple man, but our memories of him are likely to be full of half-truths and clichés. The hero must stand for a simple message that can be communicated to large numbers of people. **(17)**

As evidence for this simplicity, note that early or premature death often contributes more to a hero's lustre than does continued life. John F. Kennedy, Che Guevara and Diana, Princess of Wales, all became greater heroes through their tragic ends. Jimi Hendrix, himself the victim of an early death, correctly remarked that: "Once you are dead, you are made for life." **(18)**

Similarly, the more multicultural a society, the harder it is to have heroes. Heroes, because they serve as oversimplified caricatures, almost by definition cannot exist in a diverse, multi-ethnic, multi-racial, multi-language society. Heroes inevitably recede in influence with the rise of progress and cosmopolitanism. (19)

Many of the supposed heroes of the past, it is also worth pointing out, were brutal tyrants and butchers. Thomas Hobbes, writing the 17th century, noted that the classic heroes were honoured for their "Rapes, Thefts, and other great, but unjust, or unclean acts," including "Adulteries and Frauds." (20)

John Locke went further when he noted that "All the Entertainment and talk of History is of nothing almost but Fighting and Killing." He referred further to the "Honour and Renown, that is bestowed on Conquerours," whom he called "the great Butchers of Mankind." These heroes were bad role models in his eyes, causing youth "to think Slaughter the laudable Business of Mankind, and the most Heroick of Virtues." (21)

The very word hero illustrates the partly martial origins of the concept. The female version of the concept, heroine, alters the connotation of the word as well as the gender. The heroes of antiquity won their fame through battles and conquest. The heroines of antiquity, on the other hand, were typically known for their gifts to the human race or for mothering future heroes. (22)

Heroes often arise when times are bad. If we look at the most heroic American presidents, such as Abraham Lincoln or Franklin Delano Roosevelt, they are typically from major wars or when the survival of the nation was at stake. Other American heroes, such as Martin Luther King, or Harriet Beecher Stowe, won their fame by fighting racial oppression. Clearly it is not necessarily a good thing for a country to have a history rich in heroes. (23)

Throughout the world, heroes are losing their lustre. The American presidency no longer has the same stature it once did, in large part because of media exposure. In the 1930s, most Americans did not know that Franklin Roosevelt sat in a wheelchair. More recently, we have seen Jimmy Carter in a sweater, Gerald Ford stumbling and bumping his head, George Bush throwing up in the lap of the Japanese prime minister and the extramarital affairs of Bill Clinton. (24)

The monarchy shows a similar trend of falling prestige, largely because of modern technology. The spread of photography in the middle of the 19th century made the monarchy more accessible, and thus more popular, but also less respected. Bertie, the Prince of Wales and the son of Victoria and Alberta, created a public-relations storm when he visited North America in 1860. Because of photography, people knew what Bertie looked like and how he dressed. He was followed around by mobs and treated as a celebrity, rather than as a figure of respect. **(25)**

In later years the monarchy continued to increase its reach while losing its stature. In 1953, the coronation of Queen Elizabeth was televised and watched by 20 million Britons. In contrast, 750 million people watched the marriage of Charles and Diana in 1981, by which time the monarchy was little more than a public showpiece and a part of celebrity culture. **(26)**

As a result, we have not so much lost role models as acquired new ones and given the new role models a different use. Contrary to what many critics charge, moral discourse may operate more effectively when imperfect, blemished, individuals are in the public eye. **(27)**

Imperfect celebrities—even fictional characters in a television show—provide more complex models than do many heroes and thus may be more useful. The social vision of virtue they give rise to rests less upon the adulation of personalities and more on the critical analysis of personality traits. **(28)**

To give an example, intelligent fans might approve of Michael Jordan's quest for excellence, while disapproving of his gambling. By giving up the notion of hero, we can evaluate different aspects of a person's behaviour separately, rather than judging that person as uniformly good or bad. This more cautious moral discourse is often better, as the world of heroism is more likely to trap us in inappropriate black-and-white judgments. **(29)**

I am commonly asked whether the weak stature of heroes in a society, be it in Canada or elsewhere, involves significant costs. For instance, might the Canadian lack of interest in heroes be partly responsible for the perceived weakness of Canadian unity? Might not a few more "national myths" be a good thing? **(30)**

I believe not. In the case of Canada, it is questionable to assume that heroes further the cause of national unity. We can imagine a dissident or secessionist province that uses heroes to drum up regional support for its cause. This is common in Ireland, the Balkans and other politically unstable parts of the world. **(31)**

American history also shows heroes do not necessarily further the cause of unity. As the American nation split with the approach of the civil war, the presence of heroes was arguably more divisive than unifying. Formerly national heroes, such as Thomas Jefferson, suddenly became regional heroes. **(32)**

By paying less heed to heroes, the Canadian union might be more stable rather than less. Heroes, who serve as oversimplified cartoons and slogans, tend to raise the emotional stakes in debates. If what Canada needs now is reasoned consideration, its hero-poor culture may be exactly what is in order. **(33)**

Vocabulary

Write down the meanings of the following words:

- *valourized* heroes **(3)**
- *transcend* **(3)**
- Cultural *discernment* **(16)**
- *skepticism* **(16)**

Questions for Writing and Discussion

1. What is Cowen's thesis or overall claim? Find one or two sentences that clearly express his thesis. In paragraph 19, Cowen says, ". . . the more multicultural a society, the harder it is to have heroes." Why is this statement important for Cowen's thesis?

2. What are Cowen's purposes in this essay? Is he making a claim of fact, value, cause and effect, or policy? Does he aim to convince us of a belief or persuade us to take some action? Cite specific passages from the essay to support your answer.

3. Review the six-part classical structure in the "Shaping" section of this chapter. Does Cowen's essay follow the sequence outlined there (Introduction, Narration, Partition, Argument, Refutation, and Conclusion)? How does he revise or adapt this structure?

4. Cowen uses a variety of supporting evidence. Identify at least three types of evidence and give an example of each. Evaluate his evidence. Is it appropriate and persuasive? Is it timely and relevant? If you were giving Cowen advice about revising and improving his evidence, what changes would you suggest?

5. Cowen uses what kinds of appeal (to reason, to character, to emotion)?

6. Read Norman Doidge's response to Cowen's argument. With which writer's viewpoint do you agree? Which writer's essay is more convincing? Write a persuasive essay in support of your choice. You may want to structure your argument according to the six-part classical outline (see Question 3).

PROFESSIONAL WRITING

IN PRAISE OF HERO WORSHIP
NORMAN DOIDGE

Dr. Norman Doidge is a research psychiatrist and psychoanalyst who writes a regular column for the National Post. *This essay, challenging Professor Cowen's position on the role of celebrities, appeared in the* National Post *on June 1, 2000. As you read his rebuttal, examine Doidge's persuasive techniques. Is his argument convincing? Consider your own viewpoint on this subject prior to reading each of these essays. Is your view reinforced, or changed? Think of an additional argument Cowen and Doidge could have used to support their claims.*

Tyler Cowen, professor of economics at George Mason University, is one of those intractable enthusiasts who calls himself an optimist. His first book, *In Praise of Commercial Culture*, by Harvard University Press, was an unabashed defence of the free market as culture's greatest patron. This weekend, the *National Post* ran an excerpt from his latest book, *What Price Fame?*. I don't know what he is smoking, but I'd like to try some. **(1)**

Cowen's Blockbuster® argument is based on a fact, and an interpretation. The fact is that heroes, as virtuous ideals for young people to emulate, have all but disappeared from our society, having been replaced by "celebrities." His interpretation is that this a good thing. Heroes are famous for their virtue and the great things they have done; celebrities are, as a wit said, famous for being famous, and usually they get famous by entertaining us. **(2)**

"I am optimistic about celebrities. Fame encourages individuals to seek stardom, as nearly everyone wants recognition . . . By making more fame and more stardom possible, we spur creative performances. We have more music, more movies—and more science and entrepreneurship . . . Celebrity is simply commercialized fame . . . promoting stars for profit." Celebs are good for fans, who use "stars to advertise their tastes, distinguish themselves from others and signal their social status." It's no accident that Canada's leading celebrities, in order, are Mike Myers, Alanis Morissette, Bryan Adams and Matthew Perry, two actors and two singers. Cowen disparages heroes by arguing that most did bad things (died or killed to protect their country), and our images of them are cartoonish and one-dimensional, predisposing us to dangerous "hero worship." Even when he concedes heroes have virtue, Cowen argues that celebrities are better models precisely because they lack it: "Contrary to what many critics charge, moral discourse may operate more effectively when imperfect, blemished, individuals are in the public eye," because they are more complex. "Heroes . . . arise when times are bad." He seems utterly confident that the good times will keep on rolling. We don't need the Winston Churchills, the Abraham Lincolns, or the Raoul Wallenbergs any longer. In this Cowen promotes an indifference to politics that is downright dangerous. **(3)**

Cowen is quite correct in rooting his attack on heroes in the philosophy of Thomas Hobbes and John Locke, the founders of liberal democracy. Both men, responding to the bloody religious and civil wars they lived through, thought the bloodshed was caused by men being too willing to sacrifice their lives in the name of what they saw as the higher good. To stanch the blood, Hobbes and Locke tried to make men more squeamish by describing early death as awful, and heroes as vainglorious butchers. They made individual self-preservation and security (the pursuit of health and wealth), individual rights, and self-interest, the foundation of liberal democracy. **(4)**

Hobbes and Locke were not without their critics, though. Jean-Jacques Rousseau pointed out that the self-interested, timid bourgeois man they created felt incomplete and filled with unsatisfied longings because his life was now based on the endless calculation of self-interest. We required a corrective for what was missing, something that would satisfy our souls, rather than just our material well-being. **(5)**

As Allan Bloom argues, the corrective became "culture." It is not a commodity, but rather a remedy for a life based on the pursuit of commodities. To be "cultured" became an achievement, that required a cultivation of the self. In fact, the very word *Kultur* was given its modern significance by philosopher Immanuel Kant when discussing Rousseau's critique. (The ancient Greeks, who seem so "cultured" to us, didn't have or need such a word.) Culture is now a degraded, vague, plastic word; every human artifact is seen as a cultural artifact; but it originally had in some way to do with higher, even spiritual things. **(6)**

But as happens in every regime, soon the driving forces of the regime (here the free market, and liberal democracy with its love of equality) prove stronger than the weak corrective. In novels, grand heroes were replaced by more banal egalitarian "anti-heroes." Soon, the corrective of culture starts less and less to supplement our faults, and instead begins to express them. One goes from the sublime art of the Sistine Chapel to Warhol's soup cans, junk sculpture, and pornographic everything. Self-expression and self-gratification replace self-transcendence and sublimation. **(7)**

In Cowen's analysis, a large, diverse supply of "cultural commodities" becomes more important than the souls of those who consume them. He argues, "a world with fame and celebrity is likely to be a diverse world." **(8)**

Celebrities (Mike Myers exempted) are often the worst models for happiness. Being a lost soul—having a poorly formed identity, being aimless, malleable, needy for attention is almost a prerequisite for celebdom. These deficits allow celeb-wannabes to spend adulthood endlessly swapping identities, as did Marilyn, Madonna, Michael Jackson, and Lady Di. That so many celebrities are grotesquely unhappy in their personal lives makes them even more sympathetic to those of us—raised in a celebrity culture, devoid of true heroes with virtues to emulate—who are filled with a sense of emptiness at our core. **(9)**

The free market is an amazing invention, but it is not the answer to all our prayers. Tyler Cowen is a likeable man, and a great consumer. But his latest argument, if accepted, will help take us from heroes to zeros. **(10)**

PROFESSIONAL WRITING

THE INTERNET: A CLEAR AND PRESENT DANGER?

CATHLEEN A. CLEAVER

Cathleen Cleaver is a former director of legal studies at the Family Research Council, an organization based in Washington, D.C. She has published extensively on issues relating to children and the Internet, in newspapers and magazines such as USA Today, Newsday, *and the* Congressional Quarterly Researcher. *The following essay was originally a speech given at Boston University as part of a College of Communication Great Debate. In this speech, she argues that some industry and government regulation of the Internet is necessary.*

- Someone breaks through your firewall and steals proprietary information from your computer systems. You find out and contact a lawyer who says, "Man, you shouldn't have had your stuff online." The thief becomes a millionaire using your ideas, and you go broke, if laws against copyright violation don't protect material on the Internet. (1)

- You visit the Antiques Anonymous Web site and decide to pay their hefty subscription fee for a year's worth of exclusive estate sale previews in their private online monthly magazine. They never deliver and, in fact, never intended to—they don't even have a magazine. You have no recourse, if laws against fraud don't apply to online transactions. (2)

- Bob Guccione decides to branch out into the lucrative child porn market and creates a Teen Hustler Web site featuring nude adolescents and preteens. You find out and complain, but nothing can be done, if child pornography distribution laws don't apply to computer transmissions. (3)

- A major computer software vendor who dominates the market develops his popular office software so that it works only with his browser. You're a small browser manufacturer who is completely squeezed out of the market, but you have to find a new line of work, if antitrust laws don't apply online. (4)

- Finally, a pedophile e-mails your son, misrepresenting himself as a twelve-year-old named Jenny. They develop an online relationship and one day arrange to meet after school, where he intends to rape your son. Thankfully, you learn in advance about the meeting and go there yourself, where you find a forty-year-old man instead of Jenny. You flee to the police, who'll tell you there's nothing they can do, if child-stalking laws don't apply to the Internet. (5)

The awesome advances in interactive telecommunication that we've witnessed in just the last few years have changed the way in which many Americans communicate and interact. No one can doubt that the Internet is a technological revolution of enormous proportion, with outstanding possibilities for human advancement. (6)

As lead speaker for the affirmative, I'm asked to argue that the Internet poses a "clear and present danger," but the Internet, as a whole, isn't dangerous. In fact, it continues to be a positive and highly beneficial tool, which will undoubtedly improve education, information exchange, and commerce in years to come. In other words, the Internet will enrich many aspects of our daily life. Thus, instead of defending this rather apocalyptic view of the Internet, I'll attempt to explain why some industry and government regulation of certain aspects of the Internet is necessary—or, stated another way, why people who use the Internet should not be exempt from many of the laws and regulations that govern their conduct elsewhere. My opening illustrations were meant to give examples of some illegal conduct which should not become legal simply because someone uses the Internet. In looking at whether Internet regulation is a good idea, I believe we should consider whether regulation is in the public interest. In order to do that, we have to ask the question: Who is the public? More specifically, does the "public" whose interests we care about tonight include children? **(7)**

CHILDREN AND THE INTERNET

Dave Barry describes the Internet as a "worldwide network of university, government, business, and private computer systems, run by a thirteen-year-old named Jason." This description draws a smile precisely because we acknowledge the highly advanced computer literacy of our children. Most children demonstrate computer proficiency that far surpasses that of their parents, and many parents know only what their children have taught them about the Internet, which gives new relevance to Wordsworth's insight: "The child is father of the man." In fact, one could go so far as to say that the Internet is as accessible to many children as it is inaccessible to many adults. This technological evolution is new in many ways, not the least of which is its accessibility to children, wholly independent of their parents. **(8)**

When considering what's in the public interest, we must consider the whole public, including children, as individual participants in this new medium. **(9)**

PORNOGRAPHY AND THE INTERNET

This new medium is unique in another way. It provides, through a single avenue, the full spectrum of pornographic depictions, from the more familiar convenience store fare to pornography of such violence and depravity that it surpasses the worst excesses of the normal human imagination. Sites displaying this material are easily accessible, making pornography far more freely available via the Internet than from any other communications medium in the United States. Pornography is the third largest sector of sales on the Internet, generating $1 billion annually. There are an estimated seventy-two thousand pornographic sites on the World Wide Web alone, with approximately thirty-nine new explicit sex sites every day. Indeed, the *Washington Post* has called the Internet the largest pornography store in the history of mankind. **(10)**

There is little restriction of pornography-related activity in cyberspace. While there are some porn-related laws, the specter of those laws does not loom large in cyberspace. There's an implicit license there that exists nowhere else with regard to pornography—an environment where people are free to exploit others for profit and be virtually untroubled by legal deterrent. Indeed, if we consider cyberspace to be a little world of its own, it's the type of world for which groups like the ACLU have long fought but, so far, fought in vain. **(11)**

I believe it will not remain this way, but until it changes, we should take the opportunity to see what this world looks like, if for no other reason than to reassure ourselves that our decades-old decisions to control pornography were good ones. **(12)**

With a few clicks of the mouse, anyone, any child, can get graphic and often violent sexual images—the kind of stuff it used to be difficult to find without exceptional effort and some significant personal risk. Anyone with a computer and a modem can set up public sites featuring the perversion of their choice, whether it's mutilation of female genitals, eroticized urination and defecation, bestiality, or sites featuring depictions of incest. These pictures can be sold for profit, they can be sent to harass others, or posted to shock people. Anyone can describe the fantasy rape and murder of a specific person and display it for all to read. Anyone can meet children in chat rooms or via e-mail and send them pornography and find out where they live. An adult who signs onto an AOL chat room as a thirteen-year-old girl is hit on thirty times within the first half hour. **(13)**

All this can be done from the seclusion of the home, with the feeling of near anonymity and with the comfort of knowing that there's little risk of legal sanction. **(14)**

The phenomenon of this kind of pornography finding such a welcome home in this new medium presents abundant opportunities for social commentary. What does Internet pornography tell us about human sexuality? Photographs, videos, and virtual games that depict rape and the dehumanization of women in sexual scenes send powerful messages about human dignity and equality. Much of the pornography freely available without restriction on the Internet celebrates unhealthy and antisocial kinds of sexual activity, such as sadomasochism, abuse, and degradation. Of course, by its very nature, pornography encourages voyeurism. **(15)**

Beyond the troubling social aspects of unrestricted porn, we face the reality that children are accessing it and that predators are accessing children. We have got to start considering what kind of society we'll have when the next generation learns about human sexuality from what the Internet teaches. What does unrestricted Internet pornography teach children about relationships, about the equality of women? What does it teach little girls about themselves and their worth? **(16)**

Opponents of restrictions are fond of saying that it's up to the parents to deal with the issue of children's exposure. Well, of course it is, but placing the burden solely on parents is illogical and ineffective. It's far easier for a distributor of pornography to control his material than it is for parents, who must, with the help of software, search for and find the pornographic sites, which change daily, and then attempt to block them. Any pornographer who wants to can easily subvert these efforts, and a recent Internet posting from a teenager wanting to know how to disable the filtering software on his computer received several effective answers. Moreover, it goes without saying that the most sophisticated software can only be effective where it's installed, and children will have access to many computers that don't have filtering software, such as those in libraries, schools, and at neighbors' houses. **(17)**

INTERNET TRANSACTIONS SHOULD NOT BE EXEMPT

Opponents of legal restrictions often argue simply that the laws just cannot apply in this new medium, but the argument that old laws can't apply to changing technology just doesn't hold. We saw this argument last in the early '80s with the advent of the videotape. Then, certain groups tried to argue that, since you can't view videotapes without a VCR, you can't make the sale of child porn videos illegal, because, after all, they're just plastic boxes with magnetic tape inside. Technological change mandates legal change only insofar as it affects the justification for a law. It just doesn't make sense that the government may take steps to restrict illegal material in *every* medium—video, television, radio, the private telephone, *and* print—but that it may do nothing where people distribute the material by the Internet. While old laws might need redefinition, the old principles generally stand firm. **(18)**

The question of enforcement usually is raised here, and it often comes in the form of: "How are you going to stop people from doing it?" Well, no law stops people from doing things—a red light at an intersection doesn't force you to stop but tells you that you should stop and that there could be legal consequences if you don't. Not everyone who runs a red light is caught, but that doesn't mean the law is futile. The same concept holds true for Internet laws. Government efforts to temper harmful conduct online will never be perfect, but that doesn't mean they shouldn't undertake the effort at all. **(19)**

There's clearly a role for industry to play here. Search engines don't have to run ads for porn sites or prioritize search results to highlight porn. One new search engine even has sex as the default search term. Internet service providers can do something about unsolicited e-mail with hotlinks to porn, and they can and should carefully monitor any chat rooms designed for kids. **(20)**

Some charge that industry standards or regulations that restrict explicit pornography will hinder the development of Internet technology. But that is to say that its advancement depends upon unrestricted exhibition of this material, and this cannot be true. The Internet does not belong to pornographers, and it's clearly in the public interest to see that they don't usurp this great new technology. We don't live in a perfect society, and the Internet is merely a reflection of the larger social community. Without some mitigating influences, the strong will exploit the weak, whether a Bill Gates or a child predator. **(21)**

CONCLUSION: TECHNOLOGY MUST SERVE MAN

To argue that the strength of the Internet is chaos or that our liberty depends upon chaos is to misunderstand not only the Internet but also the fundamental nature of our liberty. It's an illusion to claim social or moral neutrality in the application of technology, even if its development may be neutral. It can be a valuable resource only when placed at the service of humanity and when it promotes our integral development for the benefit of all. **(22)**

Guiding principles simply cannot be inferred from mere technical efficiency or from the usefulness accruing to some at the

expense of others. Technology by its very nature requires uncondi-
tional respect for the fundamental interests of society. **(23)**

Internet technology must be at the service of humanity and of
our inalienable rights. It must respect the prerogatives of a civil
society, among which is the protection of children. **(24)**

Vocabulary

Write down the meanings of the following words:

- steals *proprietary* information **(1)**
- rather *apocalyptic* view **(7)**
- legal *deterrent* **(11)**
- don't have *filtering* software **(17)**
- the law is *futile* **(19)**
- cannot be *inferred* **(23)**
- usefulness *accruing* to some **(23)**
- respect the *prerogatives* **(24)**

Questions for Writing and Discussion

1. Before you read or reread Cleaver's essay, write down your own thoughts
   and experiences about pornography on the Internet. Have you run into
   sites that you find offensive? Should access to such sites be made more
   difficult? Do you think children should be protected from accessing such
   sites—either by accident or on purpose? What do you think are the best
   method(s) for such regulation: Internet software programs, parental regulation, governmental regulation? Explain.

2. Cleaver begins her essay with several scenarios describing potential
   abuses and crimes that occur online. Did you find these scenarios effective as a lead-in to her argument? Did they help you focus on her thesis?
   Should she use fewer scenarios? Why do you think she used all of these
   examples when only two dealt with child pornography on the Internet?

3. Cleaver states her case for government regulation of pornography on the
   Internet, but who is against regulation, and what are their arguments?
   What arguments opposing Internet regulation does Cleaver cite? (Are
   there other opposing arguments that Cleaver does not consider?) How
   well does Cleaver answer these opposing arguments?

4. Arguing essays make appeals to reason, to character, and to emotion. Find examples of each type of appeal in Cleaver's essay. Which type of appeal does she use most frequently? Which appeals are most or least effective? Does she rely too much on her emotional appeals (see paragraph 13, for example)? For her audience and her context (a debate), should she bolster her rational appeals with more evidence and statistics? Why or why not?

5. Imagine that you are at this debate on the Internet and that your side believes that there should be no or very little regulation of the Internet. What arguments might you make in response to Cleaver? Make a list of the possible pro-con arguments on this topic and explain which ones you will focus on as you respond to Cleaver.

PROFESSIONAL WRITING

FIELDS OF BROKEN DREAMS
SHARON BUTALA

"In wildness is the preservation of the world." Henry David Thoreau's words serve to introduce Sharon Butala's own nature ethic. Author of the best-selling book, The Perfection of the Morning, *Sharon Butala lives in Eastend, Saskatchewan. Her new novel,* Wild Stone Heart, *was published in the fall of 2000 by HarperCollins. In this essay, published in* The Globe and Mail *(March 4, 2000), Butala deplores the destruction of the small family farm, cautioning that, with its loss, we are also losing nature's diversity—and risking our souls. Butala's appeal is made convincing by her passionate voice rising from her personal connection with the land. Her evidence is set out in language which vividly captures both the beauty and the devastation of Saskatchewan's prairies and grasslands, and, in recent years, the tragedy of the land and its people wrought by the "corporatization of Western farms."*

My memories of drives in the country when I was a child in the 1940s and early 1950s, after the devastation of the 1930s, are of abandoned farmstead after abandoned farmstead, of frame farmhouses, wooden livestock sheds and optimistic hip-roofed barns collapsing slowly in their few acres of waist-high wild grasses, all of this surrounded by rows of overgrown caragana hedges and dying poplars and firs, and finished by a gap-toothed, tipsy fence lurching through wildflowers along the roadside. (1)

Then we thought such farmsteads picturesque and charming; as children we knew little of the suffering they commemorated. None of us understood that in many areas of the province, these vestiges of someone's disastrous past would hold the last relics of prairie bio-diversity. They were places where birds might nest undisturbed, where wild animals—skunks, rabbits, porcupines, weasels, foxes, badgers, gophers, mice, all kinds of insects and frogs, snakes, and deer and hunting coyotes—might find refuge from the noisy and relentless agricultural machinery, from the death-dealing chemicals, and from the monocrops of cereals where there was no place to hide from predators or to raise their young in safety, and where their natural diets, and thus the ecological cycle, had been destroyed. (2)

Refuge too, could be found in the unplowed and wild road allowances between farms, and in the grounds of the no-longer used schoolhouses, and the areas too hilly or rocky for the farming equipment of the day. Bluffs (as we call clumps of trees on the prairies) dotted the farmers' fields not so many years ago, providing shelter, food and nesting places. Where the land was wet—the sloughs, ponds and boggy areas—a farmer might shake his head in exasperation, but he had no choice but to farm around them and leave the beaver, muskrat, ducks, geese, wild swans and herons to their natural places in nature. (3)

The land was beautiful then, both the treed parkland areas in central Saskatchewan where I was raised, and the fabulous and astonishing grasslands in the southwest corner of Saskatchewan where at the age of 36 I came to live. Then Saskatchewan was a paradise of natural beauty, full of wild animals and birds, in winter where the acres of snow and ice would catch the light and glow like burnished jewels, or where the fields of grass in summer would record in moving shadow all the changes of the wild sky, and shimmer and bow and sing softly with every breeze. (4)

It was a paradise. As anyone who has lived in it knows, beauty is a requirement of the human soul. And in it is to be found truth and peace and awe—awe as the way into the world of spirit, an approach to the Creator—and the emotion on which the soul feeds in order to grow. (5)

This last few months it would be impossible not to know that we're in the middle of an agricultural crisis, this one caused by globalization subsidies resulting in the demise of the family farm: while Europe supports its wheat farmers with subsidies of more than $5 a bushel, Ottawa provides about 40 cents. Over the past three generations, the number of farms in my province has fallen steadily, from 142 000 in the 1936 census to less than 60 000 now. **(6)**

It's never a pretty sight to watch people go bankrupt. But now many are telling the story of how in late middle age they've lost everything after a lifetime of work that chiefly benefited others. The small family farm is being wiped out of existence to be replaced by monster enterprises where no birds sing. What nobody is saying is that along with the human tragedies, the corporatization of Western farms, their growth into vast acreages, means the virtual wiping out of what little biodiversity is left out here, as well as the destruction of that soul-stirring beauty. **(7)**

As the years have passed, markets grown more competitive, farms have had to get bigger and bigger to survive. This has meant that farm machinery has also gotten bigger in order that, given our short growing season, a farmer can get all his land seeded rapidly in spring and harvested before the first snowfall. Bigger means clumsier, so that going around old farmsteads or unused country schoolhouses on one's land, or squeezing by the old windbreaks planted by settlers long gone is a major irritation, as is any acre of land (or square foot) judged to be "unproductive" in terms of saleable monocrops. And so old buildings are bulldozed, burned and buried, windbreaks uprooted and carted away, the sites smoothed over as if there'd never been anything there. The following spring they're seeded to crop. Wetland is drained and filled too, and road allowances plowed and seeded. **(8)**

Thus, both plant and animal biodiversity is lost, along with the natural beauty that is the precious inheritance of all of us. But even more that is essential to our human destiny is lost. When all the small farmers are gone there will be no one left, except for those few Amerindian people living in the traditional manner, who understands how nature works in an intimate, personal, daily way over a small piece of ground. This is wisdom gleaned slowly over generations, for the most part never expressed coherently nor in writing, and thus, not saved in any way accessible to the rest of us. **(9)**

Never mind scientists: The humble ones have always admitted that their knowledge gleaned in laboratories or controlled studies on carefully engineered pieces of land could never match the wisdom of a First Nations elder or an old farmer who'd spent his life in one place in the countryside. Never mind the new environmentalists, mostly raised in the city, whose knowledge about land tends to be acquired in universities or by hearsay. Or if this environmentalist lives in the country he's likely to have retired there, with money in the bank; he doesn't need to know his land and the seasons and the weather patterns over it the way a smaller farmer or a rancher needs to know his. **(10)**

Here is perhaps the most potent reason for all to save small-scale farms: because those who farmed in this way had the time to ponder and enjoy and be instructed and inspired by nature. In their close daily encounters with nature, month after month, year after year, they came to know their few acres of earth with such loving intensity that it approached the mystical—although they'd never say so out loud. **(11)**

When there's no one left out here except people whose days on the land are spent 20 feet off the ground in the air-conditioned cabs of tractors so massive they dwarf the shacks in which a lot of prairie people were raised, when there isn't a scrap of native grass left, or any more bluffs of trees, who will remember how to be on the land—as Native people know, as old, small-scale farmers and ranchers know? Who will remember how to listen to land? **(12)**

The growing of vast acreages of crops and the global scramble for markets and money that benefits only a few costs the rest of us our birthright as members of the human race. It is a cost far too high for any nation to pay. For land is still the source of our species and the place to which we return in death. **(13)**

Vocabulary

Write down the meanings of the following words:

- *biodiversity* **(2)**
- *sloughs* **(3)**
- *demise* **(6)**
- *corporatization* **(7)**

Questions for Writing and Discussion

1. Do you consider yourself an environmentalist—someone who is in favour of preserving wilderness areas? Or do you believe that the benefits of land development outweigh those of environmental protection? Explain, using an example from your own experience or observation.

2. Which of Butala's arguments do you find most persuasive? Which are least persuasive?

3. An argument contains a *claim, reasons* that support the claim or refute the opposition, and *evidence.*

   • What sentence or sentences best illustrate Butala's overall claim or thesis for this essay? Does she make a claim of fact, value, cause, or solution—or some combination of these?

   • List the reasons she gives to support her claim. Are there opposing arguments she does not address? Suggest at least one. Why do you think Butala chooses not to confront the opposition?

   • For *one* of her reasons, list the evidence, facts, examples, or testimony that Butala gives.

4. Note passages in which Butala's *appeal to character* is evident. Where is she most reasonable? least reasonable? In your judgment, does her persona help or hurt her argument?

5. Cite an example in which Butala uses an *emotional appeal.* Does this passage make her argument more effective? Explain.

6. Assume you are the spokesperson for a global conglomerate of corporations who are responsible for the destruction Butala deplores. Write a short response to Butala justifying your position. Choose an adversarial or Rogerian strategy, whichever would work best with Butala.

ARGUING: THE WRITING PROCESS

■ **ASSIGNMENT FOR ARGUING**   For this assignment, choose a subject that interests you or relates to your own experience. You may even choose a subject that you have already written about for this class. Then examine the subject for a debatable claim of fact, value, cause and effect, or policy that you could make about it. If the claim is arguable, you have a focus for your arguing paper. Analyze your probable audience to guide your argumentative strategy. (Avoid ready-made pro-con subjects such as abortion, drinking age, drugs, and euthanasia *unless* you have clear beliefs based on your own experience.)

CHOOSING A SUBJECT

Consider the following ideas:

   • Brainstorm possible ideas for argumentative subjects from the other courses you are currently taking or have taken. What controversial issues in psychology, art, philosophy, journalism, biology, nutrition, engineering, physical education, or literature have you discussed in your classes? Ask current or past instructors for possible controversial topics relating to their courses.

• Newspapers and magazines are full of controversial subjects in sports, medicine, law, business, and family. Browse through current issues looking for possible subjects. Check news items, editorials, and cartoons. Look for subjects related to your own interests, your job, your leisure activities, or your experiences.

• Interview your friends, family, or classmates. What controversial issues are affecting their lives most directly? What would they most like to change about their lives? What has irritated or angered them most in the recent past?

COLLECTING

Narrowing and Focussing Your Claim   Narrow your subject to a specific topic, and sharpen your focus by applying the "Wh" questions. If your subject is "grades," your responses might be as follows:

Subject: Grades

• *Who:* College students

• *What:* Letter grades

• *When:* In first and second years

• *Where:* Especially in non-major courses

• *Why:* What purpose do grades serve in non-major courses?

Determine what claim or claims you want to make. Make sure that your claim is *arguable*. (Remember that claims can overlap; an argument may combine several related claims.)

Claim of Fact

• Letter grades exist. (not arguable)

• Employers consider grades when hiring. (slightly more arguable, but not very controversial)

• Grades do not measure learning. (very arguable)

Claim About Cause or Effect

• Grades create anxiety for students. (not very arguable)

• Grades actually prevent discovery and learning. (arguable)

Claim About Value

- Grades are not fair. (not very arguable: "fairness" can usually be determined)

- Grades are bad because they discourage individual initiative. (arguable)

- Grades are good because they give students an incentive to learn. (arguable)

Claim About a Solution or Policy

- Grades should be eliminated altogether. (arguable—but difficult)

- Grades should be eliminated in humanities courses. (arguable)

- Grades should change to pass/fail in non-major courses. (arguable—and more practical)

Focussing and narrowing your *claim* helps determine what evidence you need to collect. Use your observing, remembering, reading, and investigative skills to gather the evidence. *Note:* An argumentative essay should not be a mathematical equation that uses only abstract and impersonal evidence. *Your experience* can be crucial to a successful argumentative essay. Start by doing the *remembering* exercises. Your audience wants to know not only why you are writing on this particular *topic,* but also why the subject is of interest to *you.*

Remembering   Use *freewriting, looping, branching,* or *clustering* to recall experiences, ideas, events, and people who are relevant to your claim. If you are writing about grades, brainstorm about how *your* teachers used grades, how you reacted to specific grades in one specific class, how your friends or parents reacted, and what you felt or thought. These prewriting exercises will help you understand your claim and give you specific examples that you can use for evidence.

Observing   If possible for your topic, collect data and evidence by observing, firsthand, the facts, values, effects, or possible solutions related to your claim. *Repeated* observation will give you good inductive evidence to support your argument.

Investigating   For most argumentative essays, some research or investigation is essential. Because it is difficult to imagine all the valid counter-arguments, interview friends, classmates, family, co-workers, and authorities on your topic. From the library, gather books and articles that contain arguments in support of your claim. *Note:* As you do research in the library, make photocopies of key passages from relevant sources to hand in with your essay. If you cite sources from your research, list them on a "Works Cited" page following your essay. (See Chapter 11 for the proper format.)

SHAPING

As you begin your shaping activities, reconsider your audience. Imagine one real person who might be among your readers. Is this person open-minded and likely to be convinced by your evidence? Does this person represent the opposing position? Would a Rogerian strategy be effective in this case? Reread your collecting notes and *underline* the reasons and evidence that would be most effective for this reader. After reconsidering your audience and rereading your collecting notes, try the shaping strategies that follow.

List of "Pro" and "Con" Arguments   Either on paper or in a computer file, write out your *claim*, and then list the arguments for your position (pro) and the arguments for the opposing positions (con). After you have made the list, match up arguments by drawing lines, as indicated. (On the computer file, move "Con" column arguments so they appear directly opposite the corresponding "Pro" column arguments.)

Claim: Grades should be changed to pass/fail in non-major courses.

PRO	CON
Grades inhibit learning by putting too much emphasis on competition.	Grades actually promote learning by getting students to study as hard as possible.
Pass/fail grading encourages students to explore non-major fields.	Students should be encouraged to compete with majors. They may want to change majors and need to know if they can compete.
Grade competition with majors in the field can be discouraging.	If students don't have traditional grading, they won't take non-major courses seriously.
Some students do better without the pressure of grades; they need to find out if they can motivate themselves without grades, but they shouldn't have to risk grades in their major fields to discover that.	

If some pro and con arguments "match," you will be able to argue against the con and for your claim at the same time. If some arguments do not "match," you will need to consider them separately. The outlines below suggest ways of organizing your pro and con arguments.

Outlines for Arguments   For more than two thousand years, writers and speakers have been trying to determine the most effective means to persuade audiences. One of the oldest outlines for a successful argument comes from classical rhetoric. The following six-part outline is intended as a guideline rather than a rigid list. Test this outline; see if it will work for *your* argument.

Introduction:	Announces subject; *gets audience's interest and attention;* establishes a trustworthy character for the writer
Narration:	Gives *background,* context, statement of problem, or definition
Partition:	States thesis or *claim,* outlines or *maps* arguments
Argument:	Makes *arguments* and gives *evidence* for the claim or thesis
Refutation:	Shows why *opposing arguments* are not true or valid
Conclusion:	Summarizes arguments, suggests solution, *ties into the introduction or background*

Most arguments have these features, but not necessarily in this order. Some writers prefer to respond to or refute opposing arguments before giving the arguments in support of their claims. When con and pro arguments match, refuting an argument followed by the argument for your claim may work best. As you organize your own arguments, put your strongest argument last and your weakest argument either first or in the middle.

Because most short argumentative essays contain the introduction, narration, and partition all in a few introductory paragraphs, you may use the following abbreviated outlines for argument:

Outline 1	Introduction (attention getter, background, claim or thesis, map)
	Your arguments
	Refutation of opposing arguments
	Conclusion
Outline 2	Introduction
	Refutation of opposing arguments
	Your arguments
	Conclusion
Outline 3	Introduction
	Refutation of first opposing argument that matches your first argument
	Refutation of second opposing argument that matches your second argument, and so on
	Additional arguments
	Conclusion

For Rogerian arguments, you can follow one of the above outlines, but the emphasis, tone, and attitude are different:

Introduction:	Attention getter, background
	Claim (often downplayed to reduce threat)
	Map (often omitted)
	Appeal to character (crucial to Rogerian argument)
Opposing arguments:	State opposing arguments fairly
	Show where, how, or when those arguments may be valid; establish common ground
Your arguments:	State your position fairly
	Show where, how, or when your arguments are valid
Resolution:	Present compromise position
	State your solution to the problem, and show its advantages to both sides

Developing Arguments   Think of your argument as a series of *because* statements, each supported by evidence, statistics, testimony, expert opinion, data, specific examples from your experience, or a combination of these.

Thesis or Claim: Grades should be abolished in non-major courses

Reason 1	Because they may keep a student from attempting a difficult non-major course *Statistics, testimony, data, and examples*
Reason 2	Because competition with majors in the field can be discouraging *Statistics, testimony, data, and examples*
Reason 3	Because grades inhibit students' learning in non-major fields *Statistics, testimony, data, and examples*

You can develop each reason using a variety of strategies. The following strategies may help you generate additional reasons and examples:

Definition:	Define the crucial terms or ideas. (What do you mean by *learning?*)
Comparison:	Compare the background, situation, and context with another similar context. (What other schools have tried pass/fail grading for non-major courses? How has it worked?)
Process:	How does or should a change occur? (How do non-majors become discouraged? How should a school implement pass/fail in grading?)

These strategies may help you develop an argument coherently and effectively. If several strategies are possible, consider which would be most effective for your *audience.*

DRAFTING

You will never really know "enough" about your subject or have "enough" evidence. At some point, however, you must stop collecting and start your draft. The most frequent problem in drafting an argumentative essay is delaying the actual writing too long, until the deadline is too close.

For argumentative essays, start with a working order or sequence and sketch an outline on paper or in your head. Additional examples and appeals to reason, character, or emotion may occur to you as you develop your argument or refute opposing arguments. In addition, if you have done some research, have your notes, photocopies of key data, statistics, quotations, and citations of authorities close at hand. As you write, you will discover that some information or arguments simply don't fit into the flow of your essay. Don't force arguments into your draft if they no longer seem to belong.

REVISING

Argumentation is the most public of the purposes for writing. It requires that you become aware of many different points of view. You must counter the arguments of others and recognize the flaws in your own logic. Test your argument by having friends or classmates read it. Explain your claim, your focus, and your intended audience. Ask your readers to look for possible opposing arguments that you need to counter or weaknesses in your own argument or evidence. Were your appeals effective? Ask your readers if your argument should be more adversarial or more Rogerian.

Guidelines for Revision

- **When you finish your draft, reconsider your *audience*.** Persuading your audience requires that you tailor your reasons and evidence to your audience and situation. Do an audience analysis, and then reread your draft and make appropriate changes.

- **Ask a class member or friend to read your draft to determine the intended audience for your argument.** See which arguments your reader thinks would not be effective for your audience.

- **Ask your reader to tell you what kind of *claim* you are making, whether your arguments or counterarguments are logical, and whether your ethical or emotional appeals are effective for your audience.**

- **Which of your *because* arguments are most effective? Least effective?** Should you change the outline or structure that you initially chose?

- **Revise your draft to avoid fallacies or errors in reasoning.** Errors in logic create two problems: They can destroy your rational appeal and open your argument to a logical rebuttal, and they lessen your credibility—and thus reduce your appeal to character. (Review the list of fallacies below.)

- **Support your reasons with evidence:** *data, facts, statistics, quotations, observations, testimony, statistics,* or *specific examples from your experience.* Check your collecting notes once again for additional evidence to add to your weakest argument. Is there a weak or unsupported argument that you should simply omit?

- **Signal the major arguments and counterarguments in your partition or map.** Between paragraphs, use clear transitions and paragraph hooks.

- **If you cite sources in your essay, check the** *accuracy* **of your statistics, quotations, and source references.** (See Chapter 11 for the proper format of in-text documentation and the "Works Cited" page.)

- **Revise sentences to improve conciseness and clarity.**

- **Edit sentences for grammar, punctuation, and spelling.**

Revising Fallacies in Logic

Listed below are common fallacies in logic. Reread your draft and revise as appropriate to eliminate these logical errors.

- *Hasty generalization:* Conclusion not logically justified by sufficient or unbiased evidence. If your friend Leora tells you that Professor Paramecium is a hard grader because he gave her a 36 percent on the first biology test, she is making a hasty generalization. It may be *true*—Prof P. may *be* a difficult grader—but Leora's logic is not valid. She cannot logically draw that conclusion from a sample of one; the rest of the class may have received grades of between 80 and 100.

- *Post hoc ergo propter hoc:* Literally, "after this, therefore because of this." Just because Event B *occurred after* Event A does not mean that A *necessarily caused* B. You washed your car in the morning, and it rained in the afternoon. Though we joke about how it always rains after we wash the car, there is, of course, no causal relationship between the two events. "I forgot to leave the porch light on when I went out last night, and someone robbed my house": Without further evidence, we cannot assume that the lack of light contributed to the robbery. A more obvious cause might be the back door left unlocked.

- *Genetic fallacy:* Arguing that the origins of a person, object, or institution determine its character, nature, or worth. Like the post hoc fallacy, the genetic fallacy is an error in causal relationships.

This automobile was made in Oshawa. It'll probably fall apart after 10 000 kilometres.

He started Celestial Seasonings Herb Teas just to make a quick buck; it's just another phony yuppie product.

The second half of each statement *may* or *may not* be true; the logical error is in assuming that the origin of something will necessarily determine its worth or quality. Stereotyping is frequently caused by a genetic fallacy.

- *Begging the question:* Loading the conclusion in the claim. Arguing that "pornography should be banned because it corrupts our youth" is a logical claim. However, saying that "filthy and corrupting pornography should be banned" is begging the question: The conclusion that the writer should *prove* (that pornography corrupts) is assumed in the claim. Other examples: "Those useless psychology classes should be dropped from the curriculum"; "Senator Swingle's sexist behaviour should be censured by Parliament"; "Everyone knows that our ineffective drug control program is a miserable failure." The writers must *prove* that the psychology classes are useless, that Senator Swingle is sexist, and that the drug program is a failure.

- *Circular argument:* A sentence or argument that restates rather than proves. Thus, it goes in a circle: "Prime Minister Trudeau was a great communicator because he had that knack of talking effectively to the people." The terms in the beginning of the sentence *(great communicator)* and the end of the sentence *(talking effectively)* are interchangeable. The sentence ends where it started.

- *Either/or:* An oversimplification that reduces alternatives to only two choices, thereby creating a false dilemma. Statements such as "Love it or leave it" attempt to reduce the alternatives to two. If you don't love your school, your town, or your country, you don't have to leave: A third choice is to change it and make it better. Proposed solutions frequently have an either/or fallacy: "Either we ban boxing or hundreds of young men will be senselessly killed." A third alternative is to change boxing's rules or equipment. "If we don't provide farmers with low-interest loans, they will go bankrupt." Increasing prices for farm products might be a better alternative.

- *Faulty comparison or analogy:* Basing an argument on a comparison of two things, ideas, events, or situations that are similar but not identical. Although comparisons or analogies are often effective in argument, they can hide logical problems. "We can solve the cocaine problem the same way we reduced the impaired driving problem: Attack it with increased enforcement and mandatory jail sentences." Although the situations are similar, they are not identical.

The solution to the problem of impaired driving will not necessarily work for drugs. An analogy is an extended comparison that uses something simple or familiar to explain something complex or less familiar. "Solving a mathematics problem is like baking a cake: You have to take it one step at a time. First, you assemble your ingredients or your known data. . . ." Like baking, solving a problem does involve a process; unlike baking, however, mathematics is more exact. Changing the amount of flour in a recipe by 1 percent will not make the cake fall; changing a numeric value by 1 percent, however, may ruin the whole problem. The point, however, is not to avoid comparisons or analogies. Simply make sure that your conclusions are qualified; acknowledge the *differences* between the two things compared as well as the similarities.

- *Ad hominem (literally, "to the man"):* An attack on the character of the individual or the opponent rather than his or her actual opinions, arguments, or qualifications: "Susan Davidson, the crown attorney, drinks heavily. There's no way she can present an effective case." This is an attack on Ms. Davidson's character rather than an analysis of her legal talents. Her record in court may be excellent.

- *Ad populum (literally, "to the people"):* An emotional appeal to positive concepts (God, mother, country, liberty, democracy, apple pie) or negative concepts (fascism, atheism) rather than a direct discussion of the real issue.

- *Red herring and straw man:* Diversionary tactics designed to avoid confronting the key issue. *Red herring* refers to the practice of dragging a smelly fish across the trail to divert tracking dogs away from the real quarry. A red herring occurs when writers avoid countering an opposing argument directly: "Of course equal pay for women is an important issue, but I wonder whether women really want to take the responsibility that comes with higher-paying jobs. Do they really want the additional stress?" This writer diverts attention away from the argument about equal pay to another issue, stress—thus, a red herring. In the *straw man* diversion, the writer sets up an artificially easy argument to refute in place of the real issue. Former President Richard Nixon's famous "Checkers" speech is a good example. Accused of spending $18 000 in campaign gifts for personal use, Nixon described how he received Checkers, a little black-and-white spotted cocker spaniel dog. Because his daughter Tricia loved this dog, Nixon decided to keep it. Surely, there's nothing wrong with that, is there? The "Checkers" argument is a "straw man" diversion: Justifying his personal use of this gift was much easier than explaining how and why he spent the $18 000. Avoid red herring and straw man tactics by either refuting an argument directly or acknowledging that it has some merit. Don't just change the subject.

RESPONDING
TO LITERATURE

Responding to literature requires that readers participate imaginatively while they read a literary work, reread to see how the parts of the work relate to the whole, and share their interpretations of a piece of literature with other readers.

First, readers must *imagine* and recreate that special world described by the writer. The first sentences of a short story, for example, throw open a door to a world that—attractive or repulsive—tempts our curiosity and imagination. Like Alice in *Alice in Wonderland,* we cannot resist following a white rabbit with pink eyes who mutters to himself, checks his watch, and then zips down a rabbit hole and into an imaginary world.

Here are three opening sentences of three very different short stories:

> Just below Manawaka, where the Wachakwa River ran brown and noisy over the pebbles, the scrub oak and grey-green willow and chokecherry bushes grew in a dense thicket.
>
> —Margaret Laurence, "The Loons"

> As Gregor Samsa awoke one morning from uneasy dreams he found himself transformed in his bed into a gigantic insect.
>
> —Franz Kafka, "The Metamorphosis"

> There are times even now, when I awake at four o'clock in the morning with the terrible fear that I have overslept; when I imagine that my father is waiting for me in the room below the darkened stairs or that the shorebound men are tossing pebbles against my window while blowing their hands and stomping their feet impatiently on the frozen steadfast earth.
>
> —Alistair MacLeod, "The Boat"

Responding to literature does not mean passively reacting to the writer's story. As readers, we should anticipate, imagine, feel, worry, and question. A story is like an empty balloon that we must inflate with the warm breath of our imagination and experience. Our participation makes us partners with the author in the artistic creation.

Responding to literature also requires that readers *reread.* If we read a story or a poem only once, we have misunderstood the whole point of literature. Great literature is worthy of study because the more we reread, the more we learn and discover. If we assume that the purpose of a story is merely to entertain us or to provide a moment's diversion, then we should stick to television sitcoms written for an audience of couch potatoes who want only predictable, unimaginative plots and canned studio laughter.

Rereading requires two distinct but related operations. First, you should *reread for yourself,* that is, reread to write down your ideas, questions, feelings, and reactions. To heighten your role in creating a story, you should note, in the margins, your questions and responses to important events, main characters, bits of description, and images that catch your attention. Don't just underline or highlight passages. Actually *write* your responses in the margin.

Second, you should *reread with a writer's eye*. In fiction, identify the main and minor characters. Look for and note the conflicts between characters. Mark passages that contain *foreshadowing*—that urge you to think ahead imaginatively. Pinpoint sentences that reveal the narrative point of view. Use the appropriate critical terms (*character, plot, conflict, point of view, setting, style,* and *theme*) to help you reread with a writer's eye and to see how the parts of a story relate to the whole. Each critical term is a tool—a magnifying glass that helps you understand and interpret the story more clearly.

In addition to rereading, responding to literature requires that readers *share* ideas, reactions, and interpretations. Sharing usually begins in small-group or class discussions, but it continues as you explain your interpretation in writing. A work of literature is not a mathematical equation with a single answer. Great literature is worth interpreting precisely because each reader responds differently. The purpose of literature is to encourage you to reflect on your life and the lives of others—to look for new ways of seeing and understanding your world—and ultimately to expand your world. Sharing is crucial to appreciating literature. Writing about your responses and sharing them with other readers helps you "reread" your own ideas in order to explain them fully and clearly to other readers.

■ RESPONDING TO A SHORT STORY   Read and respond to Kate Chopin's "The Story of an Hour." Use your imagination to help create the story as you read. Then *reread* the story, noting in the margin your questions and responses. When you finish rereading and annotating your reactions, write your interpretation of the last line of the story.

PROFESSIONAL WRITING

THE STORY OF AN HOUR
KATE CHOPIN

Kate O'Flaherty Chopin (1851–1904) was an American writer whose mother was French and Creole and whose father was Irish. In 1870, she moved from St. Louis to New Orleans with her husband, Oscar Chopin, and over the next ten years she gave birth to five sons. After her husband died in 1882, Chopin returned to St. Louis to begin a new life as a writer. Many of her best stories are about Louisiana people and places, and her most famous novel, The Awakening, *tells the story of Edna, a woman who leaves her marriage and her children to fulfill herself through an artistic career.*

Knowing that Mrs. Mallard was afflicted with a heart trouble, great care was taken to break to her as gently as possible the news of her husband's death. **(1)**

It was her sister Josephine who told her, in broken sentences, veiled hints that revealed in half concealing. Her husband's friend Richards was there, too, near her. It was he who had been in the newspaper office when intelligence of the railroad disaster was received, with Brently Mallard's name leading the list of "killed." He had only taken the time to assure himself of its truth by a second telegram, and had hastened to forestall any less careful, less tender friend in bearing the sad message. **(2)**

She did not hear the story as many women have heard the same, with a paralyzed inability to accept its significance. She wept at once, with sudden, wild abandonment, in her sister's arms. When the storm of grief had spent itself she went away to her room alone. She would have no one follow her. **(3)**

There stood, facing the open window, a comfortable, roomy armchair. Into this she sank, pressed down by a physical exhaustion that haunted her body and seemed to reach into her soul. **(4)**

She could see in the open square before her house the tops of trees that were all aquiver with the new spring life. The delicious breath of rain was in the air. In the street below a peddler was crying his wares. The notes of a distant song which someone was singing reached her faintly, and countless sparrows were twittering in the eaves. **(5)**

There were patches of blue sky showing here and there through the clouds that had met and piled one above the other in the west facing her window. **(6)**

She sat with her head thrown back upon the cushion of the chair quite motionless, except when a sob came up into her throat and shook her, as a child who has cried itself to sleep continues to sob in its dreams. **(7)**

She was young, with a fair, calm face, whose lines bespoke repression and even a certain strength. But now there was a dull stare in her eyes, whose gaze was fixed away off yonder on one of those patches of blue sky. It was not a glance of reflection, but rather indicated a suspension of intelligent thought. **(8)**

There was something coming to her and she was waiting for it, fearfully. What was it? She did not know; it was too subtle and elusive to name. But she felt it, creeping out of the sky, reaching toward her through the sounds, the scents, the color that filled the air. **(9)**

Now her bosom rose and fell tumultuously. She was beginning to recognize this thing that was approaching to possess her, and she was striving to beat it back with her will—as powerless as her two white slender hands would have been. **(10)**

When she abandoned herself a little whispered word escaped her slightly parted lips. She said it over and over under her breath: "Free, free, free!" The vacant stare and the look of terror that had followed it went from her eyes. They stayed keen and bright. Her pulses beat fast, and the coursing blood warmed and relaxed every inch of her body. **(11)**

She did not stop to ask if it were not a monstrous joy that held her. A clear and exalted perception enabled her to dismiss the suggestion as trivial. **(12)**

She knew that she would weep again when she saw the kind, tender hands folded in death; the face that had never looked save with love upon her, fixed and gray and dead. But she saw beyond that bitter moment a long procession of years to come that would belong to her absolutely. And she opened and spread her arms out to them in welcome. **(13)**

There would be no one to live for during those coming years; she would live for herself. There would be no powerful will bending her in that blind persistence with which men and women believe they have a right to impose a private will upon a fellow creature. A kind intention or a cruel intention made the act seem no less a crime as she looked upon it in that brief moment of illumination. **(14)**

And yet she had loved him—sometimes. Often she had not. What did it matter! What could love, the unsolved mystery, count for in face of this possession of self-assertion which she suddenly recognized as the strongest impulse of her being. **(15)**

"Free! Body and soul free!" she kept whispering. **(16)**

Josephine was kneeling before the closed door with her lips to the keyhole, imploring for admission. "Louise, open the door! I beg; open the door—you will make yourself ill. What are you doing, Louise? For heaven's sake open the door." **(17)**

"Go away. I am not making myself ill." No; she was drinking in a very elixir of life through that open window. **(18)**

Her fancy was running riot along those days ahead of her. Spring days, and summer days, and all sorts of days that would be her own. She breathed a quick prayer that life might be long. It was only yesterday she had thought with a shudder that life might be long. **(19)**

She arose at length and opened the door to her sister's importunities. There was a feverish triumph in her eyes, and she carried herself unwittingly like a goddess of Victory. She clasped her sister's waist, and together they descended the stairs. Richards stood waiting for them at the bottom. **(20)**

Someone was opening the front door with a latchkey. It was Brently Mallard who entered, a little travel-stained, composedly carrying his grip-sack and umbrella. He had been far from the scene of accident, and did not even know there had been one. He stood amazed at Josephine's piercing cry; at Richards's quick motion to screen him from the view of his wife. **(21)**

But Richards was too late. **(22)**

When the doctors came they said she had died of heart disease—of joy that kills. **(23)**

TECHNIQUES FOR RESPONDING TO LITERATURE

As you read and respond to a work of literature, keep the following techniques in mind.

- **Understanding the assignment and selecting a possible purpose and audience.** Unless stated otherwise in your assignment, your purpose is to *interpret* a work of literature. Your audience will be other members of your class, including the teacher.

- **Actively reading, annotating, and discussing the literary work.** Remember that literature often contains *highly condensed experiences*. In order to give imaginative life to literature, you need to reread patiently both the major events and the seemingly insignificant passages. In discussions, look for the differences between your responses and other readers' ideas.

- **Focussing your essay on a single, clearly defined interpretation.** In your essay, clearly state your main idea or thesis, focussing on a single idea or aspect of the piece of literature. Your thesis should *not be a statement of fact*. Whether you are explaining, evaluating, or arguing, your interpretation must be clearly stated.

- **Supporting your interpretation with evidence.** Because your readers will probably have different interpretations, you must show which specific characters, events, conflicts, images, or themes prompted your response, and you must support your interpretation. *Do not merely retell the major events of the story—your readers have already read it.*

PURPOSES FOR RESPONDING TO LITERATURE

In responding to literature, you should be guided by the purposes that you have already practised in previous chapters. As you read a piece of literature and respond in the margin, begin by writing *for yourself*. Your purposes are to observe, feel, remember, understand, and relate the work of literature to your own life: What is happening? What memories does it trigger? How does it make you feel? Why is this passage confusing? Why do you like or dislike this character? Literature has special, personal value. You should write about literature initially in order to discover and understand its importance in your life.

When you write an interpretative essay, however, you are writing *for* others. You are sharing your experience in working with the author as imaginative partners in recreating the work. Your purposes will often be mixed, but an interpretative essay often contains elements of *explaining, evaluating, problem solving,* and *arguing*.

- **Explaining.** Interpretative essays about literature explain the *what, why,* and *how* of a piece of literature. What is the key subject? What is the most important event or character? What are the major conflicts or the key images? What motivates a character? How does a character's world build or unravel? How does a story meet or fail to meet our expectations? How did our interpretations develop? Each of these questions might lead to an interpretative essay that explains the *what, why,* and *how* of your response.

- **Evaluating.** Readers and writers often talk about "appreciating" a work of literature. *Appreciating* means establishing its value or worth. It may mean praising the work's literary virtues; it may mean finding faults or weaknesses. Usually, evaluating essays measure *both strengths and weaknesses,* according to specific criteria. What important standards for literature do you wish to apply? How does the work in question measure up? What kinds of readers might find this story worth reading? An evaluative essay cites evidence to show why a story is exciting, boring, dramatic, puzzling, vivid, relevant, or memorable.

- **Problem solving.** Writers of interpretative essays occasionally take a problem-solving approach, focussing on how the reader overcomes obstacles in understanding the story or how the author of a story solved problems in writing key scenes, creating characters, setting a plot in motion, and creating and resolving conflicts. Particularly if you like to write fiction yourself, you may wish to take the writer's point of view: How did the writer solve (or fail to solve) problems of setting, character, plot, or theme?

- **Arguing.** As readers share responses, they may discover that their interpretations diverge sharply from the ideas of other readers. Does "The Story of an Hour" have a "feminist" theme? Is it about women or about human nature in general? Is the main character admirable, or is she selfish? In interpretative essays, writers sometimes argue for their beliefs. They present evidence that refutes an opposing interpretation and supports their own reading.

Most interpretative essays about literature will be focussed by these purposes, whether used singly or in combination. Writers should *select* the purpose(s) that are most appropriate for the work of literature and their own responses.

RESPONDING TO SHORT FICTION

RESPONDING AS A READER

Begin by noting in the margins your reactions at key points. *Summarize* in your own words what is happening in the story. Write down your *observations* or *reactions* to striking or surprising passages. Ask yourself *questions* about ambiguous or confusing passages. Following are examples written by students that illustrate all three kinds of responses.

Summary Comments

Mrs. Mallard is initially paralyzed by the news.

Mrs. Mallard feels her sister will protect her. She weeps in her sister's arms.

From the security of her chair, she stares at life outside her window.

Mrs. Mallard is young, but the lines on her face reveal repression.

Mrs. Mallard now feels "free, free, free" of the bonds of marriage.

News of her husband's death does not kill her, but news of his life does.

Observations and Reactions

Mrs. Mallard has "heart trouble"—possible double meaning.

Although Mrs. Mallard is experiencing shock and grief, outside her window the world is full of life.

The mistaken belief that men and women have a right to impose their will on others—this may be the point of the story.

Joy that kills = monstrous joy.

She does not die of the joy that kills—she dies of killed joy.

Questions

Why does the "storm" of grief come so quickly and then disappear?

She would live for herself: Is this selfishness or just a desire to be free?

Why does Chopin make Mrs. Mallard seem powerless, as though she is overcome by a fever?

Should we admire Mrs. Mallard for wanting her freedom?

Is this the story of an hour or the story of her life?

READING WITH A WRITER'S EYE

After you respond initially and make your marginal annotations, use the following basic elements of fiction to help you *analyze how the parts of a short story relate to the whole.* Pay attention to how setting or plot affects the character, or how style and setting affect the theme. Because analysis artificially separates plot, character, and theme, look for ways to *synthesize* the parts: Seeing how these parts relate to each other should suggest an idea, focus, or angle to use in your interpretation.

Character   A short story usually focusses on a *major character*—particularly on how that character faces conflicts, undergoes changes, or reveals himself or herself. *Minor characters* may be flat (one-dimensional), static (unchanging), or stereotyped. To get a start on analyzing character, diagram the *conflicts* between or among characters. Examine characters for motivation: What causes them to behave as they do? Is their behaviour affected by *internal* or *external* forces? Do the major characters reveal themselves *directly* (through their thoughts, dialogue, and actions) or *indirectly* (through what other people say, think, or do)?

Plot   *Plot* is the sequence of events in a story, but it is also the cause-and-effect relationship of one event to another. As you study a story's plot, pay attention to *exposition, foreshadowing, conflict, climax,* and *denouement.* To clarify elements of the plot, draw a time line for the story, listing in chronological order every event—including events that occur before the story opens. *Exposition* describes the initial circumstances and reveals what has happened before the story opens. *Foreshadowing* is an author's hint of what will occur before it happens. *Conflicts* within characters, between characters, and between characters and their environment may explain why one event leads to the next. The *climax* is the high point, the point of no return, or the most dramatic moment in a story. At the climax of a story, readers discover something important about the main character(s). *Denouement* literally means the "unravelling" of the complications and conflicts at the end of the story. In "The Story of an Hour," climax and denouement occur almost at the same time, in the last lines of the story.

Narrative Point of View   Fiction is usually narrated from either the first-person or the third-person point of view.

A *first-person narrator* is a character who tells the story from his or her point of view. A first-person narrator may be a minor or a major character. This character may be relatively *reliable* (trustworthy) or *unreliable* (naive or misleading). Although reliable first-person narrators may invite the reader to identify with their perspectives or predicaments, unreliable narrators may cause readers to be wary of their naive judgments or unbalanced states of mind.

A *third-person omniscient narrator* is not a character or participant in the story. Omniscient narrators are assumed to know everything about the characters and events. They move through space and time, giving readers necessary information at any point in the story. A *selective omniscient narrator* usually limits his or her focus to a single character's experiences and thoughts, as Kate Chopin focusses on Mrs. Mallard in "The Story of an Hour." One kind of selective omniscient point of view is *stream-of-consciousness narration,* in which the author presents the thoughts, memories, and associations of one character in the story. Omniscient narrators may be *intrusive,* jumping into the story to give their editorial judgments, or they may be *objective,* removing themselves from the action and the minds of the characters. An objective point of view creates the impression that events are being recorded by a camera or acted on a stage.

Reminder: As you reread a story, do not stop with analysis. Do not quit, for example, after you have identified and labelled the point of view. Determine how the point of view affects your reaction to the central character or to your understanding of the theme. How would a different narrative point of view change the story? If a different character told the story, how would that affect the theme?

Setting   *Setting* is the physical place, scene, and time of the story. It also includes the social or historical context of the story. The setting in "The

Story of an Hour" is the house and the room in which Mrs. Mallard waits, but it is also the social and historical time frame. *Setting is usually important for what it reveals about the characters, the plot, or the theme of the story.* Does the setting reflect a character's state of mind? Is the environment a source of tension or conflict in the story? Do changes in setting reflect changes in key characters? Do sensory details of sight, touch, smell, hearing, or taste affect or reflect the characters or events? Does the author's portrait of the setting contain images and symbols that help you interpret the story?

Style   *Style* is a general term that may refer to sentence structure and to figurative language and symbols, as well as to the author's tone or use of irony. *Sentence structure* may be long and complicated or relatively short and simple. Authors may use *figurative language* (Mrs. Mallard is described in "The Story of an Hour" as sobbing, "as a child who has cried itself to sleep continues to sob in its dreams"). A *symbol* is a person, place, thing, or event that suggests or signifies something beyond itself. In "The Story of an Hour," the open window and the new spring life suggest or represent Mrs. Mallard's new freedom. *Tone* is the author's attitude toward the characters, setting, or plot. Tone may be sympathetic, humorous, serious, detached, or critical. *Irony* suggests a double meaning. It occurs when the author or a character says or does one thing but means the opposite or something altogether different. The ending of "A Story of an Hour" is ironic: The doctors say Mrs. Mallard has died "of joy that kills." In fact, she has died of killed joy.

Theme   The focus of an interpretative essay is often on the *theme* of a story. In arriving at a theme, ask how the characters, plot, point of view, setting, and style *contribute* to the main ideas or point of the story. The theme of a story depends, within limits, on your reactions as a reader. "The Story of an Hour" is *not* about relationships between sisters, nor is it about medical malpractice. It is an ironic story about love, personal freedom, and death, but what precisely is the *theme?* Does "The Story of an Hour" carry a feminist message, or is it more universally about the repressive power of love? Is Mrs. Mallard to be admired or criticized for her impulse to free herself? Do not trivialize the theme of a story by looking for some simple "moral." In describing the theme, deal with the complexity of life recreated in the story.

PROFESSIONAL WRITING

THE BOAT
ALISTAIR MACLEOD

Born in North Battleford, Saskatchewan, Alistair MacLeod went to high school in Cape Breton, then attended St. Francis Xavier University in Antigonish, Nova Scotia, the University of New Brunswick, and Notre

Dame. His short stories, many of them evocative of the difficult lives of the fishers and miners in Cape Breton, have been published in a variety of journals, including Fiddlehead *and* Canadian Fiction Magazine. *His two collections are called* The Lost Salt Gift of Blood *(1976), in which "The Boat" appeared, and* As Birds Bring Forth the Sun *(1986). MacLeod's long awaited first novel,* No Great Mischief, *published in September 1999, won Ontario's Trillium Book Award. On June 18, 2000, Alistair MacLeod won two Canadian Bookseller Awards: author of the year and fiction book of the year. Currently, MacLeod is a professor of English at the University of Windsor in Ontario.*

There are times even now, when I awake at four o'clock in the morning with the terrible fear that I have overslept; when I imagine that my father is waiting for me in the room below the darkened stairs or that the shorebound men are tossing pebbles against my window while blowing their hands and stomping their feet impatiently on the frozen steadfast earth. There are times when I am half out of bed and fumbling for socks and mumbling for words before I realize that I am foolishly alone, that no one waits at the base of the stairs and no boat rides restlessly in the waters by the pier. (1)

At such times only the grey corpses on the overflowing ashtray beside my bed bear witness to the extinction of the latest spark and silently await the crushing out of the most recent of their fellows. And then because I am afraid to be alone with death, I dress rapidly, make a great to-do about clearing my throat, turn on both faucets in the sink and proceed to make loud splashing ineffectual noises. Later I go out and walk the mile to the all-night restaurant. (2)

In the winter it is a very cold walk and there are often tears in my eyes when I arrive. The waitress usually gives a sympathetic little shiver and says, "Boy, it must be really cold out there; you got tears in your eyes." (3)

"Yes," I say, "it sure is; it really is." (4)

And then the three or four of us who are always in such places at such times make uninteresting little protective chit-chat until the dawn reluctantly arrives. Then I swallow the coffee which is always bitter and leave with a great busy rush because by that time I have to worry about being late and whether I have a clean shirt and whether my car will start and about all the other countless things one must worry about when he teaches at a great Midwestern university. And I know then that that day will go by as have all the days of the past ten years, for the call and the voices and the shapes and the boat were not really there in the early morning's darkness and I have all kinds of comforting reality to prove it. They are only shadows and echoes, the animals a child's hands make on the wall by lamplight, and the voices from the rain barrel; the cuttings from an old movie made in the black and white of long ago. **(5)**

I first became conscious of the boat in the same way and at almost the same time that I became aware of the people it supported. My earliest recollection of my father is a view from the floor of gigantic rubber boots and then of being suddenly elevated and having my face pressed against the stubble of his cheek, and of how it tasted of salt and of how he smelled of salt from his red-soled rubber boots to the shaggy whiteness of his hair. **(6)**

When I was very small, he took me for my first ride in the boat. I rode the half-mile from our house to the wharf on his shoulders and I remember the sound of his rubber boots galumphing along the gravel beach, the tune of the indecent little song he used to sing, and the odour of the salt. **(7)**

The floor of the boat was permeated with the same odour and in its constancy I was not aware of change. In the harbour we made our little circle and returned. He tied the boat by its painter, fastened the stern to its permanent anchor and lifted me high over his head to the solidity of the wharf. Then he climbed up the little iron ladder that led to the wharf's cap, placed me once more upon his shoulders and galumphed off again. **(8)**

When we returned to the house everyone made a great fuss over my precocious excursion and asked, "How did you like the boat?" "Were you afraid in the boat?" "Did you cry in the boat?" They repeated "the boat" at the end of all their questions and I knew it must be very important to everyone. **(9)**

My earliest recollection of my mother is of being alone with her in the mornings after my father was away in the boat. She seemed to be always repairing clothes that were "torn in the boat," preparing food "to be eaten in the boat" or looking for "the boat" through our kitchen window which faced upon the sea. When my father returned about noon, she would ask, "Well, how did things go in the boat today?" It was the first question I remember asking: "Well, how did things go in the boat today?" "Well, how did things go in the boat today?" **(10)**

The boat in our lives was registered at Port Hawkesbury. She was what Nova Scotians called a Cape Island boat and was designed for the small inshore fishermen who sought the lobsters of the spring and the mackerel of the summer and later the cod and haddock and hake. She was thirty-two feet long and nine wide, and was powered by an engine from a Chevrolet truck. She had a marine clutch and a high speed reverse gear and was painted light green with the name *Jenny Lynn* stencilled in black letters on her bow and painted on an oblong plate across her stern. Jenny Lynn had been my mother's maiden name and the boat was called after her as another link in the chain of tradition. Most of the boats that berthed at the wharf bore the names of some female member of their owner's household. **(11)**

I say this now as if I knew it all then. All at once, all about boat dimensions and engines, and as if on the day of my first childish voyage I notice the difference between a stencilled name and a painted name. But of course it was not that way at all, for I learned it all very slowly and there was not time enough. **(12)**

I learned first about our house which was one of about fifty which marched around the horseshoe of our harbour and the wharf which was its heart. Some of them were so close to the water that during a storm the sea spray splashed against their windows while others were built farther along the beach as was the case with ours. The houses and their people, like those of the neighbouring towns and villages, were the result of Ireland's discontent and Scotland's Highland Clearances and America's War of Independence. Impulsive emotional Catholic Celts who could not bear to live with England and shrewd determined Protestant Puritans who, in the years after 1776, could not bear to live without. **(13)**

The most important room in our house was one of those oblong old-fashioned kitchens heated by a wood- and coal-burning stove. Behind the stove was a box of kindlings and beside it a coal scuttle. A heavy wooden table with leaves that expanded or reduced its dimensions stood in the middle of the floor. There were five wooden home-made chairs which had been chipped and hacked by a variety of knives. Against the east wall, opposite the stove, there was a couch which sagged in the middle and had a cushion for a pillow, and above it a shelf which contained matches, tobacco, pencils, odd fish-hooks, bits of twine, and a tin can filled with bills and receipts. The south wall was dominated by a window which faced the sea and on the north there was a five-foot board which bore a variety of clothes hooks and the burdens of each. Beneath the board there was a jumble of odd footwear, mostly of rubber. There were also, on this wall, a barometer, a map of the marine area and a shelf which held a tiny radio. The kitchen was shared by all of us and was a buffer zone between the immaculate order of ten other rooms and the disruptive chaos of the single room that was my father's. **(14)**

My mother ran her house as her brothers ran their boats. Everything was clean and spotless and in order. She was tall and dark and powerfully energetic. In later years she reminded me of the women of Thomas Hardy, particularly Eustacia Vye, in a physical way. She fed and clothed a family of seven children, making all the meals and most of the clothes. She grew miraculous gardens and magnificent flowers and raised broods of hens and ducks. She would walk miles on berry-picking expeditions and hoist her skirts to dig for clams when the tide was low. She was fourteen years younger than my father, whom she had married when she was twenty-six and had been a local beauty for a period of ten years. My mother was of the sea as were all of her people, and her horizons were the very literal ones she scanned with her dark and fearless eyes. **(15)**

Between the kitchen clothes rack and barometer, a door opened into my father's bedroom. It was a room of disorder and disarray. It was as if the wind which so often clamoured about the house succeeded in entering this single room and after whipping it into turmoil stole quietly away to renew its knowing laughter from without. **(16)**

My father's bed was against the south wall. It always looked rumpled and unmade because he lay on top of it more than he slept within any folds it might have had. Beside it, there was a little brown table. An archaic goose-necked reading light, a battered table radio, a mound of wooden matches, one or two packages of tobacco, a deck of cigarette papers and an overflowing ashtray cluttered its surface. The brown larvae of tobacco shreds and the grey flecks of ash covered both the table and the floor beneath it. The once-varnished surface of the table was disfigured by numerous black scars and gashes inflicted by the neglected burning cigarettes of many years. They had tumbled from the ashtray unnoticed and branded their statements permanently and quietly into the wood until the odour of their burning caused the snuffing out of their lives. At the bed's foot there was a single window which looked upon the sea. **(17)**

Against the adjacent wall there was a battered bureau and beside it there was a closet which held his single ill-fitting serge suit, the two or three white shirts that strangled him and the square black shoes that pinched. When he took off his more friendly clothes, the heavy woollen sweaters, mitts and socks which my mother knitted for him and the woollen and doeskin shirts, he dumped them unceremoniously on a single chair. If a visitor entered the room while he was lying on the bed, he would be told to throw the clothes on the floor and take their place upon the chair. **(18)**

Magazines and books covered the bureau and competed with the clothes for domination of the chair. They further overburdened the heroic little table and lay on top of the radio. They filled a baffling and unknowable cave beneath the bed, and in the corner by the bureau they spilled from the walls and grew up from the floor. **(19)**

The magazines were the most conventional: *Time, Newsweek, Life, Maclean's, Family Herald, Reader's Digest.* They were the result of various cut-rate subscriptions or of the gift subscriptions associated with Christmas, "the two whole years for only $3.50." **(20)**

The books were more varied. There were a few hard-cover magnificents and bygone Book-of-the-Month wonders and some were Christmas or birthday gifts. The majority of them, however, were used paperbacks which came from those second-hand bookstores which advertise in the backs of magazines: "Miscellaneous Used Paperbacks 10¢ Each." At first he sent for them himself, although my mother resented the expense, but in later years they came more and more often from my sisters who had moved to the cities. Especially at first they were very weird and varied. Mickey Spillane and Ernest Haycox vied with Dostoyevsky and Faulkner, and the Penguin Poets edition of Gerard Manley Hopkins arrived in the same box as a little book on sex technique called *Getting the Most Out of Love.* The former had been assiduously annotated by a very fine hand using a very blue-inked fountain pen while the latter had been studied by someone with very large thumbs, the prints of which were still visible in the margins. At the slightest provocation it would open almost automatically to particularly graphic and well-smudged pages. **(21)**

When he was not in the boat, my father spent most of his time lying on the bed in his socks, the top two buttons of his trousers undone, his discarded shirt on the ever-ready chair and the sleeves of the woollen Stanfield underwear, which he wore both summer and winter, drawn half way up to his elbows. The pillows propped up the whiteness of his head and the goose-necked lamp illuminated the pages in his hands. The cigarettes smoked and smouldered on the ashtray and on the table and the radio played constantly, sometimes low and sometimes loud. At midnight and at one, two, three and four, one could sometimes hear the radio, his occasional cough, the rustling thud of a completed book being tossed to the corner heap, or the movement necessitated by his sitting on the edge of the bed to roll the thousandth cigarette. He seemed never to sleep, only to doze, and the light shone constantly from his window to the sea. **(22)**

My mother despised the room and all it stood for and she had stopped sleeping in it after I was born. She despised disorder in rooms and in houses and in hours and in lives, and she had not read a book since high school. There she had read *Ivanhoe* and considered it a colossal waste of time. Still the room remained, like a solid rock of opposition in the sparkling waters of a clear deep harbour, opening off the kitchen where we really lived our lives, with its door always open and its contents visible to all. **(23)**

The daughters of the room and of the house were very beautiful. They were tall and willowy like my mother and had her fine facial features set off by the reddish copper-coloured hair that had apparently once been my father's before it turned to white. All of them were very clever in school and helped my mother a great deal about the house. When they were young they sang and were very happy and very nice to me because I was the youngest and the family's only boy. **(24)**

My father never approved of their playing about the wharf like the other children, and they went there only when my mother sent them on an errand. At such times they almost always overstayed, playing screaming games of tag or hide-and-seek in and about the fishing shanties, the piled traps and tubs of trawl, shouting down to the perch that swam languidly about the wharf's algae-covered piles, or jumping in and out of the boats that tugged gently at their lines. My mother was never uneasy about them at such times, and when her husband criticized her she would say, "Nothing will happen to them there," or "They could be doing worse things in worse places." **(25)**

By about the ninth or tenth grade my sisters one by one discovered my father's bedroom and then the change would begin. Each would go into the room one morning when he was out. She would go with the ideal hope of imposing order or with the more practical objective of emptying the ashtray, and later she would be found spellbound by the volume in her hand. My mother's reaction was always abrupt, bordering on the angry. "Take your nose out of that trash and come and do your work," she would say, and once I saw her slap my youngest sister so hard that the print of her hand was scarletly emblazoned upon her daughter's cheek while the broken-spined paperback fluttered uselessly to the floor. **(26)**

Thereafter my mother would launch a campaign against what she had discovered but could not understand. At times although she was not overly religious she would bring in God to bolster her arguments, saying "In the next world God will see to those who waste their lives reading useless books when they should be about their work." Or without theological aid, "I would like to know how books help anyone to live a life." If my father were in, she would repeat the remarks louder than necessary, and her voice would carry into his room where he lay upon his bed. His usual reaction was to turn up the volume of the radio, although that action in itself betrayed the success of the initial thrust. (27)

Shortly after my sisters began to read the books, they grew restless and lost interest in darning socks and baking bread, and all of them eventually went to work as summer waitresses in the Sea Food Restaurant. The restaurant was run by a big American concern from Boston and catered to the tourists that flooded the area during July and August. My mother despised the whole operation. She said the restaurant was not run by "our people," and "our people" did not eat there, and that it was run by outsiders for outsiders. (28)

"Who are these people anyway?" she would ask, tossing back her dark hair, "and what do they, though they go about with their cameras for a hundred years, know about the way it is here, and what do they care about me and mine, and why should I care about them?" (29)

She was angry that my sisters should even conceive of working in such a place and more angry when my father made no move to prevent it, and she was worried about herself and about her family and about her life. Sometimes she would say softly to her sisters, "I don't know what's the matter with my girls. It seems none of them are interested in any of the right things." And sometimes there would be bitter savage arguments. One afternoon I was coming in with three mackerel I'd been given at the wharf when I heard her say, "Well I hope you'll be satisfied when they come home knocked up and you'll have had your way." (30)

It was the most savage thing I'd ever heard my mother say. Not just the words but the way she said them, and I stood there in the porch afraid to breathe for what seemed like the years from ten to fifteen, feeling the damp moist mackerel with their silver glassy eyes growing clammy against my leg. (31)

Through the angle of the screen door I saw my father who had been walking into his room wheel around on one of his rubber-booted heels and look at her with his blue eyes flashing like clearest ice beneath the snow that was his hair. His usually ruddy face was drawn and grey, reflecting the exhaustion of a man of sixty-five who had been working in those rubber boots for eleven hours on an August day, and for a fleeting moment I wondered what I would do if he killed my mother while I stood there in the porch with those three foolish mackerel in my hand. Then he turned and went into his room and the radio blared forth the next day's weather forecast and I retreated under the noise and returned again, stamping my feet and slamming the door too loudly to signal my approach. My mother was busy at the stove when I came in, and did not raise her head when I threw the mackerel in a pan. As I looked into my father's room, I said, "Well how did things go in the boat today?" and he replied, "Oh not too badly, all things considered." He was lying on his back and lighting the first cigarette and the radio was talking about the Virginia coast. (32)

All of my sisters made good money on tips. They bought my father an electric razor which he tried to use for a while and they took out even more magazine subscriptions. They bought my mother a great many clothes of the type she was very fond of, the wide-brimmed hats and the brocaded dresses, but she locked them all in trunks and refused to wear any of them. (33)

On one August day my sisters prevailed upon my father to take some of their restaurant customers for an afternoon ride in the boat. The tourists with the expensive clothes and cameras and sun glasses awkwardly backed down the iron ladder at the wharf's side to where my father waited below, holding the rocking *Jenny Lynn* in snug against the wharf with one hand on the iron ladder and steadying his descending passengers with the other. They tried to look both prim and wind-blown like the girls in the Pepsi-Cola ads and did the best they could, sitting on the thwarts where the newspapers were spread to cover the splattered blood and fish entrails, crowding to one side so that they were in danger of capsizing the boat, taking the inevitable pictures or merely trailing their fingers through the water of their dreams. (34)

All of them liked my father very much and, after he'd brought them back from their circles in the harbour, they invited him to their rented cabins which were located high on a hill overlooking the village to which they were so alien. He proceeded to get very drunk up there with the beautiful view and the strange company and the abundant liquor, and late in the afternoon he began to sing. (35)

I was just approaching the wharf to deliver my mother's summons when he began, and the familiar yet unfamiliar voice that rolled down from the cabins made me feel as I had never felt before in my young life or perhaps as I had always felt without really knowing it, and I was ashamed yet proud, young yet old and saved yet forever lost, and there was nothing I could do to control my legs which trembled nor my eyes which wept for what they could not tell. (36)

The tourists were equipped with tape recorders and my father sang for more than three hours. His voice boomed down the hill and bounced off the surface of the harbour, which was an unearthly blue on that hot August day, and was then reflected to the wharf and the fishing shanties where it was absorbed amidst the men who were baiting their lines for the next day's haul. (37)

He sang all the old sea chanties which had come across from the old world and by which men like him had pulled ropes for generations, and he sang the East Coast sea songs which celebrated the sealing vessels of Northumberland Strait and the long liners of the Grand Banks, and of Anticosti, Sable Island, Grand Manan, Boston Harbor, Nantucket and Block Island. Gradually he shifted to the seemingly unending Gaelic drinking songs with their twenty or more verses and inevitable refrains, and the men in the shanties smiled at the coarseness of some of the verses and at the thought that the singer's immediate audience did not know what they were applauding nor recording to take back to staid old Boston. Later as the sun was setting he switched to the laments and the wild and haunting Gaelic war songs of those spattered Highland ancestors he had never seen, and when his voice ceased, the savage melancholy of three hundred years seemed to hang over the peaceful harbour and the quiet boats and the men leaning in the doorways of their shanties with their cigarettes glowing in the dusk and the women looking to the sea from their open windows with their children in their arms. (38)

When he came home he threw the money he had earned on the kitchen table as he did with all his earnings but my mother refused to touch it and the next day he went with the rest of the men to bait his trawl in the shanties. The tourists came to the door that evening and my mother met them there and told them that her husband was not in although he was lying on the bed only a few feet away with the radio playing and the cigarette upon his lips. She stood in the doorway until they reluctantly went away. (39)

In the winter they sent him a picture which had been taken on the day of the singing. On the back it said, "To Our Ernest

Hemingway" and the "Our" was underlined. There was also an accompanying letter telling how much they had enjoyed themselves, how popular the tape was proving and explaining who Ernest Hemingway was. In a way it almost did look like one of those unshaven, taken-in-Cuba pictures of Hemingway. He looked both massive and incongruous in the setting. His bulky fisherman's clothes were too big for the green and white lawn chair in which he sat, and his rubber boots seemed to take up all of the well-clipped grass square. The beach umbrella jarred with his sunburned face and because he had already been singing for some time, his lips which chapped in the winds of spring and burned in the water glare of summer had already cracked in several places, producing tiny flecks of blood at their corners and on the whiteness of his teeth. The bracelets of brass chain which he wore to protect his wrists from chafing seemed abnormally large and his broad leather belt had been slackened and his heavy shirt and underwear were open at the throat revealing an uncultivated wilderness of white chest hair bordering on the semi-controlled stubble of his neck and chin. His blue eyes had looked directly into the camera and his hair was whiter than the two tiny clouds which hung over his left shoulder. The sea was behind him and its immense blue flatness stretched out to touch the arching blueness of the sky. It seemed very far away from him or else he was so much in the foreground that he seemed too big for it. **(40)**

Each year another of my sisters would read the books and work in the restaurant. Sometimes they would stay out quite late on the hot summer nights and when they came up the stairs my mother would ask them many long and involved questions which they resented and tried to avoid. Before ascending the stairs they would go into my father's room and those of us who waited above could hear them throwing his clothes off the chair before sitting on it or the squeak of the bed as they sat on its edge. Sometimes they would talk to him a long time, the murmur of their voices blending with the music of the radio into a mysterious vapour-like sound which floated softly up the stairs. **(41)**

I say this again as if it all happened at once and as if all of my sisters were of identical ages and like so many lemmings going into another sea and, again, it was of course not that way at all. Yet go they did, to Boston, to Montreal, to New York with the young men they met during the summers and later married in those far-away cities. The young men were very articulate and handsome and wore fine clothes and drove expensive cars and my sisters, as I said, were very tall and beautiful with their copper-coloured hair and were tired of darning socks and baking bread. **(42)**

One by one they went. My mother had each of her daughters for fifteen years, then lost them for two and finally forever. None married a fisherman. My mother never accepted any of the young men, for in her eyes they seemed always a combination of the lazy, the effeminate, the dishonest and the unknown. They never seemed to do any physical work and she could not comprehend their luxurious vacations and she did not know whence they came nor who they were. And in the end she did not really care, for they were not of her people and they were not of her sea. (43)

I say this now with a sense of wonder at my own stupidity in thinking I was somehow free and would go on doing well in school and playing and helping in the boat and passing into my early teens while streaks of grey began to appear in my mother's dark hair and my father's rubber boots dragged sometimes on the pebbles of the beach as he trudged home from the wharf. And there were but three of us in the house that had at one time been so loud. (44)

Then during the winter that I was fifteen he seemed to grow old and ill at once. Most of January he lay upon the bed, smoking and reading and listening to the radio while the wind howled about the house and the needle-like snow blistered off the ice-covered harbour and the doors flew out of people's hands if they did not cling to them like death. (45)

In February when the men began overhauling their lobster traps he still did not move, and my mother and I began to knit lobster trap headings in the evenings. The twine was as always very sharp and harsh, and blisters formed upon our thumbs and little paths of blood snaked quietly down between our fingers while the seals that had drifted down from distant Labrador wept and moaned like human children on the ice-floes of the Gulf. (46)

In the daytime my mother's brother who had been my father's partner as long as I could remember also came to work upon the gear. He was a year older than my mother and was tall and dark and the father of twelve children. (47)

By March we were very far behind and although I began to work very hard in the evenings I knew it was not hard enough and that there were but eight weeks left before the opening of the season on May first. And I knew that my mother worried and my uncle was uneasy and that all of our very lives depended on the boat being ready with her gear and two men, by the date of May the first. And I knew then that *David Copperfield* and *The Tempest* and all of those friends I had dearly come to love must really go forever. So I bade them all good-bye. **(48)**

The night after my first full day at home and after my mother had gone upstairs he called me into his room where I sat upon the chair beside his bed. "You will go back tomorrow," he said simply. **(49)**

I refused then, saying I had made my decision and was satisfied. **(50)**

"That is no way to make a decision," he said, "and if you are satisfied I am not. It is best that you go back." I was almost angry then and told him as all children do that I wished he would leave me alone and stop telling me what to do. **(51)**

He looked at me a long time then, lying there on the same bed on which he had fathered me those sixteen years before, fathered me his only son, out of who knew what emotions when he was already fifty-six and his hair had turned to snow. Then he swung his legs over the edge of the squeaking bed and sat facing me and looked into my own dark eyes with his of crystal blue and placed his hand upon my knee. "I am not telling you to do anything," he said softly, "only asking you." **(52)**

The next morning I returned to school. As I left, my mother followed me to the porch and said, "I never thought a son of mine would choose useless books over the parents that gave him life." **(53)**

In the weeks that followed he got up rather miraculously and the gear was ready and the *Jenny Lynn* was freshly painted by the last two weeks of April when the ice began to break up and the lonely screaming gulls returned to haunt the silver herring as they flashed within the sea. **(54)**

On the first day of May the boats raced out as they had always done, laden down almost to the gunwales with their heavy cargoes of traps. They were almost like living things as they plunged through the waters of the spring and manoeuvred between the still floating icebergs of crystal-white and emerald green on their way to the traditional grounds that they sought out every May. And those of us who sat that day in the high school on the hill, discussing the water imagery of Tennyson, watched them as they passed back and forth beneath us until by afternoon the piles of traps which had been stacked upon the wharf were no longer visible but were spread about the bottoms of the sea. And the *Jenny Lynn* went too, all day, with my uncle tall and dark, like a latter-day Tashtego standing at the tiller with his legs wide apart and guiding her deftly between the floating pans of ice and my father in the stern standing in the same way with his hands upon the ropes that lashed the cargo to the deck. And at night my mother asked, "Well, how did things go in the boat today?" (55)

And the spring wore on and the summer came and school ended in the third week of June and the lobster season on July first and I wished that the two things I loved so dearly did not exclude each other in a manner that was so blunt and too clear. (56)

At the conclusion of the lobster season my uncle said he had been offered a berth on a deep sea dragger and had decided to accept. We all knew that he was leaving the *Jenny Lynn* forever and that before the next lobster season he would buy a boat of his own. He was expecting another child and would be supporting fifteen people by the next spring and could not chance my father against the family that he loved. (57)

I joined my father then for the trawling season, and he made no protest and my mother was quite happy. Through the summer we baited the tubs of trawl in the afternoon and set them at sunset and revisited them in the darkness of the early morning. The men would come tramping by our house at four A.M. and we would join them and walk with them to the wharf and be on our way before the sun rose out of the ocean where it seemed to spend the night. If I was not up they would toss pebbles to my window and I would be very embarrassed and tumble downstairs to where my father lay fully clothed atop his bed, reading his book and listening to his radio and smoking his cigarette. When I appeared he would swing off his bed and put on his boots and be instantly ready and then we would take the lunches my mother had prepared the night before and walk off toward the sea. He would make no attempt to wake me himself. (58)

It was in many ways a good summer. There were few storms and we were out almost every day and we lost a minimum of gear and seemed to land a maximum of fish and I tanned dark and brown after the manner of my uncles. (59)

My father did not tan—he never tanned—because of his reddish complexion, and the salt water irritated his skin as it had for sixty years. He burned and reburned over and over again and his lips still cracked so that they bled when he smiled, and his arms, especially the left, still broke out into the oozing salt-water boils as they had ever since as a child I had first watched him soaking and bathing them in a variety of ineffectual solutions. The chafe-preventing bracelets of brass linked chain that all the men wore about their wrists in early spring were his the full season and he shaved but painfully and only once a week. **(60)**

And I saw then, that summer, many things that I had seen all my life as if for the first time and I thought that perhaps my father had never been intended for a fisherman either physically or mentally. At least not in the manner of my uncles; he had never really loved it. And I remembered that, one evening in his room when we were talking about *David Copperfield*, he had said that he had always wanted to go to the university and I had dismissed it then in the way one dismisses his father's saying he would like to be a tight-rope walker, and we had gone on to talk about the Peggottys and how they loved the sea. **(61)**

And I thought then to myself that there were many things wrong with all of us and all our lives and I wondered why my father, who was himself an only son, had not married before he was forty and then I wondered why he had. I even thought that perhaps he had had to marry my mother and checked the dates on the flyleaf of the Bible where I learned that my oldest sister had been born a prosaic eleven months after the marriage, and I felt myself then very dirty and debased for my lack of faith and for what I had thought and done. **(62)**

And then there came into my heart a very great love for my father and I thought it was very much braver to spend a life doing what you really do not want rather than selfishly following forever your own dreams and inclinations. And I knew then that I could never leave him alone to suffer the iron-tipped harpoons which my mother would forever hurl into his soul because he was a failure as a husband and a father who had retained none of his own. And I felt that I had been very small in a little secret place within me and that even the completion of high school was for me a silly shallow selfish dream. **(63)**

So I told him one night very resolutely and very powerfully that I would remain with him as long as he lived and we would fish the sea together. And he made no protest but only smiled through the cigarette smoke that wreathed his bed and replied, "I hope you will remember what you've said." **(64)**

The room was now so filled with books as to be almost Dickensian, but he would not allow my mother to move or change them and he continued to read them, sometimes two or three a night. They came with great regularity now, and there were more hard covers, sent by my sisters who had gone so long ago and now seemed so distant and so prosperous, and sent also pictures of small red-haired grandchildren with baseball bats and dolls which he placed upon his bureau and which my mother gazed at wistfully when she thought no one would see. Red-haired grandchildren with baseball bats and dolls who would never know the sea in hatred or in love. **(65)**

And so we fished through the heat of August and into the cooler days of September when the water was so clear we could almost see the bottom and the white mists rose like delicate ghosts in the early morning dawn. And one day my mother said to me, "You have given added years to his life." **(66)**

And we fished on into October when it began to roughen and we could no longer risk night sets but took our gear out each morning and returned at the first sign of the squalls; and on into November when we lost three tubs of trawl and the clear blue water turned to a sullen grey and the trochoidal waves rolled rough and high and washed across our bows and decks as we ran within their troughs. We wore heavy sweaters now and the awkward rubber slickers and the heavy woollen mitts which soaked and froze into masses of ice that hung from our wrists like the limbs of gigantic monsters until we thawed them against the exhaust pipe's heat. And almost every day we would leave for home, before noon, driven by the blasts of the northwest wind, coating our eyebrows with ice and freezing our eyelids closed as we leaned into a visibility that was hardly there, charting our course from the compass and the sea, running with the waves and between them but never confronting their towering might. **(67)**

And I stood at the tiller now, on these homeward lunges, stood in the place and in the manner of my uncle, turning to look at my father and to shout over the roar of the engine and the slop of the sea to where he stood in the stern, drenched and dripping with the snow and the salt and the spray and his bushy eyebrows caked in ice. But on November twenty-first, when it seemed we might be making the final run of the season, I turned and he was not there and I knew even in that instant that he would never be again. **(68)**

On November twenty-first the waves of the grey Atlantic are very very high and the waters are very cold and there are no signposts on the surface of the sea. You cannot tell where you have been five minutes before and in the squalls of snow you cannot see. And it takes longer than you would believe to check a boat that has been running before a gale and turn her ever so carefully in a wide and stupid circle, with timbers creaking and straining, back into the face of storm. And you know that it is useless and that your voice does not carry the length of the boat and that even if you knew the original spot, the relentless waves would carry such a burden perhaps a mile or so by the time you could return. And you know also, the final irony, that your father like your uncles and all the men that form your past, cannot swim a stroke. **(69)**

The lobster beds off the Cape Breton coast are still very rich and now, from May to July, their offerings are packed in crates of ice, and thundered by the gigantic transport trucks, day and night, through New Glasgow, Amherst, Saint John and Bangor and Portland and into Boston where they are tossed still living into boiling pots of water, their final home. **(70)**

And though the prices are higher and the competition tighter, the grounds to which the *Jenny Lynn* once went remain untouched and unfished as they have for the last ten years. For if there are no signposts on the sea in storm there are certain ones in calm and the lobster bottoms were distributed in calm before any of us can remember and the grounds my father fished were those his father fished before him and there were others before and before and before. Twice the big boats have come from forty and fifty miles, lured by the promise of the grounds, and strewn the bottom with their traps and twice they have returned to find their buoys cut adrift and their gear lost and destroyed. Twice the Fisheries Officer and the Mounted Police have come and asked many long and involved questions and twice they have received no answers from the men leaning in the doors of their shanties and the women standing at their windows with their children in their arms. Twice they have gone away saying: "There are no legal boundaries in the Marine area"; "No one can own the sea"; "Those grounds don't wait for anyone." **(71)**

But the men and the women, with my mother dark among them, do not care for what they say, for to them the grounds are sacred and they think they wait for me. **(72)**

It is not an easy thing to know that your mother lives alone on an inadequate insurance policy and that she is too proud to accept any other aid. And that she looks through her lonely window onto the ice of winter and the hot flat calm of summer and the rolling waves of fall. And that she lies awake in the early morning's darkness when the rubber boots of the men scrunch upon the gravel as they pass beside her house on their way down to the wharf. And she knows that the footsteps never stop, because no man goes from her house, and she alone of all the Lynns has neither son nor son-in-law that walks toward the boat that will take him to the sea. And it is not an easy thing to know that your mother looks upon the sea with love and on you with bitterness because the one has been so constant and the other so untrue. (73)

But neither is it easy to know that your father was found on November twenty-eighth, ten miles to the north and wedged between two boulders at the base of the rock-strewn cliffs where he had been hurled and slammed so many many times. His hands were shredded ribbons as were his feet which had lost their boots to the suction of the sea, and his shoulders came apart in our hands when we tried to move him from the rocks. And the fish had eaten his testicles and the gulls had pecked out his eyes and the white-green stubble of his whiskers had continued to grow in death, like the grass on graves, upon the purple, bloated mass that was his face. There was not much left of my father, physically, as he lay there with the brass chains on his wrists and the seaweed in his hair. (74)

Questions for Writing and Discussion

1. Identify the narrative point of view, selecting a phrase or two to justify your answer. What is the effect of this particular narrative strategy?

2. Examine the role of setting in the story. What do the details about each of the following—the boat, the rooms in the house, the ocean—contribute to our intellectual and emotional understanding of the narrator's experience?

3. (a) In your own words, describe the narrator's father. (b) The narrator wonders why his father had not married before he was 40 and then why he had married at all. Describe the mother. Was theirs a good marriage? Explain. (c) Why does the narrator not individualize his sisters?

4. What is the climax of the story? Why is it ironic?

5. Comment on MacLeod's style. Include reference to tone, and examples of figurative language, symbolism, and sentence structure that simulates ocean rhythms.

6. What "complexities of life" are recreated in this story; that is, what might be the theme(s)?

7. Does every choice shape our lives? Describe how a particular choice sig-
   nificantly shaped your life.

PROFESSIONAL   WRITING

THE WEDNESDAY CIRCLE
SANDRA BIRDSELL

*Sandra Birdsell was born in 1942 to a Métis father and a Russian
Mennonite mother in Manitoba. She has worked as a scriptwriter, play-
wright, filmmaker, novelist, and short-story writer. "The Wednesday
Circle" describes a specific episode in the lives of a Mennonite mother,
Mika, and one of her three daughters, Betty. The stories of the Lafronière
family are contained in* Agassiz Stories *(1987).*

Betty crosses the double planks that span the ditch in front of
Joys' yard. Most people have only one plank. But Mrs. Joy needs
two. Mrs. Joy is a possible candidate for the circus. Like sleeping
with an elephant, Betty's father says often. But Mr. and Mrs. Joy,
the egg people, don't sleep together. Betty knows this even though
she's never gone further than inside their stale smelling kitchen. **(1)**

The highway is a smeltering strip of gunmetal grey at her back.
It leads to another town like the one she lives in. If you kept on
going south, you would get to a place called Pembina in the States
and a small dark tavern where a woman will serve under-age kids
beer. Laurence, Betty's friend, knows about this. But if you turn
from the highway and go west, there are dozens of villages and then
the Pembina Hills which Betty has seen on one occasion, a school
trip to the man-made lake at Morden. Home of the rich and the
godly, Betty's father calls these villages. Wish the godly would stay
home. Can't get a seat in the parlour on Friday nights. **(2)**

Beyond her lies a field in summer fallow and a dirt road rising
to a slight incline and then falling as it meets the highway. Before
her is the Joys' crumbling yellow cottage, flanked on all sides by
greying bales of straw which have swollen and broken free from
their bindings and are scattered about the yard. Behind the cottage
is the machine shed. Behind the machine shed and bumping up
against the prairie is the chicken coop. **(3)**

Because Mika, Betty's mother, sends her for the eggs instead of
having them delivered by Mr. Joy, she gets them cheaper. **(4)**

Betty balances the egg cartons beneath her chin and pushes open the gate. It shrieks on its rusty hinges. The noise doesn't affect her as it usually does. Usually, the noise is like a door opening into a dark room and she is filled with dread. Today, she is prepared for it. Today is the day for the Wednesday Circle. The church ladies are meeting at her home. Even now, they're there in the dining room, sitting in a circle with their Bibles in their laps. It's like women and children in the centre. And arrows flying. Wagons are going up in flames and smoke. The goodness and matronly wisdom of the Wednesday Circle is a newly discovered thing. She belongs with them now. They can reach out to protect her even here, by just being what they are. And although she wants nothing to happen today, she is prepared for the worst. **(5)**

"Come on in," Mrs. Joy calls from the kitchen. **(6)**

Betty sets the egg cartons down on the steps and enters the house. Mrs. Joy's kitchen resembles a Woolworth store. There are porcelain dogs and cats in every corner on knick-knack shelves. Once upon a time, she used to love looking at those figurines but now she thinks they're ugly. **(7)**

The woman sits in her specially made chair which is two chairs wired together. Her legs are stretched out in front resting up on another chair. Out of habit, Betty's heart constricts because she knows the signs. Mrs. Joy is not up to walking back to the chicken coop with her. And that's how it all began. **(8)**

"Lo, I am with you always even unto the end of the world," her mind recites. **(9)**

These verses rise unbidden. She has memorized one hundred of them and won a trip to a summer Bible camp at Lake Winnipeg. She has for the first time seen the ocean on the prairie and tried to walk on water. The waves have lifted and pulled her out where her feet couldn't touch the sandy bottom and she has been swept beneath that mighty sea and heard the roaring of the waves in her head and felt the sting of fish water in her nostrils. Like a bubble of froth she is swept beneath the water, back and forth by the motion of the waves. She is drowning. What happens is just as she's heard. Her whole life flashes by. Her head becomes a movie screen playing back every lie and swearing, malicious and unkind deeds, thoughts, words. There is not one thing that makes her look justified for having done or said them. And then her foot touches a rock and she pushes herself forward in desperation, hoping it's the right direction. **(10)**

Miraculously, it is. She bounces forward from the depths to where she can tiptoe to safety, keeping her nose above the waves. She runs panting with fear to her cabin. She pulls the blankets over her. She tells no one. But that evening in the chapel during devotions, the rustling wind in the poplars against the screen causes her to think of God. When they all sing, "Love Lifted Me," the sunset parts the clouds above the water so there is a crack of gold where angels hover, watching. So she goes forward to the altar with several others and has her name written in the Book of Life. They tell her the angels are clapping and she thinks she can hear them there at that crack of gold which is the door to heaven. She confesses every sin she's been shown in the water except for one. For some reason, it wasn't there in the movie. And they are such gentle, smiling nice people who have never done what she's done. So she can't bring herself to tell them that Mr. Joy puts his hands in her pants. **(11)**

"Rainin' today, ain't it child?" Mrs. Joy asks. **(12)**

"No, not yet," Betty says. "It's very muggy." **(13)**

"Don't I know it," she says. **(14)**

"Are your legs sore?" Betty asks. **(15)**

"Oh Lord, yes, how they ache," Mrs. Joy says and rolls her eyes back into her head. Her jersey dress is a tent stretched across her knees. She cradles a cookie tin in her lap. **(16)**

"That's too bad," Betty says. **(17)**

A chuckle comes from deep inside her mammoth chest. "You sound just like your mother," she says. "And you're looking more and more like her each time I see you. You're just like an opal, always changing." **(18)**

God's precious jewels, Mrs. Joy calls them when she visits Mika. She lines them up verbally, Betty and her sisters and brothers, comparing chins, noses. This one here, she says about Betty, she's an opal. You oughta keep a watch over that one. Always changing. But it just goes to show, His mysteries does He perform. Not one of them the same. **(19)**

"Thank you," Betty says, but she hates being told she looks like her mother. Mika has hazel eyes and brown hair. She is blonde and blue-eyed like her Aunt Elizabeth. **(20)**

"Well, you know where the egg pail is," Mrs. Joy says, dismissing her with a flutter of her pudgy hand. **(21)**

"Aren't you coming?" Betty asks. **(22)**

"Not today, girl. It aches me so to walk. You collect the eggs and then you jest find Mr. Joy and you pay him. He gets it in the end anyhow." **(23)**

Betty looks around the kitchen. His jacket is missing from its hook on the wall. She goes over to the corner by the window and feigns interest in the porcelain figures. She picks one up, sets it down. His truck is not in the yard. **(24)**

"Where is he?" **(25)**

"Went to town for something," Mrs. Joy says. "But I thought he'd be back by now. Doesn't matter though, jest leave the money in the back porch." **(26)**

The egg pail thumps against her leg as she crosses the yard to the chicken coop. She walks towards the cluttered wire enclosure, past the machine shed. The doors are open wide. The hens scratch and dip their heads in her direction as she approaches. Hope rises like an erratic kite as she passes the shed and there are no sounds coming from it. She stamps her feet and the hens scatter before her, then circle around and approach her from behind, silently. She quickly gathers three dozen of the warm, straw-flecked eggs, and then steps free of the stifling smelly coop out into the fresh moist air. She is almost home-free. She won't have to face anything today. It has begun to rain. Large spatters spot her white blouse, feel cool on her back. She sets the pail down on the ground beside the egg cartons and begins to transfer the eggs. **(27)**

"Here, you don't have to do that outside." His sudden voice, as she fills the egg cartons, brings blood to her face, threatens to pitch her forward over the pail. **(28)**

He strides across the yard from the shed. "Haven't got enough sense to come in out of the rain," he says. "Don't you know you'll melt? Be nothing left of you but a puddle." **(29)**

He carries the pail, she carries the cartons. He has told her: Mrs. Joy is fat and lazy, you are my sunshine, my only sunshine. I would like six little ones running around my place too, but Mrs. Joy is fat and lazy. His thin hand has gone from patting her on the head with affection, to playfully slapping her on the behind, graduated then to tickling her armpits and ribs and twice now, his hands have been inside her underpants. **(30)**

"Be not afraid," a verse leaps into her head. "For I am with you." She will put her plan into action. The Wednesday Circle women are strong and mighty. She knows them all, they're her mother's friends. She'll just go to them and say, Mr. Joy feels me up, and that will be the end of it. **(31)**

She walks behind him, her heart pounding. He has an oil rag hanging from his back pocket and his boots are caked with clay, adding inches to his height. **(32)**

"I'm waiting for my parts," he says over his shoulder. "Can't do anything until I get that truck fixed." Sometimes he talks to her as though she were an adult. Sometimes as though she were ten again and just coming for the eggs for the first time. How old are you, he'd asked the last time and was surprised when she said, fourteen. My sunshine has grown up. **(33)**

They enter the machine shed and he slides the doors closed behind them, first one and then the other, leaving a sliver of daylight beaming through where the doors join. A single light bulb dangles from a wire, shedding a circle of weak yellow light above the truck, not enough to clear the darkness from the corners. **(34)**

"Okay-dokey," he says and puts the pail of eggs on the workbench. "You can work here. I've got things to do." He goes over to the truck, disappears beneath its raised hood. **(35)**

Then he's back at the workbench, searching through his toolbox. "Seen you with your boyfriend the other day," he says. "That Anderson boy." **(36)**

"He's not my boyfriend," she says. **(37)**

"I saw you," he says. His usual bantering tone is missing. "The two of you were in the coulee." Then his breath is warm on the side of her face as he reaches across her. His arm knocks against her breast, sending pain shooting through her chest. I need a bra, she has told Mika. Whatever for? Wear an undershirt if you think you really need to. **(38)**

"Do you think it's a good idea to hang around in the coulee with your boyfriend?" **(39)**

"He's not my boyfriend," she says. "I told you." **(40)**

He sees her flushed cheeks, senses her discomfort, "Aha," he says. "So he is. You can't fool me." **(41)**

She moves away from him. Begins to stack the cartons up against her chest, protection against his nudgings. Why is that everyone but her own mother notices that she has breasts now? **(42)**

"Don't rush off," he says. "Wait until the rain passes." The sound of it on the tin roof is like small pebbles being dropped one by one. **(43)**

He takes the cartons from her and sets them back on the workbench. He smiles and she can see that perfect decayed circle between his front teeth. His hair is completely grey even though he's not as old as her father. He starts to walk past her, back towards the truck and then suddenly he grasps her about the waist and begins to tickle her ribs. She is slammed up against him and gasping for breath. His whiskers prickle against her neck. She tastes the bitterness of his flannel shirt. **(44)**

She pushes away. "Stop." **(45)**

He holds her tighter. "You're so pretty," he says. "No wonder the boys are chasing you. When I'm working in here, know what I'm thinking all the time?" **(46)**

"Let me go." She continues to push against his bony arms. **(47)**

"I'm thinking about all the things I could do to you." **(48)**

Against her will, she has been curious to know. She feels desire rising when he speaks of what he would like to do. He has drawn vivid word-pictures that she likes to reconstruct until her face burns. Only it isn't Mr. Joy in the pictures, it's Laurence. It's what made her pull aside her underpants so he could fumble inside her moist crevice with his grease-stained fingers. **(49)**

"Show me your tits," he whispers into her neck. "I'll give you a dollar if you do." **(50)**

She knows the only way out of this is to tell. When the whole thing is laid out before the Wednesday Circle, she will become whiter than snow. "No," she says. **(51)**

"What do you mean, no," he says, jabbing her in the ribs once again. **(52)**

"I'm going to tell," she says. "You can't make me do anything anymore because I'm going to tell on you." She feels as though a rock has been taken from her stomach. He is ugly. He is like a salamander dropping from the sky after a rainstorm into a mincemeat pail. She doesn't know how she could ever have liked him. **(53)**

"Make you?" he says. "Make you? Listen here, girlie, I've only done what you wanted me to do." **(54)**

She knows this to be true and not true. She isn't certain how she has come to accept and even expect his fondling. It has happened over a course of four years, gradually, like growing. **(55)**

She walks to the double doors where the light shines through. "Open them, please," she says. **(56)**

"Open them yourself," he says. She can feel the presence of the Wednesday Circle. The promise of their womanly strength is like a lamp unto her feet. They will surround her and protect her. Freedom from his word-pictures will make her a new person. **(57)**

"You say anything," he says. "You say one thing and I'll have some pretty stories to tell about you. You betcha." **(58)**

"That woman," Mika is saying to the Wednesday Circle as Betty enters the dining room. "That woman. She has absolutely no knowledge of the scriptures. She takes everything out of context." Mika is standing at the buffet with a china teacup in her hand. Betty steps into the circle of chairs and sits down in Mika's empty one. Mika stops talking, throws her a look of surprise and question. The other women greet her with smiles, nods. **(59)**

"Did you get the eggs?" Mika asks. **(60)**

Betty feels her mouth stretching, moving of its own accord into a silly smile. She knows the smile irritates Mika but she can't help it. At times like these, her face moves on its own. She can hear her own heartbeat in her ears, like the ocean, roaring. **(61)**

"What now?" Mika asks, worried. **(62)**

"What do you mean, she takes everything out of context?" Mrs. Brawn asks, ignoring Betty. It's her circle. She started it off, arranging for the church women to meet in each others' homes twice a month to read scripture and sew things which they send to a place in the city where they are distributed to the poor. The women are like the smell of coffee to Betty and at the same time, they are like the cool opaque squares of Mika's lemon slice which is arranged on bread and butter plates on the table. They are also like the sturdy varnished chairs they sit on. To be with them now is the same as when she was a child and thought that if you could always be near an adult when you were ill, you wouldn't die. **(63)**

"My, my," Mika mimics someone to demonstrate to Mrs. Brawn what she means. She places her free hand against her chest in a dramatic gesture. "They are different, ain't they? God's precious jewels. Just goes to show, His mysteries does He perform." **(64)**

Betty realizes with a sudden shock that her mother is imitating Mrs. Joy. **(65)**

Mrs. Brawn takes in Mika's pose with a stern expression and immediately Mika looks guilty, drops her hand from her breast and begins to fill cups with coffee. **(66)**

"I suppose that we really can't expect much from Mrs. Joy," Mika says with her back to them. Betty hears the slight mocking tone of her voice that passes them by. **(67)**

Heads bent over needlework nod their understanding. The women's stitches form thumbs, forest-green fingers; except for the woman who sits beside Betty. With a hook she shapes intricate spidery patterns to lay across varnished surfaces, the backs of chairs. What the poor would want with those, I'll never know, Mika has said privately. But they include the doilies in their parcels anyway because they have an understanding. They whisper that this white-haired woman has known suffering. **(68)**

She works swiftly. It seems to Betty as though the threads come from the ends of her fingers, white strings with a spot of red every few inches. It looks as though she's cut her finger and secretly bleeds the colour into the lacy scallops. The women all unravel and knit and check closely for evenness of tension. **(69)**

Mika enters the circle of chairs then, carrying the tray of coffee, and begins to make her way around it. She continues to speak of Mrs. Joy. **(70)**

"Are you looking forward to school?" the white-haired woman asks Betty. Her voice is almost a whisper, a knife peeling skin from a taut apple. Betty senses that it has been difficult for her to speak, feels privileged that she has. **(71)**

"Yes, I miss school." **(72)**

The woman blinks as she examines a knot in her yarn. She scrapes at it with her large square thumbnail which is flecked oddly with white fish-hook-shaped marks. "Your mother tells us you were at a camp," she says. "What did you do there?" **(73)**

Mika approaches them with the tray of coffee. "I just wish she hadn't picked me out, that's all," Mika says. "She insists on coming over here in the morning and it's impossible to work with her here. And Mr. Joy is just as bad. I send Betty for the eggs now because he used to keep me at the door talking." (74)

Mr. Joy is just as bad. Mr. Joy makes me ashamed of myself and I let him do it. The woman shakes loose the doily; it unfolds into the shape of a star as she holds it up. (75)

"You like it?" the white-haired woman asks Betty. (76)

"It's pretty." (77)

"Maybe I give it to you." (78)

"Ah, Mika," a woman across the circle says, "she just knows where she can find the best baking in town." (79)

Then they all laugh; even the quiet woman beside Betty has a dry chuckle over the comment, only Mrs. Brawn doesn't smile. She stirs her coffee with more force than necessary and sets the spoon alongside it with a clang. (80)

"Obesity is no laughing matter," she says. "Mrs. Joy is a glutton and that's to be pitied. We don't laugh at sin, the wages of sin is death." (81)

"But the gift of God is eternal life through Jesus Christ our Lord," the woman says so softly, the words are nail filings dropping into her lap. If Betty hadn't seen her lips moving, she wouldn't have heard it. "God forgives," the woman says then, louder. She is an odd combination of young and old. Her voice and breasts are young but her hair is white. (82)

Mika stands before them with the tray of coffee. "Not always," Mika says. "There's the unpardonable sin, don't forget about that." She seems pleased to have remembered this. (83)

"Which is?" the woman asks. (84)

"Well, suicide," Mika says. "It has to be, because when you think of it, it's something you can't repent of once the deed is done." Mika smiles around the circle as if to say to them, see, I'm being patient with this woman who has known suffering. (85)

"Perhaps there is no need to repent," the woman says. (86)

"Pardon?" (87)

"In Russia," the woman begins and then stops to set her thread down into her lap. She folds her hands one on top of the other and closes her eyes. The others, sensing a story, fall silent. (88)

"During the revolution in Russia, there was once a young girl who was caught by nine soldiers and was their prisoner for two weeks. She was only thirteen. These men had their way with her many times, each one taking their turn, every single night. In the end, she shot herself. What about her?" (89)

"I've never heard of such a case," Mika says. She sounds as though she resents hearing of it now. (90)

"There are always such cases," the woman says. "If God knows the falling of a single sparrow, He is also merciful. He knows we're only human." (91)

Mrs. Brawn sets her knitting down on the floor in front of her chair, leans forward slightly. "Oh, He knows," she says. "But he never gives us more than we can bear. When temptation arises, He gives us the strength to resist." She closes her statement with her hands, like a conductor pinching closed the last sound. (92)

Betty watches as the white-haired woman twists and untwists her yarn into a tight ring around her finger. "I don't believe for one moment," she says finally, "that God would condemn such a person to hell. Jesus walked the earth and so He knows." (93)

"No, no," Mika says from the buffet. "He doesn't condemn us, don't you see? That's where you're wrong. We condemn ourselves. We make that choice." (94)

"And what choice did that young girl have?" the woman asks. "It was her means of escape. God provided the gun." (95)

Mika holds the tray of lemon squares up before her as though she were offering them to the sun. She looks stricken. Deep lines cut a sharp V above her nose. "You don't mean that," she says. "Suicide is unpardonable. I'm sure of it. Knowing that keeps me going. Otherwise, I would have done it myself long ago." (96)

There is shocked silence and a rapid exchange of glances around the circle, at Betty, to see if she's heard. (97)

"You shouldn't say such things," Mrs. Brawn says quietly. "For shame. You have no reason to say that." (98)

The white-haired woman speaks with a gaunt smile. "Occasionally," she says, "in this room, someone dares to speak the truth." **(99)**

"What do you mean?" asks Mrs. Brawn. **(100)**

"Look at us," the woman says. "We're like filthy rags to Him in our self-righteousness. We obey because we fear punishment, not because we love." **(101)**

Betty sees the grease spot on her blouse where his arm has brushed against her breast. Her whole body is covered in handprints. The stone is back in her stomach. She feels betrayed. For a moment the women are lost inside their own thoughts and they don't notice as she rises from her chair and sidles over to the door. Then, as if on some signal, their conversation resumes its usual level, each one waiting impatiently for the other to be finished so they can speak their words. Their laughter and goodwill have a feeling of urgency, of desperation. Betty stands at the door; a backward glance and she sees the white-haired woman bending over her work once again, eyes blinking rapidly, her fingers moving swiftly and the doily, its flecked pattern spreading like a web across her lap. **(102)**

Questions for Writing and Discussion

1. Betty's feelings are mixed during her encounter with Mr. Joy. Explain why.

2. What does the Wednesday Circle represent to Betty? Do the women of the Circle meet her expectations?

3. What religious and/or moral issues does the story raise?

4. Explore the symbolism of light and darkness in the story.

5. What is the overriding feeling or mood in Birdsell's story?

PROFESSIONAL WRITING

EYES

CLARK BLAISE

Born in 1940 to Canadian parents, Clark Blaise was raised in Fargo, North Dakota, the American South, the urban North and Manitoba. Inspired by his personal history of impermanence and change, Blaise's writing often explores the difficult as well as rewarding experience of belonging in many places. With his wife, author Bharati Mukherjee, Blaise wrote an autobiographical journal about their year-long stay in India, Days and Nights in Calcutta *(1977) as well as* The Sorrow and the Terror *(1987) about the Air India bombing. Many of Blaise's short stories are collected in* A North American Education *(1973),* Tribal Justice *(1974),* Man and His World *(1982), and* Southern Stories *(2000).* Time Lord, *his most recent book, is about Sir Sandford Fleming.*

Blaise is a graduate of Denison University and the University of Iowa. A student of Bernard Malamud, Blaise has taught at Concordia, York, Skidmore, Iowa, Saratoga Springs, and David Thompson University Centre, and has held the prestigious position of Director of the International Writers Program at the University of Iowa. He now lives in San Francisco with his wife Bharati Mukherjee and teaches at the University of California–Berkeley.

"Eyes," from A North American Education, *was first published in* Fiddlehead *in 1971.*

You jump into this business of a new country cautiously. First you choose a place where English is spoken, with doctors and bus lines at hand, and a supermarket in a *centre d'achats* not too far away. You ease yourself into the city, approaching by car or bus down a single artery, aiming yourself along the boulevard that begins small and tree-lined in your suburb but broadens into the canyoned aorta of the city five miles beyond. And by that first winter when you know the routes and bridges, the standard congestions reported from the helicopter on your favorite radio station, you start to think of moving. What's the good of a place like this when two of your neighbors have come from Texas and the French paper you've dutifully subscribed to arrives by mail two days late? These French are all around you, behind the counters at the shopping center, in a house or two on your block; why isn't your little boy learning French at least? Where's the nearest *maternelle*? Four miles away. **(1)**

In the spring you move. You find an apartment on a small side street where dogs outnumber children and the row houses resemble London's, divided equally between the rundown and remodeled. Your neighbors are the young personalities of French television who live on delivered chicken, or the old pensioners who shuffle down the summer sidewalks in pajamas and slippers in a state of endless recuperation. Your neighbors pay sixty a month for rent, or three hundred; you pay two-fifty for a two-bedroom flat where the walls have been replastered and new fixtures hung. The bugs *d'antan* remain, as well as the hulks of cars abandoned in the fire alley behind, where downtown drunks sleep in the summer night. (2)

Then comes the night in early October when your child is coughing badly, and you sit with him in the darkened nursery, calm in the bubbling of a cold-steam vaporizer while your wife mends a dress in the room next door. And from the dark, silently, as you peer into the ill-lit fire alley, he comes. You cannot believe it at first, that a rheumy, pasty-faced Irishman in slate-gray jacket and rubber-soled shoes has come purposely to your small parking space, that he has been here before and he is not drunk (not now, at least, but you know him as a panhandler on the main boulevard a block away), that he brings with him a crate that he sets on end under your bedroom window and raises himself to your window ledge and hangs there nose-high at a pencil of light from the ill-fitting blinds. And there you are, straining with him from the uncurtained nursery, watching the man watching your wife, praying silently that she is sleeping under the blanket. The man is almost smiling, a leprechaun's face that sees what you cannot. You are about to lift the window and shout, but your wheezing child lies just under you; and what of your wife in the room next door? You could, perhaps, throw open the window and leap to the ground, tackle the man before he runs and smash his face into the bricks, beat him senseless then call the cops. . . . Or better, find the camera, affix the flash, rap once at the window and shoot when he turns. Do nothing and let him suffer. *He is at your mercy*, no one will ever again be so helpless—but what can you do? You know, somehow, he'll escape. If you hurt him, he can hurt you worse, later, viciously. He's been a regular at your window, he's watched the two of you when you prided yourself on being young and alone and masters of the city. He knows your child and the park he plays in, your wife and where she shops. He's a native of the place, a man who knows the city and maybe a dozen such windows, who knows the fire escapes and alleys and roofs, knows the habits of the city's heedless young. (3)

And briefly you remember yourself, an adolescent in another country slithering through the mosquito-ridden grassy fields behind a housing development, peering into those houses where newlyweds had not yet put up drapes, how you could spend five hours in a motionless crouch for a myopic glimpse of a slender arm reaching from the dark to douse a light. Then you hear what the man cannot; the creaking of your bed in the far bedroom, the steps of your wife on her way to the bathroom, and you see her as you never have before: blond and tall and rangily built, a north-Europe princess from a constitutional monarchy, sensuous mouth and prominent teeth, pale, tennis-ball breasts cupped in her hands as she stands in the bathroom's light. (4)

"How's Kit?" she asks. "I'd give him a kiss except that there's no blind in there," and she dashes back to bed, nude, and the man bounces twice on the window ledge. (5)

"You coming?" (6)

You find yourself creeping from the nursery, turning left at the hall and then running to the kitchen telephone; you dial the police, then hang up. How will you prepare your wife, not for what is happening, but for what has already taken place? (7)

"It's stuffy in here," you shout back, "I think I'll open the window a bit." You take your time, you stand before the blind blocking his view if he's still looking, then bravely you part the curtains. He is gone, the crate remains upright. "Do we have any masking tape?" you ask, lifting the window a crack. (8)

And now you know the city a little better. A place where millions come each summer to take pictures and walk around must have its voyeurs too. And that place in all great cities where rich and poor co-exist is especially hard on the people in-between. It's health you've been seeking, not just beauty; a tough urban health that will save you money in the bargain, and when you hear of a place twice as large at half the rent, in a part of town free of Texans, English, and French, free of young actors and stewardesses who deposit their garbage in pizza boxes, you move again. (9)

It is, for you, a city of Greeks. In the summer you move you attend a movie at the corner cinema. The posters advertise a war movie, in Greek, but the uniforms are unfamiliar. Both sides wear mustaches, both sides handle machine guns, both leave older women behind dressed in black. From the posters outside there is a promise of sex; blond women in slips, dark-eyed peasant girls. There will be rubble, executions against a wall. You can follow the story from the stills alone: mustached boy goes to war, embraces dark-eyed village girl. Black-draped mother and admiring young brother stand behind. Young soldier, mustache fuller, embraces blond prostitute on a tangled bed. Enter soldiers, boy hides under sheets. Final shot, back in village. Mother in black; dark-eyed village girl in black. Young brother marching to the front. (10)

You go in, pay your ninety cents, pay a nickel in the lobby for a wedge of *halvah*-like sweets. You understand nothing, you resent their laughter and you even resent the picture they're running. Now you know the Greek for "Coming Attractions," for this is a gangster movie at least thirty years old. The eternal Mediterranean gangster movie set in Athens instead of Naples or Marseilles, with smaller cars and narrower roads, uglier women and more sinister killers. After an hour the movie flatters you. No one knows you're not a Greek, that you don't belong in this theater, or even this city. That, like the Greeks, you're hanging on. **(11)**

Outside the theater the evening is warm and the wide sidewalks are clogged with Greeks who nod as you come out. Like the Ramblas in Barcelona, with children out past midnight and families walking back and forth for a long city block, the men filling the coffeehouses, the women left outside, chatting. Not a blond head on the sidewalk, not a blond head for miles. Greek music pours from the coffeehouses, flies stumble on the pastry, whole families munch their *torsades molles* as they walk. Dry goods are sold at midnight from the sidewalk, like New York fifty years ago. You're wandering happily, glad that you moved, you've rediscovered the innocence of starting over. **(12)**

Then you come upon a scene directly from Spain. A slim blond girl in a floral top and white pleated skirt, tinted glasses, smoking, with bad skin, ignores a persistent young Greek in a shiny Salonika suit. "Whatsamatta?" he demands, slapping a ten-dollar bill on his open palm. And without looking back at him she drifts closer to the curb and a car makes a sudden squealing turn and lurches to a stop on the cross street. Three men are inside, the back door opens and not a word is exchanged as she steps inside. How? What refinement of gesture did we immigrants miss? You turn to the Greek boy in sympathy, you know just how he feels, but he's already heading across the street, shouting something to his friends outside a barbecue stand. You have a pocketful of bills and a Mediterranean soul, and money this evening means a woman, and blond means whore and you would spend it all on another blond with open pores; all this a block from your wife and tenement. And you hurry home. **(13)**

Months later you know the place. You trust the Greeks in their stores, you fear their tempers at home. Eight bathrooms adjoin a central shaft, you hear the beatings of your son's friends, the thud of fist on bone after the slaps. Your child knows no French, but he plays cricket with Greeks and Jamaicans out in the alley behind

Pascal's hardware. He brings home the oily tires from the Esso station, plays in the boxes behind the appliance store. You watch from a greasy back window, at last satisfied. None of his friends is like him, like you. He is becoming Greek, becoming Jamaican, becoming a part of this strange new land. His hair is nearly white; you can spot him a block away. (14)

On Wednesdays the butcher quarters his meat. Calves arrive by refrigerator truck, still intact but for their split-open bellies and sawed-off hooves. The older of the three brothers skins the carcass with a small thin knife that seems all blade. A knife he could shave with. The hide rolls back in a continuous flap, the knife never pops the membrane over the fat. (15)

Another brother serves. Like yours, his French is adequate. *"Twa lif d'hamburger,"* you request, still watching the operation on the rickety sawhorse. Who could resist? It's a Levantine treat, the calf's stumpy legs high in the air, the hide draped over the edge and now in the sawdust, growing longer by the second. (16)

The store is filling. The ladies shop on Wednesday, especially the old widows in black overcoats and scarves, shoes and stockings. Yellow, mangled fingernails. Wednesdays attract them with boxes in the window, and they call to the butcher as they enter, the brother answers, and the women dip their fingers in the boxes. The radio is loud overhead, music from the Greek station. (17)

"Une et soixante, m'sieur. Du bacon, jambon?" (18)

And you think, taking a few lamb chops but not their saltless bacon, how pleased you are to manage so well. It is a Byzantine moment with blood and widows and sides of dripping beef, contentment in a snowy slum at five below. (19)

The older brother, having finished the skinning, straightens, curses, and puts away the tiny knife. A brother comes forward to pull the hide away, a perfect beginning for a gameroom rug. Then, bending low at the rear of the glistening carcass, the legs spread high and stubby, the butcher digs in his hands, ripping hard where the scrotum is, and pulls on what seems to be a strand of rubber, until it snaps. He puts a single glistening prize in his mouth, pulls again and offers the other to his brother, and they suck. (20)

The butcher is singing now, drying his lips and wiping his chin, and still he's chewing. The old black-draped widows with the parchment faces are also chewing. On leaving, you check the boxes in the window. Staring out are the heads of pigs and lambs, some with the eyes lifted out and a red socket exposed. A few are loose and the box is slowly dissolving from the blood, and the ice beneath. (21)

The women have gathered around the body; little pieces are offered to them from the head and entrails. The pigs' heads are pink, perhaps they've been boiled, and hairless. The eyes are strangely blue. You remove your gloves and touch the skin, you brush against the grainy ear. How the eye attracts you! How you would like to lift one out, press its smoothness against your tongue, then crush it in your mouth. And you cannot. Already your finger is numb and the head, it seems, has shifted under you. And the eye, in panic, grows white as your finger approaches. You would take that last half inch but for the certainty, in this world you have made for yourself, that the eye would blink and your neighbors would turn upon you. (22)

Questions for Writing and Discussion

1. Blaise has chosen an unusual narrative viewpoint for this story. What is it? What effect is the author trying for? Does he succeed? Explain your answer.

2. Paragraphs three to eight describe an incident involving a "rheumy, pasty-faced Irishman." How is this "story within the story" a part of Blaise's central motif?

3. The final paragraphs are a detailed description of the weekly ritual of shopping for meat. Explain the symbolism inherent in this graphic portrayal and its appropriateness as an ending to the story. How does this picture serve to reinforce Blaise's theme?

4. This story would be easy to make into film. Explore its cinematic characteristics, including Blaise's use of language and dialogue.

5. Choose an experience common to most of us at one time or another; for example, the birth of a child, a job interview, a first airplane flight, a championship game. Using Blaise's narrative viewpoint and choosing language and dialogue for their cinematic potential, write two or three "scenes" describing the experience.

PROFESSIONAL   WRITING

THE LIGHT OF DISTANT PLANETS
STEPHEN GUPPY

Stephen Guppy teaches English and Creative Writing at Malaspina University-College on Vancouver Island. He has published two books of poetry and a collection of short fiction, and his poems and stories have appeared in numerous Canadian anthologies and magazines. He has been shortlisted for the Journey Prize and the Scottish International Open Poetry Competition. His most recent book is Blind Date With the Angel: The Diane Arbus Poems. *"The Light of Distant Planets" was first published in* Event.

All the way west from Alberta, I sang about the Man in the Moon. My parents, who must have been ready to strangle me by the time we reached the Rockies, tried to interest me in colouring books and dog-eared Donald Duck comics. I ignored them and went right on singing. My sister, locked in a Gravol trance, stared mutely out the window. Long journeys made her car-sick. They made me want to sing. (1)

We drove out from the air force base at Cold Lake, where my father was stationed, to Vancouver Island twice a year to visit my mother's parents. Each time, diverted by highway closures and fluctuations in the weather, we took a slightly different route. One year we climbed through Crow's Nest Pass, our ancient slug-green Chevy van slogging uphill for hours between grimy, coal-blackened snowdrifts. The next we went clear down to Montana before attempting to make our way west. America, we discovered, was full of Greatests and Firsts, as if the whole country were a trophy case or the Guinness Book of Records. We drove across the World's Longest Non-Suspension Bridge, had a picnic atop the Largest Hydro-Electric Dam on the North American Continent, saw the Tallest Mountain in the Forty-Eight States, and waved to the World's Oldest Miner. We arrived in Vancouver from Seattle, like a family of American tourists, the van laden down with pennants and crests and snow-globes full of tiny dams and bridges. The following year we looped through Jasper and Banff, where my sister, fogged with Gravol, muttered nonsense-vowels at the Grizzlies that reared up out of the roadside bush and snarled at us as we passed. My mind, by the time I was five years old, was a road map of B.C. and Alberta, with inserts for the northwestern states. (2)

This time we were driving through Kicking Horse Pass, with overnight stops at Calgary and Golden. I sang all the way through the dazzling peaks, changing keys in a snow flurry near the summit. My mother, who had withdrawn into a headache when we'd begun to climb into the mountains, surfaced as we passed beneath the famous Kicking Horse and announced that we were passing through the most important place she'd ever been. It was right here, on this very spot, she said, that she had woken up in the Skyliner Car of the CNR train in October of 1946 and had a vision about her life. **(3)**

She was wrong, of course: that was eight hundred miles south in Crow's Nest Pass, which we'd driven through five or six times in the past without her ever being reminded of anything. She was right in an aesthetic sense, however: Kicking Horse Pass was a much more suitable place for a revelation than Crow's Nest: less coal dust, better mountains, an abundance of postcard-white snow. **(4)**

Making poetic sense of everything while being hopelessly adrift in terms of logic (or geography) was one of my mother's defining characteristics. Not knowing when to end a good thing was already one of mine. As soon as my mother stopped talking, I went right back to singing my song. **(5)**

There was a man lived in the moon, in the moon, in the moon.

There was a man lived in the moon and his name was Aken Drum. **(6)**

I had learned the song I was singing during my brief and undistinguished career as a Kindergarten student. The teacher was a German named Miss Kaufman. She punished the kids by spanking them and then making them stand in the corner with a wastebasket on their heads. You could be punished for colouring the animals in your book the wrong colour: ducks were white with yellow bills; bears were brown and sometimes black; robins were brown with red stomachs. No creature that had ever existed was orange or purple or lime. On my first day in class, Miss Kaufman spanked a boy named Joey for cutting out a Mickey Mouse without allowing enough room for the outline. Joey's underpants, when she pulled down his pants, were soiled with shit where his buttocks met and torn along the waistband. He struggled against her lanky knees while she lectured the class and whacked him. The rest of us looked down at our scrap-books, where our cut-out robins, ducks, and bears, all crayoned the appropriate colours, floated in their auras of mucilage like ikons of primitive saints. After nap-time, we ate the snacks our mothers had provided while Joey sobbed into a cardboard bucket in the corner of the room. (7)

The first time Miss Kaufman spoke to me, I kicked her in the shins. I followed this manoeuvre by butting her in the crotch, then bounced a round-house right off her pelvis. She shrieked and called the Principal. My sister, red-faced with embarrassment, was hauled out of her Grade Three class and compelled to take me home. Disgraced, I spent the rest of the year cutting pictures of cars out of the liquor ads in *Argosy* and *Popular Mechanics* and pasting them into my scrap-book while my mother did the vacuuming and played her Rosemary Clooney 78's on our home-made Heathkit hi-fi. Between repetitions of "This Old House" and "Take My Heart, Take My Heart, Take Me," I sang the one song I'd learned in Kindergarten before my contretemps with the dreaded Miss Kaufman. (8)

And he played upon a ladle, a ladle, a ladle.

And he played upon a ladle and his name was Aken Drum. (9)

I could sing this song for hours on end, as it never really ended. Accompanied by the drone of the Electrolux and interrupted at irregular intervals by the shattering crashes of sonic booms as they detonated over the air base, I chanted about the Man in the Moon from breakfast until dinner, then hummed the tune to myself while the rest of the family played Snap or Go Fish and listened to Rosemary Clooney. My scrapbook grew wrinkled and fat with paste and car ads. Other kids trudged through the snow to Miss Kaufman. Sub-arctic blizzards and CF-100's roared over the roof and hammered at the windows, like the voices of quarrelling gods. When spring came and the ice finally melted, we loaded up the van and drove south. (10)

My mother was a War Bride. She met my father in Bristol, while he was staying with an aunt of his while on leave from the army base at Aldershot. They were married in August of 1942, just two weeks before my father's boat left for North Africa, Sicily, and various points north. After VE Day, the Army sent my father back across the Atlantic, crammed into a troop ship. Six months later, my mother followed. The ship she took was a passenger liner, though old and partially gutted—it had been used as a supply ship during the last months of the War. Apart from the crew, there was no one aboard but women and kids. Some of the women were kids themselves, girls who should have been in school. They leaned against the rail as Liverpool slid out on the greasy Irish Sea and dropped off the edge of the planet. After that, there were days of heaving waves and pregnant girls puking into buckets. In the gray hours between not-quite-sleep and almost-waking, my mother went out on the deck, stepping carefully in her Betty Grable heels on the wood cleats and slippery metal, and did a slithery, lurching circuit of the liner. If there was anybody else outside, she'd chat, yelling into the constant wind, and try to light a Woodbine. (11)

"Yanks," the other girl would say, sooner or later. (12)

"Over-paid, over-sexed, and over here," my mother would reply. It was a code, of course, like the one they used to fool the Jerries about D-Day. (13)

But where was here? Not this lurching deck, that much was certain, but England. The lost world. Home. They'd be looking for it, over those sloping gray waves, down the streets of Mobile or Great Falls or Saskatoon, over Iowa cornfields, for the rest of their lives. (14)

Arriving at last at Halifax, the women and their little ones were herded onto a train. The train went west, to Montreal and Toronto, where it paused in grimy, snowbound stations long enough for some of the girls—those who had married Yanks—to transfer to other trains and buses, before it broke free of civilization and drifted out into featureless space. The next day there was nothing much to see, only snow and lakes and stunted trees. Once in a while a town would appear, unexpected as a desert oasis, and one of the girls would disembark, clutching kiddies or her own distended belly. She would stand on the platform and stare at the train, as if she were leaving, not arriving. The porters would deposit her luggage at her feet, and she would wait there for something to happen. The train would pull away. (15)

The prairie towns my mother passed through were inhabited by women and cars. The few men seemed huge and distracted; like bears who had wandered in from the bush, they shuffled along the sidewalks, avoiding the knots of animated women who burst from the doors of the markets in their nylons and sleek bear-brown furs. At night, there was nothing, just nothing. The train thumped along in a tunnel made of light from its own filthy windows. Beyond was the sea, or the desert, or the infinite space between stars. There were no planes, no lights, no barrage balloons. The War was not only over, it was fiction, it had never occurred. My mother would wake from dreams of V2's thundering into the bricks of her row house, her mother and father burned alive in their beds, the windows splashing over her bed like sheets of jagged water, and find herself safe and alone in her berth. She would pull back the thick velour curtain and look out into darkness, the omnipresent rumbling of the train-wheels in her ears. When the sky cleared there were bitter stars, so white they looked like zircons. The whole of the world was liquid; it flowed west from the past to the future, like a painted diorama on the wall of the Bristol Museum. The War was in the east, near the entrance, where the ushers took tickets and passed out brochures. She would stroll toward the windows soon, loitering like a schoolgirl, and look dispassionately at the pastel scenes of the life that lay ahead. **(16)**

After three days, there were mountains. These were white and abruptly vertical, as if someone had taken the resolute plane of the prairies and tried to tip it on its side. The train passed through tunnels, the racket of its iron wheels amplified by the echoing rock of the mountain. It traversed immense crevasses in the clefts of which boiled waterfalls and rapids, clattering along quite happily on flimsy wooden trestles that seemed to have been constructed out of millions of toothpicks. It plowed through hills of snow. **(17)**

One night, as the train ascended Crow's Nest Pass, my mother awoke in her narrow berth and blinked into the dark. She lay there for what seemed like a long time and listened, though there was no sound but the thumping of the train-wheels. She believed that if she lay there long enough she would hear another woman cough, or the whimpering of one of the newborns. Then it came to her: she was all alone. This was wrong, of course, there were still a few other girls from England on the train; she wasn't the only one going on all the way to Vancouver. In the darkness, though, she felt alone—the last British War Bride on a vast empty train, thundering through solid rock toward the distant, unimaginable coastline of an ocean on the far side of the world. Getting up, she pulled on her housecoat and went out in to the corridor. Guided by the muted lights, she made her way from car to car; there was no one in the whole train, just no one. **(18)**

She was groping her way through the Skyliner Car when the train came pounding out of the tunnel. Instantly, the dome above her head, which a moment ago had been utterly black, was filled with constellations. She could see the Little Dipper and the Dragon, drifting east. The tables in the lounge were white with starlight. She sat down on a leather banquette, looking up at the

Northern Crown. She felt as if the stars were inside her, like particles of white sand in water. Her childhood, her marriage, the air raids, the war, all of these were a tunnel she had passed through unscathed. They were gone now, like the heaving gray Atlantic and the prairies. Ahead there was nothing, her husband, the coast. There was only this moment, in which she was suspended. She would live there forever, a spirit sealed in glass, reflecting empty starlight like a mirror. **(19)**

While my mother was making her laborious way from coast to coast, my father was building a house. For the past five years, he had spent his nights in rooms full of grunting, snoring soldiers. He had slept in ruined villas, next to marble walls lined with ornate frames from which the paintings had long since been stolen. He had slept in army hospitals where the nurses wore high rubber boots with their uniforms so that they could walk through the rainwater that poured between the beds. He had slept in a slit trench every night of one summer, as if he were a vole or a badger. He had curled up in the dark in a farmer's field in the Appenines and woken to find the corpse of a German, his thighs blown to streamers, not five feet from his head. He had never been alone. **(20)**

In civilian life, he seemed incapable of living in a house that had been occupied by others; unable to settle on an existing place, he was forced to build his own. This he'd do by finding materials and tools that cost him nothing or next to nothing. "Scrounging," as he called it. One of our houses he would build out of lumber he'd found floating in the waters of Georgia Strait, timbers and planks that had fallen off scows and that technically belonged to no one. Another he'd make from D-grade wood that had been rejected by a sawmill. This first house he built for my mother, he constructed out of salvaged chunks of army barracks that had been built during the war and then demolished. **(21)**

The finished product, when he brought his new wife to see it, was a patch-work of khaki and camouflage panels, some of the windows still taped against air-raids, the front porch and every room inside painted uniform Air Force-surplus gray. It was less a house than a piece of sculpture, a monument my father had built to his past, constructed from the fragments of his memory. All the barracks he'd slept in from Aldershot to Rotterdam had congealed into one compressed structure, the way that rooms from different parts of your life will coalesce into single vast and rambling structure in the murky light of dreams. **(22)**

If my father had expected his wife to refine and humanize the makeshift house he'd created, soften it with curtains and valances and re-paint it in soft pastel colours, to give it the homey, feminine touch it so obviously needed, he must have been disappointed. For the first few weeks after her arrival, she did nothing but brew herself cups of tea and complain about the damp. My father, coming home from the machine shop where he was working, would find her in the armchair that was the only stick of furniture in the living-room, bundled up in a bulky afghan, staring out of the curtainless window at the drizzle of west coast rain. At night, while he slept, she would rise and walk through the rooms of the house in a washed-out flannel nightgown, the afghan bundled around her hips and dragging along the tiles. She would go to the window of each room in turn and stare out through her own reflected face at the glistening rocks and fir trees. On clear nights, she would watch the stars, gazing up at their glassy alphabet as if she meant to decipher and read it. It was left to my father to decorate the house, which he did on his evenings and weekends, and to his sisters to run up the curtains. Other relatives donated furniture. Crockery was ordered from a catalogue, as were floormats and a radio that also told the time. (23)

By the time my mother informed my father that she was pregnant, the house was almost livable. Eight months later, my sister was born. A couple of weeks after that, my grandparents came out from England. They had travelled through the same vast Canadian landscape as their daughter, but at a different time of year. Instead of snow and lead-gray skies, their minds, when they arrived in the village where my parents lived, were full of heat and wheatfields. The rain of Vancouver Island caught them completely by surprise. Disoriented, hopelessly climate-lagged, they bundled themselves in sweaters and refused to go outside. It was my father's turn to pace and watch the moon. Rain or no rain, he went out as soon as he could every evening, walking for miles along the deserted beach, pausing for a cigarette in the shelter of the cannery wall, waiting out squalls underneath the government dock, his back against a barnacled piling. When the wind came up, the clouds would part, and the sky would take on extra dimensions, expanding into a sphere of lights—the dazzling band of the Milky Way, the Dippers, the pinprick of Vega. In the centre of it all the moon shone down, blunt and blue as the shell of an oyster. (24)

And his hair was made of roast beef, roast beef, roast beef.

And his hair was made of roast beef, and his name was Aken Drum. (25)

The rain begins in Revelstoke and doesn't let up until Vancouver. All the way across British Columbia, my sister plays listlessly with Walk Doll. Walk Doll is blonde and has long rubber legs. When you shake her, her eyelids bat furiously. She spends whole days with her hands up, as if she has been apprehended while robbing a bank. Her blue-glass eyes gaze resolutely upwards, which makes her seem oddly spiritual—a Barbie with ambitions of sainthood. **(26)**

In Alberta, we too spent our lives looking up. We stood out on the icy street to watch the Northern Lights all winter. Craned our necks as Neptune bombers thundered above the rooftops. Watched the Golden Hawks do barrel rolls and fly in tight formation, their wing-tips glinting fiercely in the stark Alberta sun. On the west coast, there is no sky, only clouds and constant rain. We walk from the car with our heads down, eyeing the puddles and pockets of slush. In restaurants, we avoid the windows. We position ourselves in the centre of the room, leaving the plush vinyl booths for other travellers. **(27)**

"Have some french fries! A burger!" our mother exclaims, trying desperately to perk up my sister. **(28)**

"What?" my sister eventually replies, her blue eyes as glassy as Walk Doll's. **(29)**

"Leave the kid alone, she's car-sick," our dad mutters, scanning the huge plastic menu. "I suppose you want one of these pirate ships?" he asks me. For a dollar, he explains, you can get a hot dog, fries, dill pickle, glass of milk or apple juice, instant chocolate pudding. He shows me the picture of the Jolly Roger Lunch, a wiener and french fries in a little cardboard ship with a cup of gooey pudding on the poop deck. **(30)**

"I'm not very hungry either, Dad," I tell him. "Maybe just a sandwich. Or some soup." **(31)**

"Oh, what the hell, live a little," Dad says. He waves the gigantic menu at the waitress. **(32)**

When my Jolly Roger Lunch arrives, I pick at the fries without enthusiasm and refrain from making contact with the hot dog. To my surprise, no one notices my lack of interest in the food. Even my mother, who usually monitors my caloric intake like a physicist counting electrons, picks glumly at her ham-on-rye and pays no attention to anyone. The other diners seem almost as disoriented as we are. This constant need to move around, this reckless jittering back and forth between one time zone and another, has irreparably damaged their senses. We were never designed to adapt ourselves to shifting climatic conditions; certainly not on such short notice, anyway. Migrations that once required eons we accomplish twice a year. (33)

"Here, honey," my father says, holding out a French fry to Walk Doll's pouting lips, "put away a few of these—you could use a little starch in your diet." (34)

The rubber doll completely ignores him. My sister is also oblivious; she watches without interest as the customers troop sniffling to the washrooms and cashier—she has evolved beyond their primitive needs, transcended the urge to travel in flocks and consume at specific locations. What nourishment she still requires is supplied by a single Gravol spansule. (35)

I take a couple of wilted chips out of my cardboard pirate ship and position them like outstretched arms on either side of my hot dog. A couple more French fries make excellent legs. The head is a cup of custard. (36)

And his eyes were made of potatoes, potatoes, potatoes.

And his eyes were made of potatoes and his name
was Aken Drum. (37)

When we arrive at our destination, the clouds abruptly part. We pull into my grandparents' driveway and step out of the car into sunlight. It is suddenly, inexplicably summer. My grandfather, bending to pull spring onions from the garden, has already taken off his gardening jacket and rolled up the sleeves of his shirt. My grandmother, a wicker basket of laundry from the line in her arms, stands waving in the sunlight on the porch. (38)

"We never thought we'd see you again!" Gran emotes. She drops the laundry basket and embraces my mom. Dad mouths her words exactly as she says them. My sister, clutching Walk Doll, staggers stiffly from the car. For the next week, we are guests in my grandparents' house. I sleep in Grandpa's bedroom, on a roll-away cot. Mom and Dad take the big bed, which Gran normally has to herself. My sister and she share the attic. In the evenings, sent to bed before anyone else, I lie straining to hear the dialogue from *Amos and Andy* on my grandparents' miraculous Electrohome TV. I doze off to the trenchant theme from *Dragnet*. When morning comes, we wander out for breakfast one by one. Mom and Gran chat mournfully over corn flakes. It takes me a few days to realize that when they talk about "home," they mean neither the coast nor Alberta, but somewhere else entirely. England, the life they've abandoned. My dad prolongs his morning shower and shave until they've finished. Grandpa, on the other hand, has been outside since dawn. **(39)**

Completely ignored by the adults, I wolf down my Post Alpha-Bits and then play with our new souvenirs. There are glossy brochures from the northwestern states. Replicas of redwood trees and tiny, ancient miners. Tyrannosaurs and mammoths from the dinosaur museum. By the time Dad appears from the bathroom, there's no room for him at the table. He has to eat his corn flakes standing up. **(40)**

"Six days of driving," my father sighs. He crosses to the kitchen sink and squints out at the sunlight. "Half my leave driving out here and the rest driving back." **(41)**

I look up from my plastic Albertasaurus just in time to catch my mother's and grandmother's contradictory expressions—Gran's furious, Mom's childishly confused. **(42)**

"Why do I bother?" my father adds, gazing up at my grandparents' budgie with a look of unalloyed despair. **(43)**

"Who's a pretty boy, then?" the bird inquires, cocking his tangerine head to one side. **(44)**

Man and bird exchange quizzical glances, then one returns to pecking at his slab of mottled cuttlebone, while the other puts his jacket on and heads out for a walk. **(45)**

By the third day of our visit, my father has developed an apparently uncontrollable urge to go for long, almost maniacally brisk walks in the sunlight. While my sister and I are still struggling out of our roll-away cots, he wolfs down his corn-flakes and bolts out the door. **(46)**

"Don't forget you're going fishing with Dad!" my mother calls after him. "Mom and I have packed you guys some lunches!" **(47)**

My father waves vaguely without turning around. Then he zigzags between hedges and canters down the street. **(48)**

My grandfather comes in with a basket of vegetables from the garden just in time to see my father heading off. **(49)**

"Can't let those trout die of old age," he remarks. "Your gaffer can always meet us at the river." (50)

I carry the picnic lunch while he brings the rods. By noon, we've hooked nothing but water. (51)

"Do you miss it?" I ask him. (52)

"What?" he says, threading a livid red worm onto my hook. (53)

"Home," I say. "Where you used to live, in England." (54)

He squints at me sideways and proffers the worm, which is wriggling forlornly in its death-throes. I pinch the line gingerly and drop it in the lake. (55)

"Not much," he says. He shrugs and then rummages around in the can for another worm. When he's pierced it with a fishhook, he tosses it into the water. Ripples spread over our faces, reflected in the surface of the pond. (56)

"Mom does," I tell him. We part and then come together on the water, his stubbled cheeks and tuft of white hair bobbing, my own face small and troubled, a tiny moon pitted with weeds. (57)

"She would," he says. He jerks his line and flicks out a bullhead. "Pass me them sandwiches, will you? My stomach thinks my throat has been cut." (58)

Next morning, I wake up not long after dawn. My head is still roaring from the furnace, but I can hear my father snoring through the wall. When I open my eyes, the first thing I see is my grandfather staring in the window. He has placed a pair of small tomatoes, green at the stem ends and banded with yellow, over his eyes and is holding them in place by frowning. Scallions sprout from behind either ear, trailing streamers of green along his cheekbones. A petit-pan squash sits on his head like a *boulevardier's* beret. Sprigs of parsley sprout from his collar. (59)

I sit up in bed and rub at my eyes. (60)

"Grandpa?" I mutter. (61)

My grandfather opens his mouth and sticks out his tongue, on which is a single red gooseberry. (62)

And his nose was made of a carrot, a carrot, a carrot.

And his nose was made of a carrot and his name was Aken Drum. (63)

On the trip back to Alberta, my parents hardly speak. Every twenty miles or so, my father turns on the radio. Four or five miles later, my mother turns it off. In the interludes between the bursts of song, they both stare straight ahead at the landscape. My sister is also silent; she sits looking out her window, her mouth slightly open, her eyes glazed and blank. I too am keeping quiet. Having unpacked the sno-globes before we left my grandparents' place, I am occupied with serious matters. Like a wizard in a fairy-tale, I am making it snow. I am bringing the winter to various worlds, sending gusts of swirling flakes between the spires of the redwoods, under the arch of the Golden Gate Bridge, over a doomed stegosaurus. Walk Doll, who is also at a loss for words, sits stiffly on the seat right between us. **(64)**

"Swallow," my mother says, . . . a propos of nothing. **(65)**

"What?" I ask, looking up from a miniature blizzard. **(66)**

"Swallow! So your ears don't pop!" **(67)**

I crane my neck and gaze into the gap between her shoulder and my father's. I can smell my mother's perfume, which is "Evening in Paris." It's eight o'clock, and getting dark. We are entering the Rockies. **(68)**

"Is this Kicking Horse Pass?" I ask. **(69)**

"Hardly," my mother says, looking accusingly at Dad. At that moment, the sun hits the mountains. The postcard horizon of jagged white peaks ignites into margarine yellow. Back-lit, my parents are stereotypes, two-dimensional as Dagwood and Blondie. My sister's face and mine are gold. So, for that matter, is Walk Doll's. All five of us gaze at the sunset, which fades as we look at it, like the treasure in a Brothers Grimm story. **(70)**

By nine o'clock, my ears have popped. It is dark. We are high in the Rockies. My sister, soothed by car-sickness pills, slumps against the arm-rest, mouth gaping. Our parents are lost in their own private thoughts, Dad driving, Mom gazing out the window at the rocks and walls of snow. Only Walk Doll and I remain vigilant. Her plastic eyes gaze upwards at the headliner of the car, on the lookout for divine inspiration. I sit with a whole solar system of sno-globes in my lap, an arctic god creating his own ice-age. Like all migrant life forms, we are filled with regret and expectation. The days of our lives are nothing more than stops along a highway, little worlds in which the snow falls for no reason. **(71)**

As we reach the summit of Crow's Nest Pass, I pretend I hear a passing train. I imagine squares of buttery light flowing past beside the highway, a Skyliner Car from another life with its dome of grimy fire. I wave at rocks and darkness, watch my reflection waving back, the small white face, the hopeless smirk of thwarted expectation. (72)

I open my mouth. I am singing. (73)

And his mouth was made of tomatoes, tomatoes, tomatoes.

And his mouth was made of tomatoes and
his name was Aken Drum. (74)

It is snowing on the Air Force Base, and the arctic sky is so heavy and dark that it may as well be midnight. The searchlights near the runways streak the clouds like veins of ore. In Miss Kaufman's room, the children are drawing outlines around the animals in their scrapbooks. Each squirrel gets a livid blue halo. Each antelope has green fire on its antlers. The animals themselves are brown, white, gray, exactly as they must be in nature. Outside the windows, the snow is clean and white. It swirls obliquely down from the sky, a sort of benediction, though as pointless and unwanted as all the other works of God. Now Miss Kaufman is leading the children in song. See her angular body sway as she waves at the class with a piece of blue chalk, as if she were an orchestra conductor. Voices drift like vapour-trails through the lemon-yellow air. (75)

There was a man lived in the moon, in the moon, in the moon.

There was a man lived in the moon and
his name was Aken Drum. (76)

Only a few blocks away from the school, I am patiently cutting out car ads. Mercurys. Chevrolets. Chryslers. Anthropomorphic Austins with glaucous, blinking eyes. Hudsons as bulbous as blowfish. In some of the cars, there are tanned, smiling men. In others, there are smiling blonde women. Some are parked in fields of lime-green grass where whole families have gathered in the nebulous shade, drinking sodas, cooking hot-dogs, having picnics. (77)

This is us, I decide, smoothing down the lumps of glue under the body of a grinning man who is sitting beside a Plymouth. His children gaze up at him in abject adoration while their mother spreads Miracle Whip on a sandwich. This is me, this boy with the bottle of pop in his hand. This is also me, this smaller boy, his brother. This girl is my sister. Our mother is Walk Doll. See her perfect blonde hair. This Plymouth is ours. This is also ours, this green shade, this sunlight. We are travelling, travelling, west to the sea. Far above us the moon shines, made vague by the light of day. The stars are all invisible now, though we know that they must be shining. They are flowing east above us as we migrate through our lives—a million small white faces, silent voices, grains of sand. **(78)**

Questions for Writing and Discussion

1. In his narration of a family vacation trip, the author vividly evokes the setting of the story. Select two or three passages that most effectively communicate the sense of time, place, and mood.

2. The author describes enclosed, small spaces and open, vast spaces. Select examples of each. What meaning may we infer from these contrasts?

3. Examine the narrator's recollection of the arrival of each of his parents to Canada. Choose some passages that are suggestive of the parents as pioneers of a new frontier.

4. Of what significance to the story is each of the following: the repeated rhyme, Miss Kaufman's kindergarten class, the narrator's scrapbook, snow, Walk Doll, the Jolly Roger lunch, and dinosaurs.

5. The title anticipates the story's primary motif. Illustrating your answer with references to "light" and "distant planets," explain the relationship between this motif and the story's theme.

6. The story is told by an adult looking back nostalgically on boyhood memories. From his mature point of view, these experiences become even more meaningful in their philosophical context. In two or three paragraphs recount a childhood incident that goes beyond the event itself to demonstrate a larger truth.

RESPONDING TO LITERATURE: THE WRITING PROCESS

■ **ASSIGNMENT FOR RESPONDING TO LITERATURE**
Choose one of the short stories from this chapter (or a work of literature assigned in your class), and read it actively, reread and annotate the work, and share your responses with others in the class. Then write an interpretative essay. Assume that you are writing for other members of your class (including your instructor) who have read the work but who may not understand or agree with your interpretation.

COLLECTING

In addition to reading, rereading, annotating, and sharing your responses, try the following collecting strategies:

- **Collaborative annotation.** In small groups, choose a work of literature or select a passage that you have already annotated. In the group, read each other's annotations. Then discuss each annotation. Which annotations does your group agree are the best? Have a group recorder record the best annotations.

- **Elements of fiction analysis.** Reread the paragraphs defining character, plot, point of view, setting, and style. Choose three of these elements that seem most important in the story that you are reading. Reread the story, annotating for these three elements. Then freewrite a paragraph explaining *how these three elements are interrelated or how they explain the theme.*

- **Time line.** In your notebook, draw a time line for the story. List above the line everything that happens in the story. Below the line, indicate where the story opens, when the major conflicts occur, and where the climax and the denouement occur. For "The Story of an Hour," student writer Karen Ehrhardt drew the following time line:

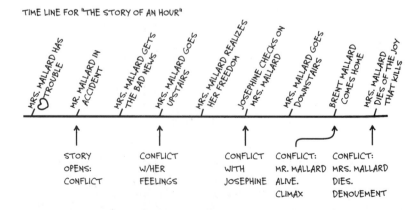

TIME LINE FOR "THE STORY OF AN HOUR"

MRS. MALLARD HAS TROUBLE — MR. MALLARD IN ACCIDENT — MRS. MALLARD GETS THE BAD NEWS — MRS. MALLARD GOES UPSTAIRS — MRS. MALLARD REALIZES HER FREEDOM — JOSEPHINE CHECKS ON MRS. MALLARD — MRS. MALLARD GOES DOWNSTAIRS — BRENT MALLARD COMES HOME — MRS. MALLARD DIES OF THE JOY THAT KILLS

STORY OPENS: CONFLICT — CONFLICT W/HER FEELINGS — CONFLICT WITH JOSEPHINE — CONFLICT: MR. MALLARD ALIVE. CLIMAX — CONFLICT: MRS. MALLARD DIES. DENOUEMENT

- **Feature list.** Choose a character trait, repeated image, or idea that you wish to investigate in the story. List, in order of appearance, every word, image, or reference that you find in the story.

- **Scene vision or revision.** Write a scene for this story in which you change some part of it. You may *add* a scene to the beginning, middle, or end of the story. You may *change* a scene in the story. You may write a scene in the story from a different character's point of view. You may change the style of the story for your scene.

- **Story picture.** Draw a picture of the story, based on the time line and conflict mapping, that represents the entire story. Use the information from your character analysis, time line, and character conflicts to help you draw a single picture of the complete story. Student writer Lori Van Skike drew a picture for "The Story of an Hour" that shows how the rising and falling action of the plot parallels Mrs. Mallard's ascent and descent of the stairs:

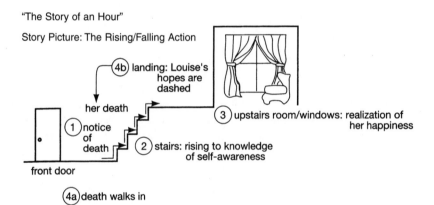

"The Story of an Hour"

Story Picture: The Rising/Falling Action

- **Character conflict map.** Start with a full page of paper. Draw a main character in the centre of the page. Locate the other major characters, internal forces, and external forces (including social, economic, and environmental pressures) in a circle around the main character. Draw a line between each of these peripheral characters or forces and the main character.

- **Background investigation.** Investigate the biographical, social, historical, or geographical context for the story. Locate a biography of the author. How are the major events of the author's life relevant to the story? Read about the historical or economic background of the story. Look at maps or descriptions of the setting for the story. How do these background sources increase your appreciation or widen your understanding of the story?

- **Reconsideration of purposes.** What idea, theme, or approach most interests you? Will you be explaining, evaluating, problem solving, or arguing? Are you combining purposes? Do these purposes suggest what kinds of information you might collect?

SHAPING

Test each of the following possible shapes against your ideas for your essay. Use or adapt the shape or shapes that are most appropriate for your own interpretation.

Explaining Relationships
Often interpretative essays analyze how the parts of a story relate to the whole. As you explain these relationships, you should show how key lines or scenes contribute to the portrait of the major character or to the overall theme of the story. Your focus might be on how *plot* or *character conflicts* affect your understanding of the major character, on how the *setting* reflects the theme, or on how *images* reveal character and/or contribute to the theme.

Introduction and thesis:	The images in story X reveal that the theme is Y.
First scene or part:	How key images contribute to theme
Second scene or part:	How key images contribute to theme
Third scene or part:	How key images contribute to theme
Conclusion:	

Evaluating
If your response suggests an evaluating purpose, you may wish to set up *criteria* for an effective short story and then provide evidence that shows how the particular story does or does not measure up to your standards. Your thesis might be "Story X is highly dramatic because the main character undergoes emotional changes, the character conflicts heighten the tension, and the theme is controversial." A similar shaping strategy might be to set a *definition* of a "hero" or "heroine" and then analyze how the main character fits your definition.

Introduction and thesis:	Story X is highly dramatic.
Criterion 1:	A dramatic short story should focus on a character who changes his or her behaviour or beliefs. Judgment and evidence for Criterion 1:
Criterion 2:	A dramatic story must have striking conflicts that lead to a crisis or a predicament. Judgment and evidence for Criterion 2:
Criterion 3:	A dramatic story should have a theme that makes a controversial point. Judgment and evidence for Criterion 3:
Conclusion:	

Arguing
During class discussion, you may disagree with another person's response. Your thesis may then take the form, "Although some readers believe this story is about X, the story is really about Y." In an argumenta-

tive structure, you counter opposing interpretations by first pointing to evidence in the story and then supporting your interpretation with evidence.

Introduction and thesis: Although some readers suggest that the story is about X, it is really about Y.

Body paragraphs: State the opposing interpretation and give evidence that this interpretation cites:
State your interpretation and give evidence (description, dialogue, images, points of conflict, incidents from the plot):

Conclusion:

Investigating Changes in Interpretation   Often, readers *change* interpretations during the course of responding to a piece of literature. Thus, your main point might be, "Although I initially thought X about the story, I gradually realized the theme of the story is Y." If that sentence expresses your main idea, you may wish to organize your essay following the *chronology* or the *steps* in the changes in your interpretation:

Introduction and thesis: Although I initially thought X, I now believe Y.

Body paragraphs: First step (your original interpretation of the story and supporting evidence):
Second step (additional or contradictory ideas and evidence that forced you to reconsider your interpretation):
Third step (your final interpretation and supporting evidence):

Conclusion:

Note: One strategy you should *not* use is simply to retell the main events of the story. A review of the plot is not an acceptable interpretation. Your audience has already read the story. They want you to state your interpretation and then use details from the story to show how and why your interpretation is credible. *Although you will cite events from the plot, you must explain how or why these events support your interpretation.*

DRAFTING

To prepare to draft your essay, read through your annotations and gather your collecting and shaping notes. Some writers prefer to write one-sentence statements of their main ideas at the top of the page to keep them focussed as they write. Other writers prefer to make rough outlines to follow, based on their adaptations of one of the preceding shaping strategies. When you begin drafting, you may wish to skip your introduction and start with the body of your essay. You can fill in the introduction after you have written a draft.

Once you start writing, keep your momentum going. If you draw a blank, reread what you have already written or look at your notes. If you cannot think of a particular word or are unsure about a spelling, draw a line _____ and keep on writing.

REVISING

Use the following guidelines as you read and revise your essay. Be prepared to make changes in your ideas, organization, and evidence, as well as to fix problems in sentences and word choice.

Guidelines for Revisions

- **Clarify your main idea or interpretation.** Ask a classmate to write, in one sentence, the main point of your interpretation. If the statement does not exactly match your main point, clarify your thesis. Your interpretation (not a statement of fact) should be clearly stated early in your essay.

- **Do not give a plot summary.** Your reader has read the story, so do not simply retell the plot. Do, however, give ample evidence. You must also explain how that evidence supports your main point.

- **Support each part of your interpretation with references to specific passages from the text.** Do not be satisfied with one piece of evidence. Find as many bits of evidence as possible. The case for your interpretation grows stronger with each additional piece of evidence.

- **Explain how each piece of evidence supports your interpretation.** Do not just cite several pieces of evidence and go on to your next point. Explain for your reader *how* the evidence supports your interpretation.

- **Define key terms in your essay.** If you are writing about the hero in a story, define what you mean by *hero* or *heroine*. If you are arguing that "The Story of an Hour" has a *feminist* theme, define *feminism*.

- **Signal the major parts of your interpretation.** Let your reader know when you shift to a new point. Use transitions and paragraph hooks at the beginning of body paragraphs.

- **Use the present tense as you describe the events in the story.** If you are describing the end of "The Story of an Hour," write, for example, "Mrs. Mallard descends the stairs and learns the 'good news' about her husband."

- **Quote accurately and cite page numbers for each reference.** Double-check your quotations to make sure they are accurate, word-for-word transcriptions. Following each direct quotation, cite page references as follows:

  > In the first sentence, Kate Chopin says, "Mrs. Mallard was afflicted with a heart trouble" (310).

  Note: The period goes outside the parentheses. See Chapter 11 for correct documentation style.

- **Revise your essay for sentence clarity and conciseness.** Read your essay aloud. Reduce unnecessary repetition. Use active verbs. Rework awkward or confusing sentences.

- **Edit your essay.** Check your essay for correct spelling, word choice, punctuation, and grammar.

WRITING A
RESEARCH PAPER

LEARNING OUTCOMES

After reading this chapter, you will have learned to

- locate sources, take notes, collect, evaluate, and shape information

- use sources judiciously

- document your sources using MLA or APA style

Although the words *research paper* sound imposing to most people, research is really a natural and enjoyable part of our everyday experience, both outside and inside college classrooms. We pride ourselves on being good detectives—whether it's window-shopping for a good bargain, finding the hottest used sports car, asking co-workers for tips on the best Mexican food in town, or just browsing in bookstores for something that's fun to read. Even in college classes, curiosity leads us to discover new ideas. Whenever we wonder about what causes ozone holes, why teenagers commit suicide, what makes the Internet work, how artists turn clay into beautiful pottery, or what the national debt means, the seed for a research idea drops into our minds. At some point, the idea becomes a question, takes root, and begins to grow. When that happens, we want to learn about something, to find out what others already know or don't know. Curiosity blooms into research when we'd rather discover the answers for ourselves than be handed an answer—an "answer" that may have the manufactured feel of a plastic flower.

Whether or not you called it by that name, the essays that you have already written in this course have involved research. The verb *research* literally means "seek out" or "search again." All writing requires research. Your observing essay, for example, required you to "look again" at your subject in order to describe it well. For your remembering essay, you recalled special events from the past, researching your mind for memories. You have also investigated topics by searching in written documents and by doing surveys and interviews. You have explained, evaluated, argued, and even explored subjects using research. In short, you are already a researcher with considerable experience in presenting the results of your research to a chosen audience. A research paper—sometimes called a *term paper*—is simply a more thorough and systematic extension of skills that you have already practised.

This chapter will show you how to write a research paper—preparing, locating sources, taking notes, collecting and shaping information, revising, and documenting your sources. As in other writing assignments, the process is recursive. Often, you will need to back up, collect new information, redraft parts of your paper, or refocus your subject during the writing process. At the end of this chapter, John Polanszky's paper, "Spies in the Sixties: The Conflicting Themes of Ian Fleming and John le Carré," illustrates the important features of a research paper. Throughout the chapter, however, samples from his research log, bibliography, notes, drafts, and documentation illustrate various stages in one writer's process of writing a research paper.

TECHNIQUES FOR WRITING A RESEARCH PAPER

Like other kinds of writing, a research paper requires that you focus on a particular subject, develop a claim or thesis, and support your position with convincing evidence: background information, facts, statistics, descriptions, and other people's evaluations and judgments. The evidence that you present in a research paper, however, is more detailed than that in an essay, and the sources must be cited in the text and documented at the end of the paper.

In a sense, a research paper is like a scientific experiment. Your readers should be able to trace your whole experiment—to see what ideas and evidence you worked with, where you found them, and how you used them in your paper. If readers have any questions about the information you've presented or the conclusions you've reached, they can start with your sources and recreate or check the "experiment" for themselves. If they want to investigate your subject further, your sources will guide their reading. As you write your research paper, keep the following techniques in mind:

- Using *purpose, audience,* and *form* as your guides for writing. Research is just a method of collecting and documenting ideas and evidence. Purpose, audience, and form should still direct your writing.

- Finding the *best that has been written or said* about your subject. Instead of trying to reinvent the wheel, discover what other people or writers already know (or don't know), and then build on what they have learned. Learn to evaluate your sources—be especially critical of Internet or Web sources.

- Using sources to make *your* point. As you gather information, you may revise your thesis in light of what you learn, but don't let the tail wag the dog. Don't allow raw information to control you or your paper.

- *Documenting* your sources, both in the text and at the end of the paper. Using ideas, information, or actual language from your sources without proper documentation is *plagiarism.*

USING PURPOSE, AUDIENCE, AND FORM AS GUIDES

Like any other kind of writing, research papers have a *purpose.* Reporting, explaining, evaluating, problem solving, and arguing are all purposes for research papers. Purposes may appear in combinations, as in a paper that summarizes current research and then proposes a solution to a problem. Research papers, however, are not just reports of other people's ideas or evidence. What you, the researcher, observe and remember and learn is important, too. Most subjects are not interesting until writers make them so. Your curiosity, your interest in the subject, your reason and intuition establish why the subject is worth researching in the first place—and why a reader would want to read the paper once it is finished.

Research papers have a defined *audience,* too. The subject you choose, the kind of research you do, the documentation format, the vocabulary and style you use—all should be appropriate for your selected audience. If you write a research paper in your field, you will write for a professor and for a community of people knowledgeable about your subject. If you are a legal assistant, a superior may ask you to research a specific legal precedent. If you work for a manufacturer, a manager may assign you a research report on the sales and strategies of a competitor.

Finally, your research paper will follow a *form* that fits your purpose and meets the expectations and needs of your audience. First, form is controlled by purpose. If you are writing a research paper evaluating some product or performance, it may look like an evaluating paper, organized around your claims, criteria, judgments, and evidence. If you are arguing for a position or claim, you will present research showing both sides of the controversy and then try to convince your reader to believe or act on your claim. In each case, however, you will cite your sources in the body or text of your paper and include a list of your sources (a *bibliography*) at the end.

The *form* for your research paper is also affected by your intended audience. If you are researching new advances in nursing for an audience of experts, you may choose an elaborate form, with an abstract or summary of your ideas at the beginning, a section reviewing and evaluating current research, subsections for each of your main points with diagrams and charts, and an appendix with supplementary materials. If, however, you are writing primarily for jogging enthusiasts, your research paper may look more like an informal essay. Magazines and journals in the field illustrate a variety of appropriate forms for research papers. The student essay by John Polanszky at the end of this chapter illustrates one form.

FINDING THE BEST SOURCES

Accessing information from both published and unpublished sources is central to all research. To find good sources, you need to hone your detective skills. Unfortunately, Hollywood has promoted the myth that good detectives follow their suspects in high-speed car chases or through glamorous affairs. Of course, that's just fantasy. Detectives must do actual research— paperwork and legwork—to track down leads. Writers are, in a real sense, also detectives, constantly researching their own experiences and the experiences of others. Journalists, lawyers, psychologists, doctors, businesspeople, coaches, scientists, novelists—all sorts of people practise their skills in locating key bits of information and tracking down good leads. Research combines careful planning with good luck, mindless drudgery and moments of inspiration, many dead ends and a few rare discoveries. As coaches sometimes say, those who prepare and work hard make their own luck.

USING SOURCES TO MAKE YOUR POINT

When your hard work does yield a source that has good information and ideas on your exact subject, don't be tempted to let that source take over your paper. If you start stringing together passages from only one or two key sources, you'll be summarizing rather than doing research. You'll be letting the sources tell you what to think, what information is important, or what conclusions to reach. Use your sources, then, to support *your* point. Write your own paper; don't let your sources write it for you.

DOCUMENTING YOUR SOURCES

Documenting your sources is an important part of writing a research paper. Documentation takes place in two stages: First, in the body or text of your paper, you give credit for any material that you have taken from your sources. Then, at the end of the paper, you include a list of "Works Cited" or "Works Consulted" that gives fuller information about these sources for your readers. If your readers doubt a fact or statistic, they can check your sources for themselves. If your readers want more information, your documentation enables them to track down the sources. *Note:* Decide on the documentation format (usually MLA or APA styles) before you begin your research. You need to know what relevant bibliographical information you need to record in your notes.

PREPARING YOURSELF FOR THE RESEARCH PROCESS

Writing a research paper involves the same process that you used in writing essays. The major difference is that each stage or dimension of the process takes longer. You may spend two weeks just collecting sources, reading articles and books, jotting down ideas, testing your ideas on classmates and friends, and narrowing and focussing your subject. And because you gather so much material, the shaping and organizing processes are also more demanding. Sometimes you may feel as if you're trying to put forty frogs in a dishpan: By the time you arrange ten, the first four have already jumped out. The revising also takes longer, partly because you have to include your documentation, but partly because the sections of the paper may not fit together as smoothly as you had hoped. There is really no way to rush research. If writing an ordinary paper is like fixing your lunch, then writing a research paper is like preparing Thanksgiving dinner. You can't microwave a research paper. Good things take time.

The first step in writing a research paper is to *readjust your inner clock*. Initially, you'll think that you're not making much progress. You'll think that you're in a slow-motion movie or that you're trying to jog through butter. However, once you readjust your inner clock, set more modest goals, and content yourself with a slower but more persistent pace, you've won half the battle. By reducing the pressure on yourself, you'll feel less frustrated when you reach a dead end and also ready to appreciate valuable information when you discover it.

To help you adjust mentally and physically to a new pace and an extended writing process, begin your preparation by making a research notebook, outlining a realistic timetable for the paper, and selecting a documentation format.

RESEARCH NOTEBOOK

Although some researchers still recommend using index cards for recording bibliographical entries and notes, for most shorter research projects (up to twenty pages), a notebook computer, a loose-leaf notebook, or a spiral notebook with pockets for additional papers and photocopies may be more functional. Divide your notebook into four sections: research log, bibliography, notes from sources (including photocopies), and drafts and ideas.

The *research log* section of your notebook serves as a scratch pad and log of your research progress. In it, you will record what you accomplish during each research session, potential references you need to check, reminders to yourself, questions to ask a librarian or your instructor, and notes about your problems, progress, and intended next steps. As you work, jot down what you did and what you still need to do. These notes about your problems, progress, questions, and next steps will help you maintain momentum on your research project. Each time you return to the library or to your research, you can check your notes to see what you need to do next.

Below is an excerpt from John Polanszky's research log:

10/26

4:30–6.00 p.m.

Still working on finding articles. Found the Booth article. It has some good stuff.

Stafford's book is missing from the shelves. UGH—I hate that.

Try to find tomorrow: <u>James Bond in the Cinema</u> by John Brosnan. When I saw the name I thought of Pierce Brosnan—coincidence or is there a connection?

Remember that 5–6 p.m. is a good time to work in the library. Everyone clears out, so I don't have to fight over the Internet computer, the photocopier, and the microfilm machines.

In the *bibliography* section of your notebook, keep a list of every source that you consult, with complete information about each source. If your library's online catalogue system shows the status of every source, be sure to print out every source you want to check. If you cannot print the source, you'll need to copy it in your notebook. Leave space between entries for additional information, such as call numbers. This list becomes *your working bibliography*. Polanszky's bibliography included the following entries:

Booth, Alan R. "The Development of the Espionage Film." <u>Spy Fiction, Spy Films and Real Intelligence</u>. Ed. Wesley K. Wark. London: Frank Cass, 1991. 136–160.

PR 888 S65S68   2 copies of the book are available in stacks on 2nd floor.

Stafford, David. <u>The Silent Game: The Real World of Imaginary Spies</u>. Toronto: Lester and Orpen Dennys, 1988.

PR 888 S65S73   Copy in stacks on 2nd floor is out; book is also on Short Term Loan.

In the *source notes* section, leave plenty of pages to record direct quotations, paraphrases of key ideas, and facts from the sources in your bibliography list. Introduce each section with a reference to the author and a short version of the title. After each note, indicate the page number or numbers. One page of Polanszky's notes contained the following entries:

Booth, "The Development of the Espionage Film."

Booth explains that both the novel and film version of le Carré's <u>The Spy Who Came in From the Cold</u> have as their central message the idea "that the sole moral law of Cold War intelligence was 'results'" (151).

Stafford, <u>The Silent Game</u>

Since the 1960s and 1970s the focus of spy fiction has increasingly turned to "conspiracy within the nation or secret service," describing a sense of loss of control over one's destiny (215).

For your source notes section, make *photocopies* of any valuable source materials. Write author, title, and page numbers on each photocopied source.

In the *drafts and ideas* section of the notebook, jot down brainstorms, looping or clustering exercises, sketch outlines, trial drafts, and examples from your own experience. During a research project, ideas can come to you at any time. When they do, take time to write them down. This section of your notebook serves as a journal devoted solely to your research paper. One example from Polanszky's drafts and ideas records his personal thoughts about his changing attitudes towards the spy film genre:

10/29

I can remember watching old Bond films on television with my dad. At the time, I only appreciated the films on the most superficial level—as great entertainment full of car chases, nifty gadgets and exotic settings. Of course, these are the elements that made, and continue to make, the Bond films so popular.

Having watched these films many times now, I see them as more contrived and campy, but I can't help still enjoying them. The Bond films from the 1960s seem especially dated, not to mention sexist and racist! Sean Connery pretending to be Japanese by putting on a stereotypical costume and wig in You Only Live Twice seems embarrassing, if not downright offensive, when you have 30 years of hindsight to your advantage. I don't even want to start with Bond's attitude towards women! On the other hand, there seems something almost innocent about the way these films portray everything in black and white. Bond, Britain, and the Western way of life are good and everything opposed to that is evil. Audiences have definitely become more sophisticated (and jaded?) over the years—I guess that can be said for society at large.

RESEARCH TIMETABLE

Before you begin your research, write out a tentative schedule. Your instructor may assign due dates for specific parts of the paper (brainstorming exercises, topic selection, working bibliography, rough draft), but you should make a schedule that fits your work habits and your weekly schedule.

The following schedule assumes that you have at least a month to work on your research paper. The amount of time required by each part depends on the amount of time you can work each day. On some days, you may have only thirty minutes. On other days, you may have several hours. The key is to do a little bit every day to keep your momentum going.

Prepare for research. Buy and organize a research notebook; set up a timetable; select a documentation format.	1–2 days
Choose a subject. Begin the narrowing and focussing process.	2–3 days
Collect sources. Find library sources; identify and find unpublished sources; do interviews or surveys; record personal experiences; browse sites on the Internet.	
Evaluate source materials; take *notes* on selected sources; *photocopy* sources.	12–14 days
Shape and outline ideas; *reread* notes and photocopies; *draft* sections of essay. Continue to *focus* thesis while rereading, planning, and drafting.	6–10 days
Revise draft. Get peer response, collect additional information, sharpen thesis, reshape or revise outline, cite sources in the text and in the bibliographical list, and edit and proofread the paper.	6–8 days

Tailor your schedule to your own temperament and work habits. If you like to work exactly to a schedule or even finish early, design your schedule so you can finish a day or two before the due date. If you are like most writers—you love to procrastinate or you are often up all night just before an assignment is due—then use your schedule to set early target dates, to get your momentum going. When you finish drafting your schedule, put a copy in the *research log* section of your notebook, so that you can check your progress as you work.

DOCUMENTATION FORMAT:
MLA AND APA STYLES

A final step in preparing for the research paper is to select a documentation style. This chapter illustrates both the MLA and APA styles. If you are writing a paper for the humanities, follow the Modern Language Association (MLA) style set forth in the *MLA Style Manual and Guide to Scholarly Publishing* (2nd ed., 1998). If you are writing a paper in the behavioural sciences, use the American Psychological Association (APA) style as described in the *Publication Manual of the American Psychological Association* (4th ed., 1994).

Leading academic and professional journals also illustrate the documentation styles customary in specialized fields. You may want to consult issues of those journals to determine the exact format for footnotes or in-text citation of sources. *Before you begin doing research, however, select a documentation style* that is appropriate for your subject, purpose, and audience. Then practise that style as you compile your working bibliography.

RESEARCH PAPER: THE WRITING PROCESS

■ **ASSIGNMENT FOR THE RESEARCH PAPER**   Choose a subject that strongly interests you and about which you would like to learn more. It may be a subject that you have already written about in this course. Research this subject in a library and, as appropriate, supplement your library research with questionnaires, interviews, Internet research, or other unpublished sources of information. Check with your instructor for suggested length, appropriate number or kinds of sources, and additional format requirements. Use a documentation style appropriate for your subject, purpose, and audience.

CHOOSING A SUBJECT

For this research paper, choose a subject in which you already have personal interest or experience. Start by brainstorming for possible research subjects. Even a personal experience may suggest an idea. If you wrote about how you fainted in the gym during aerobics or weight training, you might research the potential dangers of exercising in high heat and humidity or sitting in a sauna after hard exercise. If you worry about a friend's drinking problem, you might like to read more about the causes and treatments of alcoholism.

In addition, reread the essays that you have written to see whether one of them refers to a possible research subject. If your observing essay, for example, was about a tattoo parlour that you visited, use that essay as the starting point for further investigation and research. Who could you interview to find out more about tattooing? What is the history of tattooing? Is it becoming more popular? What controversies surround its use? What resources does your library have? What sites can you find on the Internet? You might also use a topic from your remembering, reading, or investigating essays as starting places for additional reading and research. *Build on what you already know and what already interests you rather than launch into an entirely unknown subject.*

Narrowing and Focussing Your Subject   Once you have a tentative idea, remember that you'll need to narrow it, focus it, or otherwise limit the subject. The topic of alcoholism is too general. Focus on a particular research question: "Do beer commercials on television contribute to alcoholism?" "Are there really positive effects of drinking moderate amounts of alcohol?" "What methods does Alcoholics Anonymous use to help people?" "Have laws on impaired driving actually reduced the number of fatal automobile accidents?" Your research question may lead to a **thesis statement** that you will demonstrate in your research essay: "Although some studies show a definite link between consuming moderate amounts of white wine and reduced incidence of heart disease, the negative effects of alcohol consumption far outweigh the potential benefits."

Only after you've started your research, however, will you know whether your research question is still too broad (you can't begin to read everything about it in just two weeks) or too narrow (in two weeks, you can't find enough information about that question).

Two techniques may help narrow and focus your subject. You may wish to try these now, wait until you have done some initial reading, or do them several times during your collecting and shaping.

The first strategy is simply to think about your *purpose* and *audience.* The best way to focus your paper is to reflect on your purpose: What kinds of claims do you want to make about your topic? (If necessary, review the claims of fact, cause and effect, value, and policy outlined in Chapter 9, "Arguing.") As you collect articles, think about the kinds of claims you might want to make about your topic:

> *Claims of Fact:* Are makers of hard liquor being discriminated against by not being allowed to advertise on TV? Is alcoholism a disease or just an addiction?
>
> *Claims of Cause and Effect:* Does TV advertising increase alcohol consumption or just effect the consumption of certain brands? Can students who are "recreational" drinkers become alcoholics? Do recovery programs like Alcoholics Anonymous really work?
>
> *Claims of Value:* Does beer have any nutritional value? Are microbrews really made better or fresher than beers from larger breweries?
>
> *Claims of Policy:* Do age-based drinking laws really work? Should liquor consumption be banned at college events? Residences? At any campus function? Should makers of hard liquor be allowed to advertise on television?

Asking questions about your potential audience may also help you find a focus for your essay. If you are writing for a local audience, consider what they believe and what they might be interested in. Is the topic of alcohol regulation controversial? Who are your readers? What are they likely to believe on this issue? Profile your audience and brainstorm how you can connect your research question to those particular readers.

Question analysis is a second narrowing and focussing strategy. The who, what, when, where, and why questions that you use to focus your topic are the same questions that reference librarians use to help you focus your research in the library.

Who: What group of people are interested or affected?
What: How are key terms defined? What academic discipline is involved?
When: What is the period or time span?

Where: What continent, country, province, or town is involved?
Why: What are the possible effects or implications?

Answering these questions—by yourself, in a group, or with a reference librarian—may suggest new angles, new avenues for research, or subtopics that could lead to a focus for your research paper. As you narrow your topic, you are narrowing and focussing the range of your research in the library. Polanszky, brainstorming with another class member, applied these questions to his subject about conflicting themes in spy fiction and film and came up with the following possibilities:

Spy Fiction and Film

Who?   Ans: I am interested in literary characters and their creators (authors). Specifically, I want to focus on the recurring pattern of popular themes in the spy genre in fiction and film. I will concentrate on Ian Fleming's James Bond and various characters created by John le Carré.

What?   Ans: Key terms defined—what is the historical trend or pattern in spy fiction and spy film? Do I need to define the genre itself? Probably not, it seems pretty self-evident, but I will have to explain some of the parameters that I've chosen. Academic discipline—will incorporate history, literature and film. The historical context is essential for explaining this particular genre. I have to be careful not to stray too far from my central topic. This paper is ultimately about film and literature.

When?   Ans: I really want to know why two opposed themes enjoyed such great popularity at the same time. The 1960s. I need to provide some background information—at least in regards to the authors' intelligence careers. But what about trends—was this an isolated phenomenon or is this something that started in the sixties but continues today? I should be careful not to cast too broad a net.

Where?   Ans: In the West—in Canada, in Britain, in the U.S., in Europe. I'm looking at spy fiction and film during the Cold War so this goes without saying. Of course, it could be interesting to see how these themes were received in the rest of the world. Not too well, or not at all, in the Communist bloc, but what about Japan, South America, Africa, the Middle East? What did the rest of the world think of James Bond and the other Cold Warriors? This might be another paper altogether!

Why?:   Ans: I can make a list of the factors shaping these themes:

– The political and social climate when these works were produced.

– The authors' beliefs and how these beliefs were formed.

– The historical context of the genre.

– The expectations of both film and fiction audiences.

I will try to uncover both how these themes were manifested and why.

As a result of his question analysis, Polanszky decided to focus on the novels of Ian Fleming and John le Carré and the films that grew out of these works during the 1960s, and to examine their themes in light of both their contemporary cultural context as well as the broader historical context of the spy fiction and film genres. *In any research, however, what you look for and what you find are always different. You will need to modify your focus as you read and learn.*

COLLECTING

With ideas for a tentative subject, a possible purpose, and an audience, you can focus on collecting information. Collecting data for your research paper will require identifying and locating published and unpublished sources, evaluating your sources and choosing those that are the most appropriate for your needs, and then taking notes on your selected sources. *Remember, however, that finding sources—like writing itself—is an ongoing and recursive process.* You often identify new sources after you have taken notes on others. Although you may begin your search in the online catalogue, in the reference section, or on the Internet, as you narrow and focus your topic or draft sections of your paper, you may come back and recheck the online catalogue, basic references, periodical indexes, or bibliographies.

Use *informal contacts* with friends or acquaintances as an integral part of your collecting process. Friends, family members, business associates, or teachers may be able to suggest key questions or give you some sources: relevant books and magazine articles, television programs that are available in transcript, or local experts on your subject. One student, for example, was doing research on successful techniques for job interviews. She mentioned her project during a telephone conversation with her father. As it turned out, he regularly interviewed job applicants at his company. The student was able to interview him for specific recommendations.

Unpublished Sources

Although the library may be your main source of information, other sources can be important, too. You may *interview* authorities on your subject or design a *questionnaire* to measure people's responses. (Interviews and questionnaires are discussed in Chapter 6.) *Phone calls* and *letters* to experts, government agencies, or businesses may yield background information, statistics, or quotations. *Notes from classes, public lectures,* or *television programs* are useful sources. Use a tape recorder to ensure that you transcribe your information accurately. A *scientific experiment* may even be appropriate. *Unpublished public documents,* such as deeds, wills, surveyors' maps, and environmental impact statements, may contain gold mines of information. Finally, don't ignore the most obvious sources: Your room, the attic in your home, or your relatives may have repositories of valuable unpublished data—private letters, diaries, old bills, or cheque stubs.

Primary and Secondary Sources

Some sources—accounts of scientific experiments, transcripts of speeches or lectures, questionnaires, interviews, private documents—are known as *primary sources.* They are original, firsthand information, "straight from the horse's mouth." Secondhand reports, analyses, and descriptions based on primary sources are known as *secondary sources.* Secondary sources may contain the same information, but they are once-removed. For example, a lecture or experiment by an expert in food irradiation is a primary source; the newspaper report of that lecture or experiment is a secondary source.

The distinction between primary and secondary sources is important for two related reasons. First, secondary sources may contain errors. The newspaper account, for example, may misquote the expert or misrepresent the experiment. If possible, therefore, find the primary source—a copy of the actual lecture or a published article about the experiment. Second, finding the primary sources may make your research document more persuasive through an appeal to character (see Chapter 9, "Arguing"). If you can cite the original source—or even show how some secondary accounts distorted the original experiment—you will gain your readers' trust and faith. Not only does uncovering the primary data make your research more accurate, but your additional effort makes all your data and arguments appear more credible.

Library Sources

Before you begin collecting information, acquaint yourself with the library itself. If you have not already done so, inquire at the information desk about library tours, or walk through the library with a friend or classmate. Locate the *reference section;* the *online catalogue* for books and articles; the *indexes* for newspapers, journals, and magazines; the *microfilm room;* the *stacks;* and the *government documents* section. Don't assume that because you've used one library, you can immediately start your research in a new library. Remember: *Librarians* themselves are valuable sources of information. Use their expertise early in your research.

Background Information and General Reference

Before you consult the online catalogue, you may need a *general overview* of your subject. Start with an encyclopedia, dictionary, almanac, or biography for background information. Many people associate encyclopedias with their grade-school "research"—when they copied passages out of *The World Book* or *The Canadian Encyclopedia.* But encyclopedias are an excellent source of basic information and terminology that may help you focus, narrow, and define your subject. *Use them as background reading, however, not as major sources.*

In addition to the general encyclopedias, there are hundreds of references—one or two might just save you hours of research in the library and lead you directly to key facts or important information on your topic. (You may wish to begin your collecting in the reference room or check there only after you have collected information from other books and articles. Often these references are more valuable *after* you have done some reading on your subject.) Beyond the standard dictionary or thesaurus, the *Oxford English Dictionary,* known as the *OED,* or *Webster's Third New International Dictionary of the English Language* may help you find key ideas or definitions.

There are also many specialized dictionaries for scientific terms, slang words, symbols, and a host of other specialized vocabularies. If you need facts, figures, or statistics, consult the *World Almanac,* or the *Book of Facts.* If your subject is an author, look at *Canadian Contemporary Authors,* or check one of the references that indexes collections of biographies. *Biography and Genealogy Master Index* and *Biographical Dictionaries* reference more than three million biographical sketches.

The *librarian* is still the most valuable resource for your research. At some point during your research in the library, probably after you have a focussed topic and have collected some sources, talk to a reference librarian. For many writers, asking for help can be really intimidating. To make the process of asking for help as painless—and productive—as possible, try saying something like the following: "Hi, I'm a student. I'm doing a research project for my college writing course. My topic is the evolution of spy fiction and film during the 1960s. I'm trying to find information about the history of the genre, in particular the work of Ian Fleming and John le Carré. Here's what I've found so far [explain what you've done]. What additional reference books, indexes, dictionaries, or bibliographies might help me in my research?" The resulting conversation may be the most productive five minutes of your entire library research. After you've talked to the librarian once, it will be easier to return and ask a question when you hit a snag.

The Online Catalogue   The good news for researchers as we begin the 21st century is that computerized databases have revolutionized the whole process of library research. In most university libraries, a computer terminal can, in a few seconds, give you information that used to require hours of searching card catalogues or printed indexes. You can easily locate books, articles, and government documents relevant to your topic. You can find the library call numbers and locations of sources. You can determine if a source is available or checked out. Often, you can get an abstract or a short description of a source. For some systems, you can print out the bibliographical information so that you don't have to take notes. Occasionally, you can print out whole articles right there. Often you can access most of this information from a personal computer at home.

The only bad news is that nearly every online catalogue system is different. Your school may use an online computer library system. There are many different systems currently in use, but whatever system your library uses, you need to spend time learning the tricks of that particular database. Don't try to learn the system by yourself. Take a library orientation tour. Collect the library's handouts about your computerized databases. Ask the librarians for help. And don't wait until your research paper is assigned to walk into the library. If you have to learn a new computer system *and* write your paper at the same time, you will be inviting massive frustration.

Search Strategy   As you practise with your library's online or compact disc (CD-ROM) systems, you'll discover that the *search strategy* you use and the *key words* you enter become very critical. Should you use a *word* or a *subject* search? Should you use *browse* or *express* to search your database? You need to *practise with your library's system* to see *how it works*. Next, you need to pay careful attention to the key words you enter. If you are writing an essay about teenagers' psychological problems, entering the word *teen* may get you nowhere, while entering the word *adolescent* or even *teenage* may hit the jackpot. To help with your key-word search, try the following. First, make a list in your research notebook of all the possible terms that may relate to your subject. When you do an express search, note the other possible terms or headings given on the computer terminal. Second, stop and check a print source such as the *Library of Congress Subject Headings* (LCSH) and the Dewey Decimal system. Ask the reference librarian where the LCSH is located. Usually, it will be in the reference section or near the online terminals. Look up your topic in the LCSH and copy any headings or key words that are related to your subject. When John looked in the LCSH under "Spy" he found "Spy films" and "Spy stories," among others. So he checked under "Spy films" and found several listings and cross-references.

Internet Sources

Where should you start your search for relevant sources—in the library or on the Internet? The answer to that question depends on your topic, your purpose, and your audience. But the explosion of Web sites in recent years means that, for many writers and topics, the Internet may well be the place to start. The immense variety of sources makes the Internet a great place to do your browsing—especially if you're not quite sure exactly what your topic will be or what angle you wish to investigate. Other writers—especially those who are already sure of their focus—may wish to begin with an online search in their library, and to save their Internet research for later, when they want to find sources they cannot locate in the library. Whatever choice you make, you will probably want to browse the Internet at some point during your research.

Especially if you are not an expert at Internet research, you should think about the strengths and weaknesses of Internet research. The strengths of Internet research are many:

- The Internet has a mind-boggling number of sources, Usenet groups, and Web pages.

- The Internet can have an amazing retrieval speed for sources from around the world.

- The Internet gives you the ability to chat with other people who share similar interests.

- The Internet gives you personal access—from your library or your home—to key information from libraries, businesses, organizations, and governments.

Unfortunately, doing research on the Internet does have drawbacks that are often related to its strengths. Internet enthusiasts often praise the Web for creating a democratic space where every person and site is equal. On the downside, however, librarians often shudder at doing research on the Internet simply because everything is so decentralized and disorganized. And there are other problems as well:

- The sheer number of possible sources on the Internet may make finding the exact source you need very difficult.

- Browsing on the Web may be fun, but you may spend hours going from one site to the next without making any real progress.

- The increasing commercialization of Web sites may interfere with locating relevant information.

- Waiting for a source to download from a busy site can be tedious and frustrating.

- Sources on the Internet may not be accurate or reliable—and thus not appropriate for your paper.

With realistic estimations about the Internet's virtues and faults, however, you should be able to find relevant and even exciting sources that will help you learn about your topic and communicate your findings to your audience.

Note: As you continue to read in this section of the chapter, you may want to open a connection to the Internet so you can check out several of the sites. Also, remember to start making bookmarks for any sites you want to revisit later.

Internet Browsers and Search Engines   Once you have an idea for a possible topic, you can begin searching sites on the Internet for relevant

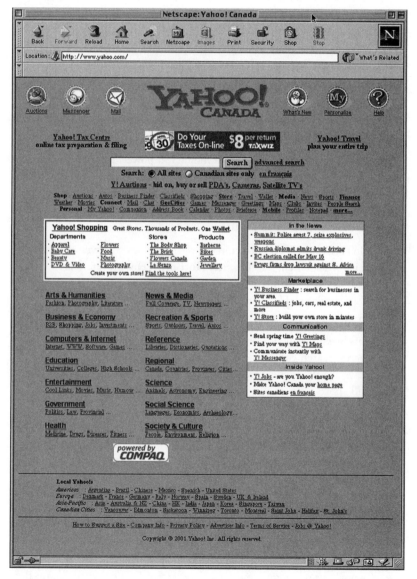

*Reproduced with permission of Yahoo! Inc.© 2000 by Yahoo! Inc. YAHOO! and the YAHOO! logo are trademarks of Yahoo! Inc.

information. If you need to review the basics of Internet research and terminology, refer to the basic Internet glossary on the next page. If you are sitting at a computer with a browser, such as Netscape or Internet Explorer, you can begin working on your topic right now by accessing one of the popular search engines described below. Of course, there are actually hundreds of such searching tools available on the Web, but the ones described here can get you started.

- **AltaVista Canada** <www.altavistacanada.com> AltaVista Canada is one of the most powerful search engines. It is especially effective if you have already browsed through subject directory searches such as Yahoo! and know your precise topic. AltaVista uses LookSmart's directory.

- **Excite** <www.excite.ca> Excite is a competent search engine with Usenet connections as well as key-word searching similar to but not as sophisticated as AltaVista's. Excite serves America Online and Netscape searches.

- **Google** <www.google.com> Google is a powerful search engine with a huge index. It analyzes and ranks sites according to the proximity of key words within the pages. Google only produces results that match all search terms, and it displays them in excerpts of the text rather than in summaries.

- **GoTo.Com** <www.goto.com> GoTo provides a convenient list of general search engines (**Excite, HotBot, WebCrawler, Search.com, Snap**), guides, white pages, and specialty searches such as Encarta. Very similar to **HotBot (hotbot.lycos.com)** and **Snap (www.snap.com)**, as all three engines use Inktomi's database.

- **InfoSeek** <www.infoseek.com> InfoSeek is a popular engine that serves **Search.com** and **WebTV** and gives easy access to Usenet news as well as standard subjects such as finance, business, health, and sports.

- **Lycos** <www.lycos.com> Lycos is similar to AltaVista in its ability to scan the text of each Web document with a text index in order to find matches to key words.

- **Yahoo!** <www.yahoo.ca> Yahoo! is an easily accessible search engine that provides a search of 14 basic categories such as Arts, Business, Computers, Education, Health, Science, Sports, and Social Science. Yahoo! is a Web crawler in that it also searches Lycos, AltaVista, and WebCrawler.

- **Electric Library** <www.elibrary.com> Infonautics' Electric Library is not a search engine but an article retrieval service available on the Web. The Electric Library will search over 150 full-text newspapers, 800 magazines and journals, and 2000 reference works and print out an entire article on your computer's printer. The main drawback to Electric Library is that its sources are appropriate primarily for current, popular topics.

Of course, Web sites and search engines are constantly changing. But the good news is that you can find comparative reviews and data about the various research tools and search engines on the Internet. Access **Search Engine Watch** at **http://searchenginewatch.com** for reviews and comparisons of popular and specialized search engines.

Basic Internet Glossary

Basic Internet Glossary The URL (uniform resource locator) is the address that identifies each Internet site. In the address that follows, for example, **http** stands for "hypertext transfer protocol," **www** stands for World Wide Web, **Yahoo!** is the manager of the Web site, and **.com** indicates a commercial site:

URL: **http://www.yahoo.com**

In addition to commercial (**.com** or **.ca**), you can access a variety of locations, including educational (**.edu**), governmental (**.gov**), noncommercial (**.org**), military (**.mil**), and networking (**.net**). Other URLs can access gopher sites (**gopher://**), ftp (**ftp://**), newsgroups (**news://**), and so forth.

Note: URLs have no spaces between any letters, periods, or slashes. URLs must be typed with complete accuracy—one missed slash or period or letter and your computer will not be able to find the correct address.

As you get started doing research on the Internet, acquaint yourself with the following key terms and definitions. If you know the basic language for navigating the Internet, you won't remain a newbie very long.

bookmark Your computer's browser (see below) will enable you to record each URL that you want to remember, so that the next time you want to visit that site, you merely have to click on the right line in your bookmark rather than type out a complete URL string. Remember to bookmark sites that look promising as you do your research!

browser Your computer needs a browser such as Netscape or Internet Explorer to help you access Telnet, gopher, or Web sites on the Internet. (A browser is not the same as a search engine such as Yahoo!, Excite, or AltaVista—see listings that follow.)

cyberspace The online world created in electronic space or on the Internet. For a history of the Internet, read Philip Elmer-DeWitt's essay "Welcome to Cyberspace," in Chapter 7, "Explaining."

FTP The file transfer protocol is the set of commands that enables you to transfer files between two sites on the Internet.

gopher A program that "goes for" or finds items in a long list or menu is a gopher. Gopher addresses begin with "**gopher://**" rather than with "**http://**." Gopher was an early search program prior to the hypertext searches supported on the Web.

home page The home page is usually the first page of any Web site, and it identifies the author of the page, the location or sponsor of the site, and the basic information about the site.

Hyperlink Often just called *links,* these are highlighted words, icons, or bits of graphic that you can click on to move to a related site. A hypertext is simply a collection of documents or graphics connected by these links.

html Hypertext markup language is the computer code used to write pages on the Web.

listserv A listserv is a mail list that enables users to conduct an ongoing e-mail conversation about a particular topic.

MOO A multiuser domain, object-oriented, provides a space in which people can meet, at a given time, to discuss a particular topic.

MUD A multiuser domain (or dungeon) enables simultaneous communication, often by role-playing a certain character or persona.

newsgroup Any group of people who post messages on Usenet. Usenet is a network that gives access to an electronic discussion group.

search engine A program that enables Internet users to find relevant sites on the Internet. Popular search engines or search tools include Yahoo!, AltaVista, Excite, and Lycos.

Telnet An electronic program that enables you to communicate with another computer with a user name and a password. If you access the Internet or the Web from your home, you probably need to "telnet" into America Online or an educational or commercial source in order to access the Internet.

This short list is just the tip of the iceberg of Internet terminology. If you want to know about **ASCII, baud rates, bytes, cookies, flame wars, MIMEs, POPs, spam, Veronica, WYSIWYG,** or literally hundreds of other terms, visit one of the dozens of Internet glossaries available online, such as the Internet Literacy Consultants' Glossary of Internet Terms at **www.matisse.net/files/glossary.html.** Check out this site and make a bookmark so you can return whenever you have a question.

Tips for Doing Research on the Internet

If you are still learning to use the Internet, here are some tips that may save you quite a bit of time during your research.

- The time of day you access the Internet may be crucial. Obviously, 3 A.M. is a good time for minimal Net traffic, but you do need your sleep. Log on at different times of the day to find out when is best for your location.

- Bring print sources to read while you wait for graphics or text to download to your computer. If you have the option on your browser or search engine, choose "text only" format for Web displays—downloading graphics adds significant time.

- If it takes more than a couple of minutes to get files from your site, click on the "Stop" button and try another source.

- Use the "bookmark" or "favourites list" to record your best sites. You may even want to organize your favourites or bookmarks into a folder designated specifically for the topic of this paper.

- Make sure your browser is set so that the location (URL), title, date, and page are recorded on the copies you print. If they do not appear, ask your laboratory monitor or teacher for assistance.

- Make sure you have enough information from your source (author, title, title of work, full URL address, and date of visit) so that you can write an in-text citation and a references citation in either MLA or APA format. (See the sections on MLA and APA citation of online sources later in this chapter.)

Useful Research Addresses   In some cases, instead of browsing through a search engine such as AltaVista or Yahoo!, you may wish to go directly to a reliable and relevant site. Here are a few you may wish to visit as you research your topic. Each of these sites offers links to other relevant sites. You should note that some databases may be licensed by your college or university. Other databases require payment.

- **ERIC** <www.cal.org/ericcll> Your library will probably have an ERIC (Educational Resources Information Center) database on CD-ROM that you can conveniently search, but if you are not at a library, you can access the ERIC site at this URL. You may even order ready-made searches on popular topics such as "English Only/English Plus," or "Teaching ESL Abroad."

- **Canadian Scholarly Electronic Journals** <http://www.schoolnet.ca/up-pv/rcis/e/ejcano.htm> This service provides information about many Canadian electronic journals such as *The Canadian Journal of Film Studies* or *The Antigonish Review*. Also check out Online Newspapers at <www.onlinenewspapers.com> for an exhaustive list of links to electronic newspapers and periodicals from around the world. You will be able to catch up with publications ranging from the *Calgary Herald* to the *Madagascar Tribune*.

- **HyperNews** <www.hypernews.org> This Web site enables you to retrieve articles and contribute responses to new articles as they are posted on the site.

- **HYTELNET** <www.lights.com/hytelnet> At this site, you can find Telnet addresses of library catalogues throughout the world (at **www.libdex.com**). You can select from among research libraries, K–12 libraries, medical libraries, and public libraries.

- **The National Library of Canada** <www.nlc-bnc.ca/> The National Library of Canada site can give you direct access to an immense range of government and library resources.

- *The Globe and Mail* <www.globeandmail.com> You can access the current paper or do a key-word search of relevant articles appearing in the paper.

- **Online Writing Centres** Check out the online writing centres at the following addresses for help with writing as well as with finding relevant research strategies and sites:

  Memorial University Faculty of Arts Writing Centre at <**www.mun.ca/writingcentre/index.shtml**>,

  University of Ottawa Writing Centre (bilingual) at <**www.uottawa.ca/academic/arts/writcent/**>,

  University of Toronto Writing Lab at <**www.utoronto.ca/writing/index.html**>,

  University of British Columbia Writing Centre's Writer's Workshop at <**www.cstudies.ubc.ca/wc/workshop/what.htm**>.

- **Popular Magazines** Many magazines, such as *Maclean's* and *Chatelaine,* have home pages that allow you to access articles and participate in online chats on current issues. Use your www search engine to find their URLs.

- **Statistics Canada** <www.statcan.ca> Want up-to-date information on demographic data from Statistics Canada? Access this site for news releases and statistics.

Evaluating Internet Sources   Evaluating sources on the Internet requires much more care and attention than judging print sources. Printed sources in the library have often been screened and filtered for accuracy and reliability, whereas often Web sources may represent simply one person's opinion, reaction, or point of view. Even more problematic is our inability to judge the context of the information. When we read an article in the *Calgary Herald,* for example, we can expect a certain level of accuracy and reliability; conversely, when we read an article in a supermarket tabloid, we know we should expect very little accuracy. We know not to quote a tabloid article about diet supplements when we are writing an academic paper about health and nutrition. Even in the television media, we know when we're watching *CBC News* and when we're seeing an infomercial. On the Internet, however, we may have very few context cues to help us judge what we're reading.

Internet sources must be evaluated with a critical eye. When we find a source, we need to ask some key questions: Who is the author? Is the author an expert, a salesperson, or a person with a reason to be biased? What organization is publishing this information? Where did the author find his or her sources? Can we verify the information in other reliable sources? How current is this information? As you read and download texts from the Internet, pay particular attention to five criteria below.

- **Authorship.** Who is the author? Is the author well known? Are the author's credentials or biographical information available on the Internet or elsewhere? Does the author have a reason to be biased? Does the site give an e-mail address so you can request more information? The less you know about the author, the more cautious you need to be about using the source. *If you decide to use the source, indicate exactly what you know or don't know about the author's credentials.*

- **Publishing organization.** Does the site indicate the organization responsible for the text? Is there information in the header or footer indicating the organization, webmaster, or designer of the home page? Is this organization recognized in its field? Is this organization's expertise relevant to your topic and your purpose? Is the organization selling something? Can you determine its bias? *If the organization or source has a clear bias, identify it if you quote from the source.*

- **Reference to other sources.** Does the author refer to other studies on your topic? Does the text contain references to other important studies? Does the text use citations or have a bibliography? Does the author acknowledge that his or her position is new or controversial? Does the author refer to alternate points of view? *Any source that has no references to other key works may simply be one writer's opinion and/or may contain erroneous information.*

- **Accuracy and reliability.** Can the information in the text be verified for accuracy? Are the methods of gathering information indicated? Has this study been replicated elsewhere? If the accuracy or reliability are questionable or unknown, either do not use the text or else qualify your use of the source. *If you have reason to believe the source is not reliable or accurate, find other sources.*

- **Currency.** Depending on your purpose and audience, currency may or may not be important. If you are writing about the reception of Shakespeare's plays, information from texts written in the 17th century may be more relevant than current ones. If you are writing about censorship on the Internet, however, you need the most current available information. Can you determine the date the text was written? Can you find the date the information was posted to the site? Are cited statistics based on recent data?

As you gather sources from the Internet, be skeptical! Question the authority of the texts you find. If you think the source is not reliable, trust your judgment and don't use it. If the text seems accurate and reliable, but you cannot verify all of these criteria, indicate the problems in the source when you introduce your citation. If you have a question about the reliability, relevance, or accuracy of any source, check with your instructor or a librarian. *If you decide to use any questionable or biased sources, you need to qualify their findings and data when you introduce the source.* Otherwise, your reader may believe that your argument is based on biased, inaccurate, or unreliable data.

Computerized Databases

In addition to the resources available on the Internet or in the library's online catalogue, many libraries have other computerized databases to assist your research project. Some of these, such as CBCA (Canadian Business and Current Affairs) or *InfoTrac* (database of general interest and current events), have no print equivalents. Your library may have one of the other popular computerized databases, such as the *Knowledge Index* or *DialogOnDisc*. *Ask your reference librarian to help you locate and use these databases.* Listed below are a few of the other commonly searched computerized databases:

- ERIC (Education Resources Information Center)
- NTIS (National Technical Information Service)
- SCI SEARCH (Science Citation Index)
- MLA (Modern Language Association International Bibliography)

Periodical Indexes

Magazines, journals, and newspapers are called *periodicals* because most are published on a daily, weekly, or monthly basis. An index is just a list of citations, organized for easy reference. Indexes may be in print or computerized form, such as CD-ROM. Just as the index of a textbook refers you to topics, ideas, or names in that book, a periodical index refers you to articles published in a certain group of magazines, journals, or newspapers. Periodical indexes, such as the *Readers' Guide to Periodical Literature,* are usually monthly, quarterly, or annual publications that refer to articles published in hundreds of different periodicals.

The library contains hundreds of periodical indexes, in print or computerized format, each referring to a slightly different subject or group of periodicals. A general index such as the *Readers' Guide* refers to approximately two hundred popular magazines. A general computerized database, such as *InfoTrac,* draws from more than one thousand current magazines, journals, and newspapers. A specialized index may focus on just one publication, such as *The New York Times Index,* or on just one subject, such as the *Art Index,* which indexes approximately three hundred periodicals in the arts.

Below is a list of frequently used indexes. When you discuss your research project with your instructor or with a reference librarian, ask which indexes will be most helpful for your topic and which are available in computerized format:

- *Applied Science & Technology Index*
- *Art Index*
- *Book Review Index*
- *Business Periodicals Index*
- *Canadian News Disc*
- *Canadian Periodical Index*
- *Consumers Index*
- *Education Index*
- *Humanities Index*
- *InfoTrac*
- *The New York Times Index*
- *Psychological Abstracts*
- *Public Affairs Information Service Bulletin*
- *Readers' Guide to Periodical Literature*
- *Social Sciences Index*

Government Documents   Many federal and provincial ministries, through The Queen's Printer, Supply and Services Canada, Statistics Canada and other agencies, offer publications covering an astonishing variety of everyday topics, many of them written in non-technical language for the general public. The largest publisher in the world is the U.S. Government Printing Office (GPO). It publishes countless articles, pamphlets, and books on history, government, and law. Your library may have a separate government documents section, and the documents librarian can help you gain access to the collection.

Evaluating Library Sources   Even with published library sources, you should appraise your sources with a critical eye, just as you do for Internet and Web sources. Just because something is published or printed does not mean that it is relevant, current, accurate, or reliable. Some will not relate specifically to your topic; others will be too superficial or too technical. Some will be out of date; others will be biased or simply inaccurate. Evaluate your printed sources based on the following criteria:

- **Sources should be relevant.** The sources you select should be relevant to your subject, your purpose, and your intended audience. If your narrowed topic is still too general, all your sources will look relevant. In that case, narrow your subject even more. Sources must also be relevant to your purpose. If you are writing an argumentative research paper, for example, you need sources representing both sides of the issue. If you are proposing a solution to a problem, look for sources describing the problem or the solution. Finally, sources should be appropriate for your intended academic audience; beware of brief and superficial articles found in popular magazines.

- **Sources should be current.** As a rule of thumb, look for the most current sources—especially those on scientific or technical subjects. Research and data on AIDS is more accurate and complete now than it was in 1990. Sometimes, however, older books and articles are important. If you are doing historical research about Hurricane Hazel in Canada, you may want to read key documents from the 1950s. In every academic discipline, some sources remain authoritative for decades. When you find that many writers refer to a single source, it may be valuable regardless of its date of publication.

- **Sources should be reliable.** Check for possible biases in articles and books. Don't expect the National Rifle Association to give an unbiased report on gun-control legislation. Don't assume that representatives of right-to-life or prochoice groups will objectively represent the full range of facts about abortion. Because at least some bias is inevitable in any source, locate and use a variety of sources representing several points of view. If you are in doubt about an author's point of view or credibility, consult experts in the field or check book reviews. *Book Review Digest,* for example, contains references to reviews that may indicate the author's reputation or reliability.

Taking Notes   Taking careful notes from both published and unpublished sources is, of course, fundamental to accurate documentation. When a source appears relevant and useful, do the following:

1. Record complete bibliographical information in the bibliography section of your research notebook (or in your computer notebook). For many online library systems, you will be able to print out the bibliographical information you need right from your computer terminal. For books, you need authors, editors, titles, volumes, publishers, places of publication, and years of publication. For articles, you need authors; article titles; magazine or journal titles; volume numbers or dates, months, and years of publication; and beginning and ending page numbers.

   If the source is unpublished—such as a telephone conversation, a letter, or public document in the county courthouse—record all the information about it that your readers will need to identify and consult the source themselves. (See the "Documenting Sources" section in this chapter.) For printed sources, remember that the information you copy from a periodical index may be missing key information, such as the author's full name or the page numbers for the article. When you actually find each source, update your bibliographical information.

2. Record notes in the source notes section of your research notebook. Identify each entry with the author's name and the title. If your notes fill two or more pages, put the author and title at the top of each page. Write on only one side of each page. Briefly summarize the main points made in the source, note specific information useful to you, paraphrase key ideas, transcribe interesting quotations, and jot down your own brief comments, questions, and memories. Place page numbers immediately following each paraphrase or quotation. Use direct quotation rather than paraphrase when the actual words in the source are more concise, author-itative, or persuasive than your paraphrase might be. Be sure that direct quotations are accurate, word-for-word transcriptions from the original.

3. Photocopy important sources for later rereading and reference. Make sure all photocopies clearly show authors, titles, and page numbers. (For some research projects, your instructor may request photocopies of every source you paraphrase or quote.) **Tip:** If you photocopy several pages, copy title pages or the magazines' covers, and staple the copies together. Then, you will have all the necessary bibliographical information, and you can underline key passages or make notes on the photocopies themselves.

Photocopying has distinct advantages. You can copy the relevant pages of a source so you don't have to lug thirty books home. (Leaving the sources in the library also helps other researchers.) Photocopies are good insurance against losing key information—in case the book or journal is checked out the next time you need it. Photocopies also allow you to reread sources *after* you have read other books or articles; often, on the first reading of a source, you're not certain what is important and what is not. Finally, photocopies allow you to recheck the final draft of your research paper against sources, to make sure that paraphrases, direct quo-tations, and page citations are accurate. You may save yourself an extra trip to the library to check a page number, a date, or a journal title. To avoid spending unnecessary amounts of money on photocopies, however, always read sources before making copies.

4. *As you read sources and take notes, record your own reactions and ideas in the drafts-and-ideas section of your research or computer notebook.* Be an active reader of your sources. When you agree or disagree with what you are reading, stop for a minute and jot down your ideas. When you think of a comparison, a process, a way to analyze or evaluate something, possible causes and effects, or examples from your own experience, *write out your ideas as completely as you can, right then, while they're fresh in your mind.* Don't get so absorbed in taking notes that you forget to record your own ideas. You don't have to collect twenty sources and *then* do a draft; instead, draft ideas *as* you collect information.

SHAPING

Once you've collected information for your research paper, you may feel overwhelmed by the task of shaping it into a coherent form. You can assert control over your data, however, and shape them into coherent form by reconsidering your purpose and thesis. *Reread your own notes and especially your draft sections from your research notebook.* Then, in the draft section of your notebook, answer the following questions:

Subject:	What is your general subject?
Narrowed topic or question:	What aspect of your subject is most interesting to you now? What question will you answer or explain?
Purpose:	Is your purpose primarily to inform, explain, evaluate, describe a problem and propose a solution, or argue a claim?
Working thesis:	What thesis, claim, or proposal do you want to impress upon your readers?
Audience:	Analyze your audience. How can you interest them in your subject? What aspects of your collected data are most appropriate for your audience?

As you shape, draft, and revise your research paper, you may continue to refocus your topic and question, refine your thesis, or revise your sense of audience.

Shaping Strategies   Your goal now is to design some order, sequence, plan, or outline for your research paper. Forcing yourself to write an outline, however, simply may not work. You should have an idea from your previous papers about how your writing process works best, but if you're stuck, feeling frustrated, or overwhelmed, try several of the following strategies:

- *Review strategies for shaping* that are appropriate for your particular purpose. If you are arguing for a certain claim, reread the shaping strategies discussed in Chapter 9. If you are evaluating something or analyzing a problem and proposing a solution, review the strategies discussed in Chapter 8.

- *Explain to a friend or classmate your purpose, audience, and working thesis.* Then try to explain how you might proceed.

- *Try freewriting, looping, or clustering* to develop a plan.

- *Reread your notes and drafts* from your research notebook.

- *Take a break.* Let your ideas simmer for a while. Go for a walk. Work on assignments for another course. Go jogging or swimming.

Let your mind run on automatic pilot for a while—the information and ideas in your mind may begin organizing themselves into an initial "sketch outline" without your conscious effort. From the sketch outline, you can then create a working outline.

Organizing Your Notes   With a rough outline as a guide, reread your draft ideas, notes, and photocopies, and label them according to headings and subheadings in your working outline. Before you remove pages from the source notes section of your notebook or unstaple photocopied articles or sections of books, *make sure each entry or photocopy contains the author, title, and page numbers.* Now you are ready to arrange your notes and copies for use during drafting. Organize your notes into groups according to each section of your working outline. Reread each group, deciding which information should come first, in the middle, or last.

DRAFTING

At this point, some of the most difficult work is behind you. Congratulate yourself—there aren't many people who know as much as you do right now about your subject. You are an authority: You have information, statistics, statements, ideas from other writers and researchers, and your own experiences and observations at your fingertips. As you write, remember your purpose and audience. What is your purpose—to inform, explain, evaluate, offer a solution, or argue? Who exactly are your audience? What arguments and evidence will convince them? Your sources will become the evidence and support for *your ideas.* Remember that your voice and point of view should unify the information for your reader.

Many writers prefer to start a draft with the first main idea, leaving the introduction until later. As you write, you may discover a quotation, example, or narrative that doesn't fit anywhere else but that would be a perfect lead-in. Or you may already know how you want to start, using an idea that will help organize and direct your thoughts. As you draft, be guided by your working outline and your notes. Avoid copying passages verbatim from your own notebook ideas; instead, reread your notes and express those ideas in language that fits the idea you're working on.

If you get stuck, go back and reread what you have drafted so far or reread the source notes and ideas that you have assembled from your notebook and photocopies. Try to maintain your momentum by writing as quickly as possible. Don't be upset if the natural flow of your writing suggests a slightly different order or deviates from your working outline. Consider the new possibility. You may have discovered a better way to shape your material. If you are missing some fact or quotation, just leave a long line and keep writing. Later you can find the source and add the material you need.

Using Sources   Proper use of sources requires both creativity and scrupulous honesty. On the one hand, you want to use other people's information and ideas when and where they serve *your* purpose and *your* ideas. A research paper is not simply a long string of quotations connected by a few transitions. On the other hand, the sources you cite or quote must be used *fairly* and *honestly*. You must give credit for other writers' ideas and information. You must quote accurately, cite your sources in your text, and document those sources accurately.

What Sources to Cite   You must cite a source for any fact or bit of information that is not *general knowledge*. Obviously, what is "general knowledge" varies from one writer and audience to another. **As a rule, however, document any information or fact that you did not know before you began your research.** You may know, for example, that the United States spends more money on defence than it does on education. However, if you state that the defence budget for the previous year is greater than the total amount spent on education for the past forty years, then cite the source for that fact.

Knowing when you must cite a source for an idea, however, can be tricky. You do not need to indicate a source for *your* ideas, of course. But if you find a source that agrees with your idea, or if you suspect that your idea may be related to ideas from a particular source, cite that source. A citation will give your idea additional credibility: You show your reader that another authority shares your perception.

How to Cite Sources   In the text of your research paper, you will need to cite your sources according to either the Modern Language Association (MLA) style or the American Psychological Association (APA) style. Remember: Choose either the MLA style or the APA style and stick with it. Don't mix styles.

According to the MLA style, the in-text citation contains the author and page number of your source (Booth 157). No comma appears between author and page number. (If the author is unknown, identify the title and page number of your source. Underline book titles; place quotation marks around article titles.)

According to the APA style, the in-text citation contains author and date (Booth, 1991). Use a comma between author and date. If you refer to a page number, it should appear after the author and date (Booth, 1991, p. 157). Use a *p.* (or *pp.* for more than one page) before the page number(s).

The in-text citation (either MLA or APA) refers readers to the end of your paper, where you give complete information about each source in a "Works Cited" (MLA) or "References" (APA) list. For illustration purposes, the following examples use MLA style. See the "Documenting Sources" section for examples of both APA and MLA styles.

Identify Cited References   Once you have decided that a fact, a paraphrase, or a direct quotation contributes to your thesis and will make a strong
impression on your reader, use the following guidelines for in-text citation.

- Identify in the text the persons or source for the fact, paraphrased
  idea, or quotation:

As the well-known novelist noted: "To keep to the middle of the road
between fantasy and realism is what we ask of any really powerful fantasy
figure . . ." (Amis 16).

> *Note:* The parentheses and the period *follow* the final quotation marks.

- If you cite the author in your sentence, the parentheses will contain
  only the page reference:

Fleming thus became, as David Stafford poignantly described him, "a propagandist of the new Elizabethan Age" (214–215).

- Use block format (separated from the text by a blank line, indented
  ten spaces, and double-spaced) for quotations of five lines or more:

Le Carré himself aptly illustrated that his work was very much a reflection
of broader public attitudes:

> I mean the world had been aware from its newspapers of this
> grey army of cold warriors, of defectors, of spies, frontier
> crossers. And what had literature produced? This candy-floss
> image of a macho man, an Etonian who really seemed not to
> have a moral doubt in his head. (qtd. in Masters 243)

> *Note:* In block quotations, the final period comes *before* the paren-
> theses containing the citation of your source.

- Vary your introductions to quotations:

It is important to consider Fleming's life before his literary career,
because, as John Pearson, Fleming's biographer, noted, the Bond novels
are "an autobiography of dreams" that offer "a reflection of Fleming's personality, fantasies and convictions" (Stafford 161).

If it is true that the Bond novels offer "a reflection of Fleming's personality, fantasies and convictions" then Fleming's life, before his literary
career, must be considered an important element in deciphering what
Fleming's biographer, John Pearson, called an "autobiography of dreams"
(Stafford 161).

- Edit quotations when necessary to condense or clarify. Use three ellipsis points or spaced periods (. . .) if you omit words from the middle of a quoted sentence:

> According to Rubenstein, the end of the Cold War "did not lead to the re-emergence of the witty spy, but rather to . . . light hearted sadism" (25).

If you omit words from the end of a quoted sentence or omit sentences from a long quoted passage, place a period after the last word quoted before the omission; follow it with three ellipsis points—for a total of four periods. (Be sure that you have a complete sentence both before and after the four periods.)

> In le Carré's <u>The Spy Who Came in From the Cold</u>, Control's menacing words succinctly describe the author's feelings towards the Intelligence community:
>
> > We do disagreeable things so that ordinary people here and elsewhere can sleep safely in their beds at night. . . . Of course, we occasionally do very wicked things. (15)

In some cases you may want to change the wording of a quotation or add explanatory words of your own to clarify your quotation. If you do so, clearly indicate your changes or additions by placing them within square brackets:

> As Masters noted: "The conclusion [of <u>The Spy Who Came in From the Cold</u>] is bleak and institutional. The success [of the novel] put him strongly in the mould of the thriller" (244).

How to Avoid Plagiarism

Plagiarism is the act of passing off another researcher's or writer's *information, ideas, or language* as one's own. Whether intentional or not, plagiarism is a serious offence. The result may be a failing grade in both the research project and the course. In the working world, people have lost jobs and political candidates have been forced to end campaigns because they have been caught plagiarizing.

To avoid such consequences, be honest and give credit for the work of others by carefully documenting *all* facts, ideas, charts, diagrams, and actual phrases or sentences borrowed from your sources. Assume, for example, that an accurate quotation from your source would read as follows:

> "The Intelligence world was considerably enraged by the poor image it was given in the Smiley trilogy" (Masters 249–250).

The most blatant form of plagiarism involves using *both* your source's information and your source's language (shown below in italics) without giving credit:

> Of course, le Carré's work was often controversial and the Intelligence world was considerably enraged by the poor image it was given in the Smiley trilogy.

A second form of plagiarism, equally serious, involves giving credit to a source for facts or ideas, but *failing to use quotation marks to indicate that you have borrowed the exact language from the source.* In essence, you are saying that these ideas and facts come from Masters 249–250, but that the language is your own. That, of course, is untrue:

> Of course, le Carré's work was often controversial and the Intelligence world was considerably enraged by the poor image it was given in the Smiley trilogy (Masters 249–250).

Avoid plagiarism by documenting the passage as follows:

> Of course, le Carré's work was often controversial and "The Intelligence world was considerably enraged by the poor image it was given in the Smiley trilogy" (Masters 249–250).

To avoid plagiarism, don't randomly copy out interesting passages. Take accurate notes and transcribe quotations *exactly* as they appear in sources. Either put quotation marks around the exact words of the source or paraphrase the main ideas in your own words.

REVISING

You have been revising your research essay since the first day of the project. You thought about several subjects, for example, but you chose only one. You started with a focus but revised it as you thought, read, and wrote more. You initially tested your ideas in the draft section of your research notebook, but you revised those ideas as you drafted. At this point, you are just continuing your revising; now, however, you have a complete draft to revise.

Start the revision of your complete draft by taking a break. Fix your schedule so that you can do something else for a couple of days. When you return and reread your draft, be prepared to be flexible. If there is something missing in your data, prepare yourself to track down the information. If a favourite source or quotation no longer seems relevant, have the courage to delete it. If an example on page 4 would work better as a lead-in for the whole paper, reorder your material accordingly. If the evidence for one side of an argument appears stronger than you initially thought, change your position and your thesis. *Being willing to make such changes is not a sign of poor research and writing. Often, in fact, it demonstrates that you have become more knowledgeable and sophisticated about your subject.*

After you have finished your rough draft, ask friends or classmates to give you their responses. Accept their criticism gracefully, but ask them to explain *why* they think certain changes would help. Would they help to make your purposes clearer? Would they be more appropriate for your audience? Don't be intimidated and feel that you must make every change that readers suggest. You must make the final decisions.

DOCUMENTING SOURCES

Both the MLA and APA documentation styles require citation of sources in the text of your paper, followed by a "Works Cited" (MLA style) or "References" list (APA style) at the end of your paper. Use footnotes only for content or supplementary notes that explain a point covered in the text or offer additional information. *Note:* MLA in-text documentation and "Works Cited" documentation are explained here. See pages 415–422 for APA in-text documentation and "References" format.

In-Text Documentation: MLA Style
In the MLA style, give the author's name and the page numbers in parentheses following your use of a fact, paraphrase, or direct quotation from a source. These in-text citations then refer your readers to the complete documentation of the source in a "Works Cited" or "Works Consulted" list at the end of the paper.

As you cite your sources in the text, use the following guidelines:

If you cite the author in the text, indicate only the page number in parentheses:

According to Chris Garbutt, "Guys don't share much of anything" (21).

If the author is unknown, use a short version of the title in the parentheses:

Most students in Canada would be surprised to learn that "the Communist Party in Russia actually sponsors rock concerts" (<u>A Day in the Life 68</u>).

If the source is unpublished, cite the name or title used in your bibliography:

In an informal interview, one university administrator noted that funding of foreign-language study has steadily decreased over the past ten years (Meyers).

If the source is from the Internet or the Web, use the author, or if there is no author, use the title:

It has been suggested that the real life Canadian spy William Stephenson served as the model for James Bond (<u>Assassins Canada</u>, 2000).

If your bibliography contains more than one work by an author, cite the author, a short title, and page numbers. The following examples show various ways of citing a reference to Anthony Masters, *Literary Agents: The Novelist as Spy:*

In <u>Literary Agents: The Novelist as Spy</u>, Masters explains that le Carré's experience with the upper classes led him to see his country in decline (240–241).

As Masters notes, "[le Carré] with his first hand knowledge of upper-class intrigue, saw Britain in desolation" (<u>Literary Agents</u> 240–241).

Le Carré's experience with the upper-classes led him to see his country in decline (Masters, <u>Literary Agents</u> 240–241).

Note: Use a comma between author and title but not between title and page number.

If a source has two authors, cite both authors' names in the text or in the parentheses:

The sequence is entirely irrelevant to the narrative of the film, yet she becomes a device to deliver a summary of the plot as segments of the film are projected onto her body (Bennett and Woollacott 153).

If a source has three or more authors, give the name of the author listed first in your bibliography followed by the abbreviation *et al.,* meaning "and others":

The James Bond film series had mass appeal thanks to healthy doses of sex, violence, action and glamour (Tahmée et al. 32).

If a source has several volumes, precede the page number with the volume number and a colon, as indicated:

Language and grammar can be taught with real-life contexts or scenarios (Valdman 3:82).

If you are citing a quotation or information from a source that itself cites another source, use the abbreviation *qtd. in* for "quoted in" to indicate that you have used an indirect source for your information or quotation. (If possible, however, check the original source.)

As le Carré himself explained, "And what had literature produced? This candy-floss image of a macho man, an Etonian who really seemed not to have a moral doubt in his head" (qtd. in Masters 243).

If you cite two or more authors as sources for a fact, idea, or plan, separate the citations with a semicolon, as follows:

> Throughout this century, spy stories, in both literature and film, have largely kept in step with public attitudes towards world politics and the intelligence community (Stafford 3; Booth 157).

Content or Supplementary Notes

You may use footnote numbers in the text of your paper to refer to a "Notes" section at the end of the paper. If you have an important idea, a comment on your text, or additional information or sources *that would interrupt the flow of your ideas in the text,* you may use that idea or comment in your supplementary "Notes" section. During **his** research, for example, Polanszky read about connections between the Bond character and various real-life figures. He didn't want to digress in his paper, so he described the controversy in a supplementary note at the end of the paper. Here is a first draft of that note:

> [1] Much has been written about the connections between Fleming's life and that of his most famous creation. It has been suggested that the real life Canadian spy William Stephenson served as the model for James Bond (Assassins Canada, 2000). Stephenson's story has also been well chronicled, most notably in William Stevenson's (no relation) A Man Called Intrepid: The Secret War.

"Works Cited" List: MLA Style

After you have revised your essay and are certain that you will not change any in-text documentation, you are ready to write your list of sources. Depending on what you include, it will be one of the following:

- A "Works Cited" list (only those works actually cited in your essay)

- A "Works Consulted" list (works cited and works you read)

- A "Selected Bibliography" (works cited and the most important other works)

- An "Annotated List of Works Cited" (works cited, followed by a short description and evaluation of each source)

A "Works Cited" list alphabetically orders, by author's last name, all published and unpublished sources cited in your research paper. If the author is unknown, alphabetize by the first word (excluding *A, An,* or *The*) of the title. As a general rule, underline or italicize titles of books, periodicals, and newspapers, but use quotation marks to enclose titles of newspaper and magazine articles. Use the following abbreviations for missing information (other than an unknown author): n.p. (no place of publication given), n.p. (no publisher given), n.d. (no date of publication given), or n. pag. (no pagination in source). The first line of each citation begins at the left margin, and succeeding lines are indented five spaces. Double-space the entire "Works Cited" list.

Following are examples of MLA-style entries in a "Works Cited" list, organized by kind of source: books, articles, and unpublished sources. Use these as models for your own "Works Cited" list. For additional information and examples, see *MLA Handbook for Writers of Research Papers* (4th ed., 1995).

BOOKS: MLA STYLE

Order the information as follows, omitting information that does not apply:

Author's last name, first name. "Title of Article or Part of Book." <u>Title of Book</u>. Ed. or Trans. Name. Edition. Number of volumes. Place of publication: Name of publisher, Date of publication.

A Book by One Author

Greey, Madeleine. <u>Get Fresh!</u> Toronto: Macmillan Canada, 1999.

Additional Books by Same Author

Mowat, Farley. <u>Owls in the Family</u>. Toronto: McClelland & Stewart, 1961.

———. <u>A Whale for the Killing</u>. Toronto: McClelland & Stewart, 1972.

A Book With Two or Three Authors

Karpinski, Eva, and Marlene LeCompte. <u>The Language We Share: A Canadian Cross-Cultural Reference for Learning English.</u> Toronto: Harcourt, 1996.

Flachmann, Kim, Michael Flachmann, and Alexandra MacLennan. <u>Reader's Choice</u>. 3rd ed. Toronto: Prentice Hall, 2000.

A Book With More Than Three Authors

Comley, Nancy R., et al. <u>Fields of Writing</u>. New York: St. Martin's, 1997.

An Unknown or Anonymous Author

<u>New York Public Library Student's Desk Reference.</u> New York: Prentice, 1993.

A Book With an Author and an Editor

Austen, Jane. <u>Pride and Prejudice</u>. Ed. Mark Schorer. Boston: Houghton, 1956.

Note: The names of well-known publishers are often shortened to the first key word. Thus, "Houghton Mifflin Co." becomes "Houghton," and "Harcourt Brace Jovanovich, Inc." becomes simply "Harcourt."

An Edited Book

Myers, Linda, ed. <u>Approaches to Computer Writing Classrooms</u>. Albany: State University of New York Press, 1993.

A Translation

Tremblay, Michel. "The Thimble." Trans. Jay Bochner. <u>Canadian Short Fiction</u>. Ed. W. H. New. Scarborough, ON: Prentice Hall, 1974. 452–453.

An Article or Chapter in an Edited Book

Urquhart, Jane. "The Death of Robert Browning." <u>Short Fiction: An Introductory Anthology</u>. Ed. David Rampton and Gerald Lynch. Canada: Harcourt, 1992. 1342–1351.

A Work in More Than One Volume

Morrison, Samuel Eliot, and Henry Steele Commager. <u>The Growth of the American Republic</u>. 2 vols. New York: Oxford UP, 1941.

A Work in an Anthology

MacLeod, Alistair. "The Boat." <u>Canadian Short Fiction</u>. Ed. W. H. New. Scarborough, ON: Prentice Hall, 1997. 348–360.

An Encyclopedia or Dictionary Entry

"Don Giovanni." <u>The Encyclopedia Americana</u>. 1994 ed.

A Government Document: Known Author

Machenthun, Kenneth M. <u>Toward a Cleaner Aquatic Environment</u>. Environmental Protection Agency. Office of Air and Water Programs. Washington: GPO, 1973.

[GPO stands for "Government Printing Office."]

A Government Document: Unknown Author

Indian and Northern Affairs. <u>The Inuit</u>. Ottawa: Supply and Services Canada, 1986.

An Unpublished Dissertation

Burnham, William A. "Peregrine Falcon Egg Variation, Incubation, and Population Recovery Strategy." Diss. Colorado State U, 1984.

A Pamphlet

<u>Guide to Raptors</u>. Denver: Center for Raptor Research, 1990.

PERIODICALS: MLA STYLE

For all articles published in periodicals, give the author's name, the title of the article, and the name of the publication. For newspapers and magazines, add complete dates and inclusive page numbers. Use the first page number and a plus sign if an article is not printed on consecutive pages. For most professional journals, add volume numbers, issue numbers if appropriate, years of publication, and inclusive page numbers.

An Article in a Weekly or Biweekly Magazine

Fotheringham, Allan. "Why Do They Do It?" <u>Maclean's</u> 1 July 2000: 76.

An Article in a Monthly or Bimonthly Magazine

Anderson, Mark. "High Wireless Act." <u>National Post Business</u> July 2000: 48–53.

An Unsigned Article in a Magazine

"You Gotta Pass the Puck." <u>Report on Business</u> January 2000: 23.

An Article in a Professional Journal

Many professional journals have continuous page numbers throughout the year. The first issue of the year begins with page 1, but every issue after that begins with the number following the last page number of the previous issue. For such journals, give volume followed by the year.

Cochran, D. D., W. Daniel Hale, and Christine A. Hisam. "Personal Space Requirements in Indoor Versus Outdoor Locations." <u>Journal of Psychology</u> 117 (1984): 132–33.

[For page numbers over 100, use only two digits for the final page citation: 2128–29.] If each issue of a professional journal begins with page 1, cite the volume number followed by a period, then the issue number and year. In the following example, the article is in Volume 9, Issue 1, published in January 1987.

Brodkey, Linda. "Writing Ethnographic Narratives." <u>Written Communication</u> 9.1 (1987): 25–50.

An Article in a Newspaper

Omit the introductory article (*Wall Street Journal* instead of *The Wall Street Journal*). If the masthead includes an edition, include it in your entry.

Nolen, Stephanie. "Harry Potter and the PR Wizards." <u>Globe and Mail</u> 29 June 2000: R1+.

An Unsigned Article in a Newspaper

"Factory Theatre Boasts Premieres." <u>National Post</u> 29 June 2000: A19.

An Editorial

Hunter, Ian. "Liberal Pundits Speak for Yesterday." Editorial. National Post 29 June 2000: A15.

An Unsigned Editorial

"Habs Shut Out." National Post 29 June 2000: A15.

A Review

Kingwell, Mark. Rev. of Sex and Real Estate: Why We Love Houses, by Marjorie Garber. Globe and Mail 15 July 2000: D2–3.

A Published Interview

Hampson, Sarah. "Saint Tommy's Torchbearer." With Shirley Douglas. Globe and Mail 9 March 2000: R3.

ELECTRONIC AND INTERNET SOURCES: MLA STYLE

The World Wide Web and the Internet itself are under constant revision, so even the latest MLA guidelines, available in the second edition of the *MLA Style Manual and Guide to Scholarly Publishing* (1998) are not definitive and will certainly continue to change. Use the specific citations following this list as models for your own citations. For more complete citation examples, consult the *MLA Style Manual*.

1. Name of author (if known)

2. Title of article, short story, poem, or short work within a book, periodical, or database

3. Title of book (underlined)

4. Name of the editor, or translator (if relevant)

5. Publication information for any print version of the source

6. Title of periodical, project, or database (underlined), or for a site with no title, a description such as *Home page*

7. Volume number, issue number of journal (if appropriate)

8. Date of electronic publication or of posting

9. Number of pages, paragraphs, or sections (if they are numbered)

10. Name of any organization associated with the Web site

11. Date when researcher accessed the source

12. Electronic address (URL) in angle brackets

A Book

Shaw, Bernard. <u>Pygmalion</u>. 1912. Bartleby Archive. 6 Mar. 1998
<http://www.columbia.edu/acis/bartleby/shaw>.

A Poem

Carroll, Lewis. "Jabberwocky." 1872. 6 Mar. 1998
<http://www.jabberwocky.com/carroll/jabber/jabberwocky.html>.

A Scholarly Project

Voice of the Shuttle: <u>Web Page for Humanities Research</u>. Ed. Alan
Liu. Mar. 1998. U. of California Santa Barbara. 8 Mar. 1998
<http://humanitas.ucsb.edu/>.

An Article in a Journal

Tuman, Myron. "Print and Its Discontents: A Review of Alan Purves's
<u>The Web of Text and the Web of God</u>." Kairos 3.2 (Fall 1998):
3 pars. 2 Feb. 1999 <http://english.ttu.edu/kairos/3.2/reviews/
tuman/purves.htm>.

An Article in a Magazine

Sigesmund, B. J. "California Flyin'." <u>Newsweek</u> 2 Feb. 1999. 3 Feb
1999 <http://www.newsweek.com/nw-srv/tnw/today/ps/
ps)1mo_1.htm>.

Shuger, Scott. "The Truman No-Show." <u>Slate</u> 2 Feb. 1999. 3 Feb. 1999
<http://www.slate.com/Code/TodaysPapers/TodaysPapers.asp>.

An Article in a Newspaper

Lohr, Steve. "U.S. Presents Documents in Case Against Microsoft."
<u>New York Times on the Web</u> 21 Jan. 1999. 2 Feb. 1999
<http://www.nytimes.com/library/tech/99/01/biztech/articles/
21soft.html>.

An Editorial

Regan, Tom. "The New 'Political Correctness' and the GOP."
Editorial. <u>Christian Science Monitor</u> 2 Feb. 1999. 3 Feb. 1999
<http://www.csmonitor.com/atcmonitor/commop/regan/>.

A Letter to the Editor

Hall, Susan. Letter. <u>New York Times on the Web</u> 27 Jan. 1999. 3
Feb. 1999 <http://www.nytimes.com/yr/mo/day/letters/
hall.html>.

A Posting to a Discussion List

Wallace, Nicole. "Parallel with Siddhartha." Online posting. 15 Oct. 1998. 3 Feb. 1999 <http://www.colostate.edu/cgibin/ceilidh/>.

A Professional Site

The Official Website of the Nobel Foundation. The Nobel Foundation. Dec. 1998. 3 Feb. 1999 <http://www.nobel.se/>.

A Personal Web Page

Palmquist, Michael. Home page. Jan. 1998. 3 Feb. 1999 <http://lamar.colostate.edu/~mpalmqui/main.htm>.

Synchronous Communications (MOOs, MUDs)

Ghostly Presence. Group discussion. Telnet 16 Mar. 1997 <moo.du.org:8000/80anon/anonview/14036#focus>.

A Publication on CD-ROM, Diskette, or Magnetic Tape

"Exchequer." The Oxford English Dictionary. 2nd ed. CD-ROM. Oxford: Oxford UP, 1992.

Godwin, M. E. "An Obituary to Affirmative Action and a Call for Self-Reliance." ERIC. CD-ROM. SilverPlatter. Oct. 1992.

An E-Mail Communication

Palmquist, Michael. "Re: Computer Classroom Tutorial." E-mail to Kate Kiefer. 23 Jan. 1999.

OTHER SOURCES: MLA STYLE

For unpublished sources, give relevant information that may help your reader identify or locate the source.

Computer Software

Microsoft Word. Computer Software. Microsoft, 1992.

A Film

The Red Violin. Dir. François Girard. Perf. Samuel L. Jackson. Lions Gate, 1999.

A Recording

Toronto Symphony Orchestra. Musically Speaking. Warner Music Canada Ltd., 1998–1999.

A Television or Radio Program

"Mountie and Soul." Due South. CTV. CFTO. Toronto. 26 Oct. 1997.

A Letter

Stershic, Sybil. Letter to the author. 4 July 2000.

A Lecture or Speech

Barlow, Maude. Address. League of Canadian Poets. Toronto. 25 May 1991.

If title is unknown, list type of oral presentation such as *Reading, Speech,* or *Lecture.*

A Personal Interview

Heller, Dr. Ricki. Personal interview. 14 Jan. 2000.

A Personal Survey

Seneca College Library Interlibrary Loan Questionnaire. Personal survey. 28 February 2000.

A Cartoon

Petricic, Dusan. Cartoon. Toronto Star 14 July 2000.

An Advertisement

Fiat Products Ltd. Advertisement. Canadian Homes and Cottages. Volume 10. Issue 3: 87.

In-Text Documentation: APA Style

In the APA style, give the author's name and date in parentheses following your use of a summary or paraphrase. If you quote material directly, give author's name, date, and page number. (Use *p.* for one page and *pp.* for more than one page.) These citations will direct your reader to your References list, where you give complete bibliographical information. As you cite your sources, use the following guidelines:

If you do not cite the author in the text, give author, date, and page in parentheses at the end of the citation. If you are specifically citing a quotation or a part of a source, indicate the page with *p.* or the chapter with *chap:*

"Fear of failure doesn't seem like much to pin your manhood on, but it is one of the masculine stereotypes provided by professional sports" (Garbutt, 2000, p. 20).

If you cite the author in the text, indicate the date in parentheses immediately following the author's name, and cite the page number in parentheses following the quotation:

According to Chris Garbutt (2000), "Guys don't share much of anything" (p. 21).

If you cite a long direct quotation (more than 40 words), indent the passage five spaces from the left margin. Omit the enclosing direct quotation marks. Place the period at the end of the passage, not after the parentheses that include the page reference:

> Dan Strickland (1996) disabuses the reader of the common notion of nature's "preplanned harmony":
>
> > Once again, the best interpretation of what we actually see in nature is that each player is (unconsciously) out for him or herself. There are certainly winners and losers in the real world but no evidence of a "plan." Nor is there any reason to think any species other than us gives—or is capable of giving—any thought to the feelings or welfare of its victims, neighbours, or "cooperators." (p. 299)

If you are paraphrasing or summarizing material (no direct quotations), you may omit the page number:

> According to Strickland (1996), "me first" is a basic instinct among all nature's creatures.

Note: Although the APA style manual says that writers may omit page citation for summaries and paraphrases, check with your instructor before you omit page references. If you have previously cited the author and date of a study, you may omit the date:

> In addition, Strickland points out that "me first" is a basic instinct among all nature's creatures.

If the work has between two and five authors, cite all authors in your text or in parentheses in the first reference. *Note:* In your text, write "Long and Long"; in parenthetical citation, use an ampersand: "(Long & Long)":

> Long and Long (1985) refer to two foreign-language teachers who noted, "We are members of a world community . . . and our fates are closely intertwined" (p. 366).

> As two foreign-language teachers noted, "We are members of a world community . . . and our fates are closely intertwined" (Long & Long, 1985, p. 366).

For subsequent citations, cite both names each time if a work has two authors. If a work has three to five authors, give the last name of the first author followed by *et al.* Include the year for the first citation within a paragraph:

> Taylor et al. (1997) found . . .

If a work has six or more authors, use only the last name of the first author and the abbreviation *et al.* followed by the date for the first and subsequent in-text and parenthetical citations:

Teachers should integrate the study of history, culture, politics, literature, and religion of a particular region with the study of language (Berryman et al., 1988).

If a work has no author, give the first few words of the title and the year:

Most students in Canada would be surprised to learn that "the Russian government has sponsored rock concerts" (<u>A Day in the Life</u>, 1988).

If the source is from the Internet or the Web, use the author, or if there is no author, use the title:

Many Web sites now provide detailed information about how to plan a study-abroad semester or year (<u>Foreign Language</u>, 1997).

If the author is a corporation, cite the full name of the company in the first reference:

Two events occurred in Europe at the turn of the 17th century that affected thought and conduct in profound and durable ways: the birth of rights and the spread of machines (University of Toronto, 2000).

If the source is a personal communication (letter, memo, interview, phone conversation), cite in text but do not include in your "References" list (personal communications are not recoverable data):

As Dr. Ricki Heller (personal interview, January 14, 2000) emphasized, "Journal writing encourages introspection."

If you are citing a government document, give the originating agency, its abbreviation (if any), the year of publication, and (if you include a direct quotation) the page number:

Newcomers to a foreign culture should "pay attention to their health as well as their grammar. What the natives regularly eat may be dangerous to a foreigner's constitution" (Department of Health and Human Services [DHHS], 1989, p. 64).

If your citation refers to several sources, list the authors and dates in alphabetical order:

Several studies (Lambert, 1996; Lange, 1987; Long & Long, 1985) have documented severe deficiencies in Americans' foreign-language preparation.

"References" List: APA Style   If you are using the APA style, you should make a separate list, titled "References" (no underlining or quotation marks), that appears after your text but before any appendixes. Include only sources actually used in preparing your essay. List the sources cited in your text *alphabetically,* by author's last name. Use only *initials* for authors' first and middle names. If the author is unknown, alphabetize by the first word in the title (but not *A, An,* or *The*). In titles, capitalize only the first word, proper names, and the first word following a colon. Ask your instructor which of the APA's two recommended formats you should use for reference list entries: first line indented five spaces, and subsequent lines full measure (as shown here), or first line full measure and subsequent lines indented five spaces. Double-space the entire "References" list.

Following are samples of APA-style reference list entries. For additional information and examples, consult the *Publication Manual of the American Psychological Association* (4th ed., 1994).

BOOKS: APA STYLE

A Book by One Author

Greey, M. (1999). <u>Get fresh!</u> Toronto: Macmillan Canada.

Additional Books by Same Author

Mowat, F. (1961). <u>Owls in the family</u>. Toronto: McClelland & Stewart.

Mowat, F. (1972). <u>A whale for the killing</u>. Toronto: McClelland & Stewart.

A Book With Two or More Authors

Flachmann, K., Flachmann, M., MacLennan, A. (2000). <u>Reader's choice</u>. Toronto: Prentice Hall.

An Unknown or Anonymous Author

<u>New York Public Library student's desk reference</u> (1993). New York: Prentice Hall.

Note: In titles of books and journals, capitalize the first word, the first word after a colon, and any proper names. (New York Public Library is a proper name.)

A Book With an Author and an Editor

Austen, J. (1956). <u>Pride and prejudice</u> (M. Schorer, Ed.). Boston: Houghton Mifflin.

Note: The APA style usually uses the full name of publishing companies.

A Work in an Anthology

> MacLeod, A. (1997). The boat. In W. H. New (Ed.), <u>Canadian short fiction</u> (pp. 348–360). Scarborough, ON: Prentice Hall.

A Translation

> Tremblay, M. (1974). The thimble. (J. Bochner, Trans.). In W. H. New (Ed.), <u>Canadian short fiction</u> (pp. 452–453). Scarborough, ON: Prentice Hall. (Original work published 1996).

Note: Titles of poems, short stories, essays, or articles in a book are not underlined or italicized or put in quotation marks. Only the title of the anthology is underlined.

An Article or Chapter in an Edited Book

> Urquhart, J. (1992). The death of Robert Browning. In D. Rampton & G. Lynch (Eds.), <u>Short fiction: An introductory anthology</u> (pp. 1342–1351). Canada: Harcourt Brace Jovanovich.

A Government Document: Known Author

> Machenthun, K. M. (1973). <u>Toward a cleaner aquatic environment</u>. Environmental Protection Agency. Office of Air and Water Programs. Washington, DC: U.S. Government Printing Office.

A Government Document: Unknown Author

> Indian and Northern Affairs Canada. (1986). <u>The Inuit</u>. Ottawa: Supply and Services Canada.

PERIODICALS: APA STYLE

The following examples illustrate how to list articles in magazines and periodicals according to APA style. *Note:* Do *not* underline or italicize or put quotation marks around titles of articles. Do underline (or italicize) titles of magazines or periodicals. Cite the volume number for magazines and omit the *p.* or *pp.* before any page numbers. If an article is not printed on continuous pages, give all page numbers, separated by commas.

An Article in a Weekly or Biweekly Magazine

> Fotheringham, A. (2000, July 1). Why do they do it? <u>Maclean's</u> <u>113</u>, 76.

An Article in a Monthly or Bimonthly Magazine

> Anderson, M. (2000, July). High wireless act. <u>National Post Business</u>, 48–53.

An Unsigned Article in a Magazine

> You gotta pass the puck. (2000, January). <u>Report on Business,</u>
> 16(7) 23.

An Article in a Journal With Continuous Pagination

Underline the volume number and do not include *pp*. Also, APA style requires repeating all number digits: Write 2552–2555.

> Cochran, D. D., Hale, W. D., & Hissam, C. P. (1984). Personal
> space requirements in indoor versus outdoor locations. <u>Journal of</u>
> <u>Psychology, 117</u>, 132–133.

An Article in a Journal That Paginates Each Issue Separately

Underline the volume number followed by the issue number in parentheses.

> Hashimoto, I. (1988). Pain and suffering: Apostrophes and
> academic life. <u>Journal of Basic Writing, 7</u>(2), 91–98.

An Article in a Newspaper

Use *p.* or *pp.* before newspaper section and page numbers.

> Nolen, S. (2000, June 29). Harry Potter and the PR wizards.
> <u>The Globe and Mail</u>, pp. R1, 3.

An Unsigned Article in a Newspaper

> Factory Theatre boasts premieres. (2000, June 29). <u>The</u>
> <u>National Post</u>, p. A19.

An Editorial

> Hunter, I. (2000, June 29). Liberal pundits speak for yesterday.
> [Editorial.] <u>The National Post</u>, p. A15.

An Unsigned Editorial

> Habs shut out. (2000, June 29). [Editorial.] <u>The National Post</u>,
> p. A15.

ELECTRONIC AND INTERNET SOURCES: APA STYLE

Since the World Wide Web and the Internet are still under revision, APA documentation styles will certainly be revised. For assistance with APA styles, go to the American Psychological Association Web site at **www.apa.org/journals/webref.html.** The APA site contains very minimal guidance and advice, but it does advise that references should begin with the same information usually provided for a print source reference. The Web information is then placed at the end of the reference—as in the MLA form.

The APA form recommends using "Retrieved from" in addition to the date. Use the following guidelines to compile your citation:

1. Name of author (if given)

2. Title of article (with APA capitalization rules)

3. Title of periodical or electronic text (underlined)

4. Volume number and/or pages (if any)

5. Retrieved from (include date here) from the World Wide Web: (give the URL here), and do not end with a period

Note: APA style does not cite personal communications such as e-mail in a reference list.

Article in a Journal

Lomas, J., & Veenstra, G. (1997). Devolving authority for health care in Canada's provinces: 1. An introduction to the issues. <u>Canadian Medical Association Journal, 156</u>(3), 371–377. Retrieved June 30, 2000, from the World Wide Web: http://www.cma.ca/cmaj/vol-156/issue-3/0371.htm

Article in a Newspaper

Lohr, S. (1999, January). U.S. presents documents in case against Microsoft. <u>New York Times on the Web</u> [Newspaper, selected stories on line]. Retrieved February 3, 1999, from the World Wide Web: http://www.nytimes.com/library/tech/99/01/biztech/articles/21soft.html

OTHER SOURCES: APA STYLE

In the APA system, unpublished letters and interviews are personal communications and do not represent recoverable data. Therefore, they should not appear in a "References" list. Do, however, cite personal letters or interviews in your text. (See "In-Text Documentation: APA Style.")

A Review

Daurio, B. (2000, May 13). Stories that cut to the bone. [Review of the book <u>19 Knives</u>]. <u>The Globe and Mail</u>, D25.

A Published Interview

Hampson, S. (2000, March 9). Saint Tommy's torchbearer. [Interview with Douglas, S.]. <u>The Globe and Mail</u>, p. R3.

Computer Software

<u>Microsoft word</u>. Vers. 5.0 [Computer software]. (1992). Microsoft.

A Film

> Girard, F. (Director). (1999). <u>The red violin</u> [Film]. Toronto: Lions Gate Films Inc.

A Recording

> Toronto Symphony Orchestra. (1998–1999). <u>Musically speaking</u> [CD]. Toronto: Warner Music Canada Ltd.

A Television or Radio Program

> Wachtel, E. (Host). (2000, February 6). <u>Writers and company</u> [Radio program]. Toronto, ON: CBC.

Editing and Proofreading   Edit your paper for conciseness, clarity, and accuracy of grammar, spelling, and punctuation. See your handbook for assistance in revising errors and improving usage. Check your direct quotations to make sure they are *accurate, word-for-word transcriptions* of the originals. Make sure that your in-text citation of sources is accurate. Proofread both the text *and* the "Works Cited" or "References" section. Finally, have someone else proofread your research paper for typos, spelling errors, missing words, or confusing sentences.

STUDENT   WRITING

SPIES IN THE SIXTIES: THE CONFLICTING THEMES OF IAN FLEMING AND JOHN LE CARRÉ

JOHN POLANSZKY

John Polanszky's final version of his research paper appears on page 423. His purpose was to describe and explain the thematic conflicts in the popular works of literature and film based on characters created by Ian Fleming and John le Carré. In this paper, he uses a variety of research to establish the cultural, historical, and biographical contexts for these works. Through this technique he illustrates the dynamic nature of the evolution of the spy story and its relationship to the real world of politics and espionage. Polanszky follows the MLA style for in-text documentation, supplementary notes, and "Works Cited" list. The marginal annotations highlight key features of his research paper.

↕ **1"**

↓ **½"**

Polanszky 2

/double space

John Polanszky

Professor J. A. Guccione

History 343F

/double space

15 December 2000

/double space

Spies in the Sixties:

The Conflicting Themes of Ian Fleming and John le Carré

Spy stories have long captivated audiences, not only in Canada, but around the world. Whether offering escapist fantasies or social critiques, the spy genre in both fiction and film has enjoyed broad popular appeal. The genre has also evolved over the years, following a readily identifiable cyclical pattern. This pattern has seen an oscillation between the two general extremes of heroic and anti-heroic depictions of espionage and intelligence activity (Booth 157). The heroic ideal reached its apex during the 1950s in Ian Fleming's super-spy, James Bond.[1] The early 1960s subsequently saw a return to a more critically minded, anti-heroic phase, most convincingly articulated in John le Carré's <u>The Spy Who Came in From the Cold</u>. This same period, however, also witnessed the emergence of a new phenomenon in the development of the genre. While the dominant literary trend, eventually echoed in cinema as well, was anti-heroic, the popularity of the explicitly heroic James Bond reached extraordinary new heights with the production of the James Bond film series.

This phenomenon at first seems rather curious, especially in light of the political climate and public apprehension regarding the intelligence community (as well as other

The superscript number refers the reader to the "Endnotes" page for comments.

1" ↔

↔ **1"**

↕ **1"**

authority structures) during the 1960s, both of which were most accurately reflected in the cynicism of John le Carré. The success of the Bond films seems to have arisen not from a response to or reflection of public attitudes, but rather in spite of them. The film series transformed the literary Bond of the 1950s into an icon of popular culture that transcended the genre of espionage film and fiction. While le Carré's work continued in the cyclical tradition of spy literature, the Bond films broke out of this cycle and no longer posited themselves as reflections of public attitudes towards, or shapers of, popular perceptions of intelligence activity.

As has been the case with many writers working in the spy genre, both Fleming and le Carré had real life involvement with intelligence activity. This involvement is essential in explaining not only the authenticity (or lack of authenticity) in the works of these authors, but also in providing a sense of perspective with which to approach the different thematic directions of their novels. If it is true that the Bond novels offer "a reflection of Fleming's personality, fantasies and convictions" then Fleming's life, before his literary career, must be considered an important element in deciphering what Fleming's biographer, John Pearson, called an "autobiography of dreams" (Stafford 161).

Fleming received his introduction to espionage and intelligence work during the Second World War with his involvement in British Naval Intelligence. Among Fleming's greatest intelligence achievements was his creation of 30 Assault Unit, also known as "Fleming's Private Army," a specialized commando unit that focussed specifically on the retrieval of enemy intelligence (Masters 153). The training of this unit included safe-blowing, lock picking, small-arms, radar, booby traps, minefields, gelginite and plastic explo-

Polanszky states his thesis at the end of the second paragraph.

Polanszky makes a claim and cites information to support it in the following paragraphs.

In-text citation for a source with author — notice the punctuation.

Polanszky 3

sives, code breaking and how to read Intelligence reports (Masters 153). The connection between 30 Assault Unit and Bond is clear; Fleming's wartime exploits provided rich background material for a fertile imagination.[2] The significance of Fleming's intelligence work, however, extends beyond its usefulness as a plot resource. Much of the Bond character was rooted in the Second World War, particularly Fleming's nationalism regarding Britain's wartime role and post-war status (Stafford 168–169). The Second World War gave many Britons hope that Britain's old position as a world power might be restored. These hopes were short-lived, however, with the onset of the Cold War and Britain's international decline chilling many soaring expectations. Fleming thus became, as David Stafford poignantly described him, "a propagandist of the new Elizabethan Age" (214–215). It is this sense of fear of decline that perhaps most accurately characterized the literary Bond—a man of the 1940s living beyond his time (Stafford 176).

Author is quoted in sentence so only the page number is required in the parenthetical reference.

As with Fleming, John le Carré's novels have also been greatly affected by his intelligence work. Indeed, it has been pointed out that the two factors that have most heavily influenced le Carré's writing are "the shadow of his confidence-trickster father, and his own involvement in the Secret Services" (Masters 230). David Cornwell (le Carré's real name) joined MI5 during the late 1950s—a time of scandals and infighting among senior officials—when the self-confidence of the British Intelligence community was seriously tested (Masters 229–239). In light of this pervading atmosphere, it is not surprising that le Carré's novels are highly cynical, reflecting a world in which anger, despair, and resignation are commonplace. These attitudes were not simply confined to the Intelligence community during the

Further evidence supporting claim.

late 1950s and early 1960s. The world at large was caught at a peculiar crossroads where the Cold War seemed to be thawing with the arrival of Nikita Khrushchev as the head of the Soviet government. Yet crisis and tension were widespread with events such as the downing of a U.S. U-2 spy plane over Soviet territory in 1960, the erection of the Berlin Wall in 1961, and the Bay of Pigs fiasco in Cuba that same year making headlines. This increase in East-West tension was further aggravated in Britain by the Burgess, Maclean, Philby, and Blunt revelations, which, for many, showed that being "a gentleman was no guarantee of sexual or patriotic orthodoxy" (Stafford 215). This attitude paralleled le Carré's belief that the old class system, still in control of the Secret Services, was the real menace to Britain (Masters 239). In light of this historical context, le Carré's work can be seen as strikingly antithetical to that of Fleming, and as the next revolution in the thematic wheel of spy fiction.

Understanding Fleming and le Carré's literary work, however, demands one look beyond their intelligence involvement. To begin with, both men held fundamentally different attitudes towards Britain's status on the world stage. Fleming believed in the future greatness of Britain while, as Anthony Masters points out, le Carré "with his firsthand knowledge of upper-class intrigue, saw Britain in desolation" (240–241). Bond conveys Fleming's sense of hope not only in his spectacular victories against Britain's enemies, but also in his tastes for such strictly British luxuries as Bentley cars and Morland cigarettes (Stafford 169). These tastes represent a very palpable consumerism, a quality that not only placed Bond squarely in the post-war era, but also facilitated a successful transition to film. Bond's opulent tastes and emphatic Britishness were not the only

Polanszky provides an historical context.

Transition to the next point of the essay.

Polanszky 5

elements that characterized the literary Bond. Despite his many triumphs, the literary Bond (unlike his cinematic counterpart) was also based in reality. The notion that a powerful fantasy-figure can not be entirely implausible is described by Kingsley Amis, in relation to the Bond books, as "the Fleming effect" (111). Bond's plausibility is created by such simple devices as having Bond train in preparation for a difficult mission, or display moments of self-doubt before or after having dispatched a villain. This aspect of the Bond novels is essential in understanding the emergence of le Carré's brand of spy fiction, as well as the cinematic incarnation of the Bond character. The small touches of reality in the Bond books were transformed into an overwhelming sense of realism, expressed in the self-examination of characters such as Alec Leamas, in le Carré's novels. Le Carré's novels portray, with excessive, authentic detail, the "interior bureaucracies" of the Intelligence community (Stafford 196). Thus, Fleming's nationalistic optimism was not only superseded by le Carré's cynicism, but "the Fleming effect" was, in a sense, completely eclipsed by a hard edged and bitter realism.

Le Carré himself aptly illustrated that his work was very much a reflection of broader public attitudes:

> I mean the world had been aware from its newspapers of this grey army of cold warriors, of defectors, of spies, frontier crossers. And what had literature produced? This candy-floss image of a macho man, an Etonian who really seemed not to have a moral doubt in his head. (qtd. in Masters 243)

Despite the cynicism, however, le Carré can not be described as unpatriotic. The anger in le Carré's fiction is

Quotes containing five or more lines should be indented 10 spaces.

not directed against Western society in general, but against a specific mentality present in the Intelligence community. This mentality is succinctly expressed by le Carré's fictional head of Intelligence, Control, who, in The Spy Who Came in From the Cold, tells the doomed protagonist, Alec Leamas, "We do disagreeable things so that ordinary people here and elsewhere can sleep safely in their beds at night. Is this too romantic? Of course, we occasionally do very wicked things" (15). Le Carré's novels, taken as a whole, go even further in suggesting that a nation's Intelligence service is a reflection of society's general moral health (Masters 229). The success of The Spy Who Came in From The Cold marked the return of the anti-heroic vein to popular spy fiction. In contrast to the anachronistic Bond, le Carré's characters such as George Smiley and Alec Leamas were created as a response and reflection to the new anxieties of the 1960s (Masters 156). Bond's fate, however, was not yet sealed as the 1960s saw the emergence of Bond as a pop cultural icon of immense proportions.

The release of the Bond films during the 1960s, beginning with Dr. No in 1962, sparked a genuine popular phenomenon as the movie-going public fell in love with Fleming's 007. While the Bond of literature was becoming increasingly dated and out of touch with the currents of the spy fiction genre, the cinematic Bond was breaking new ground. On a superficial level, the initial appeal of the Bond films was that they were highly visual, involving great action and spectacle (Brosnan 11). The films themselves were broken up into a series of "set-pieces," which the series' producer, Albert Broccoli, called "bumps" (Brosnan 12). These "bumps" eventually evolved to a point where a Bond film would consist of a series of virtually unrelated action sequences. Thus

Paraphrased material also requires proper citation.

the emphasis was shifted away from a story involving politics and espionage towards a more visceral sort of thrill.

The Bond films, however, also represent a deeper transformation of the Bond novel. A fundamental shift occurs within "the mythology of James Bond" (Bennett and Woollacott 144–145). This shift is largely due to the loss of the "Fleming effect." Examples of this deterioration of the plausible abound in the Bond films of the 1960s. The film version of Goldfinger, for instance, opens with a pre-credit scene where Bond kills a Mexican drug runner. Bond dispatches the villain with uncharacteristic cruelty, electrocuting him in a bathtub. The novel Goldfinger, however, opens with a moment of quiet introspection, as Bond reflects on having killed the Mexican with his bare hands (Bennett and Woollacott 145–152). The film Bond also displays a shallow penchant for witticisms, as he remarks after having killed the Mexican, "Shocking, positively shocking" (Bennett and Woollacott 152). The increased use of gadgetry and the trademark title sequences also set the cinematic Bond apart from his literary counterpart. The title sequence for Goldfinger portrays a scantily clad woman posing in time to the title song. The sequence is entirely irrelevant to the narrative of the film, yet she becomes a device to deliver a summary of the plot as segments of the film are projected onto her body (Bennett and Woollacott 153). Finally, the element of comedy throughout the Bond films serves to further undermine the subtle credibility of the literary Bond, as a two-dimensional comic book character replaces the glorified, yet plausible, depiction of an intelligence officer.

The transformation of Bond into an icon of popular culture effectively removed the character from the familiar cycle of the spy story genre. While John le Carré's brand of

In-text citation for a source with two authors.

The thesis is restated towards the end of the essay.

anti-heroic and morally ambiguous cynicism accurately reflected emerging public attitudes towards politics and the intelligence community, Fleming's Bond found a new niche, beyond the confines of the genre. Thus, two very different approaches to the portrayal of the intelligence community and the role of spy fiction came to not only co-exist, but flourish side by side. The 1960s recast the landscape of popular culture and with it, the unwritten rules of the spy story genre. While the cycle of the heroic vs. anti-heroic continues to move forward, and audience perceptions and anxieties are not only reflected, but also transformed by spy fiction, new writers and their creations will undoubtedly capture the public's imagination. The celluloid Bond, however, continues to hold its own as a touchstone of nostalgic, masculine fantasy from an imaginary past.

1"

Polanszky 9

Notes

[1] One of the earliest examples of the popular hero in the spy genre was John Buchan's Richard Hannay, the protagonist in such works as <u>The Thirty-Nine Steps</u>. The Scotland born Buchan, like Fleming and le Carré, led an adventuresome life eventually becoming the Governor General of Canada. For an interesting article contrasting Buchan as an artist and a man of action see Donald Mackenzie's "John Buchan: Man of Letters or Man of Affairs?"

[2] Much has been written about the connections between Fleming's life and that of his most famous creation. It has been suggested that the real life Canadian spy William Stephenson served as the model for James Bond (<u>Assassins Canada</u>, 2000). Stephenson's story has also been well chronicled, most notably in William Stevenson's (no relation) <u>A Man Called Intrepid: The Secret War</u>.

1"

1"

1"

Content notes are placed on a separate page and double-spaced. Indent the first line five spaces.

In his notes, our student includes ideas that would have been digressive in the text of his paper.

↕ **1"**   Polanszky 10

Works Cited

The "Works Cited" list begins a new page. List the entries alphabetically by the author's last name. If no author is given, list by the first word in the title. Double-space all lines.

Indent five spaces after first line of each entry.

↔ **1"**   ↔ **1"**

Amis, Kingsley. <u>The James Bond Dossier</u>. London: Jonathan
    Cape, 1965.

Aronoff, Myron Joel. <u>The Spy Novels of John le Carré:
    Balancing Ethics and Politics</u>. New York: St. Martin's
    Press, 1999.

<u>Assassins Canada</u>. The Responsible Government Index. 25
    Nov. 2000.
    <http://nflb.tripod.com/jamebond.htm>.

Bennett, Tony and Janet Woollacott<u>. Bond and Beyond: The
    Political Career of a Popular Hero</u>. Communications
    and Culture. London: Macmillan, 1987.

Booth, Alan R. "The Development of the Espionage Film."
    <u>Spy Fiction, Spy Films and Real Intelligence</u>. Ed.
    Wesley K. Wark. London: Frank Cass, 1991. 136–160.

Brosnan, John. <u>James Bond in the Cinema</u>. London:
    Tantivity Press, 1981.

Chapman, James. <u>Licence to Thrill: A Cultural History of
    the James Bond Films</u>. New York: Columbia University
    Press, 2000.

Cobbes, John L. <u>Understanding John le Carré</u>. Columbia,
    SC: University of South Carolina Press, 1998.

↕ **1"**

Polanszky 11

<u>Goldfinger</u>. Dir. Guy Hamilton. Perf. Sean Connery.
    MGM/UA Home Video, 1988.

le Carré, John. <u>The Spy Who Came In From the Cold</u>.
    New York: Bantam Books, 1983.

Mackenzie, Donald. "John Buchan: Man of Letters or
    Man of Affairs?" <u>University of Glasgow Avenue</u>
    No.19 Jan. 1996. 15 Oct. 2000
    <http://www.gla.ac.uk/Graduate/Avenue/19/
    16johnbu.htm>.

Internet Web page

Masters, Anthony. <u>Literary Agents: The Novelist as Spy</u>.
    Oxford: Basil Blackwell Ltd., 1987.

Monaghan, David. <u>Smiley's Circus: A Guide to the
    Secret World of John le Carré</u>. London: Orbis,
    1986.

Rubenstein, Leonard. <u>The Great Spy Films: A Pictorial
    History</u>. Seacaucus: The Citadel Press, 1979.

Stafford, David. <u>The Silent Game: The Real World of
    Imaginary Spies.</u> Toronto: Lester and Orpen
    Dennys, 1988.

Stevenson, William. <u>A Man Called Intrepid: The Secret
    War</u> New York· Harcourt Brace Jovanovich, 1976.

Wolfe, Peter. <u>Corridors of Deceit: The World of John le
    Carré</u>. Bowling Green: Bowling Green State
    University Popular Press, 1987.

APPENDIX:
WRITING UNDER PRESSURE

The main chapters of this text describe purposes for writing and strategies for collecting, shaping, drafting, and revising an essay. These chapters assume that you have several days or even weeks to write your paper. They work on the premise that you have time to read model essays, time to think about ideas for your topic, time to prewrite, and write several drafts. Much college and university writing, however, occurs on midterm or final examinations, when you may have only 15 to 20 minutes to complete the whole process of writing. When you must produce a "final" draft in a few short minutes, your writing process may need drastic modification.

A typical examination has some objective questions (true/false, multiple-choice, definition, short-answer) followed by an essay question or two. For example, with just 25 minutes left in your Western Civilization midterm, you might finish the last multiple-choice question, turn the page, and read the following essay question:

> Erich Maria Remarque's *All Quiet on the Western Front* has been hailed by critics the world over as the "20th century's definitive novel on war." What does Remarque's novel tell us about the historical, ideological, national, social, and human significance of 20th-century warfare? Draw on specific illustrations from the novel, but base your observations on your wider perspective on Western civilization. Good luck!

Overwhelmed by panic, you find the blood drains from your face and your fingers feel icy. You now have 22 minutes to write on the "historical, ideological, national, social, and human significance of 20th-century warfare." Do you have to explain everything about modern warfare? Must you use specific examples from the novel? Good luck, indeed! Everything you remembered about the novel has now vanished. Bravely, you pick up your pen and start recounting the main events of the novel, hoping to show the instructor at least that you read it.

You can survive such an essay examination, but you need to prepare yourself emotionally and intellectually. Following is some advice:

Read the question carefully.

Get your thoughts in order.

Write what the question asks, not what you wish it asked.

Don't ramble.

Give textual facts or specific examples.

Summarize with a clear, understandable closing.

Proofread.

Keep calm. Your life doesn't depend on one test.

KNOW YOUR AUDIENCE

Teachers expect you to answer a question exactly as it is asked, not just to give the information that you know. Because teachers must read dozens of essays, they are impressed by clear organization and specific detail. As one sixth semester student says, teachers hate babble because they cannot follow the thread of your argument. Although they demand specific examples and facts from the text, they want you to explain how these examples *relate* to the overall question. In a pile of two hundred English exams graded by one professor, margins featured comments like "Reread the question. This doesn't answer the question." "What is your main point? State your main point clearly." "Give more specific illustrations and examples." Keep this teacher in mind as you write your next essay response.

ANALYZE KEY TERMS

Understanding the key terms in the question is crucial to writing an essay under pressure. Teachers expect you to respond to *their* specific question, not just to write down information. They want you to use your writing to *think* about the topic—to analyze and synthesize the information. In short, they want you to make sense of the information. Following are key terms that indicate teachers' expectations and suggest how to organize your answer.

Discuss: A general instruction that means "write about." If the question says *discuss,* look for other key words to focus your response.

Describe: Give sensory details or particulars about a topic. Often, however, this general instruction simply means "discuss."

Analyze: Divide a topic into its parts, and show how the parts are related to each other and to the topic as a whole.

Synthesize: Show how the parts relate to the whole or how the parts make sense together.

Explain: Show relationships between specific examples and general principles. Explain what (define), explain why (causes/effects), and/or explain how (analyze process).

Define: Explain what something is. As appropriate, give a formal definition, describe it, analyze its parts or function, describe what it is not, and/or compare and contrast it with similar events or ideas.

Compare: Explain similarities and (often) differences. Draw conclusions from the observed similarities and differences.

Contrast: Explain key differences. Draw conclusions from the observed differences.

Illustrate: Provide specific examples of an idea or process.

Trace: Give the sequence or chronological order of key events or ideas.

Evaluate: Determine the value or worth of an idea, thing, process, person, or event. Set up criteria and provide evidence to support your judgments.

Solve: Explain your solution; show how it fixes the problem, why it is better than other alternatives, and why it is feasible.

Argue: Present both sides of a controversial issue, showing why the opposing position should not be believed or accepted and why your position should be accepted. Give evidence to support your position.

Interpret: Offer your understanding of the meaning and significance of an idea, event, person, process, or work of art. Support your understanding with specific examples or details.

MAKE A SKETCH OUTLINE

The key terms in a question should not only focus your thinking but also suggest how to organize your response. Use the key terms to make a sketch outline of your response. You may not regularly use an outline when you have more time to write an essay, but the time pressure requires that you revise your normal writing process.

Assume that you have 25 minutes to read and respond to the following question from a history examination. Read the instructions carefully, note the key terms, and make a brief outline to guide your writing.

• Answer *one* of the following. Draw on the reading for your answer. (25 pts)

1. Explain the arguments that the balance of power does and does not work in the nuclear age (discuss and illustrate both sides of the argument). Then take a stand—citing the evidence for your position.

2. Explain the arguments that the United Nations does and does not play a positive role in international relations (discuss and illustrate both sides of the argument). Then take a stand—citing the evidence for your position.

Let's assume that because you know more about the United Nations, you choose the second question. First, you should identify and underline key words in the question. The subject for your essay is the *United Nations* and its role in *international relations*. You need to *explain* the reasons why the UN does or does not have a positive effect on international relations. You will need to *discuss* and *illustrate* (give specific examples of) both sides of the controversy. Finally, you need to *take a stand* (argue) for your belief, citing *evidence* (specific examples from recent history) of how the UN has or has not helped to resolve international tensions.

Based on your rereading and annotation of the key words of the question, make a quick outline or list, perhaps as follows:

I. Reasons (with examples) why some believe the UN is effective

   A. Reason 1 + example

   B. Reason 2 + example

II. Reasons (with examples) why some believe the UN is not effective

   A. Reason 1 + example

   B. Reason 2 + example

III. Reasons why you believe the UN is effective

   Refer to reasons and examples cited in I, above, but explain why these reasons and examples outweigh the reasons cited in II, above.

With this sketch outline as your guide, jot down reasons and examples that you intend to use, and then start writing. Your outline will make sure that you cover all the main points of the question, and it will keep your essay organized as you concentrate on remembering specific reasons and examples.

KNOW THE MATERIAL

It goes without saying that you must know the material in order to explain the concepts and give specific examples or facts from the text. But what is the best way to review the material so that you can recall examples under pressure? The following three study tactics will improve your recall.

First, read your text actively. Do not just mark key passages in yellow highlighter. Write marginal notes to yourself. Write key concepts in the margin. Ask questions. Make connections between an idea in one paragraph and something you read earlier. Make connections between what you read in the text and what you heard in class.

Second, do not depend only on your reading and class discussion. Join or form a study group that meets regularly to review course material. Each person in the group should prepare some question for review. Explaining key ideas to a friend is an excellent way to learn the material yourself.

Finally, use your writing to help you remember. Do not just read the book and your notes and head off for the test. Instead, review your notes, *close* your notebook, and write down as much as you can remember. Review the assigned chapters in the text, close the book, and write out what you remember. If you can write answers to questions with the book closed, you know you're ready for an essay examination.

PRACTISE WRITING

As several of the fourth semester students suggested, practising short essays *before* an examination will make you feel comfortable with the material and reduce your panic. A coach once noted that while every athlete wants to win, only the true winners are willing to *prepare* to win. The same is true of writing an examination. Successful writers have already completed 80 percent of the writing process *before* they walk into an examination. They have written notes in the margins of their notebooks and textbooks. They have discussed the subject with other students. They have closed the book and written out key definitions. They have prepared questions and practised answering them. Once they read a question, they are prepared to write out their "final" drafts.

PROOFREAD AND EDIT

In your normal writing process, you can put aside your draft for several days and proofread and edit it later. When you are writing under pressure, however, you need to save three or four minutes at the end to review what you have written. Often, you may be out of time before you have finished writing what you wanted to say about the question. At this point, one effective strategy is to draw a line at the end of what you have written, write "Out of Time," and then write one or two quick sentences explaining what you planned to say: "If I had more time, I would explain how the UN's image has become more positive following the crises in Israel and Iraq." Then use your remaining two or three minutes to reread what you have written, making sure that your ideas are clear and that you have written in complete sentences and used correct spelling and punctuation. If you don't know how to spell a word, at least write "sp?" next to a word to show that you think it is spelled incorrectly.

SAMPLE ESSAY QUESTIONS
AND RESPONSES

The following are sample essay questions, students' responses, and instructors' comments and grades.

HISTORY 100: WESTERN CIVILIZATION

Examination II over Chapter 12, class lectures, and Victor Hugo's
The Hunchback of Notre Dame

ESSAY I (25 POINTS)

What was the 15th-century view of "science" as described in *The Hunchback?* How did this view tend to inhibit Claud Frollo in his experiments in his closet in the cathedral?

Answer 1

The 15th-century view of "science" was characterized by superstition and heresy. In <u>The Hunchback of Notre Dame</u>, for example, we see superstition operating when the king's physician states that a gunshot wound can be cured by the application of a roasted mouse. Claud Frollo, a high-ranking church official, has a thirst for knowledge, but unfortunately it pushes beyond the limits of knowledge permitted by the church. When he works in his closet on the art of alchemy and searches for the "Philosopher's Stone" (gold), he is guilty of heresy. Frollo has read and mastered the arts and sciences of the university and of the church, and he wants to know more. He knows that if he presses into the "Black Arts," the Devil will take his soul. And indeed, the "Devil" of passion does. Frollo feels inhibited because many of the experiments he has performed have made him guilty of heresy and witchcraft in the eyes of the church. And this seems to be the case in almost anything "new" or out of the ordinary. La Esmeralda, for instance, is declared "guilty" of witchcraft for the training of her goat. Her goat appears to have been possessed by the Devil himself, when, in fact, all the girl is guilty of is training the goat to do a few simple tricks. All in all, the 15th-century view of "science" was one not of favour, but of oppression and fear. Thankfully, the Renaissance came along!

An excellent response. Your focus on superstition and heresy along with the specific examples of the roasted mouse, the "Philosopher's Stone," and La Esmeralda's goat illustrates the 15th-century view of science and its inhibiting effect. Grade: A

Answer 2

The 15th-century view of science was that, according to the Bible, God was the creator of all, and as to scientific theory, the subject was moot. No one was a believer in the scientific method—however, we do find some science going on in Claud Frollo's closet, alchemy. At that time he was trying to create gold by mixing different elements together. Though alchemy seems to be the only science of that time period, people who practised it kept it to themselves. We even find King Louis IX coming to Frollo, disguised, to dabble in a little of the science himself. At this time people were rejecting the theory of the Earth revolving around the sun because, as a religious ordeal, God created the Earth and man, and they are the centre of all things, so there were no questions to be answered by science, because the answer was God.

Give more examples from the novel and show how the 15th-century view actually <u>inhibited</u> Frollo. Otherwise, generally good response. (Why was creating the Earth such a religious "ordeal"?) Grade: B

Answer 3

According to The Hunchback of Notre Dame, the view of "science" in the 15th century was basically alchemy, that is, being able to turn base metals into gold. Everything else that we would regard as scientific today was regarded as sorcery or magic in the 15th century. What inhibited Claud Frollo in his experiments of turning base metals into gold was that, according to the laws of alchemy, one needed "The Philosopher's Stone" to complete the experiment, and Claud Frollo was unable to find this particular stone.

Answer 4

During the period that the Hunchback took place, the attitude toward science was one of fear. Because the setting was in the medieval world, the people were afraid to admit to doing some things that were not being done by a majority of people. The overall view during that period was to keep one's own self out of trouble. The fright may be the result of the public executions which were perhaps Claud Frollo's deterrent in admitting to performing acts of science which others are uneducated in. Claud Frollo was outnumbered in the area of wanting to be "educated" and he kept to himself because he feared the people. He was in a position that didn't give him the power to try and overcome people's attitude of fear toward science. If he tried, he risked his life.

BIOLOGY 220: ECOLOGY

FINAL EXAMINATION

ESSAY II (20 POINTS)

Water running down a mountainside erodes its channel and carries with it considerable material. What is the basic source of the energy used by the water to do this work? How is the energy used by water to do this work related to the energy used by life in the stream ecosystem?

Answer 1

The process begins with the hydrologic cycle. The sun radiates down and forces evaporation. This H_2O gas condenses and forms rain or snow, which precipitates back to earth. If the precipitation falls on a mountain, it will eventually run down the hillside and erode its channel. (Some water will evaporate without running down the hill.) The energy used by water to do its work relates directly to the energy used by life in the stream system. The sun is an energy input. It is the source of energy for stream life just as it is the source of energy for the water. Through photosynthesis, the energy absorbed by the stream is used by higher and higher trophic levels. So the sun is the energy source for both running water and the life in the stream. It all starts with solar energy.

Answer 2

Ultimately, the sun is the basic source of energy that allows water to do the work it does. Solar power runs the hydrologic cycle, which is where water gets its energy. Heat evaporates water and allows molecules to rise in the atmosphere, where it condenses in clouds. Above the ground, but still under the effects of gravity, water has potential energy at this point. When enough condensation occurs, water drops back to the ground, changing potential energy to kinetic energy, which is how water works on mountainsides to move materials. As water moves materials, it brings into streams a great deal of organic matter, which is utilized by a number of heterotrophic organisms. That is the original source of energy for the ecosystems and also how energy used by water is related to the energy that is used by life in streams.

Very clear explanation of the hydrologic cycle, but response doesn't explain how source of energy for the stream ecosystem is related, through photosynthesis, to solar energy. Grade: B

Answer 3

The actual energy to move the water down the mountains is gravitational pull from the centre of the earth. The stream's "growth" from the beginning of the mountaintop to the base starts out with being a heterotrophic system. This is because usually there is not enough light to bring about photosynthesis for the plants and in turn help other organisms' survival, so the streams use outside resources for energy. Once the stream gets bigger (by meeting up with another stream), it is autotrophic. It can produce its own energy sources. When the water reaches the base and becomes very large, it falls back to a heterotrophic system because the water has become too deep for light to penetrate and help with photosynthesis.

Reread the questions. The basic source of energy is solar power. You almost discover the answer when you discuss photosynthesis, but after that, you get off track again. Grade: C-

HANDBOOK

Section 1

Review of Basic Sentence Elements

If you are unfamiliar with grammatical terms, parts of speech, or basic sentence elements, check the definitions and examples in this section.

1A Sentence Structure

1B Nouns and Pronouns

1C Adjectives and Adverbs

1D Verbs

1E Phrases and Clauses

1F Articles, Prepositions, Interjections

Section 2

Sentence Structure and Grammar

This section shows you how to revise such common problems as sentence fragments, faulty parallelism, unnecessary use of passive voice, and lack of subject-verb agreement.

2A Fragments

2B Mixed Constructions and Faulty Predication

2C Dangling Modifiers and Misplaced Modifiers

2D Faulty Parallelism

2E Active and Passive Voice

2F Nominals and *Be* Verbs

2G Subject-Verb Agreement

2H Verb Tense

2I Pronoun Agreement

2J Pronoun Reference

Section 3

Diction and Style

This section contains tips on making your writing more precise, concise, and effective. You will learn to recognize and eliminate vague words, needless words, clichés, and jargon. At the end of this section, the Usage Glossary explains distinctions between confusing pairs of words such as *affect/effect, advise/advice,* and *amount/number.*

3A Vague Words

3B Wordiness

3C Colloquial Language and Slang

3D Clichés and Jargon

3E Sexist Language

3F Denotation and Connotation

3G Usage Glossary

Section 4

Punctuation and Mechanics

If you have problems using commas, semicolons, colons, or dashes, this section will help you pinpoint errors and fix them. The examples show you how to revise comma splices and fused sentences, how to punctuate dialogue, and how to use numbers, apostrophes, italics, and capitals.

4A Sentence Punctuation

4B Comma Splices and Fused Sentences

4C Commas

4D Periods and Semicolons

4E Colons and Dashes

4F Exclamation Points and Question Marks

4G Quotation and Ellipsis Marks

4H Italics

4I Parentheses and Brackets

4J Apostrophes and Hyphens

4K Capitals and Numbers

The information in this Handbook will help you with the final stages of the revising process: editing and proofreading. Most writers and researchers agree that editing and proofreading should wait until the end of the writing process, when you are least likely to interrupt the flow of your ideas. During this final stage, you should clarify your sentences and correct any errors in grammar, usage, diction, spelling, and mechanics. As you edit, concentrate on polishing the surface blemishes in your writing, but don't get so locked in on punctuation or grammar that you ignore the meaning, organization, or development of your essay. Even when you are proofreading, you may find an occasional spot to add another bit of detail, take out a repetitious phrase, or sharpen a transition.

To be a good editor, you need to understand the *conventions* of language and the *expectations* of the reader instead of memorizing rules. In fact, the "rules" of grammar, punctuation, and usage may vary from one occasion to the next. A sentence fragment or a substandard usage such as "ain't" may be appropriate in one situation but not in another. Moreover, the notion of "rules" tends to suggest that language is static or unchanging. In fact, the opposite is true: Vocabulary, acceptable usage, even grammatical choices depend on current conventions and expectations. What is acceptable for one occasion or audience may be totally inappropriate for another. If you are not aware of these conventions, all your hard work in collecting, shaping, drafting, and revising may be wasted. A sloppy job of editing can ruin the best of essays.

This chapter describes standard conventions of editing in formal English usage. As you edit your writing, however, remember that your purpose and audience should be your final guide.

WHY EDIT AND PROOFREAD?

Most writers and readers agree that grammar, usage, spelling, and mechanics are less important than content and ideas. But writers should realize that readers react not only to the ideas in an essay but also to the clarity, accuracy, and even the surface appearance of the writing. Often, writers will say, rather defensively, "Of course there are a few typos and grammar problems in my essay, but readers can still get the message. After all, it's my *ideas* that count." Unfortunately, ideas count only if the reader *gets* them. If the reader becomes irritated by unclear sentences and errors in spelling or usage, your good ideas may never reach their destination.

Writers who say that surface errors are unimportant are either rationalizing or living in a fantasy world. In the real world, most readers react negatively if writing is not neat, accurate, and readable. If your friend or roommate leaves a scrawled note that says, "I borried your shert for too day—hope you do'nt mind!" you may worry about the "shert"—and look for a new roommate. If your bank statement has misspellings, crossed-out numbers, or pencilled-in debits, you may change banks in a hurry. If your doctor writes a note saying, "In my opinnion you should have bone serjury immediately!" you may rush to get another "opinnion" before agreeing to "serjury." The medium may communicate the real message: If the medium—your language—is flawed by surface errors, readers often suspect that the message is flawed, too.

Some readers believe that writers who do not edit or proofread are just lazy. Although you need time to polish your writing, effective editing and proofreading are not just matters of effort or willpower. Rereading your essay ten times will not necessarily resolve all the problems. Editing is often difficult because many of your errors really don't look like mistakes—primarily because *you already know what you are trying to say.* When you reread what you have written, you tend to recall the idea already in your mind instead of reading the words exactly as they are written on the page.

If you live with a friend or roommate, try this experiment. Sit in a neutral corner of the room and look at your desk. It looks relatively clean, right? A few books, papers, and pencils are scattered here and there, but you know where everything is. It has an order. It makes sense. The math book is on the corner of the desk—under the notebook, the sock, and the coffee—just where you left it last night. The psychology book is open to Chapter 4, right underneath the sweatshirt and the lecture notes that you're going to study after dinner. Stuff is kind of stacked up, but not really messy. Now look at your friend's desk. Everything looks disorganized, as if it were dumped upside down from a backpack. You count four books, two spiral notebooks, four dog-eared sheets of paper, one cup of stale coffee, a broken ballpoint pen, and a T-shirt. It's a mess, right? And sometimes it really irritates you. *How can your roommate stand to live in such chaos?* But wait. Your roommate's desk has some order to it, too, just as yours does. You just can't see the order for the mess.

Unfortunately, the same is true of writing: In your *own* writing, all you see is the meaning—the order that is in your mind. In other people's writing, you see the errors first and then, only after careful reading, the meaning. The bedrock truth is that readers will more easily see your errors than your meaning. Your writing will be more effective if your readers aren't irritated about the mistakes that they have had to read through. Errors or surface distractions may even undermine your credibility as a writer. For some kinds of writing—letters of application or essays for classes—the result of a few errors may be more than irritation; you simply may not be admitted, get the job, or get a passing grade.

HOW TO EDIT AND PROOFREAD

The purpose of editing is, of course, to keep language problems from interfering with the ideas or message—to make language work for your purpose rather than against it. Editing usually requires that you read over your work several times, checking for errors and anticipating problems that your readers might have. However, because you literally may not see many "obvious" errors, have friends or classmates look over your draft for problems or mistakes. When you use other readers, however, explain your purpose and audience. Then ask them to use conventional proofreading and editing marks to indicate their suggestions. *Remember: Your editors' marks are suggestions.* If they mark errors you've simply overlooked, make the correction. But if they mark something that you don't understand, check the appropriate section in this Handbook. If you disagree with their marks or suggestions, ask them to explain why they are suggesting the change. *You are responsible for deciding whether and how to make the change.*

Begin your editing and proofreading process for each essay by *reviewing your previous essays.* What problems and errors did your teacher mark? Keep a log of your problems in grammar, usage, punctuation, or mechanics, and review your entries. If you typically have punctuation problems and wordy sentences, reread those sections in this Handbook and focus on those specific items as you edit.

To improve your editing and proofreading skills, learn the following proofreading marks and correction symbols.

Proofreading Marks

⋀	Insert comma
cho͜sing	Insert letter or word
⋁prom⋁	Insert quotation marks
bill⌒boards	Close up
¶	begin a new paragraph
("practise"?)⊙	Add period
English#speakers	Add space
detreiorate	Transpose letters
(English‖learning)	Transpose words
~~Unnecessary~~	Delete words
"practice⌒"	Delete punctuation
subǰect	Replace a letter
retention ~~presence~~	Replace a word
Ȼommunication	Use lower case
english	Capitalize

The following paragraph illustrates how to use these proofreading marks.

The english language, spoken and written, is in decline. People seem unable to say what they mean, they make grammar errors which obfuscate meaning and they constantly mispronounce words. Even those who should be exemplary speakers, TV and radio broadcasters, are guilty of poor oral communication. Politicians probably were the first corruptors of precise language use by deliberately chosing words that fudge the issue. I would think that this policy will need to be considered at a later point in time. Notice the incorrect use of the subjunctive "would think" instead of the indicative and more definite "I think." As well, notice the weak passive voice, "will need to be considered" which, by avoiding a subject or agent, avoids accountability. "A later point in time," more succinctly, "later," adds to the unnecessary wordiness of the assertion. Many people's diction is poor. They say "prolm" instead of prob-lem. Especially in Feb-u-ary (Feb-**ru**-ary) a discussion of nu-cu-lar (nu-**cle**-ar) energy may precede the question, Jeet jet? (Did you eat yet?) No, but Tranna **(Toronto)** has some fine restaurants. Along with abusing the language, incorrect pronunciation by Englishspeakers makes (English learning) confusing for new Canadians and leads to perpetuation of the distortions. Our written Communication is in even greater danger of causing the language to deteriorate. One regular offender is the possessive "its," too often written as "it's," the contraction of "it is." This blatant error shouts out from bill boards, newspaper columns and students' final English essays, never to be highlighted by spellcheck. This technological aid, in which the language naifs place all their faith, allows the ~~presence~~ ^{retention} of any homonym, regardless of its correctness in the context (Is it "their," "there," or "they're"? Is it "practice" or "practise"?). The amount **(number)** of people who don't bother to make the verb agree with its subject are **(is)** increasing. Neither my colleagues nor I are **(am)** happy about this sloppiness. After all, correct pronunciation and grammar, like manners and rules of the road, make individual interaction smoother and society more civilized.

Editing Symbols

Your instructor may use correction marks to guide your own editing. Listed here are some of the most common symbols, with an explanation and reference to the section number in this Handbook.

adj	use adjective, 1C
adv	use adverb, 1C
cs	comma splice, 4B

d	revise diction (word choice)
dm	dangling modifier, 2C
frag	sentence fragment, 2A
fs	fused sentence, 4B
mm	misplaced modifier, 2C
//	revise faulty parallelism, 2D
p	punctuation needed, 4A–J
pn agr	make pronoun agree with antecedent, 2I
ref	pronoun referent problem, 2J
sp	spelling error
sxt	sexist language, 3E
sv agr	subject-verb agreement error, 2G
t	verb tense error, 1D, 2H
trans	needs transition
v	verb form problem, 1D
wdy	wordy—omit needless words, 3A, 3B
wc	revise word choice

Tips for Editing and Proofreading

1. Review sections of this chapter just before you begin editing. If you need to review basic grammatical terms, begin with Section 1. Otherwise, review appropriate parts of Sections 2, 3, or 4.

2. Practise your editing and proofreading skills first on others' essays. You will see others' problems much more readily than you will see your own. Becoming a good editor of their writing will, in turn, help you recognize your own problems more easily.

3. As you edit, look for one problem at a time. Concentrate, for example, just on punctuation, or just on subject-verb agreement, or just on diction or word choice.

4. Have a friend or classmate read your essay aloud. Listen as the person reads. If you notice something that is not clear, stop and revise the sentence. If the reader does not understand what he or she is reading, stop and revise.

5. If you are writing on a computer, reformat and print out your essay, double-spaced, in narrow columns, 40 to 45 spaces wide. Many obvious errors will jump out at you as you reread your writing in a new format.

6. For proofreading, place a ruler or a blank piece of paper underneath the line you are checking. If you are proofreading for typos, try reading backward, one word at a time, from the bottom of the page to the top.

Section 1

Review of Basic Sentence Elements

This section reviews the names and definitions of basic sentence elements. Other sections in this Handbook use the terms defined and illustrated in this section.

1A SENTENCE STRUCTURE

A sentence is a group of words beginning with a capital letter and ending with a period or other end mark; it has a subject and a predicate and expresses a complete thought. The *subject* is the word or group of words that is the topic or focus of the sentence. It acts, is acted upon, or is described. The *predicate* gives information about the subject: what the subject is, what it is doing, or what is done to it.

Subject	Predicate
Piranhas	bite!
The McNeils	dig clams at the seashore.
Bubble gum	can cause cancer in rats.

Sentences may contain the following elements: subject (S), verb (V), direct object (DO), indirect object (IO), subject complement (SC), object complement (OC), modifier (M), and conjunction (+).

   s   v
Piranhas bite.

   s   v   do +   do   m
Piranhas attack fish or animals in their waters.

   s   v   io   m   do
Andrea gave Carlos two piranhas.

   s   v   do   oc
Carlos considers Andrea a prankster.

   s   v   sc
Andrea is a prankster.

Subjects may be nouns, pronouns, noun phrases, or noun clauses.

Verbs may be single words *(bite)* or verb phrases *(will have bitten)*. Verbs may be transitive or intransitive; verbs have tense, voice, and mood.

Direct objects can be nouns, pronouns, noun phrases, or noun clauses. A direct object receives the action of a transitive verb. Direct objects usually answer the question "What?" or "Whom?" about the subject and verb:

Piranhas bite [whom?] *people.*

Indirect objects can be nouns, pronouns, noun phrases, or noun clauses. The indirect object answers the question "To whom?" or "For whom?" about the subject and verb:

Andrea gave [to whom?] *Carlos* two piranhas.

Complements occur in the predicate of the sentence following a *to be* or linking verb. Subject complements rename or describe the subject. Object complements rename or describe the object:

sc
Carlos is *upset.*

oc
Carlos named one piranha *Bucktooth.*

Modifiers describe or limit a subject, verb, object, or complement. They may be single words, groups of words, or entire clauses:

m
Piranhas have a nasty disposition.

Conjunctions are words that link words, phrases, clauses, or sentences. The word *conjunction* means "join together." (See Section 4A for additional examples of conjunctions.)

- *Coordinating conjunctions (and, but, or, yet, for, nor, so)* join equal sentence elements:

  Carlos is angry, *but* Andrea is laughing.

- *Correlative conjunctions (both . . . and, either . . . or)* also join equal sentence elements:

  Neither Carlos *nor* his aquarium fish are particularly happy about the piranhas.

- *Subordinating conjunctions (because, since, although, if, until, while,* and others) begin many dependent clauses:

  If Andrea plays another joke on Carlos, she may lose a good friend.

1B NOUNS AND PRONOUNS

A *noun* names a person, place, object, or idea. Nouns may be grouped in several classes:

- *Proper nouns* name specific people, places, or things:

  Lester Pearson, Cape Breton, Buick

- *Common nouns* name all nouns that are not proper nouns:

  cat, ocean, helicopter

- *Concrete nouns* name things that can be sensed:

  table, waves, coat

- *Abstract nouns* name things not knowable by the senses:

  justice, pity, freedom

- *Collective nouns* name groups:

  family, committee, team

- *Compound nouns* are several words joined by hyphens to form a noun:

  brother-in-law, commander-in-chief

A *pronoun* takes the place of a noun. Pronouns must meet three requirements:

- *Reference:* A pronoun must refer to a specific, identifiable word, phrase, or clause. This referent or antecedent occurs within the sentence or in a preceding sentence. (See Section 2J for examples of how to solve problems in pronoun reference.)

  Evelyn has the flu. *She* has missed two classes. [*Evelyn* is the referent for *she.*]

- *Agreement:* A pronoun must agree with or correspond to the noun that it replaces. A pronoun must agree in *person* (first, second, or third person), *number* (singular or plural), and *gender* (he, she, it). (See Section 2I for examples of how to solve problems in pronoun agreement.)

  Each girl should check on *her* friend. [*Her* agrees in person (third person), in number (singular), and gender (feminine) with the referent, *girl.*]

- *Case:* Pronouns must take the appropriate case (subjective, objective, possessive):

Subjective pronouns (I, you, he, she, it, we, they, who) should be the subject or the complement in a sentence:

  They have the flu. [Subject]

  Who is sleeping there? It is she. [Complement]

Objective pronouns (me, you, her, him, whom, us, you, them) should act as objects in a sentence:

  Evelyn gave *me* the flu. [Indirect object]

Possessive pronouns (my, mine, your, yours, his, her, hers, its, our, ours, their, theirs, whose) show possession:

  I am sick as a dog with *her* flu virus.

Pronouns may be grouped in several classes:

- *Personal pronouns (I, me, mine, we, us, our, ours, you, yours, she, her, hers, he, him, his, it, its, they, them, theirs)* refer to people or things:

  She bought a cat for *him.*

- *Relative pronouns (that, who, whom, which, what, whose, whoever)* introduce clauses:

  Whoever fed the cat made a mistake.

- *Interrogative pronouns (who, whose, what, which, whom)* introduce a question:

  Which cat is the mother?

- *Reflexive* and *intensive pronouns (myself, yourself, herself, ourselves,* and so on) refer back to a pronoun or antecedent or intensify the antecedent:

  She says she paid for the cat *herself.* I *myself* suspect she just found it.

- *Indefinite pronouns (all, anyone, another, anybody, both, each, few, most, some, several, none, someone, something, such,* and so on) refer to non-specific persons or things:

  Someone will turn up and claim the cat.

- *Demonstrative pronouns (this, that, these, those)* refer to an antecedent:

  On Tuesday morning, I must pay my bill. *That* will be a painful moment.

1B n/pr

1C ADJECTIVES AND ADVERBS

Adjectives are modifiers that limit, describe, or add information about nouns and pronouns:

> Maurice Richard was my *favourite* hockey player. [modifies noun, *player*]

> Even standing still, he looked *dynamic.* [modifies pronoun, *he*]

Adverbs limit, describe, or add information about verbs, adjectives, or other adverbs, and they complete sentences:

> He competed *ferociously.* [modifies verb, *competed*]

> Winning the Stanley Cup was a *very* significant victory for Richard's team, the Montreal Canadiens. [modifies adjective, *significant*]

> Richard's ability to skate *extremely* fast and to score goals made him an invaluable player. [modifies adverb, *fast*]

> *Justifiably,* he became the hero of thousands of hockey fans across Canada. [modifies whole sentence]

1D VERBS

The *verb* is the heart of most sentences. Verbs can set up equations or definitions ("A flotilla *is* a small fleet of ships"). They can describe states of being ("Fear and confusion *exist* in Lebanon"). They can explain occurrences ("The players *became* angry at the referee's call") or describe actions ("The candidate *defeated* her opponent"). When sentences communicate clearly, verbs often deserve the credit.

The great variety of verb forms creates richness in the language. This richness, however, can create confusion. Some verbs are regular; others, irregular. In some cases, combinations of verb tense, voice, and mood may entangle sentences. The following explanations and examples will help you resolve problems in verb forms so that you can communicate precisely and vividly.

Principal Parts of Verbs

Verbs have three principal parts: simple form, past tense, and past participle:

Simple Form (Infinitive)	Past Tense	Past Participle
live (to live)	lived	lived
go (to go)	went	gone

Regular and Irregular Verbs   *Regular verbs* form the past tense and past participle by adding *-ed* or *-d* to the simple form:

Simple Form	Past Tense	Past Participle
count	counted	counted
dance	danced	danced
create	created	created

Irregular verbs can cause problems because they form the past tense and past participle by changing letters, sounds, or entire words. Check your dictionary to determine if a verb is irregular. If the dictionary gives only two forms *(catch, caught)*, the past participle is the same as the past tense *(caught)*. Following are some examples of the nearly two hundred irregular English verbs:

Simple Form	Past Tense	Past Participle
sing	sang	sung
begin	began	begun
break	broke	broken
drive	drove	driven
sink	sank, sunk	sunk
sleep	slept	slept
read	read	read
eat	ate	eaten
see	saw	seen
slide	slid	slid

Linking Verbs   *Linking verbs* (*is, becomes, seems, looks,* and so on) equate subjects with predicates, so that the word or words in the predicate rename or describe the subject. A linking verb creates a subject complement (sc)—a word or words that complete the equation:

1D v

```
      s      v      sc           m
```
Lillian was president of the company. [Lillian = president]

```
      s      v        sc
```
The storm seemed threatening. [Storm = threatening]

Auxiliary Verbs

Auxiliary verbs, also called *helping verbs*, combine with main verbs to show tense, voice, or mood. The verbs *be, do,* and *have* are common auxiliary verbs:

She is running a marathon. [auxiliary verb = *is*]
They did enjoy the dinner. [auxiliary verb = *did*]
He had left before she arrived. [auxiliary verb = *had*]

Tense

Tense tells *when* a verb's action, occurrence, or state of being takes place. The six verb tenses in English are illustrated here with the regular verb *create*. The parentheses contain the *progressive* form (*-ing*) to show continual or ongoing action, occurrence, or state of being:

Present	I create (I am creating)
Past	I created (I was creating)
Future	I will create (I will be creating)
Present Perfect	I have created (I have been creating)

The present perfect tense describes actions occurring or conditions existing at an unspecified time in the past and continuing into the present: *I have created several award-winning recipes for chili.*

Past Perfect	I had created (I had been creating)

The past perfect tense describes actions occurring or conditions existing before a specific time in the past: *I had created three different recipes for extra-hot chili before I won my first award.*

Future Perfect	I will have created (I will have been creating)

The future perfect tense describes actions that have already occurred or conditions that will exist by a specific future time: *I will have created a new salsa recipe before the fair begins.*

Transitive and Intransitive

Many verbs in English can be either transitive or intransitive, depending on the sentence. *Transitive* verbs take objects. As the prefix *trans-* suggests, they carry the action across to the object:

```
      s          v           do
```
Ahmed developed the film.

```
      s      v                do
```
Slava sees the oncoming car.

1 D v

Intransitive verbs do not take objects:

<pre>   s   v   m</pre>
Ahmed developed early. [*Early* is not a direct object; it describes when Ahmed developed]

<pre>   s   v   m</pre>
Slava sees in the dark. [*In the dark* is not a direct object]

Voice   Verbs have *active* and *passive* voice. *Active voice* means that the subject of the sentence performs the action. *Passive voice* means that the subject is acted upon. A passive-voice sentence uses a form of *be* plus a past participle. (For additional discussion of active and passive voice, see Section 2E.)

Active Voice   The Inuit *build* stone and peat houses.
Passive Voice   Stone and peat houses *are built* by the Inuit.
[Contains a form of *be* + past participle: *are* + *built*]

Mood   Verbs have three moods that indicate a writer's attitude toward a statement. *Indicative mood* expresses a statement of fact or asks a question. *Imperative mood* expresses commands or directives. *Subjunctive mood* expresses a wish or condition contrary to fact:

Indicative   She has perfect pitch. [fact]
Why does she sing opera? [question]
Imperative   Pay attention to the music. [command]
Turn and face the spotlight. [directive]
Subjunctive   I wish that I were more talented. [wish]
If she were to catch a cold, she would not sing on opening night. [condition contrary to fact]

1E PHRASES AND CLAUSES

Phrases

A *phrase* is a group of related words that does not contain a subject or a predicate:

Prepositional Phrase   He wrote *on the computer.*
Noun Phrase   A *notebook computer* is handy.
Appositive Phrase   The Apple II, *the first popular school computer,* is the Model T of home computers. [An appositive phrase identifies or provides more information about the preceding noun or pronoun.]

A *verbal phrase* is a group of related words that contains a verbal: an infinitive *(to talk)*, a present participle *(talking)*, or a past participle *(talked)*. There are three kinds of verbals:

- *Infinitives* usually use *to + simple verb;* they function as nouns, adjectives, or adverbs:

Infinitive	*To talk*
Infinitive Phrase	He planned *to talk for three minutes.* [infinitive phrase = direct object] *To listen carefully* was his first objective. [infinitive phrase = subject]

- *Gerunds* are nouns made from the *-ing* or present participle form of the verb:

Gerund	*Talking* got her into trouble. [*Talking* is a gerund; gerund = subject]
Gerund Phrase	*Talking during the lecture* got her into trouble. [gerund phrase = subject]

- *Participles* are adjectives made from verb forms. As adjectives, they modify nouns or pronouns. They can use either the *-ing* (present participle) or the *-ed* (past participle) verb form:

Participle	*Coughing* students may bother the teacher. [Participle modifies *students.*] *Whispered* conversations may distract students. [Participle modifies *conversations.*]
Participial Phrases	*Rustling their papers and snapping their notebooks closed,* they prepare to leave the lecture hall. [Participial phrase modifies *they.*] Several students, *entranced by the final scene in the film,* write quietly for a few moments. [Participial phrase modifies *students.*]

Clauses

A *clause* is a group of words containing a subject and a verb. It need not be an entire sentence or a complete thought. Clauses can be independent (main) or dependent (subordinate):

- *Independent or main clause:* A group of words containing a subject and a verb that can stand by itself as a complete thought:

We drank decaffeinated coffee.

- *Dependent clause:* A group of words that contains a subject and verb but cannot stand by itself as a complete thought:

Because we drank decaffeinated coffee

- *Subordinate clauses* (sometimes called *adverb clause*s): Dependent clauses that begin with a subordinating conjunction, such as *because, if, although, unless, when, while, since, as, until, before,* and *after:*

  Although I drank coffee, everyone else drank tea.

- *Relative clauses* (also called *adjective clauses*): Dependent clauses that begin with when, where, or why, or with relative pronouns *(who, that, which, whom, whoever, whomever, whatever):*

  Driving *when you are under the influence of alcohol* may result in a mandatory jail sentence. [Adjective clause modifies *driving*.]

  Free coffee, *which the bar serves after midnight,* is part of a campaign for responsible drinking. [Adjective clause modifies *coffee*.]

  The police officer gave a ticket to the woman *who was driving the red pickup truck.* [Adjective clause modifies *woman*.]

1F ARTICLES, PREPOSITIONS, INTERJECTIONS

Articles

Articles (a, an, the) often appear before nouns. They are modifiers that limit a noun. *A* and *an* are less limiting than *the:*

> I have *a* plan to solve our problems.
> I have *the* plan to solve our problems. [*The* suggests that the plan is more definitive.]

The article *a* appears before words that begin with a *consonant sound* (not necessarily a consonant): *a* kite, *a* hammer, *a* university, *a* one-sided victory.

The article *an* appears before words that begin with a *vowel sound* (not necessarily a vowel): *an* opening, *an* egg, *an* old shirt, *an* honour, *an* E.

Prepositions

Prepositions (in, on, up, to, after, by, for, across, within, and others) usually occur in prepositional phrases with a noun or pronoun that is the object of the preposition:

> *In* the hot sun *by* the edge *of* the water, a small turtle lay perfectly still.

Note: some words can function as either prepositions or conjunctions:

> We will row home *after* lunch. [preposition]

> *After* you finish your sandwich, we will row home. [conjunction]

Interjections

Interjections (*oh, alas, yea, damn, hooray, ouch,* and others) are words conveying strong feeling or surprise. Interjections occasionally appear in informal writing or in a dialogue:

> The Blue Jays won the pennant *(yea!)* but lost the World Series *(boo, hiss).*
> *Alas,* their hitting was anemic.
> "*Oh,* she moped about it for days."

Section 2

Sentence Structure and Grammar

1 F art/prep/int

When sentences don't follow standard English conventions, readers may become aggravated, confused, or simply lost. While some deviations from established conventions barely distract the reader, others totally scramble meaning. If "sickening grammar" detracts from your meaning, your readers may react uncharitably. If you write a confusing sentence fragment, some readers will think, "This writer doesn't know what a sentence is." If you have a problem in subject-verb agreement, readers may think, "This writer didn't reread the sentence or doesn't know what the subject of the sentence is." If you write a sentence with a dangling modifier, the reader may think, "The writer doesn't know how comical this sounds." This section will help you avoid those embarrassing problems that confuse readers or invite them to think about your grammar rather than your meaning.

2A FRAGMENTS

Use sentence fragments only for special emphasis. A *fragment* is an incomplete sentence. A fragment may lack a subject or verb, or it may be only a dependent clause. *Test* for sentence fragments by taking the group of words out of context. If the group of words cannot stand by itself as a complete thought, it is a fragment.

Revise sentence fragments by adding a subject or verb or by combining the fragment with the preceding sentence:

Fragment:	I still remember the championship basketball game when I scored forty points. *Breaking the existing conference record.*
	["Breaking the existing conference record" is not a complete sentence. It cannot stand by itself as a complete thought. Combine with previous sentence.]
Revision:	I still remember the championship basketball game when I broke the existing conference record by scoring forty points.

Fragment:	At the cottage I enjoy many water sports. *Waterskiing and sailing, which are my two favourites.* ["Waterskiing and sailing, which are my two favourites" cannot stand by itself as a complete thought. Revise to make one complete sentence.]
Revision:	At the cottage, I enjoy my two favourite water sports: waterskiing and sailing.
Fragment:	She stood in line for four hours in the freezing rain. *To get tickets for the rock concert.* ["To get tickets for the rock concert" cannot stand by itself as a complete thought. Combine with previous sentence.]
Revision:	To get tickets for the rock concert, she stood in line for four hours in the freezing rain.
Fragment:	After a tough class, I took a long shower, dried my hair, and put on my underwear. Then I walked into the living room. *Because I thought no one was home.* Was I surprised to discover my mother talking to Reverend Jones! ["Because I thought no one was home" cannot stand by itself as a complete thought. It is a dependent clause or fragment.]
Revision:	After a tough class, I took a long shower, dried my hair, and put on my underwear. Because I thought no one was home, I walked into the living room. Was I surprised to discover my mother talking to Reverend Jones!
Fragment:	At the end of the game, the frustrated fans began to throw snowballs on the field. *The score being 42–0.* ["The score being 42–0" is not a complete sentence. Change *being* to *is* or *was.*]
Revision:	At the end of the game, the frustrated fans began to throw snowballs on the field because the score was 42–0.

For special emphasis, however, sparingly used sentence fragments can be effective. In context, the following are examples of effective sentence fragments:

Yes, it's true: Accents, the Plasticine bust enhancers favoured by movie stars and models alike, are now available to you, the lowly viewer. No surgery. No hideous contraptions.

—Mark Kingwell

It was not until my defection to Canada in 1987 that I truly understood the concept of privacy and the safeguards people erect to defend it.

None of which, however, made *A Leaf in the Bitter Wind* easy to write.

—Ting-xing Ye

But what did she, Kostash, make of it all, in terms of memory and thrust and the survival of the civil society? Not all good, by any means.

—Patrick Watson

Exercise

In the following passage, identify all sentence fragments. Then revise the passage to eliminate inappropriate fragments.

(1) Most people think that a library is as quiet as growing grass, but often it is the noisiest place on campus to study. (2) The worst time being finals week. (3) Some of the chatter is from people who come to the library just to visit: "How did you like the party Saturday night?" (4) "Did you get the notes from psychology?" (5) The chatter goes on continually, punctuated by coughs, gasps, and giggles. (6) Just when I start to panic about my marketing examination. (7) Someone across the table tells a joke, and they all start laughing. (8) They try to cover their laughter with their hands, but the sound explodes out anyway. (9) Irritating ten other students who are trying to study. (10) Sometimes I wish the library had its own police force. (11) To arrest those gabby, discourteous "party people." (12) I would sit there smiling as they handcuffed these party people and dragged them out of the library. (13) Ah, the sweet revenge of daydreams.

2B MIXED CONSTRUCTIONS AND FAULTY PREDICATION

Mixed Constructions

Occasionally, writers begin sentences with one structure and then switch, right in the middle, to another. Revise sentences with mixed constructions by choosing one structure and sticking to it:

Mixed: Because the repairs were so expensive is why I ended up selling the car.

Revised: Because the repairs were so expensive, I sold the car.

Mixed:	By getting behind in math classes is a quick way to flunk out.
Revised:	Getting behind in math classes is a quick way to flunk out.

Faulty Predication

Sometimes the predicate does not *logically* fit with the subject. Remember that the verb *to be* is an *equals* sign. Revise faulty predication by changing either the subject or the predicate:

Faulty:	Freestyle ski jumping is where skiers take crazy chances in midair. *Note:* "Ski jumping" is an activity, not a place. It is illogical to say, "Ski jumping is where . . ."
Revised:	Freestyle ski jumping is a sport that encourages skiers to take crazy chances in midair.
Faulty:	My dog Noodles is the reason I'm feeling depressed. *Note:* "My dog Noodles" is a specific animal, not a "reason." Missing Noodles, however, could be a cause for depression.
Revised:	I'm feeling depressed because I miss my dog Noodles.
Faulty:	Real intelligence is when you can say no to that third piece of chocolate cream pie. *Note:* "Intelligence" is or equals a mental condition, not a "when."
Revised:	Saying no to that third piece of chocolate cream pie requires real intelligence.

2B mix con/flty pred

Exercise

In the following passage, identify sentences with mixed constructions, faulty predication, or both, and then revise them.

(1) After my first year, I intend to transfer to McGill. (2) Basically, I want to attend a school that has a city environment and a diverse population of students. (3) I suppose my sister Gabrielle is a big reason I want to transfer. (4) She wants me to move closer to home. (5) Also, by attending a city school will enable me to see plays, to visit museums occasionally, and to eat out at good restaurants. (6) Finally, I'd like to meet all sorts of students. (7) A good university is when a student can meet people from all walks of life. (8) Because McGill has diversity is really why I intend to transfer.

2C DANGLING MODIFIERS AND MISPLACED MODIFIERS

Dangling Modifiers

Modifying phrases must clearly describe, qualify, or limit some word in the sentence. When the modifying phrase occurs at the beginning of a sentence, the word that is modified must appear *immediately* following the phrase. Otherwise, the modifying phrase "dangles" or is logically "unattached" to the sentence. Such sentences are confusing and often comical:

Faulty:	Rushing to get to class on time, my shoelace broke.
	[*Who* was rushing to get to class? The shoelace? Revise by indicating the person immediately after the comma.]
Revised:	Rushing to get to class, I broke a shoelace.
Faulty:	Flying at 5000 feet, the cars looked like tiny toys.
	[*Who* is flying at 5000 feet? The cars? Revise by indicating that person immediately after the comma.]
Revised:	Flying at 5000 feet, I saw cars that looked like tiny toys.
Faulty:	From birth until Grade 1, one parent should be home with the children.
	[Does the opening phrase, "From birth until Grade 1," modify *parent* or *children?* Revise by placing the appropriate word immediately after the introductory phrase.]
Revised:	From birth until Grade 1, children should have one parent at home.
Faulty:	Sue practised her freestyle stroke until she knew she could swim faster than Flipper, being a fanatical swimmer.
	[Who is the fanatical swimmer—*Sue* or *Flipper?* When modifying phrases "dangle" from the *end* of a sentence, revise by placing the phrase next to the word it modifies.]
Revised:	Being a fanatical swimmer, Sue practised her freestyle stroke until she knew she could swim faster than Flipper.

2C dm/mm

Misplaced Modifiers

Place a modifying word, phrase, or clause immediately before or after the word it modifies. In the following sentences, notice how changing the placement of the word *only* changes the meaning of the sentence:

> Only I tasted grandfather's pumpkin pie. [I was the only one who tasted it.]
>
> I only tasted grandfather's pumpkin pie. [I only tasted it; Pete actually ate it.]
>
> I tasted only grandfather's pumpkin pie. [I didn't taste anything else; I didn't even taste Aunt Margaret's pecan pie.]
>
> I tasted grandfather's only pumpkin pie. [Grandfather made only one pumpkin pie, and I tasted it.]

Confusing:	He borrowed a computer from his professor with a faulty memory.
	[*Who* or *what* has the faulty memory? Place the phrase "with a faulty memory" next to the word it modifies *(computer)*.]
Revised:	He borrowed a computer with a faulty memory from his professor.
Confusing:	The hamburgers have been horrible in the fast-food restaurants that I've eaten.
	[Did the writer eat restaurants or hamburgers? Revise by placing the clause "that I've eaten" next to the word it should modify *(hamburgers)*.]
Revised:	The hamburgers that I've eaten in fast-food restaurants have been horrible.

2C dm/mm

Exercise

In the following passage, identify sentences with dangling modifiers and misplaced modifiers, and then revise each faulty sentence.

(1) SP302, History of Film, is a worthwhile class to take. (2) Occurring on Tuesday night from 7:00 P.M. to 9:45 P.M., Professor Hancock teaches the class so that it coincides with dollar movie night at the campus theatre. (3) Normally, a long class would be boring because of the Nod Factor. (4) However, Professor Hancock keeps everyone awake and entertains the students, being very energetic. (5) Her lecture on *Citizen Kane* was a particularly good example. (6) Unfortunately, the film began before she finished her lecture. (7) Rushing across the stage just as the film was beginning, an electrical cord tripped her up, causing her to lose her balance and fall. (8) She regained her composure in

time to remind us that Orson Welles also wrote and performed the famous broadcast about the invasion of the Martians on the radio. (9) We certainly were relieved to get that important information!

2D FAULTY PARALLELISM

Repeated elements in a sentence that are similar in meaning or function should be *parallel* in grammatical form. The parallel form should, in turn, help to emphasize the meaning. Any repeated sentence elements, from subjects and verbs to prepositional phrases, may occur in parallel form:

Parallel Clauses   *I came, I saw, I conquered.*
Parallel Adverbs   He read *slowly* and *thoroughly.*
Parallel Prepositional Phrases   She walked *through the archway, across the quadrangle,* and *into the library.*

Identifying and numbering the repeated elements may help you see the parallel elements in a sentence:

2C dm/mm

She walked   (1) through the archway,
                    (2) across the quadrangle,
                        and
                    (3) into the library.

Faulty: Walking, biking, and automobiles are the three most popular modes of transportation.
[Identify and number elements that should be parallel. "(1) *Walking,* (2) *biking,* and (3) *automobiles* are the three most popular modes of transportation." Revise, choosing one pattern for all three elements.]

Revised: Walking, biking, and driving are the three most popular modes of transportation.

Faulty: Travelling abroad last summer, John increased his social awareness, his cultural knowledge, and overall sophistication.
[Identify and number elements that should be parallel. "Travelling abroad last summer, John increased (1) *his social awareness,* (2) *his cultural knowledge,* and (3) _____ *overall sophistication.*" Then revise, choosing one grammatical pattern for all three elements.]

Revised: Travelling abroad last summer, John increased his social awareness, his cultural knowledge, and his overall sophistication.
[or]

Revised:	Travelling abroad last summer, John increased his social awareness, cultural knowledge, and overall sophistication.

Faulty:	There are three commandments for college and university students: Thou shalt go to class; thou shalt read the text; and be sure to borrow your neighbour's notes.

[Identify and number elements that should be parallel. Since the first and second "commandments" set the grammatical pattern, the reader expects the third commandment to take the same "thou shalt" form.]

Revised:	There are three commandments for college and university students: Thou shalt go to class; thou shalt read the text; and thou shalt borrow thy neighbour's notes.

Faulty:	She was angry not only because he was late but also he forgot the tickets.

Note: Compared or contrasted sentence elements introduced by "either . . . or," "both . . . and," or "not only . . . but also" must be parallel.

[Identify and number elements that should be parallel. "She was angry not only (1) because he was late but also (2) _____ he forgot the tickets." Revise to make (1) and (2) parallel.]

Revised:	She was angry not only because he was late but also because he forgot the tickets.

Exercise

In the following passage, identify and revise any sentences with faulty parallelism.

(1) Alcohol abuse is a primary cause of spectator violence at college and university football games. (2) On average, the police make between five and ten arrests at each home football game. (3) These arrests are for property destruction, public intoxication, and occasionally when students conduct themselves in a disorderly manner. (4) When spectators consume too much alcohol not only do they hurt themselves but also act obnoxiously toward others. (5) Following a recent fight, ambulance attendants said that some drunken spectators or "animals" actually pelted them with sod while they tried to assist an injured man. (6) The attendants tried pleading, reason, and shouting, but to no avail. (7) To reduce these ugly incidents and restoring the enjoyment of the game,

alcohol should not be sold at football games after the beginning of the second half.

2E ACTIVE AND PASSIVE VOICE

Verbs that can have direct objects (transitive verbs) are in the *active voice* when the subject of the sentence *acts upon the object*:

The wolfhound bit Perry.

Wolfhound, the subject of the sentence, *acts upon the object, Perry.* The arrow shows that in the active voice, the action of the verb *bit* goes forward, toward the object, *Perry.*

Verbs that can have objects (transitive verbs) are in the *passive voice* when the *subject is acted upon.* The passive voice uses a form of *be (is, am, are, was, were, been, being)* followed by the past participle of the main verb (in this case, *bitten*):

2D //

Perry was bitten by the wolfhound.

The verb *was bitten* is transitive, but *Perry,* now the subject of the sentence, is acted upon. The arrow shows that the action of the verb goes backward, so that *Perry* receives the action.

Notice the following *differences* between active and passive voice:

The active-voice sentence, "The wolfhound bit Perry," uses two fewer words than the passive version, its action moves in a normal forward direction, and it clearly identifies the actor.

The passive-voice sentence, "Perry was bitten by the wolfhound," uses two more words, and it inverts the direction of the action in the sentence. In some cases, the passive voice may omit the actor altogether: "Perry was bitten on Friday." In that case, the reader does not know who or what bit Perry.

Active Voice

Usually, *active voice* is preferable because it is more direct, vivid, and concise than passive voice. Remember, however, that sentences must be judged *in the context* of the writer's purpose, audience, and focus.

Following are examples of passive-voice constructions that, in context, may be more effective in the active voice. To change from passive to active, move the actor (often identified in the *by* phrase) to become the subject of the sentence:

Passive:	Children's unruly behaviour cannot be accepted by their parents. *Note:* The actor in the *by* phrase is *parents.* Change to active voice by making *parents* the subject of the sentence.
Active:	Parents cannot accept their children's unruly behaviour. [The active-voice version makes the actor the subject of the sentence and has two fewer words.]
Passive:	It is argued by members of our class that the teacher grades too hard. *Note:* The *actor* in the *by* phrase is *members.* Change to the active voice by making *members* the subject of the sentence.
Active:	Members of our class argue that the teacher grades too hard. [This active-voice version is more direct and has three fewer words.]
Passive:	Under the current proposal, property taxes will be raised $1000 over the next two years. *Note:* The *actor* is not identified in a *by* phrase; however, the *premier* actually proposed the tax increase. Change to active-voice by making *premier* the subject of the sentence.
Active:	The premier currently proposes to raise property taxes by $1000 over the next two years. [The active-voice version reveals who, in fact, is responsible. It adds information without increasing the length of the sentence.]

Passive Voice

The *passive voice* is appropriate when the actor is unknown or is less important than the action or the receiver of the action. Use the passive voice in the following situations:

- *When the actor is unknown:*

  When her sports car swerved off the road and into the river, Carolyn was killed. [We don't know who or what actually killed her.]

- *When you want to emphasize that some person or thing is helpless or is a victim:*

  The small Alberta town was levelled by the tornado.
  Our hockey team was mauled by the Canadiens, 7–0.
  The bag lady was mugged in broad daylight.

• *When the scientific experiment and the results should be the focus of the sentence or the passage* (scientific writing typically uses the passive voice to lend objectivity to the findings):

The first recordings of humpback whales were obtained in 1952 from a U.S. Navy hydrophone installation.

The titration experiment was performed under careful laboratory conditions.

One typical *abuse of the passive voice* occurs when writers omit the actor in order to conceal responsibility:

The tuition for non-resident students was increased by $500 for the upcoming academic year.

This sentence, which was written by university officials, omits the actor or the agency responsible for the change. Because tuition increases are unpopular with students, university officials may have deliberately omitted the responsible actor or agency to avoid confrontation or blame. Careful readers should recognize such deceptive uses of the passive voice.

Caution: Don't assume that all verbs that follow the pattern, *be* verb form + past participle ["was _____ed"], are necessarily in the passive voice. In the sentence "I was scared," for example, the verb *scared* can be either transitive or intransitive, depending on the context. Only *transitive verbs* can be in either the active or the passive voice:

2E act/pass

Transitive Active	A horrible Halloween mask scared me.
Transitive Passive	I was scared by a horrible Halloween mask.
Intransitive	At the Cave of Horrors, I was upset and scared.
Transitive Active	The boss fired me.
Transitive Passive	I was fired.
Intransitive	I was tired.

Test: To distinguish between intransitive and transitive passive, try adding the word *very.* If *very* cannot logically be used, the construction is passive voice:

I was [very] tired. [*Very* works; *tired* is intransitive.]
I was [very] fired. [*Very* doesn't work; *fired* is transitive passive.]

In addition, a good dictionary will indicate whether a verb is transitive, intransitive, or both.

Exercises

Identify sentences containing the passive voice. Change passive-voice sentences into the active voice:

1. People communicate using body movements.

2. A nod, a gesture, or a glance can be interpreted by people in several ways.

3. A wave and a smile mean one thing, but a wave and a tear can be interpreted to mean something else.

4. In addition, some people may be irritated by a continual or intense stare.

5. We may also be intimidated by a person who talks to us at very close range.

Read the following passage and identify sentences that are in the active or passive voice. Then determine which sentences should be in the active voice and which should be in the passive voice. Revise the passage, leaving sentences as they are, changing active-voice sentences to passive, or changing passive-voice sentences to active—as appropriate for the context.

(1) Writing on a word processor can transform the act of writing, but only if the writer has some rudimentary typing skills. (2) Unfortunately, many men have a sexist hang-up about typing, so that their writing on a computer is inhibited. (3) Traditionally, it has been felt by most men that only females (i.e., secretaries) should type. (4) Only the macho Hemingways and Mailers of the world actually type their own novels and stories. (5) Now, however, many male business executives are caught by conflicting role images. (6) It is socially acceptable for them to be computer-literate, but it is still somehow demeaning to sit at a keyboard and practise the "female" skill of typing. (7) One more example of how notions about sexist roles can hurt men as well as women is thus provided by word processing.

2F NOMINALS AND *BE* VERBS

Nominals

Nominals (also called *nominalizations*) are *nouns* created from verbs. Nominals often make sentences less dynamic because they disguise or eliminate the action in a sentence. Frequently, nominals are nouns ending in -*ment*, -*ance*, -*ence*, -*ion*, and -*ing*. Each of the following nominals "contains" a verb: *expectation (expect), description (describe), solution (solve), resistance (resist), government (govern), preference (prefer), meeting (meet)*. For many purposes and audiences, you can make your writing more vigorous, dynamic, and readable by changing nominals into verbs:

Nominal: Bill's *expectation* was to win the marathon.
Revised: Bill *expected* to win the marathon.

Nominal: The owner's manual contains a *description* of how to adjust the timing.
Revised: The owner's manual *describes* how to adjust the timing.

Nominal:	On this campus, there exists some *resistance* among students to tuition increases.
Revised:	On this campus, students *resist* tuition increases.
Nominal:	*Dissatisfaction* with drinking-policy *decisions* is likely to be a major *contribution* to student *objections*. *Note:* When repeated nominals obscure the meaning, rewrite the whole sentence, making the primary *actor* the subject of the sentence.
Revised:	Students object to the drinking policy.

Be Verbs

Be verbs *(is, am, are, was, were, been, being)* are effective in stating conditions, definitions, or concepts:

> Edgar Allan Poe's "The Raven" *is* a literary classic.
> An iconoclast *is* one who destroys sacred images or seeks to over-throw popular ideas or institutions.

2F nom/*be* v

Often, however, *be* verbs create static, flat, or lifeless sentences. Where appropriate, make your writing more dynamic by replacing *be* verbs with action verbs.

Eliminate *be* verbs by changing passive voice to active voice, by changing nominals or adjectives into verbs, by selecting a more vigorous verb, or by combining sentences:

Be Verb:	The classical mythology course that is offered by the English department *is* fascinating.
Revised:	The English department *offers* a fascinating course in classical mythology.
Be Verb:	The driving force for many workaholics *is* their fear of failure.
Revised:	Fear of failure *drives* many workaholics.
Be Verb:	AIDS *is* a simple but sometimes lethal malfunction of the immune system. AIDS *is* a disease that can lead to the physical and mental destruction of its victim.
Revised:	AIDS, a simple but sometimes lethal malfunction of the immune system, can *destroy* its victim physically and mentally.

Exercise

In the following passage, identify *nominals* and *be* verbs. Then revise the passage to make it more vivid, energetic, and concise by eliminating inappropriate nominals and *be* verbs.

(1) As parents, we know that many young people love to ride motorcycles, motorbikes, and motor scooters. (2) Today, however, our 10-year-old kids have some attraction to those off-road three-wheelers. (3) Although kids get enjoyment from riding three-wheelers in the hills, these vehicles can be the cause of serious injury. (4) Unfortunately, these young drivers—and their parents—do not receive sufficient education from salespeople about the potential dangers. (5) As a result, some activist groups are in opposition to the sales of all three-wheelers. (6) These groups want regulations for the industry in order to make riding safer for children and adults. (7) The efforts of these groups to reform the industry are commendable to every responsible parent.

2G SUBJECT-VERB AGREEMENT

A verb must agree *in number* with its subject. Remember: -s or -es added to a noun makes it plural: *whale, whales.* Adding -s to a present-tense verb makes it singular: *whales sing; whale sings.*

2G sv agr

1. Many agreement problems occur when plural words come between a singular subject and its verb. To correct a subject-verb error, first identify the actual subject, and then use the correct verb ending for that subject:

Faulty:	A list of campaign promises often hurt the candidate. [Put brackets around any prepositional phrases. The subject of the sentence is never in a prepositional phrase. "A list [of campaign promises] often hurt the candidate." *List* is the subject and *hurt* is the verb. Read without the words inside the brackets and revise the verb.]
Revised:	A *list* of campaign promises often *hurts* the candidate.
Faulty:	This company, with few skilled mechanics and electricians, do not guarantee any repairs. [Put brackets around the prepositional phrase. "This company [with few skilled mechanics and electricians], do not guarantee any repairs." Read the sentence without the words in brackets and revise the verb.]
Revised:	This *company*, with few skilled mechanics and electricians, *does* not guarantee any repairs.

2. Two subjects connected by *and* take a plural verb. "The sergeant and his recruits march double-time across the grounds." When two subjects are connected by *or* or *nor*, however, the verb agrees with the closer subject:

Faulty:	Neither the recruits nor the sergeant know how to march.
Revised:	Neither the recruits nor the sergeant *knows* how to march. [or]
Revised:	Neither the sergeant nor the recruits *know* how to march.

3. Indefinite pronouns *(each, one, either, everyone, neither, everybody, nobody, no one, none, somebody, someone)* usually take a singular verb:

Faulty:	Each of the books cost $20. [Remove the prepositional phrase: "Each [of the books] cost $20." *Each* is singular, so the verb should be *costs.*]
Revised:	Each of the books *costs* $20.
Faulty:	Everybody in all three classes are going to see the film. [Remove the prepositional phrase: "Everybody [in all three classes] are going to see the film." *Everybody* is singular, so the verb should be *is.*]
Revised:	Everybody in all three classes *is* going to see the film.

2G sv agr

4. A collective noun as a subject usually takes a singular verb. Collective nouns *(family, committee, audience, class, crowd,* and *army)* usually refer to a single *unit* or *group* of several individuals or elements, and thus they take a singular verb:

Faulty:	The audience at the concert whistle its approval.
Revised:	The audience at the concert *whistles* its approval. *Note:* When referring to the action or condition of *several individuals* within a group, use the phrase *the members of* or the phrase *a number of* followed by the plural verb: The members of the committee argue about the policy.

5. Even when the normal subject-verb order is reversed, the verb should agree in number with the subject:

Faulty:	For such a small dormitory, there is far too many students. [Put the subject and verb in their normal order: Too many students are in the small dormitory. (*Students* is the subject, so the verb is plural: *are.*)]
Revised:	For such a small dormitory, there *are* far too many students.

Exercise

In the following passage, revise all errors in subject-verb agreement.

(1) If you have friends or a family member who smoke, I have some suggestions to help this person quit. (2) First, if the family are supportive, try talking openly about the facts. (3) There is a few public service agencies that will provide evidence demonstrating the link between smoking and cancer. (4) Next, investigate this person's behaviour: What does this person do just before he or she smokes? (5) To quit smoking, the smoker must disrupt the patterns of behaviour that leads to smoking. (6) An inventory of the activities and places that cause a person to smoke provide key information. (7) For example, if the person always smokes after dinner, suggest eating snacks over a two-hour period instead of having a sit-down meal. (8) If he or she always smoke in a certain chair in the living room, change the furniture. (9) Breaking any habit is always easier if you break the entire behaviour pattern. (10) Of course, each of these smokers need to want to stop smoking.

2H VERB TENSE

Avoid unnecessary shifts in verb tense:

Shift:	After they *ate* ice cream and cake for dessert, they *are* ready to relax.
Revised:	After they *ate* ice cream and cake for dessert, they *were* ready to relax.
Shift:	Peter *ate* dinner before you *had offered* to cook tacos.
Revised:	Peter *ate* dinner before you *offered* to cook tacos.
Shift:	At one point in this film, Gandhi *gathered* his followers together to discuss strategy. Suddenly, a British general *gave* an order to fire upon them. People then *scurry* around and *try* to protect themselves and their children from the hail of bullets. *Note:* For summaries or accounts of artistic works, films, literary works, or historical documents, use the present tense.
Revised:	At one point in this film, Gandhi *gathers* his followers together to discuss strategy. Suddenly, a British general *gives* an order to fire upon them. People then *scurry* around and *try* to protect themselves and their children from the hail of bullets.

Exercise

In the following passage, revise any unnecessary shifts in tense.

(1) In Sophocles' play, *Antigone,* two characters are tragic figures: Antigone and Creon. (2) In the play, Antigone faced a choice of conscience. (3) Should she be loyal to her family and bury her brother, or should she have been loyal to the state and obeyed the edict of Creon, the king of Thebes? (4) She assumes that she knew the best way to handle the situation and wilfully chooses her own death. (5) Creon also faced a choice of conscience. (6) Should he punish someone who has betrayed the state, even if that person is a member of his family? (7) Like Napoleon and General Wolfe, Creon thought primarily about himself and his public image. (8) In Creon's case, ego or "hubris" leads to tragic results for the people around him.

2I PRONOUN AGREEMENT

A pronoun must agree in number and person with the noun to which it refers:

Faulty: One of the scientists signed their name to the report.
[Because the subject is never in the prepositional phrase, put parentheses around the prepositional phrase ("of the scientists"). Now look for another noun that could be the subject of the sentence. *One* is the subject of the sentence, and it is a singular noun. Change *their* to the singular form, *his* or *her.*]

Revised: One of the scientists signed her name to the report.

Faulty: Each of the students felt cheated on their test.
Note: Each is singular: *their* is plural.

Revised: The students felt cheated on *their* tests.

Faulty: Everyone brought their gift to the party.

Revised: Everyone brought *his* or *her* gift to the party.
Note: Avoiding sexist language by using "his or her" can be wordy or awkward in some contexts. Rewrite the sentence with a plural subject and a plural pronoun.

Revised: The *guests* brought *their* gifts to the party.

Avoid shifts in person. Avoid shifting between third person *(people, one, they, he, she)* and second person *(you)*:

Faulty:	When you come to the party, everyone should bring a friend.
	Note: You is second person; *everyone* is third person. Revise the sentence, using either second or third person throughout.
Revised:	When *you* come to the party, bring a friend.
Faulty:	A good party should make *people* feel at ease, so *you* can make new friends.
Revised:	A good party should make *people* feel at ease, so *they* can make new friends.
Revised:	A good party should make *you* feel at ease, so *you* can make new friends.

2J PRONOUN REFERENCE

A pronoun should refer clearly and unambiguously to its antecedent:

Unclear:	Jennifer told Suki that her bank account was overdrawn.
	[Whose bank account was overdrawn?]
Revised:	When Jennifer discovered that her bank account was overdrawn, she told Suki.
Unclear:	If people do not take care of their cats, we should turn them in to the humane society.
	[Who should be turned in—the cats or their owners?]
Revised:	If people do not take care of their cats, we should report the owners to the humane society.

Exercise

In the following passage, correct problems in pronoun agreement and reference.

(1) People use the term *best friend* to describe a person who has a special warmth and friendliness. (2) I still remember when Rosa Martinez, one of my best friends, said that they really like me, too. (3) I called her my best friend; we stood by each other. (4) One time at a party, I saw her talking angrily to another woman. (5) It turned out that she had dated Tom, the guy she was going with at the time. (6) Each of them felt cheated by their boyfriend. (7) Before I knew what was happening, they were screaming at each other. (8) When I tried to stick up for her, she took a swing at me, and so I swung back with my best left hook, popping her in the right eye. (9) As a result, I was suspended from school for a week. (10) It just goes to show that when you have a best friend, everyone expects that you'll help them if you can.

Section 3

Diction and Style

Effective writing hides a curious paradox. On the one hand, good writing contains vivid detail. Good writing does not merely assert that thus-and-so is true; it supports a claim or assertion with evidence. It recreates an experience, shows exactly how the writer feels, or communicates precisely what the writer thinks. To accomplish this, writers *add* specific details, examples, facts, or other data. On the other hand, good writing is also concise. Good writers *take out* vague words, weak verbs, and empty language. Their writing is as lean and sinewy as a long-distance runner. As you edit your writing for diction and clarity of style, you should *add* specific examples but *remove* vague, imprecise language. Your details should be ample; your diction and style spare.

3A VAGUE WORDS

Replace vague words with more specific or concrete language.

1. The following *nouns* are vague or unspecific. Vague nouns encourage writers to *tell* rather than to *show* with specific details or examples. Vague nouns may also lead to wordy and imprecise sentences. In most cases, *replace* the following nouns with more specific words, details, or examples:

thing	situation	difficulty
something	type	feeling
anything	way	beauty
someone	fun	people
some	trouble	deal
area	problem	place
case	field	character
manner	nature	appearance
factor	aspect	

Vague:	During their first semester, students worry about all sorts of *things*. [Be specific: What things?]
Revised:	During their first semester, students worry about making new friends and passing their courses.
Vague:	I have taken courses in the *field* of accounting for two years, and it has changed my *feeling* toward studying in the *area* of mathematics.
Revised:	After taking accounting courses for two years, I no longer hate studying mathematics.
Vague:	Meteorologists occasionally have a great *deal of trouble* in forecasting a *situation* where an upper-

level disturbance becomes a *factor* in local weather. [Be specific: What kind of trouble? Be concise: Omit unnecessary, vague words.]

Revised: When an upper-level disturbance affects local weather, meteorologists occasionally miss a forecast.

2. The following *modifiers* are weak, vague, or unspecific. Replace them with stronger modifiers or add specific details:

very	a lot	pretty
really	good	bad
a few	certain	happy
many	nice	much
regular	similar	soon

Vague: I really liked certain classes in high school very much, but I just couldn't stand a lot of the really boring courses. [Be specific: What *certain classes?* Be specific: How or why were they *really boring?*]

Revised: I really looked forward to learning about the turtles, snakes, and birds in the biology lab, but I couldn't stand just sitting still and practising grammar hour after hour in French class.

Vague: On Canada Day 2000, CBC Television pleased its viewers with a variety of lively programs.

Revised: On Canada Day 2000, CBC Television entertained its viewers from Parliament Hill with a special hosted by Peter Mansbridge and Alison Smith that included classic Canadian talent from Bruce Cockburn to Chantal Kreviazuk to the lithe fiddler, Natalie MacMaster. *NHL Cool Shots,* another special, took a rink-side view of some of the NHL's top players.

3. The following *verbs* are weak, vague, or unspecific. Where appropriate, replace them with more active, energetic, or vivid verbs. When these verbs occur with nominals or the passive voice, change to active verbs or the active voice. Always test your revision: In your context, is the change more effective, concise, or vivid?

deals with	take	get
gets involved with	relate to	go
has to do with	make	give

Vague: He *gets* some enjoyment from sky diving.
Revised: He *enjoys* sky diving.

3A vw

Vague:	Her job *deals with* collecting rare species of lizards.
Revised:	She *collects* rare species of lizards.
Vague:	Jogging along the path, she *got involved with* a rattlesnake in a serious way. [How exactly was she "involved" with this rattlesnake?]
Revised:	Jogging along the path, she was seriously bitten by a rattlesnake.

Exercise

In the following passage, substitute specific and vivid words or phrases for all vague nouns, verbs, and modifiers.

(1) When I was separated from my girlfriend, I missed her a lot. (2) Being alone sometimes gave me a pretty empty-type feeling. (3) When I called her on the phone, we talked about all the nice times we spent together, not about all the very big fights we used to have. (4) Since there was no stress to deal with, we had a fun-filled, long-distance relationship. (5) I know that one aspect of this relationship will improve the way we get along, now that we're back together. (6) We always had difficulty talking in a serious manner about our future. (7) Now we are more involved with each other and can really talk about all sorts of things. (8) For anyone who is having troubles, I recommend this kind of separate situation because, in the long run, the relationship will be much happier.

3B WORDINESS

1. The following wordy phrases can be made more concise:

Wordy	Concise
due to the fact that	because
despite the fact that	though
regardless of the fact that	although
at this point in time	now
at the present time	now
until such time as	until
in the event that	if, when
at all times	always
there is no doubt that	doubtless
in a deliberate manner	deliberately
by means of	by
the reason is that	[omit]

2. The following phrases are redundant; they say the same thing twice or repeat unnecessarily:

Redundant	Concise
new innovation	innovation
disappear from view	disappear
repeat again	repeat
reflected back	reflected
circle around	circle
few in number	few
cheaper in cost	cheaper
oblong in shape	oblong
blue in colour	blue
consensus of opinion	consensus
important essentials	essentials
resulting effect	effect
cooperate together	cooperate

3B wdy

3. Where appropriate, make your writing more concise by omitting *there is, there are, it is,* and *this is* constructions:

Wordy:	There are seven people living in that apartment.
Revised:	Seven people live in that apartment.
Wordy:	This is the step that is crucial for getting a job.
Revised:	This step is crucial for getting a job.

4. Some *who, which,* and *that* clauses can be changed into modifying words or phrases:

Wordy:	Cheryl Harris, who is the mayor, is accused of embezzling city funds.
Revised:	Mayor Cheryl Harris is accused of embezzling city funds.
Wordy:	Then they each wolfed down a banana split that contained 500 calories.
Revised:	Then they each wolfed down a 500-calorie banana split.
Wordy:	The police officer, who was frustrated about missing a promotion, started taking kickbacks.
Revised:	The police officer, frustrated about missing a promotion, started taking kickbacks.

Exercise

Revise the following passage to reduce wordiness.

(1) One of the most recent new discoveries in medicine is the so-called diving reflex. (2) When people are subjected to temperatures that are freezing, their circulation slows down due to the fact that the air is so cold. (3) In addition, the metabolism of every cell that is in the body slows down, conserving oxygen. (4) In a recent case, Erika Nordby, who is 12 months old, wandered off outside at night time owing to the fact that a door was unlatched. (5) When her mother finally found her at long last in the snow, she was unconscious, her body temperature was cold and below normal, and her skin was greyish-blue in colour. (6) Regardless of the fact that paramedics could find no pulse or heartbeat, they began CPR (cardiopulmonary resuscitation) immediately. (7) Within a few days, Erika began to recover in a steady manner, and soon she was watching *Barney* shows on TV. (8) Although she may have some lingering effects from her ordeal that do not go away in a short period of time, the unexplainable miracle is that she survived.

3C wdy

3C COLLOQUIAL LANGUAGE AND SLANG

Your audience and purpose should determine whether conversational language is appropriate. In informal or expressive writing, colloquial language (spoken language), slang, or trendy expressions may be vivid and effective. In conversation or informal writing, we may say that something is *cool, hip, gross, weak, sweet,* or *too much*. We may call a friend *dude*, a skateboarder a *thrasher*, or someone we don't like a *wimp* or *geek*.

In formal writing, however, you should avoid colloquial expressions and slang. Your readers may not know the expressions, they may find some slang offensive, or they may think *gross* is simply too vague to describe what really happened. Slang, in fact, tends to become a shorthand for a whole experience and thus invites *telling* ("This guy was a real geek") rather than *showing* ("Rudolph had messy hair, wore adhesive tape on his glasses, and always had one green and one orange sock sticking out of his polyester pants. He lived out of a 20 kg bookpack, watched *Dr. Who* on TV every day, and used big words all the time").

3D CLICHÉS AND JARGON

Clichés

Some expressions are so commonly used that they have become automatic, predictable, trite, or hackneyed. The phrases in the left-hand column, for example, may have been fresh and original once, but now they are as stale as dirty dishwater and about as exciting as a secondhand sock. The expressions in the right-hand column, for example, are so predictable that we can easily guess the missing word:

tried and true	strong as an _____
needle in a haystack	dark as _____
easier said than done	heavy as _____
burning the midnight oil	cold as _____
didn't sleep a wink	busy as a _____
crack of dawn	happy as a _____
dead of night	white as _____
last but not least	quick as a _____
birds of a feather	blind as a _____
hit the nail on the head	sober as a _____
face the music	tough as _____
straw that broke the camel's back	gentle as a _____

Jargon

Jargon is the technical vocabulary of any specialized occupation, field, or profession. In technical or specialized writing, writers should use the vocabulary of their field. In the following passage, the specialized vocabulary *(homeotic, mutant, rudimentary,* and *thoracic)* is entirely appropriate:

> In the cockroach *Bletella germanica,* a homeotic mutant produces rudimentary wings on the first thoracic segment. No modern insect normally bears wings on its first thoracic segment, but the earliest winged fossil insects did!
> —Stephen J. Gould, *Hen's Teeth and Horse's Toes*

Jargon, however, is also a generic label for impressive words used for their own sake. Any specialized vocabulary is inappropriate when used not to *inform* but to *impress* an audience with the writer's intelligence. When writers use jargon inappropriately, they are not communicating—they're showing off.

Below is a jargon-filled parody, in legalese, of the simple, clear sentence, "Have an orange." This passage, by the editors of *Labor Magazine,* appears in Stuart Chase's essay, "Gobbledygook":

> I hereby give and convey to you, all singular, my estate and right, title, claim and advantages of and in said orange, together with all rind, juice, pulp and pits, and all rights and advantages therein . . . anything hereinbefore or hereinafter or in any other deed or deeds, instrument or instruments of whatever nature or kind whatsoever, to the contrary, in any wise, notwithstanding.

Sometimes writers use jargon not to make themselves sound impressive but to promote the *subject* they're writing about. We commonly call the result *advertising*. Here is a sample of a Nike advertisement for a walking shoe:

> Walking. To you, it's a simple matter of putting one foot in front of another. To Nike, it's an entire science.
>
> In fact, we have studied walking in one of the world's leading bio-mechanical labs. Our own. And as a result, we've designed a tech-nically advanced shoe specifically for the walking motion. The EXW. We built it close to the ground for stability. With a tri-density midsole that supports and centres your foot. A vented toe area for cool comfort. Flex grooves that bend with your foot. And a Nike-Air cushioning system that makes you feel, literally, like you're walking on air.
>
> Now, all this technology may seem a bit much. But try on a pair. You'll see that the EXW doesn't make walking more complicated. It just takes it one step further.

3D cli/jar

Nike hopes the inflated language and technical jargon in this passage will make you feel better about spending $80 for a walking shoe. "World's lead-ing biomechanical labs," "advanced shoe specifically for the walking motion," "tri-density midsole," "vented toe area," and "flex grooves"—all this jargon does seem a bit much. We may ridicule such language, but remember that if the advertisement causes us to buy the shoe, the language is appropriate for the audience.

Exercise

In the following passage, replace clichés with fresh, figurative language, and eliminate or replace inappropriate jargon.

(1) The television news media in Canada need to be reformed. (2) The bottom line is that serious news has been lost as stations rush to entertain the viewer. (3) Trying to find an informative story on the evening news is like looking for a needle in a haystack. (4) The station executives who finalize the programmatic output for the evening news believe that the average Canadian is dumber than an ox. (5) As a result, viewers see in-depth stories about a sex scandal involving a local politician, but only a few seconds explain-ing why the stock market is scraping the bottom of the barrel. (6) Newscasters attempt to maximize their humour by telling jokes that go over like a lead balloon rather than informing the viewer about the latest decision-making process on peace-keeping. (7) If station programmers actually interfaced with the public occasion-ally, they would recognize the error of their ways.

3E SEXIST LANGUAGE

Do not use language that unfairly stereotypes people or discriminates against either women or men. Just as you would avoid racist terms, you should avoid language that stereotypes people's roles, occupations, or behaviour by gender. Sentences such as "A doctor always cares for his patient" or "A secretary should always help her boss" imply that all doctors are men and all secretaries are women. Phrases such as *female logic, male ego, emotional woman,* or *typical male brutality* imply that all women are excessively emotional and all men are egotistical brutes. In fact, those stereotypes are not true. If you use sexist language, you will offend your readers. Even more important, your language should not encourage you or your reader to see the world in sexist stereotypes.

3E sxt

1. Avoid words that suggest sexist roles:

Sexist	Revised
man	people, person
chairman	chair, head
businessman	businessperson
policeman	police officer
mankind	humankind
statesman	politician, diplomat
lady lawyer	lawyer
career girl	professional
coed	student
mailman	letter carrier
old wives' tale	superstition

Note, however, that some words that link occupation with gender are still appropriate. Most writers still use *actor* and *waiter* for men and *actress* and *waitress* for women. Other words, however, such as *stewardess* or *seamstress,* are often replaced with *flight attendant* or *garment worker.*

2. Be consistent in your use of people's names. If you write *Michael Ondaatje,* then write *Dionne Brand,* not *Miss Brand.* If you write *Young* instead of *Neil Young,* then write *Arden,* not *Jann Arden* or *Jann.*

3. Avoid using the pronouns *he, his,* or *him* when you are referring to activities, roles, or behaviour that could describe either sex:

Sexist:	A doctor should listen carefully to his patient.
	Note: Use a plural if it does not alter your meaning.
Revised:	Doctors should listen carefully to their patients.
Sexist:	An effective teacher knows each of her students.
	Note: You may use *his or her* sparingly, but avoid using the construction *s/he.*
Revised:	An effective teacher knows each of his or her students.

Sexist:	Everyone hopes that he will survive the first year of college.
	Note: Often, you can revise the sentence by using first or second person or by omitting the pronoun.
Revised:	I hope to survive the first year of college.
Revised:	All of us hope to survive the first year of college.
Revised:	You hope to survive the first year of college.
Revised:	Everyone hopes to survive the first year of college.
	Note: Do *not* mix singular and plural by saying, "Everyone hopes *they* will survive the first year of college."

Exercise

Revise the following passage to eliminate sexist language.

3E sxt

(1) Everyone in college now is looking for that special job that will match his talents and yet bring him sufficient income. (2) Teaching is a low-paying but good career if you don't mind being a professor who spends his life reading papers, getting grants, and serving on committees. (3) A secretary or stewardess can begin her career with minimal training, but a nurse must dedicate herself to rigorous medical schooling. (4) In business and entertainment, girls can work right alongside the men. (5) In the entertainment field, many people dream of being a Bryan Adams or a Shania Twain, although most singers don't have Adams' talent or Shania's perseverance. (6) A businessman often works his way up the ladder and becomes chairman of the company. (7) Even staying at home and raising a family is a respectable career for either a man or his wife, though most men simply don't have the temperament to raise children. (8) Whatever your chosen career, from mailman to congressman, hard work and dedication are the keys to landing and keeping that important job.

3F DENOTATION AND CONNOTATION

The *denotation* of a word is its literal or dictionary definition. Both *house* and *home* refer, denotatively, to a structure in which people live. Many words have, in addition, a *connotation* or emotional association that can be negative, neutral, or positive. *House* has, for most people, a *neutral* or sterile connotation, whereas *home*, for most people, has a *positive* connotation, suggesting warmth, comfort, security, and family.

Choose words appropriately for their connotative value:

Inappropriate:	Dr. Aileen Brown, a *notorious* scientist, just received the Nobel Prize for her work with superconductors. [*Notorious* people are usually famous for their *misconduct.*]
Revised:	Dr. Aileen Brown, a *famous* scientist, just received the Nobel Prize for her work with superconductors.
Inappropriate:	Wai looked at her friend Ferenc and said, "Why don't you finish your dinner? You need the food—you're already a bit *scrawny* looking." [Ferenc prefers to think of himself as *thin* or *slim* rather than scrawny.]
Revised:	Wai looked at her friend Ferenc and said, "Why don't you finish your dinner? You need the food—you're already a bit *thin.*"
Inappropriate:	Lynn's father told Paul that the apartment was decorated *cheaply* but tastefully. [Paul's feelings may be hurt. He does have good taste in furnishings, and he did the best he could on his tight budget.]
Revised:	Lynn's father told Paul that the apartment was decorated tastefully but *inexpensively.*

3G gls

Exercise

The following groups of words have similar denotative meanings but vary widely in their emotional associations or connotative meanings. Rank the words in each group from most negative, to neutral, to most positive.

- social drinker, wino, lush, reveller, alcoholic, sot, party animal, elbow bender, inebriate, problem drinker, booze hound, bar hopper
- scholar, intellectual, four-eyes, walking encyclopedia, geek, savant, bookworm, genius, pedant, bibliophile
- thrifty, penny-pinching, frugal, miserly, tight-fisted, cheap, economical, prudent, stingy
- steady, loyal, stubborn, firm, unyielding, dedicated, obstinate, devoted

3G USAGE GLOSSARY

This glossary lists alphabetically words and phrases that frequently cause problems for writers. In many cases, writers disagree about the preferred usage in formal writing. If you are in doubt, check a dictionary, such as *The Gage Canadian Dictionary, The Canadian Oxford Dictionary, The Concise Oxford Dictionary,* or a guide such as *The New Fowler's Modern English Usage* or *The Canadian Style: A Guide to Writing and Editing.*

Because this glossary references only the most obvious usage errors, refer to a standard or unabridged dictionary for items not included.

a, an: Use *a* when the following word begins with a *consonant sound:* a book, a clever saying, a hat. Use *an* when the following word begins with a *vowel sound:* an apple, an old building, an honour.

accept, except: *Accept* is a verb meaning "to receive": "I accept the gift." *Except* is a preposition meaning "other than" or "excluding": "Everyone received a gift except John." Rarely, *except* is a verb meaning "to exclude": "The editor excepted the footnote from the article."

advise, advice: *Advise* is a verb: "I advise you to exercise regularly." *Advice* is a noun: "Please take this advice."

affect, effect: *Affect* is a verb: "The flying beer cups did not affect the outfielder's concentration." *Effect* is a noun: "His obvious poise had a calming effect on the crowd." *Remember:* If you can say, "The effect," then you are correctly using the noun form. Less often, *effect* is also a verb: "His behaviour effected a change in the crowd's attitude."

all right, alright: *All right,* two words, is the accepted spelling. *Alright* is non-standard, in the opinion of most experts.

a lot: *A lot* is always two words that mean "many." Wherever possible, however, *avoid* using *a lot.* Replace with a more specific description. See Section 3A.

already, all ready: *Already* means "by now" or "previously": "The essay was already completed." *All ready* means "completely prepared": "The paragraphs were all ready to be printed."

among, between: Use *among* for *three or more* people or things: "We should distribute the winnings among all the players." *Note: Between* is used for three or more items when location or a reciprocal relationship is indicated: "They found the treasure at a point equidistant between the three trees." "Through careful negotiations, a non-aggression treaty was reached between the four nations."

amount, number: *Amount* refers to quantity: "He saved a large amount of food for the winter months." *Number* refers to countable items: "She owned a large number of expensive sports cars."

anyone, any one: *Anyone* is a pronoun: "Anyone who likes Mayan art should hear the lecture." *Any one* is an adjective phrase modifying a noun: "He owns more Mayan art than any one person could possibly appreciate."

bad, badly: *Bad* is an adjective used in the predicate ("After a week of the flu, she looked bad") or before a noun ("She caught my cold at a bad time"): "She felt bad because she had a bad cold." *Badly* is an adverb: "He wrote badly because he had a high fever."

being, being that: *Being* cannot be used as a complete verb. "The seat being taken" is not a complete sentence. *Being that* is non-standard: "Being that the bus was late, we missed the show." Use *because* or *since:* "Because the bus was late, we missed the show."

beside, besides: *Beside* is a preposition meaning "next to" or "by the side of": "Peggi sat beside the senator." *Besides* is a preposition meaning "moreover" or "in addition to": "Besides, the senator likes several people besides George."

can, may: In formal writing, use *can* for ability: "I can take out the garbage." Use *may* for permission: "May I have the honour of taking out the garbage?" Also use *may* for possibility: "If I have time, I may take out the garbage."

centre around: Illogical: One can "circle around" but not "centre around." Replace with "centre on" or "focus on": "The controversy focussed on the right of the worker to a safe, smoke-free environment."

cite, site: *Cite* is a verb meaning "to quote as an authority" or "to mention": "She cited Newcastle's blue law, which forbade card playing on Sunday." *Site* is a noun meaning a "place" or "location": "The church basement was, in fact, the site of Newcastle's first bingo game."

continual, continuous: *Continual* means "frequently repeated": "Most soap operas have continual interruptions for commercials." *Continuous* means "unceasing": "Throughout the broadcast, we heard a continuous buzzing sound."

could of, should of: Non-standard. Use *could have* or *should have.*

data, media, criteria: The singular forms are *datum, medium,* and *criterion.* In formal writing, use plural verbs and pronouns with the plural noun. "Our data reveal a sharp increase in rapes and assaults since last year." "The media use their own criteria for sex and violence."

different from, different than: For prepositional phrases, use *different from:* "His chili recipe is different from yours." Although *different from* is preferred, sometimes *different than* results in a more concise sentence. "She is a different player than she used to be" is less wordy than "She is a different player from the player she used to be."

disinterested, uninterested: *Disinterested* means "objective or impartial": "As a disinterested third party, Marji resolved our dispute." *Uninterested* means "not interested": "We were uninterested in the outcome of the hall elections."

farther, further: *Farther* usually refers to distance: "How much farther are we going to jog?" *Further* refers to additional time, amount, or degree: "Furthermore, if you cannot hire me, I will go further into debt."

fewer, less: *Fewer* refers to numbers or countable items: "Fewer teenagers smoke than a decade ago." *Less* refers to amount ("less sugar") or degree ("less important"): "Teenagers spend less money on cigarettes than they did a decade ago."

3G gls

hopefully: *Hopefully* means "with hope," or "in a hopeful manner": "Charlene waited hopefully for a letter from home." Most good writers still object to the colloquial usage of *hopefully* (meaning, "I hope," or "it is to be hoped"): "Hopefully, Charlene will get her letter from home." Change to: "I hope Charlene gets her letter from home."

imply, infer: *Imply* means to suggest without directly stating: "The news report implied that the president was seriously ill." *Infer* means to draw a conclusion: "I inferred from the news report that the president was seriously ill." Writers and speakers *imply;* readers and listeners *infer.*

its, it's: *Its,* like *his* or *her,* is a possessive pronoun: "The tree is losing its leaves." *It's* is a contraction of *it is:* "It's your turn to rake the leaves."

lay, lie: *Lay* is the transitive verb *(lay, laid, laid)* meaning "put" or "place:" "Please lay the book on the table." *Lie* is an intransitive verb *(lie, lay, lain)* meaning "recline" or "occupy a place": "The books lie on the table."

like, as, as if: *Like* is a preposition: "A great race driver is like an opera singer—vain and arrogant." *As* can be a preposition ("His mission as a driver was to demonstrate his grace and courage"), but it can also introduce a clause: "Even at the end of the race, he looked as if he had just stepped off the cover of a magazine."

lose, loose: *Lose* is a verb meaning "misplace" or "be deprived of": "Good detectives never lose their nerve." *Loose* is an adjective meaning "free" or "not tight": "The psychopath got loose by climbing through the ventilating system."

principal, principle: *Principal* as an adjective means "major" or "main"; as a noun, *principal* refers either to a "chief official" or to a "capital sum of money": "The principal of the high school listed as his principal debt the $50 000 he owed on the principal of his house mortgage." *Principle* is a noun meaning "basic truth," "rule," or "moral standard": "He learned the principles of accounting and finance."

quote, quotation: *Quote* is a verb: "I quoted the passage from Thoreau's *Walden*." Do not use *quote* as a noun ("The following quote from *Walden*"); instead, use *quotation, remark,* or *passage:* "The following passage from *Walden* illustrates Thoreau's politics."

that, which: *That* always introduces restrictive clauses; *which* introduces either restrictive or non-restrictive clauses. Some writers prefer, however, to use *that* only for restrictive clauses and *which* only for non-restrictive. "The hat that has the pheasant feather was a birthday present." The clause "that has the pheasant feather" restricts, limits, and identifies which hat was the present. "The hat, which is nearly ten years old, was a birthday present." The clause "which is nearly ten years old" is only incidental information; it does not specify which hat was the present.

their, they're, there: *Their* is a possessive pronominal adjective: "She is playing with their tennis balls." *They're* is a contraction: "They're really upset that she didn't even ask." *There* is an adverb or an expletive: "She's practising over there. There are the tennis balls."

to, too, two: *To* is a preposition: "I am writing to Bev." *Too* is an adverb meaning "in addition" or "also": "You too can write her a letter." *Too* also is an intensifier meaning "very": "Dad expects me to write too often." *Two* is a number: "I have written two times this month."

used to, supposed to: Use the past tense ("used to") not ("use to"): "I used to go there every weekend." "I was supposed to be at swimming practice at 3:30 P.M. this afternoon."

3G gls

Section 4

Punctuation and Mechanics

The purpose of punctuation is to clarify meaning and promote communication. Commas, periods, semicolons, dashes, and other punctuation marks guide readers to meanings, just as traffic signals, double yellow lines, turning lanes, and one-way signs guide motorists to destinations. The conventions of punctuation create *expectations* in the reader. Just as you are surprised when a car runs a red light and nearly hits you, readers are surprised when writers fail to follow the conventions of punctuation.

Punctuation—or the lack of it—can change the entire meaning of a sentence. In actual conversation, pauses, inflections, intonation, gestures, and facial expressions do the work of punctuation. In writing, however, punctuation must provide these clues.

Read the following sentences. How many different ways can you find to punctuate each sentence? How does each version alter the meaning?

> Give the peanuts to my daughter Ella
> She said walk quietly
> Let's go see the lions eat Marcia.

Sometimes writers unintentionally create confusion by omitting important punctuation. Notice how the appropriate use of commas in the following sentences prevents a possible surprise and clarifies the meaning:

Confusing:	To keep the pipes from freezing the plumber advised us to run the water all night. [How exactly did the pipes freeze the plumber?]
Revised:	To keep the pipes from freezing, the plumber advised us to run the water all night.
Confusing:	On the menu for lunch was ham and Sam was doing the cooking. [Is Sam on the menu?]
Revised:	On the menu for lunch was ham, and Sam was doing the cooking.

The guidelines for punctuation and mechanics in this section will help you to avoid unintentional problems and to clarify your writing. Review these guidelines as you edit your own and other people's writing.

4A CONJUNCTIVE WORDS

Much of the confusion about punctuation occurs because connecting words often have similar meanings but signal different punctuation conventions. A stop sign, a red light, and a blinking red light, for example, all mean that motorists must stop, but each signals a slightly different procedure. In English, *but, although,* and *however* mean that a contrast is coming, but each requires different punctuation:

4A conj

We won the volleyball game, *but* our best hitter broke her wrist.
Although we won the game, our best hitter broke her wrist.
We won the game; *however,* our best hitter broke her wrist.

Using commas and semicolons to punctuate sentences and clauses requires knowing the three basic types of connecting or *conjunctive* words.

Coordinate conjunctions: Conjunction means "join together"; "coordinates" are "equals." A coordinate conjunction (coord. conj.) joins equals together. The acronym BOYFANS will help you remember the coordinate conjunctions:

b	o	y	f	a	n	s
but	or	yet	for	and	nor	so

Subordinating conjunctions: A subordinate conjunction (sub. conj.) joins a dependent or subordinate clause to an independent or main clause. The following are the most common subordinating conjunctions:

after	before	since	until
although	even if	so that	when
as	even though	than	whenever
as if	if	that	where
as though	in order that	though	wherever
because	rather than	unless	while

Adding a subordinating conjunction changes an independent clause (IC) to a dependent clause (DC):

                                    ic
Independent Clause   He buys a newspaper.

                         sub
                         conj   dc
Dependent Clause   *If* he buys a newspaper

                              dc   ic
Complete Sentence   If he buys a newspaper, he will see the story.

Conjunctive adverbs: A conjunctive adverb (conj. adv.) acts as a transitional phrase. Following are the most common conjunctive adverbs:

accordingly	however	meanwhile	still
also	incidentally	moreover	thereafter
consequently	indeed	nevertheless	therefore
furthermore	instead	otherwise	thus
hence	likewise	similarly	

If you are uncertain whether a connecting word is a conjunctive adverb, *test* by moving the connecting word to another place in the clause. Conjunctive adverbs can be moved; subordinating conjunctions (such as *if* or *because*) and coordinating conjunctions (*but, or, yet, for, and, nor, so*) cannot.

4A conj

- Conjunctive adverbs can be moved:

We won the game; *however,* our best hitter broke her wrist.
We won the game; our best hitter, *however,* broke her wrist.
We won the game; our best hitter broke her wrist, *however.*

- Subordinating conjunctions cannot be moved:

Although our best hitter broke her wrist, we won the game.
Our best hitter, *although,* broke her wrist, we won the game.
[Obviously, *although* cannot be moved to another position in the clause.]

- Coordinating conjunctions cannot be moved:

We won the game, *but* our best hitter broke her wrist.
We won the game, our best hitter, *but,* broke her wrist.
[Moving a coordinating conjunction scrambles the sentence.]

Follow these rules for joining independent clauses (IC) and dependent clauses (DC):

1. Join two independent clauses with a *comma* and a *coordinating conjunction:*

                coord
    ic,   conj   ic.
The pizza is good, *but* the mystery meat is disgusting.

2. Join two independent clauses with a *semicolon* and a *conjunctive adverb:*

              conj
    ic;   adv   ic.
The pizza is good; *however,* the mystery meat is disgusting.

3. Join two independent clauses with a *semicolon:*

    ic;   ic.
The pizza is good; the mystery meat is disgusting.

4. Join a dependent clause to an independent clause with a *comma:*

    dc,   ic.
Although mystery meat tastes all right, it looks disgusting.

4B COMMA SPLICES AND FUSED SENTENCES

Two common errors in joining independent clauses are the *comma splice* and the *fused sentence* (also called a *run-on sentence*). Revise by following one of the patterns in 1–3 in the rules just cited:

Comma Splice: [IC, IC.] I know that airplanes are safer than cars, I still have a fear of flying.

Revised: I know that airplanes are safer than cars, *but* I still have a fear of flying.

Comma Splice:	[IC, conj. adv., IC.] I know that airplanes are safer than cars, however, I still have a fear of flying.
Revised:	I know that airplanes are safer than cars; *however*, I still have a fear of flying.
Fused Sentence:	[IC, IC.] I know that airplanes are safer than cars I still have a fear of flying.
Revised:	*Although* I know that airplanes are safer than cars, I still have a fear of flying.

Exercise

In the following passage, correct all comma splices and fused sentences.

(1) For years, scientists have attempted to teach animals to communicate for the most part, their efforts have failed. (2) In the 1950s, psychologists failed to teach a chimpanzee to speak, the ape was able to grunt only a few words. (3) In the 1960s, however, a chimp named Washoe learned the sign language of the deaf. (4) Washoe came to understand hundreds of words, he used them to communicate and express original ideas. (5) As it turns out, the great apes have the capacity to learn language, but they cannot speak. (6) This research proved that humans are not the only animals capable of using language they are, however, the most sophisticated users of language.

4C ,

4C COMMAS

Commas for Introductory Elements

Use commas to set off most introductory elements:

Because I broke three flasks, I'm going to have a large bill for chemistry lab. [introductory dependent clause]
In the middle of finals week last semester, I became seriously depressed. [long introductory prepositional phrase]
Jogging home after classes, I see children playing in the schoolyard. [introductory participial phrase]
To save money, I often take the bus. [introductory infinitive phrase]
Incidentally, I hope my friend will be here this weekend. [introductory adverb]

Items in a Series

Use commas to separate items in a series (a, b, and c). Generally, use a comma before the *and*. In some cases, omitting the comma before the final item in the series may cause confusion:

Confusing:	She rented an apartment with a convection oven, a microwave, a refrigerator with an icemaker and a garbage disposal. [Does the refrigerator have a built-in icemaker and garbage disposal?]
Revised:	She rented an apartment with a convection oven, a microwave, a refrigerator with an icemaker, and a garbage disposal.

Exercise

Revise the punctuation in the following passage.

(1) Everyone can have fun outside in the wintertime by following some common-sense rules. (2) If you are going to be outside for several hours be sure to eat a nutritious meal before leaving. (3) On cold damp or windy days wear clothes that are warm and dry. (4) To stay warm protect yourself against moisture that builds up from the inside. (5) Most experts recommend dressing in layers. (6) The inner layer wicks moisture away from your body the middle layer provides thermal protection and the outer layer protects against rain or wind. (7) Curiously enough most people tend to put on too many clothes, underestimating their body's ability to exercise comfortably naturally and safely in cold weather.

4C ,

Non-restrictive Elements

Non-restrictive modifiers should be separated from the sentence by commas. Always *test* the phrase or clause. If it can be removed from the sentence without a change in the meaning, use commas:

Non-restrictive:	Coach Hall, who was invited to the party, celebrated the victory. [The clause "who was invited to the party" is incidental information. It does not restrict or specify which coach was celebrating. The two commas indicate that removing the clause from the sentence will not change the meaning: "Coach Hall celebrated the victory."]
Non-restrictive:	Seattle, which has a reputation as a rainy city, is actually drier than New Orleans. [Remove the clause, and the meaning of the sentence is not altered: "Seattle is actually drier than New Orleans."]

Non-restrictive:	Charles, the man in the grey suit, eats fried grasshoppers when no one is looking. [The appositive "the man in the grey suit" can be removed from the sentence without an alteration in the meaning.]
Restrictive:	Demonstrators who hurled bricks were arrested by the police. [The meaning is that *only those* demonstrators *who hurled bricks* were arrested by the police. The phrase *who hurled bricks* cannot be removed from the sentence without a change in meaning. Do *not* use commas to separate restrictive elements.]
Non-restrictive:	The class, which was taught by Roland Lapierre, met at eight o'clock in the morning. *Note:* This sentence says that the class met at eight o'clock, and Roland Lapierre was, incidentally, the teacher. (Usually use *which* for non-restrictive clauses.)
Restrictive:	The class that was taught by Roland Lapierre met at eight o'clock in the morning. *Note:* This sentence says that the particular class taught by Professor Lapierre met at eight o'clock. Other classes met at some other time. (Use *that* for restrictive clauses. Do not use commas.)

4C ,

Unnecessary Commas

Do not use a comma to separate a subject and a verb:

Faulty:	My toughest class of the day, met at eight o'clock.
Revised:	My toughest class of the day met at eight o'clock.

Do not use a comma to separate compound subjects or predicates:

Faulty:	The dean of students, and the president decided to cancel classes. [compound subject]
Revised:	The dean of students and the president decided to cancel classes.
Faulty:	Because of the heavy snowfall, I stayed inside all afternoon, and popped popcorn. [compound predicate] *Note:* When coordinate conjunctions do not join independent clauses or items in a series, a comma is usually not necessary (see Section 4A for appropriate use of commas with coordinate conjunctions).
Revised:	Because of the heavy snowfall, I stayed inside all afternoon and popped popcorn.

Coordinate Adjectives

Use a comma to separate coordinate (equal) adjectives. Test for coordinate adjectives: (1) Insert an *and* between the adjectives and (2) reverse the order of the adjectives. If the meaning of the sentence remains unchanged, the adjectives are equal or coordinate:

Example: It was a dull dark day.
          [Insert *and;* reverse adjectives: *It was a dull and dark day. It was a dark and dull day.* Since the meaning of the sentence has not changed, these are coordinate or equal adjectives. Remove the *and* and add a comma.]

Revised: It was a dull, dark day.

Example: The car had studded snow tires.
          [Insert *and;* reverse adjectives: *The car had studded and snow tires. The car had snow and studded tires.* The meaning of the original sentence is changed; therefore, the adjectives are not coordinate. Do *not* separate with comma.]

Revised: The car had studded snow tires.

4C ,

Dialogue

Use commas to set off a direct quotation or dialogue.

• Direct quotation:

The author points out, "In modern commercial society, the notion of celebrity has displaced the idea of the hero."

—Tyler Cowen

• Dialogue:

"We'll try it," the professor said to me, grimly, "with every adjustment of the microscope known to man."

—James Thurber

In fiction or non-fiction, begin a new paragraph when the dialogue shifts from one person to the next:

"Rainin' today, ain't it child?" Mrs. Joy asks.

"No, not yet," Betty says. "It's very muggy."

"Don't I know it," she says.

"Are your legs sore?" Betty asks.

"Oh Lord, yes, how they ache," Mrs. Joy says and rolls her eyes back into her head. Her jersey dress is a tent stretched across her knees. She cradles a cookie tin in her lap.

"That's too bad," Betty says.

—Sandra Birdsell, "The Wednesday Circle"

Addresses, Dates, Degrees

Use commas to set off addresses, dates, and degrees/titles:

Addresses:	Hamilton, Ontario, is his hometown.
Dates:	On October 16, 1970, Prime Minister Trudeau invoked the War Measures Act.
Degrees:	Randall Felder, D.D.S., is my orthodontist.

Exercise

Revise the punctuation in the following passage.

(1) Dinosaurs which have been extinct for millions of years are making news again. (2) At a meeting of the Geological Society of America in November 1987 scientists announced a startling discovery. (3) Dinosaurs, that lived 80 million years ago, benefitted from an atmosphere that contained nearly 50 percent more oxygen than it does now. (4) Gary Landis geochemist for the U.S. Geological Service and Robert Berner professor at Yale University reached that conclusion after analyzing, air bubbles trapped in bits of amber. (5) They found that the tiny, air bubbles contained 32 percent oxygen, compared with 21 percent in the modern atmosphere. (6) When asked whether a decreasing oxygen supply, could have caused the extinction of the dinosaurs, Berner explained "It was a very gradual change, and most organisms easily adapt." (7) "The large slow-moving dinosaurs probably became extinct" he said "following some cataclysmic, geological, event."

4D ./;

4D PERIODS AND SEMICOLONS

Periods

Use periods at the end of sentences, indirect questions, and commands:

Sentence:	Niagara Falls, Ontario, is a famous tourist attraction.
Indirect Question:	I asked my friend from Moose Jaw if he had ever been there.
Command:	Take the "Maid of the Mist" boat ride for a really close look.

Semicolons

Use a semicolon to join related independent clauses. Remember to test for independent clauses by using a period. If you can use a period at the end of each independent clause, and if the sentences are related, you may wish to use a semicolon. Remember, however, that semicolons are usually more appropriate in formal writing:

> Nowadays, says one sociologist, you don't have to have a reason for going to college; it's an institution. His definition of an institution is an arrangement everyone accepts without question; the burden of proof is not on why you go, but why anyone thinks there might be a reason for not going.
>
> —Caroline Bird

> I have been to the Falls several times; today is my friend's first visit.

Use a semicolon to separate items in a series that already have internal punctuation:

> We quickly meet the "good guys" of *Star Wars*: Luke Skywalker, played by Mark Hamill; Ben "Obi-Wan" Kenobi, played by Alec Guinness; and Han Solo, played by Harrison Ford.
>
> —Judith Crist

Do *not* use a semicolon to join dependent with independent clauses:

> Harrison Ford played the leading role in *Raiders of the Lost Ark*; which made him an instant star.

4D . / ;

4E COLONS AND DASHES

Colons

Use a colon to introduce a list or an explanation. Colons often create formal, structured sentences:

> When you go to the grocery store, please get the following items: two boxes of frozen peas, five pounds of baking potatoes, and a package of stuffing for the turkey.
> There is only one guaranteed method to lose weight: Eat less and exercise more.

Usually, a colon following a verb is unnecessary:

Unnecessary:	The best way to lose weight is: eat less and exercise more.
Revised:	The best way to lose weight is to eat less and exercise more.

| Unnecessary: | I need: peas, baking potatoes, and stuffing. |
| Revised: | I need peas, baking potatoes, and stuffing. |

Dashes

Use a single dash for an abrupt shift. Use a pair of dashes for an interrupting or parenthetical comment. Use a dash instead of a comma, colon, or parentheses when you want a sentence to have a more informal, colloquial flavour:

> Turn on your television late at night or on a weekend afternoon—even, these days, at midmorning—and the good-natured hosts, a has-been actress (Ali McGraw) or never-was celeb (Ed McMahon), are touting cosmetics or miracle car wax as if they are doing us a public service.
>
> —Mark Kingwell

Exercise

4F ! / ?

In the following passage, insert semicolons, colons, or dashes at the appropriate places. In some cases, there are several ways to punctuate the sentence correctly, so be prepared to explain your choice.

> (1) Yo-yo dieting the process of repeatedly losing and gaining weight is common today. (2) Instead of changing eating habits and exercise patterns, the yo-yo dieter uses three common strategies to lose weight taking diet pills, drinking diet liquids, and fasting outright. (3) The yo-yo dieter, however, needs to know the truth about dieting diet cycles decrease the muscle-to-fat ratio in the body and decrease the body's ability to lose weight during the next dieting cycle. (4) Quick-fix diets, in other words, will lead to rapid weight losses however, they will be followed by an even faster weight gain. (5) Ultimately, crash diets do more harm than good the body just wasn't designed to be a yo-yo.

4F EXCLAMATION POINTS AND QUESTION MARKS

Exclamation Points

Use exclamation points sparingly, for stylistic emphasis:

> Canadian and American Chinatowns set aside their family tongue differences and encouraged each other to fight injustice. There were no borders. "After all," they affirmed, "*Daaih ga tohng yahn* . . . We are all Chinese!"
>
> —Wayson Choy

Question Marks

Use a question mark after a direct question:

What is your first childhood memory?

Do not combine question marks with commas or periods:

"What is your earliest memory?" she asked me. [Do *not* use a comma and a question mark: "What is your earliest memory?," she asked me.]

4G QUOTATION AND ELLIPSIS MARKS

Quotation Marks

Use quotation marks to indicate a writer's or speaker's exact words:

Marya Mannes says, "Woman, in short, is consumer first and human being fourth."

4F ! / ?

Use quotation marks for titles of *essays, articles, short stories, poems, chapters,* and *songs*—any title that is part of a larger collection:

"Television: The Splitting Image" is the title of an essay by Marya Mannes.

Use single quotation marks for quotations within a quotation:

James said, "I know I heard her say, 'Meet me outside the east door.'"

Ellipsis Marks

Use ellipsis marks (three *spaced* periods) to indicate material omitted from a direct quotation:

Marya Mannes said, "Woman . . . is consumer first and human being fourth." [The ellipses indicate that words are omitted from the middle of the sentence.]

Use a period *plus* three spaced periods to signal either omitted words at the end of a sentence or omitted intervening sentence(s):

Marya Mannes said, "Woman, in short, is consumer first and human being fourth. . . . The conditioning starts very early. . . ."

Punctuation with Quotation Marks

The following guidelines will help you to punctuate sentences with quotation marks. Periods and commas go *inside* quotation marks:

According to biologist Julie Nichols, "Penguins are more densely covered with feathers than any other bird—nearly 180 feathers per square inch."

Colons and semicolons go *outside* quotation marks:

Recent data about the eagle's feathers may revise the old saying "light as a feather": the vaned feathers on a bald eagle weigh more than its entire skeleton.

Exclamation points and question marks go *inside or outside* quotation marks. They go *inside* if they are a part of the quoted material:

The award for the highest number of feathers, according to Nichols, "goes to the whistling swan with a staggering 25 000 feathers!" [The original sentence ends with an exclamation point.]

They go *outside* if they are not a part of the quoted material:

Is it true that, as Nichols claims, "the tiny ruby-throated hummingbird has 940 feathers"? [The original sentence ends with a period.]

4H ITALICS

Most word-processing programs allow you to *italicize* certain words for emphasis. When using a typewriter or writing by hand, use underlining to indicate words that should be set in italics.

Titles:	"The Loons," from the collection *A Bird in the House,* is an important link in Margaret Laurence's Manawaka cycle of novels and stories. [Underline (or italicize) titles of books, magazines, films, paintings, newspapers—any work published separately. Use quotation marks for titles of chapters, articles, or poems—any title that is part of some collection in a book or magazine.] *Exceptions:* Do not underline the Bible or titles of legal documents, such as the BNA Act or the Canadian Charter.
Names:	The most famous travel ships used to be the *Santa Maria,* the *Titanic,* and the *Queen Mary.* Now the great ones are the *Apollo* and the *Challenger.* [Underline (or italicize) names of ships, trains, aircraft, or spacecraft.]

Foreign Words:	He graduated *cum laude,* while his friend, who barely passed first year mathematics, graduated *magna cum laude.* "*C'est la vie,*" he thought. [Note, however, that many foreign words (burrito, bourgeois, genre, cliché, junta, and many others) have been incorporated into the language and do not need italics. Consult your dictionary if you are in doubt.]
Words or Letters:	*Suppose to* should have a *d: supposed to.* [Quotation marks are also used to indicate italics in handwritten or typed manuscripts.] *Note:* Do not underline or put quotation marks around the title of your essay when it appears on a title page or the first page of your manuscript.

Exercise

4H ital

Revise the following passage, underlining appropriate words and titles.

(1) Alice Munro is the author of several collections of short stories, among them, Something I've Been Meaning to Tell You, in which the story, The Found Boat, first appeared. (2) Several of Munro's stories have been published in The New Yorker magazine. (3) With a style more traditional than au courant, Munro deals deftly and delicately with universal themes such as love, death, sex, and growing up, the theme of Boat. (4) This is a rite of passage story in which five children discover and restore a wrecked boat. (5) They think of several names for the boat: Water Lily, Sea Horse, Flood Queen and Caro-Eve. (6) After fixing the vessel, the boys and girls take it to a secluded spot where they learn about the mysteries of puberty in a game of Truth or Dare. (7) Alice Munro is an undisputed genius in this genre of writing.

4I PARENTHESES AND BRACKETS

Parentheses

Use parentheses ( ) to set off additional information, examples, or comments:

Outside our lifeboat, let us imagine another 210 million people (say the combined populations of Colombia, Ecuador, Venezuela, Morocco, Pakistan, Thailand, and the Philippines), increasing at a rate of 3.3 percent per year.

—Garrett Hardin

Writing a film review requires that you carefully examine the criteria for your judgment (see Chapter 8).

Brackets

Use brackets [ ] to set off editorial remarks in quoted material. Brackets indicate that you, as an editor, are adding comments to the original material:

Original:	After you hear my arguement, you will reelect Chrétien.
Edited:	After you hear my arguement [sic], you will reelect [Prime Minister Jean] Chrétien. [As editor, you add information about Chrétien and indicate by using *sic* ("thus it is") that the misspelling, grammatical mistake, or inappropriate usage occurs in the original source and is not your error.]

4J APOSTROPHES AND HYPHENS

Apostrophes

Use apostrophes for contractions, possession, and some plurals:

4J ' / -

Contractions:	It's too bad you don't agree.
Possession:	The wind blew the student's notes across the front lawn. [The notes belonging to one student blew across the lawn.]
	The wind blew the students' notes across the front lawn. [The notes belonging to several students blew across the lawn.]
	Your sister-in-law's accident was someone else's fault.
	[In compounds, make the last word possessive.]
Plurals:	The 1980's [or 1980s] were the Yuppie years.
	Eliminate unnecessary *which's* in your sentences.

Hyphens

Use hyphens for compound words, compound adjectives before nouns, some prefixes, and some numbers. When in doubt, always check a good dictionary.

Compounds:	cross-reference; president-elect
Adjectives:	a 20th-century writer; the slate-blue sea; the three-year-old child
	Note: When the compound adjectives follow a noun, omit the hyphen: He is a writer well known only in Vermont.
Prefixes:	ex-Prime Minister Mulroney; self-motivation
Numbers:	twenty-six; one hundred and sixty-five; one-fifth

4K CAPITALS AND NUMBERS

Capitals

Capitalize proper nouns and adjectives, professional titles, principal words in titles of books or articles, and regional locations:

4K cap/num

Proper Names:	Judson Smith, Victoria, Halifax, Churchill River, English, Swahili, Labour Day, Christmas, Hanukkah, Wednesday, October [Do not capitalize seasons or terms: autumn, spring, summer, fall semester, first year.]
Titles:	Senator Cools, Prime Minister Trudeau, Professor Findlay, Associate Dean Natalie Renner, Uncle Don, Father [Do not capitalize family titles preceded by a pronoun: my mother, my uncle, our grandfather.]
Titles:	*Fall on Your Knees*, "My Financial Career," "Where the World Began," *Going Down the Road* [Some style manuals suggest capitalizing only the first word in a title. If you are citing titles in a bibliography or list of works cited, check your style manual.]
Regions:	the South, the Northwest, the Middle East [Do *not* capitalize directions: travelling east, walking due north.]

Numbers

Conventions regarding numbers vary. Generally, except in scientific or technical writing, spell out numbers of one digit and use numerals for the rest. Treat ordinal numbers in the same way.

> The exam is only six weeks away. I heard that one third of the questions will be multiple-choice.
> This stadium seats 50 000 people, but adding the end-zone bleachers increases the seating to 57 000.

Use a combination of figures and words to express numbers in the millions or higher:

> 16 million   2.7 billion

If a passage requires many numbers, be consistent in your usage:

> Of 27 students enrolled in the course last year, 25 wrote the exam and 8 failed.

At the beginning of sentences, spell out numbers. Alternatively, rewrite the sentence:

> Three hundred and ten students are enrolled this semester.
> In Chemistry 201, 310 students are enrolled.

Exercise

Revise the following passage for proper use of apostrophes, hyphens, capitals, italics, and numbers. Use your dictionary to help you edit this passage.

(1) The advertisement shows a skydiver floating down to earth, and the pictures caption says, "I take vitamin supplements every day, just to be on the safe side." (2) Self styled experts, from your local pharmacist to physicians from the mount Sinai hospital, encourage the public to believe that vitamins are a cure all.
(3) There are only thirteen known vitamin deficiencies (such as scurvy, which is a Vitamin C deficiency), but nearly sixty percent of the two hundred and fifty two canadian's responding to our questionnaire believed in taking vitamin supplements. (4) These days, its almost patriotic to take vitamins—even your Mother says, "Don't forget to take your vitamins!" (5) During the 1990's, vitamins popularity rose an astonishing twenty nine percent, and revenue from vitamin sale's jumped to nearly three billion.
(6) Although sales are generally higher in the west, some Eastern cities such as quebec city and Moncton have also shown dramatic increase's in sales. (7) If you want to learn more about vitamins, read The Vitamin-Pushers in a recent issue of Consumer Reports.

LITERARY CREDITS

Page 173: **Bridgid Stone,** "My Friend Michelle, An Alcoholic." Reprinted with the permission of the author.

Page 186: **Jonathan Kozol,** "The Homeless and Their Children" from *Illiterate America.* Copyright © 1985 by Jonathan Kozol. Reprinted with the permission of Doubleday, a division of Random House, Inc.

Page 187: **Phillip Elmer DeWitt,** "Welcome to Cyberspace" from *Time* (Special Issue, Spring 1995) (excerpted). Copyright © 1995 by Time, Inc. Reprinted with the permission of *Time.*

Page 195: **Pico Iyer,** "The Global Village Finally Arrives" from *Time* 142 (Special Issue, Fall 1993). Copyright 1993 by Time, Inc. Reprinted with the permission of *Time.*

Page 204: **Toni Cade Bambara,** "The Lesson" from *Gorilla, My Love.* Copyright © 1972 by Toni Cade Bambara. Reprinted with the permission of Random House, Inc.

Pages 205 and 219: **Nancie Brosseau,** "Anorexia Nervosa." Reprinted with the permission of the author.

Page 211: **Christine Bishop,** "English Only." Reprinted with the permission of the author.

Page 225: **John Gilchrist,** "The Belvedere." Written by John Gilchrist and broadcast on CBC Radio One, *Calgary Eyeopener*, May 9, 1999.

Page 228: **Grant Buckler,** "DVD Moves into the Mainstream." Reprinted from *We Compute Magazine* by permission of Grant Buckler, freelance writer/editor.

Page 232: **Peter Travers,** "Oprah . . . Oscar; Oscar . . . Oprah" from *Rolling Stone* (October 29, 1998). Copyright © 1998 by Straight Arrow Publishers, Inc. Reprinted with the permission of the publishers. All rights reserved.

Page 234: **Elayne Rapping,** "Watching the Eyewitless News" from *The Progressive* (March 1995). Copyright 1995. Reprinted with the permission of *The Progressive*, 409 East Main Street, Madison, WI 53703.

Page 241: **Patrick Watson,** review of *The Next Canada*. Reprinted by permisson of Patrick Watson, Creative Director, The Heritage Minute.

Page 245: **Mark Kingwell,** "Not Available in Stores" in *Saturday Night,* 1998. Reprinted by permission of Mark Kingwell.

Page 257: **Roger Ebert,** review of *The Red Violin* in *The Chicago Sun-Times.* Reprinted by permission of Roger Ebert.

Page 264: **Patricia Raybon,** "A Case of Severe Bias" from *Newsweek* (October 1989). Reprinted with the permission of the author.

INDEX

a, an, 457, 486
Abstract nouns, 451
accept, except, 486
Active voice, 455, 466–67
Addresses, commas in, 497
Ad hominem fallacies, 306
Adjective clauses, 457
Adjectives, 452
 coordinate, 496
Ad populum fallacies, 306
Adverb clauses, 457
Adverbs, 452
 conjunctive, 490–93
Advertisements
 MLA Works Cited list format, 415
 summarizing and responding to,
  49–52
advise, advice, 486
affect, effect, 486
Agreement
 pronoun-antecedent, 451, 474–75
 subject-verb, 472
Agreement and disagreement, in
 summary and response essays, 47,
 65–67
Allen, Gregory, 106
all right, alright, 486
Almanacs, 386
a lot, 486
already, all ready, 486
AltaVista Canada, 390
Alternating comparison-and-contrast
 structure, 255
American Psychological Association
 (APA) style, 415–22
 deciding to use, 376, 380, 402
 in-text citations, 402, 415–17
 References list, 402, 418–22
 style guide for, 380
among, between, 486
amount, number, 486
Analogies
 in explanatory writing, 182–83
 faulty, 305–6
 in investigative writing, 171
 in observational writing, 109–10

for remembering essays, 135
Analysis
 causal, 205–6, 255
 criteria, 254
 in evaluative writing, 254–255
 in explanatory writing, 179, 183–85,
  205–6
 in investigative writing, 171, 173
 process, 183–85, 205, 302
 of questions for research paper, 382–84
 in summary and response essays,
  46–47, 65–66
Annotation
 collaborative, 366
 for interpretive writing, 312
 in journals, 7
 for summary and response essays, 59
Anonymous works
 APA References list format, 418
 MLA Works Cited list format, 409
Antecedent, of pronouns, 451, 474–75
Anthologies
 APA References list format, 419
 MLA Works Cited list format, 410
anyone, any one, 487
APA style. *See* American Psychological
 Association (APA) style
Apostrophes, 503
Appeals, 268–72
 to character, 270
 combined, 271–72
 to emotion, 270, 306
 to reason, 268–70, 304–6
Appositive phrases, 455
Argumentative writing, 262–306
 appeals in, 268–72, 304–6
 claims in, 264–68, 298–99, 303
 collecting in, 298–99
 drafting in, 303–4
 examples of professional writers,
  275–96
 interpretive writing as, 314, 368–69
 revising in, 303–6
 Rogerian argument in, 272–75, 301–2
 shaping in, 300–2
 subject selection, 297–98

techniques for, 262–68
Arguments
    appeals for, 268–72
    characteristics of, 262–63
    claims for, 264–68, 298–99, 303
    developing, 302
    logical fallacies in, 210–11, 304–5
    outlines for, 301–2
    "pro" and "con," 300
    Rogerian, 272–75, 301–2
Articles *(a, an, the)*, 457
Art Index, 396
as, as if, like, 488
Audience
    analysis of, 20–21
    for argumentative writing, 302, 303
    for essay examinations, 435
    for interpretive writing, 312
    for investigative writing, 145, 173
    for observational writing, 110, 111,
        112–13, 113
    and purpose of writing, 18–27
    for research papers, 374–75, 382
    for summary and response essays, 61,
        69
Authors, in-text citation of
    American Psychological Association
        (APA) style, 415–17
    Modern Language Association
        (MLA) style, 406–8
    References list (APA style), 418–22
    Works Cited list (MLA style),
        408–15
Author tags, in summary and response
    essays, 45
Auxiliary verbs, 454

Background information
    for interpretive writing, 367
    for research papers, 386
bad, badly, 487
Begging the question, 305
being, being that, 487
beside, besides, 487
between, among, 486
Be verbs, 470
Biographical Dictionaries, 386
Biography and Genealogy Master Index,
    386
Bird, Caroline, 266
Birdsell, Sandra, 335–45
Bishop, Christine, 211–18

Blaise, Clark, 345–51
Blixen, Karen, 86
Block comparison-and-contrast
    structure, 255
Body paragraphs
    in explanatory writing, 209
    in interpretive writing, 369
Bookmarks, 391, 393
Book of Facts, 386
Books
    APA References list format, 418–19
    MLA Works Cited list format,
        409–10, 412
Brackets, 503
Brainstorming
    for argumentative writing, 297–98
    for explanatory writing, 200
    for remembering essays, 133
Branching
    for argumentative writing, 299
    for evaluative writing, 253
    for explanatory writing, 202
Brosseau, Nancie, 205, 206, 207–8,
    219–21
Browe, Sonja H., 79–81
Browsers, Internet, 165, 389–91, 393
Buckler, Grant, 228–31
Botale, Sharon, 293–96

Cameron, Chris, 254–55
can, may, 487
Capitalization, 504–5
Cartoons, MLA Works Cited list
    format, 415
Case, pronoun, 451
Catalogues, library, 387
Causal analysis
    in evaluative writing, 255
    in explanatory writing, 205–6
Cause-and-effect relationships
    claims about, 265–66, 298
    in explanatory writing, 179, 180,
        185–87, 210–11
CD-ROMs, 34–35
    key word searches for, 387
    MLA Works Cited list format, 414
    periodicals indexes on, 396–97
centre around, 487
Character
    appeals to, 270
    major/minor, 315
    of short story, 315, 367

Character conflict map, 367
Chopin, Kate, 309–12, 314–17
Chronological order, 28
    in evaluative writing, 255
    in explanatory writing, 205
    in investigative writing, 170, 173
    in observational writing, 106, 114
    in remembering essays, 117, 135–36,
        141
Ciccarello, Terri, 9
Circular argument, 305
cite, site, 487
Claims, 264–68, 303
    about cause and effect, 265–66, 298,
        382
    of fact, 264–65, 298, 382
    narrowing and focussing, 298–99
    and purpose for writing, 19
    about solutions and policies, 267–68,
        299, 382
    about value, 266–67, 299, 382
Classification
    in explanatory writing, 203, 210
    in investigative writing, 171
    in observational writing, 107–8
    for remembering essays, 135
Clauses, 456–7
    dependent, 456, 490–92, 498
    independent, 456, 490–92, 498
    relative, 457
    subordinate, 457
Cleaver, Cathleen A., 286–92
Clichés, 480–81
Climax, of short story, 316
Closed questions, 168–69
Clustering
    for argumentative writing, 299
    for evaluative writing, 253
    for explanatory writing, 202
    for remembering essays, 134
Coherence, in explanatory writing, 209
Colgrave, Sukie, 180–81
Collaborative annotation, 366
Collecting
    for argumentative writing, 298–99
    for evaluative writing, 252–54
    for explanatory writing, 201–3
    for interpretive writing, 366–67
    for investigative writing, 163–69
    for observational writing, 103–5,
        111–12
    for remembering essays, 133–34

for research papers, 384–99
for summary and response essays,
    59–62
in writing process, 37–43, 28, 30–37
Collective nouns, 451, 472
Colloquial language, 480
Colons, 498–99
    with quotation marks, 501
Commas, 493–97
    addresses/dates/degrees, 497
    conjunctive words and, 490–493
    coordinate adjectives, 496
    dialogue, 496–97
    introductory elements, 493
    nonrestrictive elements, 494–95
    question marks with, 500
    with quotation marks, 500–1
    series, 494
    unnecessary, 495
Comma splices, 492–93
Commercial products, evaluative writing
    about, 227–31
Common nouns, 450
Comparison and contrast
    alternating, 255
    in argumentative writing, 302
    block, 255
    in evaluative writing, 254–55
    faulty comparison in, 305–6
    in investigative writing, 164, 171, 173
    in observational writing, 85, 107, 114
    for remembering essays, 136
Complements, 450
Compound nouns, 451
Comprehension, in reading process, 41
Computers
    in library research, 387, 397–98
    See also Internet; World Wide Web
    in research process, 169, 387–91
    as writing tools, 5, 30
Computer software
    APA References list format, 421
    MLA Works Cited list format, 414
Conclusions
    in evaluative writing, 255–56
    in interpretive writing, 368–69
    in investigative writing, 172
    in observational writing, 110–11
    for remembering essays, 140
Concrete nouns, 450
Conflict, in short story, 315, 316
Conjunctions, 450

coordinating, 450, 472, 491, 492
correlative, 450
subordinating, 450, 491–92
Conjunctive adverbs, 490–92
Conjunctive words, 490–92
    conjunctive adverbs, 490–92
    coordinate conjunctions, 491–92
    subordinating conjunctions, 491–92
Connotations, 484–85
Conrad, Joseph, 109
Content notes, in Modern Language
    Association (MLA) style, 408
continual, continuous, 487
Contractions, 503
Coordinate adjectives, 496
Coordinating conjunctions, 450, 472,
    491, 492
Corporate author, APA in-text citations,
    417
Correlative conjunctions, 450
could of, should of, 487
Cowen, Tyler, 277–83
Criteria
    for evaluative writing, 225, 254,
        256–57
    nature of, 225, 256
criteria, data, media, 487
Criteria analysis, 254
Cross, Donna Woolfolk, 204
Cyberspace, 391

Dangling modifiers, 462
Dashes, 499
data, media, criteria, 487
Databases, electronic
    key word searches for, 387
    in library, 386–87, 397–98
    library catalogue as, 386–87
Dates, commas with, 497
Davies, Robertson, 108–9
Definitions
    in argumentative writing, 302
    in explanatory writing, 180, 181–83,
        203, 210
    extended, 181–82
    formal, 181–82, 210
    in interpretive writing, 368, 370
    in investigative writing, 164, 171
    in observational writing, 108–9
    for remembering essays, 135
Degrees, commas with, 497
Demonstrative pronouns, 452

Denotations, 484–85
Denouement, of short story, 316
Dependent clauses, 456, 490–493, 498
Description, in summary and response
    essays, 63
Descriptive process analysis, 183, 184–85
Details
    in observational writing, 84–85,
        104–5, 113
    in remembering essay, 117
    sensory, 84–85, 104–5, 113
Devlin, Dudley Erskine, 56–58, 63–67
DialogOnDisc, 396
Dialogue
    commas in, 496
    for remembering essays, 139–40, 142
Diction and style, 476–89
    clichés, 480–81
    colloquial language, 480
    denotation and connotation, 484–85
    jargon, 481–82
    sexist language, 483–84
    slang, 480
    usage glossary, 485–89
    vague words, 476–78
    wordiness, 478–79
Dictionaries, 386
    MLA Works Cited list format, 410
different from, different than, 488
Dillard, Annie, 90–93, 110
Direct objects, 449, 466
Direct quotations
    in APA style, 416
    block format for, 403
    commas in, 496
    in interpretive writing, 371
    introducing, 403
    in investigative writing, 145, 166–67,
        173
    in MLA style, 403–4
    quotation marks in, 500
    in summary and response essays, 45,
        64, 69
Discussion
    classroom, 8, 62–63
    goals of, 62–63
    in interpretive writing, 309–312
    in summary and response process,
        62–63
disinterested, uninterested, 488
Diskettes, MLA Works Cited list
    format, 414

Documentation in research papers,
    406–22
  American Psychological Association
    (APA) style, 415–22
  deciding to use, 376, 380, 402
  in-text citations, 402, 415–17
  References list, 402, 418–22
  style guide for, 380
  citation decisions in, 402–4
  determining style for, 376, 380, 402
  Modern Language Association
    (MLA) style, 406–15
  content or supplementary notes, 408
  deciding to use, 376, 380, 402
  in-text citations, 167, 402–4, 406–8
  style guides for, 380, 409, 412
  Works Cited list, 402, 408–15
Doidge, Norman, 284–86
Domain, 391
Dominant idea. *See* Main idea; Thesis
Double-entry notes
  in journals, 7
  for observational writing, 104
  for summary and response essays, 60
Douglas, Susan, 52–54
Drafting
  in argumentative writing, 303
  in evaluative writing, 256
  in explanatory writing, 209–10
  in interpretive writing, 369–70
  in investigative writing, 172
  in observational writing, 111–12
  in remembering essays, 140
  of research paper, 379, 401–5
  in summary and response essays, 68
  in writing process, 28
Drawing, 103–4

Ebert, Roger, 257–59
Edited works
  APA References list format, 418, 419
  MLA Works Cited list format, 409,
    410
Editing
  of essay examinations, 438
  importance of, 444–45
  of research paper, 422
  symbols for, 447–48
  tips for, 448
  in writing process, 29
Editorials
  APA References list format, 420

MLA Works Cited list format, 412,
    413
Education Index, 572
effect, affect, 486
Ehrenreich, Barbara, 42–49
Either/or fallacy, 305
Electric Library, 390–91
Ellipses, to indicate omissions from
    quotations, 404, 500
Elmer-DeWitt, Philip, 187–93, 209–9
  MLA Works Cited list format, 414
Emotional appeals, 270, 306
Encyclopedias, 386
  MLA Works Cited list format, 410
Entertaining writing, 18
Essay examinations, 434–41
  audience for, 435
  key terms in, 435–36
  knowledge of material and, 437–38
  practicing for, 430
  proofreading and editing, 438
  sample questions and responses,
    438–41
  sketch outlines for, 436–37
Essay map, in explanatory writing,
    207–8
et al., 593, 407. 416
Ethical appeals, 270
Evaluation
  in interpretive writing, 313–14, 368
  of sources, 374, 394–96
Evaluative writing, 224–60
  collecting in, 252–54
  about commercial products, 227–31
  drafting in, 256
  examples of professional writers,
    225–51, 257–59
  interpretive writing as, 313–14, 368
  about performances, 232–34
  revising in, 256–57
  shaping in, 254–56
  subject selection for, 251
  techniques for, 224–51
Events
  observational writing about, 88–89
  remembering essay about, 120
Evidence
  in appeals, 268–72
  for argumentative writing, 263. 302,
    304
  for evaluative writing, 225, 257
  for explanatory writing, 180

for interpretive writing, 313, 370
reading and, 40
for summary and response essays, 47, 61, 69
Examinations, essay. *See* Essay examinations
Examples, in explanatory writing, 203–4
except, accept, 486
Excite, 390
Exclamation points, 499
with quotation marks, 501
Experience, as evidence in summary and response essays, 47
Explanatory writing, 17, 171–222
analysis in, 179
collecting in, 201–3
drafting in, 208–9
examples of professional writers, 187–98
examples of student writers, 211–21
explaining *how,* 183–85, 201, 210, 313
explaining *what,* 181–83, 201, 313
explaining *why,* 185–87, 201–2, 313
interpretive writing as, 313, 368
relationships in, 179
revising in, 210–11
shaping in, 203–9
in short story, 505
subject selection for, 200
techniques for, 180–200
Expletives, 662
Exploratory writing, 18
Expository writing. *See* Explanatory writing
Extended definitions, 181–82

Fact, claims of, 264–65, 298, 382
Fallacies, 304–6
ad hominem, 306
ad populum, 306
begging the question, 305
circular argument, 305
either/or, 305
faulty comparison or analogy, 305–6
genetic, 304
hasty generalization, 304
post hoc ergo propter hoc, 210–11, 304
red herring, 306
straw man, 306
farther, further, 488
Faulty comparison or analogy, 305–6

Faulty parallelism, 464–65
Faulty predication, 461
Feature list, 367
fewer, less, 488
Field research
for evaluative writing, 254
for explanatory writing, 203
interviews in, 167, 254
questionnaires in, 167, 168–69, 254, 385
Figurative expressions. *See* Analogies; Metaphors; Similes
Films
APA References list format, 422
MLA Works Cited list format, 414
Findley, Timothy, 120
First person, writing in, 116, 316
Flashback, in remembering essay, 116
Footnotes, in Modern Language Association (MLA) style, 408
Foreign words, italics for, 502
Foreshadowing, 309, 316
Form, of research paper, 374, 375
Formal definitions, 181–82, 210
Fragments, sentence, 458–60
Freewriting
for argumentative writing, 299
for evaluative writing, 253
for explanatory writing, 202
inventory of writing, 15
for observational writing, 105
for remembering essays, 133
sample of, 9
FTP sites, 391
Furnish, Dale, 106
Fused sentences, 492–93
Fussell, Paul, 107–8
Future perfect tense, 454
Future tense, 454

Garbutt, Chris, 151–60
Gender
pronoun-antecedent agreement, 451
sexist language, 483
Generalization
hasty, 304
over-, 360
General reference information, 386
Genetic fallacies, 304
Geographic regions, capitalization of, 504
Gerund phrases, 456

Gerunds, 456
Gilchrist, John, 225–27
Goldman, Albert, 107
Gopher sites, 392
GoTo.Com, 390
Government documents
    APA in-text citations, 417
    APA References list format, 419
    locating, 397
    MLA Works Cited list format, 410
Guppy, Stephen, 352–65

Hasty generalization, 304
Helping verbs, 454
Hillen Ernest, 86–89, 206
Hoffman, Roy, 10–13
Home page, 392
hopefully, 488
HotBot, 390
HTML, 392
http, 391
Huxley, Thomas, 268
Hyperlink, 392
Hypertext, 392
Hyphens, 503

Images
    in observational writing, 85
    for remembering essays, 136–37, 141
Imperative mood, 455
imply, infer, 488
Indefinite pronouns, 452, 472
Independent (main) clauses, 456,
    490–92, 498
Indicative mood, 455
Indirect objects, 450
Indirect quotations, 585
Inductive logic, 268–70
infor, imply, 488
Infinitive phrases, 456
Infinitives, 456
Informal contacts, 384
Informative writing, 18
InfoSeek, 390
InfoTrac, 396, 397
Intensive pronouns, 452
Interjections, 458
Internet, 30, 253, 387–99
    browsers, 165, 389–91, 393
    citation of sources
    APA in-text citations, 417
    APA References list format, 420–21

MLA in-text citations, 406–7
MLA Works Cited list format,
    412–14
evaluating sources on, 394–99
glossaries of terms, 391–92
pros and cons of using, 387–88
search engines, 165, 389–91, 392
tips for doing research on, 392–93
useful sites, 165, 393–94
Interpretive writing, 308–71
    collecting in, 366–67
    drafting in, 369–70
    examples of professional writers,
        309–65
Interpretive writing, *continued*
    purposes for responding, 313–14
    responding to short fiction, 309,
        314–15
    revising in, 37–71
    shaping in, 368–69
    in summary and response essays,
        46–47, 67
    techniques for responding, 312–13
Interrogative pronouns, 452
Interviews
    in evaluative writing, 254
    in investigative writing, 167, 254
    for research papers, 385
    APA References list format, 421
    MLA Works Cited list format, 412,
        415
    tips for conducting, 167
In-text citations
    American Psychological Association
        (APA) style, 402, 415–17
    Modern Language Association
        (MLA) style, 167, 402–4, 406–8
Intransitive verbs, 454, 468
Introductions
    in evaluative writing, 255–56
    in explanatory writing, 206–7
    in interpretive writing, 368–69
    in investigative writing, 172
    in observational writing, 110
    for remembering essays, 140
Introductory elements, commas for, 493
Inverted pyramid, 170
Investigating
    for argumentative writing, 299
    for evaluative writing, 253–54
    for explanatory writing, 203
Investigative writing, 144–47

collecting in, 163–69
drafting in, 172
examples of professional writers, 145–60
example of student writers, 256
multiple sources, using, 147–50
profile of person, 150–51
revising in, 172–73
shaping in, 170–71
subject selection for, 162–63
summary of book/article, 145–46
techniques for, 144–45
Irony, in short story, 317
Irregular verbs, 453
Italics, 501–2
it is, 479
its, it's, 488
Iyer, Pico, 195–98

Jargon, 481–82
Journal articles
APA References list format, 420, 421
electronic, 393
indexes to, 396–97
MLA Works Cited list format, 411, 413
Journals, 6–13
professional writer on, 10–13
reading entries in, 7
write-to-learn entries in, 8
writing entries in, 8–9
Judgments, for evaluative writing, 224–25

Kafka, Franz, 308
Keller, Helen, 120–23
Key words, 387
King, Martin Luther, Jr., 271–72
Kingwell, Mark, 245–50
Koester, Jennifer, 77–79
Kostash, Myrna, 241–44

Laurence, Margaret, 308
lay, lie, 488
Lead-ins
in explanatory writing, 180, 206–7
in investigative writing, 144, 172
sample, 206–7
Lectures, MLA Works Cited list format, 415
Leonard, Andrew, 182–83
less, fewer, 488

Letters, MLA Works Cited list format, 413, 415
Lewis, Karyn M., 49–52
Library of Congress Subject Headings (LCSH), 387
Library research, 385–87
background information in, 386
computerized databases, 387, 396
evaluating sources, 397–98
for evaluative writing, 253
for explanatory writing, 203
general reference, 385–86
government documents, 397
for investigative writing, 164–65
librarians and, 164, 386, 387
catalogue on-line, 387
sources of information in, 164–65, 165
lie, lay, 488
like, as, as if, 488
Linking verbs, 45354
Listening skills, 167
Lists, colons to introduce, 498
Listservs, 392
MLA Works Cited list format, 414
Literature, responding to. *See* Interpretive writing
Logic
appeals to, 268–70, 304–6
fallacies in, 210–11, 304–6
inductive, 268–70
Looping
for argumentative writing, 299
for evaluative writing, 253
for explanatory writing, 203
for remembering essays, 133–34
lose, loose, 489
Lycos, 390

MacLeod, Alistair, 308, 317–34
Magazines
APA References list format, 419–20
electronic, 394
index to, 396–97
MLA Works Cited list format, 411, 413
Magnetic tape, MLA Works Cited list format, 414
Main (independent) clauses, 456, 490–92, 497–98
Main idea
in interpretive writing, 368–69

in investigative writing, 145
in observational writing, 85–86, 111, 113
and purpose for writing, 19
of remembering essays, 117, 141
in summary and response essays, 40, 45, 61
See also Thesis
Major characters, 315
may, can, 487
McNeil, Robert, 117–18
media, criteria, data, 487
Meer, Jeff, 145–46
Memories
for argumentative writing, 299
for evaluative writing, 253
for explanatory writing, 202
See also Remembering essays
Metaphors
in explanatory writing, 182–83
in investigative writing, 171
in observational writing, 109–10
in remembering essays, 135
Minor characters, 315
Misplaced modifiers, 463
Mitford, Jessica, 207
Mixed constructions, 460–61
MLA style. *See* Modern
    Language Association (MLA style)
Modern Language Association (MLA
    style), 406–15
    content or supplementary notes, 408
    deciding to use, 376, 380, 402
    in-text citations, 167, 402–4, 406–8
    style guide for, 380, 409, 412
    Works Cited list, 402, 408–15
Modifiers, 450
    dangling, 462
    misplaced, 463–464
    nonrestrictive, 494–95
    vague, 476–78
Mood, 455
MOOs, 392
MLA Works Cited list format, 414
Morrow, Lance, 171
Mowat, Farley, 94–102, 111, 183–84
MUD (multiuser domain or dungeon), 392
MLA Works Cited list format, 414
Multiple authors
    APA in-text citations, 415
    APA References list format, 418

MLA in-text citation for, 406
MLA Works Cited list format, 409
Multiple sources, in investigative
    writing, 147–50
Multivolume works
MLA in-text citation for, 406–8
MLA Works Cited list format, 409
Myths, about writing, 2–3

Names
    capitalization of, 504
    italics for, 501
    sexist language and, 483–84
    See also Authors, citation of
Narrator, point of view of, 316
Newsgroups, 392
    MLA Works Cited list format, 413
Newspapers
    APA References list format, 420–21
    indexes to, 396–97
    MLA Works Cited list format, 411–12, 413

New York Times Index, 396
Nixon, Richard
        and the *straw man* fallacy in logic
        (the "Checkers" speech), 306
Nominals, 496–70
Nonrestrictive elements, commas for, 494–95
Notes
    during interviews, 167
    in investigative writing, 166, 167
    organization of, 401
    regarding sources, 203
    in research notebook, 377–79, 398–99
Noun phrases, 455
Nouns, 450–51
    abstract, 451
    collective, 451, 472
    common, 450
    compound, 450
    concrete, 469–70
    nominals, 450
    proper, 450
    vague, 476
Number
    pronoun-antecedent agreement, 634, 657
    subject-verb agreement471–72
number, amount, 486

Numerals
    apostrophes in plural, 504
    spelling out, 504

Objective pronouns, 451
Objectivity
    in observational writing, 84, 104,
        112–13
    in summary and response essays, 45
Objects
    direct, 449, 466
    indirect, 450
    observational writing about, 88
Observational writing, 84–114
    collecting in, 103–5
    drafting in, 111–12
    about events, 88–89
    examples of professional writers,
        90–101
    for explanatory writing, 202
    about objects, 88
Observational writing, *continued*
    about people, 86–87
    about places, 87–88
    revision in, 112–14
    shaping in, 105–11
    subject selection for, 102–3
    techniques for, 85–102
Observations
    for argumentative writing, 299
    for evaluative writing, 252–53
    for interpretive writing, 315
    for remembering essays, 117, 141
Omissions, ellipses to indicate, 404, 500
Open questions, 168
Organization
    of notes, 401
    in summary and response essays, 61
Orwell, George, 136–37
Outlines
    for argumentative writing, 301–2
    for essay examinations, 436–37
    for summary and response essays,
        67–8
Overgeneralization
    in evaluative writing, 257
Oxford English Dictionary (*OED*), 386

Pagination, APA References list format,
    419
Pamphlets, MLA Works Cited list
    format, 410

Paragraph hooks, in explanatory writing,
    208
Parallelism, faulty, 464–65
Paraphrasing
    in APA style, 416
    in investigative writing, 166, 173
    in MLA style, 403
    in summary and response essays, 45,
        63–4, 69
Parentheses, 502
Parks, Brad, 103
Participial phrases, 456
Participles, 456
Passive voice, 455, 466, 467–8
Past participle, 453
Past perfect tense, 454
Past tense, 453, 454
    writing in, 117
Peer response
    to observational writing, 112–13
People
    investigative writing about, 150–51
    observational writing about, 86–7
    remembering essay about, 117–18
Performances, evaluative writing about,
    232–34
Periodicals
    APA References list format, 419–20
    electronic, 393–94
    indexes to, 396–97
    MLA Works Cited list format,
        411–12, 413
Periods, 497
    with ellipsis marks, 500
    question marks with, 500
    with quotation marks, 500
Person, pronoun-antecedent agreement,
    451, 474–75
Persona, for remembering essays,
    138–39
Personal communication
    APA in-text citations, 417
    electronic mail, 414
    from informal contacts, 384–85
    MLA Works Cited list format, 414
Personal pronouns, 451
Persuasive writing, 18, 223, 257
Petrie, Neil H., 30–37
Photocopies, in research process, 165–66,
    379, 399
Phrases, 455–56
    appositive, 455

gerund, 456
infinitive, 456
noun, 455
participial, 456
participle, 456
prepositional, 455
redundant, 479
verbal, 456
wordy, 478
Places
    observational writing about, 87–88
    remembering essay about, 118–19
Plagiarism
    avoiding, 166, 374, 404–5
    defined, 404
    in investigative writing, 166
Plot, of short story, 316, 368, 370
Plurals, apostrophes in, 503
Point of view
    for interpretive writing, 316
    in observational writing, 85, 113
    for remembering essays, 133, 141
Polanszky, John, 373, 377–79, 384,
        422–33
Policies, claims about, 267–68, 299, 382
Possessive case
    apostrophes in, 503
    pronouns in, 451
Post hoc ergo propter hoc fallacies, 210, 304
Predicates, 449
    compound, comma with, 495
    faulty predication, 461
Prepositional phrases, 455
Prepositions, 457
Prescriptive process analysis, 183–84
Present perfect tense, 454
Present tense, 454
    writing in, 117, 370
Primary sources, 384. *See also* Interviews;
        Questionnaires
principal, principle, 489
Pro and con arguments, 300
Problem solving,
    claims about solutions, 267–68
    in interpretive writing, 314
Process analysis, 183–85
    in argumentative writing, 302
    descriptive, 183, 183–85
    in explanatory writing, 183–85, 205
    prescriptive, 183–85
Profile of person, in investigative
        writing, 150–51

Progressive form of verb, 454
Pronouns, 451–52
    agreement, 451, 474–75
    case, 451
    demonstrative, 452
    indefinite, 452
    intensive, 452
    interrogative, 452
    objective, 451
    personal, 451
    possessive, 451
    reference, 451, 474
    reflexive, 452
    relative, 451
    sexist language and, 483–84
    subjective, 451
Proofreading
    of essay examinations, 438
    importance of, 444–45
    proofreading marks, 446–47
    of research paper, 422
    tips for, 448
Proper nouns, 450
Punctuation and mechanics, 490–505
    apostrophes, 503
    brackets, 503
    capitals, 504
    colons, 498–99
    commas, 490–92, 493–97
    comma splices, 492–93
    dashes, 491
    ellipsis marks, 500
    exclamation points, 499
    fused sentences, 492–3
    hyphens, 503
    italics, 501–2
    numbers, 504–5
    parentheses, 502
    periods, 497
    question marks, 500
    quotation marks, 500–1, 501
    semicolons, 490–92, 498
Purposes for writing, 17–27
    an observational writing, 113
    audience-based, 17–27
    combination of, 18–19
    examples of professional writers,
        22–27
    in interpretive writing, 312, 313–14,
        367, 368
    in investigative writing, 145, 173
    in observational writing, 111

in research papers, 374, 382
subject-based, 18–19
in summary and response essays, 60, 69
thesis/claim/main idea, 19
writer-based, 17–18
Pyramid, inverted, 170

qtd. in, 407
Question marks, 500
with quotation marks, 501
Questionnaires
for evaluative writing, 254
for investigative writing, 167, 168–69
for research papers, 385
Questions
for argumentative writing, 298
for audience analysis, 20–21
closed, 168–69
for evaluative writing, 252
for explanatory writing, 181–83, 201–2
for interpretive writing, 315
for investigative writing, 144, 145, 163–64, 167, 168–69, 170, 172, 173
for observational writing, 104–5
open, 168
reporter's, 144, 145, 163–64, 172, 173, 201–2, 298, 382–84
for research papers, 382–84
Quotation marks, 500
other punctuation with, 500–1
quote, quotation, 489

Rachels, James, 263–64
Radio programs
APA References list format, 422
MLA Works Cited list format, 414
Rapping, Elayne, 234–241
Raybon, Patricia, 264–65
Reader's Guide to Periodical Literature, 396–97
Reading, 39–82
active, 41
class discussions and, 62–63
comprehension and, 41
defined, 39
for evaluative writing, 253
for explanatory writing, 203
for interpretive writing, 308–9, 312, 315–17

journal entries based on, 6–7
rereading and interpretive writing, 308–9
techniques for writing about, 40–41. *See also* Summary and response essays
text in, 40, 47
with a writer's eye, 309, 315–17
Reading logs, for summary and response essays, 60
Reason, appeals to, 268–70, 304–6
Recordings
APA References list format, 422
MLA Works Cited list format, 414
Red herring fallacies, 306
Reference, pronoun, 451–475
References list (APA style), 403
books, 418–19
electronic and Internet sources, 420–21
other sources, 421–22
periodicals, 419–20
Reference to introduction, in observational writing conclusions, 110–11
Reflection, in summary and response essays, 67
Reflexive pronouns, 452
Regions, capitalization of, 504
Regular verbs, 453
Relationships
in argumentative writing, 265–66
in explanatory writing, 179, 180, 185–87
in interpretive writing, 368
in investigative writing, 164
in remembering essays, 117, 141
Relative clauses, 457
Relative pronouns, 451
Remembering essays, 116–142
collecting in, 133–34
drafting in, 14
about events, 120
examples of professional writers, 120–132
about people, 117–18
about places, 118–19
revising in, 141–42
shaping in, 135–40
subject selection for, 135
techniques for writing, 116–132
See also Memories

Repeated elements, 464–65
Reporter's questions
   for argumentative writing, 298
   for explanatory writing, 201–2
   for investigative writing, 144,
      163–64, 172, 173
   for research papers, 382–84
Rereading
   of draft research papers, 405–6
   for interpretive writing, 308–9
   in observational writing, 111–12, 113
   for summary and response essays,
      60–62, 69
Research notebook, 377–79
   bibliography section, 378, 398–99
   draft and ideas section, 379
   research log section, 377–8
   source notes section, 378–89
Research papers, 373–433
   collecting information for.
      See Research process
   documentation formats for. See
      Documentation in research
      papers
   drafting, 379, 401–5
   example of student writer, 422–33
   purpose/audience/form in, 374–75
   research notebooks for, 377–79
   revising, 405–6
   shaping, 400–1
   subject selection, 381–84
   techniques for writing, 373–76
   time tables for, 379–80
Research process
   computers in, 165, 387–91
   field research. See Field research
   finding sources in, 375
   in investigative writing, 163–69
   library research. See Library research
   preparation for, 376–80
   research notebook in, 377–79
   tips for, 392–3
   World Wide Web in, 165, 393–94
   See also Collecting; Research papers
Response, 46–49
   example of, 47–49
   kinds of evidence in, 47
   purposes of, 65
   shaping, 65–67
   types of, 46–47
   See also Summary and response
      essays

Reviews
   APA References list format, 421
   MLA Works Cited list format, 412
Revision
   in argumentative writing, 303–6
   in evaluative writing, 256–57
   in explanatory writing, 210–11
   guidelines for, 113–14, 141–42, 69,
      173, 210–11, 256–57, 303–4,
      370–71
   in interpretive writing, 370–71
   in investigative writing, 173
   in observational writing, 112–14
   of remembering essays, 141–42
   of research papers, 405–6
   of summary and response essays, 69
   in writing process, 28–29
Rhetoric, 2
Richler, Mordecai, 118–19
Rituals, of writers, 3–13
Rogerian arguments, 272–75, 301–2
Rogers, Carl, 272
Rosenfeld, Albert, 274–75
Royko, Mike, 275–77
Run-on sentences, 492–93

Sagan, Carl, 110
Scene vision or revision, 367
Schaef, Anne Wilson, 267–68
Scholarly projects, MLA Works Cited
      list format, 413
Scientific method, 268–70
Search engines, Internet, 165, 389–91,
      392
Search Engine Watch, 391
Secondary sources, 385. See also Internet;
      Library research
Selective omniscient narrator, 316
Semicolons, 498
   conjunctive words and, 490–92
   with quotation marks, 501
Sensory details, 84–85, 104, 113
Sentence fragments, 458–60
Sentence structure, 458–75
   active voice, 466–67
   be verbs, 470
   components of, 449–50
   dangling modifiers, 462
   faulty parallelism, 464–65
   faulty predication, 461
   fragments, 458–60
   misplaced modifiers, 463

mixed construction, 460–61
nominals, 469–70
passive voice, 455, 466, 467–68
pronoun agreement, 474
pronoun reference, 475
in short story, 317
subject-verb agreement, 471–72
verb tense, 473
Series
commas in, 494
parallelism of, 464–65
semicolons in, 491
Setting, of short story, 316–17, 368
Sexist language, 483–84
Shaping, 28, 30–37
for argumentative writing,
300–302
for evaluative writing, 254–56
for explanatory writing, 203–209
for interpretive writing, 368–69
for investigative writing, 170–72
methods of, 105–111, 135–40,
63–68, 170–72, 203–209,
254–56, 400–401.
for observational writing, 105–111
for remembering essays, 135–40
for research papers, 400–401
for summary and response essays,
63–68, 65–67
Short story, responding to, 309–12,
314–17
should of, could of, 487
Similes
in explanatory writing, 182–83
in investigative writing, 171
in observational writing, 109–10
in remembering essays, 135
Simple form of verb, 453
site, cite, 487
Sketching, 103–104
Slang, 480
Solutions
claims about, 267–68, 299, 382
Sources in research paper
documenting. *See* Documentation in
research papers
evaluation of, 374, 394–99
finding, 375
informal contacts, 384–85
Internet. *See* Internet
investigative writing, 166–67
library. *See* Library research

photocopying, 165–66, 203, 378–79,
398–99
plagiarism and, 166, 374, 404–405
primary, 385. *See also* Interviews;
Questionnaires
secondary, 385. *See also* Internet;
Library research
unpublished sources, 379, 385,
398–99
using, to make point, 374–402
See also Research process
Spatial order
in observational writing, 106–114
for remembering essays, 135
Speeches, MLA Works Cited list forma,
415
Stone, Brigid, 173–77
Story picture, 367
Straw man fallacies, 306
Stream-of-consciousness narrator, 316
Style, of short story, 506
Subject, narrowing and focusing, 135,
381–84
Subjective pronouns, 451
Subjectivity, in observational writing, 84,
104
Subject of sentence, 449–50
compound, comma with, 495
subject-verb agreement, 471–72
Subject selection
for argumentative writing, 297–98
for evaluative writing, 251
for explanatory writing, 200
for investigative writing, 162–63
for observational writing, 102–3
and purpose of writing, 17–20
for remembering essays, 133
for research papers, 381–84
for summary and response essays,
56–58
Subjunctive mood, 455
Subordinate clauses, 457, 490–92,
497–98
Subordinating conjunctions, 450,
491–92
Summary, 45–46
in APA style, 416
examples of, 45–46, 64–5, 145–6
in interpretive writing, 314–15
in investigative writing, 145–6, 166,
173
in observational writing, 111

purposes of, 45
shaping, 63–65
Summary and response essays, 40–82
about advertisements, 49–52
collecting in, 59–62
drafting in, 68
examples of professional writers, 42–45, 52–58, 70–75
examples of student writers, 49–52, 76–81
journals and, 7
response in, 46–49
revising in, 69
shaping in, 183–87
subject selection for, 56–58
summary in, 45–46
techniques for, 40
supposed to, used to, 489
Surveys, MLA Works Cited list format, 415
Symbols
editing, 447–48
proofreading, 446
in short story, 317
Synchronous communication, MLA Works Cited list format, 414

Tannen, Deborah, 70–75, 76–81
Television programs
APA References list format, 422
MLA Works Cited list format, 414
Telnet sites, 392
Tense, 454, 473
Term papers. *See* Research papers
Testimony, in investigative writing, 164
that, which, 479, 489
the, 457
their, they're, there, 489
Theme, of short story, 317
there is, there are, 479
Thesis
in argumentative writing, 302
in evaluative writing, 224
in explanatory writing, 180, 207, 210
in interpretive writing, 368–70
and purpose for writing, 19
for research papers, 381–82
in summary and response essays, 61
See also Claims; Main idea
Third person, writing in, 316
this is, 479
Thomas, Lewis, 184–85

Three-column log, for evaluative writing, 252–53
Thurber, James, 138–39
Time line, for interpretive writing, 366
Time table, for research, 379–80
Titles
capitalization of, 504
in evaluative writing, 255–56
in explanatory writing, 180
for investigative writing, 144
in investigative writing, 172
italics for, 501
in observational writing, 110
quotation marks for, 500, 501
for remembering essays, 140
to, too, two, 489
Tone
in explanatory writing, 204–205
for remembering essays, 137–38
in short story, 317
in summary and response essays, 61
Topic sentences, in explanatory writing, 209
Toufexis, Anastasia, 147–50, 206
Transitional words and phrases, in explanatory writing, 208–9, 211
Transitions, in observational writing, 114
Transitive verbs, 454–55, 468
Translations
APA References list format, 419
MLA Works Cited list format, 410
Travers, Peter, 232–34
two, to, too, 489

uninterested, disinterested, 488
Unity, in explanatory writing, 209
Unknown author
APA References list format, 418, 419
MLA Works Cited list format, 409, 310
Unpublished sources
MLA style for citation of, 406, 410, 414
using, 378–79, 385, 398–99
Unsigned articles
APA References list format, 420
MLA Works Cited list format, 411, 412
URL (Universal Resource Locator), 165, 391
Usage glossary, 485–489
used to, supposed to, 489

Vague words, 476–78
Value, claims about, 266–67, 299, 382
Verbal phrases, 456
Verbs, 449–450, 452–55
  auxiliary, 454
  be, 470
  colons following, 498
  intransitive, 454–55, 468
  irregular, 453
  linking, 453–54
  mood, 455
  principal parts of, 453
  regular, 636
  subject-verb agreement, 471–73
  tense of, 454, 473
  transitive, 454, 468
  vague, 477–78
  voice, 455, 466–68
Vocabulary, in journals, 7
Voice, 455
  active, 455, 466–67
  in explanatory writing, 204–5
  passive, 455, 466, 467–70
  for remembering essays, 137–138, 142

Walker, Alice, 124–131, 136, 140
Watson, Patrick, 241–44
Warner, Charles Dudley, 376
Webster's Third New International Dictionary for the English Language, 558
which, that, 662, 671
White, E. B., 182
who, 479
"Wh" (reporter's) questions
  for argumentative writing, 298
  for explanatory writing, 201–102
  for investigative writing, 144, 163–64, 172, 173
  for research papers, 382–83
Winn, Marie, 266
Wolofsky, Sandy, 22
Wordiness, avoiding, 478–79
Words or letters, italics for, 501–2
Working bibliography, 378, 398–99
Works Cited list (MLA style), 402–408–15
  books, 409–10, 413
  electronic and Internet sources, 413–14

other sources, 414–15
periodicals, 411–12
World Almanac, 386
World Wide Web (WWW), 391
  citation of sources
  APA in-text citations, 417
  APA References list format, 420–21
  MLA in-text citation, 406–7
  MLA Works Cited list format, 412–14
  glossaries of terms, 391–2
  useful sites, 165, 393–94
  See also Internet
Writer's block, 2
Writing
  attitude for, 5–6
  energy for, 5–6
  essay examinations, 434–41
  myths concerning, 2–3
  place, time, and tools for, 4–5
  purposes for, 17–27
  rituals of writer, 3–13
Writing process, 27–37
  for argumentative writing, 297–306
  collecting in, 28, 30–37
  computers in, 5, 30
  dimensions of, 27–29
  drafting in, 31
  editing in, 29
  for evaluative writing, 251–60
  examples of professional writers, 34–37
  for explanatory writing, 200–22
  for interpretive writing, 363–71
  for investigative writing, 161–73
  for observational writing, 102–14
  overview of, 29
  for remembering essays, 132–42
  for research papers, 381–422
  revision in, 28–29
  shaping in, 28, 30–37
  for summary and response essays, 55–82
Writing situation, 21–22

Yahoo!, 390, 391
Ye, Ting-Xing, 16

Zoellner, Robert, 25, 207